# History of the Diocese of Hartford

James H. O'Donnell

**Alpha Editions**

This edition published in 2020

ISBN : 9789354019128

Design and Setting By
**Alpha Editions**
email - alphaedis@gmail.com

# HISTORY

OF

# THE DIOCESE OF HARTFORD

BY

## REV. JAMES H. O'DONNELL

AUTHOR OF

" Liturgy for the Laity," "Studies in the New Testament,"
Etc., Etc.

BOSTON
THE D. H. HURD CO.
1900

# PREFATORY NOTE.

THE undersigned desires to express his gratitude to Right Rev. Bishop Tierney, D.D., whose words of advice and encouragement and unfailing interest in the work, often stimulated him to renewed endeavor; to Very Rev. Thomas J. Shahan, D.D., Dean of the Faculty of Divinity of the Catholic University of America, whose copious notes, collected in 1888 for a "History of the Diocese of Hartford," have been of incalculable value; to the Hon. Charles T. Hoadley, LL.D., State Librarian and member of the Connecticut Historical Society; to Mr. Albert C. Bates, Librarian of the Hartford Historical Society; to Marc F. Valette, LL.D., President of the Brooklyn Catholic Historical Society; to the Hon. William J. Onahan, Chicago, Ills.; to the Bishop's Memorial Hall, University of Notre Dame, Ind.; to the Rev. Edward I. Devitt, S. J., Gonzaga College, Washington, D. C.; to the Rev. John O'Brien, editor of the *Sacred Heart Review*, for the favor of using the admirable historical sketches of the Rev. William F. Powers; to the Price & Lee Company for permission to draw from the "History of Catholicity in Waterbury, Conn.;" to Mr. F. X. Reuss, of Philadelphia, Professor James Madigan and Professor Leo Curley, of Waterbury, for valuable services; to the Watertown Library, for free access to the library at all times, and leave to draw one or many volumes gratis; to Charles F. Chapin, editor of the *Waterbury American*, whose letter "To the Newspaper Men of Connecticut" smoothed the writer's pathway into editorial sanctums; to the many, in a word, who, by suggestion and material furnished, contributed to the accomplishment of the present work.

JAMES H. O'DONNELL.

*Watertown, Conn.*

To the Right Rev. Bishop Tierney, D.D.

to the

Rev. Clergy and Religious

and to the Laity of the Diocese

the

Following Pages are

Affectionately Inscribed.

# CONTENTS

V

Diocese of Hartford.

# DIOCESE OF HARTFORD.

## BY REV. JAMES H. O'DONNELL,

Watertown, Conn.

AUTHOR OF "LITURGY FOR THE LAITY," "STUDIES IN THE NEW TESTAMENT," ETC., ETC.

*"Historia, non ostentationi, sed fidei veritatique componitur."* —PLINY.

"One lesson we must learn ourselves and teach our children. It is to know our antecedents; to glory in our predecessors in the faith; to be ever ready to explain, but never to apologize, for the faith of our fathers."—THOMAS D'ARCY McGEE.

# THE DIOCESE OF HARTFORD

## CHAPTER I.

### THEN AND NOW.

Seal of the Colony of Conn.

THE diocese of Hartford comprises the State of Connecticut. Its area is about five thousand and four square miles. Prior to 1808, Connecticut formed a part of the diocese of Baltimore, whose jurisdiction comprised all the territory of the United States east of the Mississippi River. On April 8, 1808, Pius VII., then occupying the Papal chair, by the bull "*Ex Debito Pastoralis Officio*," erected the episcopal sees of New York, Philadelphia, Boston, and Bardstown. To the diocese of Boston was allotted the territory which now forms the New England States. The first bishop of Boston was the Right Rev. John Lefebvre Cheverus, D.D. Connecticut remained under the jurisdiction of the diocese of Boston until 1843. During these five and thirty years Bishop Cheverus and Bishop Fenwick—apostolic men both—made periodical visits to the scattered Catholics of the state, preaching, catechizing, visiting the sick, administering the holy sacraments, and offering up the august Sacrifice of the Mass. Their ministrations strengthened the faith of the few Catholics here, consoled them in their trials, and fortified them against the spiritual dangers then so prevalent. Their visits were anxiously awaited and their services accepted with an eagerness and joy understood only by those who know of the tender relationship that exists between priests and people. They have long since entered into their celestial reward; but the fruits of their apostolic labors still remain, and their example in searching for the wandering sheep of the fold exercises a stimulating influence upon their devoted successors in the same ministry. They labored faithfully and well, and prepared the ground for the foundations that were laid, and upon which has arisen, grand, stately, and majestic, a diocese second to none in our land, in all things faithful to its exalted mission, and of which its subjects, both priests and laity, are justly proud.

Bishop Cheverus ruled over the diocese of Boston from 1810 to 1823, when he was transferred to the See of Montauban, France. From 1823 to 1825, the affairs of the diocese were conducted by an Administrator, Very Rev. William Taylor. The successor of Bishop Cheverus in the episcopal office was Right Rev. Benedict Fenwick, who was consecrated on the feast of All Saints, 1825.

The rapid increase of the Catholic population of the New England States, together with his declining health, caused Bishop Fenwick to petition the Fifth Provincial Council of Baltimore (1843) for a division of his diocese.[1] In accordance with his request, a petition was duly laid before the Propaganda at Rome, with the result that on September 18, 1843, Pope Gregory XVI. erected the See of Hartford, with jurisdiction over the States of Rhode Island and Connecticut. The first bishop of Hartford was Right Rev. William Tyler, D.D.[2] Bishop Tyler and his successors resided at Providence until 1872, when that city was erected into an Episcopal See. Bishop McFarland in that year took up his residence in Hartford.

Until 1830 there was not a Catholic church in Connecticut. When Bishop Cheverus and Bishop Fenwick, and others who preceded them, visited this portion of the Lord's vineyard, they said Mass, preached, and dispensed the graces of religion in private houses and in public halls; sometimes the Holy Sacrifice was offered in barns, suitably prepared for the joyous occasion. Not infrequently bigotry dethroned reason and justice, and the minister of God, with his devoted little band, would perforce seek access to a stable wherein to celebrate the divine mysteries. But what mattered it? Was not the divine Victim of the sacrifice born in a lowly stable, and were not the dumb beasts among the first witnesses of His advent? When Bishop Fen-

---

[1] The records of the Council, May 19, contain this item:

"Consuerunt, Patres S. Sedi supplicandum esse, ut nova Sedes Episcopalis erigatur in urbe Hartford, quae Provincias Connecticut et Rhode Island includat."

[2] In a letter to Archbishop Eccleston, of Baltimore, September 30, 1843, Cardinal Fransoni, Prefect of the Propaganda, Rome, wrote as follows: "Quod spectat ad Novarum Sedium Episcopalium erectionem, Episcoporum et Coadjutorum electionem. . . . sciatis haec omnia, SS mo Dno Nostro probante, jam esse decreta, electis videlicet iis ad singulos Episcopatus, vel ad munus Coadjutoris obeundum, quos primo loco in singulis casibus proposuistis, excepto," etc.

wick visited Hartford in July, 1829, his church was a printing office and his altar an humble table. To-day we behold in Connecticut one hundred and nineteen parish churches where Mass is said regularly, and one hundred and twenty-three churches, chapels and other buildings where divine services are held frequently. On July 19, 1829, the first Sunday-school for Catholic youth in this State was opened in the office of the *Catholic Press* at Hartford, no doubt with meagre attendance. Now children, many thousands in number, gather weekly within beautiful temples to listen to words of Christian wisdom, to learn the salutary doctrines of the church, and to imbibe the sturdy, vigorous and loyally catholic spirit that shone so conspicuously in their ancestors. Prior to 1830 there was no day-school in which Catholic children could receive a religious as well as a secular training; but on November 2d of that year the doors of the first Catholic school in Connecticut were thrown open. It was for boys only, and was held in the basement of Trinity church, on Talcott street, Hartford. The master was Mr. Joseph Brigden, a convert, a gentleman of superior intellectual attainments, and possessing at that time fifteen years' experience as an educator. To-day fifty-three handsome and substantial parochial schools adorn their surroundings, and are imparting to twenty-three thousand children instruction in the secular branches and fitting them for the high and responsible duties of citizenship. These schools are erected and maintained at a sacrifice that clearly demonstrates the depth and sincerity of our convictions. They are necessary for the proper education of Catholic youth. They are nurseries in which their tender hearts are cultivated, their consciences formed on the lines of Christ's teachings. The religious element there predominates; it pervades the classroom; religious influences are ever present, for we believe with Washington that "reason and experience doth forbid us to expect that national morality can prevail in exclusion of religious principles."

In 1835 a census taken by Bishop Fenwick accredited to Connecticut seven hundred and twenty Catholics. In 1844 the Catholic population of the State was 4,817. The census of 1890 placed the Catholic *communicants* of Connecticut at 152,945, and the Protestant communicants of all denominations at 147,184, giving a Catholic majority of 5,761, with a per cent. of Catholic communicants of .51. In 1899, 250,000 souls yield generous and loyal obedience to the Bishop of Hartford. Previous to 1829, and during a part of that year, the Catholics of Connecticut were attended at intervals by priests sent hither by the Bishop of Boston. The Rev. R. D. Woodley, of Providence, visited the state from November, 1828, to July, 1829, at the request of Bishop Fenwick. In August, 1829, the first priest to reside in the State by episcopal appointment took up his abode at Hartford. This honor belongs to the Rev. Bernard O'Cavanagh. For well-nigh eleven months this zealous and talented young priest sowed alone the seeds of righteousness in a parish whose limits were co-extensive with the boundaries of the State. Beginning with this pioneer, we shall present a list of the priests who labored in Connecticut until 1850. Truly, those were the days that tried priests' souls. Their names should be perpetuated and held in grateful remembrance by their co-religionists of the present. The relation of their labors will be found elsewhere in these pages.

From August 26, 1829, till July 30, 1830, Rev. Bernard O'Cavanagh.

From July, 1830, till October 27, 1831, Rev. B. O'Cavanagh and James Fitton.

From October, 1831, till September, 1832, Rev. James Fitton.

From September, 1832, till 1834, Rev. J. Fitton, Rev. James McDermott, Rev. Edward McCool, Rev. Francis Kiernan.

1835, Rev. J. Fitton, Rev. J. McDermott.

1836, Rev. J. Fitton, Rev. J. McDermott, Rev. Peter Walsh.

1837, Rev. J. McDermott, Rev. John Brady, Rev. Peter Walsh, Rev. William Wiley, Rev. James Smyth.[1]

1838, Rev. P. Walsh, Rev. John Brady, Rev. J. Smyth.

1839, Rev. John Brady, Rev. J. Smyth.

1840, Rev. James Strain, Rev. J. Smyth, Rev. J. Brady.

1841, Rev. James Strain, Rev. J. Smyth, Rev. J. Brady, Rev. John D. Brady.

1842, Rev. John Brady, Rev. James Smyth, Rev. John D. Brady.

1843, Rev. John Brady, Rev. James Smyth, Rev. John D. Brady.

1844, Rev. John Brady, Rev. James Smyth, Rev. Michael Lynch.

1845, Rev. John Brady, Rev. James Smyth, Rev. Michael Lynch, Rev. H. Riordan.

1846, Rev. John Brady, Rev. H. Riordan, Rev. James Smyth, Rev. Charles O'Reilly, Rev. Michael Lynch, Rev. John Brady, Jr.

1847, Rev. John Brady, Rev. James Smyth, Rev. M. Lynch, Rev. John Brady, Jr., Rev. Charles O'Reilly.

1848, Rev. John Brady, Rev. James Smyth, Rev. M. Lynch, Rev. Philip O'Reilly, Rev. John Brady, Jr.

1849, Rev. John Brady, Rev. M. Lynch, Rev. Philip O'Reilly, Rev. John C. Brady, Rev. William Logan, S. J.

1850, Rev. John Brady, Rev. M. Lynch, Rev. Philip O'Reilly, Rev. John Brady, Jr., Rev. Luke Daley, Rev. M. O'Neill, Rev. James Smyth, Rev. John C. Brady. In this year, the Rev. William Logan, S. J., of Holy Cross College, Worcester, Mass., attended New London.[2]

To resume briefly: In 1830 there were two priests in Connecticut; in 1840, three, and in 1850, nine, eight resident and one visiting. In 1860 the number of priests in the Connecticut portion of the diocese was thirty-

---

[1] Not all in the State at the same time.

[2] Father Logan died at New London, May 30, 1850, aged 40 years, from small-pox, contracted from a sick call. He was born at Emmitsburg, April 10, 1810. After his elevation to the priesthood he was engaged in missionary duty at Frederick City, and afterwards as professor in Holy Cross College. He was subsequently charged with the missions of Norwich, New London and Pomfret, and in this, as in other fields of labor, he was distinguished for his piety and zeal. In a Jesuit catalogue for 1849–1850, Father Logan is mentioned as: "*Operarius; excurrit ad Norwich, Neo-Londinum et Pomfret.*"

three. In 1870 there were sixty-three ; in 1880, one hundred and twenty-three ; in 1890, one hundred and eighty-six. In this year of our Lord, 1899, two hundred and sixty priests minister to the wants of the Catholics of Connecticut.

In 1843, before the erection of the diocese, the priests of Connecticut were stationed as follows :

*Hartford,* Trinity Church. Rev. John Brady, Rev. John D. Brady, who attended also Cabbotsville.

*New Haven,* Christ's Church. Rev. James Smyth.

*Bridgeport* was attended from New Haven.

*New London* was served from Worcester by Rev. James Fitton.

### 1844.

*Hartford,* Trinity Church. Rev. John Brady.

*New Haven,* Christ's Church. Rev. James Smyth.

*Bridgeport,* St. James. Rev. Michael Lynch.

*Middletown* was served from Hartford.

*New London and Norwich* were attended from Worcester by Rev. A. Williamson.

### 1845.

*Hartford,* Trinity Church. Rev. John Brady.

*New Haven,* Christ's Church. Rev. James Smyth.

*Bridgeport,* St. James. Rev. Michael Lynch.

*Middletown* served from Hartford.

*New London and Norwich* attended from Newport by Rev. James Fitton.

*Norfolk* served from Bridgeport.

After the death of Bishop Tyler, in January, 1849, the diocese was governed by Right Rev. John B. Fitzpatrick, D. D., Bishop of Boston, until the appointment of Bishop O'Reilly, in August, 1850. The priests residing in Connecticut in 1850 were:

*Hartford,* Trinity Church. Rev. John Brady, Rev. James Smyth, Rev. Luke Daly, who attended several stations.

*New Haven.* Rev. Philip O'Reilly.

*Bridgeport,* St. James. Rev. Michael Lynch.

*Middletown.* Rev. John Brady, Jr.

*Waterbury.* Rev. Michael O'Neill.

*Norwalk.* Rev. John C. Brady, who attended also Stamford, Danbury, New Milford and Canaan.

*New London, Norwich* and several adjoining stations were attended from Worcester, Mass., by the Rev. William Logan, S. J.

Cultured and refined, with an exalted idea of their mission, profoundly interested in whatever makes for the advancement of their peoples' welfare, the clergy of the diocese of Hartford are accomplishing splendid work for God, the church, and society. Faithful to duty, prompt in responding to every demand, insistent in their efforts to promote the educational interests of the children committed to their care, charitable to the needy, tender and compassionate to the sick, the strength and consolation of the dying ; the teachers of youth, the friends and guides of age; successful in composing difficulties, the arbiters between men estranged ; aggressive in their warfare against the drink habit, that giant evil that stalks insolently over the land, bringing ruin and desolation in its wake, the priests of Connecticut have attained a position of influence in the commonwealth that redounds to the glory of the diocese.     Loved by their own charges and respected by their separated brethren, they are a mighty power for the accomplishment of high and noble purposes, a stanch barrier to the progress of evil.    Thoroughly imbued with the spirit that pervades our beneficent laws, familiar with the glorious history of this republic, realizing in its full measure the blessings that flow from the religious freedom here enjoyed, it were superfluous—a work of supererogation—to proclaim here their loyalty to the institutions of our country.     Happy and prosperous, indeed, will this republic be, if in her course down through the coming years, it will be assailed by no greater foes than the priests of the Catholic Church.    The shafts of hate and jealousy may be directed against them; the poisoned darts will fall harmless at their feet.    Their ears may be assailed by shouts that come up from hearts eaten with bigotry, but, conscious of the purity of their motives and of the rectitude of their conduct, they will remain faithful to conscientious duty assured of the continued good-will of their fellow-citizens.    "By their fruits ye shall know them."   Judged by this divine standard, the priests of Connecticut and their brethren elsewhere in this favored land of ours, need not fear the hostile criticism of those whose words are not always weighed in the scales of justice.

   The first order of religious women, the Sisters of Mercy, was introduced into the diocese of Hartford in 1852, by Right Rev. Bishop O'Reilly.    The mother-house was located at Providence, R. I.   On May 12 of that year four sisters arrived at New Haven.   They were the pioneers in Connecticut of that splendid order which was destined to achieve many and wonderful works in the cause of religion and education.   They came among strangers, but their devotion to their sacred calling, their self-sacrifice, their unobtrusive piety and gentleness, their love for children and devotedness to the sick mellowed the hearts of persons of every creed.   They opened schools where children could receive a Catholic training, and gathered the helpless orphans within their protecting arms and shielded them from the misery and hardships of the world.   From four sisters in 1852, they increased to twenty-two in 1860; and in the present year, 1899, the number of religious women, including novices and postulants, in the diocese, is seven hundred and fifty. God has singularly blessed these holy women, who have made, and are still making, so many and great sacrifices for Him, whose very names are unknown to the world, who go uncomplaining to any service, and who are as patient, zealous and resigned in the midst of contagion as in the class room. For many years the spiritual daughters of Mother McAuley were alone in the field; but in the progress of the years other orders were introduced, until now there are three mother-houses of the Sisters of Mercy, besides ten other different communities in the diocese. They are: Sisters of Mercy, Mother-house, Hartford; Sisters of Mercy, Mother-house, Meriden; Sisters of Mercy, Mother-house, Middletown; Sisters of the Assumption, (Nicolet, P. Q.); Sisters of Charity, (Convent Station, N. J.); Sisters of Charity of St. Vincent de Paul, (Mt. St. Vincent on the Hudson, N. Y.); Sisters of St. Joseph, (Chambery, France); Sisters of Charity of our Lady, Mother of Mercy, (Tilburg. Holland); Sisters of St. Francis; Sisters of St. Joseph, (Flushing, New York); Sisters of the Congregation de Notre Dame, (Villa Maria, P. Q.); Sisters of the Holy Cross, (St. Laurent, P. Q.); Sisters of Notre Dame, (Baltimore, Md.)

These devoted women instruct our youth in parochial schools; tenderly care for God's cherished little ones, the orphans; nurse the sick and provide for the comfort of the aged. They are ministering angels, and their presence exhales a benediction. They are noble, efficient auxiliaries to the priesthood and their fervent prayers ascending to the mercy seat from the silence and solitude of their sanctuaries bring down many and choice blessings upon the diocese. Twenty-three thousand of our youth are being trained under their fostering care. Who will measure the extent of the good accomplished by these holy women among this number of children—almost as large as the standing army of the United States before the Spanish-American war? Entering the various walks of life they will bring to their chosen vocations both virtue and talent. Religion will be an ever-present factor in their lives, and earthly ambitions, how strong soever they may press, will become subordinate to a higher destiny, that for which man was alone created. As the maternal influence is paramount in moulding the character of children, so are the example and precepts of our Sisters of inestimable value in shaping for good the careers of our youth. They seek no worldly encomiums; they are indifferent to the plaudits of men. Content are they to labor, hidden in Christ, from whom alone they seek reward.

The laity of the diocese of Hartford have ever been conspicuous for their loyalty to holy church, for cheerful submission to diocesan laws and for respect for parish regulations. Coöperating generously with their local clergy by suggestion, advice and financial assistance, they justly participate in the glory that belongs to the diocese. It is true, that from certain sections of the diocese discordant voices have been heard from time to time, but in every instance these miniature rebellions have received the unqualified condemnation of the vast majority of the laity. Angry passion may supplant reason and obedience; the law of obedience may be disregarded and authority set at defiance; but those who thus give rein to personal feelings find little sympathy among their brethren and are subject to an ostracism that speaks its disapproval more forcibly than could word of mouth.

Seventy years ago the first Catholic parish of Connecticut was organized. It embraced the entire State. Its members were the proverbial "handful," but strong in faith, robust of physique, self-reliant and confident that the future held much in reserve. They came to stay, to cast their lot with their fellows of other lands, and to assist, as far as they could, in laying deep and strong the foundations of what is now a prosperous Commonwealth. The Catholics of Connecticut have ever manifested deep interest in whatever concerns her welfare. Zealous in guarding her fair name and in upholding her prestige, they join willing hands with their Protestant fellow-citizens in laboring for the common weal. The interests of the one are the interests of the other. Catholic citizens should not, and do not, form a separate class. Knowing their duties, and grateful for the blessings they enjoy, they have become closely identified with whatever tends to the advancement of the State's interests. In all good work they emulate their non-Catholic neighbors, who applaud their zeal and extend not sympathy merely, but generous, practical assistance. United in effort, charitable in spirit, one towards the other, scrupulously respecting each other's rights, privileges and opinions, the Catholics and Protestants of Connecticut will constitute an invincible power and are likely to achieve still greater results in the moral, intellectual and commercial spheres than have yet been wrought among us.

Our nation is justly proud of its composite character, and of the fact that its formative elements have been drawn from such branches of the

Seal of the State of Conn.

human family as were most essential to its rapid and lasting development. The different arrivals of the constructive elements were generally contemporaneous with our most pressing needs. This is especially true in regard to the Irish immigration. The nation's development demanded hewers of wood and drawers of water; men of brawn as well as men of brain. These were the factors essential in our population in the early and middle periods of our history, and poor Ireland, that prolific "Niobe of nations," longing for freedom and emancipation, sent us thousands of her sturdy sons and pure daughters to aid in building up and developing this new and rugged land. Of this beneficial accretion Connecticut received a goodly share.

The spread of Catholicity in Connecticut has kept pace with its phenomenal growth throughout the country at large. Numbering nearly one third of the entire population of the State, this fact serves to emphasize the strong words of Cardinal Manning written in 1888: "The progress, the growth, the expansion of the church in the United States within the last century is, as far as I know, without a parallel in the history of the church upon earth." This wonderful expansion is forcibly illustrated by Right Rev. J. L. Spalding, D.D., bishop of Peoria.[1] "The thirteen American colonies," says the bishop, "which a hundred years ago declared their independence of the power by which they had been founded, were intensely and thoroughly Protestant. At the breaking out of the War of Independence there were not more than twenty-five thousand Catholics in a population of three

[1] *The Religious Mission of the Irish Race*, 1880.

millions.[1] They had no bishops, they had no schools, they had no religious houses, and the few priests who were scattered among them generally lived upon their own lands, or with their kinsfolk, cowed by the fearful force of Protestant prejudice. . . . An observer who a hundred years ago should have considered the religious condition of this country, could have discovered no sign whatever that might have led him to suppose that the faith of this little body of Catholics was to have a future in the American Republic ; whereas there are many reasons for thinking that no other religion is so sure of a future here as the Catholic." The bishop continues : " The Catholic church in the United States is no longer confined to three or four counties of a single State. It is co-extensive with the country, embracing North and South, East and West. Its members are counted by millions, its priests and sacred edifices by thousands. The arch-bishops and bishops rule over eleven metropolitan and fifty-four suffragan Sees.[2] The religious homes for men and women, its colleges, academies and schools are found in every part of the Union. It has acquired the right of domicile ; it has become a part of the nation's life. It is a great and public fact, which men cannot, if they would, ignore."

The following summary exhibits the present status of the diocese :[3]

| | | | |
|---|---|---|---|
| Bishop | 1 | Students in St. Sulpice, Paris | 6 |
| Secular priests | 238 | " Eichstädt | 3 |
| Priests of religious orders | 22 | Ecclesiastical students | 50 |
| Total | 260 | Colleges and academies for boys | 1 |
| Churches with resident priest | 119 | Students | 40 |
| Churches without resident priests | 50 | Academies for young ladies | 8 |
| | | Pupils | 660 |
| Total | 169 | Parishes with parochial schools | 53 |
| Stations | 17 | Pupils | 23,000 |
| Chapels | 56 | Orphan asylums | 2 |
| Religious women, including novices and postulants | 750 | Orphans | 327 |
| | | Total number of young people under Catholic care, about | 25,000 |
| Preparatory seminary | 1 | Hospital | 1 |
| Students | 40 | Patients | 314 |
| Seminaries of religious orders | 1 | Home for the aged poor | 1 |
| Students | 75 | Inmates during the year | 88 |
| Students in Rome | 5 | Catholic population, about | 250,000 |
| " Louvain | 3 | | |

[1] In 1785 the number of Catholics in the United States was approximated as follows : In New England, about 600 ; in New York and New Jersey, about 1700 ; in Pennsylvania and Delaware, about 7700 ; in Maryland (free), 12,000, (slaves), 8000 ; States of the South, 2500 ; in Illinois, at Kaskasia and the French establishments on the Mississippi, 12,000. Total, 44,500. *Letter to Vergennes*, Minister of Foreign Affairs to Louis XVI.

[2] There are now fourteen metropolitans and seventy-three suffragans, including a Prefecture Apostolic in Alaska, in the province of Oregon.

[3] From *Catholic Directory*, Hoffman, 1899.

# INTOLERANCE IN CONNECTICUT.

## CHAPTER II.

### BLUE LAWS AND "POPERY."

THAT the Puritans of New England were severe in their treatment of those who differed from them, will not be denied even by their stanchest apologists. Severity was a conspicuous trait in the Puritan character. They enforced obedience to their laws with a rigor that has no parallel, and their enactments militated against the prerogative of personal liberty. In fact, personal liberty was a boon but little known under the harsh system of Puritan legislation. While many of the "Blue Laws" of Connecticut are pure fiction, it cannot be denied that the spirit they were intended to exhibit actually prevailed, and caused much needless hardship and suffering. A few instances drawn from our town records will illustrate the character of the laws in vogue, and the illiberal spirit prevalent in Connecticut in colonial days.

In the last quarter of the seventeenth century, a New London fisherman, was fined for catching eels on Sunday, while another offender was mulcted "twenty shillings for sailing a boat on the Lord's day." In 1670, two young Puritans, a youth and maiden, John Lewis and Sarah Chapman, were fined for "sitting together on the Lord's day, under an apple tree in Goodman Chapman's orchard." At New Haven Captain Dennison paid a fine of fifteen shillings for absenting himself from worship on Sunday, and William Blagden, also a resident of New Haven in 1647, was "publically whipped" and declared guilty of "sloathfulness" for the same offense. Another unfortunate inhabitant of New Haven was whipped and fined because he had the effrontery to say that the sermons of the minister were unproductive of spiritual fruit. For audaciously declaring, "I would rather hear my dog bark than Mr. Bellamy preach," an irreverent resident of Windham was brought to trial and formally censured for his unchristian remark. When threatened with the direful punishment of being "shaken off" and "given up," he made a recantation with much compunction of heart, promised to "keep a guard over his tongue" for the future, and to attend regularly to Mr. Bellamy's sermons. But the New Haven offences, which appear to have been numerous, reached their climax when Madam Brewster, in 1646, proclaimed that the custom of bringing the collections to the deacon's table was decidedly "popish"—it was "like going to the high altar" and "savoured of the Mass." For this grave offence the outspoken woman was tried, and we may well believe she received condign punishment. But this illiberal spirit did not expire with the seventeenth century, nor even with the eighteenth century. In the year of our Lord 1831, a young woman was arrested at Lebanon for traveling on

Sunday to her father's home. Litigation, bitter and long, followed this high-handed action, and the victim justly received damages for false imprisonment.[1]

These instances will suffice to show the narrow and illiberal spirit that pervaded the lives and permeated the legislation of our Puritan forefathers.

But, if they were severe in their domestic legislation and rigorous in the enforcement of local enactments, they displayed indefensible severity towards those who held religious opinions different from their own. In this respect their intolerance stands out in marked contrast to the very first enactment of Thomas Dongan, the Catholic colonial Governor of New York:

"No person or persons who profess faith in God by Jesus Christ shall at any time be in any way molested, punished or disquieted; but that all and every such person or persons may from time to time, and at all times, freely have and fully enjoy his or their judgments or consciences in matters of religion throughout this province."[2]

This liberality was not appreciated, for when the law-making power fell under other control a number of odious, proscriptive laws were enacted against the religion professed by Governor Dongan. Ingratitude supplemented justice.

As in New York at this period, so throughout New England; both state and church conspired to crush freedom of worship. This union was detrimental to the highest interests of both, and was destined not to endure. It was a condition of things which we to-day utterly repudiate. "State and church were both victims of the unnatural alliance; and what was begun with purest aims and invoked in prayer heaven's benediction, bore bitter fruits of intolerance and religious declension."[3]

Apologists for the Puritans in their endeavor to lessen the force of the charge of intolerance, diligently claim for them the merit of sincerity. But some of the most misguided and unsuccessful characters of history have entered the same plea. While we may grant their claim without prejudice

---

[1] Apropos of this arrest the *Press*, September 10, 1831, contained the following:

"THE GREAT OUTRAGE IN CONNECTICUT.

"The wife of Dr. T. C. Foster, of New York, was arrested in Connecticut by a certain Deacon Eliphalet Hutchinson for breaking the Lord's Day by traveling to see her father, Dr. Sweet, who resides in the 'Land of Steady Habits.' She was nearly in sight of her father's house, and was basely arrested in violation of the Constitution of the U. S., and held in durance vile till after sundown, and then permitted to depart in consideration that she would pay a fine. We hope Dr. Foster will bring the case before the Supreme Court of the U. S., and have this Sunday question settled."

Before beginning his theological studies in 1827, the late Cardinal McCloskey, Archbishop of New York, was riding horse-back one Sunday morning, during a period of convalescence, and having crossed into Connecticut was met by a constable, and asked why he was riding on the Sabbath. As he was not riding either to or from church he was obliged to recross into New York State.—*Right Rev. Bishop Farley in Historical Records and Sketches. January, 1899.*

[2] Act of Gen. Assembly, Oct. 17.

[3] Rev. E. H. Gillet, D.D., in *Hist. Mag.*, July, 1868, p. 1.

to historical accuracy, we know not how to palliate their harshness towards adherents of different creeds, nor can we disregard their incomprehensible inconsistency. "Victims of intolerance, they were themselves equally intolerant when clothed with power. Their ideas of civil and religious freedom were narrow, and their practical interpretation of the golden rule was contrary to the intention of Him who uttered it. . . . They regarded churchmen and Roman Catholics as their deadly enemies, to be kept at a distance."[1]

The Puritans of Connecticut cannot escape the reproach of cultivating the spirit of persecution. Their enactments displayed but little of the sweetness and love that shone so conspicuously in the teachings of the Master for Whom they professed such profound attachment. Others who strove to follow the Divine Exemplar with as much devotion as they, were visited with their godly wrath and fined and imprisoned and banished. What Hutchinson said of the Puritans in general is applicable to their brethren in Connecticut: "In New England it must be confessed that bigotry and cruel zeal prevailed, and to that degree that no opinions but their own could be tolerated. They were sincere, but mistaken in their principles."[2] Equally pertinent are the words of Sir Richard Saltonstall to Wilson and Cotton, two ministers of Boston: "It doth a little grieve my spirit to hear what sad things are reported daily of your tyranny and persecution in New England, as that you fine, whip, and imprison men for conscience."[3]

On September 1, 1743, Benjamin Pomeroy, minister, and pastor of the church at Hebron, made the public declaration that the laws of the colony concerning ecclesiastical affairs were a great foundation to encourage persecution and encourage wicked men to break their covenants. He also declared that "there is no colony so bad as Connecticut for persecuting laws. I never heard nor read of such persecuting laws as in Connecticut."[4] For this exercise of the precious right of private judgment, Minister Pomeroy was condemned to pay the costs of the prosecution, and to give bonds in fifty pounds to keep the peace.

And yet it was Bancroft who wrote: "There never existed a persecuting spirit in Connecticut." And again: "That heavenly man, John Haynes, would say to Roger Williams, 'I think, Mr. Williams, I must now confess to you that the most wise God hath provided and cut out this part of the world as a refuge and receptacle for all sorts of consciences.'"[5] The great historian has not drawn a faithful picture of the religious condition of the colonies under Puritan rule. It is a matter of historical record that "all sorts of consciences" were not tolerated. From across the ocean came the voice of remonstrance against Connecticut intolerance. Dr. B. Avery, of England, a very influential Dissenter, wrote to a gentleman here: "I am very sorry to hear of

[1] Lossing's *Hist. of the U. S.*, pp. 118-119.
[2] *Hist. of Mass.*, vol. I., p 175.
[3] Lossing's *Hist. of the U. S.*, p. 118.
[4] *Public Records of Conn.*, vol. IX., p. 28.
[5] *Hist. of the U. S.*, vol. II., p. 56, ed. 1841.

the persecuting spirit that prevails in Connecticut. It is unaccountable that those who live and breathe by liberty should deny it to their brethren." [1]

Letter from the Rev. Ebenezer Pemberton, pastor of the Presbyterian church, New York, to Rev. Dr. Doddridge, Northampton, England :

" NEW YORK, Dec. 16, 1743.

" The imprisonment you mention in your letter was in the government of Connecticut, a colony bordering on New York, and was of the most favorable kind : two of their preachers (Moravians) being only confined in the officer's house, till inquiry was made into their circumstances ; and upon giving security for their good behavior, they were in a day or two dismissed. This short confinement they underwent, I doubt not, was unjust, and it is melancholy for me to be obliged to say that the government of Connecticut is daily going much greater lengths than these in persecuting, not the Moravians, but the most zealous ministers in their communion, for preaching without the bounds of their respective parishes. By a late law they have enacted that every minister who does not belong to their government who shall presume to preach in any of their towns without the consent of the minister of the parish and a vote of the major part of the society, shall be transported from constable to constable to the place whence he came ; and if any minister that belongs to this government transgress in the same manner, he forfeits all his salary. This is certainly going on with a high hand, and I am greatly afraid will lay a foundation for the loss of their civil privileges, which are by far the most valuable of any of the American plantations."

There was a religion by law established, and all were bound to conform to it under severe penalties. No one could be admitted a freeman, or free burgess, within the jurisdiction of New Haven colony, but such planters as were members of some one or other of the approved churches of New England. Union of church and state existed in its strictest sense ; indeed, so closely allied were they that the history of one is a record of the other. The salaries of the ministers were paid by assessments levied upon all.[2] " Early provision was made by law for the support of the ministry. All persons were obliged to contribute to the support of the church, as well as of the Commonwealth ; the ministers' rates were made and collected like any other."[3] If " all sober, orthodox persons " who dissented from the Congregational system were allowed by the General Assembly " peaceably to worship in their own way," they were not exempt from the obligation of supporting the established religion. The modicum of religious liberty allowed to Dissenters depended upon the good will of the General Court. So intimate was the relationship between the State religion and the civil authorities that the latter made attendance at divine worship compulsory under penalty of five shillings fine, and every family was obliged to possess " bibles, orthodox catechisms and books in practical godliness."

Among the special objects of aversion to the Puritans were " some loathsome heretics, Quakers, Ranters, Adamites, or some others like them." The Quakers, particularly, were the victims of much annoyance, and stringent laws were enacted against them. To entertain them was to incur a penalty

---

[1] *Historical Magazine*, July, 1868, p. 11.

[2] Public Records of Conn., 1636-1650.

[3] Rev. Dr. Gillett, *Hist. Mag.*, July, 1868.

of five pounds a week for any town infringing the law, and the luckless disciples of George Fox were imprisoned or expelled from the colony. If the captain of a vessel brought any such heretics into port he was compelled to transport them from the colony or pay a fine of twenty pounds in case of refusal. Quaker books and manuscripts were forbidden to all save teaching elders, under penalty of ten shillings for each offence. No one could "unnecessarily speak more or less" with Quakers without forfeiting five pounds for each conversation, and any town that harbored them paid also five pounds for each Quaker entertained. Furthermore, a person could be arrested under suspicion of being a Quaker, and, if after investigation he was so adjudged, he was either imprisoned or expelled from the colony.

Such being the drastic measures taken against the Quakers at the recommendation of the Commissioners of the United Colonies, not many of them remained within the borders, and those who did so could enjoy liberty of worship only by "soberly dissenting" in approved form before the County Court; but their obligation to pay the assessments for the support of the established church remained inviolate.

The antipathy of the Puritans to foreigners is embodied in their legislation. Who were *they*? Children of the soil? Foreigners—that and nothing more; and yet with the utmost nonchalance, and in utter disregard of the proprieties, they solemnly passed enactments against others who were born beyond the seas. At the "General Courte of Election," held on May 16, 1650, it was

Ordered "that no Forreigner, after the 29th of September next, shall retaile any goods by themselves, in any place within this Jurisdiction; nor shall any Inhabitant retaile any goods w^{ch} belong to any Forreigner, for the space of one whole yeare after the said 29th of September next, uppon penalty of confiscation of the value of one halfe of the goods so retailed, to be paid by the seller of them."[1]

The spirit of persecution was abroad. Intolerance was a cardinal doctrine of the Puritan, and the foundation upon which he builded his hopes of uninterrupted rule. "The Puritan, firmly believing that he was elect of God, and that the saints must persevere, exercised but little charity towards those whom education and circumstances had taught another creed."[2] A great Puritan figure, Johnson, declared that there was "no room in Christ's army for tolerationists," and Cotton taught that toleration made the world anti-Christian. "The church never took hurt from the punishment of heretics," said another devout teacher. "'Tis Satan's policy to plead for an indefinite and boundless toleration," cried Shepard in 1672, and a year later President Oakes made this declaration: "I look upon toleration as the firstborn of all abominations." The Simple Cobbler of Agawam wrote: "He that is willing to tolerate will for a need hang God's Bible at the devil's girdle."[3]

Such being the views of the Puritans on Toleration, it is pertinent to

[1] *Public Records of Conn.*, 1636–1665.
[2] "The Puritan Commonwealth." Oliver, p., 193.
[3] *Ibid.*

inquire how fared it with our ancestors in the faith in those days? Did they feel the heavy hand of persecution? If illiberal laws were enacted against "forreigners," Quakers and others; if Protestant ministers were punished for preaching beyond their jurisdictions without license, it need excite no surprise to learn that a deeply hostile spirit prevailed against the Pope and the Catholic church. Judged by Puritan standards, but with no semblance of reason, the Church was a foreign institution, governed by a foreign potentate, and inimical to the progress of the human mind. From their point of view, but with no shadow of justice, Catholics were idolaters, grossly superstitious, held in subjection by their clergy and enveloped in spiritual and intellectual darkness. Therefore did the pious Puritan regard the Catholic with horror, a being of inferior clay, with no religious rights which the elect should recognize. The Pope was Anti-Christ, and his "authority, as such, was from the bottomless pit."[1]

Whatever savored of Catholic practice was scrupulously barred. They would have nothing in common with "Papists," and as for ceremonial worship, it was anathematized. "The Puritans aimed to differ in their worship from the Romish ceremonies as much as possible. Instead of kneeling at prayers they made it a point of propriety—if not of conscience—to stand, and they always sat at singing. Instrumental music they excluded because it was used by the Roman and English churches. . . . They observed a public fast in the spring and a Thanksgiving fast in the fall. Especial pains were taken that the fast should never be appointed on Good Friday."[2]

Unlike Massachusetts, New York and Virginia, the statute books of Connecticut were never stained with enactments against the Jesuits or other Catholic priests. What have passed current for anti-priest laws are stupid forgeries, the creation of a clergyman,[3] who was forced to leave Connecticut on account of his offensive Tory propagandism. He was a man with a grievance, and, at the sacrifice of truth, sought to cast odium upon Connecticut. As far as enactments were concerned priests could come and go without fear of molestation, though any exercise of their ministry would be an infringement

---

[1] "Will and Doom; or, the Miseries of Connecticut," by Gershom Bulkeley. in "The Peoples' Right to Election" the same author wrote in May, 1689, to the Court or Convention at Hartford: "Consider your profession; we are all Protestants. I hope there is not a Papist in our limits."

[2] *History of the Colony of New Haven*, by Edward R. Lambert, pp. 189, 190. Apropos of this antipathy to music at divine worship: 1773, April, "Voted to sing on the Lord's day in the afternoon, according to the rules taught in the Singing Schools in this and the neighboring societies."—"Simsbury Town Records."

Soon after this a teacher of music was employed. After practising some time he appeared with his scholars in church on a Sunday, and the minister, having announced the psalm, the choir, under the instructor's lead, started off with a tune much more lively than the congregation had been accustomed to hear, upon which one of the deacons, Brewster Higley, took his hat and left the house, exclaiming as he passed down the aisle, "*Popery! Popery!*"—*Phelps' History of Simsbury.*

[3] Rev. Samuel Peters. His book is known as *Peters' History of Conn.*

of the following law enacted by the General Assembly, May, 1742, for the regulation of ecclesiastical affairs :[1]

"It is further enacted, That if any foreigner, or stranger that is not an inhabitant within this Colony, including, as well, such persons that have no ecclesiastical character or license to preach as such as have received ordination or license to preach by any association or presbytery, shall presume to preach, teach or publickly to exhort, in any town or society within this Colony, without the desire and license of the settled minister and the major part of the church and inhabitants of such town or society, provided that it so happen that there is no settled minister there, that every such preacher, teacher or exhorter shall be sent (as a vagrant person) by warrant from any one assistant or justice of the peace, from constable to constable out of the bounds of this Colony."

But granting the non-existence of proscriptive enactments against priests as such, it is undeniable that the concrete sentiment of Connecticut was bitterly hostile to Catholics, and this hostility was not infrequently manifested by men of exalted station in civil life and in high position in the church. The spirit of antagonism to all things Catholic was everywhere. Children imbibed it at the maternal breast. It pervaded the religious literature of the times and inspired the philippics of the clergy. Proscription of Catholics was officially taught as a duty "for the defence of the Protestant religion and people," while "popery and slavery" were seriously joined as twin evils of equal dye.[2]

In 1689 an interchange of letters between Captain Jacob Leisler, of New York, a man of ungovernable anti-Catholic prejudices, and the General Court of Connecticut, disclosed the hostile sentiment existing against Catholics at that period.

On May 31, 1689, Captain Leisler seized Fort James at New York. He published a declaration "to keep and guard surely the said fort, in the behalf of the power that now governeth in England, to surrender to the person of the Protestant religion, that shall be nominated or sent by the power aforesaid." On June 5th, Major Gold, of Fairfield, wrote to Leisler a letter of congratulation upon the capture of the fort. In response to Gold, Leisler,

---

[1] *Pub. Records of Conn.* Vol. VIII.

[2] *Pub. Rec. of Conn., 1689.* p. 463. An address to King William III., June 13, 1689, signed by Robert Treat, Governor, by order of the General Court of Conn.

The following letter from Jesse Root to Silas Deane, dated Hartford, May 25, 1775, furnishes us with another interesting combination of powers, which throws a side light upon the anti-Catholic prejudices of the time :

"DEAR SIR :

"The troops are continually marching for Boston. . . . May that unerring wisdom that guides the rolling spheres through the unmeasurable tract of ether, that mighty power . . . inspire your venerable Body with all that wisdom and firmness that is requisite to guide and direct the important concerns of the American empire, for its safety and preservation against all craft and power of *Tyranny, the Pope and the Devil.*"—*Conn. Hist. Soc. Coll.,* Vol. II., p. 237. A troublesome combination, in truth, one that now provokes a smile.

under date of June 7th, declared that his six captains and four hundred men unanimously "agreed to the preservation of the Protestant religion and the fort for the present Protestant power that now raigns in England." On June 13th the General Court of Connecticut ordered a letter to be despatched to Leisler, which contained among other matters this paragraph:[1]

"Gent," considering what you haue (have) don we doe adu(v)ise that you keep the fort tenable and well manned for the defence of the Protestant religion and those ends above mentioned, and that you suffer *no roman Catholick to enter the same armed or without armes, and that no romish Catholick be suffered to keep armes within your government or citty*, and that those whoe shall be betrusted with the government or command of your forte be trusty persons whome you may confide in." This document was signed

"THE GENERALL COURT OF CONNECTICOT,
" Per their order signed,
"JOHN ALLYN, Secret'y."

It was an official paper sent forth by the highest authority in the State, and was representative of the religious prejudices then extant against Catholics in Connecticut. It expressed precisely the proscriptive policy of the General Court against a class of persons who worshiped fervently and in spirit and in truth the same God as they, and who in the upbuilding and in the perpetuation of this republic gave freely of their warm, generous blood. Catholics coming into Connecticut could expect no toleration nor demand the recognition of any rights from a government that could proffer such illiberal counsel to another colony. The principle of hate was dominant.

## CHAPTER III.

### THE CONFESSION OF FAITH.

THE same deleterious influence that moved the General Court to transmit the above-named letter to Captain Leisler, actuated the Protestant Dissenters of Connecticut in their rejection of the Indulgence granted by Charles II, "that all manner of penal laws on matters ecclesiastical, against whatever sort of non conformists or recusants should be suspended."[2] This act of toleration aroused an opposition so acrimonious that Charles was forced to modify his grant, and to promise "that no Catholic should profit by the indulgence." The Protestant dissenters of Connecticut would forego the boon of freedom of worship if the privilege was extended to Catholics. The "Romish" church must be eliminated from any plan that would grant to dissenters liberty of conscience. Catholics were not members of the great family of Christ, and were beyond the religious pale. They were not of the household of the elect, nor were they fit subjects for toleration. Their political loyalty was suspected, and their religious doctrines, more precious than life itself, were branded as idolatrous and otherwise denounced with a degree of bitter-

[1] *Colonial Records of Conn.*, 1678–1689.
[2] *New Haven Hist. Soc. Papers*, Vol. III. p. 391. *Green's Hist. of the English People.*

ness incomparable in its intensity. And this pernicious spirit of intolerance found official expression in the "Confession of Faith, Owned and Consented to by the Elders and Messengers of the Churches in the Colony of Connecticut, in New England; assembled by delegation at Saybrook, September 9, 1708." The Assembly sent forth the Confession as "our firm persuasion, well and fully grounded upon the Holy Scripture, and commend the same unto all, *and particularly to the people of our Colony*, to be examined, accepted, and constantly maintained."[1]

But wherein lies the intolerance of the Saybrook Confession of Faith? In what are its decrees antagonistic to Catholic dogmas and offensive to Catholic ears? In Chapter XXIII. "Of Lawful Oaths and Vows," is the following decree:

"Papist monastical vows of perpetual single life, professed poverty, and regular obedience, are so far from being signs of higher perfection, that they are superstitious and sinful snares in which no Christian may entangle himself."

Thus at a stroke, and with an infallibility denied to the Pope, the whole economy of the monastic system was abolished. Chastity in the religious life, obedience and evangelical poverty were officially repudiated. The celibacy of the priesthood, that disciplinary law so precious in the sight of the Catholic laity, was branded as a superstition and a snare. And yet the godly framers of this Confession protested earnestly their faith in the authority of Holy Scripture "which ought to be believed and obeyed." "The whole counsel of God," they declared, "concerning all things necessary for His own glory, man's salvation, faith and life, is either expressly set down in Scripture, or by good and necessary consequence may be deduced from Scripture."[2] With this protestation in mind, it is a perplexing task to reconcile the above decree with the teachings of the Old and the New Testaments. They are not only contradictory; the decree is indefensible.[3] The higher spiritual life obtainable only by freedom from the cares of the world appealed as lightly to the Saybrook elders as did the plain, unequivocal words of St. Paul: "For I would that all men were even as myself . . . . But I say to the unmarried and to the widows: it is good for them if they do continue, even as I."[4]

The Confession abhors the Pope and is intolerant of his claims; it endeavors to perpetuate the fiction that he is Anti-Christ. Under the title "Of the Church"—Chapter xxvi.—we read that

"There is no other head of the Church but the Lord Jesus Christ; nor can the Pope of Rome in any sense be head thereof, but is that Anti-Christ, that man of sin and son of perdition that exalteth himself in the Church against Christ and all that is called God, whom the Lord shall destroy with the brightness of his coming."

[1] From the *Preface* to the *Confession*.

[2] The *Confession*. Chapter I.

[3] Continency possible, Matt. xix. 11, 12; the vow binding, Deut. xxiii. 21; the breach of that vow damnable, 1 Tim. v. 12; the practice commended, 1 Cor. vii. 7, 8, 27, 37, 38, 40; for reasons which particularly have place in the clergy, v. 32, 33, 35.

[4] 1 Cor. vii. 7, 8.

This decree which exhales so much sweetness and Christian charity was built upon a perversion of certain texts of Holy Writ [1] and is a repudiation of St. John's counsel to love one another in deed and in truth.[2]

But it is upon the Holy Sacrifice of the Mass—that Clean Oblation that is offered in every place from the rising of the sun even to the going down [3]—that the vials of their wrath are emptied. To Catholics the Mass is the most profound, the most exalted act of homage a creature can pay to the Creator. It is the center of all religious worship. Toward it converge the heart offerings of the faithful; from it radiate the choicest and purest graces and blessings; around it cluster all the sweet yet sad memories of Calvary. And yet all who sat beneath the shadow of Congregational pulpits were officially taught that

"The Popish sacrifice of the Mass (as they call it) is most abominably injurious to Christ's own, only sacrifice, the alone propitiation for all the sins of the elect." [4]

Concerning private Masses the Confession made this declaration:

"Private Masses, or receiving the Sacrament by a Priest, or any other alone, as likewise the denial of the cup to the people, worshiping the elements, the lifting them up or carrying them about for adoration, and reserving them for any pretended religious use, are all contrary to the nature of this Sacrament, and to the institution of Christ."

Of Transubstantiation it defined as follows:

"That doctrine which maintains a change of the substance of bread and wine into the substance of Christ's body and blood, (commonly called Transubstantiation) by consecration of a Priest, or by any other way, is repugnant not to the Scripture alone, but even to common sense and reason, overthroweth the nature of the Sacrament, and hath been, and is the cause of manifold superstitions, yea, of gross idolatries."

The Confession contains also decrees concerning marriage. It declares it the duty of Christians to marry in the Lord and that those who profess the reformed religion "should not marry with infidels, papists, or other idolaters." [5] Verily, the devout Puritans had a wonderful penchant for the construction of forceful combinations. They proclaimed sonorously that "God alone is Lord of the conscience," [6] and then arrogated to themselves the control of conscience. They declared effusively that it was their "duty to bear a Christian respect to all Christians, according to their several ranks and relations, that are not of our persuasion or communion," and forthwith compiled a series of un-Christian decrees against the most ancient organization in Christendom. In the light of the above decrees how inconsistent and insincere appear their grandiloquent protestations that the New England colonies "were originally formed, not for the advantage of trade, or worldly interest; but upon the most noble foundation, even of religion, and the *Liberty of their Consciences.*" Liberty of Conscience? For Protestant dissenters,

---

[1] Matt. xxiii. 8–10; 2 Thess. ii. 3, 4, 8, 9; Apoc. xiii. 6.     [2] 1 St. John iii.
[3] Malachias i. 11.     [4] Chapt. xxx.     [5] Chapt. xxv.     [6] Chapt. xxi.

granted. For Catholics, it was peremptorily refused. It was a strange toleration that made Catholicism synonymous with infidelity and idolatry. The laws permitting dissent explicitly included all Protestants, and by implication excluded Catholics. The enactment of May, 1743, is plain:

"*And be it further enacted*, That, for the future, that if any of his Majesty's good subjects, *being Protestants*, inhabitants of this Colony, that shall soberly dissent from the way of worship and ministry *established by the laws of this Colony*, that such persons may apply themselves to this Assembly for relief, where they shall be heard." [1]

## CHAPTER IV.

### ANTI-CATHOLIC SENTIMENT.

THE antipathy of the colonists to the Irish people was well exemplified in Voluntown, Connecticut, in 1722. In this instance the object of their aversion was a Presbyterian minister. Their opposition, of course, was not directed to his religion, but against his nationality. He was a son of the Emerald Isle. When hostility so pronounced could be manifested against a Protestant because he was an Irishman, to what extent would it not have gone had the person been an Irish Catholic, especially a Catholic priest?

In the above named year the Rev. Samuel Dorrance arrived in Voluntown, and was duly installed as rector of the church. The installation aroused bitter opposition. The discontented of the parish drew up a protest, which they forwarded to the officers of the church. It is a characteristic document.

"We, whose names are underwritten, do agree that one of our New England people may be settled in Voluntown to preach the Gospel to us, and will oblige ourselves to pay him yearly, and will be satisfied, honorable gentlemen, that your choose for us, to prevent unwholesome inhabitants, for we are afraid that Popery and heresy will be brought into the land; therefore, we protest against settling Mr. Dorrance, because he is a stranger, and we are informed he came out of Ireland, and we do observe that since he has been in town *the Irish do flock into town*, and we are informed that the Irish are not wholesome inhabitants, and upon this account we are against settling Mr. Dorrance, for we are not such persons as you take us for, but desire the Gospel to be preached by one of our own, and not by a stranger, for we cannot receive any benefit, neither of soul nor of body, and we would pay him to withdraw himself from us." [2]

The Rev. Mr. Lyons, of Derby, a minister of the church of England, was also the recipient of unmeasured abuse on account of his Irish birth. Writing to London, May 8, 1744, he said: "As soon as they had advice of my appointment, and from what country I came, and, indeed, before I arrived among them, they abused me, calling me an 'Irish Teague and Foreigner,'

[1] *Public Records of Conn.* Vol. VIII.
[2] Larned's "Hist. of Windham Co.," Vol. I., p. 25.

with many other reflections of an uncivilized and unchristian kind . . . . It would be too tedious to record all the abuse and insults I have received at Derby."[1]

The Puritan's opposition to the Catholic church was blind, intense; it carried him to ridiculous extremes, so far, in fact, as to deny to priests any spiritual power whatever. To him the ministrations of the priest were of no value. Not content with framing decrees that outraged the religious feelings of Catholics, and which were entirely inconsistent with the teachings of Holy Scripture, he refused to recognize the efficacy of the priesthood. In 1744, there occurred a case in point, when the Windham County Association, an organization comprising all the ministers of that county, after vigorously wrestling with the spirit, solemnly voted that "Baptism by a Popish priest is not to be held valid."[2] This sapient decision well illustrates the narrowness of the religious views then prevalent. If baptism administered by a priest conferred no grace, if it failed to cleanse the soul from original sin, which is the end for which the sacrament was instituted by Jesus Christ, then were all other spiritual acts performed by priests equally valueless. In this instance the hatred of the Windham County Association outran itself.

Further evidence of this anti-Catholic spirit that pervaded Connecticut in the early days of our history is found in an enactment of the General Assembly, May, 1724, which made it obligatory upon all members of the Assembly, and all persons who were or would be chosen on the annual days of election to the office of governor, deputy-governor, assistants, secretary, treasurer, and by all justices of the peace, sheriffs and their deputies, to make and take the declaration against "Popery" before they could become eligible to discharge the services belonging to their place, office or trust.[3]

This act breathes the identical spirit that made Irish Catholics outlaws in the seventeenth and eighteenth centuries and exposed them to the severest treatment which the hostility of their enemies could devise. This spirit crossed the water with the very framers of these anti-Catholic enactments. Proclaiming loudly and advocating strenuously the principles of religious freedom and equality, their unjust laws against all who differed from them, but particularly against adherents of the Catholic church, gave little evidence of the sincerity of their professions of equality and love of freedom, and have left upon their names the stain of intolerance. Enactments like the one in question effectually closed to Catholics all the avenues to official dignities, and kept them socially in a condition of inferiority in the estimation of their Protestant brethren. They could not aspire to positions of public trust with-

[1] Church Documents of the Prot. Episcopal Ch., Vol. I., p. 208.

[2] "Contributions to the Eccles. Hist. of Conn.," p. 338.

[3] Pub. Rec. of Conn., 1717-1725. Renunciation of the Pope was an indispensable requirement for all occupying public offices. When the General Assembly of Connecticut in May, 1669, acknowledged their allegiance to King Charles II, they "professed their duty and true allegiance to our Sovereign Lord *the King, renouncing the Pope* and all other foreign princes, states and potentates, and their jurisdiction and authority." The Public Records abound in instances of such renunciations.

out renouncing one of the holiest doctrines of their religion, and denying the existence of a mystery around which cluster all acts of divine worship. Truly this oath of abjuration and the declaration against " Popery " were, as they were intended to be, mighty agencies of proselytism, and may have wrought sad spiritual havoc among the weak in faith. The distinctively Irish Catholic names read on the colonial rosters inclines us to the belief that faith was sacrificed to position and influence, and that the Oath and the Declaration were contributing causes.

These obnoxious and un-Christian oaths are herewith appended that the Catholics of this generation may learn with how little of the milk of human kindness the Puritan heart was nourished. They will remind them of the obstacles thrown in the pathway of their co-religionists in the colonial period, and will furnish them with the knowledge of the toleration then enjoyed, and about which so much eloquence has been expended.

" Be it enacted by the Governor, Council and Representatives in General Court assembled, and by the authority of the same, that the oaths provided by Act of Parliament instead of the oaths of allegiance and supremacy, the Declaration against popery, and also the oath of Abjuration, agreeable to the form prescribed by a late act of Parliament, passed in the sixth year of his present Majesty's reign, be printed with the acts of this Assembly ; which are as follows :

" I, A. B., do swear that I do from my heart abhor, detest and abjure, as impious and heretical, that damnable doctrine and position, that princes excommunicated or deprived by the Pope, or any authority of the See of Rome, may be deposed, murthered by their subjects, or any other whatsoever. And I do declare, that no foreign prince, person, prelate, state or potentate, hath or ought to have any jurisdiction, power, superiority, pre-eminence or authority, ecclesiastical or spiritual, within the realm of Great Britain : So help me God.

" I, A. B., do solemnly and sincerely in the presence of God profess, testifie and declare, that I do believe that in the sacrament of the Lord's Supper there is not any transubstantiation of the elements of bread and wine into the body and blood of Christ, at or after the consecration thereof of any person whatever , and that the invocation or adoration of the Virgin Mary or any other Saint, and the sacrifice of the Mass, as they are now used in the Church of Rome, are superstitious and idolatrous. And I do solemnly, in the presence of God, profess, testifie and declare, that I do make this declaration and every part thereof in the plain and ordinary sense of the words read unto me, as they are commonly understood by English Protestants, without any evasion, equivocation, or mental reservation whatsoever, and without any dispensation already granted me for this purpose by the Pope or any authority or person whatsoever, and without any hope of any such dispensation from any authority or person whatsoever, or without thinking that I am or can be acquitted before God or man, or absolved of this declaration or any part thereof, although the Pope or any other person or persons whatsoever should dispense with or annul the same, or declare that it was null or void from the beginning."

These oaths had to be taken also by Catholic aliens as a condition of naturalization,[1] the taking of which *ipso facto* separated them from the communion of the Catholic church. They are conclusive evidence of the difficulties and temptations that beset the Catholic people who came to Connecticut in early times. They bear irrefragable testimony to the hostility of the

[1] See page 62.

colonies to the Catholic church and her sacred doctrines. The spirit of persecution was rife. Catholics were ostracized and denied the privileges of citizenship, unless, recreant to sacred trusts and teachings, they sacrificed the tenderest and holiest relations in life. I believe that the Catholics who may have taken these oaths, and thus abandoned the church, were moved thereto more by worldly motives than from a belief in the errancy of the church's doctrines. Aiming at success along commercial and social lines, they made their eternal interests subservient to temporal concerns and bequeathed to their descendants the legacy of a strange faith.

These oaths remained in force until the Revolution, and, if their operation was suspended, it was not from a sense of justice to Catholics, or from a conversion to the idea that Catholics had any rights which Puritans were bound to respect. The colonies needed the assistance of their Catholic brethren to successfully resist English oppression; therefore, to demand from them the taking of offensive oaths would be, to say the least, an incongruous proceeding. The Catholics residing in the colonies repaid the harsh and intolerant treatment, of which they were the victims, by rushing to the defence of the American cause. They gave generously of their strength and wealth to cast off the British yoke, and to achieve the independence of the colonies. They shed their blood and left their bodies on many battlefields as though oblivious of the fact that iniquitous laws were ever enacted against them. Here was true manliness, generosity, nobility of character. Here was manifested a spirit which the stern and narrow Puritan may have admired, but could not imitate.

Though Catholics could become naturalized during the Revolutionary period without being required to apostatize from the faith of the fathers, it was only in 1818, one hundred and thirty-five years after Governor Dongan's famous decree of toleration, that a liberal Christian spirit triumphed in Connecticut. In that year the death knell of exclusive religious privileges was sounded, and the union of church and state became a memory. The constitution of the State was then adopted by a vote of 13,918 in its favor, and 12,364 opposed to its ratification. In the Declaration of Rights, article first, section third, it was declared that "The exercise and enjoyment of religious profession and worship, *without discrimination*, shall forever be free to all persons in this State, provided that the right hereby declared and established shall not be so construed as to excuse acts of licentiousness, or to justify practices inconsistent with the peace and safety of the State."

And in section four, that "No preference shall be given by law to any Christian sect or mode of worship."

Section first of article seventh is an elaboration of these ideas and reads in part thus: "It being the duty of all men to worship the Supreme Being, the Great Creator or Preserver of the Universe, and their right to render that worship in the mode most consistent with the dictates of their consciences, no person shall by law be compelled to join or support, nor be classed with, or associated to, any congregation, church, or religious association."

The Constitution of this State is an utter repudiation of the governmental system of the Puritans, a rejection of the policy that united church and state ; it was a splendid step forward in the march of human progress. It was the recognition of a principle as old as the race, but ignored by some of the founders of the New England colonies, namely, that every individual has an inalienable right to worship God as his conscience dictates. It was, furthermore, an official rebuke to the legislation which compelled Catholics to forswear allegiance to their faith in order to acquire the privileges of citizenship.

## CHAPTER V.

### "POPE DAY."

THE spirit of hostility to Catholics that prevailed throughout Connecticut previous to the Revolution was in no way more clearly demonstrated than in the ridiculous celebration of " Pope Day," as it was designated, on the 5th of November. The celebration was intended to perpetuate the memory of the conspiracy known as the *Gunpowder Plot.* Catholics were accused of the crime of plotting to blow up King James I. and the houses of Parliament in 1605. Impartial history, however, has absolved them from the responsibility of the crime. The conspiracy was planned by Minister Cecil, a Protestant, and discovered by Lord Montagle, a Catholic peer. King James had been baptized in the Catholic church and received Confirmation from the hands of a Catholic bishop. He surrendered, at least outwardly, his religion at the bidding of the laws of Scotland, but he inwardly retained his love and attachment for the ancient faith. He spoke of the Roman church as the " mother church," and of the pope as " the chief bishop of all the western churches." This unconcealed regard for the Catholic church was offensive to his ministers, particularly to Cecil, who resolved upon a plan that would turn the king against his Catholic subjects, and perhaps alienate him from the church. Of the heinous Gunpowder Plot one author says that " he (Cecil) was either himself the author or, at least, the main conductor."[1] Another calls it " a neat device of the Secretary."[2] " Cecil engaged some Papists in this desperate Plot," says another, " in order to divert the King from making any advances towards Popery, to which he seemed inclinable, in the minister's opinion."[3] Another Protestant authority wrote " that this design was first hammered in the forge of Cecil, who intended to have produced it in the time of Elizabeth : that by his secret emissaries he enlisted some hot-headed men, who, ignorant whence the design first came, heartily engaged in it."[4] The few Catholics who were seduced into the plot were apostates and were known as such. Of them a Protestant writer says : " There were a few wicked and desperate wretches, whom many Protestants termed Papists, although the priests and true Catholics knew them not as such ; nor can any Protestant say that any one of them was such as the law terms popish recusants ; and if any of them were Catho-

---

[1] Politicians' Catechism.     [2] The author of the Political Grammar.
[3] Stowe & Echard.     [4] Short View of Hist. Eng., by Higgons.

lies, or so died, they were known Protestants not long before."[1]  Cecil, then, and not Catholics, was the prime instigator of the dastardly Gunpowder Plot, notwithstanding that the Anglican church thanked God for the king's escape "from the secret contrivances and hellish malice of popish conspirators." However, the plot was charged against the Catholics; that was sufficient; the consequences hoped for would naturally follow.  The 5th of November became a gala day.  What with processions, bonfires, the ringing of bells, denunciatory harangues and other appropriate features, the day was given up to unlimited abuse of the pope and of Catholics in general.  The spirit of the celebration crossed the sea and received a cordial welcome in the English colonies of New England.  The 5th of November became as sacred to the Englishman of the colonies as to his brethren at home, and the day was annually observed with ceremonies as grotesque as they were offensive.

> " Let's always remember
> The fifth of November,"

was their refrain, and the name " Pope Day " was substituted in New England for "Gunpowder Plot."  Guy Fawkes was set aside for the pope, whose effigy was carried in procession through the streets with another effigy of the devil amid the derisive shouts and laughter and curses of the fanatical mob. Money was demanded from every house on the route of the procession, and if refused, windows were broken, doors smashed in and other damage done to property.  The money collected in this manner was spent for liquor.

> " Don't you hear my little bell[2]
> Go clink, clink, clink ?
> Please give me a little money
> To buy my Pope some drink,"

was sung by one of the leaders as a preliminary to the collection.  When the boisterous mob became surfeited with noise and strong drink, the effigies were taken to a public square and committed to the flames.  The chief offender in this annual absurdity in Connecticut was New London.  For many years the rougher element there celebrated the 5th of November.  The town authorities strove to abolish the custom.  On December 27, 1768, the following vote was passed at a town meeting :

" Whereas, the custom that has of late years prevailed in this town of carrying about the Pope, in celebration of the 5th of November, has been attended with very bad consequences, and pregnant with mischief and much disorder, which therefore to prevent for the future, *voted* that every person or persons that shall be in any way connected in making or carrying about the same, or shall knowingly suffer the same to be made in their possessions, shall forfeit fifteen shillings to the town treasury of New London, to be recovered by the selectmen of said town for the use aforesaid."

Notwithstanding this vote the celebration was of annual occurrence, with few exceptions, for thirteen years after; and it was finally discontinued only

---

[1] Prot. Plea for Priests, 1621.

[2] J. G. Shea, in " U. S. Cath. Hist. Mag.," January, 1888 ; Caulkins' "Hist. of New London."

when Washington, with characteristic liberality, issued a general order condemning and forbidding the absurd custom in the army. His order is dated November 5th, and shows how much the Father of his Country towered above many of his fellows:

"As the Commander-in-Chief has been apprized of a design formed for the observance of the ridiculous and childish custom of burning the effigy of the Pope, he cannot help expressing his surprise that there should be officers and soldiers in this army so void of common sense as not to see the impropriety of such a step at this juncture; at a time when we are soliciting, and have really obtained the friendship and alliance of the people of Canada, whom we ought to consider as brethren embarked in the same cause— the defence of the liberty of America. At this juncture and under such circumstances, to be insulting their religion, is so monstrous as not to be suffered or excused; indeed, instead of offering the most remote insult, it is our duty to address public thanks to these our brethren, as to them we are indebted for every late happy success over the common enemy in Canada."[1]

The colonies were then fighting valiantly for independence. Catholics and Protestants stood side by side in that struggle. Moreover, a powerful Catholic nation had sent money, ships and men to aid the revolutionary patriots to throw off the English yoke. Washington rose equal to the occasion and realized how utterly incongruous were such celebrations, and how offensive it would be to his Catholic allies.

The order of the Commander-in-Chief sounded the knell of Pope Day. It passed out of existence and soon became a memory. In New London the custom of annual processions was adhered to, but the traitor Benedict Arnold was substituted for the Pope, and publicly burned in effigy on the 6th of September, the anniversary of his sacking the city.

## CHAPTER VI.

### THE CONNECTICUT "OBSERVER" AND THE KNOW-NOTHINGS.

THOUGH the provisions of the State Constitution concerning religion were redolent of true progress, the spirit of bigotry still moved on apace. Not infrequently it showed itself in high places. It was nourished and strengthened by jealousy. It could not look with favor upon the spectacle of men worshiping God in accordance with the dictates of conscience. In the first quarter of the present century the signs indicated that Catholicity had come to stay. The descendants of the Puritans looked askance upon its development, and with characteristic illiberality forebode dire evils to the State. By cruel insinuations and by open accusations expressly manufactured for the purpose, they sought to influence the lowest passions of the human breast against their Catholic fellow-citizens. The *Connecticut Observer* was the self-appointed mouthpiece of this opposition, the chief offender in this crusade against a respectable body of persons, whose only offence was their profession of the Catholic religion. It was an active member of that class, so numerous in the early days, who apprehended grave dangers to the republic from the

[1] *Washington's Works*, Vol. III., p. 144.

introduction of the Catholic faith. In July, 1829, it gave vent to the feelings that were consuming it as follows :

" *Romanism in Connecticut*—We understand that a Roman Catholic press has just arrived in this city ; whether sent by the institution propaganda *de fide*, or not, we are unable to say. How will it read in history, that in 1829, Hartford, in the State of Connecticut, was made the centre of a Roman Catholic mission?"

Bishop Fenwick was on a missionary trip to Hartford when this appeared, and in the initial number of the *Catholic Press*, picked up the gauntlet which the Rev. Mr. Hooker had thrown into the arena.

"The *Catholic Press*," said the Bishop, "had not yet issued its first number, when the above article was read in the *Connecticut Observer* of this day (July 11, 1829). The editors take this early opportunity to thank the gentleman conducting that paper for the notice he has been pleased to take of the arrival of their *Press ;* and at the same time beg leave to answer the question subjoined, viz.: 'How will it read in history, that in 1829, Hartford, in the State of Connecticut, was made the centre of a Roman Catholic mission?' The editors of the *Press* assure him that it will read exceedingly well. They have it likewise in their power to state, that the Propaganda at Rome are in no manner concerned *in their Press*—that the same was purchased with American money, and will be under the control of American talent." The Bishop then paid his compliments to the Rev. Editor of the *Observer* for his use of an offensive epithet thus : "What does the gentleman mean by the word *Romanism?* Is it intended for a sneer ? If so, we shall let the matter rest with the gentleman's own sense of propriety. Or did he really believe that the word truly designated our religious profession ? If so, he may with great propriety say to himself in the language of Sallust : *jam pridem amissimus vera vocabula rerum.*" The Bishop's gentle answer turned not away the wrath of the *Observer*. It continued its offensive tirades, each article surpassing its predecessor in virulence. To the sapient *Observer*, Catholicity was synonymous with unpardonable error, gross ignorance and disloyalty. Its one object was the elimination of the church from Connecticut life. To this end were its energies directed, but with what success is now evident. Like all things human, the *Observer* has passed from existence, while the institution it assailed still maintains its youthful vigor, glorious in the record of its achievements, and flourishing like the proverbial sweet bay tree.[1]

The anti-Catholic and un-American crusade conducted by the *Connecticut Observer* was continued with more or less acerbity by individuals and organizations, who cheated themselves into the belief that they had been invested

[1] The following card was placarded in public places in Hartford on January 13, 1831:

TO THE PUBLIC.

Be it known unto you far and near, that all Catholics, and all persons in favor of the Catholic Church are a set of vile imposters, liars, villians, and cowardly cut-throats. (Beware of false Doctrine).

I bid defiance to that villian—the Pope.          "A TRUE AMERICAN."
—*The Catholic Press*, January 22, 1831.

with a mission to hamper the progress of Catholicity in the State. One organization in particular, very properly called the *Know-Nothings*[1] were violent enemies of Catholics and the Catholic church. Their platform was, "No quarter to Catholics;" their slogan, "None but Americans on guard to-night." One of their objects was to prevent Catholic citizens from holding office, and they sought to frame a law that foreign-born citizens should reside twenty-one years in the country before being invested with the privilege of franchise. The insensate rage of their predecessors against Catholics carried them to the extreme of burning churches and other Catholic buildings in Philadelphia and a convent in Charlestown, Massachusetts.[2] Their hatred was particularly directed against defenceless women, Catholic nuns, those angels of mercy, whose tender ministrations have soothed the final moments of thousands of Catholics and Protestants alike, and who have always commanded the profound respect and veneration of men worthy of the

[1] The Know-Nothings were the successors of the Native American party of 1844. Its ritual, was entitled "The Know-Nothing Ritual, or Constitution of the Grand Council of the United States. Adopted unanimously, June 17, 1855, the anniversary of the Battle of Bunker's Hill."

Article I. was as follows: "This organization shall be known by the name and title of the Grand Council of the United States of North America, and its jurisdiction and power shall extend to all the districts and territories of the United States of North America."

Article II. A person to become a member of any subordinate council must be twenty-one years of age ; he must believe in the existence of a Supreme Being as the Creator and Preserver of the universe ; he must be a native-born citizen, a Protestant, born of Protestant parents, reared under Protestant influence and not united in marriage with a Roman Catholic."

The objects of the organization were: "To resist the insidious policy of the Church of Rome and other foreign influence against the institutions of our country by placing in all offices in the gift of the people, or by appointment, none but native-born Protestant citizens."

### THE OATH.

"You, and each of you, of your own free will and accord, in the presence of Almighty God and these witnesses, your right hand resting on this Holy Bible and cross, and your left hand raised toward heaven in token of your sincerity, do solemnly promise and swear that you will *not make known* to any person or persons any of the signs, secrets, mysteries or objects of this organization ; . . . that you will in all things, political or social, comply with the will of the majority. . . . . You furthermore promise and declare that you will not vote, nor join your influence, for any man for any office in the gift of the people, unless he be an American-born citizen, in favor of Americans' born ruling America, nor if he be a Roman Catholic ; and that you will not, under any circumstances, expose the name of any member of this order, nor reveal the existence of such an organization. To all the foregoing you bind yourself under the no less penalty than that of being expelled from this order, and of having your name posted and circulated throughout all the different Councils of the United States as a perjurer and as a traitor to God and your country, as a being unfit to be employed and trusted, countenanced or supported in any business transaction, as a person unworthy of the confidence of all good men, and as one at whom the finger of scorn should ever be pointed. So help you, God."

[2] In Philadelphia on May 6, 1844, a riot broke out, during which two Catholic churches, one Catholic seminary, two Catholic parsonages, and a Theological Library were destroyed by fire.

name. In Connecticut the Know-Nothings burned no churches or convents, though they did direct their poisoned shafts against the Catholic Sisterhood. They aimed at political power and having obtained it, to the humiliation of the State, in 1855, made use of it to outrage their fellow Catholic citizens. Faithful to their policy of proscription, they secured the passage of a law disbanding all the Irish volunteer companies in the State.[1] One of the companies affected by this iniquitous law was the Washington-Erina Guards of New Haven, all of whose members were intelligent, respectable and loyal Catholic American citizens. They had been charged with no breach of military discipline. They had given no sign of disloyalty to the state or the nation; nor were they paid the poor compliment of facing a manufactured accusation. They were Irishmen and Catholics. Surely these were offences grave enough in the eyes of the patriotic Know-Nothings then in power. That it was the race and creed of the Guards that brought about their disbandment is evident from the fact, that the German companies then in the State were not molested. Had they been Catholics, they, too, would have shared the fate of their New Haven brethren.

The summary disbandment of the Guards was accomplished by the following order :

"ADJUTANT-GENERAL'S OFFICE,
"*Hartford, Sept. 25th, 1855.*

" *Thomas W. Cahill, Esq., Captain Commanding Company E, 2d Regt. Connecticut Militia :*

"SIR : By order of the Commander-in-Chief, Infantry Company E, 2d Regt. Connecticut Militia, is this day disbanded.

"In pursuance of the above order you are hereby directed to deliver all of the property belonging to this State, in your possession, to the Quartermaster-General at the State arsenal, at Hartford.

"Yours, &c.,      "J. S. WILLIAMS, *Adjt.-Genl.*"

For six years this obnoxious law remained upon the statute books of Connecticut, a stain upon the escutcheon of the State. For six years the Irish Catholics of the State lived with the official brand of suspicion upon them. They were regarded as unfit persons to carry arms. But grim war is a great leveler of distinctions. It brought to Connecticut a realization of the

---

[1] The Know-Nothings were successful this year also in Massachusetts and New Hampshire. In the former State Governor Gardiner, faithful to his principles, disbanded the Irish military organizations of the State. John Mitchell was at that time editor of the *Citizen*, and had this to say of the Governor's action :

"Since the *Citizen* was established, seeing that the existence of separate Irish, German and Native-American companies could not be helped, we have earnestly impressed upon the Irish soldier that he bears arms solely for his adopted country, whose laws he is bound to obey, and whose flag and constitution he is to defend with his life. We have loudly condemned the anomaly and absurdity of what is called the 'Irish' vote (another mischief invented and used by American politicians), and exhorted our countrymen not to vote in masses or batches as Irishmen, nor suffer electioneering intriguers to 'make capital' of them by a few blarneying phrases. . . . But to submit to no brand of inferiority, no shadow of disparagement at the hand of these natives. . . . We are happy to find that Colonel Butler, of Lowell, refuses to brook the outrage. He declines to transmit the order for disbandment, invites a court-martial and appeals to the law. And the Shields Artillery, of Boston, have taken like action in the case."

gross injustice it had done to a numerous and respectable body of its citizens, and the famous war Governor, William A. Buckingham, was prompt to repair the great wrong of his predecessor, William T. Minor.

In 1861, at the outbreak of the Rebellion, Connecticut was called upon for its quota of troops. The military branch of the State government was at that time in a condition of deplorable inefficiency. Fully cognizant of this state of affairs, it occurred to Governor Buckingham to appeal to his Irish fellow-citizens to organize a regiment of their own. But with the memory of the law of 1855 still fresh would they accept the invitation? The governor's request was made known to Captain Cahill, who returned this dignified reply: "Six years ago I was captain of a company of volunteer militia and a native of New England. I was, with my comrades, thought to be unfit to shoulder a musket in time of peace, and the company was disbanded by order of the then governor of the State, under circumstances peculiarly aggravating to military pride. The law by which we were disbanded still stands on the Statute Book, and so long as it is there my fellow-soldiers and myself feel it to be an insult to us, and to all our fellow-citizens of Irish birth and Catholic faith. If we were not fit to bear arms in time of peace, we might be dangerous in time of war." When this reply of the distinguished captain was brought to the governor he caused a bill to be introduced into the Assembly repealing the Know-Nothing law of 1855. It passed the House by a unanimous vote, and in the same morning it met with equal success in the Senate. Justice was done to the Irish Catholics of the State, and an infamous enactment was stricken from the records. On September 3, 1861, Governor Buckingham commissioned Captain Cahill to organize a regiment, and the glorious, fighting Ninth, known in the military annals of the State as "the Irish Regiment" went to the front to fight, and, if need be, to die for the maintenance of the Union. The Irish people of Connecticut forgot the harsh treatment to which they were subjected, as *seven thousand nine hundred* of them donned the blue and went to the Southland in response to their country's call. In this way they repaid the ostracism inflicted upon them by their Know-Nothing contemporaries.

The hostility displayed towards Irish Catholics by Governor Minor's administration was the last official recognition in Connecticut of the odious principle that because an individual is a Catholic, therefore must his loyalty to the republic be suspected. Never again shall such a law as the one above referred to, blot the public records of our commonwealth. Since then, however, various organizations have from time to time sprung into being, all animated with a common purpose, whose platform may be summarized in the single word *Hate*. They exist for no other purpose than to harass their Catholic fellow-citizens and to exclude them, if possible, from position of public trust. But their proscriptive policy has met with only rebuke from the intelligent, respectable and cultured portions of our Protestant brethren. Professing loyalty to the Federal Constitution, they, nevertheless, seek to nullify one of its grandest provisions, that "No religious test shall ever be required as a qualification to any office or public trust under the United

State." But such organizations cannot long survive, a disturbing element, among a people so devotedly attached to the cause of education as are the citizens of this republic. They fear the light of intelligence and seek the cover of darkness for the accomplishment of their fell designs. Like the Know-Nothings of other days, the un-American organizations of the present "love darkness rather than the light because their works are evil, for every one that doth evil hateth the light, and cometh not into the light, that his works may not be reproved!"

We shall close this chapter with some reflections which will present the Puritan character as it was, and not as it has been portrayed by historians, who see in the Puritans nothing save what is commendable, who exalt them above the founders of all other States and who enthusiastically proclaim them the salt of the earth, the very elect of God. As we recede from the age which their influence dominated the halo that has been painted around them disappears as the motives of their conduct become more apparent. Their successors in the governments of the different States of New England have done well in freeing themselves from the influence of their narrow legislation ; and though the puritanical spirit is still in evidence here and there, more especially in some rural districts, it is unquestionable that in the not distant future it will have totally disappeared. What remains of it must succumb to the advance of liberty and progressive ideas.

"And now what shall be said of Puritanism? That it erected one monument to the glory of God, or exemplified the duty of obedience to the civil magistrate? That its altar was set up in the wilderness, consecrated by the prayers and blessings of the savage? That its usurped powers were used to quell strife, to calm dissension, to strengthen peace, or to enforce equity? That it presented an example of humility and patience, for the guidance of those simple ones who were fascinated by its solemn pretense? That, in all its doings, it had only in view 'Glory to God in the highest, and on earth peace and good-will to men?' Or are the eulogies it has received from history like the epitaphs upon tombstones?

"Since the dawn of creation, the praises of the Supreme Being had been chanted in the wilderness of New England. The forest teemed with gorgeous life, and not a brook babbled its sportive way, but glistened with the gambols of innumerable fish. Nature, animate and inanimate, was full of joyous freedom, and the lord of the domain roved about unmindful of the glitter of gold or the splendor of courts. This system of Nature Puritanism subverted; but its powers of substitution sprang from the muzzle of its guns, and not from the kindly affections of the heart. It subjugated nature, but the wild harmonies it destroyed were not replaced by the creations of divine art. It sought exclusively its own good, or, at least, it made that paramount. Deriving its genius from the theocracy of stubborn Israel, it promised its disciples the *prestige* of temporal success and prosperity. It had an eye to the things of Cæsar as well as to those of Heaven. Join my ranks, was its promise, and you shall be rich ; for the promised land belongs to the saints : you shall be powerful, for God will fight your battles. Wherever it penetrated, its work was to destroy and create anew. *It defaced the moral landscape of Catholicism, but was unable to substitute anything so fair and so beautiful.* The church presented a vast area, on whose surface could be seen rocks and caverns and pitfalls ; but then there were also quiet nooks and peaceful, gladsome vales, smiling in the brightness of an eternal sun. Puritanism was like a dreary waste overhung by a wintry sky, where, if a gleam of light were perchance discernible, it but irradiated desolation."

"Ignorance and presumption, ever hand in hand, have united to break down that noble Tree *planted* by *Christ himself,* because, forsooth, it has borne some decayed branches. But amidst all the desolation of this world it *still lives,* exhibiting a miracle more wonderful than that performed at the humble cave in Bethany. For its roots are cherished by mortal hand and eternal sunshine lingers upon its fragrant foliage.

"In a religious sense it (Puritanism) left nothing behind but its warnings. The synods, the confessions, the platforms and the heresies which distinguish its reign in New England, are in marked contrast with this noble church it presumptuously hoped to displace, and which, since the days of its Catholic defenders, has neither altered an article of its creed nor a principle of its government." [1]

---

# EARLY CATHOLICITY IN CONNECTICUT.

### CHAPTER VII.

#### IRISH SETTLERS.

IT is not improbable that the first European to sail along the shores of Connecticut, and perhaps, to stand upon its soil, was the great Catholic navigator, John Verrazano. Accepting a commission in the service of Francis I., King of France, he sailed in the frigate "Dauphin" in 1524, and after a tempestuous voyage, reached the coast of Florida. He sailed along the continent as far north as Newfoundland. To all this territory he gave the name of *New France.* It is claimed that the honor of discovering New York Bay belongs to him. If such be the facts, it is not unreasonable to infer that the prow of his stanch ship cut the waters of Long Island Sound ; and as vessels of exploration were always provided with priests, whose mission it was to preach the glad tidings of the gospel in newly-discovered lands, it may be that well-nigh four centuries ago the virgin forests of Connecticut re-echoed with the chant of holy monks, and that some spots were hallowed by rude altars upon which was offered the Holy Sacrifice of the Mass, and over whose table towered the symbol of man's redemption, the everlasting Cross.

[1] *The Puritan Commonwealth* by Peter Oliver, pp., 484–493.

There is an interesting tradition to the effect that the first resident Catholics of Connecticut were a band of seventeen Indians, who were carried to Southern Europe about two hundred and fifty years ago by a shipmaster, who sailed the Thames, there instructed in the Catholic faith, baptized and brought back to their native land. This tradition was handed down to the time of the venerable missionary, Rev. James Fitton, who firmly believed in the accuracy of the story. His belief received confirmation from the discovery in his own time in the eastern section of the State, probably near Norwich, of an ancient Indian cemetery. In one of the mounds were discovered, among other articles commonly found in Indian graves, some rings upon which were engraved two hearts and glass bottles partially filled with water. Father Fitton had in his possession one of these rings, and held in his hands the mysterious bottles. These he concluded contained holy water, which had been given to the Indians when leaving Europe, while the rings, he contended, represented the sacred hearts of Jesus and Mary, and had been placed upon the fingers of the converts at their baptism.

Such is the narrative as told by Father Fitton at the dedication of St. Patrick's church, Norwich. The conversion of the Indians, if true, would be a remarkable fact in the ecclesiastical history of Connecticut; but I have made diligent inquiries among the recognized authorities on Indian history in the State, and have failed to verify Father Fitton's relation. As to the rings representing the sacred hearts of Jesus and Mary, it may be stated, that it was in 1675 that the revelation was made to Blessed Margaret Mary Alacoque that she with her holy confessor was to obtain the institution of the Feast of the Sacred Heart. Did the rings anticipate the devotion, or did the alleged conversion take place afterwards?

It is a fact incontestably established that Irish people in respectable numbers were residents of New England less than a quarter of a century after the Pilgrims set foot on Plymouth Rock. In Connecticut they were contemporaries of Theophilus Eaton, who was Governor of New Haven colony from 1639 till his death, in 1657. They rendered signal services in the Pequot war in 1637. Captain Daniel Patrick, an Irishman, was dispatched from Boston with forty men to assist the Connecticut troops in that struggle.[1] He next appears in 1639, when, with Robert Feake, he purchased Greenwich from an Indian sachem, thus becoming the first settlers of that town.[2] The title of purchase, however, was not transferred formally until April of the following year. The Dutch Governor Kieft immediately protested against the cession of this territory to Patrick and Feake, and declared his purpose to dislodge them unless they yielded submission to the New Netherland government. Patrick withheld his submission, though he declared he would do nothing in the least prejudicial to "the rights of the States General." For two years he held possession despite the protest of the Dutch Governor. In

[1] Sanford's "*Hist. of Conn.,*" p. 24; Carpenter's "*Hist. of Conn.,*" p. 54; Broadhead's "*Hist of New York,*" Vol. I., p. 272. It is asserted that Patrick's name was originally Gilpatrick.—*Linehan's "Sketches"*

[2] The original name of Greenwich was Petuquapam.

II—3

1642 the English colonists were thrown into a state of alarm by the reports of an uprising of the Indians of Connecticut. Uncas, the great chief of the Mohegans, had assiduously circulated rumors regarding an intended massacre of the Colonists by Miantonomoh, chief of the Narragansetts. Connecticut and New Haven Colonies perfected a league of defence.

Fearing the consequences of his isolation should hostilities break out Patrick yielded submission to the Dutch Government, declaring that he was moved thereto by "both the strifes of the English, the danger consequent thereon, and these treacherous and villainous Indians of whom we have seen sorrowful examples enough." His formal submission was consummated on April 9, 1642, when at Fort Amsterdam he took the oath of allegiance to the States General, the West India Company and the authorities of New Netherlands. He demanded, however, adequate protection from enemies and all the privileges "that all patroons of New Netherland have obtained agreeably to the Freedoms."

Late in the following year the Indians of Stamford and neighborhood, inspired by their powerful and haughty chief, Mayano, became troublesome and gave the Colonists cause for grave alarm. On one occasion Mayano, coming suddenly upon "three Christians," fiercely attacked them. Patrick was one of the little band. The chief killed one of the three, but was himself dispatched after a desperate struggle. Patrick cut off his head and sent it as a trophy of victory to Fort Amsterdam with a detailed account of the atrocities perpetrated by Mayano and his tribe. An expedition consisting of 120 men was immediately dispatched from Manhattan against the hostiles. They marched through Greenwich to Stamford, but failed to discover any signs of the Indians. The Dutch soldiers became incensed at their failure, and one of them in an outburst of rage upbraided Patrick with having brought them on "a fool's errand." Patrick indignantly repelled the implied charge of treachery and spat in the soldier's face. Then turning to leave his irate accuser, the latter "shot him behind in the head, so he fell down dead and never spake."[1]

So perished one of the first Irishmen to enter the State of Connecticut. Patrick "had married a Dutch wife from the Hague," Annetje van Beyeren. He had little sympathy for the cold, severe dogmas of the Puritans, and we are told that "he seldom went to the public assemblies." He was a strong, daring, adventurous spirit, a sturdy character who left his impress upon his time. His name is perpetuated in "Captain's Island," on which stands the light-house off Greenwich.[2]

One of the first towns in Connecticut in which the Irish people became permanent residents was Windsor. John Dyer is mentioned in the town records as a "Pequot soldier."[3] Edward King, "an Irishman, one of the oldest settlers in this vicinity,"[4] probably settled here about 1635. The

[1] Winth. II , 151.
[2] Broadhead's "*Hist. of New York*," Vol. I.
[3] Stiles' "*Ancient Windsor*," p. 41.
[4] Ibid, pp. 55, 93. He speaks of King elsewhere as "the Irishman."

name of John Griffen appears in 1648, but he resided there, no doubt, before that time. Another Celtic name found in the records of the town is Edward Ryle. King was Ryle's host, and for this exercise of fraternal charity both became amenable to a peculiar law then on the statute books. To protect themselves against worthless characters who might sow the seeds of vice and crime, and become burdens on the towns, it was enacted by the General Court in 1637, that

"No young man that is not married, nor hath any servant, and be no public officer, shall keep house by himself without consent of the town where he lives, first had, under pain of 20 shillings per week."

"No master of a family shall give habitation or entertainment to any young man to sojourn in his family, but by the allowance of the inhabitants of said town where he dwells, under a like penalty of 20 shillings per week."[1]

With these enactments before them the sage fathers of Windsor, in town meeting, June 27, 1658, took cognizance of the fact that divers persons, from time to time, resorted to the premises of Edward King, and that such recourse was prejudicial to the town if not summarily prohibited. Accordingly, it was voted that, unless King gave security for his good behavior and gave serious consideration to the orders of the town before the 1st of October following, a fine of 20 shillings would be inflicted. It was "also ordered that Edward Ryle shall continue there no longer than the aforesaid time appointed, upon the same penalty."[2]

It was not alleged that Ryle was a vagrant, or that he was liable to become a charge on the town; nor was King charged with any offense grave in itself. Such laws were restraining forces that operated to the prejudice of personal liberty. They furnished, moreover, occupation for unscrupulous persons whose zeal in the public weal was commensurate with the size of the fine.

In the Great Swamp Fight in King Philip's War in 1675, five Connecticut Irishmen are on record as having won distinction by their gallant conduct, and as receiving as the reward of their services, generous grants of land. The names of these brave men deserve to be perpetuated. They were the sturdy pioneers in this land of a race that has ever been its defenders; and as the records of the infant nation are emblazoned with the brave deeds of Erin's sons, so will the annals of the mighty giant in the future be enriched with their brilliant and valorous achievements. Our heroes of the Great Swamp Fight were James Murphy, Daniel Tracy, Edward Larkin, James Welch[3] and John Roach. The Norwalk town records contain this entry concerning Roach:[4]

---

[1] "Colonial Records of Conn.," 1636–1665, p. 8. The first section of this law was in force as late as 1821; the second until 1702.

[2] "*Ancient Windsor*," pp. 54, 55.

[3] T. H. Murray in "Rosary Mag.," March, 1896.

[4] P. 63.

'JOHN ROACH, A SOLDIER IN THE 'DREFUL SWAMP FIGHT.'

"Whereas, the town of Norwalk having given and granted unto John Roach as a gratuity, being a soldier in the late Indian War, the parcel of land consisting of twelve acres more or less, layed out upon the west side of the West Rocks, so called," etc.

Were these heroes Catholics? Very likely. The same names may be read in the census list of every considerable Irish Catholic parish in New England.

## CHAPTER VIII.

### EMIGRATION, COMPULSORY AND VOLUNTARY.

WHEN the public records of colonial times are carefully scanned we discover abundant reasons to account for the presence then of large numbers of Irish people in Connecticut. We cease to be surprised at the number of Celtic names that greet the eye when we reflect upon the causes that forced them to bid farewell to the green hills and pleasant rivers and crystal lakes of their native land. Exiled from Erin, they were brought to our shores in thousands, sold as slaves and scattered over the various colonies of America. Official documents tell a heart-rending story of how the sons and daughters of Ireland became so numerous in the English colonies at so early a period of our history. They proclaim loudly the existence of unparalleled brutality on the part of men who had God ever on their lips, and whose boasted knowledge of the Divine Word was their choicest accomplishment. Professing godliness, they perpetrated crimes at which humanity stands appalled, and upon which they invoked the benediction of heaven. To exterminate the Irish Catholic race was their aim, and all means were alike legitimate if the end could be attained. Let us pass down to future generations the names of those godly man-hunters and pious traffickers in human lives. Let us place on record again some of the "orders" that cover their authors with infamy, and which consigned to living deaths thousands of pure, innocent little ones, who were torn from the hearts of those nearest on earth and sent into strange lands.

The names of some of those man-catchers have come down to us. They were merchants of Bristol, England: Messrs. David Sellick and Leader, Robert Yeomens, Joseph Lawrence, Dudley North and John Johnson.[1]

It was these holy men, zealous in spreading the light of the gospel, who conceived the idea of relieving the British government of a serious embarrassment in which it found itself after the compulsory exile of 40,000 soldiers who fell into the hands of the devout Protector. How to dispose of their wives and children became a grave problem. "They could not be sent to Connaught, as women, with children only, could not be expected to 'plant' that desolate province; they could not be allowed to remain in their native place, as the decree had gone forth that all the Irish were to 'transplant' or be transported; it would have been inconvenient and inexcusable to do what had been so often done in the war—massacre them in cold blood—as the war was over."[2]

[1] Prendergast's "*Cromwellian Settlement in Ireland.*"
[2] Thebaud's "*Irish Race.*"

The piety of the above-named merchants, however, furnished a way out of the difficulty. Had they not ships engaged in trade with the American Colonies? Why not put them to the devout use of transporting these surplus wives and children, the enemies of the kingdom, and distributing them among the English Colonies of the New World? Here was a solution of the problem, even though it entailed misery and wretchedness unspeakable. Accordingly "The Commissioners of Ireland, under Cromwell, gave them (the British merchants) orders upon the governers of garrisons to deliver them prisoners of war . . . upon masters of workhouses to hand over to them the destitute under their care 'who were of an age to labor,' or, if women, those 'who were marriageable, and not past breeding;' and gave directions to all in authority to seize those who had no visible means of livelihood, and deliver them to these agents of the Bristol merchants; *in execution of which latter directions Ireland must have exhibited scenes in every part like the slave-hunts in Africa.*" [1]

The following orders are extracted from the "Calendar of Colonial State Papers," 1571–1660, and 1661–1665. They reveal a depth of depravity that stains the escutcheon of no other nation :

"*April 1st, 1653, Order of the Council of State.* For a license to Sir John Clotworthy to transport to America 500 natural Irishmen."

"*Order of the Council of State, Sept. 6th, 1653.* Upon petition of David Sellick, of Boston, New England, merchant, for a license for the 'Good Fellow,' of Boston, Geo. Dalle, Master, and the 'Providence,' London, Thomas Swanlly, Master, to pass to New England and Virginia, where they intend to carry 400 Irish children, directing a warrant to be granted, provided security is given to pass to Ireland, and within two months to take in 400 Irish children and transport them to these plantations."

"Captain John Vernon was employed for the Commissioners for Ireland, and contracted in their behalf with David Sellick and Mr. Leader, under his hand bearing date 14th of Sept., 1653, to supply them with 250 women of the Irish nation above 12 years and under the age of 45 ; also 300 men above 12 years and under 50, to be found in the country within twenty miles of Cork, Youghal, Kinsale, Waterford and Wexford, to transport them into New England." ("*Cromwellian Settlement of Ireland,*" 1875, p. 90.)

Captain Vernon's five hundred and fifty unfortunates were Catholics, devoted disciples of the faith which St. Patrick taught the Irish people. How bitterly intense was England's hatred for the Catholic religion !

One shudders to think of the fate that awaited these poor and virtuous children among their stern New England task-masters. But what mattered it; were they not but children of Irish parents, who had no rights their conquerors were bound to respect? Sentiment, begone !

In the same Collection of State Papers we find (1628) the proposal of Sir Pierce Crosby to transport for £5000 *ten companies of a certain Irish regiment* to a place in America not yet settled.

"*June 10, 1655. Order of Council of State.* Upon petition of Armiger Warner praying indemnity against his bond of £800 entered into with John Jeffreys, Merchant, for transporting 100 *Irish* to Virginia, etc."

---

[1] "*Cromwellian Settlement.*"

"*Oct. 2, 1655. Order of the Council of State. 1000 Irish girls* and the *like number of boys* of 14 years or under, ordered to be sent to Jamaica. The allowance to each one not to exceed *20* shillings."

"*May 22, 1656. Order of Council of State* for the transportation of *120* men from Knockfergus in Ireland and Port Patrick in Scotland to Jamaica."

The above "Orders" explain the presence in New England of such large numbers of Irish people a century before the Colonies threw off the English yoke. From April, 1653, to May, 1656, 4250 of Ireland's men and women were transported to the New World by Messrs. Sellick & Co.; and it is asserted by the Rev. Aug. J. Theband, S. J., "that in four years those English firms of slave-dealers had shipped 6,400 Irish men and women, boys and maidens, to the British Colonies of North America."[1]

The number of young boys and girls alone transported to the West Indies was 6000, while the total number sent there has been estimated at 100,000.[2]

"After the horrors of a civil war, horrors unparalleled, perhaps, in the annals of modern nations, the children and young people of both sexes are hunted down over an area of several Irish counties, dragged in crowds to the seaports, and there jammed in the holds of small, uncomfortable, slow-going vessels. What those children must have been may be easily imagined from the specimens of the race before us to-day. We do not speak of their beauty and comeliness of form, on which a Greek writer of the age of Pericles might have dilated, and found a subject worthy of his pen; we speak of their moral beauty, their simplicity, purity, love of home, attachment to their family and God, even in their tenderest age. We meet them scattered over the broad surface of this country—boys and girls of the same race, coming from the same countries—chiefly from sweet Wexford—the beautiful, calm, pious south of Ireland. Who but a monster could think of harming those pure and affectionate creatures, so modest, simple and ready to trust and confide in every one they meet? . . . They were to be violently torn from their parents and friends—from every one they knew and loved—to be condemned, after surviving the horrible ocean-passage of those days, the boys to work on sugar and tobacco plantations, the girls to lead a life of shame in the harems of Jamaica planters !

"Such of them as were sent North were to be distributed among the 'saints' of New England, to be esteemed by the said 'saints' as 'idolaters,' 'vipers' 'young reprobates,' just objects of 'the wrath of God;' or, if appearing to fall in with their new and hard task-masters, to be greeted with words of dubious praise, as 'brands snatched from the burning,' 'vessels of reprobation,' destined, perhaps, by a due imitation of the 'saints' to become some day 'vessels of election,' in the mean time to be unmercifully scourged by both master and mistress with the 'besom of righteousness,' probably, at the slightest fault or mistake."[3]

The eloquent Jesuit has not overdrawn the picture. Among all the sad episodes in the history of Ireland, the expatriation of these unfortunate people has no equal. Their religion was their only crime. To eradicate from their tender hearts the precious seeds of faith implanted at their baptism, the merciless agents of the British Government found "homes" for thousands of poor Irish children among men and women who would see to it that not a vestige of Catholic faith remained; and in robbing them of their dearest treasure would think they were doing a service to God. It is of no consequence now

[1] "*The Irish Race in the Past and Present*," p. 385.
[2] Sullivan's "*Story of Ireland*," p. 391.
[3] Theband's "*Irish Race*," pp. 388-'89.

to speculate as to which of the masters was the more cruel, the libertine tobacco planter of the West Indies or the rigorous, narrow-minded Puritan of New England. Both dealt harshly, mercilessly with the faith of their white slaves, and instilled into their hearts a spirit of animosity to the Catholic religion that is discernible even in the descendants of these hapless exiles to-day.

The year 1652 was a dark and dolorous one for unhappy Ireland. It witnessed the close of a fierce and terrible struggle against Cromwell, "when," says Mr. Prendergast, "there took place a scene not witnessed in Europe since the conquest of Spain by the Vandals." "Indeed," he continues, "it is injustice to the Vandals to equal them with the English of 1652; for the Vandals came as strangers and conquerors in an age of force and barbarism; nor did they banish the people, though they seized and divided their lands by lot; but the English of 1652 were of the same nation as half of the chief families in Ireland, and had at that time had the island under their sway for five hundred years." [1]

To Spain were banished 40,000 of the stoutest arms and bravest hearts of the Irish soldiery. Orphan girls, as we have seen, were sent in shiploads to the West Indies, while upon the inhospitable shores of New England were landed thousands of both tender and mature age, who were destined to eke out an unhappy existence among a people "alien in race, in language and in religion."

The American poet, Longfellow, has, in the poem of "Evangeline," immortalized the story of Acadia. How many a heart has melted into pity, how many an eye has filled with tears, perusing his metrical relation of the transplanting and dispersion of that *one* little community "on the shore of the basin of Minas!" But, alas! how few recall or realize the fact, if, indeed, aware of it at all—that not *one*, but *hundreds* of such dispersions, infinitely more tragical and more romantic, were witnessed in Ireland in the year 1654, when in every hamlet throughout three provinces "the sentence of expulsion was sped from door to door." [2]

The seventeenth century closed without witnessing any cessation from persecution and transportation. Expatriation, with all its horrors, continued. It seemed an impossible task to glut the hatred of the British government for the people of Ireland. What with the destruction of the Catholic faith, the Bristol and other rapacious merchants reaped a rich harvest from the continuation of the nefarious traffic; so that underlying all ostensible reasons for dealing so barbarously with the Irish people were the motives of pecuniary profit and religious perversion. For a century longer English vessels were crowded with wretched human freight which they carried with all possible speed to distant shores. The history of Ireland during this long period is written in brutal penal enactments against the Church and in the banishment of her children.

And Connecticut became the scene of the labors of many of these white

[1] *Cromwellian Settlement in Ireland.*
[2] Sullivan's "*Story of Ireland,*" pp. 389-90.

slaves. "The purest native Celtic blood of Ireland was to be infused into the primal stock of the American people," for, though many were placed on a footing with the slaves from Africa, others became the wives of their Puritan masters; and some of those who now proudly boast of their Puritan lineage might be averse to admit that through their veins courses the blood of some fair, virtuous and healthy young Irish woman, whom British ship-owners transported for a monetary consideration.

Irish people were sold as slaves in Connecticut, as in other colonies of New England. In testimony whereof the following is submitted: On January 5, 1764, this advertisement appeared in the *Connecticut Gazette*:

"Just Imported from Dublin in the Brig Darby, A Parcel of Irish Servants, both men and women, and to be sold cheap by Israel Boardman, at Stamford."

Not only were the humble, religious homes of Ireland robbed of their inmates to satisfy the avarice of British agents; the very prisons were scoured for victims and emptied. These also were scattered along the Atlantic coast, some of whom were disposed of in Connecticut.

"The brig 'Nancy,' Captain Robert Winthrop, of New London, Conn., sailed from Dublin in June, 1788, having the convicts indentured in New Prison, and took out 201. The vessel arrived in the middle of the month at New London. He disposed of some there by sale as indentured servants, and sent the remainder to market in the ports to the southward." Truly, a godly business for pious, God-fearing Puritans.

Another vessel, the "Despatch," sought to land 183 Irish exiles at Shelbourne, Nova Scotia, but the loyalists having prevented the disembarkation, the captain headed his ship for a remote and unsettled part of the Bay of Machias, where he cast adrift his wretched passengers. Those who survived the hardships of that experience begged their way through the New England and Southern States, telling a woeful story of starvation and unchristian treatment.

Among the unfortunate people sold at New London was Matthew Lyon, a native of the Green Isle. He was a "Redemptioner," or one who was sold into service by the captain of the vessel in order to obtain compensation for his passage. He was destined to rise to eminence in the land that first gave him a slave's home. His native genius, his indomitable pluck and energy, so characteristic of his race, soon broke the fetters of slavery and he became a free man in what was to be a free country. On his arrival at New London he was bound out to service to Jabez Bacon, of Woodbury, Conn. Having remained here for some time he was transferred to Hugh Hannah, of Litchfield, the consideration being a pair of bulls, whose value was estimated at sixty dollars. This was the origin of his famous expression of later years: "By the bulls that redeemed me!" From servitude he advanced steadily over the rugged pathway of trials and hardships to positions of renown and influence. He became the first member of Congress from Vermont, and subsequently represented Kentucky in the National House of Representatives. He was arrested under the "Alien and Sedition" law, and fined, but Congress remitted the fine.

Not all the Irish who reached our shores in the eighteenth century were hunted down by man-catchers and sold by British agents as indentured slaves. At various periods of this century there came to America thousands of Irish men and women, voluntary exiles, who were heartsick with the intolerable existence they were compelled to undergo "at home." They were driven from the Green Isle not by the lash of the man-hunter, but by the force of circumstances which flowed naturally from the iniquitous laws and barbarous treatment of former years. Insensibly, but none the less steadily, did this exodus begin and continue. The first faint traces of it are discernible in 1728. At first the emigration was confined to the Protestants of the North. Not willingly and with cheerful hearts buoyed up with the prospects of a prosperous future did they turn their faces towards the young land in the West. Reluctantly they bade farewell to the old land. They, as well as their Catholic fellow-countrymen, were gathering the bitter fruits of a century's baleful legislation. Matthew O'Connor, in "Irish Catholics," says:

"The summer of 1728 was fatal. The heart of the politician was steeled against the miseries of the Catholics; their number excited his jealousy. Their decrease by the silent waste of famine must have been a source of secret joy; but the Protestant interest was declining in a proportionate degree by the ravages of starvation. . . . Thousands of Protestants took shipping in Belfast for the West Indies. . . . The policy that would starve the Catholics at home would not deny them the privilege of flight. Nine years later multitudes of laborers and husbandmen in Ireland, unable to procure a comfortable subsistence for their families in their native land, embarked for America."

The emigration of Irish Catholics in any considerable numbers began to set in in 1762. "No resource remained (at this time) to the peasantry but emigration. The few who had means sought an asylum in the American plantations."[1] New England received a goodly share of this output. The Protestant Irish poured into the Southern and Middle States chiefly, while the Catholics settled principally in New England, though many found a refuge in Maryland. As the dominant religion in all the colonies, save Maryland for a time, was Protestant, the strangers from the North of Ireland received a cordial welcome. They felt as much at home in the cheerless meeting-houses of the colonies as in their churches beyond the sea. Religion was the bond that united the British colonists and the Irish Presbyterians.

Not the same fared the Catholic Irish. They, too, had strong hands and clear brains. They were willing to labor in order to wrest from the soil its hidden treasures. They were honest and feared God as well as their Puritan neighbors; but a brand was upon them, a cloud over-shadowed them. The antipathy that burned in the hearts of the Puritan and Covenanter in the old world against Catholics, had preceded them to their new homes, and they found themselves the same objects of contempt and derision as when on their native hillsides. Love of their neighbors, much less love of their enemies, was not a prominent trait in the Puritan character, and though religion was ostensibly the greatest force in his life, it produced but little fruit in charity. He contemplated the Catholic Irishman as a

[1] O'Connor's "*Irish Catholics.*"

creature of inferior clay, a being to be religiously contemned. He lived in an atmosphere of intolerance of even the ordinary natural rights of Catholics. The English colonists of other States had no finer regard for personal rights and liberty than their brethren of New England. In New Jersey "liberty of conscience was granted to all but Papists,"[1] says Bancroft. In 1708 the mild-mannered Penn forbade Mass to be said in Pennsylvania. Rhode Island at first granted full freedom of conscience, but after 1688 "interpolated into the statute books the exclusion of Papists from the established equality." Religious Massachusetts generously permitted "every form of Christianity except the Roman Catholic." In the Southern colonies a State religion, the Anglican, prevailed. Bancroft says of Maryland: "The Roman Catholics alone were left without an ally, exposed to English bigotry and colonial injustice. They alone were disfranchised on the soil which, long before Locke pleaded for toleration, or Penn for religious freedom, they had chosen, not as their own asylum only, but, with Catholic liberality, as the asylum for every persecuted sect. In the land which Catholics had opened for Protestants, the Catholic was the sole victim of Anglican intolerance. Mass might not be said publicly. No Catholic priest or bishop might utter his faith in a voice of persuasion. No Catholic might teach the young. If the wayward child of a Papist would but become an apostate the law wrested for him from his parents a share of their property. . . . Such were the methods adopted to prevent the growth of Popery."

And what of Connecticut? Was she more liberal than her sister colonies? Hardly. When William of Orange ascended the throne his loyal subjects in Connecticut forwarded him an address, a part of which read as follows: "Great was the day when the Lord who sitteth upon the floods did divide his and your adversaries like the waters of Jordan, and did begin to magnify you like Joshua, by the deliverance of the English dominions from Popery and slavery." The Puritan's predilection for scriptural allusions did not preclude the use of offensive combinations. Popery and slavery! Evils of great heinousness in the eyes of the godly Puritan.

Such was the condition of affairs that confronted the Irish Catholic emigrant as he stepped upon the soil of America. Whithersoever he turned he was met by adherents of a hostile creed, and refused the privileges of citizenship unless he renounced his faith and affiliated with the church by law established. But, notwithstanding this isolation of the Catholic Irish in the Colonies, the stream of emigration continued to flow steadily westward. In 1771 and 1772, 17,350 landed on our shores from Ireland. In August, 1773, 3,500 emigrants arrived at Philadelphia. How many of these 20,850 emigrants found homes in New England, but especially in Connecticut, it is impossible at the present time to say. It is probable they scattered over all the Colonies. That a large percentage of them were Catholics we infer from the fact that notwithstanding their numbers, their arrival "had no tendency to diminish or counteract the hostile sentiments towards Britain which were daily gathering force in America."

[1] "History of the U. S."

## CHAPTER IX.

### NAMES THAT SPEAK.

FROM what has been adduced it must be patent to the reader that the Irish were in Connecticut in respectable numbers very early in our history. Additional evidence is found in the many names that have come down to us in the colonial records that are distinctively Irish; and while there is no direct, local evidence, save in some cases, that their owners ever knelt before Catholic altars, the time of their advent here and the places whence they emigrated are sufficient proof that they yielded allegiance to Holy Mother Church. The Protestants of Ireland were not subjected to the barbarous treatment inflicted on their Catholic countrymen.

Mingled with the Irish names herewith presented are those of other nations, whose children, it is conceded, are, for the most part, at least, adherents of the ancient faith.

It is not claimed that the following is a complete list of the Irish and other foreign people in Connecticut in colonial times. These names are here given to teach those not of the household of Catholic faith that the brains and brawn and the virtue of the children of Ireland and other Catholic nations contributed, as well as others, to the laying strong and deep of the foundations of this our beloved commonwealth.

From a "List of the Settlers in New Haven from the Year 1639 to 1645:"[1]

| | | |
|---|---|---|
| John Griffin, | Thomas Nash, | Mathew Rowe, |
| William Gibbons, | John Nash, | Ambrose Sutton, |
| Timothy Forde, | Joseph Nash, | John Thompson, |
| John Dyer, | Anthony Thompson, | John Vincon, |
| William Harding, | Mathew Pierce, | Andrew Ward, |
| Timothy Nash, | William Russell, | George Ward, |
| Peter Mallory, | James Russell, | Thomas Welch. |

In 1639 Dr. Brian Rosseter, "a man of fine education," was the first town clerk of Windsor. He appears in Guilford in 1652. His name needs no elucidation.

| | |
|---|---|
| Thomas Dunn...............New Haven, 1647 | Lawrence Ward..................Branford, 1654 |
| John Riley........................................1649 | Thomas Welch....................Milford, 1654 |
| Dr. Chayes, a French physician.......... | John Reynolds....................Norwich, 1655 |
| New Haven, 1653 | John Mead.........................Stamford, 1656 |
| Mr. Benzio...................New Haven, 1654 | John Norton. .....................Branford, 1656 |
| Thomas Stanton ....... ........Stamford, 1654 | Henry Nicholson....... ........Stamford, 1656 |

[1] The dates appended to the names in this list are those in connection with which the names appear in the records from which they are taken. In the majority of instances, the persons were in the localities assigned much earlier than the dates given.

Stephen Pearson................Stamford, 1657
Lawrence Turner............New Haven, 1657
Thomas Mullen ...........................1657
John Kelly ...............................1658
Richard Hughes............New Haven, 1659
Robert Poynere...............Stamford, 1660
John Cotey ..............................1660
Daniel Lane................New London, 1661
William Gibbons...........New Haven, 1662
Thomas Ford.................Milford, 1662
Edward Fanning..............Mystic, 1662
Mary Reynolds ............Norwich, 1664
George Hylend.................Guilford, 1664
William Keeney...New London (about) 1664
Franchway Bolgway....................1667
Christopher Crow..............Windsor, 1669

Thomas Ford.....................Windsor, 1669
Richard Butler...............Stratford, 1669
Hugh Griffin..................."    1669
William Meade..........New London, 1669
Thomas Sha (Shea), Sr.....Stonington, 1669
Thomas Tracy.................Norwich, 1669
John Reynolds..................."    1669
Timothy Ford............New Haven, 1669
Thomas Welsh .................Milford, 1669
Michael Taintor..........Branford, 1669
Henry Crean ...............Guilford, 1669
Andrew Ward ............Killingworth, 1669
William Venteras.....................
Necolas (Nicholas) Acly................
John Kirby ......Middletown (about) 1675-6

The following record shows the presence in Connecticut of a Catholic, a Spaniard, in 1670. He was held as a slave by a Mr. Hill, and was probably here previous to this year. Kidnapping was not unknown in those devout days, and this poor Spaniard may have been the victim of the greed of some unscrupulous ship-master. The record is: "This Court doth hereby impower the Court at New London to examine the matter concerning Mr. Hill's Spanyard, and if it doth appear that the sayd Spaniard was legally purchassed, then the sayd Court of New London are to order him his freedome, and to empower some person to take order for his transportation home, provided what is reasonable for his time out of the public treasury be ordered to Mr. Hill."—*Pub. Rec. of Conn.*, 1665-1677.

Richard Jennings and Elizabeth
   Reynolds...........................[2] 1675
Thomas Gould...............Hartford, 1677
James Reynolds.............. "    1677
John Purdy.....................Rye, 1679
John Ryly (Reilly) ....................1681
Jeremiah Blake...........New London, 1681
Ambrose Thompson .................1682
Captain Ohely (O'Healy) ..........[3] 1682
James Kelly................New London, 1682
Margaret Crow.............Windsor, 1683

Chris. Crow ....................."    1683
John Crow ...............Middletown, 1683
John Nash.................New Haven, 1683
William Dyer.............New London, [4] 1685
Peter Bradley.............. "    "    1687
Thos. and John Butler... "    "
       (about), 1686
Owen McCarty.............New London, 1693
Thomas Mighill (McGill)................1696
Peter Demil.........................1703
George LeFevre. .........New London, 1705

[1] "The Court granted liberty to Edward Turner to assigne over his right in Franchway Bolgway, his French boy, to any such person in this colony as two assistants shall approve of, for twelve years from June next."—General Assembly held at Hartford, October, 1667.—"Pub. Rec. of Conn. Col.," 1665-1677., p. 76.

[2] They were married "the beginning of June, 1678." They were both emigrants from Barbadoes. Their children's names were Samuel, Richard, and Elinor.— Caulkins' "*History of New London.*"

[3] Ohely was captain of a privateer.

[4] Dyer was Surveyor General of the plantation, and was made Deputy Collector and Searcher for Conn., March 9, 1685.

[5] Shipwright; had his building yard in 1696 near the Fort Land.—"*History of New London.*"

| | | | |
|---|---|---|---|
| Daniel Collins.....................1706 | John Nevil................Glastonbury, 1737 |
| Fergus McDowell.................[1] 1709 | Henry Delamore..........New London, 1738 |
| James Poisson......................1710 | Thomas Nash.............Fairfield Co., 1739 |
| Capt. Rene Grignon ...........Norwich, 1710 | Samuel and Sarah Daley.....Killingly, 1740 |
| Peter Crary........................1710 | John Neal................... Danbury, 1743 |
| James Welch.......................1710 | Timothy Bonticou.........New Haven, 1748 |
| John Collins ......................1711 | Thomas Thompson........ " 1748 |
| Daniel Carroll.....................1711 | Daniel Russell...... ........ " 1748 |
| Thomas Short ............New London, [2] 1712 | John Row(e)................ " 1748 |
| Thomas Ennis......................1714 | John Ford................Milford, 1748 |
| Joseph Keeney ....................1714 | Richard Flynn.............Woodstock, 1749 |
| Mary Corbitt.......................1715 | Benjamin Frizzel............. " 1750 |
| Joseph Kelly .................Norwich, 1716 | Jeremiah Kinney.........Windham Co., 1751 |
| Thomas Carey.................Stamford, 1720 | John Lane, Jr...............Killingworth, 1752 |
| Stephen Boutenet..........New Haven, 1720 | Patt O'Conele, a soldier in the Crown |
| Joseph Purdy............Stamford, 1723 | Point expedition.....................1755 |
| George Chartres....................1726 | John McMunnun, the same............... |
| William McNall.......) | David Lacy....................Fairfield, 1755 |
| John Lawson........... } ........Union, [3] 1727 | James Tracy..................Windham, 1755 |
| James Sherrer.........) | James McGunnigle, 1st lieutenant........1760 |
| Robert Kennedy ...............Norwich, 1730 | Patrick Walsh, adjutant..................1760 |
| Patrick Streen and family.....Glaston- | Patrick Thompson and Son........New |
| bury.........................1731 | London...........................[4] 1761 |
| John Creesey (Creey ?).....Woodbury, 1731 | Dennis Maraugh and wife..Coventry, [5] 1767 |
| Anthony Demil (D'Emile?)..Stamford, 1734 | John Tully ................. Saybrook, 1769 |
| John Farley.................Ellington, 1734 | John Cochran................... " 1769 |
| Richard Kating (Keating)..........New | Mr. Kelly....................Simsbury, 1769 |
| London...........................1736 | Patrick Butler..................Goshen, 1770 |
| John Hamilton..............New London, 1736 | Stephen Tracy..............New London, 1770 |
| Dennis Dehortee (Doherty)........New | Michael Ball..................Colchester, 1770 |
| London........................1736 | Patrick Fleming...........Waterbury, 1770 |
| Daniel Collins..............New London 1736 | William Larrows.............Stratford, [6] 1770 |

[1] Alexander de Ressegnie, formerly of Ridgefield, settled in Norwalk in 1709. He was a descendant of Dominigue de Resseguier, who in 1579 resigned his position as Secular Abbot of the Church of St. Afrodise de Beziers, Languedoc.

[2] Year of his death. Short was the first printer in the colony of Connecticut.— "*History of New London,*" page 351.

[3] The founders of the town of Union and were from Ireland.

Rev. Timothy Collins was ordained a minister, June 19, 1723, and was located at Litchfield. Dismissed October 14, 1752. He was of Irish, and, probably, of Catholic parentage.

In 1743 there was one "Papist" in Stratford; so wrote the Rev. Samuel Johnson to the London secretary in his *Notitia Parochialis,* April 6th.

[4] Sellers of merchandise.

[5] The former died in December, 1767; the latter in October. Both were buried from the "First Church." Married December 29, 1763. The records of births, baptisms and marriages of the First Church, Coventry, contain many Irish names that are suggestive of Catholic antecedents, as John W. Murphy, Daniel, Cornelius and Cornelia Loomis, Elizabeth Murphy, Timothy Dunmick, Mary Boynton, Dennis Maraugh, Abraham Collins, etc.

[6] Described in the public records as a French transient, probably one of the Acadian exiles.

| | |
|---|---|
| Louis Cooley (Coullie) .................. 1770 | John Farley....................Hartford, 1772 |
| Michael Magee.................. Hartford, 1770 | Morte Murtagh or Mortimer) Sulli- |
| Two Catholics in..........Simsbury, 1771 | van ................New London, 1773 |
| Timothy Roes....................Coventry, 1771 | William McCauley..........New Haven, 1773 |
| Timothy Reynolds...........Greenwich, | John Lamb................New London, 1774 |
| lieutenant.............................. 1771 | Frederick Barene............Waterbury, 1776 |
| Thomas Fanning......Groton, captain, 1771 | Captain Richard McCarthy.........New |
| John McDonald................Hartford, 1772 | London............................ 1779 |
| Daniel Burns.............New London, 1772 | John Meramble.............Woodbury, 1780 |
| Anna Maloney............. " 1772 | Mr. Phillips................ Litchfield, 1780 |
| William Orr....................Hartford, 1772 | Barney Kinney..........New London, 1781 |
| Patrick Robertson........New London, 1772 | Patrick Ward................Groton, 1781 |
| Captain Callaghan....... " 1772 | Timothy Coleman..............Coventry, 1785 |

On record as a French captive and either an Acadian or one of the prisoners in the wars against Cape Breton.

Rev. Mr. Viets, of Simsbury, Connecticut, on December 20, 1771, wrote to London: "I know of but two professed Papists and one Deist in Symsbury. All of them come often to church, and one of the Romans lately procured me to baptize one of his children, and behaved with much devotion during the occasion." *Hist. P. E. Ch. Conn.,* page 172.

Described in the records as a "foreigner." He died some time previous to 1767. His name appeared in connection with a note for £308, which he held against a certain David McCullum, of St. Croix. Before his death he placed the note in the hands of William Potter, at whose house he died. The result was considerable litigation, and the case was finally brought before the General Assembly for adjudication. "*Pub. Rec. of Conn.,*" Vol. IX., p. 114.

He was subsequently captain of a brig called the "Irish Gimblet."

In the list of names of the persons killed by the British troops at New Haven, July 5 and 6, 1779, is that of *John Kennedy.* "*Hist. and Antiquities of New Haven,*" p. 125.

*Lawrence Sullivan,* from Connecticut, was taken prisoner at the battle of Bunker Hill and was released February 24, 1776.

At the period of the American Revolution, James Mooklar, an Irishman, was engaged in business on Main street, Hartford. He was a barber by occupation, and, probably the first to follow that vocation in this State. His shop was located between Currier's cabinet shop and a school house. Adjoining the school was the first Society Meeting House. The first printing office in Hartford was in a room over Mooklar's shop. In this office, owned by Mr. Green, Mr. George Goodwin, for many years the senior editor of the *Hartford Courant,* served his apprenticeship, which he began at the age of eight or nine years. Almost directly opposite Mooklar's shop was the residence of John Chenevard, a Frenchman, by occupation a sea captain. "*Conn. Hist. Coll.*"

Wrecked in a storm off Plum Island, May 27, 1779, when himself and five sailors perished.

Described as "an Irishman."

Both were killed at the massacre of Fort Griswold by the British, 1781.

Kinney was buried in the "First Ground," at New London. Ward was a lieutenant. His remains were interred in the "Old Ground," at Poquonoc. On a stone over his grave was inscribed these words:

> "In memory of Mr.
> Patrick Ward, who
> fell a victim to
> British cruelty in Fort
> Griswold, Sept. 6th
> 1781 in the 25th
> year of his age."

| | | | | |
|---|---|---|---|---|
| Joseph Manly | Coventry, 1786 | Daniel O'Brien | New London, | 1795 |
| Patrick Butler | Hartford, 1793 | John Callahan | " " | 1796 |
| Richard Kearney | New London, 1793 | Henry McCabe | " " | 1796 |
| Patrick Thomas[1] | | John Sweeney | Hartford, | 1799 |
| Joanne (Jeanne) Duboin | Hartford,[2] 1791 | Patrick Munn | " | 1799 |
| Daniel Vibert | East Hartford, 1791 | Pierce Marshall | " | 1799 |
| Pierce O'Neil | Simsbury, 1793 | Hugh McFadden | New London, | 1801 |
| Signor Rosetti | Hartford,[3] 1794 | John McGinley | " " | 1801 |
| Patrick Lucas | New London, 1794 | Michael Dawley | " " | 1801 |
| James Mageness | " " 1794 | Hugh Ward | " " | 1801 |
| John Fogarty | " " 1794 | John McGuire | Pomfret, | 1801 |
| The son of a Mrs. Garvan | 1794 | John Conley | Glastonbury, | 1801 |
| Timothy Gurley and Mary Mead | | Terrance O'Brien | New London,[5] | 1804 |
| | Coventry,[4] 1794 | Captain O'Brien | " " | 1804 |
| Widow O'Brien | New Haven, 1794 | Captain Haley | " " | 1804 |
| Brian Dougherty | West Hartford, 1794 | John Quinn | " " | [6] 1804 |
| John O'Brien | New London, 1795 | John Burke | " " | [7] 1804 |
| Nancy O'Brien | " " 1795 | John Owen | " " | [8] 1804 |

[1] In the list of expenses paid by Connecticut for the capture of Ticonderoga and adjacent posts occurs the name of an Irishman, and, no doubt, a Catholic : "To Patrick Thomas, for boarding prisoners, £1. 5s." "*Rev. War.*" III., p. 663.

On July 2, 1788, Captain Chapman, with nine emigrants from Ireland, were drowned a short distance from the shore of Fisher's Island. He had just arrived with about twenty emigrants, some of whom were ill. In attempting to land them at a spot where they were to be placed in quarantine, they all perished.

The Schooner "St. Joseph," Captain Thomas Guion of Hartford, left Cape Francois, 1790. This captain was undoubtedly a Catholic.

Arrived Mrs. Hall and Mr. Keating in Brig "Patty" from Dublin, August, 1790, at New London. The Brig "Patty" was advertised as sailing from New Haven bound for "*Dear Ireland.*"

Died at Cork in Ireland, on the 5th of March, 1791, Captain Forbes, in the 58th year of his age. He was a native of Hartford, but had resided in Ireland for many years previous to his death.

Major John Byrne, Norwich, 1790—was a printer. About this time he went to Windham, where he began the publication of the *Phœnix*, or *Windham Herald*. In 1795 he was the postmaster of Woodstock, and in 1807 a member of the Aqueduct Company of Windham.

[2] Was from St. Domingo, and was buried from North Church, Hartford.

[3] An Italian miniature painter.

[4] Married March 6th, in "First Church," Coventry.

[5] From the *Connecticut Gazette.*—Mr. Terrance O'Brien, a native of Ireland, but who had been a resident of New Haven for several years past, was set upon in New London harbor by a Lewis Willcox and severely "maimed and bruised." Willcox was imprisoned at Simsbury, for six years, in October, 1804.

[6] The *Gazette* of Nov. 28, 1804, has this advertisement : "John Quinn, a tailor, offers to make a coat for 2 dollars, a great coat for 1 dollar and 50 cents, pantaloons for 1 dollar, a vest for 75 cents. He will cut a coat for 42 cents, a pantaloons for 17 cents and a vest for 17 cents."

[7] Married at Hebron, October 17, 1804, to Sally Turrell.—*Gazette.*

[8] "Oct. 24, 1804. Married at Port Principe, Cuba, Mr. John Owen, of New London, to Dona Maria del Rosario de Quesuada."—*Ibid.*

| | | | | |
|---|---|---|---|---|
| Don Joseph Wiseman | New London, | [1] 1804 | John Mynean (Moynihan) | |
| William Kelly | " " | 1805 | | New London, 1805 |
| William Burke | " " | 1805 | Benjamin Sullivan | " " 1805 |
| Joseph Healy | " " | 1805 | | |

From lists of advertised letters published in the *Connecticut Gazette* between 1793 and 1797, I have copied some names that indicate the residence of a number of Catholics in New London in those years. The names following with those given elsewhere show that a respectable congregation of Catholics could have been assembled in that town during the closing years of the eighteenth century :

October 7, 1793: Charles Bassentene, M. Chevalier, M. Contage, Mons. Dechans, M. Dupon, MM. Delpull and Lilet, Louis Mamene, M. Ressaud, M. Raydessile, Peter Doyle, Richard Kerney.

April 24, 1794:—Le Comte de Bannay, M. Pierre, M. Saudrey, M. Peterin, M. Icara, July 14th.

January 21, 1796: M. Dutue, Madam de Leger, M. E. le Vergenl, John Maloney.

January 16, 1797: M. Godefroy, M. Bennoi Lecroix.

July 1st: M. Mauconduit, M. Dupony, Richard Brennan, Pardon Ryon (Ryan).

The following names taken from tombstone inscriptions indicate probable Catholic descent:

*From New Haven :—*

    Peter Perit, died April 8, 1791. Aged 84.
    Thaddeus Perit, died August 3, 1806. Aged 51.
    Anthony Perit, died July 15, 1816. Aged 72.

*From Guilford :—*

    Mrs. Dorothy Breed, died Sept. 3, 1777. Aged 48.
    Daughter of Patrick McLaren, of Middletown.
    She was born Sept. 25, 1728; died at Branford.

If names be any criterion upon which to base a judgment, the above list may be summoned as evidence that Catholics were a numerous, though a scattered body, in Connecticut upwards of two hundred and fifty years ago. With some exceptions, these names are redolent of the Green Isle and deeply suggestive of the faith preached by Ireland's glorious apostle. Like thousands of their fellow-countrymen since, they may have voluntarily fled from the despots that were spreading desolation broadcast over their beloved native land ; or, what is more probable, they, or some of them, may have been among the hapless exiles whom the cruelty of Cromwell, and Ireton, and Ludlow, deported to the shores of the New World. Their names exhale a Catholic fragrance. They have nought in common with Covenanter or Puritan. Strangers in a strange land, but with faith deeply implanted in hearts loyal to holy church, recognizing the existence of

[1] This note appears in the *Gazette* of June 24, 1804:

Don Joseph Wiseman, "Vice Consule de L. M. C. para los estados de Rhode Island, Connecticut, Massachusetts, New Hampshire et Vermont, "communicates certain information to the public from Newport." It is not improbable that this Spanish official was a relative of Cardinal Wiseman, who was born at Seville of an Irish family who settled in Spain.

a life beyond the grave and fully conscious of the responsibilities of the present life, we may fondly cherish the belief that in the midst of trials and sorrows they held fast to the faith of their fathers, though deprived of the salutary ministrations of its anointed teachers. If they were disciples of the ancient faith, and I believe they were, they lived, moved and had their spiritual being without the consoling presence of their spiritual guides and deprived of all the consolations of religion, save those that come from faithful adherence to the teachings of childhood. And what a trial this must have been to the devoted, loyal Catholic heart! But, all circumstances considered, we may, and not without reason, fear that some of them parted company with their spiritual mother, the church, and formed other affiliations. Deprived of the joy, and strength, and encouragement which the presence of a priest ever inspires in the faithful Catholic, living in the midst of a people deeply hostile to the old faith, environed by influences that tended to chill, if not to utterly destroy, Catholic fervor, it would not be surprising, humanly speaking, if some unfortunates wandered from the fold into strange pastures.

But I am not of the number who believe that the early Irish Catholic immigrants went over in large numbers to Protestantism or lapsed into infidelity. Notwithstanding the influences by which they were surrounded, I am convinced that the vast majority of our immigrant ancestors sturdily maintained intact the priceless gift of faith. They had suffered too severely on account of their religion to surrender it easily. The Puritans of New England, whose antipathy to Catholics and the Catholic church was deeply rooted and inexplicable, were not more successful in their assaults upon the strongholds of faith erected in their hearts than were Cromwell and his successors. "The immigrants themselves never lost the faith. Although living for years without any exterior help, without receiving a word of instruction or advice, without the celebration of any religious rite whatever, or the reception of any sacrament, yet faith was too deeply rooted in their minds and hearts to be ever eradicated, or shaken even.

"But though they themselves clung fast to their faith in the midst of so many adverse circumstances, what of their children?

"There is no doubt that many of them did, individually, everything possible to transmit that faith to their children; but all they could do was to speak privately, to warn them against dangers, and set up before them the example of a blameless life. Not only was there no priest to initiate them into the mysteries granted by Christ to the redeemed soul; there was not even a Catholic schoolmaster to instruct them. Even the 'Hedge School' could not be set on foot. Books were unknown; Catholic literature, in the modern sense, had not yet been born; there was no vestige of such a thing beyond, perhaps, an occasional old, worn, and torn, yet deeply prized and carefully concealed prayer-book, dating from the happy days of the Confederation of Kilkenny."[1]

These pathetic words find corroboration in the Birth and Marriage Records

---

[1] Thebaud's "*Irish Race.*"

II—4

of the Colonies. They bear witness to the not unfrequent union of Catholic and Puritan names; and these unions were contracted not in the presence and with the blessing of the priest, but in accordance with the formulas of the religion by law established. The children of these marriages were regenerated, if at all, by waters poured by other than anointed hands. No bishop was here to sign their foreheads with the chrism of salvation, nor was there for them the gladsome day of first communion. They saw no sacred enclosure in which the prodigal might with sorrow kneel and humbly petition for the blessing and mercy of his heavenly Father. The sick went out from life unshriven and unanointed, and the dead were consigned to the grave with no solemn chant or liturgy, with no lights, or incense, or holy water, and with no lips—save in secret—to breathe forth a prayer for the eternal repose of their souls. "There is no reason, then, for surprise in the fact that, although the families of these first Irish settlers were numerous and scattered over all the district which afterward became the Middle and Southern States, only a faint tradition remained among many of them that they really belonged to the old church and ' ought to be Catholics.' "

The religious atmosphere that permeated the New England Colonies was deleterious, not merely to the growth, but even to the preservation of the Catholic spirit; and if defections are to be recorded, they are attributable not to any desire to surrender the ancient faith and yield assent to strange doctrines, but solely to the absence of all those spiritual influences so dearly cherished by their ancestors.

## CHAPTER X.

### EVIDENCES OF EARLY CATHOLICS.

IN the following pages we shall submit detailed evidence that Catholics were both transient and permanent residents in Connecticut in very early times. The public records furnish abundant testimony that the Irish, French, Spanish and Portuguese not only were frequent visitors to our harbors as traders with the colonists, but that many of them found here permanent homes. We shall witness a large number coming within our borders under compulsion and residing in homes that were not their own. Brought hither by the cruel fortunes of war, they were compelled to employ their God-given faculties of mind and body to increase the worldly possessions of men who had no claim whatever upon their services; and the sole compensation for their toil were the crumbs that fell from their masters' tables. The unchristian manner in which they were disposed of is a melancholy commentary on the animus then prevalent against Catholics and throws a flood of light on the anti-Catholic legislation of that period of our history.

Though the facts which we shall now present to the reader have no connection with one another, they are set down as events worthy of preservation.

In 1662 a French family, Modlin by name, appears in the town records of Stratford. They were in straitened circumstances, but the means employed to mitigate their sad condition were not in accordance with the methods that now prevail in similar circumstances. The following entry, extracted from the Stratford Town Records, tells a plaintive story:

"This indenture made the 24th of June, 1662, witnesseth that we the townsmen of Stratford upon good and serious considerations moving us thereunto, doe bind out one Modlin, a little girl about six years of age, that formerly did belong to a Frenchman that was in necessity upon the town of Stratford; we say, to John Minor of Stratford, to him, his heirs and assigns, till the aforesaid girl shall attayne the age of twenty-one years; we say we bind her with her father's consent; also a lawful apprentice to the aforesaid John Minor till the aforesaid term of tyme shall be fully and completely ended.

"The aforesaid John Minor engages to provide her with apparel and diet and bedding as may be suitable for such an apprentice.

"That this is our act and deed, and witnessed by subscribing the day and date above written.

|  |  |  |
|---|---|---|
| "RICHARD BOOTH. | JOHN BRINSMADE, | }  |
| "WILLIAM CURTIS. | CALEB NICHOLAS, | } Townsmen." |
| "JEREMIAH JUDSON. |  | } |

In the same records we find evidence of the presence in Stratford in 1679 of an Irishman bearing the familiar name of Daniel Collins. In the local legislation, of which he was the object, he was the victim, probably, of a law then in vogue, forbidding unmarried young men to keep house by themselves, and prohibiting masters of families giving them entertainment:[1]

"Memoranda, that upon the 20th day of September, 1679, Sergt. Jeremiah Judson, constable, by order of the Selectmen was sent and forewarned Phillip Denman and his mate Collins out of the town or from settling or abiding in any part of our bounds.

"And upon the 12th of November, 1679, Phillip Denman and Daniel Collins by the townsmen, were warned as above."

In 1679 the English Committee for Trade and Foreign Plantations wrote to Governor Leete of the Colony of Connecticut, requesting him "to transmit a clear and full account of the present state of said Colony." Among the queries propounded was this: "What number of Privateers or Pyratts do frequent your coast?" Governor Leete replied: "It is rare that ever comes any here on these dangerous coasts, only about two years agoe there came a French Captain called Lamoine[2] with 3 ships, one of which wintered at New London, and in ye Spring went off to sea; (*and one of them he carryed to Yorke; the other was sunk at Yorke.*")[3]

The ship that "wintered at New London" was in command of Captain Lamoine, and was a man-of-war. As it was customary for ships of war of France and other Catholic countries to carry chaplains, we may infer that the captain and his crew during their winter's sojourn at New London experienced the consolations of assisting at the Holy Sacrifice of the Mass and of receiving the precious graces of the sacraments.

---

[1] See p. 35.

[2] "About fifteen years ago," wrote Edw. Randolph to the Lords of Committee in May, 1689, "Captain l'Moin, a Frenchman, brought in two or three very rich Dutch prizes worth above one hundred thousand pounds." "Documents rel. to Hist. of N. Y.," III., 582.

[3] "Colonial Records of Conn.," 1678-1689, p. 296.

The most prominent Catholic layman to visit Connecticut in the seventeenth century was Colonel Thomas Dongan, Governor of the colony of New York. He came to Milford in 1685 to confer with Governor Treat concerning the eastern boundary line between the two colonies. Commissioners had been appointed by New York and Connecticut to adjust the boundaries, and their report had been submitted. On February 23d their agreement received the signatures of the two governors in ratification. During his brief stay in Milford Governor Dongan, whom Governor Treat called "a noble gentleman," was the recipient of honors befitting his high station, as appears from a curious item in the *Public Records of Connecticut*, May, 1685 :

"This Court grants Sam¹¹ Adkins five pounds, as their charity towards the damage he received in shooting of a great gun when Gov. Dongan was last at Milford."

In 1700 a party of Frenchmen traveled through the State from Milford to Albany. This was probably the Canadian embassy which arrived at the Onondaga Castle July 24, 1700. Its object was to adjust some differences that had arisen between the whites and the Indians. The embassy comprised Mons. de Maricourt, Rev. Father Bruyas, a Jesuit, and eight others, some of whom were officers. Maricourt was one of the principal men of Canada. He and Father Bruyas were familiar with the Indian languages.[1] While in Connecticut the embassy were the guests of the colony, as we learn from the following enactment of May, 1700:

"Ordered by this Assembly, etc., That the charges expended about the French-mens entertainm' that travailed from Milford towards Albanie shall be paid out of the treasury of the Colonie, so farre as the bills signd correspond with the law."

On August 3, 1704, New London was thrown into a state of fear by the appearance of a great ship and two sloops, said to be seen at Block Island, and supposed to be French.[2] If these vessels were French men-of-war, they were officered and manned by Catholics and Catholic devotions were practiced.

At a meeting of the Governor and Council at New London, November 11, 1710, it was ordered that the Commissary, Richard Christophers, pay to *John Lane*, of Middletown, a soldier in the expedition against Port Royal, for his extraordinary care and service in tending several sick soldiers, the sum of twenty shillings.

At a meeting of the same Council on November 18th the Commissary was ordered to pay to *Simon Murfe* twelve shillings as part of his wages as a sailor on board the "Mary Gally," one of the colony's transports in the same expedition.[3]

Lane and Murfe (Murphy) are familiar names, and there should be no difficulty in establishing their origin.

[1] *Doc. rel. to Col. Hist. of N. Y.*, Vol. IV.
[2] Caulkins' *Hist. of New London*.
[3] *Council Journal of Conn.*, 1710, pp. 191–192.

The minutes of the meeting of the Council in New London, February 17, 1710, contain this interesting item :

"Two Frenchmen, with six attendants, who came from Canada, in company with Major Leviugstone, with a message from the Governour of Canada to the Governour of Massachusetts, came to this place the last night ; for whom it was ordered that eight horses be provided at the Colony's charge, to carry them into the government of Rhoad Island, and that their necessary charges while they are in this place and upon the road, until they get into the government of Rhoad Island be also defrayed by the Colony." [1]

The two envoys, Messrs. Dupius and Rouville, one of whom was probably a priest, [2] and retinue, were Catholics. Their itinerary included also Hartford and Colchester. The expenses incurred by their sojourn were borne by the Colony of Connecticut, as we gather from the records :

"*Ordered*, that the treasurer pay out of Colony's money unto Captain John Prentts the sum of nine pounds thirteen shillings, which is granted him upon the account of the French messengers from the Governour of Canada, their entertainment at his house.[3]

The visit of the envoys to Hartford entailed expense as follows :

"March 19th, 1710–11.
"To Thomas Jiggels of New London, for the bearing and paying the charge of himself, John Plumb, and the ten horses they came hither with on the 11th instant to bring the French gentlemen, viz., their charges in going back to New London, £o. 12. oo."[4]

In 1717, René Cossitt,[5] or Cossit, or Cossette, a Frenchman, settled at Granby, Connecticut. He was born in France, about the year 1690, in the Place Vendome, it is said, and was educated at the University of Paris. After a visit to Three Rivers, in Canada, he reached New Haven, where he met Ruth Porter, whom he subsequently married. She accepted Cossitt on the condition that he would never return to France. He was educated a Catholic, but after his marriage united with the Protestant Episcopal Church. Cossitt purchased land in Simsbury in 1725. His death occurred August 11, 1752.[6]

At this distance of time it is idle to speculate as to the causes that led to René Cossitt's defection from the faith of his ancestors. The absence of priests, the dearth of Catholic neighbors, the total lack of Catholic influences and the spirit of hostility to Catholics then prevalent, as exemplified in vicious legislation, were, no doubt, among the causes that led many, at least into material apostasy. The anti-Catholic spirit was particularly active in Cossitt's home. In December, 1741, it was voted at Simsbury "that any orthodox minister who has a right to preach the gospel, may, upon the desire of any considerable number of persons, with the consent of two of the Society's

---

[1] "*Pub. Rec. of Conn.*," 1706–1716, p. 197.

[2] It was customary with the government of Canada to appoint a priest on all embassies of importance.

[3] "*Pub. Rec. of Conn.*," 1706–1716, p. 198.

[4] "*Pub. Rec. of Conn.*," 1706–1716, p. 202.

[5] "The Cossitt Family," by Pearl S. Cossitt, pp. 6, 7.

[6] Phelps' "History of Simsbury, Granby and Canton," from 1642 to 1845, makes no allusion whatever to Cossitt.

Committee, have liberty to preach in the meeting house on any day, not disturbing any other religious meeting otherwise orderly established." At a subsequent meeting "popish priests" were excluded from this license.

In the case of René Cossitt there was the additional cause of perversion in his marriage with a member of a hostile church conditional upon the complete severance of the ties that bound him to the tender and sacred influences and scenes of his youth, where, no doubt, like other French children of his age, he had received his first Holy Communion and had been enrolled among the soldiers of Jesus Christ in Confirmation by the venerable Cardinal de Noailles, Archbishop of Paris.

An interesting entry is found in the marriage records of New London:

"Allan Mullins' chirurgeon (surgeon) son of Doctor Alexander Mullins of Galway Ireland, was married to Abigail, daughter of John Butler of New London, April 8th 1725."

There are reasons to believe that the parties to this marriage were Catholics, or, at least, of Catholic descent.

About three miles from New London, in a southwesterly direction, lies the town of Waterford, whose first settlers were Thomas and John Butler, about 1684. The name of Waterford was, no doubt, given to their new home in honor of the old, the beautiful city on the banks of the Suir. As the population of the Irish city was then, as now, overwhelmingly Catholic, it is not unreasonable to infer that the founders of the Connecticut Waterford were Irish Catholics. Thomas Butler died December 20, 1701, aged 50 years; John Butler died March 26, 1733, aged 80 years. "Very few of the descendants of Thomas and John Butler are now (1852) found in the vicinity; but the hills and crags have been charged to keep their name, and they have hitherto been faithful to their trust. In the western part of Waterford is a sterile, hard-favored district, with abrupt hills, and more stone and rock than soil, which is locally called *Butler-Town*, a name derived from this ancient family of Butlers."

## CHAPTER XI.

### FRENCH PRISONERS IN CONNECTICUT.

THE wars waged by the English against the French were instrumental in increasing the Catholic population of Connecticut. The victors returned with many of the vanquished. The conquered were to witness no generosity; experience no magnanimity from their conquerors. Their cup of humiliation was full; they must drain its very dregs.

When Cape Breton, which now forms part of Nova Scotia, was taken by the English in 1745, a number of French prisoners fell into the hands of the Connecticut troops, and were subsequently brought into the State. They

Phelps' *History of Simsbury*, p. 167.

Mullins' name appears afterwards as Master in the "Bartlett School" of New London for the year 1734. *Hist. of New London.*

*Hist. of New London.*

were domiciled at New Haven in July, 1745, in the custody of Samuel Miles, captain of one of the Colony's transports. As no provisions had been made for the support or disposal of prisoners of war, the General Assembly in July, 1745, directed Miles to transfer the prisoners to the custody of Joseph Whiting, Esq., who was empowered to bind out to service such of the prisoners as were willing to labor at such places and with such persons as would seem to him proper. The prisoners, however, who were unwilling or unable to go out to service were to be confined in the common jail at New Haven at the expense of the Colony.

It was further provided that when any prisoner was ordered out to service by Whiting, the person taking him was to give a bond to the Governor and Company of the Colony—the amount to be named by Whiting—to the effect that as long as the prisoner remained at service the government was exempt from all expense in maintaining him, and that such prisoner should be returned to be exchanged or otherwise disposed of as soon as an order to this effect was received from the Governor. In the event of the prisoner effecting his escape, his master was to notify the Governor immediately.

In anticipation of the arrival in future of French and Spanish prisoners from Cape Breton and other places, provision was made, July, 1745, for their safe keeping and disposal as follows:

" *Be it enacted by the Governor, Council and Representatives in General Court Assembled, and by the authority of the same,*

" That when and so often as any French or Spanish prisoners shall be brought into any port or harbor in this colony, the master of the ship or vessel in which such prisoners shall be brought shall forthwith inform the Governor of the colony, for the time being, thereof; and his Honor, the Governor, is hereby desired and fully impowered to make such orders as he shall think proper, either for confining such prisoners in gaol or ordering him out into service in this colony." [1]

The number of prisoners brought to New Haven from Cape Breton is not known. No doubt, it was a numerous band, and as Whiting had authority to bind them out at will to service, they were, probably, distributed in the various sections of the State. In 1748 we find them in Hartford, New Haven, New London, Fairfield and Windham counties in numbers sufficiently strong to call forth a proclamation from King George II., wherein he forbade his subjects in the Colonies to engage in trade and commerce with the subjects of the King of France "during the time of open war." The royal proclamation was forwarded to the sheriffs of the above-named counties, "so his Majesty's subjects may be made acquainted therewith." [2]

In 1756 war was again declared between France and England. In this struggle Connecticut furnished 5,000 men. At the fall of Fort Niagara in 1759, a number of French prisoners were captured by our forces, brought into Connecticut, and immured in his Majesty's gaols at Hartford and New Haven. They were kept in confinement until early in 1761. [3] The keeper of the Hartford prison bore a familiar name, John Coleman.

[1] " *Pub. Rec. of Conn.,*" Vol. IX., p. 152.
[2] " *Pub. Rec. of Conn.,*" Vol. IX., p. 360.
[3] Ibid, Vol. XI., p. 558.

About this time another contingent of French prisoners was brought into New London by a vessel which violated the laws regulating the control and disposal of prisoners of war.[1] To prevent them from roaming at large they were incarcerated in the common gaol of New London county.[2]

The prisoners captured in both wars with the French, and who were imprisoned or bound out to service at Hartford, New Haven, New London and elsewhere, were undoubtedly Catholics, and, we are privileged to believe, loyal to the church of whose holy ministrations they were deprived. Under other and more favorable circumstances the advent at that time of so many Catholics, who, no doubt, were competent to give a reason for the faith that was in them, would have exercised a mellowing influence upon the stern and uncompromising subjects of his British Majesty; but the influence that environed them as captives were not favorable to the dissemination of Catholic ideas. What became of them is not known. Some of them were probably exchanged, while others served long terms of imprisonment or remained bound out to service, until, under the influence of time and environment they became resigned to their lot, intermarried with women of the prevailing creed and gradually drifted away from the faith into which they had been baptized. We know that many of them were the wards of the government from 1759 to 1761. During that period were they faithful to the salutary teachings of mother, priest and church? Deprived of the consolations and graces of the Mass and sacraments were they in their hours of trial and humiliation possessed with the desire to be nourished and strengthened by these channels of divine grace? God alone knows. We would fain hope that tried in the crucible of suffering they were purified and remained in intimate union with God; that, faithful in adversity they received after death the crown of a blessed immortality.

## CHAPTER XII.

### AN UNHAPPY EVENT—KIDNAPPING.

IN November, 1752, "an unhappy event[3] took place, dishonorable to the Colony, injurious to foreigners, and which occasioned a great and general uneasiness and many unfriendly suspicions and imputations, with respect to some of the principal characters of the Colony." A Spanish vessel, the "St. Joseph and St. Helena," of which Don Joseph Miguel de St. Juan was supercargo, bound from Havana to Cadiz, being in distress, put into the port of New London. On entering the harbor the ship struck upon a reef of rocks and became so badly damaged that it became necessary to unload her. She carried a crew of forty men. Her cargo consisted of indigo and other tropical products, besides a large quantity of gold and silver in coin and bullion; when the vessel was relieved of her cargo, forty chests of money were consigned to

---

[1] *"Pub. Rec. of Conn.,"* Vol. IX., p. 152.
[2] *"Pub. Rec. of Conn.,"* Vol. XI., p. 504.
[3] Trumbell's *"Hist. of Conn.,"* Vol. I., p. 250.

the care of Colonel Saltonstall and the remainder was entrusted to Joseph Hull, collector of the port. When ready to sail in the following spring Don Miguel discovered that much of his cargo, but particularly the money consigned to Saltonstall, could not be found. After months of vain endeavor to recover his missing property or obtain compensation therefor, he addressed a memorial to the General Assembly, October 16, 1753, praying " for remedy and relief." [1] Here also he was doomed to disappointment. Failing to obtain redress Don Miguel officially notified the King of Spain of his grievances. The Spanish government lodged a complaint at the English Court against the representatives of the English Crown at New London. A British man-of-war, the " Triton," carrying forty guns, was despatched to New London to be ready for any emergency. Prior to the arrival of this vessel the General Assembly enacted the following :

" *Resolved by this Assembly,* That his Honour the Governor be, and he is hereby, desired to prepare a representation of the case relating to the Spanish ship *St. Joseph and St. Helena,* which came in to the harbor of New London in distress in November, 1752, with the necessary evidences relating thereto. And in case a ship of war be sent hither on that occasion, Jonathan Trumble and Roger Wolcott, Jun^r., Esq^r., are appointed to repair to New London with such instructions from his Honour the Governor as shall appear to him necessary to be given for the conduct of the affair ; and the above mentioned representation and evidences to be properly delivered to the captain of the ship, to be transmitted to his Majesty's Secretary of State, to be laid before his Majesty, with such other matters and things as shall appear needful on receipt of such letters as may be sent on the occasion." [2]

The result of the Commissioners' labors was the sailing from New London in a vessel secured by the Spaniards themselves with the remainder of their cargo in January, 1755.[3]

" It was generally known that the Spaniards had been robbed ; or, at least, that an important part of a rich and very valuable cargo had been stolen, embezzled, or, by some means, lost, or kept back from the owners ; and it occasioned a great ferment through the colony." [4]

The nationality of this vessel, and especially its name, are direct evidences that its officers and crew were Catholics. Being a merchantman, it is not probable it carried a chaplain ; nevertheless we are satisfied that the Sundays and principal feasts of the year were duly observed with religious exercises during their two years' enforced residence at New London. If faithful to the customs of their native land, we feel assured that the " St. Joseph and St. Helena" was the scene of fervent Catholic devotions on the feast of St. James, the patron of Spain.[5]

It occasionally happened that ship masters with an eye more to pecuniary profit than consideration for sentiment or common honesty indulged in the vicious practice of kidnapping youths when in distant ports and bringing them

---

[1] " *Pub. Rec. of Conn.,*" Vol. X., p. 235.
[2] " *Pub. Rec. of Conn.,*" Vol. X., pp. 485–486.
[3] " *Hist. of New London.*"
[4] Trumbell's " *Hist. of Conn.,*" Vol. I., p. 251.
[5] July 25th.

home to sell as slaves. Sometimes the victims brought their grievances before the colonial authorities, which resulted in the severe but just punishment of the offender. An instance occurred in 1755, which well illustrated the avarice of the shipowner and the justice of the General Assembly.[1]

In this memorial to the Assembly Joseph D'Ming (or Demink) declared that he was a native and free-born subject of the King of Portugal, and an inhabitant of the island of Bravo, one of the Cape de Verde Islands; that being on the island of Bonavista, another of the Cape de Verde Islands, in March, 1755, and having spent some time there, was desirous of returning to his home on the island of Bravo. At Bonavista he met one Phineas Cook, of Wallingford, who informed him that, as his vessel was bound for the Barbadoes, he would put in at Bravo and land D'Ming. The captain offered him a free passage which the unsuspecting Portuguese accepted. Cook, however, refused to land D'Ming at Bravo, but brought him to Wallingford, where he was sold as a slave. In February, 1757, D'Ming petitioned the Assembly for redress. The Assembly promptly acceded to his request by appointing one Captain Thomas Seymour of Hartford, to take D'Ming into his care and keeping, and to secure him from any violence or ill-usage at the hands of Cook until the next meeting of the Assembly. Cook was ordered to appear before said Assembly to plead to the charges preferred against him.

The Assembly convened in May of the same year. Having fully heard the allegations and pleadings of both parties, the Assembly judged that D'Ming was cruelly deceived and treated with outrage. It was, therefore, ordered that Cook pay over to D'Ming twenty pounds for damages, a fine of fifteen pounds to the treasurer of the Colony for his misdemeanor, as well as the cost of the prosecution, amounting to £7. 13s. 4d, lawful money. Captain Seymour, before mentioned, was appointed D'Ming's guardian—as he was a minor—to take care of his person and possessions, and in a reasonable time to procure for him a passage home.

Let us hope that the unfortunate youth who put his trust in honeyed words was soon again in the fond embrace of his sorrow-stricken parents, and that, consoled by their presence and strengthened by the practice of his religious duties, the memory of his captivity gradually faded or gave place to fervent prayers for the conversion of his captor.

## CHAPTER XIII.

### EARLY CATHOLICS IN NEW LONDON.

BEING a port of entry and the centre of considerable maritime activity, New London at all times had a larger proportion of foreign residents within its borders than other towns in Connecticut. Many sailors who came to exchange their cargoes for what New London could give in return, settled there permanently, and became identified with the commercial interests of the town. Ships of war of France and England frequently put into port, where for various reasons they often remained for a

[1] "Pub. Rec. of Conn.," Vols. X. and XI., Feb'y and May.

considerable period of time. There is strong probability that the major part of these foreign residents were Catholics. The Spaniards certainly were. Among the French population there were a few Huguenots, but the greater number were, no doubt, members of the Catholic church. Ireland's contributions to the population were, with, perhaps, a few exceptions, children of St. Patrick.

In 1767–68, the British war-ship "Cygnet," wintering at New London, lost its purser. He was the owner of the unmistakably Irish name of John Sullivan. Preferring the peaceful pursuits of civil life and captivated by the gay society of the port, he married Elizabeth Chapman and made New London his home.[1]

Among the notable characters of New London in the last quarter of the eighteenth century was a Thomas Allen, proprietor of a public inn known as the "City Coffee House," the rendezvous for those convivially inclined. A feature of his business that secured for him considerable patronage was his "Marine List," which appeared at regular intervals in Green's *Gazette*. The List was not a dry recital of sailing dates, arrivals and departures. With devotional maxims intended for the spiritual benefit of seamen, it was enlivened with bright flashes of wit and humor, interspersed with other matter wholly irrelevant to maritime intelligence. The List first appeared in 1770. It is probable that Allen was an Irishman, and some of the reasons for this belief are: the manner in which he advertises in his List the sailing of the Brig, "Patty," for "*Dear Ireland:*" his printing on March 17th, "ST. PATRICK'S DAY," in capitals; his deep hostility to the English. On one occasion, he, with others, forcibly took a minister of the Church of England from his pulpit and expelled him from the church for praying for King George; from the manner in which he printed the name of Bishop Carroll, who visited New London in 1791:

"Sailed, Monday, June 20, Packet Hull for New York, with whom went passenger the Right REV. FATHER IN GOD, JOHN, Bishop of the United States of America."[2]

Furthermore, there was a tradition current at New London for many years that Allen was an Irishman from the Island of Antigua. At the time of which we write he was a communicant of the Episcopal faith and one of the wardens of St. James' church. If Thomas Allen was always a Protestant, his manner of speaking of Bishop Carroll is the more surprising. Such acts of courtesy to Catholic clergymen were rarely witnessed in that period of our history. Indeed, it would be a source of surprise even in these days of greater liberality of religious views to hear a non-catholic speak of a Catholic bishop in the terms used by Thomas Allen.

From very early times the French were represented at New London by respectable numbers. With the probable exception of the Irish, they maintained their supremacy in numbers over other foreign elements. They came as sailors in merchant vessels and in ships of war. We infer they

---

[1] *"Hist. of New London."*      [2] *Connecticut Gazette.*

were numerous from Thomas Allen's standing advertisement of his inn, translated into French, inviting them to partake of his hospitality. Desertions from the vessels in the harbor were frequent, and when they occurred, the *Connecticut Gazette* was employed to assist in the capture of the culprits. In 1778, a French man-of-war, the "Lyon," commanded by Captain Michel, entered the port and remained about three months. Concerning this ship, this advertisement appeared in the *Gazette*, May 28, 1778:

"Deserted from the French Ship, "Lion" (or Lyon), in the Harbor of New London, Labe (L'Abbe) Galand, who was under the character of a Priest on Board, and has taken with him a quantity of silver and gold and paper currency, not his own. He has been missing about three weeks ; is a short, thick, well-built man, of light Complexion, large black Eyes, short strait black Hair, looks like a Jew. Speaks very little English. Can speak French, German, and Latin, has a good notion of Slight of hand, rode a small black Horse, had on when he went away, a brown Coat, black Jacket and Breeches, and blue Great Coat ; has a small gold watch with a small bell to the chain, which he is very fond of showing. Whosoever shall apprehend said pretended priest and return him on board said Ship shall have a reward of Two Hundred Dollars paid by me.

"J. MICHEL,

"New London, May 28, 1778.                                   "Commander of said Ship"

Was Galand a priest, or a pretended priest, as the advertisement seems to insinuate? It would be interesting to know what became of him. To return to France would incur the danger of arrest and imprisonment. If a true priest, did he perform any sacerdotal functions in the colony? Or, if a pretended priest, did he continue the deception to the detriment of his own and the souls of unsuspecting victims? There is no record that he was ever apprehended and punished for his crime. The ship "Lyon" sailed from New London, June 14, 1778, for Virginia. On her return voyage to France she was captured by a British man-of-war.[1]

Previous to and during the years (1789-1794) when France experienced the awful horrors of the Revolution ; when she suffered the bloody atrocities of men frenzied with the spirit of infidelity, many of her citizens fled and sought an asylum in the new world, some of whom settled at New London. Here they built up new homes, and accumulated new fortunes, secure from the insensate fury of their kinsmen across the sea. As the priesthood of France was the special object of the Revolution's hatred, it may be that some of its members found a refuge in Connecticut, as they did in other sections of New England. John de Cheverus, who became the first Bishop of Boston, and his saintly co-laborer in the same field, Francis Matignon, D.D.; Ambrose Marechal, who was consecrated Archbishop of Baltimore in 1817; Gabriel Richards, of western fame; and Francis Ciquard, missionary to the Indians on the Penobscot, are but a few of the victims of that political cataclysm, who came hither to spend themselves for the salvation of souls.

In 1786 the number of French residents in New London must have been

[1] Caulkins' *"History of New London."*

considerable, as in that year Phillip de Jean was appointed by the French Government naval agent at that port. He remained for about eight years, when he was transferred to San Domingo. Other names that appear in New London about this time are Badet, Bocage, Boureau, Constant, Dupignac, Durivage, Girard, La Borde, La Roche, Laurence, Laboissiere, Mallet, Montenot, Berean, Poulin, Renouf, Rigault and Rouget.[1]

However, not all the French residents of New London were from France. They came in great numbers from San Domingo, driven thence by an internal warfare that fiercely raged between the whites, blacks and mulattoes from 1791 to the end of the century—a struggle that "may well be characterized as the most vindictive on record, a struggle which, before the close of the eighteenth century, led to the extermination of the once dominant Europeans, and the independence of the colored insurgents." During these years of riot, insurrection, and bloodshed, a steady stream of exiles flowed into New London. They were of every age, class and condition, and all were Catholics. After the destruction of Cape Francois[2] in 1793, a number of French refugees were landed at New London from the brig "Sally," Captain Tryon commanding. Later in the same year thirty-four more arrived in the brig "Prudence."[3] Among the hapless exiles to reach New London was an abbess of a Convent in Cape Francois.

The residents of New London received these homeless wanderers with unbounded hospitality. Their sufferings and trials, the loss of their worldly possessions appealed strongly to the charity of their hosts. Public inns and private dwellings became their homes, though many of the refugees had nothing wherewith to make recompense. This generous welcome compensated in a measure for the cruel hardships they had endured. Captivated by the hospitality lavished upon them, many settled among their benefactors and established permanent homes. Others wandered here and there through the State, weary, heart-broken and penniless, in the endeavor to stifle the memory of their misfortunes.

The unfortunate exiles from San Domingo deserved a better fate. They were a virtuous people, peaceable, industrious, grateful and devotedly attached to their faith. Like their co-religionists, the Acadians, who also suffered the hardships and cruelties attendant upon compulsory exile, their hearts ached for home, for scenes upon which their eyes would never more rest. They were accompanied by devoted priests, who shared the anguish of their souls. One of these faithful shepherds was the Rev. Mons. Cibot, Superior-General[4] of the clergy of San Domingo. On August 4, 1793, he preached a sermon

---

[1] "*Hist. of New London.*"

[2] Now Cape Haytien ; nearly seven-eighths of the town was destroyed.

[3] *Conn. Gazette*, July and August, 1793.—In 1791 the Marquis Bragelogue with his wife and family and a retinue of seventeen servants arrived at New London. *Conn. Gazette.*—It is estimated that in 1793, 40,000 whites fled from San Domingo to escape the fury of the blacks ; many of them landed at the various ports of the United States.

[4] *Conn. Courant*, September 2, 1793. More likely, Vicar-General.

at Baltimore,[1] in which he gave fervent and eloquent expression to the feelings of gratitude that welled up in his heart. After saying that their own sins had drawn upon them their sufferings, he continued: "It is painful to you, perhaps, to hear me speak these truths in a foreign land and in the midst of a people, mild, affable, generous and beneficent, who compassionate your sufferings and try to erase the memory of them from your minds, and have succeeded, at least, in softening their rigor by their generous and unanimous consent in affording you relief. Oh! worthy and generous inhabitants of Baltimore! Oh! all you who dwell on this continent! Oh! our brothers and benefactors! may this heroical act of benevolence be told and proclaimed amidst all nations of both hemispheres."

The names of Don Manuel de Valladores, Don Francisco Xavier de Arriola, Don Juan de Campderros and Don Gabriel Sistera bear witness to their owners' nationality and religion. They were residents of New London in 1773 and later.[2] Sistera was naturalized in 1773, and became a subject of the King of Great Britain. To do so it was necessary for him to renounce the Pope and deny the Real Presence of Christ in the Blessed Eucharist. He was obliged to take the oaths of allegiance and supremacy, the declaration against "Popery" and the oath of abjuration. The record is as follows:[3]

"An Act for the Naturalization of Don Gabriel Sistera. May, 1773.[4]

"Whereas Don Gabriel Sistera, a native of Barcelona in the Kingdom of Spain, now resident in New London, hath by his petition preferred to this Assembly, prayed to be admitted to the privileges of his Majesty's subjects within this colony; therefore

"*Be it enacted by the Governor, Council and Representatives in General Court assembled, and by the authority of the same,* That the said Gabriel Sistera, having taken the oaths of allegiance, supremacy and abjuration by law appointed, be, and he is hereby declared to be naturalized and entitled to all the privileges, immunities and advantages of his Majesty's English subjects born within this colony, as fully and effectually, to all intents, construction and purposes whatsoever, as though he, said Gabriel Sistera, had been born within the dominions of and subject to the King of Great Britain; excepting only such privileges and immunities as by law are not competent to foreigners who have been or are naturalized."

Gabriel Sistera was a sea captain, and carried on an extensive trade between Spanish ports, New London and the West Indies. He came to New London from Barcelona in 1771 with his son Gabriel. One of his descendants, Charles Sistera, was graduated from Trinity College, Hartford, in 1848, while another, Joseph C. Sistera, was among the first to find a resting place in Cedar Grove cemetery, New London, November 23, 1851.[5]

[1] On the 9th of July, 1793, fifty-three vessels arrived at the port of Baltimore, carrying about 1,000 whites and 500 mulattoes from San Domingo. "Beside the emigration from France, a very large number of the most respectable inhabitants of San Domingo, flying from the massacre of 1793, found refuge at Baltimore. Many of these refugees were endowed with eminent piety."—DeCourcey Shea's "*History.*"

[2] "*Pub. Rec. of Conn.,*" Vol. XIII., p. 655.

[3] See page 22 for these oaths.

[4] *Ibid.,* Vol. XIV., p. 91.

[5] "*Hist. of New London.*"

## CHAPTER XIV.

### THE ACADIANS IN CONNECTICUT.

WE come now to the saddest page in the history of early Catholicity in Connecticut. We are to follow the footsteps of the exiled Acadians in their sorrowful wanderings from their peaceful and happy homes in Nova Scotia to the shores of Connecticut, where, by legislative enactment, they were distributed throughout the State. The sufferings endured by this kindly, industrious and religious people vividly recall the persecution of their coreligionists in Ireland by the same despotic power. Seven thousand Acadians were scattered along the coast from New Hampshire to Georgia. Of this number, four hundred reached Connecticut. In ruthlessly expelling these unfortunate people from their homes and forcibly transporting them into exile, the British Government maintained its reputation for severity when dealing with its Catholic subjects. Its hostility to the Catholic religion led it to perpetrate crimes from which humanity recoils, not the least of which was the expulsion of the French Neutrals and the barbarous destruction of their churches, harvests and homes.

What wrong had these people done, what crime had they committed, that they should be visited with such appalling chastisements? Were they rebellious, disloyal? Had the odious charge of treason to the crown been proved against them? No; the impartial, justice-loving historian, will bring no such accusation against the inhabitants of Acadia. In British hate and avarice will be found the reasons for the inception and execution of a scheme, which unbiased witnesses declare to have no parallel in the annals of the world. It is true, that those who were directly interested in bringing about the expulsion of the Acadians accused them of refusing to take the oath of allegiance to George II., but we shall see that their refusal was justifiable. "Nothing," says Garneau, "could tempt the honorable minds of Acadians to take an oath of fealty to aliens, repugnant to their consciences; an oath which it was and is the opinion of many Britain had no right to exact. The Acadians were not British subjects, for they had not sworn fidelity; therefore they were not liable to be treated as rebels; neither ought they to be considered prisoners of war, or rightly be transportable to France, since, during half a century, they had been left in possession of their lands on the simple condition of remaining neutral. But numerous adventurers, greedy incomers, looked upon their fair farms with covetous eyes. Smoldering cupidity soon burst into flame. Reasons of state polity were soon called in to justify the total expulsion of the Acadians from Nova Scotia. Although the far greater number of them had done no act which could be construed into a breach of neutrality, yet, in the horrible catastrophe preparing for them, the innocent and the guilty were to be involved in a common perdition."

The charge of disloyalty brought against the Acadians has not been sustained. They were Neutrals in fact as well as in name. It is true, that when Verger, who was in command of Fort Beausejour, was hard pressed by Lieutenant-Colonel Winslow, he called upon the Acadians for reinforcements, and that three hundred went to his assistance under penalty of death if they refused. But when the fort surrendered to the British these were pardoned. They had fought the British under compulsion; in fact, some of them had deserted, while others had pleaded in vain for permission to lay down their arms. At the surrender it was "stipulated," says Minot, "that they should be left in the same situation that they were in when the army arrived, and not be punished for what they had done afterwards." The most violent enemy of the Acadians cannot adduce another instance of their taking up arms against the British. Why, then, were 15,000 people made to suffer the most barbarous treatment because three hundred of them were compelled to engage in conduct disloyal to the government? Was it a reason sufficient to justify the wholesale banishment of thousands? Why punish an entire nation for an offence committed by some, and which, committed under duress, had been condoned? The reason must be sought elsewhere than in the disloyalty of the Acadians. They were not conspirators. They had no grievance against the British crown. In 1742, nearly thirty years after the treaty of Utrecht, which ceded Acadia to England, Governor Mascarene wrote to the Duke of Newcastle that, "The frequent rumors we have had of war being declared against France have not as yet made any alteration in the temper of the inhabitants of the Province, who appear in a good disposition of keeping to their oath of Fidelity." In a letter to the Lords of Trade, Governor Lawrence wrote : " I believe that a very large part of the inhabitants would submit to any terms rather than take up arms on either side."

When the English government determined upon the deportation of the Acadians, it resolved to make their expulsion as thorough as possible. To deport them to Canada was to transfer them among a people of kindred language, religion and sympathies; moreover, the addition of 7,000 persons to the population would have added to its military strength. Furthermore, the English professed to believe that as Canada had no cleared lands to distribute among them they might take up arms against Nova Scotia and other English colonies. "After mature consideration it was unanimously agreed that to prevent as much as possible their attempting to return and molest the settlers that may be set down on their lands, it would be most proper to send them to be distributed among the smaller colonies on the Continent, and that a sufficient number of vessels should be hired with all possible expedition for that purpose."

The transports were quickly obtained and orders were given them to assemble in the Basin of Minas and in Annapolis Basin. The vessels whose rendezvous was in the Basin of Minas were to transport to North Carolina 500 persons, to Virginia 1000, and to Maryland 500, "or in proportion, if the number to be shipped off should exceed two thousand persons." The transports in Annapolis Basin were ordered to carry 300 persons to Philadelphia, 200 to New York, to Connecticut 300, and to Boston 200, "or rather more in proportion to Connecticut, should the number to be shipped off exceed one thousand persons."[1]

The masters of the vessels were strictly enjoined to be "careful and watchful" during the whole voyage, lest the exiles attempt to seize the ships. To prevent this they were to permit only a small number on deck at a time. Moreover, they were to be "particularly careful" that the prisoners carried on board with them "no arms nor other offensive weapons." "You will use," continues Governor Lawrence in his Instructions, "all the means proper and necessary for collecting the people together so as to get them on board. If you find that fair means will not do with them, *you must proceed by the most vigorous measures possible, not only in compelling them to embark, but in depriving those who shall escape of all means of shelter and support, by burning their houses and destroying everything that may afford them a means of subsistence in the country.*"[2]

The Governor's instructions were literally obeyed. The unsuspecting Acadians were lured to the parish church at Grand Pré to the number of 1,293 souls. "The church," says Smith,[3] "was a large edifice, sufficient for the needs of that extensive parish. It was sacred to the hearts of this simple people; it was the place where, at the stated gatherings of the populace, the venerable Father La Blanc was wont to break to them the bread of life: it was the scene of their christenings, the solemnization of their marriages, and above all, hallowed by the recollections of the last rites in memory of deceased loved ones."

Gathered within the sacred precincts they listened to no discourse from the lips of their venerable father and pastor, but heard instead from Colonel Winslow the astounding declaration that they were the King's prisoners. What a cruel sentence to pronounce in the house of the God of Mercy! What a mockery of justice it all was! Some, more courageous than others, made a bold dash for liberty, but from their hiding places soon saw the flames devouring their homes. At Cumberland the terrified people, overcome with despair, took refuge in flight. Two hundred and fifty-three homes there were reduced to ashes, and the entire harvest, the fruit of months of patient industry, was ruthlessly destroyed. "In the district of Minas alone," says Haliburton, "there were 255 houses, 276 barns, 155 out-houses, 11 mills and one church destroyed. The people were so paralyzed at such wholesale destruction that they appeared quite resigned. . . . . Their resignation, however, was the resignation of despair; and when, on the 10th of September, they were driven on board the transports, nature found relief in loud lamentations at their fate." "I know not," says Bancroft, "if the annals of the human race keep the record of sorrow so wantonly inflicted, so bitter and so perennial as fell upon the French inhabitants of Acadia." "We have been true," said the broken-hearted exiles, "to our religion, and true to ourselves; yet nature appears to consider us only as the objects of public vengeance."

[1] *"Nova Scotia Archives,"* p. 274.
[2] *"Nova Scotia Archives,"* p. 276.
[3] *"Hist. of Acadia."*

We shall now trace, as far as existing records will permit, the wanderings of the unfortunate exiles who were consigned to Connecticut.

Five months before their arrival at the port of New London, intimation of their contemplated expulsion reached the Colony. Remote preparations were begun for their reception and distribution. In October, 1755, the General Assembly at New Haven enacted the following:

"Whereas, public measures appear to be taking for evacuating the Province of Nova Scotia of its French inhabitants, and removing or dispersing them to other places more consistent with the safety of his Majesty's American dominions,

"*Resolved by this Assembly*, That if, in pursuance of such design, any of them happen to be brought into any place in this colony with expectation of being received and cared for, his Honour the Governor is desired on such their arrival, to issue forth such orders for their being received, taken care of and disposed of, in such place or places in this government and under such circumstances, as may be judged most expedient, or otherwise for their removal elsewhere having regard to such order or authority as may attend their conveyance hither."[1]

On January 21, 1756, three hundred Acadians were landed at New London. On May 22, another transport arrived at the same port, after a long and tempestuous experience, with many hapless exiles sick and dying of the smallpox. What was now to be done for these four hundred luckless victims of British avarice and bigotry? What measures were to be taken for their maintenance and distribution, for it was felt that so large a number would become a burden upon the Colony? Stripped of their worldly possessions, they were now paupers among strangers, the wards of a people foreign in race, religion, language and customs, a people who had little sympathy with their devotion and loyalty to the ancient faith. "The exiles were anything but welcome in New England," says Palfrey. "Their support was an uninvited burden, and their presence, by reason of national and religious animosity, was a vexation and offence."

Though unwelcome guests, the General Assembly of Connecticut gave evidence of its desire to provide for the maintenance of its hapless charges. The conduct of Connecticut in dealing with the exiles was in marked contrast with the cold, cheerless and unchristian methods adopted by Massachusetts.

At its session in January, 1756, the General Assembly at New Haven passed:

"*An Act for distributing and well ordering the French People sent into this Colony from Nova Scotia*, as follows:[2]

"Whereas, there is a number of French people sent by Governour Lawrence into this Colony, and more daily expected, to be disposed of here, supposed to be about four hundred in the whole,

"*It is therefore resolved and enacted by this Assembly*, That a committee be appointed, and Hezekiah Huntington, Gourdon Saltonstall, Christopher Avery and Pygan Adams, Esqrs., or any three of them, are hereby appointed a committee to receive

[1] "Col. Rec. of Conn.," Vol. X., p. 425.
[2] "Col. Rec. of Conn." Vol X., pp. 452-453.

said people and distribute them in the towns hereafter mentioned, in the following manner, *viz.*:

| | | | |
|---|---|---|---|
| In New London ..12 | In Wallingford....12 | In Hebron.......... 5 | In Voluntown...... 3 |
| Groton . ......... 8 | Woodbury...... 9 | Suffield .......... 5 | Weathersfield.. 9 |
| Saybrook. ...... 7 | Norwalk.........12 | New Haven....19 | Farmington......14 |
| Lebanon.........12 | Danbury......... 6 | Milford........... 9 | East Haddam.. 6 |
| Pomfret.......... 6 | Norwich.........19 | Durham......... 4 | Bolton............ 3 |
| Plainfield. ...... 4 | Preston.. ........ 6 | Fairfield.........17 | Enfield........... 3 |
| Hartford.........13 | Killingsworth 4 | Stanford......... 9 | Guilford.........11 |
| Middleton ......16 | Coventry........ 5 | Newton.......... 4 | Derby ............ 4 |
| Tolland .......... 3 | Killingly........ 8 | Stonington......11 | Waterbury...... 6 |
| Colchester...... 7 | Canterbury..... 5 | Lyme............ 8 | Stratford.........14 |
| Symsbury ...... 6 | Windsor.........13 | Windham....... 8 | Greenwich...... 6 |
| Ashford.......... 3 | Glassenbury... 4 | Mansfield ....... 5 | |
| Branford......... 8 | Haddam......... 3 | Woodstock...... 6 | |

"And the selectmen of each of said towns are hereby directed and required to receive of said committee the number set to such town as above, or as near as may be a like proportion of the whole number, whether greater or less, and with the advice of the civil authority in such town to take care of, manage and support them as tho' they were inhabitants of such town, according to the laws of this Colony. And if said committee shall judge that any of said French people by reason of age, sickness, etc., shall be unable to travel, or cannot be conveyed from the town where they are or may be landed, that in such case said committee shall provide for and support such aged, sick or otherwise infirm persons, at the charge of the Colony.

"And, to prevent such French people making their escape out of this Colony,

"*It is resolved and enacted*, That none of them be allowed to depart out of the respective towns where they belong without a writing under the hand of some of the civil authority of such town allowing of such departure. And if any of said French shall be found in any other town than that in which they were ordered to dwell, without liberty in writing as aforesaid, it shall be the duty of the civil authority where such persons shall be found, to confine such persons until upon examination it can be known from what town they departed, and when known, to convey them back from constable to constable to the towns where they belong, there to be confin'd and not suffered any more to depart without liberty as aforesaid. And said committee are hereby directed to take care in distributing said people, that no one family of them be separated and sent into two or more towns."

The expenses incidental to the support of the French exiles, from their arrival at New London till they had reached their respective destinations, were borne by the Colony, as provided by an act of the General Assembly February, 1756, viz.:

"*Resolved by this Assembly*, That such accounts of expence and charge as have been occasioned by the distributing the Neutral French and providing for their support till they were conveyed to the respective towns to which they were assigned, be laid before the Committee of the Pay-Table, who are hereby directed to adjust the same and give orders on the Treasurer accordingly."[1]

[1] "*Colonial Records of Conn.*," vol. X., p. 461.

Colony of Connecticutt for sundry Charges on the French People brot. from Nova Scotia pr Capt. Rockwell, & distributed in this Colony by order of General Assemblye
To G. Saltonstall     Dr[1]

1756                                                                                                                £. S. D.

Jany. 28th    To 56 lb Rice 9   4—1 Cordwood out of yard 8   4..........£    17 8
———    paid Shaw for 1 bb. fresh beef unsalted.............................    1 13 4
———    Muton 8   11 1   4—ditto 6   7   Cabages 4   2..........................    19 8¼

                                                                                                     3 10 8¼

To 2 Tierces bread deld Capt. Rockwell     ⎫
    1 ditto        "       "      Peter Haris        ⎬   9   0 1 @ 18  6..    8   6 8
    3 ditto        "       "      Tinker & Lester   ⎭
                    the 6 Tierces......@ 2   6.............................    15
    3 barels Beef dd. Tinker & Lester bound up Connecticut
        River......@ 3   pr...................................................    5   5
    4 bushels Beans deld. Tinker & Lester @ 4   ..........  ........    16
Feby. 12.    To Cash paid Tailor & Daniels, transporting 7 French
                persons, & their bagage to Colchester in 2 Carts,
                some being Sick, & travel Charges, per accot ........    2   5 2
March 6.    To Cash pd. Tinker, hire of Sloop Hanah from Feby. 1,
                to 25th.   Inclusive, 26 days @ 8   4 pr Ton pr
                month, being 30 Ton, the owner victualg & maning ..    12 10
                paid Ditto for Sloop Dove (Capt. Lester) from 3d Feby.
                to 20th Inclusive 18 days @ 8   4 pr Ton pr month
                being 20 ton.........................................................    5
    1,300 bread he bout. of Wylys & Co. at Middletown @ 20/    1 15
    91½ lb Porke he bout. @ 3½d 26  8¼  ½ bus. beans @ 2   1    1   8 9¼

                                                                                                    41 12 5¼

To days time 2d, 3, 4, 5, Feby. in distributg. the French, &
    makg. out the Rule..............................................    1   8 0
a Journey to Norwich on rect. of Govr. Fitch's orders to
    Confer with the Comte............................................    0   7 6
postage Gov Lette 6d...................................................

                                                                                                    43   7 9¼
To my Commissions...................................................    0 10

                                                                                                £43 17 9¼

New London March 11th, 1756.
G. SALTONSTALL
Errors Excepted.

Colony of Connecticutt for Sundry Charges on the French People Brot into this Colony per Capt Rockwell & Distributed pr order order of the General Assembly
To Hez. Huntington Dtr

**To** 4 Days Spent at New London @ 7/.......................................£   1   8 0
To Capt. Peter Harrisses Bill Transporting.............................    1   8
107 of them to Norwich..............................................  ...........    8 10 0
To man and Horse at Norwich to provide teem to Transport the people..    0   5 0
To Thomas & Saml Leffingwell their Bills Transporting to Canterbury
    Plainfield &c............................................. .........................    2   2
To Transporting these to preston as pr Bill...............................    0   8

[1] *State Archives*, War. Vol. V.

To Dito to Volluntown and Killingly by Selectmen of Plainfield as pr
    Bill.................................................................................................... £  1  1  2
To Ditto those to Windham & mansfield as pr Bill of Saml Gifford....  1 15 8
To Abell Griswold these to Lebanon Mansfield &c. as pr his Bill......  3  5 3
To Ditto James Flint to Ashford..............................................................  1  5 0
To my Vittiling the People at Norwich as per bills........... 0 11 3
                                        2  2 9½
                                        —————    3  7 5½
                                      0  4 5
                                         6

To by Expence on the Rhoad to Canterbury........................................  1  7 6
To Capt. Skiner Bill transporting from Rocky Hill.........................  2 15 0
To Selectmens Bill Transporting to Stonington...........................  0 15 0
To Expence at Capt Kingsbury Norwich.............................................  0 15 6
Entertaining teems to Windham.............................................................
To Mansfield Selectmen Bill....................................................................  0 16 0
To Mr Stores Transporting to Coventry.............................................  1  8 2
To Dee Williams Transporting to Woodstock..................................  0  6 0
To Capt Konts Bill Transporting from Winsor to Suffield & Enfield...  0 10 0
To Woodbury Selectmen Bill Transporting their people from Infield—
    38 miles..........................................................................................  4  2 0

        Amt Brot over                             £36  3 2½
To my time & Trouble in Contracting With the People and Collecting
    the amt and to pay them off......................................................  1 00 0
To Norwalk Selectmens Bill Transporting french people from Fairfield  1  6 0
To Waterbury Selectmen Do for Do..................................................  3  3 0
To Danbury Selectmen Do for Do.....................................................  2 13 0
To Simsbury Do.........................................................................................  0  8 0

                                       £44 13 2½
To Canterbury Selectmen.......................................................................  1 11 9
To Gilford Selectmen...............................................................................  2 11 8
Windsor Bill ...............................................................................................  1  3 8
Collo. Avery & Pygan Adams Esqrs...................................................  6  6

                                        56  6 3
Collo. Saltonstall pr Bill........................................................................ 43 17 9¼

                                       100 04 2¼

Thus were these unhappy people scattered throughout Connecticut.
Family ties were shattered, wives were separated from husbands and tender
children were deprived of their natural and God-given protectors. Strange
faces met them wherever they wandered. Depressed in spirit, broken in
body, their thoughts ever reverted to distant Acadia, the scene of so much
peace and happiness and contentment, and, alas! of so much sorrow. There
they were surrounded with abundance; here they had become the objects of
public charity. A less virtuous and religious people would have broken into
open rebellion at the sight of their chains, even though against overwhelm-
ing odds; but their religion, to which they were fervently attached, supported
them amid their trials, gave them strength to bear their exile and taught
them holy submission to the will of Him who, for His own all-wise purposes,
permits His children to be burdened with heavy crosses.

In Connecticut the Acadians were not only frequently treated as paupers, they were bound out to the most menial service.

The legislation of the General Assembly, January, 1756, directed and required each town to take care of and support them as though they were inhabitants. The aged and infirm were to receive ample provision from the treasury of the Colony. But some of the towns were not faithful to the humane spirit embodied in these enactments. The town of Wallingford received twelve exiles, and the manner in which it discharged its trust is exemplified by an entry in the records of the town under date of December 21, 1756. It was voted, "That the Selectmen be impowered to proceed with the French people in this town as with *other town's poor, respecting binding them out*, etc., etc."

The town of Plainfield recognized its duty to the strangers within its borders. It listened to the voice of humanity pleading for these impoverished people, and it has the honored distinction of being the only town in Windham county to make official and public provision for them. They were furnished with wood and meat, and medical attendance was provided.

In Hartford the French were comfortably housed. The Selectmen were directed by a vote of the town to erect a building suitable for the accommodation of the thirteen people sent there, as no house with the necessary room could be rented. Two years after this vote was passed the records show that a Robert Nevins was allowed 20s., partly for rent and partly for damages his house sustained during its occupancy by the French.[1] Of the nine allotted to Woodbury the names of four have come down to us. Petre Beaumont, Henrie Sciseau, Alexander Pettigree and Philemon Cherevoy. The descendants of Cherevoy were, until recently, residents of the town.[2] The name of Sibyl Sharway, or Shearaway, has been preserved as that of one of the Acadians assigned to Litchfield. She had come to Connecticut from Maryland, and was one of the persons forming the "two families" referred to in an act of the General Assembly, passed February, 1757. The enactment vividly recalls the wanderings, the unsettled and dependent condition of the French exiles. With no spot they could claim as home, subsisting on charity—too often reluctantly bestowed—and depending upon severe masters, they excite our profound commiseration and arouse feelings of indignation against their oppressors. The Act of 1757 is as follows:

"Upon the memorial of Elisha Stoddard and others,[3] selectmen for the town of Woodbury, representing to this Assembly that there has lately come to said town of Woodbury two families of the French neutrals from Maryland, three persons in each family; and also shewing to said Assembly that said town of Woodbury had their proportionable part of the French neutrals to support, sent to this government by Governor Lawrence; praying to said Assembly to order concerning said neutral families: Whereupon it is resolved by this Assembly, that one of said families be immediately trans-

[1] "*Memorial Hist. of Hartford Co.*" Vol. I., p. 302.

[2] A child of Philemon Cherevoy, name unknown, died at Woodbury, August 22, 1790. Philemon Cherevoy died March 1, 1801, aged 52 years; Nathaniel Cherevoy died April 29, 1813, aged 28.

[3] "Col. Rec.," Vol. X., p. 615.

ported to the town of Litchfield, and the other of said families to the town of New Milford, by the direction of the selectmen of Woodbury, and that the selectmen of said towns of Litchfield and New Milford are hereby ordered and directed to receive said French families and provide for their support and deal with them from time to time according to the directions of an act of Assembly of this Colony made respecting the French sent to this government by Governor Lawrence, and that the expence of transporting said French families from said Woodbury to said towns be at the expence of this Colony."

Litchfield provided for its Acadian charges in a manner consonant with the spirit of Christianity. In the records of the town we find these entries: In January, 1759, it was "voted that the Selectmen may provide a house or some suitable place in the town *for the maintenance of the French.*" In the County Treasurer's record is the following: "To paid John Newbree for keeping William Dunlap *and the French persons,* 54s. 6d., which the County allowed, and R. Sherman, Justice of the Quorum, drew an order dated April 25, 1760, as per order on file."

We have seen that fourteen Acadians were assigned to Stratford. Among them was William Rose, a gardener.[1] Rose married Jeannette Mann. His children were Peter, Mabel, Charity and Polly. He died April 21, 1812, aged 90 years.

The Stratford Acadians remained steadfast to the Catholic faith, though strenuous efforts were put forth to proselytize them. The Church of England minister at Stratford bears witness to their unconquerable fidelity in the midst of the spiritual dangers that environed them. Writing to the Home Secretary, the Rev. Mr. Winslow said: " Besides these (Dissenters), there are no other sectaries among us, except a few families of French neutrals, of inconsiderable notice, who were in the beginning of the war dispersed from Nova Scotia, and remain inflexibly tenacious of their superstitions (?). But there is not the least danger of any influence from them. *It is rather hopeful that if they are not themselves, their posterity may in time be brought off from their errors (!), though hitherto they will not suffer any efforts of this kind.*"[2]

These lines throw a flood of light upon the anti-Catholic sentiment then prevalent. The unfortunate Acadians became the objects of unpardonable ridicule, were branded as superstitious and as the disciples of error. Socially they were outcasts, destitute of influence among their fellows, and solely because they worshiped God according to the manner of the church founded by Jesus Christ. If they had abandoned their religion; had they set their faces against all they had previously held sacred at the "efforts" of proselytizing clergymen, they would not have been superstitious, but children

---

[1] This anecdote is told of Rose. It was his custom to fish in the harbor of Bridgeport in a boat, accompanied only by his faithful dog Lyon. One day he lost his balance and fell overboard, and was on the point of being drowned when his dog swam to him. He grasped the dog's tail and directed him to swim for the shore. When the faithful animal had brought his master almost to the shore, he turned about and began to swim out again, when Rose, in his broken French, called out : "Tudder way, Lyon." The dog obeying the command, towed his master to the shore.—Orcutt's *" Hist. of Stratford and Bridgeport."*

[2] Church Documents of the Prot. Ep. Ch. in Connecticut, Vol. II., p. 31.

of light, nor would they have been "of inconsiderable notice." The last few lines of the above are a melancholy commentary on the spirit that animated some of the Protestant clergy of colonial times. As it was then, so is it now. If perversions cannot be made among the parents, strike the church in her children. But as the elder Acadians of Stratford manfully resisted all "efforts" to seduce them from the path of duty, we would fain believe that "their posterity were not in time brought off from their errors," but, stimulated by the noble teachings and heroic example of their parents, they refused to bow assent to a creed that held them in abhorrence.

In 1759 we find traces of a small band of these helpless people at Newington, though they were not originally assigned there. They were provided for by the selectmen, who, in 1762, built a house for them near Howard's Pond. It is probable, they were a part of the Hartford contingent.

As we have seen, Waterbury's allotment was six, all members of one family. In 1763 the town "Voted, to give the French family in this Town, in order to Transport sd. French Family into the Northward Country, not exceeding Ten pounds, including Charitable Contributions."

The paucity of authentic records makes it no easy task to follow the wanderings of the Acadian exiles in Connecticut. In 1767, however, some persons, evidently of influence and authority, gathered the scattered remnants of their people at Norwich, whence 240 of them were carried to Quebec by Captain Leffingwell in the brig "Pitt." The historian of Norwich, Miss Caulkins, asserts that "*their priest*" returned with them. If priests were with the expatriated French, they were not numerous. It is traditional, that two Acadian priests resided near Hartford. The Neutrals at Baltimore were consoled by the ministrations of a fellow-exile, Father Le Clerc, and we know that the priests of Mines, Piziquid and Annapolis were put on board of transports bound for New England. But, notwithstanding, it was not the intention of the English oppressors that the Acadians should remain loyal to the Catholic faith. Every means was employed to deprive them of this precious treasure. Every obstacle that might cause them to forget their religion was thrown in their way. When some of the broken-hearted people craved the privilege of being allowed the presence of priests in their exile, they were heartlessly refused the boon, as we gather from a paragraph in a letter written by the arch-conspirator, Governor Lawrence, to the Board of Trade: "As the three French priests, Chevereuil, Daudin and Le Maire, were of no further use in this province after the removal of the French inhabitants, Admiral Boscowan has been so good as to take them on board of his fleet and is to give them a passage to England."

Presuming, however, upon the presence of Acadian priests in Connecticut at this period, it is probable they did not extend the sphere of their ministerial labors beyond the limits of their immediate domicile, owing to the law enacted by the General Assembly, January 21, 1756, which forbade any Acadian to depart from the town to which he had been assigned without written permission from the civil authorities of such town. The law comprehended both clergy and laity, and the enforcement of it would preclude the exercise of sacerdotal functions beyond the towns in which the priests resided. Moreover, ignorance of the English language would make traveling from town to town both difficult and dangerous. Laws of similar purport prevailed also in Massachusetts, where opposition to Catholic priests was more violent and more openly pronounced than in Connecticut. It may be stated without reserve, that no Acadian priest in Massachusetts, if any such there were, ever officiated publicly at divine worship. "No exception was taken to their prayers in their families, in their own way, which I believe they practiced in general, and sometimes they assembled several families together; but the people *would upon no terms have consented* to the public exercise of religious worship by Roman Catholic priests."[1]

The existence of these prohibitory laws, the sentiment of hostility entertained against Catholic priests and the entire absence of priests in many places, were, no doubt, among the reasons for the appointment and authorization of Acadian laymen in New England and elsewhere to join their fellow-exiles in marriage rather than have the ceremony performed by clergymen of alien creeds. The parties to the marriage expressed their consent in the presence of their assembled families and the old Acadian people, with the understanding and promise, however, of renewing their consent and having their union blessed by a priest, should they ever have the happiness to meet one. The Abbé Cyprian Tanguay, the Canadian genealogist, in his work, *A Travers les Registres*, Montreal, 1886, publishes an entry taken from the register of the parish of Deschambault anent the renewal of consent of marriage by Michel Robichau and Marguerite Landry before the curé of the parish, Rev. Jean Menage, on October 27, 1766:

" . . . Who (Michel Robichau and Marguerite Landry) presented a writing by which it is said that, having been taken prisoners by the English and expelled from their country, for want of receiving the teachings and the doctrines of the English ministers, they married themselves in the presence of their assembled families and of the old Acadian people, in New England, in the hope of renewing their marriage, if ever, after their captivity ended, they fell into the hands of French priests."

Among those mentioned by the Abbé Tanguay who were authorized to receive the consent of persons wishing to be married was "Louis Robichaud, husband of Jeanne Bourgeois, Acadian refugee in Quebec, who was at Salem, New England, in 1774. He was then aged 71 years. This respectable old man had received the extraordinary power of dispensing the publications of the banns and the impediments to marriage, etc., (meaning those purely ecclesiastical) for Catholics who could not have recourse to the ministry of priests in New England."

"The form of acts of marriage given by Louis Robichaud was as follows:

SALEM, . . . 1774.

"By virtue of the powers given me, Louis Robichaud, by Mons. Charles Francois Bailly, priest, Vicar General of the Diocese of Quebec, at present at Halifax, missionary to the Indians and to the French, to receive the mutual consent of Catholics desiring to unite themselves in marriage, in this Province, as also to grant dispensations to those

[1] Hutchinson's "*Hist. of Mass. Bay.*"

who would be married within certain degrees of affinity or of consanguinity, and who are in need of such. I confess to having received the mutual consent of marriage of . . . . . of the 3d to the 4th degree of consanguinity . . . . . the said parties have promised and do promise, on the first occasion that they shall find a priest approved by the Holy Catholic, Apostolic and Roman Church, to receive the nuptial benediction.

"The said act made in the presence . . . . . "[1]

We shall bring this chapter to a close with the testimony of historians who cannot be charged with pro-Catholic sympathies. Their words are the eloquent expression of hearts stirred to their depths with sorrow for the unparalleled sufferings of the French Neutrals, as well as a severe but righteous indictment of their oppressors; and their sentiments, so honestly and fearlessly recorded, will serve to dispel, in some degree, at least, the mists of prejudice raised against the hapless Acadians by apologists of English cruelty and vindictiveness.

Says Haliburton : Tradition is fresh and positive in the various parts of the United States where they were afterwards located, respecting their guileless, peaceable and scrupulous character ; and the descendants of those whose long-cherished and endearing local attachments induced them to return to the land of their nativity, still deserve the name of a mild, frugal and pious people.

. . . . Upon an impartial review of the transactions of the period, it must be admitted that the transportation of the Acadians to distant colonies with all the marks of ignominy and guilt peculiar to convicts, was cruel; and although such a conclusion could not then be drawn, yet subsequent events have disclosed that their expulsion was unnecessary. It seems totally irreconcilable with the idea of justice entertained at this day, that those who are not involved in the guilt shall participate in the punishment; a whole community shall suffer for the misconduct of a part. It is, doubtless, a stain on the Provincial Councils, and we shall not attempt to justify that which all good men have agreed to condemn.

From Smith's *Acadia:* History is replete with instances of the readiness of man, in every degree of enlightenment, to lay down his life in defense of his right to worship God as he chooses: the Neutrals *were denied the services of their priests,* when such deprivation meant, according to the light of their faith, the loss of their hope of happiness in the world to come. . . . . The banishment from one's country has ever been adjudged one of the most severe penalties known in jurisprudence; this, and the other extremes of human misery, the poor, exiled Acadians suffered, by the voluntary acts of men differing only in language and religion.

From Lossing's *History of the United States:* The cruel sequel (of the war) deserves universal reprobation. The total destruction of the French settlements was decided upon under the plea that the Acadians would aid their

[1] Quoted by U. S. Cath. Hist. Mag., Jan'y. 1887. Similar faculties were granted to and exercised by a Canadian layman, Pierre Mallett, at Vincennes, Ind., between the departure of Rev. P. Gibault in October, 1789, and the arrival of Rev. Benedict Flaget in 1792.—"*Hist. of the Diocese of Vincennes.*" Alerding.

French brethren in Canada. The innocent and happy people were seized in their homes, fields and churches and conveyed aboard the English vessels. Families were broken, never to be united; and to compel the surrender of those who fled to the woods, their starvation was insured by a total destruction of their growing crops. The Acadians were stripped of everything, and those who were carried away were scattered among the English colonies, helpless beggars, to die heart-broken in a strange land. In one short month their paradise had become a desolation and a happy people were crushed into the dust.

The words of Smith form an appropriate comment on this passage of the American historian: This incursion, aided and abetted and paid for by England, consummated by New England troops, under a Massachusetts commander bred in a Puritan atmosphere, in the name of religion, was conducted in so heartless a manner, that as though by common consent, the reports of details have been purposely destroyed, and historians have passed over it with only an allusion, as if unable to record the shame of the transaction.

We shall supplement this testimony with the words of Most Rev. William Walsh, Archbishop of Halifax, who, on the centennial of the expulsion, issued a pastoral letter in which he reviewed the sad history of the Acadians. The letter, dated September 8, 1855, is addressed "To Our Dearly-Beloved Brethren, the Acadians of the Archdiocese of Halifax." We submit an extract:

"DEARLY BELOVED BRETHREN.—On the 10th of September, 1755, nearly two thousand Acadian Catholics were barbarously driven from their happy homes by the ruthless hand of persecution. For their attachment to the faith of their fathers were they thus pursued; and the voice of posterity has proclaimed the foul injustice of the act, and the cold-blooded hypocrisy and cruelty with which it was accomplished. The annals of history scarcely record a more heart-rending scene than that which was witnessed at the mouth of the Gaspereau, and on the shores of the Basin of Minas, on the memorable day alluded to. No doubt it was fondly hoped that the wholesale deportation of this innocent people, and the confiscation of their property would effectually extinguish the Catholic religion in Nova Scotia. Here, however, the impious calculations of the persecutor have been defeated by the mercy of heaven, thank God. After a long and gloomy interval of suffering, proscription and exclusion the Acadian Catholic still survives in the cherished land of his fathers, and the glorious faith for which the exiles and victims of 1755 endured the loss of property and life, still flourishes in the heart of nearly one-third of the people of Nova Scotia. . . . . . It is now a matter of history that the children of these Confessors of the Faith who were driven forth from Nova Scotia in 1755, and most cruelly dispersed over the American Continent, made frequent attempts to return to their native land, that their bones might rest in the bosom of their beloved Acadia. A few, at length, happily succeeded,[1] and established themselves in the midst of the untrodden forest, and along the virgin shores of that beautiful bay which their piety delighted to honor with the endearing name of the Immaculate Mother of God. Here, whilst the spacious and fertile lands of their fathers in the most luxuriant spots of Acadia were possessed by strangers, who had never toiled to reclaim them from the dominion of the wilderness, those new settlers made secret progress. Fostered by the protecting hand of Him who will not suffer ' the just man to be abandoned, nor his seed to want bread,' they throve apace, and with the patient spirit of their ancestors, they made the wilderness blossom as the rose. The children of confessors and martyrs, they were sure to merit the protection of Heaven. The ' little flock ' soon increased to hundreds, and from hundreds to thousands, and their children and children's children are

[1] See page 72.

now to be found in various parts of Nova Scotia and the neighboring provinces, speaking the language of the country from which they boast of being descended, and glorying in the profession of that Catholic faith which their forefathers prized beyond life itself.

"In these few words, cherished portion of our beloved flock, we have traced your melancholy but glorious history. You are the descendants of those who passed through the Red Sea of persecution, and were marked with the sign of suffering, because they were the faithful disciples of Christ crucified; of those who in 'the former days being illuminated' with peace from the Father of lights, endured a great fight of affliction."

# THE FRENCH ARMY IN CONNECTICUT.

## CHAPTER XV.

### PRELIMINARY CONFERENCES.

THE services rendered by the soldiers and sailors of Catholic France to the Colonies in their struggle for independence form a brilliant chapter in American history with which every student is familiar. Washington gratefully acknowledged their assistance in his Reply to an Address from the Roman Catholics of the United States. The address was signed by Right Rev. John Carroll, Bishop of Baltimore, on behalf of the clergy, and by Charles Carroll, of Carrollton; Dominick Lynch, Thomas Fitzsimmons and Daniel Carroll, on behalf of the laity. Washington said: "I presume your fellow-citizens will not forget the patriotic part which you took in the accomplishment of their revolution and the establishment of their government—*or the important assistance which they received from a nation in which the Roman Catholic faith is professed.*"

The names of Lafayette and De Grasse, of Rochambeau and De Choisey—names "that were not born to die," and which are synonymous with chivalry, dauntless courage and nobility of character—are wreathed with undying lustre and are held in benediction by a grateful nation. It is no part of our purpose to relate the story of their heroic achievements on land and on sea; ours it is to follow them in their march through Connecticut, to place on record here the impressions their magnificent appearance and superb discipline made upon this portion of the American people, and to recall the fact that it was within the present limits of our diocese, a few miles only from the episcopal residence, and by the aid of the experienced counsels of the French generals, that the plans were arranged which resulted in the defeat of Cornwallis at Yorktown, and the termination of British power in the Colonies. Brave and generous sons of a Catholic nation and devoted children of the Catholic church, they are a part of the history of early Catholicity in Connecticut. They fought no battles on our soil, nor performed here great deeds of valor. Their meetings were with friends, not with foes. Their passage across the State was as rapid as the circumstances would permit, for theirs was a mission of tremendous importance to the American cause. Nevertheless, they left upon the

State an impress that is yet undimmed and have bequeathed to us, their co-religionists, a record of which we are justly proud. Their route from New-port to the Hudson abound in memories that are ineffaceable. Wherever they passed they became the idols of the populace and were everywhere acclaimed the noble champions of American liberty.

The first Frenchman to offer his services to the Continental Congress was the youthful, generous and chivalrous Marquis de Lafayette, then nineteen years of age. Congress at first refused his tender, but finally bestowed upon Lafayette the rank and commission of a Major-General in the army of the United States. Having served with distinction in the Virginia and Rhode Island campaigns, he returned to France impressed with the purpose of secur-ing aid from his sovereign, Louis XVI. His plea for reinforcements was successful. In consequence of his intervention a French fleet carrying 6,000 soldiers under the command of Admiral de Ternay[1] and the Count de Rochambeau arrived at Newport on July 10, 1780. They came at a time when the army and finances of the Colonies were in a deplorable condition, and were received with unbounded enthusiasm. By order of the French government the new reinforcements were placed under the command of General Washington, the Commander-in-Chief of the American forces.

After his arrival, Count de Rochambeau, as the commander of the French land forces, sought an interview with General Washington, but military duties prevented a meeting until September 20th. The allied commanders met at Hartford.

Rochambeau set out for the rendezvous on the 17th, with Admiral De Ternay as traveling companion. As the admiral was afflicted with the gout, they made the journey in a carriage. On the evening of the 17th, when near Windham, the conveyance broke down, and they were unable to proceed. Rochambeau sent one of his aides, de Fersen, in search of a blacksmith to make the necessary repairs. The aide found one about a mile from the scene of the accident, but so ill that he declared he would not work at night if he received a hat full of guineas. Undaunted by the refusal, both Rochambeau and De Ternay—the latter with difficulty—went to the smith, and importuned him to repair their carriage. They informed him that Washington was about to arrive at Hartford to confer with them, but that the conference would not take place if the carriage were not repaired. It was a pressing argument and prevailed. "You are not deceivers," said the smith. "I have read in the *Connecticut Journal* that Washington is expected to confer with you, and I recognize that this is in the public service. Your carriage will be ready at six o'clock in the morning."

[1] Charles Louis D'Arsac de Ternay was born in 1722. He died in December, 1781, at Newport. The *Conn. Courant* of December 22, 1781, contained the following notice :

NEWPORT. Buried in Trinity Churchyard, His Excellency Charles Louis de Ternay, Knight of St. John of Jerusalem, late Governor of the Islands of France and Bourbon, and Chief Commander of the French Squadron in the American Seas. His talents, zeal, and distinguished services have merited him the confidence and favor of his government and country.

On their return journey another accident befell their carriage almost at the same place. Appealed to again for aid, the smith said: "Well, you wish me to work at night again?" Rochambeau informed him that the English Admiral Rodney had arrived with a naval force three times as large as their own, and therefore, it was necessary for them to press on in order to oppose his operations. "But," interposed the loquacious disciple of Vulcan, "what will your six vessels do against the twenty ships of the English? At any rate, you are a brave people. You shall have your carriage at five o'clock in the morning. But, without wishing to know your secrets, tell me, were you pleased with Washington and he with you?"[1]

At this conference Washington was accompanied by General Lafayette and General Knox, while with Rochambeau were Admiral de Ternay, General Chastellux and the aides-de-camp, Count de Fersen, Marquis de Damas and M. Dumas,[2] and his son, the Viscount de Rochambeau.

The execution of the plans then agreed upon depended upon the arrival of a second division of French troops or in an increase of the naval forces. It was also decided to despatch an envoy to France to solicit new reinforcements from the ministry; and for this mission the Viscount de Rochambeau, son of the commander, was chosen.

The meeting-place of the French and American generals is thus described. Speaking of Lafayette's departure from Bennet's hotel, on the occasion of his visit to Hartford, in 1824, a writer says:"[3]

"On this very spot where stood his carriage, General Washington first met General Rochambeau, after his arrival from France to aid in the cause of the Revolution. Here Washington and several other American officers first shook hands, in the presence of Lafayette, with the officers of the French army. This place, too, was in front of the mansion Col. Wadsworth's, now the Athenæum").

[1] "*Les Français En Amérique*, 1777-1783." Balch.

[2] Count de Fersen's account of this conference is thus detailed in a letter to his father, dated October 16, 1780: "I was about fifteen days ago at Hartford, forty leagues distant from here (Newport) with M. de Rochambeau. We were only six, the Admiral, his Chief of Engineers, his son, the Viscount de Rochambeau, and three aids-de-camp, of whom I was one. He had an interview there with Washington. M. de Rochambeau sent me in advance to announce his arrival, and I had time to see this man, illustrious, if not unique in our century. His handsome and majestic, while, at the same time, mild and open countenance perfectly reflects his moral qualities; he looks the hero; he is very cold; speaks little, but is courteous and frank. A shade of sadness overshadows his countenance, which is not unbecoming, and gives him an interesting air. His suite was more numerous than ours. The Marquis de Lafayette, General Knox, Chief of Artillery, M. de Gouvion, a Frenchman, Chief of Engineers and six aids-de-camp accompanied him. . . . As there is no traveling by posting in this country, every one must journey with his own horses, and nearly always on horseback, because of the bad roads. However, every body was in carriages, except our two aids de camp. We were three days making the journey. General Washington as many. . . . The two Generals and the Admiral were closeted together the whole of the day we passed at Hartford. The Marquis de Lafayette was called in as an interpreter, as Washington does not either speak French or understand it. They separated mutually pleased with each other—at least they say so."

[3] "*An Account of the Tour of General Lafayette through the United States in 1824-25*" (Hartford: Silas Andrus & Son, 1855.)

The plans arranged at this conference were frustrated by the treason of Arnold. At the very hour in which Washington and Rochambeau were engaged in council to promote the cause of the Revolution, an American officer, born of the soil, was conspiring with the enemy to betray his country.

Rochambeau's main army, numbering about 4000 men, remained at Newport. To determine upon a plan of campaign a second conference was arranged between Washington and his French ally. This meeting was held on May 21, 1781, at the "Webb house," in Wethersfield.[1] Rochambeau was accompanied by General Chastellux, and Washington by General Knox and General Du Portail.[2] We quote a few entries from Washington's diary, containing this conference. His headquarters were at New Windsor, on the Hudson:

"May 18th. Set out this day for the interview at Wethersfield, with the Count de Rochambeau and Admiral Barras. Reached Morgan's Tavern, forty-three miles from Fishkill Landing, after dining at Colonel Vanderberg's.

"19th. Breakfasted at Litchfield, dined at Farmington, and lodged at Wethersfield, at the house of Joseph Webb.

"20th. Had a good deal of private conversation with Governor Trumbull, who gave it to me as his opinion that if any important offensive operations should be undertaken, he had little doubt of our obtaining men and provisions adequate to our wants. In this Colonel Wadsworth and others concurred.

"May 21st. Count de Rochambeau, with the Chevalier Chastellux, arrived about noon. The appearance of the British fleet under Admiral Arbuthnot, off Block Island, prevented attendance of Count de Barras.

"22d. Fixed, with Count de Rochambeau, the plan of the campaign.

"23d. Count de Rochambeau set out on his return to Newport, while I prepared and forwarded dispatches to the Governors of the four New England States, calling on them, in earnest and pointed terms, to complete their Continental battalions for the campaign, at least, if not for three years or the war," etc.[3]

At the May session, 1781, the General Assembly appropriated £500 to defray the expense "to be incurred in quartering General Washington, General Knox, General Duportail, Count de Rochambeau, Count de Barras, and the Chevalier de Chastellux, and their suites, in Wethersfield."

On his arrival at Hartford on the 21st, Rochambeau was met by Washington and his retinue and escorted to Wethersfield. According to tradition, the meeting occurred near what was the east end of the State House, now the site of the Post Office building. Rochambeau came from the ferry up

---

[1] The Webb house at Wethersfield is still standing. It was the common resting-place for American officers and gentlemen of distinction in their passage through Connecticut, and was known among them, from the generous courtesy of its occupants, as "Hospitality Hall." Its chief interest to the historical student is derived from its having been the spot elected for the conference held between Washington and Rochambeau." "*Mag. of American Hist., June, 1880.*"

[2] Du Portail was a French officer holding a commission in the American army. Other French officers serving with the Continental forces were Lieutenant-Colonel Gimat and Major Galvan. Gimat was wounded at Yorktown.

[3] In Washington's private account appears this item:

"May. To the Expence of a journey to Wethersfield, for the purpose of an interview with the French Genl & Adml, specie expended in this trip, £35. 18s."

Market street, while Washington rode up Main street from his headquarters at Colonel Wadsworth's.[1]

It was agreed at the Conference that the French forces should effect a junction with the American army on the Hudson as soon as circumstances would permit.

## CHAPTER XVI.

### THE MARCH THROUGH CONNECTICUT.

ROCHAMBEAU left Hartford for Newport on the 23d. On the 9th of June, the army began its march westward. Arrived at Providence on the 11th, they rested there until the 18th, when they started on their march across what the Abbé Robin calls "The Province of Connecticut." The following are the names of the principal officers with the regiments that passed through the State:[2]

Lieutenant-general, COUNT DE ROCHAMBEAU.

Aides-de-Camp—Count de Fersen, Marquis de Vauban, Marquis de Damas, Chevalier de Lameth, M. Dumas, De Lauberdière, Baron de Clozen. Marechaux de-Camp—Major-general Baron de Viomenil, Major-general Marquis de St. Simon, Major-general Viscount de Viomenil, Major-general Chevalier de Chastellux.

M. DE CHOISY, Brigadier-general.

Intendant—M. de Tarlé. Quartermaster-general—M de Béville. Commissary-general—Claude Blanchard. Medical Department—M. de Coste, Physician-in-chief; M. Robillard, Surgeon-in-chief; M. de Mars, Superintendent of Hospitals. Engineers—Colonel Desandrouins, Lieutenant-colonel de Querenet, Major de Palys and nine line officers.

### ARTILLERY.

Colonel Commandant d'Aboville, Adjutant Manduit. Director of the Park, M. Nadal. Rank and file, 600.

### CAVALRY.

*Lauzun's Legion* (or Volunteers)—Duke de Lauzun, Count Arthur Dillon.[3] Rank and file, 600.

### INFANTRY.

BRIGADE BOURBONNOIS.—*Regiment Bourbonnois*—Colonel Marquis de Laval, Second-colonel Viscount de Rochambeau, Lieutenant-colonel de Bressolles, Major de Gambs. Rank and file, 900.

*Regiment Royal Deuxponts*—Colonel Count de Deuxponts, Second-colonel Count Guillaume de Deuxponts, Lieutenant-colonel Baron d'Ezbeck, Major Desprez. Rank and file, 900.

BRIGADE SOISSONOIS.—*Regiment Soissonois*—Colonel Marquis de St. Maime, Second-colonel Vicomte de Noailles, Lieutenant-colonel d'Anselme, Major d'Espeyron. Rank and file, 900.

[1] *Memorial Hist. of Hartford Co., Vol. I.,* p. 298.

[2] This roster of French officers is taken from the lists printed in the Mag. of Am. Hist., Vol. III., No. 7, and by Blanchard in his "Journal."

[3] Count Dillon was the second in command at the siege of Savannah, October 4-9, 1779. He brought with him from France his own Irish regiment.

*Regiment Saintonge*—Colonel Marquis de Custine, Second-colonel Count de Charlus, Lieutenant-colonel de la Vatelle, Major M. Fleury. Rank and file, 900.[1]

The army left Providence in the following order, which was observed until their departure from Newtown, when, instead of marching in regiments, the army marched in brigades: On the 18th (June) the Bourbonnois (Count de Rochambeau and General Chastellux); the 19th, the Royal Deux-Ponts (Baron de Viomenil); the 20th, the Soissonois (Count de Viomenil); the 21st, the Saintonge (M. de Custine). The regiments followed one another at intervals of a day's march, or at a distance of about fifteen miles.

The first camp after leaving Providence was at *Waterman's Tavern*, which was reached on the evening of the 18th. The second encampment, and the first in Connecticut, was at *Plainfield* on the 19th; the third at *Windham* on the 20th; the fourth at *Bolton* on the 21st; the fifth at *Hartford*, the Bourbonnois on the 22d, the Deux-Ponts on the 23d, the Soissonois on the 24th, and the Saintonge on the 25th. The regiments rested two days each, leaving Hartford in the same order on the 25th, 26th, 27th, and 28th, respectively. The advance regiment made its sixth camp at *Farmington* on the 25th. June 26th saw them at *Baron's Tavern* near Southington, since known as *French Hill*. On the 27th, they camped at *Breakneck* in *Middlebury*, and on the 28th at *Newtown*, where the army rested until July 1st. It was Rochambeau's intention to remain here till the 2d, but urgent orders from Washington caused him to hasten towards the Hudson. At Newtown the Bourbonnois and the Royal Deux-Ponts united, as did also the Soissonois and the Saintonge. In this order both brigades set out on July 1st for *Bridgebury* (Ridgebury), which they reached that evening. This was the last camp in Connecticut of Rochambeau's divisions on this march. At this point the army was diverted from the route originally planned on account of information received from General Washington. It was the intention to continue westward to Crompond and thence to King's Ferry on the Hudson, but instead, Rochambeau turned southward from Ridgebury and reached his eleventh camp at *Bedford*, New York, on July 2d, where he was joined by the legion of the Duke de Lauzun. The march was continued until July 7th, when a junction with the American forces was effected at *Phillipsburg*.

An eye-witness described Rochambeau's army as it marched across the State as "magnificent in appearance, superb in discipline." They conducted themselves as became brave soldiers of His Christian Majesty, the King of France. They committed no acts of forage, but paid liberally for the sup-

[1] The following regiments were not in Connecticut, but were engaged at Yorktown under Rochambeau. They were brought from the West Indies by St. Simon in De Grasse's fleet:

BRIGADE AGENOIS.

*Regiment Agenois*—Colonel Marquis d'Audechamp, Lieutenant-colonel Chevalier de Cadignan, Major Pandin de Beauregard. Rank and file, 1000.

*Regiment Gatenois*—Colonel Marquis de Rostaing, Lieutenant-colonel de L'Estrade, Major de Tourville. Rank and file, 1000.

*Regiment Touraine* (not brigaded)—Colonel Vicomte de Pondeux, Lieutenant-colonel de Montlezun, Major Ménonville. Rank and file, 1000.

II—6

plies furnished them; indeed, their liberality became a household word. They carried 2,500,000 livres for Washington's poorly paid troops, besides an abundance of silver money for their own requirements. Wherever they halted for the day, they were cordially received by officials appointed by the governor and escorted to suitable sites for encampment. During the march fifteen soldiers deserted—ten at Windham[1] and five at Newtown[2]—not a large number, when we consider that they were marching in the hottest season of the year in a foreign land and under great difficulties. There was no rest save what was imperatively necessary, and the army, as a body, responded nobly to the demands made upon them. A contemporary chronicler who accompanied Rochambeau says: "It is impossible for the army to march better than it has done the entire distance, or to show greater willingness; it is true that Messieurs de Custine and the Viscount de Noailles set the example by marching the entire distance on foot at the head of their regiments."[3]

At Bolton an incident occurred which furnished a subject of conversation for some time. Count de Rochambeau was the guest of the Congregational minister, the Rev. George Colton, "six feet three inches," but according to another authority, "six feet seven inches in height." He had been married twice, but had no children. To secure an heir to his fortune he offered to adopt the child of a grenadier, whose wife accompanied him, and to bestow upon the mother for herself thirty Louis in money; but she resolutely refused.

The camp at Hartford was pitched on a field north of the house of the late Nathaniel Warren, on Silver Lane.[4] Rochambeau's headquarters was at the residence of Elisha Pitkins, Esq. The other officers were domiciled at Joseph Goodwin's, Sr., at the Warren house, south of the Hockanum bridge, and at other public and private houses. The old meeting-house near Elisha Pitkin's residence was used as an hospital. The officials of the town were lavish in their attentions to their French guests. To facilitate their transportation across the Connecticut river a number of scows, which served as bridges, were pressed into service. Silver Lane takes its name from the large number of kegs that were opened here to pay the troops. The soldiers spent their money freely, among the boys for errands and among the women for sewing and mending uniforms, and for cakes, pies and other delicacies.

Tradition has been very busy with stories of this encampment; of their cattle-roasts in the meadows and the barrels of soup made in Elisha Pitkin's yard; of the frolicsome dancing parties in Ashael Robert's orchard near Silver Lane; of the "Belle-Bonne" (Beautiful and Good) apples—a name given by the French to the fruit of a tree in this orchard. Tradition tells us also that the French officers paid a visit of courtesy to some English prisoners confined at South Windsor, and were served by Governor Franklin with sour punches,

[1] Nine from the Soissonois and one from the Royal Deux-Ponts.

[2] From the Bourbonnois.

[3] The Soissonois and Saintonge.

[4] Many of the details given here of the Hartford encampment are drawn from Trumbull's *Memorial History of Hartford Co.*, and from *East Hartford: Its History and Traditions*, both admirable works.

whose sweet and sour ingredients were so pleasantly blended as to draw from the French the name "one grand contradiction."

The stay of the army in Hartford, though of brief duration,[1] was characterized by cordiality and generosity, by culture and good-breeding. Prejudice against Catholics was in a measure dispelled, and otherwise the beneficial effects of their visit were visible for many years after. That this friendly feeling did not pass away with the objects of it, but became more firmly cemented, is evident from the felicitations forwarded by the State of Connecticut to the King of France on the birth of his son, the Dauphin. His Majesty's thanks were conveyed to the people of the State through the Minister of France to the United States, the Chevalier De La Luzerne.

PHILADELPHIA, January 10, 1783.

*To his Excellency the Governor of the State of Connecticut:*

SIR:—His Majesty has been informed of the marks of joy which the State of Connecticut has shewn on the occasion of the birth of the Monsigneur the Dauphin. He views with a great deal of satisfaction the part that the citizens of your State have taken in this happy event. The King orders me to testify his sensibility on this subject, and at the same time charges me to assure the citizens and inhabitants of the State of Connecticut of his attention, and of the particular interest which he shall always take in their prosperity.

I have the honor to be, with respectful attachment, your Excellency's very obedient humble servant, LE CHEVALIER DE LA LUZERNE.

Leaving Hartford the army passed through Farmington, Southington (Baron's Tavern) and Waterbury to their eighth encampment at Breakneck Hill. They were delayed in Southington on account of freshets, which necessitated the repairing of a bridge which had become dangerous for travel. At Waterbury they made a fine impression. "It was on or about June 21st (it was June 27th) that the French army under General Rochambeau marched through Waterbury on its way to meet Washington's army near King's Bridge. What welcome travelers the bonny Frenchmen must have proved themselves as they journeyed on, for they paid all their expenses in hard money, committing no depredations, and treating the inhabitants with great civility and propriety. The officers wore coats of white broadcloth trimmed with green, white under-dress, and hats with two corners instead of three (like the cocked hats worn by American officers)."[2] They marched two and two, and when the head of the column had disappeared beyond the hill at Captain George Nichols' residence, the other extremity had not come in sight on West Side Hill.[3]

The army experienced great difficulty in reaching Breakneck in Middlebury. The roads were steep and very rough, so that the artillery was consid-

[1] On the day preceding the regiment's departure from Hartford, an officer wrote: "I went to see a charming spot called Weathersfield, four miles from East Hartford. It would be impossible to find prettier houses and a more beautiful view. I went up into the steeple of the church and saw the richest country I had yet seen in America. From this spot you can see for fifty miles around."—*Baron du Bourg.*

[2] *Hist. of Waterbury,* Price & Lee Company—1896. Vol. I, p 453.

[3] Bronson's *Hist. of Waterbury,* 1858.

erably delayed. The diarist, before quoted, says: "Breakneck is the English for *Casseeou*,[1] it well deserves the name from its difficult approach. The village is frightful and without resources." Rochambeau and his suite lodged at Israel Bronson's tavern, while the troops pitched their camp about a mile north of the church. While here the troops baked and washed to such an extent that all the wells of the neighborhood were drawn dry. To supply the deficiency all the men in the vicinity with their conveyances were employed to bring water from Hop Brook.[2]

Marching to Newtown the army passed through Woodbury. Their halt there is thus described by the distinguished historian of the town: "During this year 1781, the French army, under General Lafayette,[3] passed through this town on their journey south to join General Washington in his operations against Cornwallis. They came through White Deer Rocks, where they were obliged to cut away trees and remove stones in order to transport their heavy baggage through the defile. The army encamped for the night in town in such companies as suited their convenience, and when they pitched their tents they extended all the way from Middle Quarter to White Oak, a distance of three miles. That part which encamped near the house then occupied by David Sherman, and since by the late Gideon Sherman, ate for him, with his consent, twelve bushels of apples, as is related, and drank seven or eight barrels of new cider at his mill. During the evening they had a dance in which some of the Woodbury damsels joined with the polite French officers in their gay uniforms, while others looked on. Multitudes of the inhabitants pressed about the tents of those patriotic foreigners, who had come so far to fight the battle of freedom for a suffering people, and destined to act so distinguished a part in bringing the long and bloody contest to a close. Lafayette,[4] with his chief officers, lodged at the house of Hon. Daniel Sherman, and was waited on by all the principal men of the town."[5]

The following are the route and camps of the army of Count de Rochambeau in the campaign of 1781 from Providence, Rhode Island, to Bedford, New York:[6]

| DATES OF ARRIVAL | CAMPS | DISTANCES Miles | DATES OF ARRIVAL | CAMPS | DISTANCES Miles |
|---|---|---|---|---|---|
| June 18. | Waterman's Tavern, R. I. | 15 | June 26. | Baron's Tavern, Conn. | 13 |
| " 19. | Plainfield, Conn. | 15 | " 27. | Breakneck, " | 13 |
| " 20. | Windham, " | 15 | " 28. | Newtown, " | 15 |
| " 21. | Bolton, " | 16 | July 1. | Ridgebury, " | 19 |
| " 22. | Hartford, " | 12 | " 2. | Bedford, N. Y. | 13 |
| " 25. | Farmington, " | 13 | | | |

---

[1] "Breakneck " derives its name from the circumstance of one of the cattle falling and breaking its neck in descending the hill while employed in transporting the baggage of the troops."—Cothren's "*History of Woodbury.*"

[2] Bronson's "*Hist. of Waterbury.*"

[3] Mr. Cothren is in error here; Lafayette was not with this army.

[4] *Rochambeau.*

[5] The Abbe Robin, General Chastellux and the Baron du Bourg, who accompanied Rochambeau, say nothing of this encampment.

[6] The distances are taken from journals written during the march, and in some instances may not be strictly accurate.

Seven months before Rochambeau's troops started on their march across Connecticut, the Legion of the Duke de Lauzun, consisting of 1,000 infantry and 500 mounted Hussars, went into camp at Lebanon, the home of Governor Trumbull.[1] They were here from December 1, 1780, to June 23, 1781. Their camp was situated a short distance west of the governor's residence, and near the Congregational church. "A gay June for Lebanon was that," says a local historian, "when these six brilliant French regiments, with their martial bands and gorgeous banners, were daily displayed on this spacious and lovely village green."[2] While encamped here the Legion was reviewed by General Washington, who highly commended the efficiency of the commander and the discipline of the troops. During the encampment here a soldier was shot for desertion. The unfortunate man was tried by court-martial at 9 P.M. and executed before daybreak.

While in camp at Lebanon, De Lauzun and his officers made a visit to Norwich. The historian of Norwich[3] thus describes the event: "Colonel Jedidiah Huntington invited the officers to visit him, and prepared a handsome entertainment for them. They made a superb appearance as they came into town, being young, tall, vivacious men, with handsome faces and a noble air, mounted upon horses bravely caparisoned. The two Dillons, brothers, one a major and the other a captain in the regiment, were particularly distinguished for their fine forms and expressive features."

A local historian[4] has reflected severely upon the private character of the Duke de Lauzan. Perhaps, he was not a model for imitation, but I do not believe he was the profligate he has been painted. I prefer to form my judgment of him from the testimony of those who shared the hardships of the camp with him and who knew him best. Such a one was the Count de Fersen, aid-de-camp to Count Rochambeau. In a letter to his father from Newport, October 16, 1780, he wrote:

"I have already informed you, my dear father, that I am extremely intimate with the Duc de Lauzun. Opinions are very much divided concerning him. You will hear good and bad reports of him. The first are right, the second are wrong. If those who say them knew him, they would change their minds and do justice to his heart."

The history of the operations of the French army sustains the assertion that its assistance was indispensable to the success of the American arms. With the single exception of D'Estaing's withdrawal from Newport, in which, however, he felt justified, the French allies caused no friction with the American forces; but, on the contrary, co-operated intelligently, bravely and constantly with the plans of the Commander-in-chief. They were exponents of liberty in its highest sense, and their sole aim was to aid in securing the precious boon for their fellow-men across the sea. For this they abandoned the ease and comforts of aristocratic life, sacrificed position and fortune and

---

[1] Gov. Trumbull was the original "Brother Jonathan."

[2] "*Early Lebanon.*"

[3] F. M. Caulkins.

[4] "*Hist. of Norwich.*"

sundered the holy and tender relations of home and friendship. Washington recognized their splendid services, and in his congratulatory order to the allied army tendered this graceful acknowledgment:

WASHINGTON'S CONGRATULATORY ORDER TO THE ALLIED ARMY.

"*After Orders, 20th Oct., 1781.*

"The General congratulates the army upon the glorious event of yesterday. The generous proofs which His Most Christian Majesty has given of his attachment to the cause of America must force conviction on the minds of the most deceived among the enemy relative to the good consequences of the alliance, and inspire every citizen of these states with sentiments of the most unalterable gratitude. His fleet, the most numerous and powerful that ever appeared in these seas, commanded by an admiral whose fortune and talents insure great events, an army of the most admirable composition, both in officers and men, are the pledges of his friendship to the United States, and their co-operation has secured us the present signal success.

"The General on this occasion entreats his Excellency, Count de Rochambeau, to accept his most grateful acknowledgements for his counsel at all times; he presents his warmest thanks to the Generals Baron de Viomenil, Chevalier Chastellux, Marquis de Saint Simon, and Count de Viomenil, and to Brigadier General de Choisy (who had a separate command), for the illustrious manner in which they have advanced the common cause. He requests that Count de Rochambeau will be pleased to communicate to the army under his immediate command the high sense he entertains of the distinguished merits of the officers and soldiers of every corps, and that he will present in his name to the regiments of Agenois and Deuxponts the two pieces of brass ordnance captured by them (as a testimony of their gallantry) in storming the enemy's redoubt on the night of the 14th inst., when officers and men so universally vied with each other in the exercise of every soldierly virtue.'

## CHAPTER XVII.

### MASS IN THE FRENCH ARMY.

AS Rochambeau's army were Catholics, with, probably, a few exceptions, and as it is the custom of Catholic nations to provide chaplains for their armies and navies, we are certain that the French forces, who aided us in the Revolution, were sufficiently provided with priests. Indeed, the names of some of them are known, viz.: the Abbés Robin, Glesnon, Lacy, St. Pierre and Claude Florent Bouchard de la Portieré. A Capuchin friar was also in the service. After the war the Abbé Portieré remained at Boston until 1790, when he sailed for the West Indies. The Abbé Lacy, as his name indicates, was an Irish priest; and as he was an hospital chaplain, it is probable that he accompanied the army on its entire march.[2] If so, he performed service in Hartford, as the old meeting-house was transformed into a temporary hospital for the soldiers who had fallen ill on the route. The Abbé Glesnon was at Newport and Providence for some time, and, no doubt, said Mass in those places regularly, and, in all probability, accompanied Rochambeau's, or some other regiment, across Connecticut.

The army spent two Sundays in the State, at Hartford (June 24th) and Newtown (July 1st), and it may be averred that on those days—if on no others

[1] Lieutenant Sanderson's MS. Diary. Yorktown Orderly Book.
[2] He is spoken of as "an Irish priest, the Abbe Lacy, the Chaplain of our hospital."

—the Holy Sacrifice of the Mass was offered up by one or more of the chaplains. We cannot, however, speak with the same degree of certainty of the celebrants of the holy services. The Abbé Robin, General Chastellux and others, who wrote about their campaign experiences, are exasperating in their silence on religious matters. They, probably, regarded the saying of Mass as a function of ordinary occurrence and as having no special bearing on present or future history. This would account for the dearth of information on a subject that is of vital importance to us.

However, so firmly is the belief grounded that Mass was said in Hartford during the encampment of Rochambeau's divisions, that its Centennial was celebrated with imposing ceremonies in St. Peter's church, Hartford, on Sunday, June 26, 1881. In speaking of the historic event, the historian of the occasion says:[1] "The great thoroughfare of travel between New York and Providence or Boston was across the Ferry from East Hartford through Ferry and Front streets, crossing Little River by a ford, where the Front street stone bridge now stands, to the Meadow; thence up to and across Main street to the south roads leading in different directions to Middletown, to New Haven and to Farmington. It was on these beautiful meadows, now within the limits of St. Peter's parish, near where the Memorial Church of the Good Shepherd now stands, that the Abbé Robin, chaplain of the French troops, offered up the first Mass said in Connecticut, just one hundred years ago. Since that event two entire generations have not passed away. There are people still living in Hartford whose fathers were present at the Mass said by Abbé Robin for the soldiers alone."

The historical basis upon which these statements rest is that in 1830, almost a half century after the event is said to have taken place, the spot was pointed out to the missionary, Rev. James Fitton, then stationed at Hartford, by one who had attended the Mass, and remembered all the circumstances.

It may be accepted as a fact that Mass was said at that encampment; and, as it is certain that the Abbé Robin accompanied the army through the State, in the absence of direct proof to the contrary, we may assent to the traditions of a century, and yield to him the honor of being the celebrant on that memorable occasion.

I believe, furthermore, that Mass was said at Newtown also, and, perhaps frequently on the march, inasmuch as army chaplains always carry the articles necessary for the saying of Mass, even under unfavorable circumstances.[2]

Another question of interest here arises: Was the Legion of De Lauzun provided with a chaplain during his sojourn of seven months at Lebanon? The probability is very strong that a priest was there, at least at intervals,

---

[1] "Centennial Celebration of the First Mass in Connecticut."

[2] "The march of Rochambeau's army through several States where Mass had never before been said, brought to light Catholics in many places where they were not known to exist; and the army chaplains were often surrounded by the descendants of Irishmen or Acadians, who now saw a priest for the first time, and implored them to stay."— De Courcy and Shea's "*Hist. of the Cath. Church.*"

duly commissioned to minister to the spiritual wants of the troops. The French army was provided with five or six chaplains. The commander could, without impairing the efficiency of the ecclesiastical force, assign a chaplain to De Lauzun's Legion. The French soldiers were Catholics, and like the Catholic soldiers of our own nation, desired the frequent ministrations of their spiritual guides; and those in authority were then, as they should be now, alive to the necessity of the presence of chaplains in camp. To me it is incredible that the Legion of the Duke de Lauzun spent seven months at Lebanon deprived of religious services. And the probability of the presence of a chaplain is made all the stronger from the fact that the great feast of the Nativity of our Lord occurred during the encampment. I am convinced, therefore, that on that festival, so precious to the hearts of Catholics the world over, and particularly to Catholic soldiers in a strange land, far from home and kindred, but with memories of the mid-night Mass fresh and dear, the holy sacrifice of the Mass was celebrated—a military Mass it was, perhaps with becoming ceremony, and that the hardy soldiers enjoyed the unspeakable happiness of receiving Holy Communion.

And still further, it is improbable that the commander would permit the unfortunate deserter to be sent before the Judgment Seat unshrived, or deprived of the opportunity of making his peace with God.

We have seen that the Legion of the Duke de Lauzun remained in camp at Lebanon during the winter of 1780–81. On June 23 he began his march to the Hudson, but took a more southerly route. His first camp was between Colchester and Middlehaddam, the second at *Middletown*, the third at *Wallingford*, the fourth at *Oxford*, the fifth at *New Stratford*, the sixth at *Ridgefield*, and the seventh at Bedford, New York, where he united with Rochambeau's divisions.

## CHAPTER XVIII.

### LAFAYETTE IN CONNECTICUT.

THE most distinguished French Catholic of the Revolution to honor Connecticut with his presence was the Marquis de Lafayette. During the war he passed frequently through the State on missions of vast importance. In the summer of 1778, Washington dispatched him to Rhode Island to assist General Sullivan in repelling the British forces at Newport. The campaign resulted in failure, and Lafayette returned to Fishkill on the Hudson. On these marches he followed the main highway from New York, running through Newtown and Waterbury to Hartford and Middletown, and thence to Providence and Newport. At Breakneck, in Middlebury, he was the guest of Captain Isaac Bronson. The host honored his illustrious visitor by placing at his disposal his finest room and his best bed. Lafayette, however, removed the upper feather bed, saying : "Straw for the soldier," and slept upon the straw under-bed.[1] He is described at this period as "a slender, handsome youth, who sat a horse beautifully, and altogether made a fine appearance."[2]

[1] Bronson's "*History of Waterbury.*"          [2] *Ibid.*

Lafayette was in Hartford with Washington when the latter conferred with Rochambeau the first time, and returned to the Hudson with him to learn of the treason of Benedict Arnold.

His visit to Norwich is thus described:[1] "There were some who long remembered the appearance of the noble Lafayette, as he passed through the place on his way to Newport. He had been there before, and needed no guide; his aides and a small body-guard were with him, and he rode up to the door of his friend, Colonel Jedidiah Huntington, in a quick gallop. He wore a blue military coat, but no vest and no stockings; his boots being short, his leg was consequently left bare for a considerable space below the knee. The speed with which he was traveling, and the great heat of the weather, were sufficient excuses for this negligence. He took some refreshment and hastened forward. At another period, he passed through with a detachment of 2000 men under his command and encamped them for one night upon the plain."

In 1784 Lafayette paid a visit to this country, whose liberties he had helped to achieve. Though his sojourn was brief—he arrived during the summer and departed in December,—he visited Hartford on October 5th. An elaborate dinner and an address of welcome by the Mayor were among the features of his reception.

In 1824 Lafayette again crossed the waters to mingle once more with the people who held him in veneration. After his reception by the citizens of New York, he set out for Boston. When he reached the Connecticut line he was formally welcomed by State officials and escorted through the State with every demonstration of affection and joy. Bridgeport, New Haven, New London and Norwich paid distinguished honors to their guest. On his return he stopped at Hartford and proceeded thence by boat to Middletown. Resuming his trip by water, he reached New York on Sunday, September 5th. Lafayette was accompanied on this visit by his son George and his secretary, M. Levasseur.[2]

---

[1] *"History of Norwich."*

[2] In 1855 Prof. Morse ascribed to Lafayette the utterance that "if the liberty of the United States is ever destroyed, it will be by Romish priests." He also contended that Lafayette was a convert to Protestantism. Right Rev. Martin J. Spalding, Bishop of Louisville, Ky., disposed of Prof. Morse in a public letter Aug. 14, 1855, which will be found subjoined.

## LAFAYETTE'S PRETENDED WARNING AGAINST THE CATHOLIC PRIESTHOOD.

I am in no way committed to the opinion that he (Lafayette) was always a good Catholic and a regular communicant during his long and tempest-tossed life. Reared up piously in the Catholic faith, he received before his death the last rites of the church from the hands of the curate of the Assumption, and he was interred with the full Catholic ceremonial, as Cloquet testifies. Having passed the most of his life as a soldier, a politician and a professed revolutionist—though not a Radical or a Red Republican—he was not a religious man, and was probably for a time tinctured with the religious indifferentism, or infidelity, so prevalent in France. He admits as much in the affecting letter in which he speaks of the last illness and pious death of his wife; but that he had not wholly lost the Catholic faith may be inferred from his promise to that devoted Catholic wife that he would read with recollection certain works which she had recommended, and the perusal of which she had hoped would lead to his conversion. During his last visit to this country he attended Catholic worship in the churches of Baltimore and Philadelphia, and, probably, elsewhere; and I have been informed at Baltimore that he excused himself to the sexton for not kneeling during the service, on the ground that he had a stiff knee. No one had ever dreamed that he was a Protestant except Professor Morse and poor Dr. Vanpelt, who so distinctly and vividly recollected his conversion. All that my present purpose strains me to mention is that he was not a hypocrite; that he had not the meanness to pass as a Catholic in France—so far as he was a Christian at all—and then at the same time to speak and act in this country as a Protestant, and as a hater of that Catholic priesthood whom he respected, and whose ministry he cheerfully employed in his family at home. This is my position, and neither Professor Morse nor his witnesses have shaken it in the least. From his Memoirs we learn that he espoused the cause of the faithful French clergy, who had refused to take the iniquitous constitutional oath. Notwithstanding "the great unpopularity" which was for a time attached to these devoted priests, the worship performed by them "never ceased to be publicly practised by the family of Lafayette." ("Memoirs," Vol. III., p. 80, Paris edition.) This proves that he had no sympathy with any but duly recognized priests.

Professor Morse insists upon the successful exertions of Lafayette in favor of religious liberty, as an evidence of his hostility to the Catholic priesthood. Did he ever chance to read in the Memoirs of the French patriot his important declaration on this subject that his motion for full religious liberty to the small Protestant minority in France "would have probably failed had it not been supported by the Bishop of Langres?" (Vol. II., p. 178.) Did he ever happen to read the bill itself, drawn by the hand of Lafayette? If he did, he would have perceived that the French General therein makes a distinct profession of faith in the Catholic as the true religion, and speaks of Protestants as persons "who have not the happiness to profess the Catholic religion." Can it be that the Professor failed to notice this important act when he referred for another and sinister purpose, to this identical passage in Lafayette's life? Probably he did not condescend to notice all this, but "waived it as impertinent."

The passage of the bill of 1787 to which I refer is the following: "A portion of our fellow-citizens who have not the happiness to profess the Catholic religion, finds themselves stricken with a sort of civil death. The bureau knows too well the heart of the king not to be persuaded that he desires the true religion to be loved by all his subjects, of whom he is the common father; he knows that truth sustains itself by its own force; that error alone has need of employing constraint, and that his Majesty unites the disposition of a benevolent toleration with all the virtues which have merited for him the love of the nation." (Memoirs, II., 179-180.)

If Lafayette urged him so repeatedly and so earnestly to give the warning contained in the motto to the American people as early as 1831, why did he delay giving it until 1836 or '37 (he gives both dates), five or six years afterwards, and about three years after the death of the French patriot? He alone can answer this question.

If this was really the sentiment of Lafayette, why is not the famous motto found in those twelve volumes, consisting in great part of his own writings? And why is no trace of it to be discovered in any of the published lives of the French patriot? Why, especially, does his physician, Cloquet, who was so intimately acquainted with his inmost thoughts, say nothing whatever on this subject in the elaborate work in which he treats of the private life and conversion of the patriot?

How does the Professor reconcile the two manifestly inconsistent facts of Lafayette's using the motto to American Protestants and at the time passing for a Catholic in France, praising the tender piety of his devoted Catholic wife, and wishing to be buried by her side? How explain the solemn Catholic funeral service, so beautifully described by Cloquet, and the interment in the Catholic cemetery of Picpus, with a large

Catholic cross near his grave? Think you the priests would have assisted in such numbers at the funeral if he had been in the habit of abusing them? Or did Lafayette have one language for American Protestants and another for French Catholics?

In his chateau or castle at Lagrange, Lafayette, like other French Catholics of rank, had a chapel. Now, what was the use of this chapel if his enemies, the "Roman priests," were not to officiate therein? Was this, too, a mockery, or was it sheer hypocrisy?

I again ask an explicit answer to the dilemma I before proposed, which I repeat here, as the Professor seems to have forgotten it. Either Lafayette was a Catholic or he was an infidel: he certainly was not a Protestant. If a Catholic, he could not have originated the motto ascribed to him by Morse, without being a hypocrite, which no one will venture to assert. If an infidel, then his testimony against Catholics has no more weight than Voltaire and Tom Paine, and, like them, he may have meant, and probably did mean by priests, the ministers of all Christian denominations. Whichever horn of the dilemma our adversaries may choose to select, the Catholic church still remains unscathed.

I conclude this letter—already longer than I had intended—by the testimony of a distinguished Protestant gentleman, who ranks among the first of our historians, and whose testimony on a historical subject possesses at least as much weight as that of any man in the country. Though a Protestant, he does not allow religious prejudice to sway, much less run away with his judgment, and he was never yet known to put men's names to sentences they never wrote, and the "identical words" of which he could not remember. Need I name Jared Sparks? I publish this letter to me in answer to certain inquiries which I had made; and it will be perceived that in the first part he disposes of Dr. Vanpelt, who was, however, sufficiently settled before; and in the last part he furnishes an opinion which will go far towards refuting Professor Morse. Though Mr. Sparks did not request it, it is delicate and proper for me to state that he merely answered my questions, and that I do not seek to involve him in this discussion

"CAMBRIDGE, July 27, '55.

"DEAR SIR: On my return home, after a long absence, I find your letter of June 30 from Niagara Falls.

"As to the first of your questions, I believe no historical fact can be more better established than that Washington was not in Boston between the years 1776 and 1789, and that he was never there with Lafayette.

"That Lafayette said, 'If the liberty of the United States is ever destroyed it will be by Romish priests,' is so improbable that I could not believe it except on the affirmation of some person that heard him say so, and even then I should suspect misapprehension. Any reflecting man may conjecture many causes much more likely, to say the least, to destroy our liberties than the Romish priesthood.

"I often saw Lafayette in Paris in the year 1829. On one occasion I attended by invitation the wedding of a granddaughter in one of the principal churches of the city. The ceremony was performed by Catholic priests, and Lafayette appeared to attend to it throughout with as much solemnity as any person present. At Lagrange, where I passed two or three weeks with him, he conversed about the schools in that neighborhood, in which he seemed to take a strong personal interest. I remember hearing him say that he thought scholars too exclusively under the direction of ecclesiastics, and that laymen ought to take more active part in them; but I never heard him speak disrespectfully of the Catholic church or clergy.

"I am, dear sir, very respectfully yours,

"JARED SPARKS."

LOUISVILLE, August 14, 1835.                                    M. T. SPALDING.

## CHAPTER XIX.

### THE MARQUIS DE CHASTELLUX IN CONNECTICUT.

IN 1780, 1781 and 1782 the Marquis de Chastellux, a major-general in the French army under the Count de Rochambeau, made a number of tours through the New England and Middle Atlantic States, going as far as Wilmington, Delaware. He recorded in a familiar style his impressions of persons and places.[1] His first tour through Connecticut occurred in November, 1780.

De Chastellux disembarked at Newport on July 11th, and was detained there by military duties until November 1st. "This was the moment," he writes, "when I found myself able to withdraw from the army, but I did not wish to show too much eagerness, and I wished to see established the discipline and the arrangements relative to the cantonments; therefore I delayed starting on my long journey on the continent until the 11th." He was accompanied by his aides, M. Montesquieu and M. Lynch, whose name indicates his Celtic origin. The Marquis had three servants, the aides one each. Their first stop in Connecticut was at Voluntown, which they reached on the 13th. Here he was the guest of a Mr. Dorrance, whose household he thus describes: "He is an old gentleman of seventy-three years of age, tall and still vigorous; he is a native of Ireland, first settled in Massachusetts and afterwards in Connecticut. His wife, who is younger than him, is active, handy and obliging. But the family is charming. It consists of two young men, one twenty-eight and the other twenty-one years old, a child of twelve, and two girls from eighteen to twenty." The eldest son was a Greek and Latin scholar, and well versed in general literature. The travelers left Voluntown on the 15th at 8 A.M., stopping at Plainfield, "a small town, but a big place, for it has nearly thirty houses to support the meeting-house." The Marquis was deeply impressed with Plainfield as a military stronghold. "The situation of it is agreeable, but it offers also the very best possible military position, the first I have observed. One could camp here on the lesser heights, behind which the mountains rise like an amphitheatre, and thus present successive positions almost to the great woods, which would serve for the last retreat. The foot of the heights of Plainfield is fortified by pools of water, which can only be crossed by one causeway, and would force the enemy to defile in order to attack. . . . The left and the right are supported by escarpments. . . . This camp would be good for six, eight, or even ten thousand men; it would serve to defend Providence and the whole State of Massachusetts against troops which had passed the Connecticut River."

Leaving Plainfield, our tourists passed through Canterbury to Windham, which is described as "a pretty little town, or, rather, the germ of a pretty

[1] "*Voyages de M. Le Marquis de Chastellux dans L'Amerique, Septentrionale les annees. 1780, 1781 and 1782.*"

town." At Windham De Chastellux dined with the Duke de Lauzun, who was encamped there with his Legion, awaiting the construction of his winter quarters at Lebanon. At "a little lonely tavern" six miles from Windham, the generous Marquis acted the part of the good Samaritan by defraying the expenses of a penniless Continental soldier, who was ill there, besides giving him a sum of money to continue his journey.

De Chastellux and his companions arrived at Hartford on the 16th, and, with the Duke de Lauzun, who had passed him on the road, lodged at the hospitable mansion of Colonel Wadsworth. M. Dumas, Lauzun's aide, Messrs. Lynch and Montesquieu secured lodgings in the neighborhood. Early on the 17th De Chastellux left Hartford and the Duke de Lauzun, "but it was after breakfast, for if there is one thing absolutely unheard of in America, it is to depart without one's breakfast." The next stop was at Farmington, "a pretty little town, where they have a fine meeting-house and fifty houses standing close together, all neat and well built." Leaving Farmington at 8 A.M. on the 18th, the Marquis continued his journey through Harwinton until he reached Litchfield. His host here was a Mr. Philips, "an Irishman transplanted to America, where he has already made a fortune; he appears to be a man skillful and adroit; he speaks with caution to strangers, and fears to compromise himself: for the rest he is of a gayer mood than the Americans, even a little of a joker, a kind but little known in America."

Washington and New Milford are the last towns in Connecticut of which De Chastellux makes mention in this journey. Of this former he writes: "They gave it this respectable name, of which the memory, no doubt, will last much longer than the town intended to perpetuate it."

On his return journey De Chastellux passed through Canaan, Norfolk, New Hartford to Hartford, thence to Lebanon, to which place he returned after an absence of two months. During this visit at Lebanon he dined again at the quarters of the Duke de Lauzun, and on this occasion witnessed a scene familiar to Catholics the world over, and in which Governor Trumbull was the chief actor. "You have only to represent to yourself this little old man," writes De Chastellux, "in the antique dress of the first settlers in this colony, approaching a table surrounded by twenty Hussar officers, and without disconcerting himself, or losing anything of his formal stiffness, pronouncing in a loud voice, a long prayer in the form of a *benedicite*.[1] Let it not be imagined that he excites the laughter of his auditors; they are too well trained; you must, on the contrary, figure to yourself twenty *Amens* issuing at once from the midst of forty mustaches."

In October, 1782, a year after the surrender of Cornwallis at Yorktown, De Chastellux, commanding the first division of Rochambeau's army, marched through Connecticut to Hartford. Wishing to visit northern Massachusetts and New Hampshire, the Marquis relinquished his command at Hartford, and on November 4th set out in company with Messieurs Lynch, Montesquieu, Baron de Talleyrand, and M. Vaudreuil. On this tour they passed

---

[1] *i. e.*, grace before meals.

through Coventry, Ashford and Woodstock into Massachusetts. At Coventry the tourists fell in with a French Canadian laborer, "who had frequently changed habitations, and had seven children."

His third tour took place in December, 1782, when he followed the route taken two years before, that is, to Voluntown, through Hartford and Farmington, to Litchfield and Washington.

## CHAPTER XX

### CONNECTICUT IRISHMEN IN THE REVOLUTION

"THE French armies which co-operated with the American forces contained many thousands of Irishmen; and the second in command of the besieging force defeated at Savannah was no other than Count Arthur Dillon, who had brought with him his own Irish regiment which he had commanded in France."[1]

We have seen that the land and naval forces of the king of France assisted the American Colonies to break the chains that bound them to Great Britain; we are now to show that the brave and generous sons of Ireland contributed no less to the humiliation of their traditional enemy, the English government. What the English king said of Irish valor at Fontenoy, George III. might well have said of every battlefield from Lexington to Yorktown: "Cursed be the laws that deprive me of such subjects." The Irish emigrants could not forget the accumulated wrongs of centuries. The memories of penal laws rankled within them, and the hideous spectre of insensate cruelties was ever before them. They remembered the barbarities, by government ordered, of which they were victims, and when the opportunity was offered to strike their relentless foe they eagerly embraced it, and marched to battle with hearts throbbing with joy and pulses beating high, animated with the single purpose of driving a hated flag from the American Colonies. Urged on by the same invincible ardor that brought low in the dust the English standard at Fontenoy, and which makes the Irish soldier a splendid acquisition to any army, they fought the battles of American Independence with a gallantry unsurpassed and with such intense devotion to the cause of liberty as to evoke the admiration of their commanders. The Irish emigrant knew not the blessings of liberty at home; he would fight for it in the young land of the West.

The achievements of Ireland's sons in the War of the Revolution have received but scant recognition from the pens of American historians. Where recognition has been made at all, it has been bestowed upon a myth, a figment and nothing more. Fulsome adulation has been given to what in fact has no concrete existence. Much eloquence has been expended to exploit the deeds of the "Scotch-Irish" in the Revolution, and a maximum of energy has been dissipated in the endeavor to minimize the part taken by the genuine Irish—the Irish that need no prefix to attract attention; and this concerted attempt to defraud the true sons of Erin of the glory that is justly their meed, is all the more absurd from the fact that the individual, yclept "Scotch-Irishman," can trace no ancestry, has no local habitat, and exists only in the imaginations of a certain school of foreign and domestic apologists.

When Lord Mountjoy made his famous declaration that America was lost by the Irish emigrants, he had no thought of the being subsequently developed, the "Scotch Irishman." He had in mind the hundreds of thousands of the Irish-Irish, who streamed into this country from 1629 to 1774. In retrospect he saw the crowds who fled from Cromwell's assassins and man-hunters in 1653, and he witnessed again the exodus to the colonies from 1700 to 1774. All these sturdy emigrants, compulsory and voluntary, regarded the British crown as a symbol of tyranny, and their sympathies went out freely to the colonists who were manfully, and patriotically, but against fearful odds, resisting the burdensome laws of the mother country.

The historian Marmion pronounces the emigration from Ireland to this country during 1771, 1772, 1773, to have been without a parallel. "During these three years eighty-eight vessels carried 25,000 Irishmen from three Irish ports to the United States." "They arrived," he continues, "at a critical moment, joined Washington's armies, and contributed by their numbers, courage and conduct, to separate that country from the British crown." To the same effect writes the historian Gordon. "Many thousands left Ireland and settled in America," he says, "and contributed powerfully by their zeal and valor to the separation of the American Colonies from England." "The services rendered by the Irish in America during the war of the Revolution," says Bagenal, "were of almost equal importance in the history of that prolonged and bitter struggle as at Fontenoy, at Cremona, in the Peninsular War, or in the Crimea."[1]

Indeed, testimony confirmatory of the predominance of the Irish element in the American Revolutionary forces is abundant and unimpeachable, as much of it is the evidence of men high in station and who could not be charged with pro-Irish proclivities. In a speech in the Irish House of Commons on the 2d of April, 1784, Colonel Luke Gardiner[2] paid generous tribute to the assistance rendered by the Irish to the cause of American freedom; and his testimony is the more valuable from the fact that he was a Loyalist and an Anglo-Irishman. He was a member of the Irish peerage and died at far-famed Vinegar Hill, fighting his patriotic countrymen under an English banner.

"America," said Colonel Gardiner, "was lost by Irish emigrants. These emigrations are fresh in the recollection of every gentleman in this House, and when the unhappy differences took place, I am assured from the best authority that the major part of the American army was composed of Irish, and that the Irish language was as commonly spoken in the American ranks as English. I am also informed *it was their valor determined the contest*, so

[1] "*The American Irish.*"
[2] "*Irish Debates,*" III., p. 130.

that England not only lost a principal protection of her woolen trade, but also
had America detached from her by the force of Irish emigrants." It is no
purpose of mine to depreciate the aid given to the colonies by the men from
the Presbyterian North, but it is simple justice to state here that they spoke
not the Irish, but the English language.

Major-general Robertson, who served in the British army in America,
bore still more striking testimony to the numerous body of Irishmen who
joined their fortunes with the Continental army. In an official inquiry, he
was asked by Edmund Burke: "How are the Provincial (*i. e.* American)
Corps composed? Are they mostly Americans, or emigrants from various
nations of Europe?" He replied: "Some corps are mostly natives; the
greater number such as can be got. . . . . General Lee informed me that
one-half of the rebel army were from Ireland."[1]

Robertson's testimony was corroborated by Galloway before the same
committee. "What were the troops in the service chiefly composed of?" he
was asked. "I can answer with precision. There were scarcely one-fourth
native Americans, about one-half were Irish and the other fourth English and
Dutch." What says Plowden, the English historian? "It is a fact beyond
question that most of the early successes of the patriots of America were
owing to the vigorous exertions and power of the Irish emigrants who bore
arms in that cause." And Lecky? "Few classes were so largely represented
in the American army as Irish emigrants." The words of Viscount Town-
shend are a touching plea for the suffering Irish people:[2] "My Lords, con-

[1] The
DETAIL AND CONDUCT
of the
AMERICAN WAR,
under generals
GAGE, HOWE, BURGOYNE,
and
Vice-Admiral Lord HOWE:
with
A very full and correct state
of the whole of the
EVIDENCE,
as given before a
COMMITTEE OF THE HOUSE OF COMMONS:
and the
CELEBRATED FUGITIVE PIECES,
Which are said to have given rise to that
IMPORTANT ENQUIRY,
The whole exhibiting a
CIRCUMSTANTIAL, CONNECTED AND COMPLETE HISTORY
of the
Real Causes, Rise, Progress and Present State
of the
AMERICAN REBELLION.

MDCCLXXX.
[2] "*Hansard's Parliamentary Debates*," Vol. XIX., p. 860.

sider, in God's name; in time, consider what you owe to gallant and suffering Ireland. Suffer not your humiliating proposal and offerings to be laid at
the feet of the Congress in whose front of battle these poor Irish emigrants
perform the hardest service."

We shall supplement this testimony with evidence from American
sources. The Father of his Country realized the nation's debt of gratitude to
Ireland's sons and generously gave it public acknowledgment. When the
British evacuated Boston on March 17, 1776—a day of sacred memories to
Washington's Celtic soldiers—the countersign for the day was a graceful
tribute to the race and creed of Ireland's glorious Apostle:

"SPECIAL ORDER OF THE DAY.

"HEADQUARTERS, March 17, 1776.

" *Parole*—' Boston.'

"Countersign—' *St. Patrick.*'

"The regiments under marching orders to march to-morrow morning.

" *Brigadier of the Day,*

"GENERAL SULLIVAN."

In his letter accepting the honor of an election to membership in the
"Society of the Friendly Sons of St. Patrick," December 17, 1781, he referred to the organization as "a society distinguished for the firm adherence
of its members to the glorious cause in which we are embarked." And
when in March, 1790, he replied to an address from the Roman Catholics of
the United States, which bore the Celtic names of Carroll, Lynch and Fitzsimmons, he wrote thus: "And I presume your fellow-citizens will not forget the patriotic part which you took in the accomplishment of their revolution and the establishment of their government."

We shall close this testimony with the eloquent words of Washington's
adopted son, George Washington Parke Custis: "Of the operations of the
war—I mean the soldiers—up to the coming of the French, Ireland has furnished in the ratio of one hundred for one of any other nation whatever.
Then honored be the good services of the sons of Erin in the War of Independence. Let the shamrock be entwined with the laurels of the Revolution, and the truth and justice guiding the pen of history inscribe on the
tablets of America's remembrance eternal gratitude to Irishmen."

The Irish people at home and in the Colonies were staunch friends of
America in the darkest hour of her history. When valiantly struggling to
throw off the heavy yoke her oppressors sought to fasten upon her, they
brought to her feet their money, their brains, and their good, loyal, stout
arms. "Ireland was with America to a man," said William Pitt, Earl of
Chatham.[1] An observant traveler felicitously wrote in 1787: "An Irishman, the instant he sets foot on American ground, becomes *ipso facto,* an
American; this was uniformly the case during the whole of the late war.
Whilst Englishmen and Scotchmen were regarded with jealousy and dis-
trust, even with the best recommendations of zeal and attachment to their

[1] " *Life of Pitt.*"—Thackeray.

cause, a native of Ireland stood in need of no other certificate than his dialect; his sincerity was never called in question; he was supposed to have a sympathy of suffering, and every voice decided, as it were intuitively, in his favor. Indeed their conduct in the late revolution amply justified this favorable opinion; for whilst the Irish emigrant was fighting the battles of America by sea and land, the Irish merchants, particularly at Charlestown, Baltimore and Philadelphia, labored with indefatigable zeal, and, at all hazards, to promote the spirit of enterprise, to increase the wealth and maintain the credit of the country; their purses were always open and their persons devoted to the common cause. On more than one imminent occasion Congress owed their existence, and America probably her preservation, to the fidelity and firmness of the Irish."[1]

A search through the war records of Connecticut will disclose a profusion of names of distinctively Irish origin, names that indicate beyond doubt, that their owners first saw the light in Ireland or were the descendants of those who were born there. The State has preserved in her archives the names of more than one thousand men through whose veins coursed the warm, generous blood of the Emerald Isle. The statement may appear startling, but in substantiation thereof we submit herewith a list of 800 names whose origin seems to be beyond cavil. Two hundred and more names were not copied, as their claims to Celtic origin might possibly be challenged, though they are still borne by many who are proud to claim the green isle beyond the sea as the land of their birth or of their ancestors. But do I claim for them membership in the Catholic church? There are no records to enable one to speak with certainty; nevertheless, inferentially, I believe a large majority of these names originally represented adherents of the ancient faith, and this inference is not unreasonable in view of the facts, that it was against the Catholics of Ireland the most stringent enactments were directed; that they in far greater numbers than others were the victims of England's policy of expatriation, and that, when arrived on our shores they scattered throughout the New England Colonies, where they settled in large numbers. However, should the temptation arise in the mind of any reader to call in question the Catholicity of the names here given, let him, without denominational bias, consult the baptismal, marriage, burial, pew rent or collection records of any thickly populated Catholic parish, or make a personal canvass of names, and he will recognize that the inference here drawn rests upon a solid foundation.

Many of their descendants, and possibly some of themselves, may have lost the precious gift of faith, as the prevailing conditions made it well nigh impossible to keep alive the sacred flame. Occasionally a solitary priest passed through the State in quest of the lost sheep; but after all, what was one laborer in so vast a field? He could accomplish but little. The seed of the divine Word could be but sparsely sowed; the ground became fallow. Writing in 1834, Bishop Purcell, of Cincinnati, said: "There are places in

---

[1] The translator of Dr. Chastellux's "*Travels in North America*," an English gentleman residing in America at that period, 1780-1782.

which there are Catholics of twenty years of age who have not yet had an opportunity of performing one single public act of their religion. How many fall sick and die without the sacraments! How many children are brought up in ignorance and vice! How many persons marry out of the church, and thus weaken the bonds that hold them to it." [1]

Similar conditions existed here. What with the passing years with no sight of priest, the intermarriages with Protestants, and the social disabilities under which Catholics labored, they ceased to practice the duties of their religion. And this may account for the fact that in 1835 Bishop Fenwick found only 720 Catholics in Connecticut, notwithstanding the influx of presumably Catholic emigrants during the preceding century.

The names that constitute this Roll of Honor are drawn from the "Record of Service of Connecticut men in *the War of the Revolution*," compiled by order of the General Assembly.

The Revolutionary record of Connecticut opens with her response to the historic Lexington alarm of April 19, 1775, and closes eight and a half years later with the disbandment of her last regiment after peace, November, 1783.

There is no doubt that many, who have hitherto given little or no attention to the subject, will be astonished to know that over 1000 men from Connecticut, bearing distinctively Irish names, patriotically contributed their services, and many of them their lives, to the cause of independence. And with so many of unequivocally Irish distinction, there were undoubtedly many hundreds of Irish soldiers whose names do not as clearly indicate their Irish origin.

During the famous skirmishes of Lexington and Concord, Wednesday, April 19, 1775, which precipitated the Revolutionary War, an "alarm" was immediately spread in every direction, and reached Windham county by Thursday noon, the 20th, and through Connecticut to Stamford by Friday night, the 21st. About 4000 men started from Connecticut to Boston in response to the alarm, and among them we readily distinguish the following Irish names, and yet several of the lists are not complete:

IRISHMEN IN THE "LEXINGTON ALARM LIST" FROM CONNECTICUT, APRIL 19, 1775.

Joseph Gleason, East Haddam; Jas. McKenney, East Windsor; Andrew Kennedy, East Windsor; James Green, Enfield; Daniel Prior, Enfield; Thomas Murphy, East Haddam; Wm. McKenney, East Windsor; Daniel Green, East Windsor; Peter Reynolds, Enfield; Daniel Terry, Enfield; James Maden, Glastonbury; Wm. Griffin, Hartford; Robert McKee, Hartford; Stephen Killborn, Hartford; Thomas McCartee, Hartford; Stephen Cummins, Mansfield; Ross. Griffin, New Haven; John McKall, captain, Norwich; Joseph Griffin, Norwich; John Carey, sergeant, Preston; John Gordon, Voluntown; Thos. Gordon, Voluntown; David Kennedy, Voluntown; George Gordon, Jr., Voluntown; Daniel McMullen, fifer, Wallingford; Daniel Bailey, Wallingford; Thos. Russell, Wethersfield; Timothy Killborn, Wethersfield; Thos. Fitzgerald, Windham; Levi Carey,[2] Windham; John Carey, 3d, Windham; Nath'l Carey,[2] Windham; Wm. Martin, Windham; John Flyn; John Reynolds, Hartford; Joseph McKee, sergeant,

---

[1] "*Annals of the Propagation of Faith.*" Vol. VIII.

[2] Baptismal names like these indicate, probably, the issue of mixed marriages, as such names are very rare when both parents are Irish or Catholics.

Hartford; Joseph Keeny, Jr. Hartford; Peter Philips, Hartford; Benj. Collins, Mansfield; Nath'l Collins, New Hartford; Jeffrey Murray, Norfolk; John Martin, Norwich; John Welch, Plainfield; Jas. Gordon, Voluntown; Joseph Kennedy, Voluntown; John Gordon, 3d Voluntown; Samuel Collins, Wallingford; Simon Griffin, Wethersfield; John Jackson, Wethersfield; Ackley Riley, Wethersfield; Dan Manning, Windham; James Carey, corporal, Windham; Wm. Carey, Windham; Stephen Cummings, Windham; Michael Jackson, Woolstock; John Green, Thomas Barret.

### First Regiment. General Wooster's. 1775.

*Second Company.*—Augustus Collins, ensign; James M. Griffin, private; Wm. Murray, private.

*Third Company.*—James Ganer (Gaynor), private; Martin Clark, private; Amos Collins, private.

*Fourth Company.*—John Welch, private.

*Tenth Company.*—Angus McFee, John Grimes.

### Second Regiment. General Spencer's.

*First Company.*—Wm. Cox, drum major; Joseph Gleason, drummer.

*Second Company.*—Wm. McCorney, fifer; James Carey, Patrick Colbert, James Lord, Daniel Clark, Herman Higgins, Patrick Leonard.

*Third Company.*—Cornelius Russell.

*Fourth Company.*—Timothy Powers, George Carey, John Dodd.

*Fifth Company.*—Samuel Gleason.

*Sixth Company.*—Wm. McBride, Michael Eggins (Higgins).

*Seventh Company.*—Edmund Murfy (Murphy), Jos. Grimes, Jr.

*Eighth Company.*—James McCartey, Jesse Higgins, John Fox, Thos. Martin.

*Ninth Company.*—Michael Baree, Roger Fox, Jas. Murphy, Jas. McLean, John Jackson, Lawrence Sullivan.

*Tenth Company.*—John Conly, fifer; James McCae.

### Third Regiment. General Putnam's.

*Second Company.*—Stephen Cummins (Cummings), David Kelley, Joseph Martin.

*Third Company.*—James Carr, sergeant; John Huges (Hughes), Joseph Griffin, Jas. McDonald, Daniel Preston.

*Fourth Company.*—Daniel Carryl (Carroll), John Carey, John McCartey.

*Fifth Company.*—Alexander McNeal (McNiel), Daniel Owen, Wm. Moor (Moore), Wm. Waters.

*Sixth Company.*—Benj. Kinny, Benj. Ford, John Terry, Benj. Gary.

On the receipt of the Lexington news, Governor Trumbull summoned the General Assembly to a special session at Hartford to convene on April 26th. The Massachusetts authorities sent urgent appeals to Governor Trumbull for aid and support from Connecticut. On April 20th, the Committee of Safety at Cambridge wrote:—"As the troops have now commenced hostilities, we think it our duty to exert our utmost strength to save our country from absolute slavery. We pray your honors would afford us all the assistance in your power, and shall be glad that our brethren who come to our aid may be supplied with military stores and provisions, as we have none of either more than is absolutely necessary for ourselves." Again, on April 26th, they wrote:—"The distressed condition in which we are, and the danger to which the liberties of all America, and especially the New England Colonies are exposed, will be the best apology for the importunate application to you for immediate assistance. We pray you as regards the safety of your country, that as large a number of troops as you can spare may immediately march forward."

The Assembly met on the date indicated, and during the ten days' session refrained from aggressive declarations, but made preparations for a determined resistance. The leading measure of the session was "An Act for assembling, equipping, etc., a number of the Inhabitants of this Colony for the Special Defence and Safety thereof." It provided that one-fourth part of the Colony militia should be forthwith enlisted, accoutred and assembled, to be led and conducted as the General Assembly should order. About six thousand men who were to be distributed in six regiments of ten companies each, with a full complement of officers, were represented in this apportionment. At a third special session, convened July 1, 1775, the Assembly provided for two more regiments, making eight in all, consisting of about seven thousand, four hundred men. In October of the same year an act of the Assembly transferred those regiments from Colony regiments, who were subject only to Connecticut, to Continental regiments under the authority of the Continental commanders. The following names, notable for their Celtic flavor have been selected from the list of staff officers and rosters of the regiments for 1775, and other sources. They were represented in every prominent action from the siege of Boston to the surrender of Yorktown, including Ticonderoga, Quebec, Long Island, Trenton, Princeton, Brandywine, Germantown, Stony Point, Saratoga and the massacre at Fort Griswold.

### THIRD REGIMENT.

*Seventh Company.*—Thos. Barret, Michael Flynn, Oliver Barret, John Fox, John Green, John Lyon, Abbron Reynolds, Cyrus Powers, Michael Jackson, Jas. Murray, Nathan Powers.

*Eighth Company.*—Michael Richmond, James Reynolds, Jacob Reynolds.

### FOURTH REGIMENT. COLONEL HINMAN'S.

*First Company.*—John Garret, Luke Welch.

*Second Company.*—Alexander Keney, sergeant; Stephen Fox, Thos. Byrne, corporal; Ruben Kenny, Theodore Kenny.

*Tenth Company.*—John Carr, Michael Beach, Jere. McCartee.

### FIFTH REGIMENT. COLONEL WATERBURY'S.

*First Company.*—Andrew Powers, sergeant; Chas. Stewart, Peter Mead.

*Second Company.*—James Huges, sergeant (Hughes); Bryan Killkelly, John Downing, James Lenniham (Lennihan), lieutenant.

*Third Company.*—Patrick Kenney.

*Fourth Company.*—Joseph Hays.

*Fifth Company.*—Mathew Mead, captain; Wm. McKee, Michael Bourn, James Reed, Michael Wells.

*Sixth Company.*—Miles Cauty, Wm. Griffin, Francis Jackson.

*Seventh Company.*—Chas. Powers, Michael Morehouse, Mathew Mead.

*Eighth Company.*—Geo. Murray, Robert Welch.

*Ninth Company.*—John F. Lacy, Thos. Preston, Jeremiah Calahar.

*Tenth Company.*—Morris Griffin, Jerry Riand (Ryan), Joseph Jackson.

### SIXTH REGIMENT. COLONEL PARSON'S.

*First Company.*—John Hackett.

*Second Company.*—Peter Burn, Mathew Coy.

*Third Company.*—Daniel Carthy, corporal; Jas. Griffin, Cornelius Griffin.

*Fifth Company.*—Thos. Carney, Anthony Wolf, Benj. Kelley, David Quinley, Michael Ryen (Ryan), Jas. Butler, Thos. Lyon.

*Sixth Company.*—Benedict Carey, Joseph Gordon, Joseph Kenedy, Asa Phillips, Josiah Carey, Samuel Carey, Wm. Knight, Michael Phillips, Timothy Shea.

*Seventh Company.*—John O'Brian, Michael Torrey, Daniel Thomas.

*Eighth Company.*—Daniel McLean, Jas. Casey.

*Ninth Company.*—Joseph Corbitt, James More (Moore), John Malary, Phillip Dorus.

### SEVENTH REGIMENT. COLONEL CHAS. WEBB.

*First Company.*—William Dunn, John Macannathy, Archibald McLean.

*Second Company.*—Wm. McQueen.

*Third Company.*—James Dennis, David McDowell, John Dennis, Lawrence Martin.

*Fourth Company.*—John Kenney.

*Fifth Company.*—Michael Hunn.

*Sixth Company.*—John Cockran.

*Seventh Company.*—Joseph Murry.

*Eighth Company.*—Beriah Kelley, Roger Crow.

*Ninth Company.*—Neal McNeal, Isaac Collins.

*Tenth Company.*—Wm. Barrett, Cyrenus Collins.

### EIGHTH REGIMENT. HUNTINGTON'S. THOMAS HAYDEN, Sergeant-Major.

*Second Company.*—John Bartlett, Richard Price.

*Third Company.*—James Burn, Jeremiah Connel.

*Fourth Company.*—Wm. Hayes, corporal; Luke Hayes.

*Fifth Company.*—Jas. Green, Timo. Malloy (Timothy), Thos. McKnight.

*Sixth Company.*—John Conley, Isaac Ford.

*Seventh Company.*—Joseph Cummins, John Moors, John Murray.

*Eighth Company.*—Thos. Dennis, fifer; Thos. Ryan, drummer.

*Ninth Company.*—Cornelius Higgins, sergeant; Wm. Bevins, Silvanus Higgins.

*Tenth Company.*—Thos. Reed, sergeant; Michael Barre (Barry), Thos. Cushin.

Patrick Nugent and Peter Heady were taken prisoners at the defeat of Quebec, December 31, 1775.

### COLONEL BURRALL'S REGIMENT. BEFORE QUEBEC DECEMBER, 1775.

John Rielly, lieutenant; Thomas Fleming, drummer; James Clarey,[1] John McGoon,[1] John Green,[1] Michael McGee,[1] John Wren,[1] James Laughlin.[1]

### IN COLONEL ELMORE'S REGIMENT. AT FORT SCHUYLER. WINTER OF 1775-76.

Robert Cochran, major; John Moody, John Redmonds, John Oneal (O'Neil), Thos. Powell, David Brady, Thomas Owen, John Cain (Kane), Jeremiah Ryan, Michael Kirkland, Michael Caern, Cornelius Lynch, ensign; Daniel Owen, John Shield

### "KNOWLTON RANGERS."

Daniel Conner, Chas. Kelley.

### BIGELOW'S ARTILLERY COMPANY. FIRST IN CONNECTICUT DURING REVOLUTION.

John Reynolds, corporal; George McCarty.

The failure of the Canadian expeditions and the campaign around New York demonstrated the need of a permanent disciplined army to cope with

---

[1] Taken prisoners at the Cedars, Canada, May 19, 1776.

the veteran British regulars. All enlistments on the American side were for short terms, and the continual discharging and recruiting of new men played sad havoc with army discipline. To remedy this state of affairs Congress provided that the entire American army be re-organized January 1, 1777. This re-organization provided that eighty-eight regiments be raised for continuous service to the end of the war, unless otherwise ordered, proportioned among the States according to population. Connecticut's portion was eight regiments, and its quota was designated as the "Connecticut Line," which with the other State "Lines" formed one grand "Continental Line." It was these State "Lines," inspired in a common cause, under the leadership of the immortal Washington that bore the burden of the war for the succeeding six years to the grand close. In these regiments we find additional evidence of Irish participation.

### FIRST REGIMENT CONNECTICUT LINE.

Daniel Collins, lieutenant ; Patrick Donally, sergeant ; Wm. Collins, corporal ; Geo. McKenzy, corporal ; John Connolly, Wm. Griffin, Patrick Hynes, Thos. Jackson, Alexander McCoy, Mathew Connor, Joseph Fox, James Griffin, John Joy, John Martin, John Ryan, John Roach, John Whealy, Pell Collins, Michael Stochy, Walter Carey, Thos. Roach.

### SECOND REGIMENT. CONNECTICUT LINE.

Patrick Hynes, John Kelley, John McNulty, Thos. Mitchell, Jas. Gleeson, Thomas McKnight, Ab. Mooney, James Powers, John Ryley, Mathew Reynolds, Wm. Kennedy, John McGarry, John McKinny, Mathew Reynolds, Thomas Kelley, John Mooney, Wm. McFall, Benj. Reynolds, Sim. Reynolds, Reubin Reynolds, Daniel Stewart.

### THIRD REGIMENT. CONNECTICUT LINE.

Wm. Higgins, quartermaster ; Thomas Hayden, lieutenant ; James Reynolds, sergeant ; John Laflin, corporal ; Jas. Gordon, musician ; Daniel Powell, musician ; Ashbel Riley, musician ; James Slater, musician ; Wm. Bryan, Jas. Burn, Chas. Bryan, Jas. Bayley, Abel Collins, Martin Canary, John Conner, Asher Carty, Wm. Cummins, Darby Connell, Richard Crary, Richard Cary, Wm. Duncan, John Delaney, Thos. Durfy, John Fay, William Fay, Timothy Fay, John Griffin, John Grogan, David Haydon, Jesse Higgins, Richard Jackson, James Kenney, Benj. Kenney, Jas. Laflin, Patrick Lyons, Jas. Linden, Andrew Morrison, Wm. Moor, Andrew McKee, Abel McEntire, Wm. Mathews, Patrick Murphy, Joseph McHook, Michael McNiel, James McElvay, Daniel Miles, James Mahar (Maher), Patrick Marr, James McKeys, Edmond Murphy, John McMullen, Thomas Owen, Stephen Owen, Oliver O'Kean, David Reynolds, Jacob Reynolds, Owen Reurk (Rourke), Michael Ribley, Daniel Rivers, Timothy Stevens, Patrick Thomas, Peter Thomas, Thadeus Barre (Barry), George Farrell, Thos. Fox, Samuel Fox.

### FOURTH REGIMENT. CONNECTICUT LINE.

Thos. McLure, sergeant ; John Reynolds, musician ; Simion Reynolds, musician ; Chris. Brady, Roswell Croker, Roger Cary, Benj. Cary, Dennis Dins, Chris. Downing, Thos. Fitzgearal, Mathew Golden, Wm. Glenny, Cornelius Griffin, Joseph Griffin, John Gary, Jas. McDonald, Jno. McLaughlin, Alex. McCoy, Jas. Mallony, James McCarty, Wm. McFall, Geo. Martin, Manuel O'Daniel, Thos. Powers, Jeremiah Reed, James Shields, Patrick Thomas, Daniel Thomas, Daniel Ward, Phillip Martin.

### FIFTH REGIMENT. CONNECTICUT LINE.

Cornelius Higgins, lieutenant; Cornelius Russell, lieutenant; Daniel Cone, corporal; Timothy Cone, corporal; Wm. Cummings, corporal; John Branigan, Thomas Burns, John Bragan, Jas. Burns, Patrick Brown, Luke Brown, Samuel Barret, Moses Barret, Jeremiah Barret, Cornelius Cahale (Cahil), John Carrel (Carroll), Dennis Clark, Dennis Collins, John Downing, Joseph Green, Thomas Green, James Green, Jack Green, Thos. Hughes, John Hayes, John Kelley, Henry Keeler, Thomas Keeler, Jeremiah Keeler, Jas. Laughlin, Kit Moore, Michael McKee, Wm. McLane, Edw. McClaning, Wm. McCluster, Jeremiah Mead, John Mathews, Wm. Murphy, Jas. Patrick, Joseph Reed, Thomas Reed, John Ryan, Chris. Welch, Andrew Gleason, Wm. Cummings, Abel Collins, Thos. Green.

### SIXTH REGIMENT. CONNECTICUT LINE.

John McLean, Sam. Collins, John Clary, Wm. Collins, Henry Fitzgerald, Daniel Fourd, James Gainer (Gaynor), John Griffing, Jas. Keley (Kelley), Joshua Keley (Kelley), John Lines, Angus McFee, Donrson Melone, Anthony McDaniel, John O'Briant, Jas. Power, Jonathan Riley, Wm. Rennals, Joseph Stark, Jas. Clary, Jeremiah Kelley.

### SEVENTH REGIMENT. CONNECTICUT LINE.

John F. Lacy, Chas. McDonald, Patrick Downs, Thos. Finn, Boston Ford, Edward Griffin, John Green, Andrew Hays, James Higgins, Benj. Kelly, Oliver Kelly, Joseph Lynes, Morris Maloney, Henry McIntire, Andrew McClary, Edward Murphy, George Murry, John Moor, Antony Moor, Chas. Riley, Miles Ryon, Darby Sullivan, Robert Welch, Daniel Collins.

### EIGHTH REGIMENT. CONNECTICUT LINE.

Thomas Dyer, lieutenant-colonel; Thos. O'Brian, lieutenant; John Green, corporal; James Bailey, corporal; Peter McFarlane, corporal; Jas. Carr, Abel Cuff, Martin Ford, Amos Ford, Patrick Fling, Samuel Kelley, Joseph Martin, John McKinzy, John McManners, Jas. McDonald, David McLane, Jas. Russell, David Reynolds, Justice Reynolds, Stephen Rany, James Ryon, Michael Robins, Daniel Vaughn, John Vaughn, Morris Welch, Luke Welch, Moses Rilley, George Griffin, Joseph Lyon.

### COLONEL S. B. WEBB'S REGIMENT. KNOWN AS THE NINTH.

John Riley, captain; Thos. Quigley, John Burns, Thos. Doyle, Stephen Fox, John Fay, Wm. Fay, Timothy Fay, Gershon Fay, John McLean, John McKensie, Matthew Melonee (Maloney), Patrick McDonald, Wm. Martin, Geo. O'Bryan, Daniel Ward, Moses Ward, Daniel Gilmore, Daniel Lane, David Welch, Nehimiah Higgins, John Welch, James Brown, John Bailey, David Ward, Timothy Higgins, Jos. Goldsmith, Francis King, Malachi Corning, Niel McLean, Jas. Kirkland.

### CONNECTICUT MEN WITH COLONEL SHERBURN'S REGIMENT. LIGHT INFANTRY.

Ebenezer Blake, sergeant; Stephen Bartlett, corporal; Thos. Fanning, corporal; Roger Welsh, private; David Fanning, private; Elesha Fanning, Michael Freeman, Edward Freeman, Peter Freeman, Joseph Freeman, Hezekiah Carey.

### CONNECTICUT MEN IN COLONEL SETH WARNER'S REGIMENT STATIONED AT BENNINGTON AND SARATOGA.

Alexander McLowry, ensign; Joseph Bennet, sergeant; Wm. Collins, corporal; John Campbell, Benj. Gleason, Robert McKnight, George McCarthy, Allen Reynolds, Daniel Welch.

COLONEL MOSES HAZEN'S REGIMENT. BRANDYWINE, GERMANTOWN, MONMOUTH AND YORKTOWN.

Samuel Cochran, sergeant; James Ward, sergeant; John Burk, James Dawah (Dowagh), David Kelley, Michael Kirkland, Peter Lines, Michael Welch, John McCoy.

COLONEL DURKEE'S WYOMING VALLEY COMPANY.

Thomas McClure, Stephen Preston, John Cary, Wm. Dunn, James Bagley, Chas. Bennet.

CAPTAIN RANSOM'S WYOMING VALLEY COMPANY.

Timothy Pierce, lieutenant; Lawrence Kinney, Wm. McClure, Thos. Neal, John O'Neal, Thos. Pickett, Michael Foster.

FIRST TROOP. LIGHT DRAGOONS.

Richard Dowde (Dowd), John Butler, James McDavid, Edward Hayes, Michael Hannon, Eph'ron Kirby.

SECOND TROOP.

Michael Couney, John Conly, Dan'l Buckley, John Carroll, Geo. Couney, Thos. Neal, Stephen Taylor, Wm. Bennet, Jno. McMullen, Jno. McKinsey.

FOURTH TROOP.

Wm. McBride, Daniel Cashman, Daniel Clary, Thos. Cushman, Peter Hare.

FIFTH TROOP.

Joseph Conner, Robert McColloch, Henry Martin, David Ross, David Martin, Jas. Connolly.

SIXTH TROOP.

Wm. Lane, Jos. McClanon, John Bennet, John Henry, Wm. Denivan (Donovan), Thos. Dongall, Jas. Reed, Jas. Murphy, Aron Fox.

RECRUITS.

John Kilborn, John Welch, Martin Stiles, John White, Jos. King.

COLONEL LAMB'S ARTILLERY.

Henry Cunningham, lieutenant; Jas. Hughes, lieutenant; Daniel Meloney (Maloney), Edmond Sweaney (Sweeney), gunners; Jeremiah Ryon (Ryan), bombardier; John Welch, John McCloud, Samuel Gibson, Andrew Dowling, Cornelius Gordon, Daniel Melone (Malone), David Slater, Patrick Snow, James Newall, Peter Rose, Michael Barley, John Powers, matrosses.

COLONEL CRANE'S ARTILLERY.

Daniel Pierce, John Reynold, sergeants; Niel McNiel, corporal; John Brown, Jos. Murphy, matrosses; Joseph Griffin, Stephen Murry, Chas. Reynold, Geo. Cary, Moses Collins, Joseph Green, John Matthews, James Dougherty, Daniel Tracey, Oliver Carey.

CAPTAIN PENDLETON'S COMPANY OF ARTIFICERS. ONLY COMPANY SERVED SOUTH OF VIRGINIA DURING REVOLUTION.

Phillip Barrett, John Martin, Dennis Knox, Oliver Grafton, Wm. Glisson (Gleeson), Maurice Cummins Patrick Rodney, Thomas Clark.

INVALID CORPS.

John Finnegan, Patrick Mahar, John Kelley, Owen Rewick (Rourke).

John Burnett, Daniel Durfee, Thos. McClure, Thos. Fanning, Benj. Hayes, John

Fox, John Casey, drummer; Jas. Mahar, Jas. Shields, John Briant, Stephen Bennet, Joseph McHood, Martin McNary.

### CONNECTICUT PENSIONERS OF THE REVOLUTION.

Jeremiah Bennett, private; Daniel Buckley, private; Daniel Collins, lieutenant; James Downs, corporal; Richard Flood, private; Martin Ford, private; John Fanning, sergeant-mate; Thos. Fanning, private; Daniel Griffin, private; John Griffin, private; Cornelius Higgins, lieutenant; Timothy Higgins, private; Wm. Hughes, private; John Laflin, private; Daniel Murray, private; Peter McGuire, Joseph Martin, private; Thos. Powers, private; Daniel Preston, private; Joseph Preston, private; Michael Phillips, private; Thos. Quinley, private; Owen Ruick, private; Thos. Ruig, private; Timothy Scranton, private; Jas. Slater, musician; Wm. Tracy, private; Thos. Ward, private; John Welch, private; Joseph P. Martin, private, residing in Maine; Chris. Blake, private, residing in New Hampshire; William Cummings, Joseph Cushman, William Prior, George Martin, privates, residing in Vermont; Jas. Phillips, John Russell, privates, residing in Massachusetts; James Bennet, John Butler, Patrick Bugbee, privates, residing in New York; William Collins, private; James Dailey, first private; David Dorrance, captain; Wm. Fay, private; John Fay, private; Jack Green, private; John Green, private; Wm. Kennedy, private; John Killborne, private; Paul McCoy, private; Martin McNeary, private; Andrew McKee, private; John Martin, private; John Phillips, private; John Reed, musician; Richard Reed, private; John Reynolds, sergeant; Stephen Reed, private; Robert Welch, private; Lawrence White, private; James Connolly, private, residing in New Jersey; John Ryon, sergeant, residing in Pennsylvania; Stephen Fox, private, Wm. Manning, sergeant, Robert McCullough, private, Justus Reynolds, musician, John Halfpenny, private, residing in Kentucky; Wm. Carr, James Grant, privates, residing in East Tennessee; Daniel Welch, private, residing in Indiana.

### INVALID PENSIONERS.

James Slater, James Wayland, privates, Andrew Mead, ensign, Fairfield County; Michael Deming, Jr., Matthew Cadwell, privates, Hartford County; Daniel Preston, private, New Haven County; John Bailey, Jr.; Wm. Bailey, Jr., Daniel Cushman, John Chilson, John Downs, Isaac Higgins, Fred. Moore, Thos. Pickett, Thos. Phillips.

---

# EARLY PRIESTS IN CONNECTICUT.

### CHAPTER XXI.

#### REV. GABRIEL DRUILLETTES, S. J.

THE first representative of the priesthood to enter Connecticut was the Rev. Gabriel Druillettes, a priest of the Society of Jesus. Father Druillettes was the spiritual guide and father of the Abenaki of Maine, whose mission he founded in 1646. He remained with them, however, for a brief period only, his object being to lay the foundation for a subsequent permanent mission. During his residence among the Abenaki the New England Colonies manifested a desire to enter into a commercial alliance with New France. Having in the meantime returned to Quebec to report to his ecclesiastical superiors concerning the prospects of the Abenaki mission, Father Druillettes was appointed ambassador by the Governor of New France, and invested with authority to treat with the Grand Court of Massachusetts, whose sessions were held at Boston.

On September 1, 1650, the reverend ambassador set out from Quebec in company with John Guerin and Noel, an Indian chief, as guide. After a voyage in which hardships and sufferings formed the chief features, the little band arrived at Augusta, Maine, where Father Druillettes met Commandant John Winslow. Between these two men a bond of friendship was formed that was severed only by death. So strong was their attachment for each other that Winslow could pay the priest no higher compliment than to call him his Xavier, while Father Druillettes affectionately designated the Commandant as his Pereira, in allusion to the friend of the great apostle to the Indies.

In the prosecution of his mission Father Druillettes had conferences with the Commissioners of Boston and Plymouth Colonies. He sought to perfect a league offensive and defensive. He was informed, however, that the four English Colonies were confederates, and that all treaties and leagues concerning war and peace with neighboring nations or colonies were referred to the "consideration and conclusion" of the Commissioners of the United Colonies of New England, who met annually in September, and that the next annual session would be held at New Haven.

Plymouth Colony, recognizing the commercial benefits that would accrue to it from a league with the French, were from the beginning well disposed towards Father Druillettes and his mission,[1] and its acquiescence in the representations of the reverend ambassador operated as a spur to the Colony of Massachusetts to enter into the compact.

Father Druillettes' reflections on the probable result of his mission are here set forth in his own words:

1st. "I presume," he says, "as something quite certain that the English of the four colonies, Boston, Plymouth, Connecticut and Kwinopeia (Quinnipiac or New Haven) have power to exterminate the savage nations. They have exterminated two tribes.[2] They are so powerful and numerous that 4,000 men could be gotten ready in the Colony of Boston alone. There are at least 40,000 souls in these four Colonies, and, moreover, the road to the Iroquois grounds is very short and easy of travel.

2nd. "I presume, according to the articles of agreement, no Colony can commence an offensive war without the consent of the four Colonies. Furthermore, the deputies must assemble to deliberate on the matter, and three colonies must consent to extend aid ; so that the decision shall be given by a majority. This gives reason to hope for assistance through the intervention

[1] As an instance of kindly feeling, it is related that Father Druillettes was invited to dine by Governor Bradford of Plymouth, who paid his guest the delicate compliment of serving a fish dinner, as it was Friday.—Fitton's *Sketches*.

[2] The Pequots and Narragansetts.

of the English, and sufficient certainty that three of the four Colonies will consent. The Governor of Plymouth, with his magistrates, is not only favorable, but urges the matter; and all are in favor of the Abenaki, who are under the protection of this Colony.[1] The Colony has a considerable interest in this matter on account of the seignorial rights by which it will receive the sixth part of all that will be received from this treaty along the Kennebec river. The Governor himself, and the four other principal men would lose much in forfeiting all hope of commerce with Kennebec and Quebec, because of the Abenaki; and this would inevitably occur if the Iroquois continue to kill and hunt to death the said Abenaki, as they have been doing for several years. The Governor has a strong reason for extending this aid, as all the colonies waged war in favor of a savage nation, named 'Morchigander,' which is on the river Pecot, and that on the demand of the Colony of Connecticut, which had that nation under its protection."

Father Druillettes returned to Quebec on June 4, 1651. On the 22nd he set out again, having received increased powers to confer with the Commissioners of the United Colonies, who were to meet at New Haven in September. His departure is thus noted in Lallemant and Ragueneau's *Journal:*

"*June 22, 1651.* Father Druillettes, Mr. Godefroy and John Guerin set out with the Abenaki and one Sokoquinois (Saco Indians) for New England in seven or eight canoes. Noel Tekwerimat was of the party."

In the Registers of the Ancient Council of Quebec there is this entry, June 20, 1651:

"The Council assembled at nine o'clock in the morning. Present: the Governor; the reverend Father Superior; Messieurs de Manze, de Godefroy and Menott. On the proposition made to the Council touching a certain rescription made by the Council in the year 1648, to the end that a union be made between the Colonies of New France and New England to carry on commerce with each other, the Council, desiring to meet their wishes, has nominated and nominates Sieur Godefroy, one of the Councillors of the Council established by his Majesty in this country, to proceed with the Reverend Father Druillettes to the said New England, to the said Commissioners, to treat and act with them according to the power given to them by the Council."

The Governor of New France addressed a letter to the Commissioners of the United Colonies, as follows:

"Louis d'Ailleboust, Lieutenant-General for the King and Governor of all New France, etc., Greeting:

"Having been solicited and entreated, both by the Christian Indians depending on our government and by the Abenaquinois, living on the River Kinibeqine, and others, their allies, to protect them against the incursion of the Iroquois, their common enemies, as it has been heretofore practiced by Sieur de Montmagny, our predecessor in this government; and having anew shown us that all their nations were on the point of being totally destroyed unless he speedily brought a remedy—We, for these causes and the good of the colony, and following the express orders given us in the name of the Queen Regent, mother of the King, to protect the Indians against their said enemies, have deputed and depute, with the advice of the Council established in this country and some of the most notable inhabitants, the Sieurs Gabriel Druillettes, preacher of the gospel

[1] The Abenaki were within the jurisdiction of Plymouth Colony.

to the Indian Nations, and John Godefroy, one of the Councilors of said Council, ambassadors for them to the gentlemen of New England, to treat either with the Governors and Magistrates of New England or with the General Court of Commissioners and Deputies of the United Colonies, for assistance in men and munitions of war and supplies to attack the said Iroquois in the most proper and convenient places ; and also to agree upon articles which shall be deemed necessary to assure this treaty, and to grant to the said people of New England the trade which they have desired from us by their letters in the year 1647, with the articles, clauses and conditions which they shall therein see necessary ; awaiting the arrival of the Ambassadors whom we shall send on our behalf to satisfy and establish finally what they have agreed upon.

"We accordingly pray all governors, lieutenant-generals, captains and others to let them pass freely," etc.

The letter of the Council of Quebec to the Commissioners breathes the same spirit, expresses an earnest desire for closer commercial relations, calls attention to the insolent hostility of the Iroquois, and solicits aid in crushing their common enemy.

"GENTLEMEN : It is now several years since certain gentlemen of Boston proposed to begin commerce between New France and New England. The Council established by His Majesty in this country sent answers as well as letters written by our Governor to those gentlemen. The tenor of these messages was that we are desirous of this commerce ; also of a sincere union between your colonies and ours, and at the same time we wish to form an offensive and defensive league against our enemies, the Iroquois, who are ruining our commerce, or, at least, retarding it. It seems to us that your obligation is to crush the insolence of these savage Iroquois, who are killing the Sokonois (Saco Indians) and the Abenaki, your allies ; and, moreover, the facilities you have to begin this war are two reasons which induce us to carry on these negotiations with you in your Court of Commissioners. We have requested your Governor to write us on the subject. We join our efforts with his to assure you of our desire, and that of all New France for this commerce with New England and this war with the Iroquois, who should be our common enemy. With the Rev. Pere Druillettes, who began last winter to negotiate in this matter, we are pleased to associate Mons. Godefroy, as Councillor of our Commission. The merits of these two deputies lead us to hope for success. They are clothed with all the necessary powers, that is to say, to efficaciously arrange matters relative to commerce, and to divide the expenses necessary for the war with the Iroquois. We earnestly solicit you to listen to them, and to act with them as you would with us, and with that frankness that is as natural to the English as to the French. We cannot doubt that God will bless your arms and ours, since they will be employed in the defence of Christian savages who are your allies as well as ours, against infidel barbarians who have neither God nor faith. They do not evince the slightest justice in their proceedings, as you will learn from our deputies, who will assure you of our sincere desire that Heaven will always bless your provinces and bestow on you its favors.

"Drawn up in the Chamber of the Council established by the King at Quebec, in New France, June 20, 1651."

Arrived at Boston, Father Druillettes forwarded a letter to the Commissioners for Connecticut and New Haven, requesting a conference at Boston. In this letter he advanced several arguments to persuade the English Colonies to join with the French in a war against the Iroquois, alleging that it was a just war, inasmuch as the Mohawks had broken solemn covenants made for the continuance of peace ; that they conduct their wars with great cruelty ; that it was a holy war waged in behalf of Christianized Indians, who were persecuted and cruelly treated on account of their religion when captured by the Mohawks; that the war was a matter of common concern, as the inroads of the Mohawks tended to the destruction, or, at least, to the great disturbance of trade in which the French and the English of Massachusetts and Plymouth Colonies were mutually interested. It was further represented that the French had no convenient passages either by land or by sea to carry on war against the hostile Indians. Therefore in the name of the Governor and Council of New France and of the Christian Indians, he petitioned the English colonies to join in the war, and promised a "due consideration or allowance for charges" (expenses). In the event, however, of the English refusing to actively participate in the war, Father Druillettes besought for the French the privilege of enlisting volunteers among the English colonists; that they be furnished with food supplies for the service, and that they might pass through the English jurisdiction by land and water, as occasion would require.

Father Druillettes' request for a conference at Boston was refused on the plea of inconvenience. To his arguments and petitions he received unfavorable replies from the Commissioners for Connecticut and New Haven Colonies. Nothing daunted, Father Druillettes, Mons. Godefroy and suite, in the company of the Commissioners of Massachusetts, visited New Haven in September, 1651, only thirty-seven years after Adriaen Block sailed upon the waters and gazed upon the beautiful shores of Connecticut. The reverend ambassador presented his credentials to the Commissioners with a commission addressed to himself, whereby he was empowered to preach the Christian religion to the Indians.

Father Druillettes immediately opened negotiations. He was an orator of very graceful and persuasive address[1] and improved his abilities to the utmost to persuade the Commissioners that the English Colonies should give aid in the war against the Mohawks. If, however, the Commissioners did not wish to engage actively in war against the Indians, he solicited the privilege of recruiting volunteers and asked for the grant of a passage by land and water through their jurisdiction. He requested also, that the baptized Indians and catechumens be taken under the protection of the United Colonies. These favors granted, Father Druillettes promised in return a treaty establishing free trade between the French and the English.[2]

The efforts of the eloquent Jesuit availed nothing. Sincere in his motives, calm in the expression of his views, manly and straightforward in the presentation of his petition for aid, pleading only for the welfare of his Indian charges, with no thought of personal gain, we can imagine his disappointment when he realized the futility of his efforts. Standing before the venerable Commissioners in his "black gown," his rough belt encircling his body, his rosary hanging by his side; the first of the sacerdotal order to tread the soil of Connecticut; a member of a society whom every Puritan was taught to regard as the advance guard of Anti-Christ; an honored fellow of a body of

[1] Trumbull's *Hist. of Conn.*; Hollister's *Hist. of Conn.*
[2] *Acts of the Com. of the U. Col.*

men whom an insensate legislation threatened with fines, imprisonment and death for the sole crime of being priests of the Catholic church; this humble, saintly priest, the cultured ambassador, presented a striking picture as he stood before the Commissioners, whose co-religionists held his creed in abomination; indeed, says a historian, "he must have been the fruitful theme of conversation at New Haven for many days."[1] Father Druillettes' Indian converts and neophytes were refused the protection he sought for them, and were left a prey to the marauding, bloodthirsty Iroquois. "In vain did the governor of Canada call on New England for aid. The Puritan felt unable to help the Papist; and the Commissioners of the United Colonies, alleging that the Mohawks were neither in subjection to, nor in any confederation with themselves, turned a deaf ear to the appeal."[2] The Commissioners displayed a more liberal spirit towards the Dutch four years later. When they heard that the Indians had taken many Dutch prisoners, they agreed to send "two or three meet messengers to endeavor their redemption;" but their intercession was not required.

As we have seen, Father Druillettes had confidently relied upon the co-operation of three of the English Colonies, Massachusetts, Plymouth and Connecticut, and had hoped also to be successful with the colony of New Haven. "The principal Magistrate in the Colony of Connecticut, Mr. Winthrop," wrote Father Druillettes, "was the first to write to Quebec in regard to this commerce. He is much in favor of the French and will, probably, do all in his power to help this expedition, particularly after having received the letter, which I wrote to him, requesting him to complete what his father had begun. As for the Governor[3] of Kwenopeia (Quinnipiac), everybody says that he is very reasonable. It is quite probable that if he does not actively interest himself in this matter, at least, he will not oppose it, knowing especially that Boston and Plymouth, which are influential colonies, or, as it were, the guide of the others, are strongly in favor of it."

### LETTER OF FATHER GABRIEL DRUILLETTES TO JOHN WINTHROP, ESQUIRE.

To the Most Illustrious Seigneur, John Winthrop, Esquire, at Pequott River.

*Distinguished and Most Honorable Sir*—As in consequence of the deep snows of winter I was debarred from the pleasure of seeing you, and from communicating to you orally and at length the great hopes reposed in your singular kindness by the most illustrious Governor of New France in Canada, at Kebec—who appointed me his Envoy to all the magistrates of your New England—I now approach you by letter in order to beseech and implore you, by that spirit of exceeding benevolence toward all, but especially toward our New France, which Sieur Winthrop, whose memory is both happy and grateful to all, bequeathed to you, the heir to all that he possessed, not to refuse your protection to the cause that has brought me to these shores. That cause is the same as that which your Father, of most grateful memory, by the letters which he sent, in the name of your commonwealth to Monsieur our Governor in New France, at Kebec, took up as far back as the year 1647, and which he would have long since brought to a happy conclusion

---

[1] Hollister.

[2] Broadhead's *Hist. of New York.*

[3] Theophilus Eton. Edward Hopkins was Governor of the Colony of Connecticut.

had not death prevented him, as I have learned from many responsible persons. This, I believe, was wrought by God, most good and great, with the design of making us indebted to you for the happy issue of the cause, the beginning and origin whereof we owed to your most honorable Father. After having orally explained the whole matter to the Governor of Boston and Pleymouth, I desired with all my heart to travel to the country wherein you now reside; and it was not so much the troublesome snows that prevented me as the authority of several persons of importance, to whom I owe deference and who dissuaded me therefrom, which recalled me from Pleymouth to Boston. So great was the hope held forth to me by your kindness toward Strangers, however Barbarian they may be, that to me—who have lived for the past nine years among Barbarians, whom it has been my duty to instruct in their forests, far from the sight of Europeans—it seemed that you would have nothing to dread from my barbarism. Nay, more, I saw nothing that I might not hope for from your well-known kindness and your unusually Compassionate and Conscientious feelings toward the Savages who are Catechumens of the Christian Faith and Profession. These are, in truth, beyond all other mortals, that Hundredth Sheep straying and forsaken in the Desert, which alone the Lord Jesus Christ (Luke 15th), after having left the ninety and nine others, anxiously seeks, and, having found it, joyfully places on his shoulders; that is to say, he who burns with the most ardent zeal toward the same Lord Jesus Christ must likewise embrace, with the most tender affection of his heart, that hundredth sheep in which alone that best of Shepherds, the Lord Jesus, seems to place his whole delight. Now, this most tender affection of your heart toward your delight, because it is that of Christ our Lord—I mean toward the Barbarian Catechumens—easily leads me to believe that the testimony shown by this letter of my gratitude and of my confidence in you, however small it may be, will not be displeasing in your sight. Wherefore suffer that I implore by letter your protection, in which, after God, I consider that nearly all my hopes rest, in favor of the cause of the Lord Jesus Christ—in other words, of the defense of the Christian against the Moaghs. These not only have long harassed the Christian Canadians near Kebec, and most cruelly tortured them by slow fire, out of hatred of the Christian faith, but they even intend by a general massacre to destroy my Catechumens dwelling on the banks of the Kenebec River, because they have been for many years allied to the Canadian Christians. It is chiefly for this reason that our most illustrious Governor of Kebec commanded me to offer you in his name the most ample Commercial advantages and considerable compensation for the expenses of the war, in order to obtain from New England some Auxiliary troops for the defense of the Christian Canadians (which he has already begun against the Moaghs), and which, through his affection for the Christian savages, he wishes to promote at the same time and by the same undertaking in favor of the Akenebek Catechumens, their allies, who are inhabitants of New England, and the special clients of Pleymouth Colony.

He therefore hopes that, in the same manner as your Colony of Kenetigouk subdued the ferocity of the Naraganses, in favor of its dependents who live on the Pecot River—that is to say, the Mohighens—so likewise the colony of Pleymouth will undertake to wage war, with the consent of the Assembly called that of the Commissioners, against the Moaghs, the most cruel enemies of their Akenebek dependents, as well as of their allies, namely, the Canadian Christians near Kebec.

This twofold commission of mine, to wit: in the name of Monsieur the Governor of New France, at Kebec, and separately in the name of the Savages, both the Christians and the Akenebek Catechumens, after having been summarized and translated into the English tongue from my barbarous Latinity, will be joined to my present letter, I think, by a man who is an excellent friend of mine, and to whom, with that object, I gave a copy to be sent to you. For this reason I add nothing further; but I implore you to display your kindness toward the Barbarians and your signal compassion toward the poor of the Lord Jesus; not to disdain in your General Assembly—which, I hear, is usually held in the month of June in Hartford—to expose the whole matter at length; to urge it upon your magistrates, and, finally, to recommend a favorable settlement of the whole affair to the two personages who are called the Commissioners of your Colony, when they go to the place where the Assembly of the Commissioners is to be held Meanwhile, wheresoever on earth I may be detained by the Lord Jesus, who has called me to devote my life and death to labors among the Barbarians, who need instruction, I shall live and die the most devoted servant, in the Lord Jesus, of your entire Family, and above all, Distinguished Sir, of yourself, in the Lord Jesus, for whom, because it is for his brethren, the Christian Barbarians, I execute this Commission.

GABRIEL DRUILLETTES, S. J.,
Priest and Instructor at Kenebek.

The visit of Father Druillettes to New Haven suggests a query which is of capital interest to the Catholic historian, as well as to the entire Catholic body of Connecticut : Did he, during his sojourn there, offer the Holy Sacrifice of the Mass ? If he did, he was the first to celebrate the divine mysteries in the State. The records, however, give no answer. But the silence of Father Druillettes should not be construed as favoring a negative answer. As the saying of Mass was of daily occurrence when favorably situated, it is probable that the ambassador would not regard a Mass celebrated even in a strange locality as an unusual event. But few actors in daily events ever realize that they may be making history, and, therefore, frequently fail to place the facts on record ; so that Father Druillettes might have offered the Holy Sacrifice and make no mention of the fact in his Narrative.

When at Boston the year previous Father Druillettes was the guest of Major-General Gibbon, who, says the priest, "gave me the key of an apartment in his house where I could easily perform my devotional exercises."[1] There is strong probability that he said Mass on this occasion. Whether he celebrated the divine mysteries in New Haven would depend, in a measure, upon the lodgings placed at his disposal. An ambassador, it is consistent to believe that the authorities of the colony assigned him to apartments befitting his dignity. Such being the case, it is within the range of probability to say that Father Druillettes said Mass, not once only, but daily during his sojourn in New Haven. An eminent Jesuit authority[2] says : "As the Jesuit missionaries of those days were accustomed to travel with all the requisites for private celebration and under difficult circumstances, I should incline to the opinion that he (Father Druillettes) did celebrate in Connecticut." Father Druillettes was a holy and zealous priest, a true missionary. The all-absorbing desire of his heart was the conversion to Christianity of the Indians committed to his care. Consumed by this desire he would employ every legitimate means to bring the red children of the forest under the benign and salutary influences of the Gospel. But the most precious means at his disposal to effect the conversion of the Indians was the Mass. Nowhere else could he plead so effectually, pray so devoutly, and exercise his zeal so fervently as at the altar where the Blood of Christ is offered to the Eternal Father for the souls of men. A holy priest, fully conscious of human frailty, Father Druillettes would ascend the altar daily, and would regard that day as lost wherein was not offered up

[1] "Narrative of Father Druillettes."
[2] Rev. E. I Devitt, Gonzaga College, Washington, D. C., a letter to the author.

the august Victim. To prevent such spiritual loss and to enjoy the sweet consolations of the Mass, he would carry from place to place the vestments, sacred vessels, linens, and the matter for the Sacrifice. The faithful Guerin was with him to fill the role of acolyte. In a word, all the circumstances point to the conclusion that the reverend ambassador stood before an humble altar in New Haven and petitioned the Most High in behalf of His beloved children.

## CHAPTER XXII.

### FATHER DRUILLETTES' SUCCESSORS.

AFTER the departure of Father Druillettes from New Haven, over twenty years elapse ere we discover trace of any other priest in Connecticut. About 1674 the Rev. Jean Pierron, a priest of the Society of Jesus, made a missionary tour throughout New England, expounding the tenets of the Catholic faith to the Indians. There is a well-grounded tradition that he traversed Connecticut, and it is certain that he went as far south as Maryland and Virginia in the arduous but glorious quest for souls.[1]

Father Pierron arrived in Canada from France on June 24, 1667. Eager to begin immediately his missionary labors, he set out from Quebec on July 14th following with two Jesuit companions for the Mohawk missions in the State of New York. The scene of his labors was "Tionnontoguen," the capital of the Mohawk nation. By dint of industry and perseverance he soon became sufficiently conversant with the Mohawk language to address his savage hearers intelligently. To impress more deeply his teachings upon the minds of the Indians, he made use of small paintings, the work of his own hands.

"His representations of a good and a bad death had marvellous success. While he was one day explaining the mysteries of the faith, he saw some old men and women close their ears with their fingers. When he questioned them, they replied that they had heard nothing. He profited adroitly by this incident to represent the death of an old woman, who would not listen to the Missionary, nor look at Paradise. A demon was by her side, who had taken her fingers and forced them into her ears. As soon as the missionary had exhibited and explained this picture, no one dared again to reply: "I did not hear."[2]

Father Pierron also translated the Ten Commandments and several prayers into Iroquois verse, that the Indians might be more readily impressed by singing them.

As the Indians were greatly addicted to the vice of gambling, Father Pierron introduced a game in which they were instructed in the principal doctrines of the church. The game was "From point to point," meaning from birth to death and eternity.

The greatest evil Father Pierron had to contend with was, as the Indians

[1] Broadhead's "*History of New York*," Vol. II.
[2] "The Pilgrim of Our Lady of Martyrs." Sept., 1898.

expressed it, " a foreign demon." This demon was liquor, which the English supplied in the form of rum from the West Indies, and the French in the form of brandy from Rochelle. To eradicate the evil several sachems presented a petition and a letter from Father Pierron to Governor Lovelace requesting his aid in stopping the vicious traffic. Lovelace at once honored the petition and wrote to Father Pierron : " I have taken all the care possible, and will continue it under the most severe penalties, to restrain and hinder the furnishing of any excess to the Indians. And I am very glad to learn that such virtuous thoughts proceed from infidels, to the shame of many Christians. But this must be attributed to your pious instructions ; you, who, being well versed in a strict discipline, have shown them the way of mortification, as well by your precepts as your practice."

Father Pierron left the Mohawk missions in 1671 and returned to Quebec. The winter months of 1673 were spent in Acadia. It was after this he traveled through the New England Colonies, and going, as has been said, as far as Virginia. Of this experience he wrote that he saw nothing " but desolation and abomination among those heretics." At Boston " the uncommon knowledge he exhibited" caused him to be suspected of being a Jesuit, though he was " much esteemed." He was desirous of founding a mission among the Indians of Maryland, but his superior, Father Dablon, not wishing to encroach upon the jurisdiction of the English Jesuits, transferred him to the Seneca missions in New York. Here ended Father Pierron's missionary labors in the Colonies, as hostilities having broken out between the Senecas and the French, he retired to Canada. He returned to Europe in 1678.

In 1683, nine years after Father Pierron visited Connecticut, we catch a glimpse of two priests, the Rev. Thomas Harvey, S. J., and the Rev. John Gordon, D.D., who traveled overland from Nantasket to New York. In their journey they passed through Connecticut to the Sound, which they crossed to Long Island, and thence proceeded to their destination. They probably entered the State at Windham county and took shipping for Long Island at New London. Father Harvey and Father Gordon had been commissioned as chaplains to the troops stationed in New York, and accompanied Colonel Thomas Dongan, a Catholic, who had been appointed Governor of that Colony. They arrived at Nantasket on August 10, 1683, and reached New York on the 25th. There is no record that they performed any sacerdotal functions during their passage through the State.

On the 18th of July, 1788, a priest arrived at New London under particularly sad circumstances. He was from the Island of Guadeloupe, the Rev. Arnoux Dupré, Chaplain of a Convent of Charity. He left his tropical home in search of health, and was attracted to New London, no doubt, by the representations of the French, Spaniards and Portuguese, who flitted in and out of that harbor. He was far in decline when he reached New London. Whatever the nature of his illness, he did not long survive the voyage. He died on Friday, August 31, 1788. The day following his remains were attended to the place of burial by a respectable number of the residents of the city and decently interred.[1]  There was at this time in New London a considerable number of Catholics, both transient and permanent residents, who, no doubt, manifested their devotion to the priesthood by following the remains of Father Dupré to the grave, and by offering fervent prayers for the repose of his soul.  Poor, lonely priest!  He came a stranger burdened with affliction, but there is reason to believe that he experienced the generous hospitality of the people of New London.  His stay among them was of short duration, but they had learned to know his sorrows and to sympathize with his infirm condition.  The notice of his death printed at the time breathes an air of gentleness and sorrow for the sad fate of this servant of God, dying among strangers and far from the presence of his sacerdotal brethren, who could administer to him the salutary rites of the church, for which, no doubt, he ardently yearned.  Did he say Mass during his six weeks' illness at New London?  It is improbable that he did, though his heart must have craved the privilege both for his own and the spiritual welfare of his co-religionists.  Nothing more is known of him.  Diligent inquiries have failed to reveal the secrets that went with him into the grave, and his final resting-place is beyond identification.

The most illustrious ecclesiastic to visit Connecticut during the colonial period was the Right Rev. John Carroll, D.D., bishop of Baltimore. The apostolic zeal of this great pioneer bishop carried him into every part of his vast diocese, saying Mass, administering the sacraments, preaching the Gospel, expostulating with the weak, encouraging all.  In June, 1791, the Bishop visited Boston to investigate the conduct of the Rev. Father Rousselet, then pastor of the church of that city.   The investigation resulted in the suspension of Father Rousselet from his ministerial functions and the appointment of the Rev. John Thayer as his successor.[2]  Bishop Carroll left Boston on Thursday, June 16th, no doubt timing his departure so as to arrive at New London on or before Sunday, as he had probably heard that a respectable number of Catholics had there congregated.  As it is improbable the Bishop would undertake so long a journey unprepared to say Mass, at least on Sundays, we may infer that the Catholics of New London then enjoyed the rare privilege of assisting at the Holy Sacrifice and of partaking of the Bread of Angels from the anointed hands of their chief pastor.

Of his experience in Boston, Bishop Carroll thus wrote : " It is wonderful to tell what great civilities have been done to me in this town, where, a few years ago, a Popish priest was thought to be the greatest monster in creation. Many here, even of their principal people, have acknowledged to me that they would have crossed to the opposite side of the street rather than meet a Roman Catholic some time ago.  The horror which was associated with the idea of a papist is incredible ; and the scandalous misrepresentations by their

[1] *Connecticut Courant,* Sept. 3, 1778.
[2] " Conn. Courant " and " Conn. Gazette." 1791.

ministers increased the horror every Sunday. If all the Catholics here were united, their number would be about one hundred and twenty."[1]

Bishop Carroll sailed from New London Monday, June 20, to New York, bound homeward.

Norwich was the next city of Connecticut to receive a visit from a Catholic priest. He was the Rev. John Thayer, a name synonymous with sacerdotal energy and zeal for souls.[2] Father Thayer was a native of Boston, and a convert from Congregationalism. He was ordained to the priesthood in the world-famed Seminary of St. Sulpice, Paris, in 1789. After his ordination he labored in Boston, and was the first priest born on the soil to labor in New England. In the beginning he had a co-worker in the Rev. Father Rousselet, but from June, 1791, he was alone until the Rev. Dr. Matignon began his ministry in Boston, August 20, 1792. At this juncture, Father Thayer, anxious for a larger field, began a missionary tour through New England. He visited all the principal towns in Massachusetts, preaching and strengthening the few Catholics he met. New Hampshire, Rhode Island and Connecticut also were the scenes of his zealous labors. It was during this tour, in November, 1793, that he appeared in Norwich. At the invitation of the Rev. Joseph Strong, rector of the First Congregational church of that town, Father Thayer preached a sermon to a large audience in which he essayed to establish the divine institution of the church. On the following Tuesday evening he delivered a discourse in the same place on the invocation of the saints and the efficacy of prayers to them. In granting to Father Thayer the use of his pulpit Mr. Strong evinced a spirit of fraternal charity rare in those days. It was an exceptional act, a bright light amid the darkness of intolerance then so prevalent.

It is probable that during this missionary tour Father Thayer visited also New London, Hartford, New Haven and other towns in which it would be reported that Catholics resided.

There is an ancient tradition[3] in Hartford that two French priests resided there between 1756 and the Revolution, one on the Bloomfield, the other on the Windsor road. Tradition further says that the Rev. Francis Matignon, D.D., of Boston, visited a French priest, who was residing on the latter road,

[1] *Apropos* of Bishop Carroll's visit to Boston, the following items taken from the "Gazette of the United States" will be of interest: "Boston, June 4.—The Right Rev. Bishop Carroll, of the Roman Catholic church, arrived in town a few days since, and he confirmed the baptism of a number of Catholics. This gentleman, justly esteemed for his piety, learning and benevolence, will preach to-morrow at the Roman Catholic church."—June 15, 1791.

"Boston, June 7.—On Sunday morning the Right Rev. Bishop Carroll preached an eloquent and candid sermon at the Catholic chapel in School street. His Excellency the Governor, and Lady, and the Hon. Edward Cutts were among a crowded and very respectable audience, who appeared highly gratified by the charity, the benevolence, the piety which graced the discourse of the Right Rev. preacher."—June 18, 1791.

[2] "*The Norwich Packet,*" Nov. 14, 1793.

[3] This tradition is well grounded. It was told to Very Rev. Dr. Shahan by Mr. Henry Barnard, who had received it from Admiral Ward. The Admiral heard it from his father, whose knowledge covered the period before the Revolution.

when he passed through Hartford in 1813. In 1796, a French priest paid a visit to New Haven, probably to gather around him the French refugees, who at the end of the eighteenth century were in great numbers in Connecticut. To make his presence known he inserted this advertisement in the Connecticut *Journal*, a newspaper published at New Haven:

NEW HAVEN, January 28, 1796.

The Roman Catholics of Connecticut are informed that a priest is now in New Haven, where he will reside for some time. Those who wish to make use of his ministry will find him by inquiring at Mr. Azel Kimberly's, Chapel street.

The printers of this state are desired to insert this advertisement:

"Les François sont advertis qu' il y a un Prêtre Catholique en ville. On le demandera chez Monsieur Kimberly, Rue de la Chapelle, New Haven."

Probably this was the priest who resided on the Windsor road, and who published the following advertisement in the Connecticut *Courant*, March 1 and 8, 1796:

"A VENDRE.

"Une maison situe en Windsor vis a vis l'Eglise nouvelle, remote de la quatre vingt vergis, et de la rivière ea meme, accomode avec une grange et une maison de cabriolet avec un fort beau Jardin, il n'a tous sorts de commodities, les batiments sont tous nouveaux and entièrement fini. Il n'est pas que sept milles de Hartford situe dans un voisinage fort agreable. Pour les conditions appliquez a Richard L. Sell demenrant sur les premises.

"Fevrier 20, 1796."

*Translation.*

FOR SALE.

A house located in Windsor opposite the new church, distant from there eighty yards, and the same from the river. The place is provided with a barn and a carriage house, and has a very fine garden. There is every accommodation; the buildings are all new and entirely finished. It is only seven miles from Hartford, and situated in a very pleasant locality. For terms apply to Richard L. Sell, living on the premises.

February 20, 1796.

The Rev. Jean Ambrose Songé appears next upon the scene. A lifelong friend of the proto-Bishop of Boston, John de Cheverus, he shared with him the hardships of exile. Victims of the French Revolution, they sought an asylum in England in 1792, where they labored in the jurisdiction of the Bishop of London. With characteristic zeal and energy the Abbé Songé discharged the various duties imposed upon him, but his thoughts ever reverted to the rising young nation of the west, where the harvest was great, but the laborers few. After five fruitful years on the English mission, he sailed for America in February, 1797, bearing the following letter to Bishop Carroll, of Baltimore, from the Bishop of London.[1]

"MY LORD: Monsieur L'abbé Songé, Canon and Theologian at the Cathedral of Dol, who will hand or send you these lines, is on the point of setting off for America to be Chaplain in the family of the Vicomte De Sibert Cornillon, which family is settled near Hartford in Connecticut. . . . . He is a gentleman strongly recommended to me for his learning, piety and zeal, and he is intimately connected with Monsieur Cheverus, whom I recommended to your Lordship last Autumn. Mr. Songé has been employed

[1] "*Amer. Hist. Researches*," Oct., 1890.

here, viz., at Dorchester, an antient Bishop's See, though now a village in Oxfordshire, and has testimonial letters for your Lordship from Mr. Charles Leslie, Missionary at Oxford.

As he setts sail from London, I have given him all the necessary faculties for the Sacred Ministry, till he can apply for the same at Your Lordship's.

Presuming on Your Condescention to Your Lordship's Friend and Brother in Jesus Christ,
†JOHN DOUGLASS.

*Castle Street and Holborn, London,* February, 1797."

The Rev. Dr. Matignon of Boston added the weight of his testimony to the commendation of Bishop Douglass. He informed Bishop Carroll that Sougé was conversant with the English language, and had done much good by his preaching and in the direction of souls.

Immediately upon his arrival at New York he applied to Bishop Carroll for the faculties necessary to discharge the duties of his sacred ministry in Connecticut. The Abbe Sougé was associated for a brief period at Hartford with the Abbé J. S. Tisserant, who became the spiritual director of the saintly Mother Seton, the foundress of the Sisters of Charity in the United States. Father Cheverus wrote to Mrs. Seton of the Abbé Tisserant that he was "a most amiable and respectable man, equally conspicuous for his learning and piety."

There is no record of the duration of the Abbé Sougé's labors in Hartford. It is presumed that he remained with the Cornilion family until 1801, for in April of that year we find him at St. Joseph's, Talbot Co., on the eastern shore of Maryland. In Bishop England's *Diurnal,* mention is made of a Rev. Mr. *Sujet.* Of Locust Grove, in Georgia, the bishop writes: "First Catholic Congregation in Georgia. It was fixed in 1794 or '5 by the settlement of Mrs. Thompson's family and others from Maryland. Bishop Carroll sent Rev. Mr. Le Mercier to attend them. After 18 months he went to Savannah. Mr. *Sujet* remained 17 months, and returned to France."

This Mr. *Sujet,* probably, was our Sougé, as there was no other priest at that period in the United States with a name resembling his. *Sujet* was the euphonic spelling from hearing the name pronounced.

After his return to his native land, the Abbé Sougé became the Curé of Notre Dame, Mayenne, where he died, October 31, 1823. Bishop Cheverus, who had returned to France but a short time before to assume charge of the Diocese of Montauban, and was on a visit to his native city, Mayenne, preached the funeral sermon. The biographer of Bishop Cheverus thus speaks of his last tribute to his friend: "The Curé of this parish (Notre Dame, Mayenne) had died the preceding Friday. This Curé was Mr. Sougé, the friend of his childhood, and his companion in exile when he left Mayenne, and for some time in England. He wished to honor his memory by pronouncing his funeral oration. The subject of his eulogy was a Priest, distinguished alike for virtue and talent, and he spoke his praises with all the interest that such a subject was calculated to inspire, and all the sensibility of the most affectionate heart—expecting to embrace his friend, but finding only his cold remains."

The departure of the Abbé Sougé for the Maryland mission synchronizes with the close of the eighteenth century. In 1813 Rev. Francis Matignon,

D. D., of Boston, on his way to New York, arrived at Hartford on a Saturday, and, as a law[1] then in vogue prohibited traveling on Sunday, he remained perforce till Monday. The Rev. Dr. Strong, the rector of the Congregational church, upon learning of Father Matignon's presence in town, cordially invited him to occupy his pulpit on the morrow. Dr. Matignon accepted the proffered hospitality. But the liberal-minded minister either did not count the cost, or, knowing it, dared to be courteous. On Monday his worthy, but wrothy deacons, in solemn delegation, stoutly protested against the presence in their pulpit of a "popish priest," and formally censured their pastor for his act of courtesy to a Christian gentleman of another creed. But Dr. Strong felt that his course would receive the sanction of a strong element in his congregation, and to the remonstrants made answer: "Well, gentlemen, do your best, and do your worst; make the most of it. I have the ladies on my side."

At this time Connecticut was under the jurisdiction of the diocese of Boston, whose bishop was John de Cheverus, D.D. This apostolic man was tireless in bringing the graces of the Mass and the sacraments to his widely-scattered children. In 1823 he visited Hartford and preached in the old State House. Besides Hartford he paid visits to East Hartford, Vernon, New London, saying Mass, preaching, catechizing, encouraging his flock, and administering the sacraments. Records of baptisms administered in this visitation will be found in the history of these places.

There is a tradition that the famous convert, Rev. Virgil Barber, S. J., made a missionary visit to Hartford some time between 1823 and 1828. The tradition furthermore says, that he remained there for several days and said Mass in private houses.

The construction of the Enfield canal brought to the neighborhood of Windsor Locks a respectable number of Irishmen, who proved loyal to the faith, though they had no opportunity of performing public acts of worship. In illness the thought that overrules all others is the earnest, heartfelt desire for the priest. A Catholic, either from perverted choice or from necessity, may live without the ministrations of the priest; but at the approach of death, or even in serious illness, the recollections of other and holier days crowd in upon him; his faith is re-animated and rises grandly supreme over all other forces, and he calls upon God's anointed for the sweet consolations of

---

[1] *"Be it enacted by the Governor, Council and Representatives, in General Court assembled, and by the authority of the same,* That every assistant in this Colony, and every justice of the peace, within the limits of their authority, are hereby impowered and directed when they shall have plain view or personal knowledge thereof, either with or without a written warrant, to cause all persons unnecessarily travelling on the Sabbath or Lord's day to be apprehended, and to examine them, and if need be to command any person or persons to seize, arrest and secure any such person unnecessarily travelling on the Lord's day as aforesaid, and them to hold till judgment may be had thereon. And every sheriff, constable, grand juryman and tything man, are hereby impowered and directed without warrant to apprehend and carry before the next assistant or justice of the peace all persons trespassing said law as aforesaid, provided they be taken upon sight or present information of others and to command all necessary assistance." "*Act of October, 1751. Public Records of Conn.,*" vol. X., p. 45.

religion. And the sturdy laborers of Windsor well illustrated this truth. They were, by the fault of no one, deprived of the presence of a priest, but when one of their number was stricken with illness in August, 1827, they despatched a messenger to New York for one to hasten to their suffering comrade. And a priest then, as now and always, promptly responded to the summons. He was the Very Rev. John Power,[1] Vicar-General of New York. Learning in this manner of the presence there of a goodly number of Catholics, the zealous priest returned in October of the same year, said Mass and preached for them, thus stimulating their faith and infusing into them new courage to overcome their spiritual difficulties and new determination to persevere. It was on one of these occasions, probably the latter, that Father Power said Mass for the Catholics of New Haven. He had arrived there from Windsor Locks after the boat had sailed for New York, and, as it was Saturday, he remained over Sunday, greatly to the joy of the faithful little band. The building in which Father Power officiated on this occasion is said to have been No. 5, Long Wharf.

The Rev. R. D. Woodley, a young priest, now enters the field. In 1828 Bishop Fenwick assigned to him Rhode Island and Connecticut as the theatre of his labors with his residence at Providence. In November of this year he visited Hartford, and no doubt exercised his ministry in other places where Catholics were known to be located. In the following year, July 9, we find him again at Hartford, whence he carried the divine message to the laborers on the Enfield canal. He visited also New Haven and New London, the former on July 13 and 14, 1829.

We have thus traced the presence of every priest who entered Connecticut from the historic occasion when the saintly Druillettes pleaded in vain for his red children before the Commissioners of the United Colonies of New England in 1651. If others came, there is no accessible record of the fact, nor even a vague tradition of their presence. The ministrations of those who came, brief and widely separated though they were, were not unproductive of good. Some of the seed sown fell upon good soil, as is evidenced by the stately tree that has grown up, beneath whose peaceful shades two hundred and fifty thousand faithful souls find shelter. They planted, Apollo watered; it was God who gave the increase.

With the departure of Father Woodley we enter upon a new era, an epoch

---

[1] Very Rev. John Power, D.D., was born in the County Cork, Ireland, in 1792. He was educated at Maynooth, where he was a classmate of Archbishop McHale of Tuam, and Father Mathew, the apostle of temperance. He arrived in New York in 1816, and was made pastor of St. Peter's parish. On the death of Bishop Connelly he was appointed Administrator of the diocese, which position he occupied until the installation of Bishop Dubois. He was then appointed Vicar-General, which office he retained until his death. A contemporary said of him: "He was a man of great learning, piety and talent; as a scholar he was pre-eminent, being intimately acquainted with the Greek, Latin, French, Spanish and Italian languages; as the zealous defender of his faith, as a writer he had but few equals and no superior. Great benevolence and sweetness of disposition won for him the affection of all." He possessed great controversial powers, and as an orator he excelled in extempore discourses. His death occurred on April 14th, 1849.

destined to become glorious by reason of the splendid achievements it was to accomplish in music and painting, in sculpture and architecture, as well as in the beneficent works of mercy and charity, of education and religion that are its joy and its crown; this era is ushered in with the advent of the Rev. Bernard O'Cavanagh, who, under the guidance of the indefatigable Bishop Fenwick, laid strong and deep the foundation of the first parish in Connecticut.

---

# THE BISHOPS OF THE DIOCESE.

*"The Holy Ghost hath placed you bishops, to rule the Church of God, which He hath purchased with His own blood."* ACTS XX. 28.

## RIGHT REV. WILLIAM TYLER, D.D.,

### FIRST BISHOP OF HARTFORD.

RIGHT REV. WILLIAM TYLER, the first incumbent of the See of Hartford, was descended from a family distinguished alike for the heroic sacrifices it made for religion and for its subsequent splendid services in the cause of Christ. Converts all to our holy faith, they brought into their new life renewed spiritual vigor, increased love for God and His church, and an intense desire, which nothing could overcome, to devote themselves unreservedly to the service of the Master. Reared amidst the chilling influences prevalent in the early days of this century, their hearts yearned for something better, higher and nobler; for that which would unite them in love with their blessed Saviour; for something more substantial, more supernatural, than that which cold, formal, rigorous and barren Puritanism afforded. Their souls craved the full light of Christ's teachings, their hearts hungered for the Real Presence of their Redeemer. "I know that my Redeemer liveth," perhaps could each one say; but for him He was a far-off Being, ever enveloped in ineffable majesty and dwelling in light inaccessible, an inexorable Judge clothed always in the prerogatives of His justice. He reigned amid the thunders and lightnings of Sinai or amid the devastation that will attend the world's destruction. Of the meek and lowly Christ, but still infinite God, how limited was their knowledge! Apparently unfamiliar with the sad yet ever-consoling story of Calvary; as though oblivious of the transcendent words: "Many sins are forgiven her because she hath loved much," or "Son, thy sins are forgiven thee," or "This day thou shalt be with me in Paradise;" unmindful that Christ came to call a poor, sin-stricken race, not the just, to repentance, they longed to know the Christ as He is, and not as a narrow, distorted theology portrayed Him, and to live in intimate union with Him; therefore, casting away the trammels of rigorism that held them captive to earth, they soared into the clear atmosphere of Christ's love.

*Yours sincerely in Christ*

*✠ Wm Tyler Bp. of Hartford*

The Rev. Virgil Barber, a minister of the Congregational, and later of the Episcopal church, was the first to enter the Catholic church. His wife and five children, one son and four daughters, shared with him the hardships of the sacrifice, for their conversion meant not only the deprivation of emoluments, but the loss also of social recognition. His father, also a clergyman in the Congregational and Episcopal denominations, the Rev. Daniel Barber, followed him in proclaiming allegiance to the ancient faith. His devoted aunt, also, Mrs. Tyler, with her husband, four sons and four daughters, illumined by the light that shone round about them, yielded cheerful obedience to the divine call. Nor did the sacrifices which these families made for conscience sake go unrewarded. In His mercy God bestowed upon all the members of Virgil Barber's family the exceptional grace of religious vocations. By special dispensation the husband and father became a priest of the Society of Jesus. The wife and mother entered the Visitation convent at Georgetown, District of Columbia, and died a holy religious after forty-three years in the service of her divine Master. Their only son, Samuel, followed in his father's footsteps and became also a Jesuit priest. Of their four daughters, three became Ursuline nuns, one at Boston, another at Quebec and the third at Three Rivers, Canada, while the fourth became a Visitandine nun at Georgetown. Of Mrs. Tyler's family, one son received a vocation to the priesthood and was subsequently elevated to the episcopal dignity, while the four daughters retired from the world and within the peaceful cloisters of a convent at Emmittsburg served God as gentle, patient and faithful Sisters of Charity.[1]

William Tyler was born in Derby, Vermont, on June 5th, 1806. In his childhood his parents removed to Claremont, New Hampshire. His early life was spent amid the various occupations incidental to farm life, and while engaged in these humble labors he gave evidence of possessing in a marked

[1] Bishop Tyler's family consisted of Noah, his father, and Abigail, his mother; his brothers were Ignatius, George and Israel. His sisters were Rosette Tyler—Sister Genevieve—who entered the Emmittsburg community in 1820. She led a holy and edifying life and died at St. John's Institution, Frederick, Md., July 2, 1839. In his letter to Father Tyler announcing her death, the Rev. John McElroy, S. J., said: "She was one of those of whom the world was not worthy, and the Holy Virgin to whom she was tenderly devoted would, on this festival (the feast of the Visitation of the B. V. M.) present her pure soul to her divine Son." Catherine Tyler—Sister Mary James—entered the same community in 1827, was sent on the mission to St. Vincent's Orphan Asylum, Washington, D. C., and died there, November 24, 1839. Martha Tyler—Sister Beatrice—also entered in 1827, and after a few years withdrew to embrace a cloistered life. Sarah Maria Tyler—Sister Mary de Sales—entered also in 1827. She still survives at St. Joseph's Academy, Emmittsburg, Md. On the 16th of the present month (April, 1899) she completed her ninety-fifth year, in the full possession of her faculties.

The Bishop's father died April 23, 1845, at Elgin, Kane county, Ill. After her husband's death, Mrs. Tyler resided for a time with her daughter, Sister Mary Beatrice, at the Visitation convent, St. Louis. She died at her home, which at the time was in a small place bearing an Indian name, in the neighborhood of South Bend, Indiana.

The writer is indebted for the facts in this note to Mother Mariana Flynn, Superior and Visitatrix of the Sisters in the U. S., who received them from Sister Mary de Sales.

degree the sterling qualities that distinguished his career as priest and bishop —zeal and industry, tireless energy and profound sympathy with suffering, fidelity to purpose and conscientiousness in the discharge of duty, how onerous so ever. Master Tyler was sixteen years old when he embraced the Catholic faith. Of studious disposition and ambitious of acquiring an education that would enable him to carve out success in later years, he entered the classical school which the Rev. Virgil Barber had established at Claremont. He was the first student to become enrolled. Entering upon his studies with enthusiasm and bringing to his work systematic application he soon became as proficient in his classes as he was regular in his conduct. His reward came in a short time in his appointment as Prefect of Studies, a position which his native energy enabled him to fill to the satisfaction of his Superior and fellow-students. He was fond of athletic sports and joined freely in the amusements which the school afforded. Music was a favorite pastime in leisure moments, and he not infrequently played the cornet at divine service. But the trait that appears the most prominent at this period of his life was his devotion to prayer, his intense love for the sacraments, which he received at frequent intervals. "From the moment of his conversion to the true faith," said a contemporary, "the late bishop was distinguished by his modest virtues, and by the eminent sanctity of his life."[1] He was a profoundly religious young man, and the sentiments that ruled his heart and regulated his mind are disclosed in a letter which he wrote to a brother in Georgia:

"Now, my dear brother, let me warn you not to place too much affection and dependence on the things of this life. Although you now are prosperous, still you may meet with a reverse of fortune; and even if you could be sure of prosperity and all the blessings this world could afford, what comparison could they bear to the happiness or misery of eternity? Our time here at the longest is but short, and we are daily liable to the strokes of death. At the longest our life here is but short; a striking proof of this lately occurred in Cornish: A young man, who had lived in a Catholic family, and had obtained a knowledge of the Catholic religion, but for reasons known to himself deferred his conversion. But the tyrant Death did not wait for him, and he was ushered into the other world, unprepared as he was. I hope that you find some leisure from your business for serious meditation; and there is one time which, of all others, is, perhaps, the most productive of meditation: I mean the silent hours of night, after we retire to rest. Of this you cannot be deprived, and I hope you employ it for the benefit of your soul. How do you pass the season of Lent? As a Catholic, or as a Protestant? I know that it is difficult for one in the situation you are in to live a regular life, but I hope that God will give you grace to walk in the path of duty."

Master Tyler remained under the fostering care of the Rev. Virgil Barber for four years. With him at Claremont were two young men who were distined to be also crowned with the honors of the priesthood, and who in after years saluted him as their bishop, William Wiley and James Fitton. While at school here young Tyler acquired a good knowledge of Greek, Latin and French, besides becoming well grounded in the common branches. As Latin was the ordinary language of the school and spoken by the students at all times it is not surprising that the future bishop became proficient in its use.

[1] "Catholic Observer," June, 1849.

The religious atmosphere in which he moved exercised a controlling influence over him and directed his mind and heart to the Lord's sanctuary. He felt an irresistible attraction to the service of God in the sacred ministry. He longed for the opportunity to present himself as a candidate for the priesthood wherein he could employ his God-given talents for the salvation of his fellow-men. But his worldly possessions were few, his financial resources limited. The grim figure of Poverty stood between him and the realization of his desires. To his mother he revealed the anxiety that pressed upon his heart in a letter from which we give an extract:

"How often do we meet with disappointments, when our hopes and expectations are at their highest point! You have seen how various and changeable the course of life is, how vague and fluctuating fortune, and how great inconstancy among friends. You have been made acquainted with my intention of becoming a priest, and that the means by which I expected to attain this was by the assistance of the Rev. Superior, Mr. Barber, in retaining and promoting me as his assistant in the school. I have already informed you of the loss of expectation. Now, what course shall I pursue? For myself, I know not where another year will find me. Pa thinks that I had better agree with Uncle Daniel to procure me a situation in a store at Boston, where he is soon going. This is far from my wishes, since I have so seriously engaged my mind in the pursuit which appeared to me to be the one pointed out for me by Divine Providence. I do not like to give out; but if it is the Divine will that I should become a priest, there will be some way for my attaining it."

His confidence in Divine Providence was not misplaced. God, who had called him to the ecclesiastical state, and whose voice he sought to obey, provided the young student with the ways and means of accomplishing his high and holy purpose. Difficulties vanished, obstacles were surmounted, and hope and joy supplanted anxiety and gloom. In Bishop Fenwick's *Memoranda* under date of September 13, 1826, we read this precious entry:

"Mr. Daniel Barber, the father of Virgil Barber, arrived from Claremont on a visit to the Bishop, bringing with him Mr. Wm. Tyler, whom he introduces and recommends to him as a candidate for the ecclesiastical state. The Bishop is pleased with the progress made by him in his studies, and having received a good account of him on other points, admits him. Young Mr. Tyler is a relative of Mr. Barber, and has received the principal part of his education from Rev. Virgil H. Barber in his academy at Claremont."

Master Tyler thus became a member of Bishop Fenwick's household under whose tuition he completed his classical education in June, 1827. With a respite of only two days, as he informs us in his diary, he began his theological studies with the bishop as his instructor. He received Minor Orders on December 24, 1826; Subdeaconship, December 21, 1827, and Deaconship the day following. He was ordained to the Priesthood by Bishop Fenwick on June 3, 1829.

Father Tyler had now attained the goal of his ambition; he was a priest of the Most High. He entered upon his new and arduous duties with an enthusiasm that brooked no failure. "From that moment forward," said a writer in the *Catholic Observer*,[1] "it may be said in truth, that 'he had been delivered through the grace of God, unto the work, which he accomplished.'"

[1] June, 1849.

All who knew him felt at once, and may testify that, unmindful of himself, and of all human applause and of all worldly advantages, he had constantly but one object in view—the salvation of souls and the greater glory of his Divine Master; and the Catholics of Boston may well remember how, during many years, in sickness and in health, by night and by day, he was ever ready to serve their souls in a never-changing spirit of meekness and of zeal; and how he kept back nothing that was profitable to them, but preached it to them and taught them publicly, and from house to house, testifying to all penance towards God, and faith in our Lord Jesus Christ."

After Father Tyler's ordination he served the Cathedral parish until August 23, 1829, when he was appointed to the mission of Canton. In 1830 he was sent to Sandwich. He also served a year on the Aroostook mission, Maine. With the exception of these brief appointments the theatre of Father Tyler's labors was chiefly in Boston as an attache of the Cathedral of Holy Cross. From here he attended other missions, among them being Benedicta, Maine, in 1843. He was appointed vicar-general, which position he occupied until his elevation to the See of Hartford.

The multiplication of duties, the weight of years and increasing infirmities induced Bishop Fenwick to request the Fifth Provincial Council, assembled at Baltimore, May, 1843, to petition the Holy See for a division of his diocese. Pope Gregory acceded to the request, and on September 18, 1843, erected the States of Rhode Island and Connecticut into a diocese with the Episcopal seat at Hartford. The choice of Bishop Fenwick was confirmed at Rome, and Very Rev. William Tyler was appointed the first bishop of the new See. The official Bulls notifying him of his election were received on February 13, 1844, and on February 21st he proceeded to Frederick, Maryland, to make a retreat preliminary to his consecration. It was with the greatest reluctance that he accepted the episcopal dignity. He bowed to the wishes of Bishop Fenwick, whom he revered as a father, and submitted to the decision of his spiritual director, Very Rev. Francis Dzierozinski, S. J., Provincial of the Maryland Province. He was consecrated on Sunday, March 17, 1844, in the cathedral at Baltimore, amid the impressive ceremonies prescribed by the Roman Pontifical. The officers of the consecration service were as follows:

Consecrator—Right Rev. Benedict Fenwick, D.D., Boston.
Assisting Bishops—Right Rev. Richard V. Whalen, D.D., Richmond, Va., and Right Rev. Andrew Byrne, D.D., Little Rock, Ark.
Preacher—Rev. Henry B. Coskery, Cathedral, Baltimore, Md.
Master of Ceremonies—Rev. Francis L'Homme.
Assistants—Messrs. Thomas Foley[1] and R. J. Lawrence.

On Sunday, March 21, Bishop Tyler was one of the assistant bishops at the consecration of Right Rev. John B. Fitzpatrick, D.D., at Georgetown.

The personal appearance of Bishop Tyler at that time is thus described by his physician, Dr. Edward Le Prohon, A.M.: "At my first view of the

[1] Afterwards Bishop of Chicago.

worthy prelate I recognized in him the lymphatic temperament which dominated in him, a delicate white skin, narrow shoulders, high stature, about six feet, the body long and thin, a well-featured countenance, sweet and calm, the cheeks slightly roseate, and constantly wearing spectacles, though he has not yet reached his forty-fifth year. The entire external appearance of Mgr. Tyler showed symptoms of latent consumption; Mgr. Tyler himself felt the necessity of taking care of his feeble health the better to exercise the laborious functions of the foundation of a new diocese. . . . Mgr. Tyler's appearance took everybody's attention. He bore the expression of sanctity on his countenance, the seal of the man of God was to be seen on it."

Accompanied by Bishop Fenwick, Bishop Tyler arrived at Hartford on April 12, 1844. The church of the Holy Trinity became his cathedral, as in that historic edifice he was installed Bishop of Hartford on Sunday, April 14th—*Dominica in Albis.* Extensive preparations had been made for the worthy and dignified reception of the new prelate. Rev. John Brady, the rector, was the celebrant of the Mass, and Bishop Fenwick preached the sermon of installation, in the course of which he eulogized his colleague and congratulated the people upon the erection of the new diocese. At the Vesper service Bishop Tyler preached his first sermon as Bishop of Hartford.

Bishop Tyler's first visit was made to Middletown, Conn., on April 15th. He inspected the new church then approaching completion. His next visit was to New Haven.

When Bishop Tyler was consecrated the population of his diocese was estimated from a census taken at the time at 9,997 souls, of whom 4,817 were in Connecticut, and 5,180 in Rhode Island. In the two States there were six priests and eight churches; three priests and four churches in Connecticut, and as many in Rhode Island. Writing on March 1, 1845, to Monsieur Choiselat Gallien, a distinguished member of the Propagation of the Faith, residing in Paris, Bishop Tyler said:

"There are ten or twelve other places where there are small congregations of Catholics, whom we occasionally visit to afford them the benefits of religion. I have with me in the whole diocese only six priests to assist me in administering to the wants of all these. So you will easily perceive that we are in great want of zealous clergymen; and we have little prospect of any addition to our numbers soon." Bishop Tyler's spiritual children were mostly emigrants, poor, despised, with nothing but faith and health, unprovided with churches and priests, scattered up and down an extensive territory from Providence to Norfolk. Some may yet be spared who remember the Old Guard of Catholicity in these parts, the venerable, laborious and self-sacrificing pioneers who sowed the seed by the water courses and on the hillsides and along the coast line, which has fructified and multiplied until at the present writing there are 435 priests and 265 churches, where fifty-five years ago there were six priests and eight churches.

After his consecration Bishop Tyler took up his residence in Hartford, the place named in his Bulls as the episcopal seat. At that time Hartford contained about 13,000 inhabitants, from 500 to 600 of whom were adult

Catholics. The only church, a wooden structure, which had been purchased from the Protestants, was about 75 feet long by 40 feet wide; moreover, there were only a few feet of land on each side of the church belonging to it. In the villages within eighteen miles of Hartford there were three or four small congregations of Irish Catholics, who were occasionally attended by the resident pastor. Providence, on the other hand, had 23,000 inhabitants of whom 2,000 were Catholics. It had two churches, and either of them was larger than the one in Hartford. In the neighboring villages the Catholics were more numerous than in the towns near Hartford. "In consideration of these things," wrote Bishop Tyler to Mgr. Vincent Edward, Prince and Archbishop of Vienna, March 1, 1845, "and after having consulted with Dr. Fenwick, Bishop of Boston, and others upon whose judgment I could rely, I resolved to make my residence in Providence, and at the Council of the Bishops of the United States to petition Rome to remove the See from Hartford to Providence." Bishop Tyler took up his residence in Providence in June, 1844.

He selected as his Cathedral the elder of the two churches in Providence, SS. Peter and Paul, of which the Rev. James Fitton was pastor. Of this church the bishop wrote to the Archbishop of Vienna on the date above mentioned: "It is a stone building 80 feet long by 40 feet wide. It is very unpleasantly situated on account of the narrowness of the land on each side of it. It has only four feet on one side and not two on the other. Thus we are liable to have our windows darkened by buildings that may at any time be put up by the owners of the land near the church; and the buildings that now are near the church are very offensive, being stables in which are kept cows and horses. We desire very much to buy out these grounds that we may be secure of enjoying the light of heaven and be freed from these nuisances."

The zeal of the new bishop was hampered, but not overcome by the poverty of his diocese. His people were loyal to every request and faithful to the discharge of every religious duty. They were day laborers, devoted and God-fearing; and their willingness to contribute to the advancement of religion was a striking characteristic. But they were comparatively few in number and manifold were the needs of the new diocese. "My best chalice," wrote Bishop Tyler to Mons. Gallien, Paris, "is brass, and I have but one other at the Cathedral, and only four or five more *in the whole diocese* which belong to it. On last Christmas (December 25, 1846) I said my first Pontifical Mass, though with but one priest to assist, and very destitute of suitable ornaments. But these are small matters. The great ones are what give me concern." In a letter acknowledging the receipt of a generous allocation from the Leopold Society of Vienna, Bishop Tyler opened his heart in gratitude to the illustrious Archbishop of that ancient See:

"*Most Reverend and Venerable Sir:*

"I have not words to express my feelings of gratitude towards you and the Leopold Society. Your donations have been of incalculable benefit to me. When I was appointed to this diocese I was poor, and the church here was destitute of everything. I was overwhelmed with the sad prospect before me, and I knew not where to look for assistance."

Indeed, so widespread was the knowledge of the poverty of the Diocese of Hartford that the Bishop of Philadelphia, Right Rev. Francis Patrick Kenrick, wrote to Rev. Dr. Cullen on June 5, 1846, then rector of the Irish College at Rome, that "the unfortunate haste with which Little Rock and Hartford were made Sees in a former Council, should cause us to pause when a new See is to be erected." [1]

But God had willed through His Vicegerent, and obstacles apparently insurmountable gave way before the faith and energy of Bishop Tyler. It was his mission—and a glorious one it was—to delve and lay the foundations deep and solid, and faithful was he to the trust confided to him. He had no sooner taken up the reins of government than he bent all his energies to advance the spiritual condition of his diocese. He sought for priests at the world-famed missionary college of All Hallows, Drumcondra, Dublin. He solicited and received financial assistance from the Society for the Propagation of the Faith at Paris and the Leopold Society at Vienna to erect churches and to provide teachers for the youth of his diocese. The condition of the children appealed strongly to his affectionate and sympathetic nature. The love for them that consumed him and the anxiety that weighed upon him are exhibited in a letter he wrote to Paris in January, 1847:

"We are in a lamentable want of schools for our children. There are, I suppose, in this city alone (Providence) 1000 children of Catholic parents between six and fourteen years of age, and I am grieved to know that in spite of what I can do, they are growing up in deplorable ignorance of religion, and this through want of suitable means of being instructed. As a beginning in this matter, I wish very much to put a small colony of Sisters of Charity from Emmittsburg, Maryland. For more than ten years I witnessed in Boston the good they did in rearing the girls in that city. This is one object that I shall strive for. Then, alas! our boys are equally destitute. And then, all the children of Catholic parents in the other towns and villages! What shall I do for them?"

His love for the children of his diocese took tangible form in the organization of the "Confraternity of the Blessed Virgin Mary to Befriend Children." It was established in Providence, 1847, and its object was two-fold, to promote the spiritual welfare of its members, and to assist in providing for the spiritual and corporeal wants of children. Its members were required to say once every day this short prayer: "*O! Holy Mary, Mother of God, be a mother to me, and to the children of this Congregation; take them under thy special protection.*"

In the same letter the zealous bishop speaks of another matter that was dear to his heart; but with the hope expressed there was a vein of sadness, born of his poverty:

"Next summer," he says, "I expect three priests from the College of Drumcondra, Dublin, Ireland. I have not vestments, chalices, etc., for them. I wish to send these newly ordained priests to several places where there are bodies of poor Catholic laborers, and in some of these places there is not the semblance of a church. How happy would I be to be able to assist each of these with a few hundred dollars to begin small churches and abodes for themselves; and what encouragement would it not give the poor people among whom they go and upon whom they must depend for everything!"

[1] "*Records of the Cath. Hist. Soc. of Phila.*," Vol. VII., p. 329.

Bishop Tyler cared little for the creature comforts of life. His ambition was to provide for the welfare of his priests and people. Self gave way to the neighbor. He petitioned for assistance for the poor congregations over whom he was placed and for the heroic priests who came and went at his call; but for himself he asked nothing. He was content with the humblest accommodations. Let his devoted physician speak again :

"The little house inhabited formerly by the venerable Father Fitton became the episcopal palace of Mgr. Tyler, a residence in which many of his parishioners would have refused to lodge; but Mgr. Tyler, whose mind was occupied only with the desire of serving God, considered this miserable residence as suitable and established himself in it. Being just beside the sacristy, and only a few steps from his Cathedral, he chose this miserable abode because his dominant thought was never fixed on the comforts of human life. The episcopal residence *could easily have been drawn by oxen from one end of Providence to the other;* the stables of a hundred citizens in easy circumstances were better protected against the seasons; but Mgr. Tyler gave only a secondary consideration to whatever related only to the comforts of the man of the world. . . . . Wishing to avoid carefully the sentiments of human respect, he dispensed with a carriage and made his journeys afoot in the city; only the most necessary articles of furniture were to be seen in his house, which was not carpeted; his table was common and his meals plain; he would have been satisfied with the commonest metal had not Madame Carney of Boston generously provided the silver which she wished to have on Mgr. Tyler's table"

Bishop Tyler attended the Sixth Provincial Council which assembled at Baltimore on May 10, 1846, a Council redolent of honors bestowed upon the Immaculate Mother of God. The late Very Rev. Edward McColgan, Vicar-General, and rector of St. Peter's church, Baltimore, was assigned as his theologian. It was this Council that added to the Litany of our Lady of Loretto, with the approbation of the Holy See, the invocation, " *Queen, Conceived without Sin, Pray for us.*" To this Council also belongs the honor of having *Mary the Mother of God, Conceived without Sin,* made the patroness of the Church in the United States; thus anticipating by eight years the solemn and infallible definition of the doctrine of the Immaculate Conception.

The Seventh Provincial Council of Baltimore, which convened on May 5, 1849, also saw Bishop Tyler in attendance; but on this occasion he brought with him a certificate from his attending physician that his health was in a precarious condition. He was accompanied by the Rev. James Fitton as his theologian. Bishop Tyler, realizing the deadly encroachments of his disease, wished to resign the episcopal dignity into hands stronger than his to bear the burden. With that detachment from earth that ever characterized him, he fully realized that his days were few. But the Fathers of the Council, instead of accepting his resignation, declared in favor of the appointment of a coadjutor, who would lighten his burden. Wherefore, on the motion of the Bishop of New York,[1] Right Rev. John Hughes, D.D., the Council petitioned the Holy See to appoint a coadjutor to the Bishop of Hartford, and the name of Very Rev. Bernard O'Reilly, Vicar-General of the diocese of Buffalo, who was

---

[1] The minutes of the Council, May 8th, read: " Postulante Revmo D. Episcopo Neo-Eboracensi, censuerunt Patres supplicandum S. Sedi ut Coadjutor detur Revmo D. Gulielmo Tyler, Episcopo Hartfordiensi, ob ejusdem valetudinem minus firmam."

present at the Council as the theologian of Bishop Timon, was sent to Rome for the office. The Fathers also recommended the erection of New York into an archbishopric, or province, with Boston, Hartford, Albany and Buffalo as suffragan sees.

On the adjournment of the Council, May 13th, Bishop Tyler set out for his beloved diocese. On the steamer from New York to Stonington, he contracted acute articular rheumatism owing to a cold and damp state-room which he occupied. "The gravity of this terrible malady was depicted on the countenance of the Bishop," says his physician. "Notwithstanding his sufferings, not a word of complaint escaped his lips; his patience and resignation were superior to the sufferings of the flesh." As the condition of the illustrious patient continued to grow worse, the Rev. William Wiley, rector of St. Patrick's parish, Providence, requested the immediate presence at his bedside of the Bishop of Boston, Dr. Fitzpatrick. In the meantime a condition of delirium had ensued in which the sufferer failed to recognize any of his attendants. When Bishop Fitzpatrick arrived the patient gave no sign of recognition. Kneeling in prayer he fervently invoked the divine assistance for his dying colleague; he petitioned that reason might be restored; that the bishop might not only be enabled to receive the last sacraments with full consciousness, but also that he might give instructions about the affairs of his diocese. No sooner had Bishop Fitzpatrick concluded his prayer than the delirium vanished, consciousness fully returned, and with a smile of recognition, the dying prelate greeted his colleague. We quote again from his physician: "The sudden change that had taken place in my presence, from the state of confusion of his intellectual faculties to a return to a clear mind capable of distinguishing the true from the false; this sudden transition struck me with astonishment when I saw the two bishops conversing freely on the affairs of the diocese of Hartford." Bishop Tyler received the last sacraments with every manifestation of love and faith and resignation. He made his profession of faith and blessed his diocese, "at the end of which," wrote the Rev. James Fitton, who was present, "he closed his eyes and never spoke audibly more, save at times those pious aspirations and holy ejaculations of a departing saint.'

Bishop Tyler died on June 18, 1849, at the age of forty-five years. "The first bishop of Hartford died poor," says Dr. Le Prohon, "but he left no debts, or if there were any, they were exceedingly small."

Two days later his remains were laid at rest in the basement of the cathedral of SS. Peter and Paul under the high altar, but are now side by side of those of Bishop Hendricken in the vault of the new cathedral. Right Rev. Bishop Fitzpatrick officiated at the obsequies in the presence of a numerous concourse of priests and people. The funeral sermon was preached by Rev. William Wiley, and was a splendid tribute from a devoted son and subordinate to an affectionate father and superior.

Mgr. Tyler was an apostolic bishop, who brought to his high office the virtues that have ever characterized the converters of nations. He heard the confessions of his people and baptized the little ones of his flock. The sick were the special objects of his pastoral solicitude, and though there were priests about him to attend to such calls, his sympathetic nature brought him to their bedside, no matter what the condition of the weather, to administer the consolations of religion. He visited officially all parts of his diocese, preaching, confirming, strengthening the faith of the people and consoling his priests amidst the arduous labors of their extensive missions. Truly, was he a good and faithful shepherd and his flock entertained for him a personal love that followed him beyond the grave. The poor found in him a father and friend and benefactor. Every week he distributed food and money to his indigent charges, and in so doing, he felt that, besides ameliorating their condition, he was rendering a service to God. With St. Paul could he say in very truth : "*I was free as to all. I made myself the servant of all, that I might gain the more . . . To the weak I became weak, that I might gain the weak. I became all things to all men, that I might save all. And I do all things for the gospel's sake · that I may be made partaker thereof.*" In his preaching Bishop Tyler was plain, practical, persuasive, convincing. He cared little for the ornaments of oratory, and he embellished his discourses with few flights of rhetoric. His sermons that are extant show careful preparation, as well as a full realization of the dignity of the preacher's office. His was an age when clear and solid instruction, more than mere eloquence, was imperatively required ; and this need he seemed to have kept ever before him. On the more important occasions he read his sermons, no doubt from the belief that this method of teaching was more impressive and convincing.

Bishop Tyler, as we have seen, was hampered in the prosecution of his designs by the poverty of his diocese. Though without the means of accomplishing great works—works that would attract the attention and evoke the admiration of the world—he, nevertheless, wrought well and solidly with the slender contributions which his faithful people placed at his disposal, and with the pecuniary assistance he received from European societies. At his consecration the whole diocese contained eight priests, seven churches and four stations. At his death, five years later, the churches had increased to twelve and the priests to fourteen. There were seven ecclesiastical students and a Catholic population of about 20,000.

We shall close this sketch with words of tribute from a few of his contemporaries. In an editorial, the Boston *Pilot*, June 23, 1849, said : "Bishop Tyler, by general consent, was allowed to be one of the most devout and saintly of the episcopal order. . . . . . The saintly bishop is lamented by the church and by all the faithful who ever came in contact with him in the course of his ministrations." The *Catholic Observer*, June 30, 1849, said : "In the episcopacy, he was distinguished by the same unassuming worth, the same deep wisdom, the same untiring zeal which marked his career in the priesthood. Under his prudent care, and by his assiduous labor, religion grew up with silent, but rapid growth in every part of his extensive diocese, and his piety, his union with God, drew from Heaven those graces which gave increase to that which he had planted and matured with apostolic toils." "The life of the late Bishop Tyler," wrote a contributor to the *Pilot*, March 1, 1851, "is one of the brightest examples which our holy religion can lay before us, and he will long remain in the hearts and minds of those over whom he has unceasingly watched and prayed."

Bishop Fitzpatrick paid this tribute to his friend and colleague.[1] "His talents were not brilliant nor was his learning extensive, though quite sufficient. But he possessed great moderation of character, sound judgment, uncommon prudence and much firmness. His life as a priest was truly a model for ecclesiastics. Not one hour was given to idleness nor vain amusements or visits. He was methodical in the distribution of his time, and every portion of it was well spent. Zeal for the glory of God and the salvation of souls, true humility, total indifference to popular favor or applause, and a perfect spirit of poverty, were his peculiar virtues, and his whole life was spent in the practice of them. His aversion to honors and distinctions of any kind was so great that he could hardly be induced to accept the episcopacy to which he was appointed in 1843. . . . . . His career as bishop, like his priesthood, was humble and unassuming, but laborious and fruitful. His natural constitution was not strong, and for five years before his death his medical adviser endeavored to dissuade him from taking part in the active labors of the ministry. But he persevered to the end, taking always upon himself the larger portion of the work in the confessional and the pulpit, sparing the young men who were his assistants. He even continued to attend the sick to within the last year of his life. When the period of the last Council of Baltimore approached, he felt that he had not long to live, consumption having already made deep inroads into his lungs. He nevertheless attended the Council and applied for a coadjutor. On the return from the Council he contracted inflammatory rheumatism. He tried to say Mass on Pentecost Sunday, the day after his arrival, but was obliged by pain and debility to stop at the foot of the altar. He remained, however, to hear Mass, as he could not celebrate, and afterwards took to his bed from which he never rose."

"The divine Master was satisfied with the labors already performed. Twenty years, of which every day and every hour had been devoted to the great and only work of the bishop and the priest, the sanctification of souls, gave sufficient evidence of the purity of his faith, the fervor of his love. For him the heat and burden of the day were over. The good Master for whom he had labored called him to his rest ; and, already, we trust he has heard from the lips of Jesus the words that beatify eternally the wearied soul: *Well done thou good and faithful servant ; enter into the joy of thy Lord.*"

---

[1] From his Diary.

## RIGHT REV. BERNARD O'REILLY, D.D.,

AROUND the name of the second Bishop of Hartford lingers the sad memory of a mysterious tragedy of the sea. With soul intent upon the spiritual blessings that were to accrue to his diocese from his sojourn abroad; with heart eager to embrace again the precious children of his flock; buoyant with hope for the bright future he had conjured up for his diocese,—Bishop O'Reilly in an ill-starred moment sailed out into the unknown to his death. Without a moment's warning, perhaps, and deprived of the sacred rites which impart strength and hope and consolation to the soul during its final moments on earth, the one hundred and eighty-six voyagers of the doomed *Pacific* sank beneath the devouring waves of the Atlantic. No survivor ever returned to tell how the ship met its cruel fate. An iceberg, it may be, raised its massive form suddenly from the deep to sullenly dispute the passage of the throbbing steamer as it sped onward with its precious burden. Sudden the summons may have been, but we can imagine with what calmness and resignation and constancy the prelate went down to death. He who had braved the terrors of death a hundred times during the great cholera scourge that decimated the city of New York, was not now to quail before this mysterious visitation. The same unalterable confidence in God and His Blessed Mother that upheld the priest in those days of trial was not to desert the bishop in this hour of hopeless peril.

The subject of this sketch was born in the Townland of Cunnareen, Parish of Columbkille, County of Longford, Ireland, in 1803. He inherited the piety and patriotism that in after years were prominent traits of his character. The naturally good qualities which adorned his early years were carefully nurtured and developed amid the truly Catholic influences which environed him. Having completed his classical studies at the age of twenty-two years, he felt within him the divine call to devote his life to God's holy service in the sacred ministry. Disclosing to his devoted parents the cherished desire of his heart, he declared his willingness to remain at home and labor for souls amid the scenes of his childhood and youth; but his thoughts ever reverted to the young nation of the West where freedom of worship reigned, a glorious provision of our Constitution. Securing the consent of his parents and receiving their fervent "God bless you!" he sailed for America on January 17, 1825. Intent upon the accomplishment of his mission he entered almost immediately the seminary at Montreal. He completed his theological studies at St. Mary's Seminary, Baltimore, that nursery of bishops, and was ordained to the priesthood at New York City on October 13, 1831, by Right Rev. Bishop Kenrick, of Philadelphia.

The young priest began his labors in New York City, visiting Brooklyn once a month. In 1832 the Asiatic plague broke over New York and carried hundreds to sudden death. "It was an awful time," wrote his brother, Very

+ Bernard O'Reilly, Bp. of Hartford

Rev. William O'Reilly. "The eyes that sparkled with all the vivacity of youth in the morning, were often sealed in the darkness of the grave in the evening, or dimmed by tears for the loss of some dear one." But appalling as were the scenes Father O'Reilly witnessed, awful as was the carnage of death, fearful as was the desolation spread everywhere, he remained at his post, bringing temporal and spiritual blessings to his cholera-stricken fellows. So devoted was he during the epidemic, that his name has come down through the years in affectionate remembrance. For many years the survivors told "how, like a true soldier of the cross, he rushed into the face of danger at all times, in season and out of season, by day and by night, wholly reckless of self, provided he could assist the dying, console the afflicted, take in the orphan, or dry up the widow's tears." Twice a victim to the scourge he, nevertheless, was spared, perhaps, as a reward for his Christian charity. *"Greater love than this no man hath, that a man lay down his life for his friends."* He had freely, generously, offered himself upon the altar of charity; but God had other designs upon him, other fields were to witness his labors among the poor, the sick and the suffering, and the sacrifice was not demanded.

Unwilling to seek rest after the cholera had subsided in order to recuperate his impaired health, he was transferred in December, 1842, to St. Patrick's parish, Rochester, on which mission he labored for fifteen years. His jurisdiction extended from Auburn west to Niagara Falls. Of this identical region in the early days of the century, Thomas D'Arcy McGee thus speaks:[1] "The merchants of New York desired to unite Lake Erie to the Hudson for their own profit. An army of Catholic laborers is marshalled along the line. They penetrate from end to end of this great State. Their shanties spring up like mushrooms in the night, and often vanish like mists in the morning. To all human appearances they are only digging a canal.[2] Stump orators praise them as usual spades and shovels, who help on the great work of making money. But looking back to-day, with the results of a third of a century before us, it is plain enough those poor, rude men were working on the foundations of three episcopal sees, were choosing sites for five hundred churches, were opening the interior of the State to the empire of religion, as well as of commerce."

Father O'Reilly was confronted in this field with many difficulties, but his zeal overcame every obstacle, while his gentleness of character and conciliatory spirit overthrew the barriers which unreasonable prejudice had erected. A large portion of his territory was an unbroken wilderness, and the few who there resided were scattered and separated by great distances; but they were sought out, restored to the fold and their faith rekindled with a patience and energy worthy of an apostle. "To the untiring energy of Father Bernard O'Reilly, next to God, we must attribute the wonderful

[1] *"Catholic History of America."*

[2] The Erie Canal was begun in 1817 and completed in 1825. It connects the Hudson river at Albany and Troy with Lake Erie at Buffalo. It is 363 miles in length, and cost $7,602,000.

change wrought in favor of Catholicism and the triumphant victory which our holy faith achieved in Rochester and the surrounding country. The grateful citizens of that place, seeing his stainless, steady career, admired the man, and honored the priesthood in his name." [1]

Some of the difficulties experienced by Father O'Reilly are disclosed by a letter written by the Bishop of New York concerning the church at Saugerties, Ulster County.[2] "The Rev. Mr. O'Reilly has been authorized by the Bishop of this diocese to offer himself a second time to the benevolent consideration of the public in the State of New York in behalf of the above named church. After exhausting, in a measure, the liberality of his Protestant neighbors and the proverbial generosity of the poor and widely scattered congregation of Irishmen for whose use its erection was undertaken, this church, though roofed, is as yet destitute of doors, windows, and even a floor. The Rev. Pastor is, therefore, again compelled to solicit from his countrymen."

When the diocese of Buffalo was erected, April 23, 1847, Rochester fell within its jurisdiction, and Father O'Reilly became a subject of its newly-consecrated prelate, Right Rev. John Timon, D. D., C.M. The new bishop, recognizing the superior work of Father O'Reilly, elevated him to the office of Vicar-General on October 19, 1847, and appointed him also Superior of his seminary. His brother, the Rev. William O'Reilly, became his successor in St. Patrick's parish, Rochester. In these spheres Father O'Reilly won new laurels as a reliable counsellor and energetic priest, to whom hard work was a tonic, and as a wise guide for the young clerics committed to his care. And as though his duties as superior of the seminary, with his manifold parochial labors, were not enough to absorb his time and attention, he was assiduous in his attendance at the hospital of the Sisters of Charity of St. Joseph. Father O'Reilly had supervising care of this institution, and systematically and sympathetically did he discharge the duties of this exacting position. A physician, who resided in Buffalo in 1849–'50–'51 and occasionally attended the hospital, in a recent letter to the writer, says of Father O'Reilly: "His words were few, but his presence seemed to be pleasing, and to act as an inspiration to the sick. . . . He was thoroughly posted in medical lore, and if everything was not right the physician would be called to account. . . . He was a gentleman of a very dignified, but approachable presence, and particularly pleasing in his speech. His reputation in Buffalo was, as expressed by all, 'an admirable man, of few words.' The Know-Nothing element was then very strong in Buffalo, and the young physician was ostracized by it on account of a favor he had received from Father O'Reilly. These exponents of the gospel of hate and disturbers of public peace, directed their cowardly assaults against the hospital and the saintly women who, as ministering angels, brought health to the sick and consolation to the dying. But the chief offender, Rev. John C. Lord, a Presbyterian clergyman, found in Father

[1] Very Rev. William O'Reilly in "*Catholic Almanac*" for 1857.
[2] "*N. Y. Catholic Diary*," Oct. 10, 1835.

O'Reilly a redoubtable antagonist, a valiant champion of charity. He was driven from the arena of discussion and his conqueror was hailed with glad acclaim by the justice-loving element of the city. "No clergyman was ever more beloved by people than he was by the inhabitants of the diocese of Buffalo. The Bishop of Buffalo has oftentimes done justice, through the press, to the talents and merits of the deceased."

Father O'Reilly's star was in the ascendant. Honors greater still were to be his; still greater burdens were to be placed upon his shoulders. He was soon to hear from the highest authority on earth: "*Amice, ascende superius,*" Friend, go up higher. The reward of well nigh twenty years of dangerous, unceasing toil in the Master's vineyard was at hand.

At the request of Bishop Tyler, the Seventh Provincial Council of Baltimore, which convened May 5, 1849, nominated Father O'Reilly as his coadjutor. Pius IX. was then in exile at Gæta. On the return to Rome of the Sovereign Pontiff the nominations of the council were acted upon. Father O'Reilly was appointed coadjutor, with the right of succession to Bishop Tyler, by brief of July 23, 1850. By another brief of the same date he was created bishop of Pompeiopolis *in partibus infidelium.* Finally, by a brief of August 9, 1850, he was appointed Bishop of Hartford.[1] On October 14th he received, through Right Rev. John B. Fitzpatrick, bishop of Boston, the Bulls of his apppointment. The Bishop's Journal discloses the anxiety that weighed upon him at this period :

"*Oct.* 15. Spent this day in great anxiety as to accepting the appointment or refusing."

"16. After offering the Holy Sacrifice of the Mass to obtain light and aid in the matter from God, I concluded to accept, and felt relieved of much anxiety."

"18. I will, God helping, labor faithfully in this awful office. I have nothing at heart but God's glory in it."

Bishop O'Reilly was consecrated in St. Patrick's church, Rochester, on Sunday, November 10, 1850, by Bishop Timon of Buffalo, assisted by Bishop Fitzpatrick, of Boston, and Bishop McCloskey, of Albany. Right Rev. Peter Lefevre, D.D., bishop of Zela, Administrator of the diocese of Detroit, was present. The sermon was preached by the Rev. John McElroy, S.J. The new bishop celebrated pontifical vespers, during which Bishop McCloskey preached the sermon. He was installed bishop of Hartford in the cathedral at Providence on Sunday, November 17th, by Bishop Fitzpatrick, who preached the installation sermon. On this occasion Bishop O'Reilly sang his first pontifical Mass. The preacher at the vesper service was Bishop Timon of Buffalo.

Bishop O'Reilly brought to the episcopate a varied experience—a mis-

[1] It is noteworthy that seven priests who labored in the diocese of New York in 1843 became bishops, namely, Andrew Byrne, Bishop of Little Rock ; David Bacon, Bishop of Portland ; John J. Conroy, Bishop of Albany ; John Loughlin, Bishop of Brooklyn ; John McCloskey, Bishop of Albany, and later Cardinal-Archbishop of New York ; William Quarter, Bishop of Chicago ; Bernard O'Reilly, Bishop of Hartford.

sionary priest alone in an extensive territory—nothing singular, the reader may say; vicar-general and rector of a cathedral in a new diocese; superior of a new seminary and supervisor of an hospital ever increasing in size and influence; were not these positions, with their exacting and manifold duties, an admirable training-school for the dignity as well as for the burdens of the mitre? He had studied human nature in all its phases. In the various positions of trust to which he had been called, he had known how to obey; and those only who know how to obey know how to command. Trials were before him in his new office; he met them with unflinching courage.

"If we have to lament," said a contemporary, "over the death of one who is reaping the reward due to his exalted virtues (Bishop Tyler), we have also to rejoice at the appointment of his successor, the Rt. Rev. Bernard O'Reilly, who has already won our admiration for his zeal, piety and watchfulness. We hail his presence amongst us as the true messenger from God; we congratulate him as the harbinger of many blessings already commenced."[1]

Among the great works that engrossed the attention of Bishop O'Reilly immediately upon his accession to the episcopal throne was the adoption of means to increase the number of priests in his diocese. "A short time since," he wrote in 1852, "our affliction was very great, when from almost every section of the diocese the faithful asked for priests, and we had none to give them." To provide for future needs he established a theological seminary in September, 1851. The episcopal residence was the seminary, and it opened with eight students of theology and two of philosophy. The bishop himself taught his students the first week. The Rev. Hugh Carmody, D.D., was the first Superior of St. Mary's Theological Seminary. The institution progressed apace, as we gather from a Pastoral Letter addressed to the clergy and laity on the feast of the Annunciation, 1852: "This good work is now in a most prosperous condition, and promises the most happy results to religion in the diocese." An accession of eighteen priests during the previous year, carried consolation into many a desolate section of the diocese. "But a little time," said the Pastoral, "with the divine aid, and the instrumentality of the seminary, and every section of this diocese will be supplied with its pastor to offer the most Holy Sacrifice, and administer the Sacraments, preach the truths of God, and extend His empire on earth."

"The bishop is burdened with the solicitude of his diocese; he must provide pastors for the faithful, and ever be prepared to meet every contingency that may possibly diminish the number of his priests. He conceives it to be his duty, not only to provide the larger congregations with pastors, but to have seasonably afforded the consolations of religion to the smaller sections, and even, where it is possible, to isolated families. All his anxieties are about his priests and people; for God and for them he lives and labors, and is prepared to exhaust himself in promoting their spiritual interests and happiness."

With these thoughts uppermost in his mind, Bishop O'Reilly visited

[1] Pilot, March 1, 1851.

Europe in 1852, sailing on October 16th on the steamer *Atlantic*. To secure priests he visited that nursery of Irish missionaries, All Hallows College, Dublin, on November 7th, where he received several priests and in which he had students preparing for the sacred ministry. Among the students whom Bishop O'Reilly met during his visit to All Hallows was a young man, Thomas Hendricken by name, who was his guide about the college. The young student declared his intention of joining the Society of Jesus, and after his ordination of entering the Japan missions. The bishop, however, prevailed upon the future bishop to enter the American field. Thomas Hendricken with others destined for his diocese was ordained by Bishop O'Reilly at All Hallows on April 26, 1853, after his return from a tour of the continent.

The energy of Bishop O'Reilly was restless. It was bent not only upon multiplying the priesthood of his diocese; he sought auxiliaries who would provide the children of his flock with a religious education; who would tenderly care for the precious orphans; who would visit and nurse the sick and console the poor. To this end he introduced into the diocese the Sisters of Mercy in May, 1851. The mother-house was at Providence, and the first Superioress was Mother Xavier. At this period, bigotry was rampant throughout New England; in Rhode Island it was particularly virulent—bigotry in its reckless, anti-Christian and hateful form. Governor Anthony was the leader of this un-American crowd. Lies the most cruel, slanders the most foul, were directed against the church, the priests—but, characteristic of Know-Nothing warfare, especially against the devoted sisters. Calumny was the chief weapon employed by these moral assassins, and to such an extent did the leaders inflame the passions of their ignorant dupes that a frenzied mob in 1855—the year of the Know-Nothing triumphs—surrounded the Convent of Mercy and threatened destruction to the building and death to the sisters. All eyes turned to the bishop to protect his charges. He rose equal to the occasion. Undismayed by the ferocity of the mob the intrepid prelate stood before the convent and fearlessly addressed the angry crowd: "The sisters are in their home; they shall not leave it for an hour. I shall protect them while I have life, and if needs be, register their safety with my blood." The mob was cowed by the presence and words of the bishop, who, single-handed, stood before a brutal mob bent upon murder and plunder.

Bishop O'Reilly attended the First Plenary Council of Baltimore, which convened on May 8, 1852. He had as theological adviser the Rev. John McElroy, S. J. After the adjournment of the Council he visited Washington and had an interview with President Fillmore.

Bishop O'Reilly's attitude on the religious education of children was consonant with the teachings of the church in all ages. He believed in the necessity of a thoroughly Catholic education, if the children were to be saved to the church and to society. He held, as his colleagues in the American episcopate have ever held, that the better Catholic a man is the better citizen he will be. In a pastoral letter addressed to his diocese on January 4, 1851, he thus admonishes the laity: "Watch, with sleepless vigilance, over the education of your children, those precious deposits which God has confided to you, and which He will require at your hands. The enemy, aware that the matured in faith and practical in religion are, generally, beyond the reach of his seduction, endeavors, amidst us, to sap the germ of faith in the rising generation, through the instrumentality of an uncatholic education. As effect succeeds to cause, so will it be, in too many instances, with those precious deposits trained in uncatholic schools; they will lose the faith, the faith of God, for which their fathers perilled everything. Ordinary care, under influences more favorable, might, and doubtless would, save them to religion; but where all influences bear adversely on their faith, it is clear that great care and constant attention to their proper educational and religious training will alone save them to the faith. 'A young man, according to his way, when he is old, he will not depart from it.' Thus the Divine Spirit calls your attention to the early and proper training of your children. Be guided in a matter of such infinite importance by His counsel, that you may not have to answer before God for the loss of your children. I wish you to remember, that, as vitiated food would endanger their physical life, so uncatholic education perils what is more important, their moral and eternal life. Watch then over them, with the solicitude of Christian parents, fully impressed with the greatness of your responsibility in their regard, that they may grow up edifying members of the church of God, and transmit to others, as your fathers did, the blessed inheritance of faith. Your faith, so firm and abiding, your zeal in the cause of God, induce to the belief that you will be generous and active in accomplishing this great purpose. You will not qualify, as a sacrifice too onerous, when considered in connection with your other obligations, the procuring your offspring an education promotive of their best interests, but rather consider it a pleasing and indispensable duty. You are willing to subject yourselves to much privation, and refuse no toil that may provide them with food and raiment; and you will not be less zealous, I trust, in providing them, under the guidance of your pastors, an education free from error in faith and morals, and promotive of their future well-being. Were they, by the mysterious providence of God, deprived of your parental protection, and thrown, parentless, on this world, they would still be amply provided, by legal provision, with all things essential to physical subsistence and comfort, whilst no effort would be spared to deprive them of the faith inherited from you, evidence at once of the surpassing importance of their Christian education, and your obligation to provide for them. Educate them fully in a knowledge of their divine religion, train them early in the practice of all it enjoins, that they may comprehend its majesty and strength, and taste the consolation and sweetness consequent on this practical profession."

The love of Bishop O'Reilly's heart went out in its fullness to the orphans, those helpless yet precious charges of holy church. Deprived of their natural protectors they become the wards of religion; and as the chief pastor of the diocese he accepted the responsibility. Furthermore, as the contributions for the orphans conclusively proved, his faithful diocesans absorbed his ideas and generously seconded his efforts. We quote from the pastoral letter above mentioned :

' Venerable brethren and dearly beloved children, I most earnestly invoke your protection for the orphans that may be found in your midst. There is no work more worthy of a people devoted to the service of God than the care-taking of the poor and the orphan. If any of those parentless little ones should be lost through our parsimony or neglect, we cannot consider ourselves guiltless before God ; he will hold us to a rigid accountability for the loss of the soul that might have been saved to Him by our charitable interposition. Our divine Saviour has imposed this as a duty on his people. He will exact its fulfillment and severely punish its omission. It is not a less great work to save to God those who are of us than to convert to Him those who are not ; it is rather a prior duty, enforced by well-ordered charity. Let, then, the united action of pastors and people save to religion the helpless orphan. God will not fail to aid in the performance of the duty He imposes ; He invariably crowns with success the labors of the willing instruments of His mercy."

While Bishop O'Reilly was providing priests and sisters for his diocese, erecting schools and asylums for his children and visiting his scattered parishes, he was not oblivious of the attacks made by United States army officers on the rights of conscience. He fought successfully for the rights of Catholic soldiers who had been imprisoned by officers for non-attendance at Protestant services. On Sunday, May 28, 1851, twenty-one Catholic soldiers were imprisoned at Fort Columbus, N. Y., by Lieutenant Winder for refusal to attend Protestant worship. One of the "offenders," Private James Duggan, of Co. A, 4th Artillery, was placed on trial. The charge was: disobedience of orders; his plea was: not guilty. The finding and sentence of the court were: "The Court finds the prisoner guilty as charged, and does sentence him, James Duggan, to forfeit to the United States $5 of his pay per month for six months; two months in solitary confinement on bread and water; the other four at hard labor, with ball and chain at his leg." This sentence, in part, was confirmed by Major-General Wool. The case was appealed to the War Department with the result that the then Secretary of War, the Hon. C. M. Conrad, rebuked the bigotry displayed at Fort Columbus, and declared the soldier's right to full liberty of conscience. In the following correspondence Bishop O'Reilly wrote over the pseudonym of "Roger Williams," a name to conjure with, believing, no doubt, that the time was not ripe for a " Popish " bishop to " interfere " officially in a grave matter in which officers of the United States Army were involved:

To the Editor of the *Boston Pilot :*

Sir : As there are just now complaints from many quarters, of Catholic soldiers being punished for non-attendance at Protestant worship, I wish to say that there is no law known to the military department by which soldiers can be punished for non-compliance with an order to attend a worship at variance with their conscientious convictions.

There being no law in this matter, a commanding officer has no right to issue such an order ; and there being no right on the part of the commandant to issue such an order, there is neither a moral or legal fault in the non-compliance with it on the part of the soldier. I am satisfied that imprisonment or punishment in any form for non-compliance with such an unmilitary and illegal order would be found a misdemeanor, punishable by the civil law. Were a court-martial convened, and I think the authorities at Washington should order one in this case, for the trial of the twenty-one soldiers imprisoned at Fort Columbus, N. Y., on Sunday, 28th ult., by Lieutenant Winder, for refusal to attend Protestant worship, I am satisfied that the court would decide that the soldiers were guilty of no fault.

During the war in Florida, the commandant issued a general order for all to attend Protestant service; this order was disobeyed by some Catholic soldiers, who were immediately placed under arrest; they were tried by court-martial, and the court decided that the soldiers had committed no fault. This decision settled that matter during the entire period of that campaign, and saved the Catholic soldiers from painful annoyance on the part of some narrow-minded and bigoted officers.

Captain O'Brien, lately deceased at San Antonio, Tex., was put under arrest whilst Lieutenant at Old Point Comfort, by orders of General Kalbach, because he refused to attend Protestant worship, and the court-martial decided that he was guilty of no fault.

It is now time that this vexed and annoying question should be settled by an order from the department, recognizing the soldier's right, as that of other citizens, to worship God in accordance with the dictates of conscience.

This order from the proper department is, in this case, necessary, as the precedents of courts martial acknowledging the soldier's right to liberty of conscience, are set at naught by the petty despots of the service, who would be more in their place as tract peddlers than officers of our army.

In all these cases where our rights are invaded, we have but to apply for redress, in proper form, to the proper authority, and I am confident that these rights will be respected and guaranteed.

As soldiers cannot well move in their own defence in this matter, without exposing themselves to many other annoyances, I would ask some citizen in the vicinity of Fort Columbus, N. Y., where the facts in this case are at hand, to call the attention of the Executive to the tyranny exercised over the consciences of the Catholic soldiers in the service, and take time to agitate the matter, until all officers are directed to recognize the fact that soldiers have a conscience, and that in matters religious, they are free as the civilian to worship God as conscience directs.

I would say to the soldier, pending the continuance of this tyranny and oppression of conscience in military service, be faithful to your God and religion, resist by noncompliance all orders invading the rights and liberty of conscience, and, if punished for non-observance of these arbitrary, illegal and unmilitary orders, spread the fact before the world, and appeal for justice, in matters religious, to your fellow-citizens

ROGER WILLIAMS, Providence, R. I.

June 14, 1851.

To THE EDITOR OF THE *Boston Pilot:*

SIR:—The late action of the military authorities at Fort Columbus, New York harbor, invites to every legitimate effort to put an end to the cruel, heartless oppression of conscience practised at this fort.

Our military service, so honorable and efficient up to the present, is on the eve of being seriously injured and dishonored, if such monstrous wrong as that I now protest against be sanctioned, or permitted to escape with impunity.

That I may not be suspected of exaggeration, or "setting aught down in malice," I will give the finding of the court in the case now complained of, with the confirmation, in part, of the sentence of the court, by Major-General Wool: "Before the general court martial, which assembled at Fort Columbus, New York harbor, on 22d ult., agreeable to 3d department order, No. 8, current series, and at which Brevet Colonel J. L. Gardiner, Major 4th Artillery, is president, was tried Private James Duggan, of Company A, 4th Artillery. Charge: disobedience of orders. Plea: not guilty." Finding of the court and sentence: "The court finds the prisoner guilty as charged, and does sentence him,

Private James Duggan, to forfeit to the United States $5 of his pay per month for six months ; two months in solitary confinement on bread and water ; the other four at hard labor, with ball and chain at his leg."

This, you will admit, is a dishonoring and severe sentence, as also that the alleged "disobedience" must have been prominent and injurious to the service, to warrant it.

The disobedience charged against Duggan, deserving, in the opinion of Colonel Gardiner and the court over which he presided, the severe sentence pronounced against him, is simply his refusal to attend Protestant service. This, sir, is the front of his offending. This is the offence, if any man dare before the country to call it an offence, which we find transformed into "positive, wilful disobedience of orders." Colonel Gardiner has no right—the articles of war give him no right—to compel attendance at Protestant or any other worship ; refusal to comply with it cannot be tortured into "positive, wilful disobedience of orders."

Where the articles of war speak of religious service, they simply "recommend" or counsel both officers and men to attend religious worship ; "it is recommended" are the words used in that military code, when treating on the subject of religion, "that both officers and men attend religious worship."

The veriest bigots only could torture a right to recommend, or counsel, to the right to coerce and punish, as in this instance.

The sentence of the court, sir, is illegal ; being without any authority in military law, and with a view to coerce Catholic soldiers into apostacy, by leaving them no alternative but Protestant worship or the luxury of bread and water, with a ball and chain at the leg.

Colonel Gardiner and his court at Fort Columbus have established there a monstrous precedent, intended to justify every oppression of conscience, but a precedent which will never be copied by another court martial, unless, as the veriest slaves, we tamely submit to the unmitigated despotism of these military bigots.

The will to be terribly severe is here clearly evidenced ; the will of the scowling, hateful, heartless bigot, prepared, did it but dare, to write its edict of intolerance with Catholic blood, and persecute to the death.

The court is silent as to the alleged offence of James Duggan, qualifying it as disobedience of a grave kind ; and we and the world would have remained ignorant of the nature of his offence, were it not for the review of the sentence by General Wool. If the court were not aware of the illegality of its proceedings, and fearful to place its intolerance before the country, it would have frankly and honestly stated that his refusal to attend Protestant worship was the cause of his being court-martialed, and severely punished ; and not, as they have had the hardihood to state, "positive and wilful disobedience to orders."

Colonel Gardiner may be, as he is known to be, most anxious to revive the waning glory of Protestantism, and his chaplain not unwilling to preach to men forced to listen to him under the severest penalties ; but both will, I trust, soon learn that the soldiers of our country have consciences, and consciences, too, which both officers and chaplains must respect.

The severe sentence in the case of Duggan was submitted on the 12th inst., to General Wool, and, I regret to say, was in part approved by him. The following is his order in the matter, taken from the record :

"It appears in the testimony that the prisoner had been previously notified that, if he desired to be excused from going to church, on account of religious scruples, he should make application to that effect to the commanding officer at the Fort. In refusing to do so, and in leaving the Company without permission, he not only disobeyed orders, but showed an insubordinate spirit, which deserves punishment ; therefore, so much of the sentence as subjects the prisoner to forfeit $5 a month for six months, is approved ; the remainder of the sentence is remitted."

Painful it is to me to know that General Wool has so far approved of the finding of the court in the case of Duggan ; he should have at once annulled the whole proceedings ; it deserved severe reprobation from the commanding officer, and should have received it.

The ground assumed by General Wool for approving the sentence, in part, is the refusal of Duggan to acquaint the commander of his "religious scruples." This, most assuredly, does not justify the General's confirmation of the sentence, in part. 1st. The articles of war gave no right to command religious attendance; consequently, the commandant had no right to look for explanation for non-attendance, whether the absence proceeded from religious scruples or other causes; and, consequently the confirmation of the sentence is not justifiable on this ground.

2d. It is asserted that "in leaving the Company without permission, he not only disobeyed orders, but showed an insubordinate spirit, and, on this ground, the sentence of the court against him is, in part, confirmed." This allegation is, I think, unfair, and calculated to deceive; affording no justifiable ground for the confirmation of the sentence.

It is not alleged that Duggan deserted, but "that he left the Company without permission." Now, Duggan did not, I apprehend, leave the Company, but simply refused to march into the Protestant church, where his conscience forbid him to go, and where his country gave no authority to any person to order him to march; consequently, the charge of disobedience and insubordination cannot be sustained, and General Wool gives no reason in justification of his confirmation of the bigoted sentence passed on Duggan for non-attendance at Protestant worship.

If the actors in this dishonorable affair were satisfied that they were right, why not speak out as men, and at once say that Duggan would not attend Protestant worship, and, consequently, "must forfeit his pay for six months, live on bread and water for two months and in solitary confinement; the other four at hard labor, with ball and chain at his leg," and all would understand at once the severity of the punishment, and the object in inflicting it, which is this: that the Catholic soldiers might know that either they must attend Protestant worship at Fort Columbus, or be prepared to yield up their pay, and bear severe physical punishment. Were a Catholic officer to thus punish Protestant soldiers for non-attendance at Catholic worship, would the country tolerate it for a moment? Would not a shout of reprobation ring out from one end of the land to the other?

Is not persecution, whether Catholic or Protestant, still persecution? and should not, in this instance, the public voice denounce the intolerant actors in this disgraceful affair at Fort Columbus? In pleading the cause of the persecuted Catholic, I am but pleading the cause of the oppressed, and expressing, in the indignant terms of a freeman, the guilt which the country will soon place to the account of the oppressors of conscience at this military Fort. When Lieutenant O'Brien was court-martialed by General Kalbach at Old Point Comfort, for refusal to attend Protestant service, the Department ordered the proceedings to be quashed. The Executive did not then consider that refusal to attend Protestant service constituted disobedience, but considered that there was neither disobedience nor ground for action, and ordered the case to be quashed. This is the highest authority in matters military, and maintains the view I have taken in this case—that there is no authority to command the attendance of the soldiers at religious worship, and no disobedience when the soldier refuses compliance with such illegal orders.

During the Florida campaign a case in point occurred, and was decided favorably to the rights of conscience. An order was issued for all soldiers to attend religious worship on a certain occasion; two soldiers refused to march to the place appointed for the service; they are court-martialed, and the court finds them guilty of no offence, no disobedience.

I had supposed that our officers were men of this stamp—generous lovers of human freedom, and as ready to fight for the rights of conscience guaranteed us by the constitution, as for civil liberty. Am I mistaken? Are we retrograding? Or are the Gardiners and other officers at Fort Columbus an exception to the officers in the service generally?

I ask the Executive to interpose its authority at once, and save our gallant little army from dishonor; to rebuke so sternly this ill-advised and cruel oppression of conscience, that the bigots of the service may know that they will not be permitted to persecute Catholic soldiers in the United States service.

This, believe me, is an opening wedge, intended to cleave to the very heart, the sacred right of liberty of conscience, and should be met sternly and firmly by every friend of human freedom, until bigotry will have disappeared from our army, and the soldier's right to serve God according to the dictates of conscience will be as fully recognized as that of other citizens.

Bigotry now assails its hateful work on the poor soldier, who cannot, it appears, even serve God, if his commander should order the contrary, without exposing himself to severe punishment. Will we tamely submit to this whilst a remedy is at hand? Will we submit the sacred liberty of conscience to be annulled whilst it is in our power to strengthen and preserve this invaluable right? In Fort Columbus, New York Harbor, within a few hundred feet of the great city of New York, there is a sufferer for conscience. Have the rights of conscience, human liberty and unjust oppression no friend in New York? Yours,

ROGER WILLIAMS.

PROVIDENCE, R. I., June 23, 1851.

WAR DEPARTMENT,
Washington, July 15, 1851.

SIR: Complaints have been made to this department that a soldier at Fort Columbus, who is, or was, a Roman Catholic, was ordered to attend a Protestant church, and on his refusal to obey the order, he was punished for disobedience of orders. It is doubtful how far an officer has the right to compel officers and men under his command to attend divine service. It is evident, however, that no one ought to be compelled to attend a church of any other persuasion than that to which he belongs. Every means of persuasion should be employed to induce soldiers to attend some church, but they should be permitted to select the one they prefer; and when they profess to have conscientious scruples about attending any particular church, all compulsory measures violate the rights of conscience, and should be avoided.

Very respectfully,
Your obedient servant,
C. M. CONRAD, Sec. of War.

BREVET MAJOR-GENERAL JOHN E. WOOL.

EDITOR OF THE *Pilot:*

SIR: The above is a copy, which I have been privileged to take, of the instructions of the Secretary of War to Major-General Wool, in the matter of the right of soldiers in the military service to liberty of conscience. These instructions are consequent on complaints made to the department of war against the commandant at Fort Columbus, New York Harbor, Brevet Col. J. L. Gardiner, for the severe punishment of a Catholic soldier, through a court-martial over which he presided, for non-attendance at Protestant worship, in obedience to his order. The sentence pronounced in this case by this court-martial, is marked with a severity which would not have been prompted but by the narrowest bigotry on the part of all concerned. Private James Duggan was sentenced to forfeit to the United States $5 a month of his pay, for six months; to spend two months in solitary confinement and on bread and water; the other months at hard labor, with ball and chain at his leg. The alleged offence of Duggan was his refusal to attend Protestant worship, at the bidding of Brevet Col. J. L. Gardiner. The formal charge against him at the court was a pure fiction, well calculated to dishonor those who presented it. It was this: "Positive, wilful disobedience of orders."

The court knew well that there was not, and could not be, disobedience in this case, the order being contrary to law, and must, consequently, have used the allegation "disobedience" as a mask to their intolerance, and with a view to deceive all unacquainted with the facts in the case.

Brevet Major-General Wool has disappointed expectation in his approval, in part, of the severe and illegal sentence of this court. There are other facts connected with his action in this case, which must go far to change the opinion of many enlightened men relative to the motives that could have induced his action in this case.

The court-martial to try Duggan was ordered by Brevet Brigadier-General Walbach,

II—10

and the proceedings of the court were, in season, placed before him for approval. The General declined acting in this case, and sent them to General Wool for his decision. General Wool returned them with instructions to General Walbach, "suggesting that the sentence be remitted, with the exception of the fine of $5 for six months." General Walbach again returned them to General Wool, with a request that the proceedings be submitted to higher authority.

It is clear that General Walbach considered the finding of the court illegal, and not to be approved of, from the fact of his refusal to act on the proceedings even under instructions to remit the sentence, "with the exception of the fine of $5." The request of General Walbach should have been acceded to by General Wool; it was proper and reasonable that, as they differed in opinion, on a matter which was seriously to affect liberty of conscience, the department should be consulted. Moreover, General Walbach had ordered the court-martial, and, as it appears from his action in the matter, must have been of opinion that the finding of the court was illegal, that Duggan committed no fault, and consequently was entitled, at least of courtesy, to have the question submitted to the department. Independent of the liberal and enlightened views in religious matters entertained by General Walbach, he knew that the department would have at once annulled the proceedings of the court, and wished them referred there, that all pretense of right to oppose conscience in our military service might be removed.

General Wool will not accede to this reasonable request; he will not trust the liberality of the department; the intolerance long festering at Fort Columbus must have the authority of a precedent, and General Wool grants it. Walbach does all that is possible on his portion, as inferior officer, to protect the soldier in his dearest rights, the liberty of conscience; he spurns the demand made by the court to have their illegal and bigoted sentence approved, and when General Wool, his superior officer, returns him the finding of the court with instructions, diminishing the punishment, but sustaining the right to oppress conscience, then he properly requests the controverted point be submitted to the department.

Great praise is due to General Walbach for the generous stand he took in favor of the soldier's rights of conscience, whilst a great dishonor will ever be attached to General Wool for his ungenerous aid to the bigots of Fort Columbus, to strip the soldier of his sacred and inestimable rights. General Wool committed a fault which will not fail to lower him, in the estimation of the high-minded and generous, when he took under his protection the bigotry rampant and long festering at this military post. He should have been found on the side of military law and the constitutional right of the subject, but in this instance he is found leagued with bigots, to strip the soldier of his dearest and most valued right, liberty of conscience.

Much credit is due to Hon. C. M. Conrad, Secretary of War, for his vindication, in his instructions to General Wool, of the soldier's right to full liberty of conscience. The honorable secretary has not disappointed expectation; he met the complaint presented in the case in generous spirit, and without hesitation decided in favor of the oppressed soldier. Soldiers will appreciate his generous interposition in favor of their rights, and citizens generally will applaud a decision in favor of justice and the rights of conscience.

I am this moment privileged to copy the following order of General Wool, transmitted by the Secretary of War, remitting the sentence of Duggan, for his refusal to attend Protestant service.

> HEADQUARTERS EASTERN DIVISION,
> Troy, N. Y., July 12, 1851.
>
> SPECIAL ORDER, No. 30.
>
> Upon the recommendation of the commander of the 3d department, the unexecuted portion of the sentence of private Duggan, of Co. A, 4th Artillery, promulgated in the Eastern Division, orders No. 11, current series, is remitted.
>
> By command of     MAJOR-GENERAL WOOL.
>
> O. J. WINSHIP, Ct. A. G.

The soldier's rights to liberty of conscience being fully vindicated by the proper officer, and the sentence of Duggan being remitted, my correspondence on this subject terminates with this letter. As I have contended but for the common rights of all soldiers in the matter of the worship of God, I would ask all our Catholic editors, and the editors of papers generally, to spread the Secretary's letter before the country.

ROGER WILLIAMS.

August 2, 1851.

In 1854 Pius IX. proclaimed a universal Jubilee. In a pastoral letter announcing the holy season Bishop O'Reilly, alluding to the hostility openly manifested towards Catholicity in this country, said :

"The Church of the living God, as is usual where prejudice gets the better of reason, and passion alone is priviliged to rule, is now visited with the most gross misrepresentation; doctrines which it abhors, and practices which it is occupied in repressing, are unblushingly attributed to it; its priests, occupied in the duties of their sacred calling and offering offense to none, are assailed with the lowest and grossest reviling, whilst its best and most devoted members are ungenerously pursued with calumny and hatred that know no bounds.

"Divine Charity, so essential to the peace and happiness of men, and so strongly and frequently enforced of God, is, to a great extent, ignored and apparently eradicated from the hearts of great numbers. This amiable virtue will, doubtless, survive the shock it is receiving, and yet comfort those who are systematically opposed to it."

We have adverted to the zeal of Bishop O'Reilly in providing for the educational interests of his diocese. To increase existing advantages he sailed for Europe on December 5, 1855, to secure a Colony of Christian Brothers. The last entry in his Journal is under date of *December 4th:*

"Leave at 4 P.M. for Boston *en route* for Europe under God's protecting Providence."

Though the season of the year made ocean travel a hazardous undertaking, Bishop O'Reilly was too resolute when necessities pressed upon him to postpone action. He had partially succeeded in his purpose; and after an affectionate visit and farewell to his aged parents, he sailed for home on January 23, 1856, on the steamer *Pacific.* Knowing that his visit to Europe was made solely in their interests, his faithful diocesans awaited anxiously his return. Days, weeks, months passed with no tidings of the *Pacific.* In Europe and America the delay to reach port caused the gravest alarm. Hope, fear and doubt alternated in the breasts of the prelate's friends. His brother in Ireland was communicated with, and the result confirmed the fears of many that Bernard O'Reilly had gone down with the ill-fated steamer. It was only in April, however, that the loss of the *Pacific* with all on board was regarded as certain. "Finally," said his reverend biographer, "the silence of any hopeful circumstance became so deep that all pronounced it the silence of death, and the death-knell of Bishop O'Reilly rang from Georgia to Maine and echoed through the world."

When all hope was abandoned funeral services were held in all the churches of Rhode Island and Connecticut; but the principal service took place in the Cathedral of SS. Peter and Paul, at Providence, on June 17, 1856. The clergy of the diocese of Hartford, with but very few exceptions, were present at the solemn rite, as were also the Most Rev. Archbishop Hughes of New York, and the Right Rev. Bishops of Boston, Brooklyn, Newark and Portland.   The dioceses of New York, Boston and Albany were represented by a large number of their clergy.   Among the distinguished laymen present was the French Consul at Newport, Mons. Gourand Fauvel de la Martinique. Pontifical Mass for the dead was sung by Right Rev. Bishop Fitzpatrick of Boston, assisted by Very Rev. James Hughes of Hartford, as Deacon, the Rev. Matthew Hart of New Haven, as Subdeacon, the Rev. Patrick Delaney and the Rev. Patrick Lamb, as assistant deacons, and the Rev. John McElroy, S. J., Archdeacon.   The Rev. John Quinn, D. D., and the Rev. Patrick Gaynor officiated as Masters of Ceremonies.   At the conclusion of the Mass the Most Rev. Archbishop, of New York, preached the funeral discourse, taking his text from the *Apocalypse* xiv. 13: "*And I heard a voice from heaven saying to me: Write: Blessed are the dead who die in the Lord.   From henceforth now, saith the Spirit, that they may rest from their labors, for their works follow them.*"

The eloquent prelate began his discourse with a few observations upon the Christian religion as an alleviator of human sorrow and suffering, and remarked upon the beautiful symbolism of the church as it was then presented to him in the church and altar and episcopal throne shrouded in black, while immediately around those emblems which spoke most forcibly of the frailty of humanity, all was brilliant with the blaze of many tapers.   Thus does holy church in her wisdom keep the glories of eternity before our eyes even while she accommodates herself to our weakness by permitting us to indulge in natural grief.   Continuing, the preacher gave a brief sketch of the deceased bishop.   He spoke of the virtues, the humble piety and the energy of the deceased, who left an enduring monument in the numerous religious and charitable institutions which he founded or projected during his short episcopate.   He enlarged upon the inscrutableness of the event which had deprived the church of this diocese of its head and upon the mystery which must ever surround the fate of those who perished on that ill-fated ship.   Of one thing, however, he thought all might be certain—that the last few minutes, or hours it may have been, when death was seen to be inevitable, were spent in the service of that divine Master to whom the holy bishop had so repeatedly offered his life in labors and perils and pestilences, during an unblemished career of more than a quarter of a century of active service.

"Now that all hope has ceased," said a contemporary, "for the safety of the ill fated *Pacific*, a Solemn Requiem Mass was all that could be offered in memory of him who sank with her to rise no more in time.   There is a melancholy in death,—nature loves itself, and the horror of death never becomes intense till ashes return to ashes, and dust is consigned to dust. But this becomes more bitter when the wail of sorrow is raised only above the empty bier or the decorated catafalque; when the burning tapers that surround it seem only to show that nothing but a symbol is there.   How happy was the widow of Nain, that she had even the body of her only child—for then she became certain of a miracle from the instant our blessed Saviour touched the bier.   Poor widow! blessed was your sorrow. . . . .

"But to-day widows and orphans crowd around an empty bier and a splendid catafalque. All the gorgeous pomp that love could give was bestowed, but it was empty. The mind could not rest on that splendid pageant of hollowness, but bounded from the glitter and the glance of that mournfully bright solemnity to the Atlantic Ocean—to the steamer *Pacific* and her unfortunate passengers, and asking itself a thousand questions as to how they went down ; till back to the catafalque, with its questions unanswered, it had to come ; that *steamer* sank, and the waters closed over her ; the treacherous waves came smoothly together, no mark remained on their bosom to tell where she wounded them, and no mark can point to the spot or awake a prayer or a sigh from the passing traveler." [1]

When Bishop O'Reilly was installed bishop of Hartford his diocese contained—

Churches . . . . . . . . . . . . . . . . . . . . . . . 12
Clergymen . . . . . . . . . . . . . . . . . . . . . . 14
Ecclesiastical students . . . . . . . . . . . . . . . . 7
Catholic population, about . . . . . . . . . . . . . 20,000

Of these, five churches and seven priests were in Connecticut. At the time of the bishop's death, five years later, the diocese had

Churches . . . . . . . . . . . . . . . . . . . . . . 46
Stations . . . . . . . . . . . . . . . . . . . . . . 37
Clergymen . . . . . . . . . . . . . . . . . . . . . 42
Clerical students . . . . . . . . . . . . . . . . . . 22
Male academies . . . . . . . . . . . . . . . . . . . 2
Female academies . . . . . . . . . . . . . . . . . . 3
Parochial schools . . . . . . . . . . . . . . . . . . 9
Orphan asylums . . . . . . . . . . . . . . . . . . . 3
Catholic population, about . . . . . . . . . . . . . 60,000

Of the churches, Connecticut had twenty-seven ; of the priests, twenty-six ; of the female academies, two, at New Haven and Hartford ; of the orphan asylums, two, at New Haven and Hartford ; of the parochial schools, three, one at Hartford and two at New Haven, St. Patrick's and St. Mary's. Besides these there were male and female schools at Norwich, New London, Bridgeport and Birmingham.

## RIGHT REV. FRANCIS PATRICK McFARLAND, D.D.,

### THIRD BISHOP OF HARTFORD.

THE third bishop of Hartford, Right Rev. Francis Patrick McFarland, was born in Franklin, Pa., April 16, 1819. His parents were from Armagh, Ireland, and were John McFarland and Nancy McKeever. In his youth his father had intended to enter the priesthood, and to this end had made considerable advancement in his studies when the political troubles of 1798 compelled him, as it compelled many another aspirant for Holy

---

[1] The *American Celt*, June, 1856, quoted by Richard H. Clark in his *Lives of the Deceased Bishops*.

Orders, to abandon the great desire of his heart. In 1806, the parents of Francis bought a home in the young republic of the West and settled in Waynesboro, Pa., where they engaged in agricultural pursuits until 1840.

Reared amid the holy influences of a thoroughly Catholic home, a daily witness of the Christian conduct of parents who recognized their obligations to religion and knew their duties to the children with whom God had blessed them, young Francis in early youth gave manifold indications that God had designed him exclusively for his holy service. During all his early career he appeared to have had but one object in view, the holy priesthood. His contemporaries speak of him as a manly young man. He was devout, but his piety was unobtrusive. He was diligent in study and anxious to excel, but it was not ambition to become merely conspicuous, and among his class-mates he occupied the position conceded only to students of conspicuous merit. Faithful in his reception of the sacraments, he was a devout client of the Mother of God, a trait that distinguished his priestly and episcopal life. His religious impulses were developed, and his desires for the ecclesiastical state encouraged by his parents, who deemed it a surpassing grace to give a son to the church. Having acquired a good education in the public schools at home, with commendable spirit and energy he began the career of teaching in the humble village schools of the neighborhood. While thus engaged, he reaped the benefits of the ripe scholarship of Mr. James Clark, an alumnus of West Point Military Academy, but after his conversion a Jesuit priest and professor in the University of Georgetown, D. C. Still attracted to the priesthood, Mr. McFarland entered Mount St. Mary's College, Emmittsburg, an institution which has given to the American church many illustrious prelates. One of his professors at Mount St. Mary's was the venerable Father Joubert, the founder of the Oblate (Colored) Sisters, of Baltimore, whose parents had been massacred by the blacks in the revolution at Hayti, at the close of the last century. He completed his theological studies at the "Mount," and for a brief period occupied a professor's chair. Leaving the seminary he was ordained to the priesthood on May 18, 1845, in old St. Patrick's Cathedral, by Archbishop Hughes, in the twenty-sixth year of his age. Immediately after his ordination he was assigned to St. John's College, Fordham, N. Y., where he remained as professor nearly a year. One of his pupils at St. John's was the late Very Rev. James Hughes, Vicar-General. During his residence at Fordham, Father McFarland frequently attended sick calls at Stamford, Connecticut. As his inclinations were for practical work he retired from St. John's College and was assigned as assistant to St. Joseph's Church, New York City, where he remained until May 6, 1846, when he was appointed pastor of Watertown, N. Y., by Bishop Hughes. Attached to Watertown were several missions to which the zealous young priest gave unremitting care and attention. It was a field of duty full of difficulties and hardships, and when we reflect that the means of travel had not reached the degree of perfection enjoyed by the missionary of to-day, we can realize somewhat the arduous tasks performed by Father McFarland. During Father McFarland's pastorate at Watertown the diocese of Albany was erected. He thus became

+ F. P. McFarland
Bp. of Hartford

a subject of the Bishop of Albany, Right Rev. John McCloskey, D. D., who transferred him to St. John's parish, Utica, N. Y., on March 1, 1851. Of his labors in this field, one of his successors, Very Rev. T. S. M. Lynch, D.D., LL.D., says: "His work was lasting. He made an impression in the parish which remained long after the hallowed walls of that church which he loved so well, had been razed to the ground. His memory is still green in Utica, the blessing which he left upon our church is still with us, and long, long, will his name be revered in the parish which had the happiness of being the witness of his saintly labors." [1]

While pastor of St John's Church, Utica, the Holy See, recognizing his superior executive ability, honored him with the appointment of Vicar Apostolic of Florida, January 9, 1857. [2] This honor he declined. In March, 1858, two years after the death of Bishop O'Reilly, he was elected bishop of Hartford in the thirty-ninth year of his age. "Bishop McFarland is an American," said the *Providence Journal*, March 14, 1858, "a native of Franklin, Pa., and quite a young man, not much beyond the canonical years. He is a gentleman of good presence and bears the impress of that intelligence and cultivation for which he is distinguished in the church that has now conferred upon him its selectest honors. We are assured by a Catholic gentleman—than whom none is more competent to judge—that his scholarship is of a high order, surpassed only by his zeal and devotion for the church to which he has now renewedly and solemnly consecrated his life."

The first official act of the bishop-elect was the re-appointment of Very Rev. William O'Reilly as Vicar-General. Bishop McFarland left Utica for Providence, March 6, 1858. The hearts of his devoted parishioners were oppressed with sorrow at his departure, and on March 14th, the congregation assembled and passed a series of resolutions in which they expressed their regret at the loss of their beloved pastor, who had ever been to them a judicious counsellor, a kind and sympathizing friend, and a watchful and zealous shepherd. These resolutions were transmitted to him with a substantial purse. To these expressions of good will, Bishop McFarland returned the following felicitous response:

"PROVIDENCE, 24th March, 1858.

"GENTLEMEN: I have received your letter and the accompanying check. You are aware that I did not wish to accept any present on this occasion. Yet, the manner in which this comes, and the feelings which have prompted it, leave me no choice. I accept your offering with many thanks. It was not needed as a proof of the kind feelings of St. John's congregation towards me ; but it places me under a new obligation to them, which I can repay only by offering for them my best wishes and my poor prayers. Accept my thanks for the kind manner in which you are pleased to speak of my labors whilst amongst you. Your partiality has, however, betrayed you into attributing to me many qualities which I am not conscious of possessing. The only merit which I can at all lay claim to is that while with you I had a sincere desire to see you and your families advance in virtue, and that, from day to day, as the occasion arose, I was willing to labor with you, in my own poor way, for the advancement of your congregation in religion, in knowledge, and in the doing of works of charity. I will endeavor to visit you at no

[1] *The Rosary*, September, 1895.
[2] A division of the diocese of Savannah.

distant day. My duties here will be numerous, and such as entail great responsibility; yet I hope soon to escape from them long enough to enable me to meet you for a day, and to express, orally, what I do not find time to write.

Begging you to pray for me, that I may have strength to do the work which God has given me to do, I remain, with the best wishes,

Your much obliged and devoted friend,

F. P. McFARLAND,

Bishop of Hartford.

To Messrs. Michael McQuade, U. Burke, M.D.; F. Kernan, O. O'Neill, Wm. Clarke, John Carton, Timothy Cronin, Francis X. Manahan, committee.

The consecration of Bishop McFarland took place on Sunday, March 14, 1858, at St. Patrick's church, Providence, R. I., and was an imposing ceremony. The consecrator and celebrant of the Mass was the Most Rev. Archbishop Hughes, of New York.

Assistant Bishops—Right Rev. Bishop Fitzpatrick of Boston; Right Rev. Bishop Timon of Buffalo.

Assistant Priest—Very Rev. William O'Reilly, V. G. of the diocese.

Assistant Deacon—Rev. M. Hart, New Haven.

Second Assistant Deacon—Rev. P. Delaney, Pawtucket.

Deacon—Very Rev. J. Hughes, Hartford.

Sub Deacon—Rev. P. Lamb, Providence.

Archbishop's Cross-Bearer—Rev. John Smith, New Haven.

Processional Cross-Bearer—Rev. Peter Kelly, Danbury, Conn.

Chanters—Rev. Dr. Mulligan, Falls Village, Conn.; Rev. A. Wallace, LL.D., East Greenwich.

Thurifer—Rev. Hugh O'Reilly, Norfolk, Conn.

Acolytes—Rev. M. McCallion, Warren, R. I.; Rev. P. O'Dwyer, Collinsville, Conn.

Mitre-Bearer—Rev. M. McCabe, Woonsocket.

Crosier Bearer—Rev. Thomas Drea, Stonington, Conn.

Book Bearer—Rev. James Gibson, Crompton.

Chaplain to the Archbishop—Rev. Fr. Brennan, St. Joseph's Seminary, New York.

Chaplain to the Bishop-elect—Rev. George McCloskey, New York.

Chaplain to Bishop Fitzpatrick—Rev. E. J. O'Brien, New Haven.

Chaplain to Bishop Timon—Rev. Fr. Lynch, of the Seminary of Buffalo.

Master of Ceremonies—Very Rev. J. Conroy, V. G., Albany.

The following prelates assisted at the ceremony:

The Right Rev. John McCloskey, D. D., Bishop of Albany.

"    "    " Louis de Goesbriand, D. D., Bishop of Burlington.

"    "    " James R. Bayley, D. D., Bishop of Newark.

"    "    " John Loughlin, D. D., Bishop of Brooklyn.

"    "    " D. W. Bacon, D. D., Bishop of Portland.

The following clergymen were also present:

Rev. Wm. Quinn, Rev. Richard Brennan of the archdiocese of New York.

Rev. A. McGough, Rev. B. F. McLaughlin, Rev. Patrick Caragher, Rev. M. Powers, Rev. J. U. Herbst of the diocese of Albany.

Rev. James A. Healey, Rev. J. Sheridan, of the diocese of Boston.

Rev. D. Kelly, Rev. E. J. Cooney, Rev. J. Quinn, D.D.; Rev. P. Brown, Rev. P. Gillick, Rev. T. Quinn, Rev. Thomas Synnott, Rev. J. Sheridan, Rev. Patrick Gaynor, Rev. T. F. Hendricken, Rev. J. Gibson, Rev. Wm. Duffy, Rev. J. F. O'Neill of the diocese of Hartford.

The sermon was preached by the Right Rev. Bishop McCloskey, of Albany. The text was from the Gospel of St. John 1: 14, "And the Word was made flesh and dwelt among us, and we saw his glory, the glory, as it were, of the only begotten of the Father, full of grace and truth." It was brief, but eloquent and appropriate. He sketched rapidly the birth, life, and ascension of Jesus Christ. The apostles whom he commissioned, and with whom he promised to be until the end of the world, were now represented on earth only by the Catholic church. She alone is the mother of the saints and the martyrs, whose lives were blessed, and whose deaths have sanctified the world. Bishop McCloskey closed his sermon by an address to the new bishop, which was finely conceived and impressively delivered.

Among the prominent laity present were Dr. Brownson, Mayor Rodman of Providence, and Monsieur Gouraud Fauvel de la Martinique, vice-consul of France.

In the evening Bishop McFarland sang pontifical vespers, and Archbishop Hughes preached the sermon from the parable of the grain of mustard seed.

As the bishops of Hartford had resided in Providence since 1844, Bishop McFarland continued the residence in that city until 1872. He introduced into Connecticut the Franciscan Friars and the Sisters of the Third Order of St. Francis, who located at Winsted; the Christian Brothers, the Sisters of Charity, and the Sisters of the Congregation De Notre Dame. He was instrumental in having the following

"Act Concerning Communities and Corporations," made part of the statute law of Connecticut June 30, 1866:

*Be it enacted by the Senate and House of Representatives in General Assembly convened:*

SEC. 1. That the Bishop and Vicar-General of the diocese of Hartford, together with the pastor and two laymen of any Roman Catholic church or congregation in the State of Connecticut, upon complying with the requirements of this law, shall be, and are hereby constituted, a body corporate, with power to sue and be sued, to purchase, hold and convey real and personal property, and to enjoy all other rights and franchises incident to bodies corporate in the State of Connecticut.

SEC. 2. The Bishop, Vicar-General and pastor of such congregation shall be members, *ex officio*, of such body corporate, and upon their death, resignation, removal or preferment, their successors in office shall become such members in their stead. The two lay members shall be appointed annually, by the committee of the congregation, to hold office for one year, or until their successors be chosen.

SEC. 3. Such body corporate shall have power to receive and hold, by gift, grant or purchase, all property, real or personal, that may be conveyed thereto, for the purpose of maintaining religious worship according to the doctrine, discipline and ritual of the Roman Catholic church, and for the support of the educational or charitable institutions of that church; *provided*, that no one corporated congregation shall at any time possess an amount of property, excepting church buildings, parsonages, school-houses, asylums and cemeteries, the annual income from which shall exceed three thousand dollars.

SEC. 4. Such body corporate shall at all times be subject to the general laws and discipline of the Roman Catholic church, shall receive and enjoy its franchises as a body politic, solely for the purposes mentioned in the third section of this act; and upon the violation or surrender of its charter, its property, real and personal, shall vest in the Bishop of the diocese and his successors, in trust for such congregation, and for the uses and purposes above named.

SEC. 5. Such body corporate shall organize by the appointment of the lay members before mentioned, and upon filing in the office of the Secretary of State a certificate signed by the several corporators, stating that they have so organized, and have adopted this law as their charter, and will be concluded and bound hereby, shall have and enjoy all rights by this law conferred.

Sec. 6. Three members of this corporation, of which one shall be a layman, shall constitute a quorum for the transaction of business.

Bishop McFarland attended the Vatican Council, which convened in the Basilica of the Vatican on the feast of the Immaculate Conception. December 8th, 1869. He was then in declining health. While in Rome he sought permission either to resign or to secure a coadjutor. His American colleagues opposed both measures, but proposed as a solution of the matter a division of his diocese. Accordingly, Rhode Island was erected into a diocese with Providence as the episcopal seat, while Bishop McFarland retained his original title as Bishop of Hartford.

Bishop McFarland preached his farewell discourse in Providence on February 25, 1872. He was deeply affected by the announcement, as were his auditors. When speaking of the division of the diocese he said in part: "I thought then and still think, that this is for your interest, as you will have a younger and more zealous bishop to labor among you. The new diocese will be an ample one—indeed, more so than the present one when first erected. Many of you remember well when Bishop Tyler came, and know the rapid progress Catholicity has made here since ; the eight thousand Catholics have become two hundred thousand, with a hundred churches and one hundred and eleven priests."

On his departure from Providence Bishop McFarland received many testimonials of esteem from his devoted clergy and the faithful laity ; but the gift that touched him the most deeply was the presentation of a beautiful edition of Haydock's Illustrated Bible, bound in a sumptuous manner, with a stand of the most exquisite pattern. It was the gift of the boys of the Christian Brothers' school. It was an acceptable offering and was kindly received, the bishop being profoundly moved by the expressions of his faithful charges on the occasion.

On his arrival in Hartford Bishop McFarland took up his residence in a spacious house on the corner of Woodland and Collins streets. His dignified bearing, urbane manner and tactful methods soon gained for him many friends, "who were by no means restricted to his own flock, but included every citizen who had the good fortune to enjoy his acquaintance."

Though Hartford had been the title of an Episcopal See since 1843, Bishop McFarland found there no cathedral nor episcopal residence, nor school nor convent which he could call his. Not a foot of ground in his episcopal city did he own upon which he could lay a stone. After twenty-seven years in the priesthood and fourteen in the episcopate, he must now begin again and build up from the foundation. Nevertheless, he entered upon his new work with courage and zeal born of faith in God.

The works which Bishop McFarland contemplated were the erection of a cathedral, a mother-house for the Sisters and an episcopal residence. Where would he secure a suitable site? We quote from the Hon. Thomas McManus' admirable *Sketch of the Catholic Church in Hartford:* "The Bishop saw at a glance the growth of the city westward, and the future necessities of his people. When St. Patrick's church was built in 1851, it was substantially at the west line of the city. Asylum Hill and the territory west of its summit were then sparsely dotted with occasional residences. Twenty-one years of unusual prosperity had gathered a large population here, and St. Patrick's church had been left far to the east of the geographical centre. St. Peter's church was still farther east. The new territory had a very large proportion of Catholics in its population, comprising very many servant girls, the best of Catholics and most liberal of supporters to the church. . . . . Carefully and quietly the bishop examined the various eligible locations for a cathedral, and finally selected the old Morgan homestead, a lot of between three and four acres on Farmington avenue, belonging to Major James Goodwin, and purchased the same at a price of $70,000." The erection of the convent was the work first commenced, as its chapel was to serve as a pro-cathedral. When the Sisters importuned the bishop to begin his cathedral and defer the building of the convent, the fatherly prelate prophetically replied: "The church will be built without the least fear, but I must and will build a home for my poor, scattered Sisters, who have been left homeless since the division of the diocese. I have ever found them faithful, hard-working, and devoted, heart and soul, to the elevation of our children in every part of the diocese blessed with their presence."[1] The corner-stone of the convent was laid on Sunday, May 11, 1873, and on November 29th following the chapel was dedicated to God under the benign patronage of St. Joseph. The celebrant of the Pontifical Mass on this occasion was Right Rev. Bishop de Goesbriand of Burlington and Bishop O'Reilly of Springfield, preached the dedicatory sermon. To draw upon his diocese the divine blessing, Bishop McFarland announced that all the parishes within his jurisdiction would be dedicated to the Sacred Heart of Jesus on the feast of the Immaculate Conception following, December 8th.

The date of the dedication of St. Josephs' chapel marks the origin of the cathedral parish.

The constant supervision of the work on this convent and chapel soon reduced Bishop McFarland to the condition of an invalid. Complete rest and change of scene became an imperative necessity. He sought the healing air of Aiken, S. C., but his sojourn there was too brief to produce any permanent relief. He visited also Richland Springs, Va., in company with his brother, a physician of Tiffin, Ohio, and his niece; but home, the convent and the chapel were ever in his thoughts. They possessed for him, even in his enfeebled condition, an irresistible attraction. Realizing, no doubt, that the end was nigh, and wishing to breathe his last surrounded by his beloved associates, he soon returned home. During his final illness he experienced great suffering. In early manhood he had made an offering of himself to God. His life as a priest and as a bishop were but a constant renewal of this obla-

---

[1] *Lives of the Deceased Bishops.*

tion. And now as he lay with the shadows of death falling about him, he repeated the offering which he made on the day he entered the sanctuary: "*The Lord is the portion of my inheritance and of my cup.*" He expired on the evening of October 2nd, retaining consciousness to the last, in the fifty-fifth year of his age, the twenty-ninth of his priesthood and the sixteenth of his episcopate. Bishop McFarland left no personal property nor real estate, having some time before his death deeded the house given him when he arrived in Hartford to the corporation of the diocese. His remains were laid in state in the pro-cathedral. The funeral services were held on the 15th, with Right Rev. John Loughlin, D.D., Bishop of Brooklyn, as celebrant of the Mass; Very Rev. James Hughes, V. G., assistant priest; Rev. James Lynch, deacon; Rev. Lawrence Walsh, sub-deacon; Rev. M. A. Tierney and Rev. M. F. Kelly, masters of ceremonies. The bishops present were

The Rt. Rev. John Loughlin, Brooklyn, N. Y.
"    "    "    Bernard J. McQuaid, Rochester, N. Y.
"    "    "    Stephen V. Ryan, Buffalo, N. Y.
"    "    "    P. T. O'Reilly, Springfield, Mass.
"    "    "    Francis McNierney, Albany, N. Y.
"    "    "    E. P. Wadhams, Ogdensburg, N. Y.
"    "    "    M. A. Corrigan, Newark, N. J.
"    "    "    James F. Wood, Philadelphia, Pa.
"    "    "    P. N. Lynch, Charleston, S. C.
"    "    "    John J. Conroy, Albany, N. Y.
"    "    "    T. F. Hendricken, Providence, R. I.
"    "    "    John J. Williams, Boston, Mass.
"    "    "    William O'Hara, Scranton, Pa.

One hundred and twenty-two priests assisted at the obsequies.

The funeral panegyric was pronounced by Right Rev. Bishop Hendricken of Providence. He announced his text from *Daniel ii. 23: "To Thee, O God of our fathers, I give thanks, and I praise Thee; because Thou hast given me wisdom and strength."*

The Bishop said in part: "Right Rev. Bishops and Reverend Members of the Clergy: When I look around me and see so many eminent bishops present in this temple, so many venerable priests from all parts of the country, see this immense congregation, and these emblems of mourning, it is evident that death has taken from us a distinguished victim. The mourning is not confined to this temple; but wherever true worth is acknowledged and men have sympathy for deep learning and piety, there are those who mourn the death of Bishop McFarland." The Right Reverend preacher then briefly related the chief incidents of the deceased bishop's life, from his birth to his elevation to the episcopate. He then said: "Every good gift that comes to us is from God. The gifts of wisdom and fortitude were the gifts that shone resplendent in Bishop McFarland. He was born in evil days, when to be pious in the eyes of the world, it was only necessary to be decently vicious. He was early marked out for the episcopate. Seventeen years ago—and it looks like yesterday only—he was consecrated as Bishop of Hartford. The inconveniences and burdens which he bore for the scattered flock over which he ruled showed his great and wise zeal. In this large diocese his success and the durable works which survive him, proved he had wise zeal in perfection. Under his fostering care churches have sprung up, convents and schools have multiplied.

"We ask for the cause of his success, and we find it in the method of his labor. The sublime virtues of your lamented bishop will be remembered when the most ancient lineages will be forgotten. In his relations with men he was kind, affable and condescending. To his own merits he was apparently unconscious. He was no dumb pastor, but hastened everywhere to preach the gospel. His hearers were chiefly the poor, but now and then the learned came to hear him and were charmed by the plainness, but force of his arguments. He was consulted by both the priests of his own diocese, and by priests and bishops of other dioceses. He was a man of extraordinary piety. I have known him from the morning of his consecration, and could not detect in him a venial fault; and here, I said, is a bishop on whom rests, in fullest amplitude, the seven-fold gifts of the Holy Spirit. The poorest member of his flock or diocese could approach him without hesitation and would receive the kindest treatment. He was a learned scholar in the best sense of that term; he was a most profound theologian. The doctrine of the Immaculate Conception, when decreed by the Holy Pontiff as the belief of the church, he found no difficulty in receiving; nor would he have hesitated to receive this doctrine, so declared, had he before been inclined to doubt it. As readily did he give his adhesion to the doctrine of the Infallibility of the Holy Father when speaking *ex-cathedra* as the Head of the Church. As a citizen, he was a valuable one to both this city and State, and also to Rhode Island when he resided there. During the late war, he was not wanting in patriotism and in a proper method of showing it. In regard to the school question, his position was unequivocally declared and well understood. He was no lover of the modern common-school system, for he regarded the system of teaching that lacked in denominational character as wanting in the Christian element.

"His simplicity of life and character are known and remembered by you. I could tell you of numberless instances of his generosity. When the claim without a proper title to a certain church was made by a congregation in the city of Providence, harsh words were spoken against him. When he had satisfied the people that they were in error, and apologies had been made to him, he took no revenge, for he forgave the congregation a debt of $5,000 they owed to him, and then sold them the church in question for one-half what it had cost to erect it. He was unwearied in labor, and submissive to the will of God. I asked him only a few days before his death if he was willing to die. He replied in Latin, '*Non recuso laborem, sed quid-quid vult Deus ego volo;*' to the effect that he had never refused to labor, but if it was the will of God he would be resigned—he wished whatever God wished; literally, 'I refuse no labor, but whatever God wills I will.'"

The funeral procession was formed in the following order:

Platoon of police.
Carriages containing the Bishops.
Two carriages with bearers.

Sisters of Charity    H E A R S E    Sisters of Mercy

Children of Mary from St. Peter's church.
Relatives in carriages.
Clergy in carriages wearing cassocks and surplices.
St. Peter's Band.
St. Patrick's Society.
St. John's Society.
St. Peter's Society.
Citizens.

The bishop was interred in the habit of the Franciscan Order, and his grave was made in the grounds in front of the convent and pro-cathedral. In May, 1892, his remains were transferred to the crypt in the cathedral.

In its issue of October 22, 1874, the *Pilot* paid this tribute to the deceased bishop: "The episcopate and clergy mourn the loss of a distinguished co-worker, the Order of St. Francis a devoted member, and the Catholic church, in New England especially, the rich zeal which for sixteen years directed a diocese comprising, at one time, two States. Even those outside the church, from whom he received the highest regard and coöperation consistent with his position as an uncompromising Catholic prelate, have manifested their feeling for his loss. The deceased bishop was deserving of all these manifestations; for he was one of uncommon ability and self-sacrificing zeal, the untiring projector of churches and charities, and a father at once to the clergy of his diocese, whom he stimulated by faithful attention, and the little ones whom he gathered under his religious care. It is known that much of his episcopal duty was done at some personal sacrifice, and he did not spare himself even during ill health."

"The bishop was a learned scholar. His private library was remarkably fine—especially in the completeness of its theological collections. As an orator, he was singularly plain, yet precise in his expression, and possessed the rare faculty of never speaking for effect. His sermons were easily understood and (rare quality) easily remembered. He is said by those whose opinions are entitled to weight, to have had no superior as a theological student in the country. His intellectual gifts were many and brilliant; but the kindness, humility, and child-like docility of his character, his resignation during the long and painful illness that afflicted him, and his calm submission to the decrees of death will be remembered with reverent affection long after his other qualities are consigned to oblivion."[1]

[1] *Connecticut Catholic Year Book*, 1877.

## RIGHT REV. THOMAS GALBERRY, O.S.A., D.D.,

### FOURTH BISHOP OF HARTFORD.

THOMAS, the son of Thomas Galberry and Margaret White, was born at Naas, County Kildare, Ireland, in 1833. When three years of age his parents emigrated to the United States and established their home in Philadelphia. Young Galberry was a witness of the outrages perpetrated by the Native American party between 1842 and 1844, and the acts of sacrilege committed during these turbulent years must have made an indelible impression upon the mind of one so observant as the subject of this sketch. His parents early perceived in him striking marks of a vocation to the sanctuary, and with self-sacrifice, characteristic of Catholic parents, sent him to Villanova College, near Philadelphia, in 1847. This institution was, as it is now, conducted by the Augustinian Fathers, an order upon which the young student was to reflect so much honor, and of which he was to become its most conspicuous ornament. Of serious, but not morose disposition, of placid temperament, a painstaking, conscientious student, his mind and heart now fixed upon his one great desire, Thomas Galberry pursued his studies with success and achieved the honor, dear to the heart of every student, of being selected by the faculty to deliver the commencement oration at the completion of his classical course in 1851. "While at college," says one who knew him well, "he was given to retirement and solitude, which was evinced in his love for long walks in the beautiful neighborhood of Villanova. Some of his earliest friends, those with whom he had contracted that most lasting of friendships —the privilege of college life—often recall him to mind as a gentle and modest lad, who avoided anything like harshness or anger—always cheerful, collected and studious."[1]

His classical course completed, he bestowed months of serious consideration upon the all-important question—old, yet ever recurring—*What must I do to possess eternal life?* His inclinations, all the yearnings of his soul, were for the ecclesiastical state. He would take up the cross and follow whithersoever the Master led. Accordingly, he entered the novitiate of the Augustinian Order at Villanova, January 1, 1852. Under the experienced and efficient direction of the Rev. William Hartnett, O. S. A., the young novice made rapid advancement in all that goes to make a holy religious. Submissive to severe trials, patient under difficulties, prompt in obedience to every order, docile under reproof, it was his sole aim to please his divine Master and to become a good priest. Voluntarily had he chosen a life secluded from the world. He knew that self must be submerged, and it is the testimony of his contemporaries that well and faithfully did he fulfill his obligations. On January 4, 1853, he made his solemn profession, taking the vows of poverty, chastity, and obedience. After his profession he began the usual course of dogmatic and moral theology, sacred Scripture, canon law, church history, sacred eloquence, etc., which comprised a period of three years.

[1] *The Connecticut Catholic Year Book,* 1877.

An Augustinian priest, who has achieved merited distinction as a historian, wrote of our subject at this time :[1] " As I remember him (he was over me, my prefect, and in some branches my teacher), we boys respected Mr. Galberry. He was very attentive to his tasks, prompt at rising early, as we well knew, and exact in discipline. He was rather strict, yet that was his business, and a model of propriety, cool-tempered, self-possessed, and at a pinch, rather inclined ' to let a fellow,' as we used to say, ' out of a scrape.' At the same time, we lads didn't try often to impose on him, as boys often will. Though I can't say that we exactly loved him, as he didn't enter quite as merrily into our games and sports as some others, we all, I believe, revered him in his quiet, unassuming demeanor. I believe none hated him ; the roughly-disposed, perhaps, feared him ; a good number liked him, and all respected him. In class he was well prepared for his tasks, and we knew before entering the room we had better know our lessons."

The same observant writer continues: " Young Galberry was pious, kind of heart, attentive to his work, and noted for his thorough performance of the same, and his general steadiness. Intellectually, he was not what might be called brilliant or erudite. He knew his business ; was sound on principles; open to conviction; not given to prejudices; loving that which was best and most equitable; was rather slow in forming his judgments ; studied the matter, took counsel, and viewed whatever he had on hand from all points of view; and when his mind was ' made up,' stuck to it like a limpet to the rock. Was very firm, some might say, obstinate, but I think not. Firmness is the word, or strong determination. This characteristic was marked during his whole life-time."[2]

On the completion of his theological studies, Thomas Galberry was elevated to the dignity of the holy priesthood by Bishop Neumann on December 20th, 1856, in St. Augustine's church, Philadelphia. After his ordination, Father Galberry was assigned to a professor's chair in Villanova College, a position he filled with eminent success for two years. From the college he entered into the practical work of the sacred ministry, having been appointed rector of St. Denis' church, West Haverford, Pennsylvania, a short distance from Villanova. This little church has acquired a unique prominence from the number of illustrious priests who have been its rectors, or who have served it, no less than seven of them having been elevated to the episcopal dignity: Most Rev. Archbishop Hughes of New York, Most Rev. Peter Kenrick, Archbishop of St. Louis, Right Rev. Michael O'Connor, Bishop of Pittsburg, Right Rev. Thaddeus Amat, Bishop of Monterey and Los Angelos, Right Rev. William O'Hara, Bishop of Scranton, Right Rev. Michael Domenec, Bishop of Pittsburg, and Bishop Galberry.

In this peaceful and congenial field, Father Galberry labored until January 27th, 1860, when he was transferred to Lansingburg, New York. Here the metal of the young priest was to be tested. The church which he found there, old St. John the Baptist's, was a time-battered structure and falling

[1] *Lives of Deceased Bishops.*
[2] Ibid.

✝ Thomas Galberry OSA
Epus Hartfordiensis

into ruin. It was not an edifice suitable for the celebration of the divine mysteries. He determined to erect a temple that would be a fitting abode for Him who dwells amid the silence of the tabernacle, a prisoner of love. His financial prospects were poor, but confiding in the unfailing assistance of heaven, he appealed to the generosity not only of his own little flock, but of Catholics elsewhere. His confidence and zeal were rewarded; the corner-stone of the new church, which he placed under the patronage of the founder of his beloved order, St. Augustine, was laid on June 17th, 1869, by Bishop McCloskey of Albany, afterwards Cardinal Archbishop of New York. In December, 1865, the magnificent edifice was completed, and the first service within its walls—a service of joy and gratitude to the Giver of all gifts—was a midnight Mass on the feast of the Nativity. To crown the success of the indefatigable pastor all the indebtedness incurred had been liquidated when the first service was held. "This church, I think," writes the distinguished historian before quoted, "is the most beautiful of its kind, Gothic, so greatly does it excel others I have seen in its perfect proportions, its delicate though simple decorations, and the almost uncontrollable spirit of devotion it breathes, as it were, into the worshipers at its altars. This may be an inappropriate eulogy. However, take it as the sincere conviction of your humble servant, who has seen many wonders in architecture, but was never really in love with any so much as with St. Augustine's at Lansingburg."[1]

But the erection of this beautiful temple was not the only work that redounds to the honor of Father Galberry during his pastorate at Lansing-burg. He introduced the Sisters of St. Joseph from Carondolet, Missouri, for whose use he purchased a spacious dwelling. He enlarged his school and purchased a cemetery known as "St. John's-on-the Hill." In the midst of these exacting labors he received notification of his appointment to the responsible position of Superior of the Augustinians in the United States, November 30th, 1866. His official title was "Superior of the Commissariat of our Lady of Good Counsel." Of Father Galberry as Superior, a confrère said: "His old-time, business-like traits seemed to improve. He was very watchful as Superior, very self-sacrificing and industrious. He aimed somewhat high, in fact, higher than was expedient in his requirements from candidates for the Order, and from us all he expected prompt, thorough and unwavering obedience. While his hand was pretty heavy, no one called into question the rectitude of his views; he was too hard a worker himself, and never asked one to do what he would not do himself; he was very correct in his own conduct, very punctual in his hours of appointment of duty, and very mortified. I really think he wore himself away to death."[2]

Though Superior of the Augustinians, Father Galberry retained his position as rector at Lansingburg until February 24th, 1870, when he succeeded the Rev. L. M. Edge, O. S. A., as rector of St. Mary's church, Lawrence, Massachusetts. In 1872, Father Galberry became President of Villanova College, succeeding the Rev. Dr. Stanton, O. S. A. As President he infused new

---

[1] Clark's *Lives of Deceased Bishops.*     [2] *Ibid.*

II—11

life into the college. The growing importance of the institution demanded better and more modern accommodations. To provide these he began the erection of suitable buildings on April 1st, 1872, and which he had the happiness to see ready for occupancy early in 1874. He restored the strict yet paternal discipline of the Augustinians, and by his systematic methods, his well-directed energy and his intelligent counsel, brought the course of studies to a high educational standard. "This was his greatest work, and though perhaps better enabled to prosecute his designs, still the anxiety and toil entailed on him, soon began to imprint their seal on his years. One would believe that after so many years of constant labor—of almost ceaseless vigilance over the affairs of his several positions, that even now a respite from work would have been grateful to him. But Providence had not so ordained. He had scarcely begun a life of comparative quiet—hardly had he confined himself to the enjoyment of his college home, than a demand upon his services came from elsewhere." [1]

On September 14, 1874, a letter was received from Rome from the General of the Order notifying the Fathers at Villanova of a change in the form of government of the Augustinians in the United States. The Commissariat of Our Lady of Good Counsel, founded in 1796, was by a resolution of the General Council, transformed into a province. Accordingly, the first chapter of the newly-created province convened at Villanova December 15, 1874. For the first time in their history, the Augustinians in the United States could select their own Superior. The unanimous choice of the electors was Father Galberry ; and this free selection was a graceful and spontaneous tribute to the manner in which he had hitherto governed the Order.

But other and still greater honors were to fall upon the devoted religious. His work for Christ and souls was to be crowned with the dignity of the episcopate. As a reward for his fidelity to his sacred calling, for his zeal and uninterrupted successes in the Master's cause, he was to receive the plenitude of priestly power. He was to leave the ranks in which he had served with so much distinction to be numbered among those whom the Holy Ghost has appointed to rule the church of God. Professor, parish priest, superior, and provincial, he was to become an honored member of that distinguished body that traces its origin in an unbroken line back to the apostles.

In February, 1875, he received, unofficially, the intelligence that he had been nominated by the Holy Father to the See of Hartford. The official notification of his election soon followed. "And now in his own estimation was the cup of his sorrow filled. Too retired and unassuming, he desired not the purple. He was a religious, and as a religious sought not dignity nor honor. His wish was to remain with his *confrères* enjoying the sweets and peace which monastic life alone can bestow. Notwithstanding his reluctance to accept the honors and responsibilities of the episcopal dignity, still he judged not hastily, he acted not alone. He gave this important subject mature deliberation ; he counselled with those in whom he could confide, hearkened to their words and besought their sympathy."

---

[1] *Connecticut Catholic Year Book, 1877.*

The appointment of Father Galberry to the See of Hartford was hailed with delight by all, and by none more than by the clergy of the diocese. Those who knew him regarded the Bishop-elect as a worthy successor of the apostolic men who had gone before. Among the first to extend a cordial welcome to the diocese was the Very Rev. Administrator *ad interim*, the Rev. James Hughes, V. G.:

"Very Reverend and Dear Sir: From telegraphic news to the *Freeman*, we are informed of your appointment to the See of Hartford, and, being personally acquainted, I hasten to offer you my personal congratulations and tender you a most cordial welcome. I believe the priests of the diocese are almost strangers to you ; but, nevertheless, I am sure you will find them earnest and zealous workers and obedient co-operators in all your desires.

"We shall look every day for the arrival of your Bulls, and hope either to see or hear from you soon after.

"Wishing you every blessing of your office, and a long and happy life in the episcopate, believe me, dear Father Galberry,

Yours very sincerely,

James Hughes,
Administrator, Diocese of Hartford.

Hartford, Conn., Feb'y 22d, 1875.
Very Rev. Thomas Galberry, O.S.A."

Rumors of his contemplated intention to decline the honor conferred upon him began to spread abroad, and, in consequence, no little anxiety was created among the priests of the diocese. His brethren appealed to him to bow to the will of the Sovereign Pontiff and accept the burden he had placed upon him. Unwilling to sever the holy ties of brotherhood, humanly speaking, they, nevertheless, recognized in his election the call of God. *The finger of God was there.* From the diocese was despatched a letter from two of the senior clergy urging his acceptance of the episcopal office :

"Very Reverend and Dear Sir:—Hearing it reported and seeing it extensively circulated in the newspapers that you contemplate resigning the charge of the Diocese of Hartford, we, the undersigned, being among the oldest priests of the diocese, take the liberty of addressing you a few words in reference to the subject.

"In the first place, we assure you that your appointment gave universal satisfaction to the priests of the diocese. They lived in peace and harmony with our late revered and saintly bishop. They sincerely loved him and gave him a hearty co-operation in everything he undertook for the good of religion. From the accounts received from various sources they hoped to find in you a worthy successor of Bishop McFarland, and were anxiously looking forward to the day of your consecration in Hartford. These, we assure you, are the sentiments of the priests of the diocese towards you.

"We hope, therefore, you will not be discouraged nor deterred from assuming the charge of this diocese, where you will receive the hearty welcome and faithful co-operation of a united and devoted priesthood.

Very respectfully yours,

James Lynch,
Pastor of the Church of the Immaculate Conception, Waterbury, Conn.
Thomas J. Synnott,
Pastor of St. Augustine's Church, Bridgeport, Conn.

Bridgeport, Conn., April 30, 1875.
Very Rev. Thomas Galberry, O.S.A."

The humility of the monk, the disinclination to leave the classical shades of his *alma mater*, and with which he had now become so intimately associated, and, above all, the fear of his unworthiness to enter the episcopal ranks overcame all solicitations, and Father Galberry forwarded his resignation to Rome with the reasons that impelled him thereto. Rome gave due consideration to the reasons advanced for his resignation, and on February 17, 1876, a *mandamus*—a Papal mandate—was forwarded by Cardinal Franchi, Prefect of the Propaganda, to the Most Rev. Archbishop Williams, of Boston, the Metropolitan, enjoining the acceptance of the See of Hartford by Father Galberry. The contest with self was at an end. He who had commanded obedience from others, now bowed to the command of the Supreme Pastor. The clergy and laity of the diocese breathed a sigh of relief and sent up fervent prayers of thanksgiving that God, through His Vicegerent, had bestowed upon them so worthy a ruler.

Right Rev. Thomas Galberry was consecrated Bishop of Hartford, the fourth in succession, in St. Peter's church, Hartford, on March 19, 1876. The officers of the Solemn Mass of Consecration were as follows :

Consecrator—Most Rev. John J. Williams D.D., Archbishop of Boston.
Assistant Bishops—Right Rev. P. T. O Reilly, D.D., Bishop of Springfield, and Right Rev. E. P. Wadhams, D.D., Bishop of Ogdensburg.
Archpriest—Very Rev. James Hughes, Administrator.
Notary—Very Rev. P. A. Stanton, O.S.A.
Deacons of Honor—Rev. M. Hart and Rev. L. Daly.
Deacon of the Mass—Rev. James Lynch.
Sub-Deacon—Rev. Thomas Walsh.
Master of Ceremonies—Rev. M. A. Tierney and Rev. M. F. Kelly.
Assistant Chaplain—Rev. T. J. Synnott.
Cross Bearer—Rev. P. F. Goodwin.
Chanters—Rev. J. F. Campbell and Rev. E. Gaffney.
Censer Bearer—Rev. J. F. Campbell.

The preacher on the occasion was Right Rev. P. N. Lynch, D.D., Bishop of Charleston, S. C., who selected his text from the *Acts of the Apostles, xx. 28*: "*Take heed to yourselves and to the whole flock wherein the Holy Ghost hath placed you bishops, to rule the church of God which he hath purchased with his own blood.*"

The Bishops in attendance were the Right Rev. Bishops Lynch, of Charleston ; De Goesbriand, of Burlington ; Loughlin, of Brooklyn ; Conroy and McNierney, of Albany ; O'Reilly, of Springfield ; Wadhams, of Ogdensburg ; Corrigan, of Newark ; Hendricken, of Providence, and Healy, of Portland. In addition there were about one hundred and twenty-five priests from this and other dioceses, besides large delegations of sisters of various communities. The newly consecrated bishop sang Pontifical Vespers, during which Bishop Healy of Portland preached the sermon.

Bishop Galberry selected St. Peter's church, Hartford, as his pro-cathedral. The erection of a cathedral suitable to the dignity of the diocese over which he had been placed, now became the object of his thoughts. To stimulate the zeal of the clergy and laity of the diocese, he issued a Pastoral Letter in which he set forth the urgent need of a Mother Church, and recounted the work accomplished in this direction by his lamented predecessor. The new cathedral would be placed under the patronage of the Spouse of Mary Immaculate, the Patron of the Church Universal, St. Joseph.

On May 5, 1876, Bishop Galberry sailed from New York *en route* for Rome to make his visit *ad limina Apostolorum*. While abroad he visited the Grotto of Lourdes, whither he journeyed as a devout pilgrim of our Blessed Lady. His return to the diocese in the autumn was accompanied by many demonstrations of joy, affection and thanksgiving on the part of his devoted priests and people.

Bishop Galberry's unceasing labors and responsibilities as an Augustinian monk with the additional burdens of the episcopal office soon began to undermine his health. To obtain much-needed rest, he set out on October 10, 1878, for his beloved home of many years, Villanova College. On the train to New York he was taken suddenly ill with hemorrhages of the bowels. Arrived at New York he was tenderly carried to the Grand Union Hotel and surgical and spiritual assistance dispatched for. Very Rev. Dr. Xeno, O.S.A., Provincial of the Augustinians, was soon at the bedside of his stricken colleague. The last sacraments were administered by priests who had been summoned from neighboring parishes. With perfect resignation to the holy will of God, and realizing that death was nigh, he imparted his episcopal benediction to his diocese and to those who knelt sorrowfully about him. He sank rapidly, and died in the evening of October 10th.

A Sister of Mercy thus wrote of him: "Bishop Galberry was a saintly prelate. He seemed to resemble Bishop McFarland in his untiring zeal in the cause of religion and in the education of children. I often heard it said, 'Bishop Galberry acts so like Bishop McFarland;' you would think he lived with him, studied his life, copied his virtues, particularly his gentleness of heart, his zeal for souls, his love for the poor, and untiring kindness and anxiety for the welfare of our dear Parent House and Boarding School on Farmington avenue."[1]

During his brief episcopate of twenty months, Bishop Galberry accomplished much for his diocese. He founded the *Connecticut Catholic*, the first number of which was issued on April 29, 1876, and which recently became the *Catholic Transcript*. He made one visitation of the diocese, during which he confirmed 10,235 persons, besides administering confirmation in St. Denis' church, Haverford, Pa. (July 30, 1876). The number of priests in the diocese was increased by seventeen.

Bishop Galberry's vicars-general were Rev. James Lynch, rector of St. Patrick's church, New Haven, and Rev. Thomas Walsh, rector of St. Rose's church, Meriden.

A contemporary drew this pen picture of Bishop Galberry: "His dignified appearance, his very look and bearing call to mind the old prelates of the early church. . . . The expression of his countenance is that of cheerfulness and buoyancy of spirit, still having something about it denoting a love of

---

[1] *Lives of the Deceased Bishops.*

retirement. He is of a practical turn of mind, his long experience on the mission considerably inclining him to business pursuits. He has displayed great taste in building. Oftentimes with a low treasury at the outset, he has by wondrous exertion filled it before completing his designs. The strong and noticeable trait of his character is his deep reflective turn of mind; it is this which gains him success in whatever he undertakes. As a pulpit orator he is plain and impressive, never seeking ornament nor figure to express his ideas. In conversation he is cheerful and frank, nay almost familiar in his converse with his friends, and his company never leave his presence without a new love, a new sympathy towards him. With all under his care he is gentle, yet firm when necessary; forgiving, yet inflexible if called for, and fatherly and lenient to all who strive to do good. It is to this combination of manly virtues that prosperity and success have attended all his enterprises. And were it not for the influence of a deep, unshaken faith in the Omnipresence of God, he would never have ascended, step by step, the royal road of holiness and perfection."

The obsequies of Bishop Galberry took place on October 15th. The celebrant of the Mass was Most Rev. Archbishop Williams, of Boston; assistant priest, the Rev. Hugh Carmody; deacon, the Rev. P. A. Murphy; sub-deacon, the Rev. P. P. Lawlor. The deacons of honor were Very Rev. P. A. Stanton, O.S.A., and Rev. T. J. Synnott. Right Rev. Bishop De Goesbriand of Burlington, preached the funeral sermon. Present in the sanctuary were :

> Right Rev. John Loughlin D.D. Brooklyn.
> Right Rev. L. De Goesbriand, D.D. Burlington.
> Right Rev. P. N. Lynch, D D. Charleston.
> Right Rev. W. O'Hara, D.D. Scranton.
> Right Rev. P. T. O'Reilly, D D. Springfield.
> Right Rev. Francis McNeirny, D D. Albany.
> Right Rev. M. A. Corrigan, D D. Newark.
> Very Rev. John E. Barry, V.G., of Portland, representing Bishop Healy, who was in Europe.

Priests were present from the arch-dioceses of New York, Philadelphia, and Boston, and from the dioceses of Hartford, Albany, Buffalo, Scranton, Providence, and Springfield.

## RIGHT REV. LAWRENCE STEPHEN McMAHON, D. D.,

### Fifth Bishop of Hartford.

BISHOP McMAHON was the second child of Owen and Sarah McMahon, and was born in St. John, N. B., on St. Stephen's Day, December 26, 1835. He was brought a child in arms the following May to Charlestown, now part of Boston, where he resided until he entered Holy Cross College, Worcester.

After completing the grammar-school course, he entered the Charlestown High School at the age of twelve years, and was one of two boys who comprised the first graduating class. United States Senator, the Hon. Samuel

Yours truly in Christ
+ Laurence S. McMahon
B'p of Hartford

Pasco, of Florida, was a pupil of the school at the same time, but was graduated later. In 1898 the school celebrated its golden jubilee; just before that there was much discussion about closing the school and transferring the pupils to the Boston High and Latin schools. Mayor Quincy, the present Chief Executive of Boston, in a speech opposing this transfer, said that a school which could graduate two such scholars as Bishop McMahon and Senator Pasco had justified its erection and existence by the useful and splendid careers of these early graduates, and it would be a great wrong to close it.

At the age of fifteen young McMahon entered Holy Cross College, Worcester, but was forced after a brief stay to leave there on account of a fire, which destroyed the main building of the college. He then entered Montreal College, where he won the first prize in all his classes, taking even the honors in French from his Canadian classmates. He was then sent to St. Mary's Seminary, Baltimore, where he remained for a short time. In that year Bishop Fitzpatrick, of Boston, who was making his *ad limina* visit to Rome, arrranged that Mr. McMahon should enter the College of the Propaganda Fide, there to continue his studies; but at that time political troubles were so rife and revolution and political feeling so hostile to the Pope-King, that the young student changed his destination to Aix, in the south of France, near Marseilles, where he studied theology for three years. While at the Seminary of Aix he, with many of his fellow-seminarians, paid a visit to the Rev. Jean Baptiste Vianney, known the world over as the Curé d'Ars, and since pronounced blessed by the church. The Curé singled him out from the others, and told him that he had a true vocation to the priesthood, and would be of great service to the church of God in America, a prediction which was amply and fully verified by the after life of the young ecclesiastic.

As he was too young to be ordained to the priesthood, he asked and obtained permission to make an additional year of study at Rome. While here he lived at the French Seminary of St. Clara, as the American College was not yet open, and attended the lectures at the Apollinare, the diocesan seminary of Rome, and also at the Gregorian University, better known, perhaps, as the Roman College, the highest teaching institution in the world, taught by the Fathers of the Society of Jesus.

While preparing for the doctorate examination he was peremptorily summoned home by Bishop Fitzpatrick, who was in great need of priests for the mission. He was ordained in the cathedral of Rome, St. John Lateran, by Cardinal Constantine Patrizi, the Vicar-General of His Holiness, Pope Pius IX., on March 24, 1860.

On his return to Boston, Father McMahon was appointed an assistant at the Cathedral, to which was attached the Succursal Church of St. Vincent on Purchase street, which was attended by nearly 5,000 Catholics. In one or the other of these churches he preached every Sunday, and in one or the other heard confessions three days in the week; also in either one or the other he conducted a first communion class of children and adults twice a week. The sick calls were numerous, and as many of the parishioners lived at a great distance from the church, this was a laborious and trying duty, as there were no means of conveyance, and all journeys had to be made on foot, and not a night passed without some, and often urgent cases. The number of priests in the diocese was small, and few of the churches had assistants. In case of a sudden illness, one of the cathedral priests was despatched to assist on Sunday the sick pastor, and he was expected to keep up at the same time, as far as possible, his own work at the cathedral. Father McMahon attended also the penal and pauper institutions in Boston harbor.

Shortly after his return to Boston the Civil War broke out, and he undertook, as a voluntary duty, the work of visiting the Catholics of each regiment in the camps around Boston, hearing their confessions, speaking words of cheer and comfort, and administering holy communion before they went to the front.

Early in the war there came to Bishop Fitzpatrick an urgent letter from the officers and men of the Twenty-eighth Massachusetts, lying in the swamps of South Carolina, saying that they were dying in large numbers and more sick who were soon to die, and begging for a chaplain. The administrator of the diocese, in the absence of the bishop, read the letter at table, and said that as it was beyond the limits of the diocese and out of his jurisdiction, he could not order any one to go. Father McMahon, the youngest of the clergy present, waited modestly for the others to speak, but hearing no response to the administrator's appeal, placed himself at the disposal of his superior. This was Friday night. The next day he received his commission from Governor Andrews at the State House. The following day, Sunday, he preached at the High Mass, and that same night went to New York to embark on the government transport, and within the week was landed at Hilton Head, South Carolina. Almost immediately on his arrival was fought the battle of James' Island. Before the forward movement began, the tent of Father McMahon, the only Catholic priest present, was filled with soldiers who had been prevented for a long time, through no fault of their own, from attending to their spiritual duties. All that night and early next morning he heard confessions until the drum beat had called the men to move forward; and he went with them. After the battle of James' Island, as the only Catholic chaplain in the command, he ministered to all the Catholics.

Father McMahon was with Foster at Newbern, with Burnside at Fredericksburg; with Pope at the Second Bull Run, and with McClellan at Antietam. He met the broken and defeated army after the seven days' fight at Richmond, and his regiment was one of the covering regiments of the rear guard just come up from the South, through which the beaten Army of the Potomac, just after the fight at Malvern Hill and the seven days' fight at Richmond, dashed to safety. At the Second Battle of Bull Run, Father McMahon's regiment, with a few others, held the pass through which the defeated army retreated, and here the General of the Division, the Brigadier-General, and two of the field officers were killed.

Father McMahon thus campaigned in four States, when and where the war was fiercest and most bloody. Owing to the small number of Catholic chaplains, he was often the only chaplain in a division, and often in an army corps, and had to travel a distance of over fifteen miles, compelled to take long rides on horseback, often through a dangerous and hostile country, to minister to the scattered Catholic soldiers. The frequent change of camp, the continual forward and rearward movements, the strain of hard and continuous and saddening work (he was once, after one of the great battles, three days with hardly any food or sleep, attending the wounded), brought on an attack of intermittent fever, and he was sent to the army hospital at Washington, where for a long time he hovered between life and death. One day when he was a little better than usual and fully conscious, he playfully asked the attending physician if he could go to Boston. The physician replied: "If you go to Boston the journey will most likely kill you, and if you remain here you will surely die." He came north with some soldiers, and what little he could do for them he did willingly and cheerfully, rousing them from their despondency and giving them fresh courage. When he arrived at the bishop's house, which was only a short distance from the depot, he had just strength enough to pull the bell, and when the servant opened the door he fell on his face in the vestibule. He was carried to bed, from which he did not arise for eleven months. On his recovery, as his regiment was without a chaplain, he rejoined his old comrades, and marched with them in the great review before the President which closed the war. For all this service in the army Father McMahon never received a cent of pay.

The war ended, Father McMahon was named the first pastor of Bridgewater, at that time a small country village twenty-eight miles from Boston. He had also two missions to attend, East Bridgewater and Middleboro, the one distant seven, the other ten miles from his residence. He had no assistant, and each Sunday he said two Masses ; he also attended the almshouse at Middleboro, and gave the same faithful service to those hapless ones as he had given to the parishioners and to the army. Partly from his work, which was highly prized by the officials of the almshouse, and partly by his subsequent efforts, the State of Massachusetts gave open welcome by statute law to Catholic priests to officiate in all state and county institutions ; thus he served to secure not only civil, but religious liberty.

From Bridgewater he was sent to New Bedford. He found here a small, old church, which had been bought some years before from the Protestants. Of this congregation from one-third to one-half were Portuguese, the men mostly following the sea for a livelihood in the whaling fleet. To discharge his duty to them, busy as he was, he took up the study of Portuguese without a teacher, and learned it well enough to hear their confessions and their piteous tales of distress. For two years he wrote letter after letter to the bishops of Portugal, and to priestly acquaintances of some Portuguese parishioners in the hope of securing a priest for his parishioners of that nationality. One came, only to die in his house a short time after.

In the meantime Father McMahon set apart their small contributions, and when a priest came at last, he built and turned over to them a large handsome church, well furnished and almost without debt.

Later came the French emigration from Canada; he attended them until he was able to procure a Canadian priest.

Meanwhile he began the erection of the French church, which was afterwards opened by the French pastor. For two years he was the only priest in that part of the diocese, his jurisdiction covering the territory which stretched from New Bedford to Fall River, including the small town of Dartmouth, where there was a small sprinkling of Catholics, and on the ocean side to Nantucket, including the island of Martha's Vineyard, sixty miles distant. On one occasion when the steamer was not running he was summoned on a sick call to Nantucket, and so stormy became the weather that the boat was capsized when about half way to the destination, and if he had not been a good swimmer, he would never have reached land.

Father McMahon celebrated the first Mass said on Martha's Vineyard, which he did in a private house.

A short time after a French gentleman of New York City, living on Lexington avenue, gave him a plot of land for a new church, which was afterwards built.

The old frame church purchased from the Protestants, bare, cheap and small, and not conveniently located, he found inadequate to the needs of the people of New Bedford. A small piece of land on County street had been bought by one of his predecessors for a new church; to this he added by purchase three times as much land, sufficient for church, house and school. On a portion of this land he erected a magnificent granite church, and which was at that time the finest church in the diocese of Boston. This splendid edifice cost $150,000. The corner-stone was laid on November 1, 1866, and the church was dedicated in honor of St. Lawrence on August 10, 1871.

Father McMahon also purchased a large piece of land, on which stood a commodious mansion of stone, which he opened as a hospital—the first institution of the kind in the city—under the charge of the Sisters of Mercy whom he brought to New Bedford, and who acted as nurses, while he furnished the funds for its maintenance and was responsible for its debts.

He was the first Vicar General of the Diocese of Providence, and in that capacity prepared the ground and had the basement ready when Bishop Hendricken returned from Rome to lay the corner-stone of the Cathedral.

In 1873 Father McMahon received the degree of Doctor of Divinity from Rome in recognition of his services to religion.

Owing to the feeble health and frequent indisposition of the Bishop of Providence, a large share of the administration of the affairs of the diocese fell upon Dr. McMahon. Between him and Bishop Hendricken there existed always the fullest confidence and respect, which continued until the death of Bishop Hendricken.

Dr. McMahon labored in New Bedford for fourteen years, and the many works accomplished were evidence at once of his zeal and of the strong faith of his people. The success that attended his labors was not unnoticed by his ecclesiastical superiors, and when the See of Hartford became vacant by the death of Bishop Galberry, the prelates of the province recognized in Dr. Mc-Mahon a priest worthy to be his successor. Accordingly, he was appointed Bishop of Hartford on May 8, 1879. On Sunday, July 20, 1879, he delivered his farewell address to his congregation of New Bedford. The scene was unusually affecting, and the concourse present manifested the great grief they experienced in the separation. Seldom, if ever before, was a parting between pastor and people so unanimously regretted. Dr. McMahon said in part: " The relations existing between us have been pleasant—pleasant to me and I hope pleasant to you. That they were pleasant to me is sufficiently proved by my long stay with you. Fourteen years ago last January, I came to New Bedford, and have been here constantly ever since, not having taken even a month's vacation. I found on coming here a great deal to do. I was told by my ecclesiastical superiors that I should have a church to build and much work to do. But I found little difficulty in accomplishing what I undertook, because I had the people behind me ; I had something to lean upon. My work has been successful, thanks to your coöperation. Every man is satisfied to remain where his work succeeds; therefore I was satisfied to remain here, and looked forward to closing my life among you and mingling my dust with that of your people and of my predecessors. But Providence has ordered otherwise. The great head of the church has seen fit to summon me to more laborious duties, and after careful consideration and taking counsel of those to whom I should look for advice, I can only believe that the voice of Peter is the voice of God.

"In leaving you I am happy to say that the affairs of the church were never so prosperous in any previous time. I need not specify details, but I think there is scarcely a place of the same size in the United States where so many visible works, evidencing the progress of faith, have been accomplished during the same time as has been the case in this city. And this has not been attained at the expense of the spiritual progress. . . .

"And now, there remains but a parting word to be said. I thank you again most sincerely, most feelingly, for all your acts of kindness. I shall always retain pleasant memories of New Bedford, and whatever the vicissitudes of my life may be, I shall always look back to the years spent here with feelings of gratitude and pleasure. I shall be abundantly satisfied if I find as good people as I leave behind me. May God grant you individually and collectively every possible blessing ; may He give you all the happiness and prosperity you desire, and I wish you from my heart an affectionate farewell."

Bishop McMahon was consecrated Bishop of Hartford on Sunday, August 10, 1879, in St. Joseph's cathedral, Hartford, in the presence of a vast concourse of priests and people. Special trains were run on all the roads leading into the city. Seventy car-loads were brought from Waterbury, New Haven, Springfield, Willimantic and other cities. The celebrant of the Mass and consecrating prelate was the Most Rev. Archbishop Williams, of Boston.

*Assistant Consecrators*, RIGHT REV. BISHOP LOUGHLIN, of Brooklyn, and RIGHT REV. BISHOP
O'REILLY, of Springfield.

*Deacon of the Mass*, REV. M. MORAN, Boston.

*Subdeacon*, REV. WM. DALY, Boston.

*Deacons of Honor*, REV. M. McCABE, Woonsocket, and REV. PHILIP GRACE, D.D., Newport.

*Assistant Priest*, VERY REV. THOMAS WALSH, Meriden.

*Notary*, VERY REV. JAMES HUGHES, Hartford.

*Masters of Ceremonies*, REV. M. A. TIERNEY, Hartford, and REV. M. F. KELLY, Windsor Locks.

*Chanters*, the REV. FATHERS CAMPBELL, KENNEDY, JOYNT, BRODERICK, O'KEEFE, FAGAN
McCABE, SHEFFREY, W. ROGERS, B. O'R. SHERIDAN and E. GAFFNEY.

*Mitre Bearer*, REV. J. COONEY.

*Crozier Bearer*, REV. L. J. O'TOOLE.

*Censer Bearer*, REV. J. ROGERS.

*Candle Bearer*, REV. T. T. McMAHON.

*Acolytes*, REV. P. LAWLOR and REV. P. SHAHAN.

*Book Bearer*, REV. J. A. MULCAHY.

*Assistants at the Faldstool*, REV. E. VYGEN and REV. M. LAWLOR.

The preacher on the occasion was Right Rev. Bishop Healy, of Portland, Me. His text was drawn from the fifth chapter of the epistle to the Hebrews: "*Called by God a High Priest, according to the order of Melchizedec, of whom we have much to say and hard to be intelligently uttered.*" The Bishop said in part:

"The priest exerts an authority compared to which that of the early disciples seems to be almost nothing. Who can estimate the dignity of the priesthood? Kings and princes must bow to his authority. Recently, over the seas, there has been a bloodless but cruel persecution against the priesthood because they claim an authority beyond this world and reaching even to heaven. They rule the souls, others the bodies. The priest is an ambassador, occupying a middle place between God and man. Consider lest you judge us too severely. There must be an angelic life. We bear the mysteries of God. The priest represents none other than Christ Himself. What can be beyond that? Yet there is another glory and dignity conferred upon man, the collation of which you have just seen. You have seen how the church surrounds this dignity with elaborate ceremonial; the solemn examination of the candidate; the building up in vestments of wonderful variety; the giving of a staff to represent that he is a shepherd; the ring, signifying that he is the spouse of the church; the book of the Gospels, laid like a burden upon his neck; his head anointed, signifying that he is a king among men; his hands anointed, because from them are to flow the most wonderful blessings of God. But the supreme moment was the placing of consecrated hands upon his head and the words, 'Receive the Holy Ghost.' The Christian is the temple of the Holy Ghost; the Christian can bring his fellow-men to the portals of the church, but no further; the priest can confer miraculous favors upon his inferiors; both the simple Christian and the priest have limited authority. For the perpetuation of the people of God there is a necessity for another one who can go further. 'The Father is greater than I,' said Christ. I want to make it plain that if the priest be another Christ, the bishop is the representative of God himself, and can produce others like unto himself. Then is it wonderful that the church, by her ceremonies, endeavors to make this truth more evident? This father must possess a dignity of grace higher than the tongue can describe. When our Saviour came up out of Jordan, the Holy Ghost descended like a dove, and the voice came from heaven: 'Hear ye Him!' When this candidate arose from his prostrate condition, and the consecrated hands were placed on his head, may it not have been that the heavens were indeed opened, and that a voice came, 'This is my beloved Son, hear ye Him?' Now, this one having risen and possessing the divine prerogative, every blessing and peace flow from his hands: the ruler among those who have rule and authority. Let me stop here, leaving the impression that the pontiff represents to you none other than the Father in his original and divine fecundity. Remember what responsibility he bears, and endeavor by obedience and prayer to hold up the fainting heart that bears so great a burden."

Bishop Healy concluded his sermon with an address to the newly consecrated prelate: "To-day you have the *Te Deum* chanted in this church of Hartford, which has been so often widowed. I thank God that you have witnessed the apostolic lives of those who have ruled you. And you, venerable brother, just now inducted into the office of the episcopacy, bear your authority tempered with mercy. May you rule many years, and bear this authority and sway as one who represents God the Father. Let us all unite in prayer that this power may continue for many years (*multos annos*) and for a crown and everlasting glory in heaven."

The prelates present were: Most Rev. John J. Williams, D. D., Boston, Mass.; Right Rev. John Loughlin, D. D., Brooklyn, N. Y.; Right Rev. Patrick T. O'Reilly, D. D., Springfield, Mass.; Right Rev. J. F. Shannahan, D. D., Harrisburg, Penna.; Right Rev. S. Chatard, D. D., Vincennes, Ind.; Right Rev. T. Hendricken, D. D., Providence, R. I.

Immediately after his consecration Bishop McMahon undertook the legacy bequeathed to him of continuing the building of the cathedral. In this stupendous work he was not only wonderfully successful, but he lived to witness the consecration of the magnificent temple. He found it burdened with an indebtedness of $60,000, and his first labor was to liquidate this and then to bring to completion the plans of his predecessors. After thirteen years of unremitting attention and labor and anxiety, he had the happiness to witness the full realization of his hopes. The cathedral was erected at the sacrifice of his own income, and by the voluntary contributions of his diocesans, as no tax or assessment was placed upon any parish. Within ten years he expended over $500,000 in its construction and embellishment. In accomplishing this work Bishop McMahon not only sacrificed his means, but also his health. In the hope of restoring the latter he visited Europe in April, 1891, accompanied by the Rev. Thomas Broderick, rector of St. Peter's church, Hartford. He returned on Thursday, November 19, 1891, and never in the history of New England had a bishop been so enthusiastically welcomed. The people requested that the cathedral be opened and illuminated for the first time in honor of the man whose untiring energy and business capacity had completed it. Although the seating capacity of the edifice is about 2200, there were nearly 4000 persons in the interior, and as many more on the outside. As the bishop looked from his throne in the sanctuary out into the vast enclosure and witnessed what had been accomplished during his seven months' absence, he could not fail to realize that he stood within one of the most gorgeous temples on the American continent. The organ was used for the first time to assist the chorus of 150 voices to chant the inspiring *Te Deum* in honor of the bishop's safe return to his diocese. Rev. William A. Harty, rector of the cathedral, delivered an address of welcome in behalf of the clergy and people, to which the bishop made a felicitous and feeling response.

But other works than the erection of the cathedral absorbed the time and engaged the attention of Bishop McMahon. Between the years of his consecration and the completion of the cathedral, he organized forty-eight new parishes, dedicated seventy churches, and established sixteen convents and sixteen parochial schools. He attended the Third Plenary Council of Baltimore, whose sessions were held in November and December, 1883. In 1880, when wide-spread destitution prevailed in many parts of Ireland, Bishop McMahon was among the first to raise his voice in an appeal in behalf of the suffering poor of that unhappy country. His was a practical sympathy as evinced by the following circular which he addressed to the pastors of his diocese:

"HARTFORD, January 19, 1880.

"*Rev. Dear Sir*: You are doubtless not unacquainted with the reports which have come to us through the public press in reference to the alleged distress in the unhappy land whence most of us have sprung.

"The accounts which we have received from responsible parties would indicate that these reports have by no means been exaggerated, but, on the contrary, it is feared that all that our charity may be able to do will prove inadequate to the terrible necessities of the case.

"The sufferings of our fellow-men in any quarter of the globe should excite our warmest sympathies; but when we are called upon to rescue from hunger, sickness and death the unfortunate people of our own native land, or the land of our fathers and mothers, every consideration of religion and patriotism combine to render the call doubly imperative.

"In order, therefore, that our flocks may have an opportunity of contributing to so worthy an object, you will please to announce to your congregation that a collection will be taken up in all the churches of the diocese of Hartford on Sunday, February 1st, for the above mentioned purpose.

"As the necessity is a pressing one, you are requested to transmit as quickly as possible the sum collected to the chancellor of the diocese, in order that the money contributed may be sent to the Irish bishops of the distressed districts without any unnecessary delay.

"Yours truly in Christ,

"† LAWRENCE S. McMAHON,

"Bishop of Hartford."

The result of this appeal was a generous contribution for the relief of Ireland's distress, the amount forwarded to the Irish bishops being $23,764.81.

Bishop McMahon's exacting and unceasing labors to promote the welfare of his diocese, in the construction of the cathedral, in making frequent visitations of the parishes within his jurisdiction, preaching and confirming, and in personally attending to the innumerable and perplexing duties of a great and growing diocese, soon began to make serious inroads upon his health. He was not in robust health during the last few years of his life; nevertheless he complained not, and attended to the manifold affairs of the diocese with scrupulous punctuality. No work was too arduous for him to undertake, though the body, a prey to disease, might rebel. He was a sufferer from uræmia, and with patience and holy submission to the divine will he bore his affliction. He may have had premonitions that his tenure of life was short; at any rate, the summons found him prepared to pass hence into the life beyond. When the angel of death came it was as a thief in the night, but the bishop resigned his dignities and his burdens in the same spirit in which he assumed them—a spirit of unalterable desire to comply with God's will.

The news of Bishop McMahon's death fell like a shock that affected all classes irrespective of creed. While for a few years previous it was known that he was not immune from disease, it was not thought that death would withdraw him from the scene of his activity so suddenly. But a few weeks before he had celebrated the fourteenth anniversary of his consecration in the presence of a large concourse of people and in the midst of his devoted clergy, who had assembled to do him honor from every part of his diocese ; so that when the information was received that the diocese was again bereft of its chief pastor, it was received with sentiments of incredulity. With the hope of securing relief from the sufferings incident to his ailment, the bishop set out for Saratoga Springs to take a course of the waters. But death overtook him on the way. Desiring to break his journey and thus diminish the dangers attendant upon fatigue, he stopped at Lakeville, Connecticut, where he intended to sojourn for a few days only. On August 17th, his illness had assumed a form serious enough to confine him to the house. The best medical skill obtainable proved futile to prolong the life so precious to the diocese. He expired on the night of Monday, August 21, 1893, in the fifty-eighth year of his age. At the dying prelate's bedside were his devoted sister, Miss Rose McMahon, and the Rev. Fathers Leo, O. S. F., Shanley, Bannon and O'Connor.

The remains of the deceased prelate were brought to his episcopal city on the 23rd. As all that was mortal of Bishop McMahon was solemnly borne to the residence which he had left only a few days previously, many eyes were moistened, and many fervent, heartfelt prayers ascended to the Mercy Seat in behalf of him who had ever been to priests and people a father, guide and friend. Clothed in his pontifical robes, the body of the bishop was carried by anointed hands to the Cathedral where it was placed upon a catafalque before the main altar. His genius and executive ability had carried to completion the majestic pile which had become his mausoleum. Before the magnificent altar which he had solemnly consecrated to the living God fifteen months before, lay the lifeless body of as just, devout, unselfish and pure-minded a prelate as ever wielded a crozier. The splendid temple, the superb ornamentation everywhere visible, the beauties of brush and pencil and chisel, all combined to make St. Joseph's a fitting resting place for the great heart that throbbed only with a father's love, but which was now silent with the stillness of death.

The obsequies of the deceased bishop took place on August 26th, with the Most Rev. Archbishop Williams of Boston as celebrant of the Mass.

*Assistant Priest*, VERY REV. FR. LEO DA SAERACENA, O. S. F.
*Deacons of Honor*, REV. FLOR. DE BRUCKYER AND REV. M. A. TIERNEY.
*Deacon of the Mass*, REV. T. BRODERICK.
*Sub-deacon*, REV. T. J. SHAHAN, D. D.
*Crosier Bearer*, REV. E. BRODERICK.
*Masters of Ceremonies*, REV. A. HARTY AND REV. T. CROWLEY.

The panegyrist was Right Rev. Bishop Beaven of Springfield. He selected his text from St. Paul's First Epistle to the Thessalonians iv. 13: "*And we will not have you ignorant, brethren, concerning them that are asleep, that you be not sorrowful even as others who have no hope.*"

"To-day we feel ourselves in the presence of an occasion when neither voice nor expression attunes itself to the deep sympathy of the sorrowing heart. We find that some vibrations of the heart chords cannot be evidenced by word or sob. The trappings of death meet our gaze on every side, for he whom we loved is gone. The reward of his virtues awaits him. O! Lord, give rest to his soul.

"When the terrible form of death stalks unbidden across our threshold and takes such a one, as it has in this case, you cannot but reel and stagger at the blow. Not only does the chapel bell ring out its sorrow, but the bells of the city toll for the honor of its noble dead. He is dead, but his spirit still lives. He still lives in every home in this diocese, vivifying by his spirit, his prudence, and his zeal, every influence of religion. At his tomb we render thanks for his work, especially of the last fifteen years. At the foot of his bier may we not say he has consummated his work, he has run his course and a crown awaits him?

"His labors and works have become a sacred inheritance for us. He has built us a monument that will evoke a prayer from every Christian heart that he will enter into the joy he has won from his Master. Each may select from his character some trait applicable to himself. I might select his undeviating tenacity of purpose. You might envy his prudence. I would rather contemplate his generosity and his unassuming religious devotion to duty.

"The dominant emphasis of all Bishop McMahon's relations with his clergy and people was an adamant will, determined to do what was right in his opinion on all occasions. Look for a criterion over this rich and prosperous diocese. Look at the unity that prevails and all the other indications of good government due to the bishop's great executive ability. As we contemplate the results of his work we can indeed say that God placed in his soul a determination to do according to his conscience and to leave the rest to Almighty God. In our last episcopal gathering, he, speaking of the administration of his diocese, remarked: 'I have difficulties, I presume you have, I try to keep a clear conscience, do what I can and leave everything else to God.'

"We can only express our desire that the excellent condition of the diocese may bring to him in his heavenly abode a completion of all those blessings he brought to his fellow-men. The past in his life brings to us many treasures. Shall we guard them, so that what he has done will be an encouragement to us? Labor without stint, labor with generosity, then we may enjoy all that God has for us in life and in the future. Let us quietly and silently waft to the throne of God a silent prayer that God be merciful to one who so loved and so worked."

The final absolution over the remains was pronounced, first by Mgr. Griffin, of Worcester, Mass.; the second, by Bishop Beaven; the third, by Bishop Michaud; the fourth, by Bishop Bradley; the fifth, by Archbishop Williams.

The remains of Bishop McMahon rest in the crypt in the rear of the cathedral near the dust of his predecessors, Bishops McFarland and Galberry, where they await the glorious dawn of the resurrection morn.

The memorial tributes paid to Bishop McMahon testified to the universal esteem in which he was held. All who knew him loved the man as they revered the bishop. Reserved in manner, his was withal a gentle, kindly and affectionate nature. A lover of all that was good he was an assiduous promoter of whatever tended to the welfare of religion. No one who represented a good cause ever made a vain appeal to Bishop McMahon. From among the many tributes tendered to his memory we append the following: At a special meeting of the Board of Trustees of the Catholic Summer School of America held on August 22d, at the Catholic Club, New York City, the following resolution was ordered to be entered on the minutes:

" *Resolved*, that the Board of Trustees of the Catholic Summer School of America have learned with heartfelt regret of the unexpected demise of Right Rev. Lawrence S. McMahon, D.D., of Hartford, Conn., and deem it a duty of gratitude to give expression to their recognition of the eminent character of the deceased and the invaluable services rendered by him to the Catholic Summer School at its first session in New London, 1892."

" The Catholic Total Abstinence Union, in convention assembled (August 29, 1893), embraces this first public opportunity of formally expressing its heartfelt regrets for a death that removes a wise counsellor, a tender friend, an understanding and sympathetic advocate of its material and spiritual good, and one from whose guidance the union derived sincere comfort and benefit and to whom it was indebted for a watchful and assiduous care that faltered not nor wearied.

"Light, comfort, strength and peace flowed from the full fountain of his enlightened mind, a soul to thousands whose faces he never saw, yet to whom he was a kind, a generous and all-seeing father.

" Brief was his life, but vast his achievements. Strong and clear, his voice called on each and all to prepare in time to tread the way of the Lord. Deeply consecrated as the human agency of divine energy, he was a conspicuously worthy channel of divine will and blessings ever receptive. His care, ever alert to obey and carry out the mandate, ever eager by sympathy and service to fulfill the useful and the holy. His was a practical and pious nature. He recognized that he serves God best who serves Him by prayer, by precept and by work."

" Bishop McMahon was essentially a successful financier and organizer. He was a scholar, too, deeply versed in the problems of theology and philosophy and widely read in the works of the best literary, scientific and scriptural writers. It was a rare treat for one who was himself somewhat acquainted with classic writings to spend a social hour with Bishop McMahon, and to drink in the wonderful streams of knowledge that flowed from his mind. He was not an extensive writer, nor yet a frequent preacher, and many thought because of that he was not a profound scholar; but he was. His principal application, owing to the peculiar conditions with which he found himself surrounded on assuming the administration of the diocese, was in the direction of its material development; and in this direction his work will live after him. The magnificent cathedral of St. Joseph, which he found an irregular and shapeless pile on his arrival in Hartford, was finished and consecrated under his administration, and stands to-day a monument to his wonderful executive powers and financial resources. It was a stupendous work, this bringing to completion such a magnificent edifice within a dozen years, paying everything as the debt was contracted, and consecrating it to its divine use with no hand of mammon free to call it back from its worshipful objects.

"In another way, however, Bishop McMahon will be most sincerely mourned by all. He was the father of his flock, and his kindly heart brought him into the closest and tenderest relations with them all. He was the friend of the priest, and no man who ever wore the cloth found in him other than a tender counsellor, a sincere adviser and a kindly father. There is many a priest who can testify to his spontaneous generosity, his tender sympathy and his unswerving kindness, and who owes much of his success in a material and spiritual way to the guidance and advice of the departed prelate. To the laymen of his charge he was ever kindly and considerate, watchful of their interests, solicitous of their wants and prodigal of his service. He watched over them as tenderly as ever shepherd in Israel guarded his flocks, and he was perhaps nearer to them in a personal sense than any of the prelates who had preceded him in the administration of the diocese."

Wisdom, kindness, and justice marked the administration of Bishop McMahon. Under his prudent, paternal rule the diocese flourished and reached a degree of prosperity that placed it among the first dioceses of the United States. Humble, modest and unassuming, he quietly advanced the interests of religion and made many and generous sacrifices for the spread of the truth. He was courageous and patient in the face of great obstacles and unshaken in his confidence in divine Providence. He endeared himself to the clergy and laity, who regarded him as an able, upright ruler, a wise counsellor and a kind father.

## RIGHT REV. M. A. TIERNEY, D.D.,

### THE PRESENT BISHOP OF HARTFORD.

THE sixth and present Bishop of Hartford was born at Ballylooby, County Tipperary, Ireland, on September 29, 1839. At the age of eight years he came to this country with his parents, who settled at Norwalk, Connecticut. At an early age he entered St. Thomas' College, Bardstown, Ky. He completed his theological studies at St. Joseph's Provincial seminary, Troy, N. Y., where he was ordained to the holy priesthood by Bishop Conroy, of Albany, on May 26, 1866. After his ordination he was stationed in Providence, R. I., where he discharged the duties of rector of the cathedral. He occupied also the position of Chancellor to Right Rev. Bishop McFarland. While at Providence he erected the school of the Christian Brothers. From Providence he was transferred to New London to succeed the Rev. Father O'Connor as rector of St. Mary's, Star of the Sea. While here Father Tierney continued the work of building the church, but before the edifice was completed he was removed to Stamford, where he labored with great success for three years. St. Peter's parish, Hartford, now became the theatre of his labors, and his zeal was manifested in the erection of the convent and in building an addition to the parochial school. After a residence in Hartford of more than six years, Father Tierney was appointed pastor of St. Mary's parish, New Britain, in 1883, in succession to the Rev. Hugh Carmody, D.D. Here he built a magnificent stone church and purchased ground for a new cemetery.

James Rinardy with
+ M. Tierney
Bp of Hartford

Father Tierney received from the Apostolic Delegate, Mgr. Satolli, the formal notification of his appointment as Bishop of Hartford on Thursday, January 18, 1894. The solemn ceremony of consecration took place in St. Joseph's cathedral on February 22, 1894, in the presence of an assemblage of thousands who had gathered to do honor to the new prelate. The officers of the consecration services were :

Consecrator.—Most Rev. Archbishop Williams, Boston.

Assistant Bishops.—Bishop Beaven, of Springfield, and Bishop Harkins, of Providence.

Assistant Priest.—Rev. John Edwards, New York.

Deacon.—Rev. John Duggan, Waterbury.

Subdeacon.—Rev. William Slocum, Norwalk.

Notary.—Rev. Florimond De Bruckyer.

Chaplains to the Bishop-elect.—Rev. J. A. Mulcahy, Waterbury, and Rev. T. Broderick, Hartford.

Master of Ceremonies.—Rev. J. B. Dougherty, Mystic

Assistants.—Rev. M. May, New Britain, and Rev. M. Sullivan, New Haven.

Crozier Bearer.—Rev. R. Carroll, Bridgeport.

Mitre Bearer.—Rev. C. McCann, Bridgeport.

Candle Bearer.—Rev. T. Shanley, New Haven.

Book Bearer.—Rev. E. O'Connell, New Haven.

Gremiale Bearer.—Rev. J. Curtin, New Haven.

Censer Bearer.—Rev. T. Keena, Stamford.

Acolytes.—Rev. J. Broderick, Meriden, and Rev. M. McGivney, Middletown.

The preacher of the consecration sermon was Right Rev. Bishop Bradley, of Manchester, N. H. In concluding his eloquent discourse, he thus addressed the new bishop:

" And, Right Rev. Father and co-laborer in this cherished ecclesiastical province, having elected, as you have, to be consecrated to the episcopate on the day on which the church commemorates the founding by St. Peter of the ancient See of Antioch, let us pray that in taking ' heed of the flock over which the Holy Ghost hath placed you bishop,' you may be found a faithful imitator of the Prince of the apostles, so that when the time will have come when in God's providence you will lay down the pastoral staff, you may receive from the Prince of pastors, ' a never-fading crown of glory.' "

In June, 1895, Bishop Tierney made his *ad limina* visit to Rome, leaving the administration of the affairs of the diocese in charge of Very Rev. John A. Mulcahy, whom he had appointed his Vicar General on September 11, 1894. Since his return from Rome he has made a canonical visitation of the parishes of the diocese. Among the institutions founded by Bishop Tierney, and which are evidence of his zeal, are St. Thomas' Little Seminary and St. Francis' Hospital, both of Hartford.

At the convention of the National Total Abstinence Union held at Boston in August, 1898, Bishop Tierney was unanimously elected National President.

# PARISH AND MISSION CHURCHES.

WE enter now upon a most important section of our work. Much of the information given in the following pages came to the writer through the kindness of local rectors to whom his sincere thanks are cordially tendered. In many instances there is a woeful absence of records bearing on early Catholic history; where such is the case the writer has been obliged to rely upon the testimony of those who were a part of the stirring and epoch-making events of half a century ago. "Every year the means of remedying the deficiency in historical records of the early days of Catholicity grows more difficult," said the *Freeman's Journal*, March 31, 1883. "Old men decay like old landmarks; and important facts never reduced to writing are forgotten with the remembrance of the men who knew them. Most of us are too busy now to realize the preciousness of these perishing records. But in time to come, when a complete history of the Catholic church in the United States will be demanded, it will be too late to make anything but a patchwork out of half-remembered traditions.

"A knowledge of the history of the church in this country would be most useful to the rising generation, whose reverence and love would be quickened by the knowledge of past sufferings and triumphs. To know of the sacrifices which each stone in the old churches cost would make them sacred in many thoughtless eyes that now regard their existence as "matters of course." It is not a smattering of history—a record of impossible battles, in which the British always lost thousands to ten Americans, or when in later years, the Federal troops always conquered, even when defeated, or *vice versa*—that we need in our Catholic schools, but the teaching of facts relating to the growth of the church. Of course, the history of battles and political changes must have its place; but what would we say of the Christian schoolmaster, in the reign of Constantine, who would tell only of the eagles, not of the victories of the catacombs?

"The teachers of our children tell them at times of the saints and martyrs who lived and died long ago, of the great men who reflected the spirit of the church, but of the great men who are nearer to them, and whose presence left its marks on the life around them, there is little said.

"But we are told we must build up; then we can proceed to ornament and embellish. The process of building is ever going on; the time of bricks and mortar is not yet past. But shall we bury them under all this brick and mortar? Shall the progress of the church be only a material progress—a progress over which the statistician shall rejoice when he writes of so many churches, so many institutions? If no heed is given to the encouragement of learning and of research, there will be no ornament when the time for embellishment comes, for there will be no artists; nor can we consider the work of the Catholic historian or publicist as merely ornamental. It is vital; for the purpose of defence, of keeping zeal warm, of exciting imitation, it is most important."

The Rev. A. A. Lambing, the historian of the diocese of Pittsburg and Allegheny, has given expression to the common experience of all searchers after early Catholic historical information.

"Materials (for a diocesan history) are meagre, are scattered in many places and collected with difficulty; for the first priests on the mission were content to labor and to leave the record of their deeds to God, and there was yet no local Catholic periodical by which they might have been permanently recorded and transmitted to future generations. Hence we have to depend upon tradition for many things, and while there are few persons left to transmit it from the beginning, even their accounts do not always agree, and tradition is found at variance with tradition. In our own day the history of the church in our midst is being made, events are transpiring before our eyes, and it is difficult to estimate them at their proper value. The actors are yet on the stage, and it is a delicate matter to speak of them always in such a manner as to give entire satisfaction and generally impossible not to speak of them at all.

"Another difficulty is the impossibility of avoiding a certain degree of sameness in the description of the churches and the sketches of the congregations, which must of necessity resemble each other in many respects."

In the presentation of the following sketches we deem it conducive to clear arrangement to divide the diocese into eight districts, corresponding to the number of counties in the State, namely, Hartford, Fairfield, Litchfield, Middlesex, New Haven, New London, Tolland and Windham districts. In each district we shall present first the church or churches located in the county seat, and then take the remaining parishes in alphabetical order.

### I. HARTFORD DISTRICT.

| | | | |
|---|---|---|---|
| Hartford. | Plainville. | Hazardville. | Thompsonville. |
| Bristol. | Poquonock. | Kensington. | Unionville. |
| Broadbrook. | Southington. | Manchester. | Wethersfield. |
| Collinsville. | South Manchester. | New Britain. | Windsor Locks. |
| East Hartford. | Tariffville. | | |

---

The first Catholics to reside in Hartford of whom there is any record, were thirteen Acadian refugees or French Neutrals, who were allotted to the town by an Act of the General Assembly, January, 1756. The selectmen of the towns in which these hapless exiles were billeted were directed to care for them and not to permit them to leave the towns to which they had been assigned without written permission. By a vote of the town, December 6, 1757, the selectmen of Hartford were directed to build a house for the French strangers and to furnish them with employment, if possible. The local records are otherwise silent concerning these poor people, with the exception of an entry of date December 26th, 1759, which informs us, that Mr. Robert

Nevins was awarded twenty shillings for rent and damages which his building sustained during its occupancy by the French. What became of them? History furnishes no information. We can only hope that they were among the two hundred and forty Acadians, who found their way back to Nova Scotia. There is an interesting tradition that two Acadian priests lived near Hartford, one on the Bloomfield, the other on the Windsor road.

It is also a matter of historical record that a number of French prisoners captured in the wars against Canada were immured in prison at Hartford for some time.

We have also elsewhere adverted to the presence in Hartford at the close of the last century of a priest, the Rev. Ambrose Jean Sougé, who was the chaplain of the family of the Visconnte De Sibert Cornillon, an exile of the French Revolution. The Rev. John Thayer also visited Hartford, as did the Rev. Francis Matignon, D. D., and the Rev. Virgil Barber.

In 1823, the Catholics of Hartford were sufficiently numerous to forward a petition to Bishop Cheverus of Boston with the request that he honor them with a visit. They were evidently attached to their faith, and eagerly desirous of receiving the consolations of religion. To their petition the bishop sent the following reply:

BOSTON, February 7th, 1823.

To the Roman Catholics residing at and near Hartford. My beloved friends and children in Jesus Christ :

Your letter of the 3d inst. has been duly received, and has afforded me great gratification. I wish I could go immediately and pay you a visit, but it is out of my power to go till after Easter. I shall give you notice a fortnight before my going. In the meantime, you will do well to procure a room and meet every Sunday to perform together your devotions. Let one who reads well and has a clear voice, read the prayers of Mass, a sermon, or some instruction out of a Catholic book. If you are destitute of books, let me know, and I shall send some at the first opportunity.

During the ensuing Lent, which is to begin next Wednesday, flesh meat is allowed Sundays, Mondays, Tuesdays and Thursdays, except the last, or Holy Week, but only once a day except on Sundays.

I am happy to hear that you openly profess your religion. Never be ashamed of it, nor of its practices ; and above all, do honor to it by irreproachable conduct. Be sober, honest and industrious ; serve faithfully those who employ you, and show that a good Catholic is a good member of society, that he feels grateful to those who are kind to strangers, and sincerely loves his brethren of all persuasions, though he strictly adheres to the doctrines of his own church. It is thus, my beloved friends, that you will silence prejudice and win the esteem and favor of all the inhabitants of this hospitable country. Be assured that nothing I can do will be wanting on my part to promote your spiritual welfare. At my first visit we may fix upon regular periods when one of my reverend brethren, or myself, will go to administer to you the sacred rites of our holy religion. With affectionate and paternal regard, and fervently imploring upon you all the blessings of the Father, the Son, and the Holy Ghost,

I remain your friend and pastor,

✝ JOHN CHEVERUS, Bishop of Boston.

Bishop Cheverus was soon able to redeem his promise to the unbounded joy of his petitioners. In May, 1823, he paid a visit to Hartford, and offered the holy sacrifice of the Mass in the Hall of Representatives, now the Common Council Chamber. For this courtesy, the bishop was indebted to the kindness and liberality of Col. James Ward and Mr. Samuel Tudor. God, indeed, works in wondrous ways. Each of these gentlemen gave a descendant to the religion whose consecrated representative they befriended on that occasion. From the baptismal register of Bishop Cheverus we learn that at this time he conferred the sacrament of baptism in Hartford, Vernon, and East Hartford. The records are as follows:

*Hartford, May 25, 1823.* I baptized Francis Joseph Clerc, born April 18th, son of Laurent and Elizabeth Clerc. Sponsors—Francois Clerc, an uncle, for Calvin White, by proxy, and ———. † JOHN CHEVERUS.

*Vernon, May 25, 1823.* I baptized Mary, born 20th, daughter of John and Bridget Mulligan. Sponsors—Patrick McManus and Mary Mulligan. † JOHN CHEVERUS.

*East Hartford, May 25, 1823.* I baptized Robert, born February 26th, son of Isaiah and Phœbe Webb. Sponsors—Patrick McManus and ———. † JOHN CHEVERUS.

Laurent Clerc was born in La Balme, near Lyons, France, December 26, 1785. He was the son of the mayor of the commune, and when a year old, was badly injured by falling into the fire. By the accident he lost the sense of smell and hearing. When twelve years old he was placed under the tuition of the Abbé Sicard in Paris, under whose instruction he made rapid progress. In 1805 he was appointed a tutor, and in 1806 received the appointment as professor. In 1815 he visited England, where he met the Rev. Dr. Gallaudet, who induced him to come to the United States and establish a deaf-mute institution. He arrived in New York in August, 1816, and on April 15, 1817, opened his institute at Hartford. He retired from the control of the asylum in 1858. In 1819 he married Elizabeth Boardman, a deaf mute, by whom he had several children, none of whom was afflicted. The eldest son became an Episcopalian clergyman.[1]

Besides those mentioned above, the Catholics who resided in Hartford and vicinity at the time of Bishop Cheverus' visit were James Chaswell, John Martin and wife, Thomas, Mary, Ann and Bridget McKiernan (or McCarron). Among the Catholics who came to Hartford soon after were Mrs. Alice Mulligan and her sister, Catharine Preston, who came to Glastonbury in 1824, Betsy and Thomas Crosby, Hugh McNamara, Arthur, Elizabeth and John McAstee, James and William Cody, Mary Twomey, Denis Callahan and wife, Mrs. Sarah Willey, Mrs. Margaret Moore, Edward Monahan, Thomas Cranny, Michael Kelly, Owen Shields, Edward McNally, James McManus, his wife and his brother Thomas and wife.[2]

Mrs. Alice Mulligan, mentioned above, had the honor of giving the first Hartford young man to the holy priesthood, the Rev. John Mulligan, D. D. Graduating from Holy Cross College in 1850, he began his studies at St. Mary's Seminary, Baltimore. In 1852 he was sent to the College of the Propaganda at Rome, where, having received the Doctorate in Divinity, he was

[1] *Appleton's Cyclopædia of American Biography.*

[2] Some of these names are taken from the Hon. Thomas McManus' *Historical Sketch of the Catholic Church in Hartford,* 1880.

ordained in 1856. He served successively in Providence, Falls Village and Norwalk, where he died in 1862.

The Catholics of Hartford were again consoled and strengthened by the ministrations of their holy religion in 1827, when the Very Rev. John Power, D.D., of New York, who stopped at Hartford on his way to and from the canal at Enfield, whither he had been called to attend a sick laborer. "He said Mass in a house that stood opposite the head of Grove street," says the Hon. Mr. McManus, "in the rear from Main street and overlooking the old Centre church burying-ground. He baptized some children and visited several Catholics living at Wapping, on the east side of the river."

The year following the visit of Rev. Dr. Power, 1828, the Rev. R. D. Woodley was dispatched to Hartford by Bishop Fenwick, of Boston. He offered the Holy Sacrifice in the house of John Mulligan, which still stands, No. 34 Village street. Father Woodley informed Bishop Fenwick by letter that the gentleman who sold the church lot to Mr. Taylor, and which was afterwards conveyed to the Bishop in trust, could not give a good deed of the same; consequently, it was relinquished and another purchased in a more eligible location—a better lot in every respect. A satisfactory deed of this lot was made out and forwarded to Bishop Fenwick.

The close of 1828 saw Connecticut without a priest: Father Fitton was at Pleasant Point, Maine; Father Woodley was at Providence, and Father Wiley at Boston.

On the 9th of July, 1829, Father Woodley paid another visit to Hartford, and proceeded to the Enfield canal. Notice of his arrival amongst them having become widely circulated, a large concourse of all denominations attended Mass on Sunday. He baptized several children, admitted a considerable number to the Holy Communion, and the greater number received the sacrament of penance. He returned to Hartford on Monday, 12th, where he baptized several children. He set out on the same day for New Haven and New London. From his report to Bishop Fenwick we glean that during these missionary visits Father Woodley baptized at Hartford, adults and children, twenty-five; at New Haven, two; and at New London, two.

Synchronous with the last visit of Father Woodley to Hartford, was that of Bishop Fenwick, who arrived on July 10, 1829, and took lodgings at the City Hotel. The chief object of his visit was to examine the old church of the Episcopalians, of which they were desirous of disposing, as their new church was nearly completed. The trustees asked $500 for the church and $400 for the organ. Having examined the church the bishop was pleased with it.[1] He held conferences with Mr. Deodat Taylor, a convert, and with Mr. Samuel Tudor, a vestryman of the church. Bishop Fenwick urged the latter to donate the old church to the Catholics, but his overtures met with failure,

---

[1] Bishop Brownell, the Protestant Episcopal bishop, was present when Bishop Fenwick was examining the church. In the course of the conversation, Bishop Brownell remarked: "Well, Bishop Fenwick, as we have a fine new church building we will let you have the old one." Bishop Fenwick retorted, "Yes, and you have a fine new religion, and we will keep the old one."

as Mr. Tudor, while well disposed to make the gift, respectfully informed the bishop that he was only one of many concerned.

On July 11th, Bishop Fenwick approved of the *Catholic Press*, the first number of which appeared on that date. He wrote two articles for this issue, one in reply to an article in a Protestant journal of the same date, entitled *Romanism in Connecticut*. On Sunday, 12th, Bishop Fenwick offered the Holy Sacrifice of the Mass in the office of the *Catholic Press*, No. 204 Main Street, corner of Pearl, at which nearly all of the Catholics assisted, and preached on the gospel of the day. In the evening, at 6 o'clock, he repaired to the State House, which he rented for two dollars, and preached an eloquent discourse on the forgetfulness of God as being the cause of man transgressing the law. The discourse produced a happy effect. It was delivered in the very apartment in which the celebrated Hartford convention was held.

Under date of July 13th, the bishop wrote in his Journal: "The spirit of inquiry increases; people enter warmly into the subject of religion. They come to the printing office every night to confer with the bishop. Splendid prospect for religion in Hartford."

During this sojourn in Hartford Bishop Fenwick was not altogether occupied in spiritual duties, and in completing arrangements for the purchase of the church. He found time to defend the church in the *Catholic Press* from sectarian attacks. From a editorial in the second number of that journal, July 18, 1829, we quote a paragraph which discloses the conciliatory attitude of the bishop:

"The editor of the *Episcopal Watchman*, in last Saturday's paper, seems to be greatly disposed to pick a quarrel with us; but on our part we do assure him, that we are not inclined to any such business. Our views are altogether pacific. We wish, if possible, to live on good terms with all our neighbors, and especially with those of his communion. They have generally treated us kindly, and we shall endeavor to prove to them that their kindness has not been thrown away, and that we, too, can be kind."

On July 14th, the bishop was visited by the principal men in town. He requested a town meeting, as he understood that no building could be moved without the consent of the selectmen. They granted the desired permission. This matter arranged, he authorized the Messrs. Taylor, Francis and Deodat, to purchase the church and the organ and whatever it contained, the bell only excepted, for $900. They were also to purchase a lot nearly opposite as a site for it, paying the price demanded, $1200. He also empowered them to engage a man to move the church to the lot designed. The bishop was informed that the Episcopalians would surrender the church in November, 1829.

The following letter, written forty-seven years after, throws additional light upon this historic event:

*Chancellor Square, Utica, N. Y.,* Decbr. 3, '76.

RT. REV. DR. GALBERRY, O. S. A.

Venerated Bishop :—I do not know how to apologize for intruding upon you except my letter will plead my excuse. I read in the last *Freeman's Journal* an account of the dedication of St. Patrick's magnificent church ; this recalled to my mind a circumstance that occurred in the fall of 1825 or '26—I do not exactly remember which year—(it was 1829) when my late husband, Mr. Nicholas Devereux, and myself spent a Sunday in Hartford. After breakfast a slip of paper was pushed under our door with "Mass at such a number and street." I was then an Episcopalian and attended my own church. In the evening Mr. Imlay, a banker, called, bringing with him a Mr. Ward. Col. James Ward, a Protestant gentleman of very liberal principles. After a while the conversation turned upon religion, and Mr. Devereux, whose first thought was always the church, declared how much he regretted the Catholics were not able to purchase a small Protestant church then for sale; but the Catholic priest, whose name, I think, was Fitton (Father O'Cavanagh), said it was impossible on account of the bigotry[1] and also of want of funds. The conversation ended by Mr. Ward offering to buy the church in his own name and convey it to the Catholics if Mr. Devereux would furnish the money. This was done, and afterwards the money was repaid. . . . . I thought it might be pleasant for you to hear from one who was living of the beginning of the church in Hartford.

With great respect, I remain, obediently yours,

MRS. N. DEVEREUX.

While in Hartford the bishop baptized several children, visited the Deaf and Dumb Asylum, the Insane Hospital and the Episcopalian College. He departed on July 15th, for Boston, having spent five days in the city laying the foundations of what fifteen years later was destined to be an Episcopal See.

It was during this epoch-making visit that the impetus was given for the organization of the first Catholic Sunday-school in Hartford, and the first also in Connecticut. The following notice appeared in the first issue of the *Catholic Press*, July 11, 1829.

### "CATHOLIC SUNDAY-SCHOOL.

"The Catholics of Hartford are informed that a Sunday-school will be opened next Sunday week (July 19th) in the room of the *Catholic Press*, at 9 o'clock, A. M., and 1 o'clock, P. M. It is hoped parents will be careful in sending their children at the appointed time as every care will be taken of their instruction."

As the Catholics of Hartford were soon to rejoice in the possession of a church, Bishop Fenwick gave them the additional happiness of a resident priest, the Rev. Bernard O'Cavanagh, who arrived in Hartford on August 26th, 1829, having been appointed pastor of the Catholic congregation of that city and missionary for the State of Connecticut in general. He was the first priest ever stationed within the limits of the present diocese of Hartford. Within the same territory in which Father O'Cavanagh exercised the sacred ministry alone seventy years ago, two hundred and sixty priests now minister to 250,000 souls. Father O'Cavanagh completed his theological studies at Mount St. Mary's College, Emmitsburg, and was elevated to the priesthood in the cathedral of the Holy Cross, Boston, by Bishop Fenwick, on Sunday, July 19th, 1829. The young priest began almost immediately the visitation of his extensive parish. His first visit was to the Catholics on the Enfield Canal, where he baptized several children, and administered other sacraments, and received some generous contributions towards the liquidation of the debt contracted by the Catholics of Hartford for their church and lot. During his visit, Father O'Cavanagh was the guest of a Protestant gentleman of marked

[1] The religious papers were very hostile to the Catholic religion.

liberality of views, Colonel Norris, in whose hospitable mansion he also preached and offered the Holy Sacrifice of the Mass.

On September 5, 1829, the following notice appeared in *The Catholic Press* of Hartford :

"☞ The Catholics of this city are informed that Mass will be celebrated on Sundays in future, at 10 o'clock A.M., in the room on the third story of Mr. Ellsworth's building. Entrance, 3d door, corner of Main and Asylum streets. Confessions will be heard on Saturday afternoons in said room."

The work which chiefly engrossed the attention of Father O'Cavanagh was the transforming of the old Episcopal church into a house of Catholic worship. While this transformation was being accomplished, Mr. Daniel Barber of Claremont, N. H., an uncle of Bishop Tyler, thus wrote to the *Catholic Press :*

"It is singular to reflect on the difference between the spirit of former and the present time—the Episcopal church (church of England) in Hartford, was once destroyed by a mob at the head of which was a Col. T—t. Now a Catholic church is shooting upwards, with but little noise or opposition. I have lived seventy-three years, in the course of which many changes have taken place. Everything, indeed, but the Catholic faith is liable to change. The Protestant Episcopal church, of which I was a minister thirty-two years, has in that time so changed, that what was truth thirty years ago, according to their doctrine, is now false ! ! ! In my ordination, the bishop with his hands on my head, used these words, ' Whose sins you forgive, they are forgiven ;' this was Protestant doctrine at that period ; but I find none among them who believe it at this day.

" That your pious exertions together with those of your Catholic brethren in Hartford, may prove successful in chasing away that spiritual darkness, which has so long held its complete empire over the souls of men, is the most sincere wish of your very devoted servant.                DANIEL BARBER."

*Sept. 3d, 1829.*

From the time of Father O'Cavanagh's arrival till the dedication of the renovated church, the Catholics attended divine services in Masonic Hall near the corner of Main and Asylum streets.

In June, 1830, the church was completed and ready for dedication. It was spacious, really beautiful, and situated on a fine lot in the centre of the town, on the corner of Main and Talcott streets. It was 68 feet in length and 48 feet in width ; had a fine organ, two sacristies, a spacious basement for a Sunday school and a variety of apartments. Moreover, it had ample accommodations for two clergymen, if necessary. The church was named "The Church of the Holy and Undivided Trinity,"[1] and was solemnly dedicated to the service of one God in Three Divine Persons, on Thursday, June 17th, 1830, by Bishop Fenwick. The pastor, Rev. Father O'Cavanagh, was the celebrant of the Mass. The congregation filled the edifice and was composed principally of Protestants. The newly organized choir sang Demontis' Grand Mass. A remarkable fact and one worthy of remembrance is that the organist on that occasion was a young girl of *thirteen years of age.* She not only played the organ, but sang the leading soprano parts during the entire service. She was assisted by her teacher and her sister, who was only one

---

[1] It had formerly been "Christ's Church."

year older. She was engaged as organist by Father O'Cavanagh for one year at a salary of ninety dollars.

Bishop Fenwick preached the dedication sermon, selecting his text from the Book of Paralipomenon, seventh chapter and sixteenth verse: "*I have chosen and sanctified this place, that my name may be there forever, and my eyes and my heart remain there perpetually.*"

The contributions amounted to thirty dollars. The dedication of this, the first Catholic church in Connecticut was a bright and happy event for the devoted children of the faith in Hartford. It was a harbinger of future blessings, a presage of other and still more precious favors from heaven. With mingled emotions of pleasure and delight did that heroic little band hail the event, and to us and to those who will take up our burdens, this day, June 17th, 1830, should ever remain a day of cherished and sacred memory. Commenting on the dedication of the church, *The Jesuit*, in its issue of June 26, 1830, said: "From what we can learn, we have every reason to feel grateful to Providence for the rapid diffusion and unequivocal demonstration of liberality and truly Christian sentiments in that part of the diocese. The day, we trust, is fast approaching when even the local prejudices of sectarian bigotry will be dissolved by the glorious sun of civil and religious freedom."

The first marriage ceremonies performed by Father O'Cavanagh at Hartford are the following, copied from the marriage Record:

| Hugh Woods and Clarinda F. Taylor. | "*1829, December 13th.* Married Hugh Woods to Clarinda F. Taylor. Witnesses, Deodat Taylor and A. M. Tally.[1] B. O'CAVANAGH." |
|---|---|
| Rob't O'Hara and Nancy McLane. | "*1829, Dec. 13th.* Married Rob't O'Hara to Nancy McLane. Witnesses, Ddt Taylor and A. M. Tally. B. O'CAVANAGH." |

On Saturday, July 31, 1830, the Rev. James Fitton arrived at Hartford as assistant to Father O'Cavanagh.

Becoming dissatisfied with his situation at Hartford, Father O'Cavanagh frequently solicited his *excat* from Bishop Fenwick. After giving the matter due consideration his request was granted, and permission to enter another diocese was forwarded to him on October 27, 1831. On November 5, 1831, Bishop Fenwick received a letter, signed by fifty-four Catholics of Hartford, petitioning him to recall Father O'Cavanagh's *excat*, and threatening, in case of a refusal, to re-establish him as pastor and withdraw all support from Father Fitton, his successor. The bishop returned a pacific answer, exhorting the petitioners to peace, union and charity, but refused to accede to their request.

Leaving Hartford, Father O'Cavanagh affiliated with the Diocese of Detroit, where, about 1832, he was attached to St. Anne's cathedral, his labors being chiefly among the English-speaking Catholics. He was afterwards received into the diocese of Cincinnati. On November 11, 1845, he was re-admitted into the diocese of Boston, having a short time previously

[1] The editor of *The Catholic Press*.

returned from Rome. He was assigned as an assistant to Rev. John D. Brady at Cabottville, Mass.

The writings of Father O'Cavanagh, some of which are extant, are evidence of broad scholarship. As a controversialist he probably had few superiors among the junior clergy of his time. By his published explanations of Catholic teachings no less than by his sermons did he dispel ignorance and remove prejudice. He was well versed in patristic lore, and his theological knowledge was an honor to the priesthood.

The successor of Father O'Cavanagh was the Rev. James Fitton (October 27, 1831), a classmate of the first bishop of Hartford, Right Rev. William Tyler, D.D. The three friends, Tyler, Fitton and Wiley, received minor orders on December 24, 1826; were ordained subdeacons on December 21, 1827, and deacons the day following. Messrs. Fitton and Wiley were ordained to the priesthood on December 23, 1827.[1]

When Father Fitton began his pastorate the number of Catholics in Hartford was still small. On June 19, 1832, he reported to Bishop Fenwick that he had in that year one hundred and twenty-six communicants. On July 29, 1832, Bishop Fenwick confirmed twenty-four persons, and, as far as the records show, this was the first time that confirmation was administered in Connecticut. It will not be without interest to place on record the names of the recipients.

MALES.

| | |
|---|---|
| Deodat Augustine Taylor, | James W. Sutton, |
| David B. Flower, | James Henry Moore, |
| Ebenezer Griffin, | John Thomas Rodden, |
| Thomas Kelly, | Peter Andrew Walsh. |

FEMALES.

| | |
|---|---|
| Mary Buckley, | Elizabeth A. Kelly, |
| Mary Monica Lesseur, | Juliana Carter, |
| Arathusa Rose McGuire, | Sarah Johnson, |
| Sarah Griffin, | Catharine Elizabeth Parsons. |
| Martha Agnes Johnson, | Sarah Ann McBride, |
| Mary Sarah Griffin, | Ellen Traynor, |
| Mary Ann Cleary, | Susan Cecilia Sutton, |
| Elizabeth Delia Kelly, | Juliana Kelly. |

The malcontents were still fomenting discord. Bishop Fenwick remained in Hartford at this time ten days, during which he made an exhaustive examination of the status of the parish and drew up a series of regulations which would govern the future relations of pastors and people. He promulgated these new regulations at a meeting of the entire congregation, Sunday evening, August 5, 1832, and caused a new committee to be appointed for the administration of temporal affairs. Discontent still continued, however, but the bishop, by the exercise of patience, and a conciliatory spirit, by firmness mingled with kindness and charity, overpowered all opposition; so that on October 11th Father Fitton wrote, "All well at Hartford."

During his pastorate at Hartford, Father Fitton became involved in the

---

[1] This was the first ordination by Bishop Fenwick in Boston.

famous Hughes and Breckenridge religious controversy which at the time agitated the whole country. It had been alleged that "a young priest from some part of the Connecticut valley" had warned the people from the pulpit of St. John's church, Philadelphia, against reading the controversy. This statement brought forth the following letter:

To the Rev. John Hughes—

*Rev. and Dear Sir:* As I am the only "young priest of the Connecticut Valley" who has visited Philadelphia during the current year, I consider myself justified in calling upon Mr. Burtt for an explanation of the very mysterious statement relating to me, which appeared over his signature in the *Catholic Herald* of the 23d inst.

Referring to the 11th No. of the *Herald*, I find that the Rev. Mr. Breckenridge holds the following language: "I have been informed that Bishop Kenrick did, on the 17th of February last, in St. Mary's church Philadelphia) publicly warn the people against reading the controversy." This misstatement having been corrected by the Rt. Rev. Dr. Kenrick, was acknowledged by the Rev. Mr. Breckenridge in the 13th No. of the *Herald*, though he insisted, upon the authority of a respectable gentleman, that the hearing was given on "the day named" by a Roman Catholic priest. The very respectable informant of this mysterious affair is now reduced to a Miss M——, who, though educated among Catholics, mistook the "young priest of the Connecticut Valley" for a bishop, being informed he was such by "the audience of whom she made inquiry." So says the article of the 23d inst. Let me now, for the edification of the Rev. M. B., and for the information of Mr. Burtt and Lady M——, observe that there was NO "Connecticut Valley Priest" in Philadelphia on the 17th February. I, on that day, was in the city of Washington, and offered up the Holy Sacrifice of the Mass in St. Patrick's church at half past eight o'clock A M., and preached to a highly respectable audience under the pastoral care of the Very Rev. Mr. Matthews, in the afternoon of the same day. If this proves not the entire tale to be a forgery, it certainly reduces it to a paradox.

I remain respectfully yours,     JAMES FITTON.
*Hartford, Conn., May 27, 1833.*

During his tour through various dioceses at this period Father Fitton collected $507.40 to liquidate part of the indebtedness of the church. Father Fitton had for assistants, first, the Rev. James McDermott, who received his appointment on September 15, 1832. He remained at Hartford until his transfer to New Haven in 1832. He was accepted by Bishop Fenwick on September 2, 1831. He received Minor Orders on February 24, 1832, and was ordained sub-deacon, deacon, and priest on August 16th, 17th and 19th, respectively, of the same year. The second was the Rev. Edward McCool, who had been received into the diocese on February 20, 1834, from Charleston, S. C. He was sent to Hartford on February 28th, but returned to Boston on May 31st of the same year, and received his *exeat.* The third was the Rev. Francis Kiernan, a native of the diocese of Ardagh, Ireland. He was received by Bishop Fenwick on October 3, 1832, and sent to Chambly, France, to prosecute his studies. He received Minor Orders on December 21, 1833; sub-deaconship, May 21, 1834; deaconship, May 23d; on May 24th he was ordained to the priesthood. He was sent to Hartford on July 3, 1834, and returned to Boston on December 8th of the same year. Father Kiernan expired suddenly in Washington, D. C., on July 30, 1838.

The first marriage ceremony performed by Father Fitton at Hartford was the following:

"EDW. CASEY and ) 1830, *Sept.* 26. Married, Edward Casey to Ann Phalen. Witnesses, ANN PHALEN ) Corn'l O'Brien and Margery O'Brien.     JAMES FITTON."

The Rev. Peter W. Walsh, who had previously been attached to the cathedral of New York city, and whom Bishop Fenwick received on April 18, 1836, was appointed to Hartford on April 27th of this year, as successor to Father Fitton. Father Walsh reported the number of souls in Hartford as 350 in summer and 250 in winter; in New Britain and Farmington, 12; Tariffville, 24, and in Thompsonville, 20. On June 11, 1837, Bishop Fenwick administered confirmation to twenty-five persons. Father Walsh remained in Hartford until the appointment of his successor, the Rev. John Brady, August 5, 1837. Father Brady was ordained sub-deacon on July 25, 1833, deacon on the 26th, and priest on the 27th. On November 28, 1837, Bishop Fenwick defined the limits of Father Brady's mission to be the counties of Hartford, Middlesex, Litchfield in Connecticut, and the counties of Hampden and Berkshire in Massachusetts. His jurisdiction extended to Middletown and Portland on the south; on the west to the boundary line of New York; on the north into Massachusetts and Vermont. At intervals for many years Father Brady attended Springfield, Cabottville, Northampton, Middletown, Norfolk and other stations. In 1840 he purchased a lot on the east side of the church, upon which he erected a parochial residence. Father Brady displayed great activity in providing for the religious and secular education of the children of his charge. Among the tutors of his school was a Mr. Edward Gillen, whose proficiency as a musician had secured for him more than local fame. Leaving Hartford he went through the West as agent for Catholic publications. Reaching Notre Dame, Indiana, he entered the congregation of the Holy Cross, and in due time was ordained to the priesthood. During the war of the Rebellion he served as chaplain in the Army of the Potomac. He died at an advanced age on October 20, 1882.

During his triumphant tour through the States the illustrious apostle of temperance, Rev. Theobald Matthew, visited Hartford, and for a week was the guest of Father Brady. The Hartford Catholic Temperance Society was organized, and it had the meritorious distinction of having on its roll of membership the name of every male Catholic in Hartford. To promote the social, intellectual and religious condition of the young men of his charge, Father Brady organized the Hibernian Institute, which flourished under his supervision.

During Father Brady's absence in Europe from October, 1845, to April, 1846, the parish of the Holy Trinity was administered by the Rev. T. G. Riordan, a young priest from the diocese of Boston. Father Riordan was an accomplished clergyman, brilliant, eloquent, cultured, a man of great dignity. Prompt in the discharge of duty in every field of sacerdotal labor, he was particularly zealous in the important work of Catholic education. For many years the name of Father Riordan was held in benediction by the Catholics of Hartford; not until the passing of the last contemporary of the young priest did his name cease to be mentioned.

The rapid increase of Catholics in Hartford made a new church edifice an imperative necessity. Immigration had brought hither large numbers of devoted disciples of St. Patrick, a desirable class for church and for state.

"Irishmen were called in to dig the deep foundations of huge factories, to blast the rocks, to build the dams; and when the great structures arose, the children of Irishmen were called in to tend the spindles of the furnace. The Irish are absolutely necessary to the manufacturing success of the new world. Without them the railroads would be uncut, the canals undug, the factories unbuilt.

"Poor, poor unhappy Ireland! the flower of your population, the bone and sinew of your national strength are exiled, and applied to develop strange lands and mix in dust with stranger earth. And yet, perhaps, Ireland is fulfilling her mission appointed in the great system of the Almighty by sending forth to distant lands the agents of a mild and charitable Christianity, as she did in the days of national influence, when her zealous missionaries and polished scholars won for her from Europe, by their great labors and their great talents, the distinctive appellation of *Insula Sanctorum et Doctorum;* Island of Saints and Doctors. Yes, unhappy nation, your very sufferings now conduce, as your affluence and zeal conduced in former ages, to spread the glory of God.

"Wherever the Irish penetrate, they carry in their bosoms the living fire of the faith; they are the votaries and the missionaries of the Cross. They are the same wherever they go—whether to the manufacturing districts of the East, or the untracked wilderness of the West. Their ever-pressing want in a new place is a priest, and when they have enjoyed this comfort for some time in a series of visits, few, perhaps, and far between, their next aspiration is a church, and then a home for the priest. All this they at last accomplish by the force of their warm faith and untiring perseverance, and it is not until they have established their faith, their church and their priest, in the midst of a prejudiced community—not until the priest is *located* among them, ready and able to deal, when necessary, with the surrounding stupidity, ignorance and prejudice, that they may say to themselves: 'We are now at last free; we are now at last independent;' for then the people around begin to open their eyes, come into their churches, hear, and see, and think, and treat their Catholic neighbors almost as 'fellow-citizens.'"[1]

In 1849, Father Brady purchased a lot from J. M. Niles, situated on the corner of Church and Ann streets. The dimensions of the site were 305 feet in length on the Church street side, and 150 feet on Ann street. The amount paid was $3,660. The erection of the new church was begun immediately, and the work progressed so rapidly, that it was dedicated under the patronage of St. Patrick on December 14, 1851. The Church of the Holy Trinity, our first cathedral, was little used thereafter, save for an occasional marriage and baptism. On May 12, 1853, the historic old structure was destroyed by fire. As the conflagration occurred during the period when the Know-Nothing element was dominant in the State, it was attributed to an incendiary. The baptismal register was lost in the flames, but the marriage record was saved and is extant. The lot on which the church stood was sold in June, 1866, to John Poindexter.

[1] *"The Pilot,"* Nov. 25, 1848.

The assistant priest who served with Father Brady was the Rev. James Strain, who was received into the diocese on April 4, 1840. He was sent to Hartford on April 21st, where he remained until February 25, 1841. His successor was the Rev. John D. Brady, who attended also Cabottville, of which mission he was appointed pastor in 1844. The Rev. Philip O'Reilly assisted Father Brady from April until July, 1848. The Rev. James Smyth, the Rev. Luke Daly, the Rev. Lawrence Mangan and the Rev. Peter Kelly were also assistants.

The strained relations that existed between Bishop O'Reilly and Father Brady during the two last years of the latter's life resulted in his removal from the pastorate of St. Patrick's parish in November, 1854. He died on November 16, 1854, after an illness of a few days. His remains rest in front of St. Patrick's church, Hartford.

"In person, Father Brady was of medium height, squarely built, with a clear, light olive complexion, raven black hair, a remarkably sonorous voice, a firm step; and his appearance and demeanor quite attractive. He was precise about his dress, scrupulously neat, not over social in his associations with his parishioners or fellow-citizens, yet by no means haughty or arrogant. All loved and reverenced him with a genuine affection that had no trace of flattery. He hated a flatterer. As a preacher he was plain, persuasive and effectual; always preaching on Sundays, both at Mass and Vespers, precise as to his hours of duty, unremitting in the discharge of all obligations; he never complained of being over-worked."[1]

# PARISH HISTORIES.

### ST. JOSEPH'S CATHEDRAL.

THE history of the Cathedral parish embraces a period of twenty-six years. Its certificate of incorporation was filed on September 2, 1872. The Rev. Joseph B. Reid was the first rector of the Cathedral parish, and John Franey and Edward Lancaster were the first lay members of the corporation. When Bishop McFarland arrived in Hartford after the erection of the See of Providence in February, 1872, he took up his residence in a house situated on the corner of Woodland and Collins streets. The necessity of a new parish in the city was at once obvious to the Bishop; but where to secure a suitable location for the future cathedral became an absorbing question. St. Patrick's and St. Peter's parishes were in the eastern and southern sections of the city, and afforded the Catholics of their respective localities ample opportunities for attending divine worship. Like the course of empire, the population of Hartford was advancing westward. The Catholics of this section were already numerous, were steadily increasing, and consisted chiefly of servants and others who had sundered sectarian ties to enter the Catholic fold.

An examination of various sites resulted in the selection of the property on which stand the cathedral, convent, and episcopal residence. It belonged to James Goodwin, and on July 16, 1872, he conveyed it to George Affleck

[1] *"Connecticut Catholic Year Book,"* 1877.

by warranty deed for $70,000; $10,000 in cash was paid down, and Mr. Affleck gave a mortgage bond for $60,000; six notes of $10,000 each, payable one every six months with interest. On the same day Mr. Affleck conveyed the property to Bishop McFarland. On September 11, 1872, Bishop McFarland conveyed the same site, together with his residence on the corner of Woodland and Collins streets, to St. Joseph's Cathedral corporation. On April 12, 1873, Messrs. N. B. Stevens, Charles W. Cook, and Chester G. Munyan conveyed to St. Joseph's Cathedral corporation a strip of land ten feet wide and two hundred and fifty feet deep, lying next west of and adjoining the cathedral property. The original piece of land purchased from James Goodwin on July 16, 1872, is about 433½ feet deep on the west line, about 416 feet long on the rear (north) line, about 279 feet on the east side, and 401 feet on Farmington avenue. The mortgage of $60,000 was entirely paid and quit-claimed by James Goodwin to St. Joseph's Cathedral corporation on May 10, 1873.

The first work to which Bishop McFarland bent his energies was the erection of a convent whose chapel would serve as a pro-cathedral. The corner stone was laid on Sunday, May 11, 1873, and the chapel was dedicated on November 26th following. Although Bishop McFarland planned the cathedral, he did not live to see the beginning of this stupendous work. He died October 2, 1874. The rectors of the cathedral who served under Bishop McFarland were the Rev. E. M. Hicky, who had charge from December, 1873, to February, 1874, and the Rev. Michael Kelly, from March, 1874, to March, 1878.

The honor of beginning the erection of the cathedral fell to Bishop McFarland's successor, Right Rev. Thomas Galberry, O. S. A., who broke ground on August 30, 1876, on his return from Rome. On September 13th, the same year, he laid the first stone, and the work progressed so rapidly that the corner-stone was laid in the following spring. This event occurred on Saturday, April 29, 1877, in the presence of a vast concourse of people, who had assembled from every section of the State. It was estimated to be the largest gathering of Catholics that had ever assembled within the limits of Hartford, the number being placed at 15,000. When the procession, which had formed at the depot, had reached the convent, the clergy proceeded from the pro-cathedral to the corner-stone with the following officers of the ceremony:

*Master of Ceremonies*—Rev. M. F. Kelly.

*Cross-Bearer*—Rev. J. Mulcahy.

*Acolytes*—Rev. P. McCabe and Rev. M. Galligan.

*Chanters*—Rev. Father Leo da Saracena, O.S.F.; Rev. J. Campbell, Rev. Father Collins, Rev. Father Gilmore, O.S.A.; Rev. J. Fagan, Rev. T. W. Broderick, Rev. J. B. Dougherty.

*Officiating Prelate*—Most Rev. John J. Williams, Boston, attended by Very Rev. Thomas Walsh and Very Rev. Thomas Hughes as deacons. The bishops present were: Right Rev. Bishop Conroy, Albany; Right Rev. Bishop O'Reilly, Springfield; Right Rev. Bishop Shanahan, Harrisburg; Right Rev. Bishop Galberry, Hartford, and Right Rev. Bishop Loughlin, Brooklyn, who preached the sermon, taking his text from St. Paul's Epistle to the Ephesians, ii. 19, 20.

Mount St. Joseph's Convent of Mercy

ST. JOSEPH'S CATHEDRAL

Hartford, Conn.

Bishop's Residence

On a platform near the stone were seated many prominent citizens, civic dignitaries, State and city officials, together with a large assemblage of priests from this and neighboring dioceses. The following is a diagram of the stone:

ST. JOSEPH'S          CATHEDRAL.
Sept. 13,                1876.

DEDICATION OF THE BASEMENT.—The basement of the cathedral was dedicated on Sunday, February 10, 1878. Bishop Galberry officiated at this impressive ceremony, attended by Very Rev. Thomas Walsh, V. G.; the Rev. M. F. Kelly, master of ceremonies; the Rev. S. P. Sheffrey and the Rev. J. F. Campbell, chanters. The celebrant of the Mass was Right Rev. E. P. Wadhams, D. D., Bishop of Ogdensburg; assistant priest, Very Rev. Thomas Walsh, V. G.; deacon, Rev. J. Campbell; sub-deacon, Rev. M. A. Tierney; masters of ceremonies, Rev. M. F. Kelly and Rev. J. B. A. Dougherty. Present in the sanctuary were Right Rev. L. De Goesbriand, D. D., Burlington, and Right Rev. P. O'Reilly, D. D., Springfield. The former delivered the oration from the following text: "I have glorified thee on earth; I have finished the work which Thou gavest me to do; and now, O Father, glorify Thou me with Thine own self, with the glory which I had with Thee before the world was."

Pontifical vespers were celebrated in the evening by Bishop Galberry. Rev. Thomas Broderick preached the sermon from Psalm xlvii. 9, "As we have heard, so we have seen in the city of the Lord of Hosts, in the city of our God. God hath founded it forever."

The venerable Father Fitton also delivered an address replete with interesting reminiscences of religion in early Hartford.

We append a description of the basement of the cathedral:

The height of the basement is 23 feet above the foundations, 16 feet clear. Like the cathedral proper, it has a seating capacity for 2000 persons. The sanctuary, immediately under the upper sanctuary, contains four altars, the high altar in the centre, St. Joseph's on one side and the Blessed Virgin on the other. The sanctuary is 88 feet wide and 39½ feet in depth. There is also a marriage altar and baptistery. In the rear is a crypt containing 16 vaults for the burial of deceased bishops.

The basement contains 18 heavy granite pillars and 34 iron ones, to support the floor of the cathedral. There are 16 feet 3 inches of space between each of the pillars north and south, and 17 feet 3 inches east and west. There are 54 windows, 41 in the body, 8 in the vestry, and 5 others.

The Grotto of Lourdes has been made to represent the celebrated shrine in France as far as possible. The statues of the Blessed Virgin and St. Joseph were imported specially from Paris by Bishop Galberry.

The altars are finished in imitation of Sienna marble, and are very beautiful. The panels of the reredos are beautifully ornamented in diapered work of gold, upon blue and purple grounds. The altar of the Blessed Virgin has a very beautiful statue of our Blessed Lady robed in blue, and figured in gilt, which falls in graceful drapery to her feet. She stands upon a sea of silver, her right foot resting upon and crushing the head of the infernal serpent. The Virgin holds her right hand against the Sacred Heart, and the Infant Saviour with His left hand points to His Sacred Heart, and with His right gives a benediction to the world. In a recess to the west of this altar is the statue of Christ revealing His Sacred Heart to the blessed Margaret Mary Alacoque, who kneels before Him in her religious habit. Upon St. Joseph's altar, the patron of the church is represented as holding the Infant Jesus on his left arm, and in his right a lily. At the feet of St. Joseph is a representation of the Papal Tiara, symbolical of his protection of the Pope and the Church.

The interior finishing of the basement is plain, the walls pure white, relieved only at intervals by terra cotta figures representing the stations of the cross. The seats are of heavy oak handsomely panelled. The sanctuary is ninety-three feet in length by forty feet in width. The ceiling is sixteen feet high. The cost of the building when the basement was dedicated was $100,000.

THE CONSECRATION OF THE CATHEDRAL.—Fourteen years after the basement was dedicated, the magnificent cathedral pile was consecrated to God to be His holy temple forever. The occasion was one of joy and thanksgiving. Through many years the construction of St. Joseph's cathedral had progressed, and the Catholic population of Connecticut had looked forward eagerly to the day, when, the work completed, it might be consecrated to the holy uses for which it was designed, absolutely free from any indebtedness. Sunday, May 8, 1892, marked the culmination of the project of the splendid mother church that was first conceived by Right Rev. Bishop McFarland a quarter of a century ago. It fell to the fortune of Right Rev. Bishop McMahon to complete the great undertaking and to consecrate to the worship of the Most High a beautiful temple, which for solidity of construction, splendor of decoration and grandeur of effect is surpassed by few similar edifices on the American continent. St. Joseph's cathedral is in very truth a magnificent structure, worthy of the importance and fast-expanding proportions of the diocese of which it is the mother church. A notable fact in connection with the occasion deserves to be treasured as a unique incident of the day. It was the simultaneous consecration of six altars in one church. So far as known and ascertained from the most careful investigations such an occurrence was unprecedented in the history of the church in America. It is something, therefore, to be treasured by the Catholics of the diocese of Hartford, and to be impressed on their children, that in their day and generation a ceremonial occurrence probably never before known to the Catholic Church in the United States marked the consecration of St. Joseph's cathedral.

The order of services on that historic occasion was the following:

6 A.M., CONSECRATION OF CATHEDRAL AND ALTARS.
10.30 A.M., SOLEMN PONTIFICAL HIGH MASS.
4 P.M., ORGAN RECITAL.
7.30 P.M., SOLEMN PONTIFICAL VESPERS.

The prelates and priests who officiated at the consecration of the church and the various altars were as follows:

### CONSECRATION OF THE CATHEDRAL AND OF ST. JOSEPH'S ALTAR.

*Consecrator,* RIGHT REV. LAWRENCE S. MCMAHON, D D., Hartford.
*Deacon,* REV. HENRY J. LYNCH, Danbury.
*Sub-Deacon,* REV. DENIS CREMIN, Bridgeport.
*Deacon of the Door,* REV. PATRICK DUGGAN, Torrington
*Cross Bearer,* REV. THOMAS KEENA, Stamford.
*Censer Bearer,* REV. THOMAS PRESTON, Danielson.
*Custodian of the Holy Oils,* REV. JOSEPH GLEESON, Thompsonville.
*Custodians of the Holy Relics,* REV. WILLIAM ROGERS, Stamford; REV. PETER KENNEDY, Norwich; REV. MICHAEL DALY, Thomaston; REV. JOHN COONEY, Colchester.
*Director of Chant,* REV. WALTER J. SHANLEY, Hartford.
*Chanters,* REV. JOHN LYNCH, Hartford; REV. JEREMIAH CURTIN, New Milford; REV. HENRY WALSH, Plainville; REV. WILLIAM LYNCH, Windsor Locks.
*Acolytes,* MICHAEL OWENS, WILLIAM MAGUIRE.
*Holy Water Bearer,* GEORGE DUNN.
*Crozier Bearer,* JOHN DALY.
*Mitre Bearer,* JOHN BOYLE.
*Masters of Ceremonies,* REV. JAMES H. O'DONNELL, Waterbury; REV. JOHN D. COYLE, Stafford Springs; REV. THOMAS A. R. NEALON, Hartford.

### ALTAR OF THE BLESSED SACRAMENT.

*Consecrator,* MOST REV. EDWARD CHARLES FABRE, D.D., Archbishop of Montreal.
*Deacon,* REV. M. RODDEN, Bristol.
*Sub-Deacon,* REV. J. E. BOURETT, Waterbury.
*Censer Bearer,* REV. TIMOTHY SWEENEY, Portland.
*Custodian of Holy Relics and Holy Oils,* REV. JOHN VAN DEN NOORT, Putnam.
*Chanter,* REV. TERRENCE SMITH, Bridgeport.
*Cross Bearer,* JOHN MCDONOUGH.
*Acolytes,* THOMAS MULCAHEY, MATTHEW COUGHLIN.
*Holy Water Bearer,* EDWARD WHITE.
*Mitre Bearer,* JOHN MCKONE.
*Master of Ceremonies,* REV. CHARLES MCELROY, Birmingham.

### ST. PATRICK'S ALTAR.

*Consecrator,* RIGHT REV. PATRICK LUDDEN, D. D., Syracuse, N. Y.
*Deacon,* REV. PATRICK MULHOLLAND, New Haven.
*Sub-Deacon,* REV. MICHAEL MCKEON, New Haven.
*Crozier Bearer,* REV. JAMES O'BRIEN, Bridgeport.
*Custodian of Holy Relics and Holy Oils,* REV. JOHN SYNNOTT, Baltic.
*Chanter,* REV. R. SHORTELL, Danbury.
*Cross Bearer,* WILLIAM FARRELL.
*Acolytes,* WILLIAM MORAN, JAMES LYONS.
*Holy Water Bearer,* ROBERT SHEA.
*Mitre Bearer,* JOSEPH KENNEDY.
*Master of Ceremonies,* REV. JOHN BRODERICK, Meriden.

### ST. BRIDGET'S ALTAR.

*Consecrator,* RIGHT REV. L. F. LAFLECHE, D. D., Three Rivers, Canada.
*Deacon,* REV. MICHAEL TIERNEY, New Britain.
*Sub-Deacon,* REV. JOHN A. MULCAHY, Waterbury.
*Censer Bearer,* REV. JAMES THOMPSON, Taftville.
*Custodian of Holy Relics and Holy Oils,* REV. PATRICK FOX, Newtown.

*Chanter*, REV. F. J. LALLY, East Hartford.
*Cross Bearer*, JOHN MULCAHEY.
*Acolytes*, HENRY KELLY, OWEN McCABE.
*Holy Water Bearer*, FRANCIS CHRISHOLM.
*Mitre Bearer*, JOSEPH LACY.
*Master of Ceremonies*, REV. MICHAEL SULLIVAN, New Haven.

## ST. FRANCIS' ALTAR.

*Consecrator*, RIGHT REV. MATTHEW HARKINS, D.D., Providence
*Deacon*, REV. JOHN RUSSELL, New Haven.
*Sub-Deacon*, REV. A. V. HIGGINS, O. P., New Haven.
*Censer Bearer*, REV. THOMAS KELLY, Ansonia.
*Custodian of the Holy Relics and Holy Oil*, REV. THOMAS COONEY, Grosvenordale.
*Chanter*, REV. ROBERT EARLY, New Haven.
*Cross Bearer*, DAVID MULCAHEY.
*Acolytes*, PATRICK COSGROVE, EDWARD SILK.
*Holy Water Bearer*, KEARON FINN.
*Mitre Bearer*, THOMAS MORIARITY.
*Master of Ceremonies*, REV. ANTHONY McCARTHY, O. S. F., Winsted.

## ST. BERNARD'S ALTAR.

*Consecrator*, RIGHT REV. CHARLES E. McDONNELL, D.D., Brooklyn.
*Deacon*, REV. BERNARD O'R. SHERIDAN, Middletown.
*Sub-Deacon*, REV. JAMES O'R. SHERIDAN, Windsor Locks.
*Censer Bearer*, REV. THOMAS SMITH, Greenwich.
*Custodian of the Holy Relics and Holy Oils*, REV. WILLIAM DULLARD, Hartford.
*Chanter*, REV. WILLIAM GIBBONS, New Britain.
*Cross Bearer*, JOHN MANNIX.
*Acolytes*, JOHN OWENS, EDWARD SHEA.
*Holy Water Bearer*, PATRICK J. O'MEARA.
*Mitre Bearer*, EDWARD HOWLEY.
*Master of Ceremonies*, REV. JAMES FAGAN, Naugatuck.

## SOLEMN PONTIFICAL HIGH MASS.

*Celebrant*, MOST REV. JOHN J. WILLIAMS, D.D., Boston.
*Assistant Priest*, VERY REV. JAMES HUGHES, V.G., LL.D., Hartford
*Deacon*, REV. THOMAS W. BRODERICK, Hartford.
*Sub-Deacon*, REV. THOMAS J. SHAHAN, D.D., Catholic University, Washington, D. C.
*Acolytes*, REV. JAMES WALSH, Tariffville; REV. JOHN CORCORAN, New Haven.
*Censer Bearer*, REV. WALTER J. SHANLEY, Hartford.
*Pontifical Cross Bearer*, REV. FRANK MURRAY, Bristol.
*Masters of Ceremonies*, REV. JAMES H. O'DONNELL, Waterbury; REV. JOHN D. COYLE, Stafford
Springs; REV. THOMAS A. R. NEALON, Hartford; REV. WILLIAM MAHER, D.D., Hartford
*Preacher*, MOST REV. JOHN J. HENNESSY, D.D., Dubuque, Iowa.

## SOLEMN PONTIFICAL VESPERS.

*Celebrant*, MOST REV. M. A. CORRIGAN, D.D., New York.
*Assistant Priest*, RIGHT REV. MGR. JOHN FARLEY, New York.
*Deacon*, REV. JOHN EDWARDS, New York.
*Sub-Deacon*, REV. JAMES J. DOUGHERTY, New York.
*Acolytes*, REV. N. SCHNEIDER, New Britain; REV. C. LEDDY, Hartford.
*Censer Bearer*, REV. FREDERIC MURPHY, Waterbury.
*Masters of Ceremonies*, REV. JAMES H. O'DONNELL, REV. JOHN D. COYLE, REV. THOMAS
A. R. NEALON.
*Preacher*, REV. WALTER ELLIOTT, C. S. P., New York.

INTERIOR ST. JOSEPH'S CATHEDRAL.
Hartford, Conn.

## PRELATES PRESENT.

*Archbishops,* MOST REV. JOHN J. WILLIAMS, D.D., Boston; MOST REV. EDWARD C. FABRE, D.D., Montreal; MOST REV. MICHAEL A. CORRIGAN, D.D., New York; MOST REV. JAMES VINCENT CLEARY, D.D., Kingston, Canada; MOST REV. JOHN J. HENNESSY, D.D., Dubuque, Iowa.

*Bishops,* RIGHT REV. JOHN SWEENEY, D.D., St. John's, New Brunswick; RIGHT REV. LOUIS F. FAFLECHE, D.D., Three Rivers, Canada; RIGHT REV. WILLIAM O'HARA, D.D., Scranton, Pennsylvania; RIGHT REV. BERNARD J. McQUADE, Rochester, N. Y.; RIGHT REV. FRANCIS McNEIRNEY, D.D., ALBANY, N. Y.; RIGHT REV. JAMES A. HEALY, D.D., Portland, Me.; RIGHT REV. MICHAEL J. O'FARRELL, D.D., Trenton, N. J.; RIGHT REV. DENIS M. BRADLEY, D.D., Manchester, N. H.; RIGHT REV. RICHARD PHELAN, D.D., Pittsburg, Pa.; RIGHT REV. P. A. LUDDEN, D.D., Syracuse, N. Y.; RIGHT REV. MATTHEW HARKINS, D.D., Providence, R. I.; RIGHT REV. JOHN BRADY, D.D., Boston, Mass.; RIGHT REV. CHARLES McDONALD, D.D., Brooklyn, L. I.; RIGHT REV. HENRY GABRIELS, D.D., Ogdensburg, N. Y.; RIGHT REV. JOHN J. CONROY, D.D., Curium; RIGHT REV. J. MICHAUD, D.D., Burlington, Vt.

*Monsignors,* RIGHT REV. MGR. JOHN M. FARLEY, P. A., New York; RIGHT REV. MGR. PETER HEVEY, P. A., Manchester, N. H.; RIGHT REV. MGR. G. ELY BROCHU, P. A., South bridge, Mass.; RIGHT REV. MGR. THOMAS GRIFFIN, D.D., Worcester, Mass.; RIGHT REV. MGR. D. J. QUIGLEY, V. G., Charleston, S. C.; VERY REV. MGR. DeREGGE, Rochester, N. Y.

## BENEFACTORS OF THE CATHEDRAL.

*Deceased,* VERY REV. THOMAS WALSH, V. G., Meriden; REV. PHILIP J. McCABE, Hartford; REV. HUGH CARMODY, D.D., New Britain; REV. PATRICK DONAHUE, Lakeville; REV. MAURICE CROWLEY, Collinsville; OWEN and SARAH McMAHON.

*Living,* RIGHT REV. PATRICK MANOGUE, D.D., Sacramento, Cal.; REV. DOMINICAN FATHERS, St. Mary's, New Haven; REV. FRANCISCAN FATHERS, St. Joseph's, Winsted.

*Societies,* HOLY NAME SOCIETY, St. Joseph's Cathedral; ANCIENT ORDER OF HIBERNIANS, Connecticut; SISTERS OF MERCY, Hartford Diocese.

*Parishes,* ST. PETER'S, Danbury, for window.

*Sunday School Children,* ST. JOSEPH'S, Winsted; ST. THOMAS'S, Southington; ST. BRIDGET'S, Manchester.

*Individuals,* VERY REV. JAMES HUGHES, V. G., LL.D., Hartford; REV HUGH P. SMYTH, Boston; REV. W. A. HARTY, Hartford; REV. H. J. LYNCH, Danbury; REV. D. J. CREMIN, Bridgeport; REV. P. P. SHAHAN, Norwich; REV. J. C. O'BRIEN, Bridgeport; REV. FLOR DE BRUYCKER, Willimantic; REV. JOHN SYNNOTT, Hazardville; REV. T. W. BRODERICK, Hartford; REV. JOHN RUSSELL, New Haven; REV. JOHN A. MULCAHY, Waterbury; REV. B. O. R. SHERIDAN, Middletown; REV. T. P. JOYNT, New London; REV JOSEPH M. GLEESON, Thompsonville; REV. P. F. McALENNEY, Meriden; REV. M. M. KEOWN, New Haven; REV. THOMAS A. R. NEALON, Hartford; JAMES AHERN, Hartford; A. H. CHAPELL, New London; JOHN HIGGINS, Hartford; EDWARD LANCASTER, Hartford; CATHERINE McCARTHY.

DESCRIPTION OF THE CATHEDRAL.—The cathedral is cruciform in shape and early Gothic in design. The building occupies a beautiful site on Farmington avenue, removed from the street, and approached by well-laid walks to its three entrances. Its entire length is 268 feet; width 178 feet in the transept, and 93 feet in the nave. It has a frontage of 123 feet. The magnificent square towers are now 150 feet high, but the spires will add 100 feet to this height. The height of the church from the center of the ceiling to the floor is 90 feet. The exterior is of Portland rough brown stone, with cut stone ornamentation, and is not strikingly attractive, the beauty of the edifice being confined to the interior furnishings. Three large double doorways enable one to enter the building, and disclose the tiled vestibule. The square towers, surrounded by their low battlements, recall those of the church of Notre Dame, Montreal.

THE UPPER CATHEDRAL.—*Description of the Ceiling.*—The most prominent feature of the interior is the magnificent ceiling, striking and effective when viewed from the floor, and rich and stately in its beauty when more closely inspected from the galleries.

The ceilings of the nave, transepts, chancel, and over the galleries are constructed from different colored woods divided into sections of oblong panels. The sections are separated from each other by a continuous beam running lengthwise from the center of the nave, and by ribs and arches at the transepts.

The sheeting of the panels is filled and stained, shaded and varnished in light olive, and the planes of the sides and soffits of the arches are of dark olive. The quarter rounds in the angles of the arches are beautifully decorated in mosaic patterns, stained, and shaded with ebony, African wood, and gold. The same materials, with mahogany, are used in the flower decorations at the intersection of the ribs and arches, the case mouldings and the soffits.

The sheeting in the panels between the four great arches at the transept is handsome diaper work, richly decorated with mosaic. The soffits of the great arches are treated in a similar manner. The frames around the picture painted on the ceiling are decorated with ebony, African wood, and gold, while some of the quarter rounds are gilt in full.

The sheeting on the grounds of all the center pieces on the ceiling under the galleries are of African wood neatly diapered in gold. The flowers and center pieces at the intersection of the vaults are decorated with ebony, oak, mahogany and gold.

The wood-work of the ceiling under the organ gallery and front vestibule and in small chapels at the sides of the chancel, are of light English oak finished in diaper work. The sides, soffits, and rib mouldings are of dark oak. The colors are in beautiful harmony in all the door decorations, and add to the individual effects of their treatment.

*Decoration of the Walls.*—Looking from the chancel to the walls of the church, the plain plastering in the nave, transept, under the galleries, as well as in the vestibule, towers, and chancel chapels, is found to be finished in a light olive, while the stucco mouldings are green and gold. The prominent members of the mouldings are finished in ashes of roses, and the ornamental work in the same tint with the prominent parts nearly white. The spandrels of the tracery on the walls around the large rose windows in the transepts, and the one in the chancel, are filled with foliage, painted in light and shade. The walls themselves are painted in olive green and banded with gold. The stucco mouldings and ornaments on the walls and ceilings are painted in light shades, so that the members are bold and effective when viewed from any portion of the floor of the church. The back wall of the sanctuary immediately attracts the admiration of the beholders. It is executed in stucco work.

The wainscoting of the wall is four feet in height. The lower section is of Tennessee marble, matching the pillars. The neck moulding is of twenty-two karat nugget gold, with rough finish.

*The Stained Glass Windows.*—The stained glass windows were imported from Innspruck in a perfect condition, and were presented by societies, churches, and private individuals throughout the diocese. The outlines of the figures are discerned through the outer windows from either side, but it gives but little idea of their beauty as viewed from the interior. The features are so perfect and true to nature that the figures appear like statues in mid-air. Every window is symbolic of Scriptural ideas, and the arrangements and designs are a study, pleasing, instructive, and intensely interesting.

There are thirty-two windows in all, representing eighty-two figures life size, and thirty-two angels. It has been said that St. Mungo's cathedral in Glasgow has a similar but larger collection, but the windows in Hartford when the sun is gradually sinking in the west is a sight never to be forgotten. Those who are interested in excellent glass work will be well repaid for the journey to the city to view them.

The seven lancet windows in the chancel are filled with large figures which appear life-size from the floor, and represent the saintly associates of Jesus Christ. The central figure is the Sacred Heart of Jesus, and on the right, in the order named, is the Blessed Virgin Mary, St. John the Evangelist, St. James the Less, on the left, St. Joseph, St. Peter, and St. Paul. There are two large rose windows in each transept, and a similar one in the facade.

The large rose window in the eastern transept represents scenes taken from the life of our Lord. The arcade openings, eight in number, present the history of the Crucifixion, and include—The Apostles asleep; Jesus apprehended; Jesus thrice denied by Peter; Herod and Pilate made friends; Barabbas released and Jesus delivered to be crucified; Jesus scourged; "Ecce Homo;" Jesus bearing His cross.

The rose window in the western transept is devoted to St. Joseph. The eight arcade openings present scenes from the life of the patriarch Joseph in the Old Law, and include—The Dream of Joseph; Joseph sold to the Ishmaelites; Joseph in prison; the dream of Pharaoh; Joseph established by Pharaoh over the land of Egypt; Joseph enthroned; Joseph embracing his brothers. The life of St. Joseph in the New Law, and the Virgin Mary, form the themes of the sixteen pentafoil openings in this rose window—The Presentation of the Blessed Virgin in the Temple; the Marriage of St. Joseph and the Blessed Virgin; the dream of St. Joseph; the Visitation; Presentation of the Child Jesus in the Temple; the Flight into Egypt; the Child Jesus in the workshop of St. Joseph; the death of St. Joseph. An angel freeing St. Peter from prison is the subject of the central opening. In the central opening of the rose window in the facade King David is pictured playing the harp, and surrounding him are sixteen angels playing upon musical instruments.

The Chapel of the Blessed Virgin has two lancet windows presenting in the four sections the birth of the Blessed Virgin; St. Ann teaching her; St. Dominic advocating the Immaculate Conception.

The chapel of the Blessed Sacrament has likewise two lancet windows. The blessed Julianna of Liege, the last communion of St. Jerome, the miracle of Bolsena, St. Thomas writing the Mass of Corpus Christi, are the themes.

St. Francis's chapel has two smaller lancet windows, one for each side of the altar,—St. Francis of Assisi and St. Thomas of Villanova.

St. Bernard's chapel has two also of the same size representing the martyrs, St. Stephen and St. Laurence.

*The Paintings.*—The vaulted ceiling springs from four tri-clusters of marble pillars. At the intersection of the arches, in the center of the ceiling, is a massive frame of oak, decorated with gilt, containing a circle twenty-one feet in diameter, on which is painted, by the celebrated German painter, Lamprecht, one of the most beautiful works of art in the cathedral, "The Sermon upon the Mount." Thirty figures are represented, life size, and were painted by Lamprecht reclining on his back on a peculiarly constructed scaffolding. The best view of the painting is obtained from one of the triforium galleries. Standing directly underneath this painting in the main aisle of the church you may gaze upon the chapels, chancels, galleries, and all the interior beauties.

The entire rear wall in the shrine of the Blessed Virgin has the largest painting in the building, representing the coronation of the Blessed Virgin Mary. The painting represents Mary, life size, surrounded by God the Father, God the Son, and the Holy Ghost in the form of a dove. On the eastern wall of the shrine is yet another handsome painting, and one that Lamprecht considers his best work in the building. It represents St. Dominic giving the Rosary to the Blessed Virgin Mary. The original of the picture is in Rome. The Assumption of the Blessed Virgin forms the subject of the painting over the entrance to the shrine.

The rear wall of the chapel of the Blessed Sacrament has two paintings. The lower, showing distinctly behind the altar, represents Christ breaking bread before His disciples, while the upper section represents the Day of Judgment. On the western wall of the chapel is another painting representing Christ appearing to Mary Magdalen. Over the entrance to the chapel our Lord is pictured as appearing to the blessed Margaret Mary. There is a painting over each of the four confessionals. The two in the corners of the eastern transept show our Lord performing the miracle of restoring the man sick of the palsy, and the Prodigal Son; the two in the western transept, St. Peter receiving the command of our Lord to feed His lambs, and the woman taken in adultery. Over the entrances at the two side aisles from the vestibule to the nave are two paintings plainly discerned as you are leaving the sacred edifice—St. Elizabeth, of Hungary, distributing gifts to the poor, and St. Vincent de Paul administering to the wants of poor children. Both pictures are intended to inculcate the lesson of charity and generosity to the poor.

*Marble Pillars and their Statuary.*—Twenty-six pillars, no two exactly alike, including four clusters of three, support the galleries and arches. They are of rich Tennessee marble.

The subjects for the capitals in the chapels are: The Baptism of our Lord, the Christian Baptism, Preparation for Confirmation, the Bishop Confirming, the Bishop Blessing, the Bishop Ordaining, the Marriage of St. Joseph and the Blessed Virgin, the Christian Marriage, the Forgive-

REV. WILLIAM H. ROGERS.

REV. PAUL F. McALENNEY

REV. WALTER J. SHANLEY.

REV. THOMAS J. KEENA.

REV. JOHN T. WINTERS.

ness of Sin, Receiving Holy Communion, Renewing the Baptismal Vows, Receiving Extreme Unction.

The twelve pillars that are clustered at the transepts have forty-eight groups in them. At the east side they represent scenes taken from the lives of the prophets Daniel and Jeremiah. The western side is filled with scenes from the life of St. John the Baptist and Melchizedec. The groups are constructed according to Scripture. Over the capitals on the eastern side are emblems of the old sacrifice entwined in the foliage, flowers, and fruit, and on the western side the emblems of the new sacrifice are shown. Each corner presents one construction from the top of the pillar capitals to the base of the statue in the niche.

*Choir Gallery.*—The choir gallery projects in the form of a semi-circle between the triforium galleries.

The gallery front is divided into sections, the middle consisting of a series of twelve-inch panels and the ends of a series of eighteen. The sheeting of the panels, like those in the magnificent ceiling, is light olive oak, stained, shaded, and varnished, while the sides are of polished dark oak.

Handsome Mosaic patterns in ebony, African wood, and gold decorate the panels, and bright gold the ribs and arches. The treatment is finished by a wide band of olive, which separates the panels from the railing, and rosettes deeply lined with gold.

*The Triforium Galleries.*—The triforium galleries, which may be used as chapels for the celebration of the Mass at the same time that service is being held in the lower part of the church, add very much to the beauty and design of the edifice. The ceiling is made of different colored woods, matching in design and arrangement the main ceiling. There are seven arches, supported by a cluster of pillars with capitals of foliage work. Opposite each arch is a double window of stained glass, with designs corresponding to those in the smaller windows in the other part of the church, and in the center of each arcade is a large candelabra fitted with gas and electric lights, which adds a great brilliancy to the galleries and displays the ceiling when the church is illuminated.

*The Organ.*—The magnificent organ of the cathedral was made by Hook & Hastings, at Boston. It is of unusual size, and ranks among the largest American organs. It occupies a commanding position in the front gallery, and presents an imposing front 40 feet wide and nearly 40 feet high, comprising groups of many pipes of largest size, richly decorated, and casing of oak of elaborate and interesting design. No effort has been spared to make the instrument as perfect and complete as possible, and in material, workmanship and tone it has no superior.

*The Episcopal Throne.*—This is situated on the left side of the sanctuary. It is carved out of quartered oak. The front elevation from the floor is fifteen feet nine inches, and it has an outside width of eight by sixteen inches. The center of the throne is a canopy recess, divided into sections of panels. The tracery of the panels is filled in with suitable patterns, and bands finish the arches. The recess is supported by a cluster of three columns and a part of a

fourth added on, making a three-quarter column with partly open and partly
closed panels. Each column ends in a pinnacle decorated with bands and
finials. The columns are partly connected. The canopied hood of the throne
was the most difficult part of the entire throne to execute, as it required more
than ordinary skill to curve its lines and bands and do it artistically. The
oak was modelled out to procure the serpentine lines which ornament it on
the face, while a series of ascending buttresses decorate the sides. The hood
terminates in a finely carved cross, which surmounts the throne. It is of
Gothic architecture and cost $1,800.

The episcopal chair, which stands on the floor of the throne, is three and
one-half feet high and two feet wide on the outside. It is an excellent specimen of the carver's artistic skill. The arched back is divided into two parts;
the upper section consists of two tracery panels, and the lower part is divided
into four sections, each being filled by quatrefoil panels. The cost was $200.

*The Stations of the Cross.*—The stations of the cross are placed between the
windows in the nave and on the side-walls of the transepts and chancel. They
are all in *alto relievo*, and shaded in ivory and bone. The consecration-crosses
are of dark fancy marble, and are inserted in the wall below the stations of
the cross. A candle bracket is attached to each to hold the candles, which
were lighted at the consecration ceremonies, and will be lighted upon each
recurring anniversary.

*The Pulpit.*—The pulpit is placed at the tri-cluster of pillars at the intersection of the transepts and arches, and is an excellent specimen of the carver's skill, in antique oak. The side-panels are of mosaic and diaper effects,
surrounding rosette centers. The pulpit is approached by a broad flight of
steps, with a highly ornate balustrade. The canopy, which also serves as a
sounding board, supports six statues. It ends in a pinnacle surmounted by a
statue, which, like the others, is of carved oak.

*The Sanctuary.*—The set of oak stalls, six in number, extend between the
tri-cluster of pillars and the chancel walls, thus separating the chancel from
the side-chapels. They occupy eleven feet eight inches of space, and are
about four feet high. They have low backs, consisting of two quatrefoil
panels. The kneelers in front of these stalls are very elaborate in design.
Looking upon them from the front, they are three and one-half feet in height.
Each section is built up of four arches supported by columns and filled in
with open tracery, which has such unique and varied designs that the general
effect is unusually pleasing. The treatment is finished by a wide band which
caps the railing.

The entire sanctuary and all the chapels are carpeted with a rich green
carpet.

*St. Joseph's Altar.*—The high altar of St. Joseph's cathedral is a magnificent piece of work, constructed in harmony with the splendid fittings of
the cathedral. It was built by Charles E. Hall & Co., of Boston, from plans
furnished by P. C. Keeley, at a total cost of $12,000.

As one enters the cathedral and the eye drinks in the dazzling effects of
the interior, wandering from the marvellous work of the sculptor's chisel and

artist's brush to the decorated ceiling and stained windows, the altar stands in attractive silhouette, and fills the beholder with wonder at its beauty. The cold, chaste marble, carved in harmonious designs, and relieved with graceful touches of gold, from which the subdued lights are reflected in a mass of brilliant splendor, rises in majestic grandeur to fill out the harmony of detail that characterizes the whole interior. St. Joseph's altar is one of the brightest gems in the coronet that crowns the interior of the beautiful edifice.

The altar is three stories in height. The first story is taken from the floor to the top of the altar-table, the first being enriched by detached pillars with moulded bases and handsome caps. Between these are deep medallions with pillared jams and enriched hoods, all finished with a moulded cornice. The ends and rear of the altar-table have Gothic panels, base, and cornice to harmonize with the front. The second story has a tabernacle, with the safe and metal door, the steps for the candlesticks, flower-vases, and sculptural works. The ends of this story form bases for the niches and pedestals for the sculptural work. Both ends of each niche are moulded in exact imitation of the front elevation. The entire rear of this story has moulded Gothic panels between the buttresses, all being finished on top with a plinth to receive the moulded base of the screen. The third story is constructed with a tower for the exposition, open tracery, screens, and niches on the ends. These niches have vaulted ceilings. The spire over the canopy of the exposition tower is open work, and is the same in design on the four elevations. The entire altar is built on a solid foundation, and the work was done in the most careful manner.

The entire altar front is of the finest white American statuary marble, except the shafts of the detached pillars, which are of the most perfect onyx. The ornaments of the pillar-caps are taken from the foliage of the cedar, oak, and pine. The carving is done with excellent taste and effect, the centre being enriched with the Alpha, Cross, and Omega. These are a full half inch in the face and panels, and exquisitely polished. The background of all these panels is well diapered with pressed vine-leaf grapes, wheat and water-lily, all sunk about half an inch deep, and the face of all being carved with nature. The monograms are half an inch over the face of this diaper work. The faces of the two large round panels at the ends of the altar have Gothic tracery. The panel around this tracery is diapered with foliated tooth flowers, all beautifully carved. The enrichments in hoods over the panels are the foliated tooth flower neatly carved, the ornaments in the spandrels of the circle being carved also. All the plinths, pillars, bases, small pillar-shafts, mouldings, cornice, and plains are hand-polished. The end of the altar-table is one solid piece of American white marble one inch and a half thick, with five crosses sunk in the top and a sepulchre for the sacred relics cut in the slab.

The second story of the altar, containing the Tabernacle, is made of light Sienna marble beautifully polished. The main body of the Tabernacle is of white American statuary marble, with tracery panels of light Sienna marble. The Tabernacle door and safe are in keeping with their surroundings. The door is gold plated and has the letters I. H. S. in the centre panel. The risers of the three steps at each side of the Tabernacle are of white statuary marble. All the tracery and ornaments are neatly carved. The mouldings, carvings and diaper work on this story add to the general beauty and harmony of the whole. The entire work of the second story is of white American statuary marble.

The pedestal and inside of the bower for the exposition is of Italian marble. All the mouldings and plain parts are highly polished, and the carvings and ornaments are flat from the tool. The enrichments are taken from nature, the diaper work in the bower of the exposition being the passion flower done in one inch deep of relief. The virgin rose is carved on all the pillar caps and band at the springing of the bower arch. The crochets and finials of the canopy over the bower are lilies carved in exquisite harmony with nature.

The effect of this wondrous creation is beautiful in the extreme, and the exquisite harmony and splendor of the whole is enhanced by the myriads of lights twinkling from its different stories when the altar is in use. One stands entranced, bewildered, in contemplating the marvelous magnificence of the throne on which the Living God gives His sacred body and blood into the hands of His creatures to be worshiped in the adorable sacrifice of the Mass. St. Joseph's altar is the most sacred portion of the edifice; it is also the most beautiful. It is the brightest setting in all the glittering picture that St. Joseph's Cathedral presents.

*Seating Capacity.*—The large, heavy doors of oak are stained and deeply polished, matching the shade of the pews. The aisle which you enter from the door is seven feet wide. The two side aisles are about five feet.

Between the central and each side aisle are forty-two double oak pews. The building is intended to seat 2,000 persons, but can by close sitting accommodate 2,252.

There are sedelia in the transepts to afford increased sitting accommodations when needed.

*The Chapels.*—At the extreme right of the church, separated from the sanctuary by the wood screen, is the Chapel of the Blessed Sacrament. This also contains a white altar with pillars of Mexican onyx. The reredos does not extend any higher than the tabernacle, and is finished with battlements. The tabernacle has no niche.

The shrine of the Blessed Virgin is on the left of the sanctuary. In its centre, on a marble pedestal placed on an onyx platform, is a very beautiful statue in white marble of the Blessed Virgin Mary. The statue is a gift of Rev. W. A. Harty, then rector of the cathedral.

The chapel in the western transept is St. Francis's Chapel, and contains a white marble altar which has in its panels of the high reredos some beautiful specimens of Mexican onyx. The tabernacle supports a niche for the statue of St. Francis. The altar is the gift of the Very Rev. Father Leo da Saracena, O. S. F., of Winsted, Conn.

The chapel in the eastern transept is St. Bernard's Chapel. It has also an altar of the same size and design as St. Francis, but varying in its decorations  The niche contains a very handsome statue of St. Bernard.  The altar is erected in memory of the late Bishop O'Reilley, by his two nephews, the Very Rev. James Hughes, V. G., LL.D., of Hartford, and the Rev. Bernard O'Reilley Sheridan, of Middletown.  Both chapels are lighted by standards of lights erected in the transepts.

On the right side of the sanctuary is St. Bridget's altar, of white marble and Mexican onyx, of smaller size, but similar in design to the high altar. The wall back of the altar is finished in gold work, and the niche over the tabernacle has a gold crucifix.  The altar was presented to the cathedral by the Sisters of Mercy of the diocese.  The altar on the left side is consecrated to St. Patrick, and was the gift of the Ancient Order of Hibernians.  It is similar in size and design to St. Bridget's altar.

The architect of the cathedral was Mr. P. C. Keeley.

The priests who have been rectors of the cathedral after the administration of Rev. M. F. Kelly are Rev. William A. Harty, March, 1878, to September, 1882 ; Rev. Philip J. McCabe, September, 1882, to December, 1885 ; Rev. William A. Harty, January, 1886, to March, 1894 ; Rev. Walter J. Shanley, the present rector, since March, 1894.

The clergymen who have been assistants at various periods at the cathedral are: Rev. J. H. Ryan, D. D., Rev. J. Larkin, Rev. P. J. McCabe, Rev. J. H. Carroll, Rev. G. J. O'Farrell, Rev. T. W. Brady, Rev. R. E. Shortell, Rev. W. J. Shanley, Rev. A. F. Harty, Rev. F. P. Havey, Rev. W. J. McGurk, Rev. Thomas A. Nealon, Rev. P. H. McClean, Rev. J. O'Brien.  The present staff of assistants consists of Rev. Thomas Duggan, Rev. John L. McGuiness and Rev. Felix O'Neil.  The chancellor and secretary is the Rev. James P. Donovan, D.D.

The population of the cathedral parish is estimated at 5,700 souls, Irish and American.  They are a people devoted to their faith, active in the promotion of every good work and of high social and intellectual standing. Contributing cheerfully and generously to the support of religious works, frequent recipients of the sacraments, faithful in attendance at the various devotions of the church, they reflect honor upon the diocese and are a source of consolation to their clergy.

St. Joseph Parochial School.—The lot on which the Cathedral school is erected on the corner of Broad street and Capitol avenue, was purchased by Right Rev. Bishop Galberry in the summer of 1878.  He began the erection of a school, but died before it was completed.  It was opened for the reception of children in 1879.  The school has eight grades with 830 children. It is conducted by eleven Sisters of Mercy under the direction of Sister M. Benedict.  The school takes high rank among the educational institutions of Hartford.  No better evidence of the scholarship of its pupils need be adduced than the great success that invariably attends their examinations for entrance into the high school of Hartford, and the honorable positions they maintain there throughout their course.  Like many other parochial schools of the diocese, St. Joseph's is under the supervision of a priest specially appointed for that purpose. A contemporary writer says of this school: "The system of education carried on here is one of the best in vogue in any of the public schools in New England. Work is begun in the kindergarten and primary grades and extends through the grammar grades. The boys and girls from the primary up are taught in separate rooms, and so much interest is taken in their studies that even in the most inclement weather but a small percentage of the children are absent. We had the pleasure of listening to a singing exercise in the kindergarten, which was very cleverly rendered and showed that the teacher in charge knew well the work she was handling. In every room, from first to last, there is an atmosphere of culture and refinement, stimulated by the presence and influence of the worthy Sisters in charge of the school. No blackboard nor wall is without its decorative drawings in vari-colored crayon, the handiwork of artists and a stimulus to the furthering of artistic talent in the pupils."

THE CATHEDRAL LYCEUM.—The cathedral lyceum, an organization of Catholic young men, was organized by the Rev. Walter J. Shanley, rector of the cathedral, on August 12, 1894. Increasing rapidly in membership it was deemed advisable in March, 1895, to erect a building for lyceum purposes. This was made feasible by the generous donation by Mr. William F. O'Neil of a piece of land 112x150 feet on Lawrence street. Ground was broken on June 4, 1895, and the corner-stone was laid before a large concourse of people on July 21, 1895. The lyceum was blessed on April 11, 1896, and was formally opened on April 13th. The building affords the members a suitable place to spend their evenings and furnishes them with means of varied amusement.

The object of the lyceum is the moral, intellectual and physical development of its members. Its endeavor is to strengthen them in the practice of their religion, to make them good citizens and useful members of society. A large library of choice works has been formed, and connected with it is a fine, commodious and well-furnished reading-room. The gymnasium has been dedicated to Mr. William O'Neil as a recognition of his generosity. Every effort is made to elevate the members of the lyceum; to this end courses of lectures have been established and classes have been formed in draughting, free-hand drawing and vocal music.

## ST. PATRICK'S PARISH,

### HARTFORD.

THE history of St. Patrick's parish is chiefly the history of the pastorate of the late Very Rev. James Hughes, V. G., LL. D. When Father Hughes received from Bishop O'Reilly at Hartford on November 9, 1854, his appointment as the successor of Father Brady, he began the longest pastorate in the history of the diocese of Hartford. For two score years or more Father Hughes was a prominent figure in the ecclesiastical and civil life of Hartford. During all the vicissitudes of this long period he wielded an influence among all classes that reflected honor on the sacerdotal character.

VERY REV. JAMES LYNCH, V.G.

VERY REV. JAMES HUGHES, V.G

VERY REV. THOMAS WALSH, V.G

and which was always employed for the best interests of church and state. His was preëminently an active life. His term in the priesthood abounded in works that will long survive him and serve to keep his memory green for generations yet to come. Of noble and stalwart appearance, he was every inch a priest. He loved the church, and sought by every legitimate means to conserve and promote her highest interests. Of deep and abiding faith in the sacredness of his vocation, self was submerged in his congregation, and the wishes of the latter became paramount. Father Hughes was a man of strong, sturdy character, and his individuality was evident in all the parochial works of his pastorate. From the time of his ordination, almost, he occupied high official positions in the diocese. As vicar-general and administrator he displayed superior executive powers, and that which rests upon his memory as a glorious crown are the justice and impartiality that characterized his rule. His name will long linger in the hearts of the people of Hartford, and the impress of the master hand upon the works he accomplished will be visible to children yet unborn.

Father Hughes discharged the office of vicar-general during the episcopates of Bishop O'Reilly, Bishop McFarland, Bishop McMahon and Bishop Tierney. He was administrator during the absence of Bishop McFarland at the Vatican Council, and after the Bishop's death in October, 1874, he served in the same capacity until the consecration of Bishop Galberry. Again he was called to the helm during Bishop McMahon's seven months' absence in Europe; and, finally, he governed the diocese during the interregnum between the death of Bishop McMahon and the appointment of Bishop Tierney.

In recognition of his services to religion his Alma Mater, St. John's College, Fordham, N. Y., conferred upon him the degree of Doctor of Laws; and as the Catholic chaplain of the Connecticut National Guard during a summer's encampment at Niantic, he won high encomiums from the civil and ecclesiastical authorities. But the recognition that would have been an appropriate reward of an active, useful and successful career in the priesthood came when the shadows of death were beginning to fall over the form of the venerable priest. Aware of the zeal of Father Hughes in promoting the interests of religion, the Holy See elevated him to the dignity of domestic prelate, but death summoned him hence before the ceremony of investiture. When Father Hughes passed away there went out from the diocese a true priest, a father to his people, one of nature's noblemen. The material works accomplished are still in evidence, and speak eloquently of the brain that conceived and of the hand that directed them.

When Father Hughes came to Hartford he found St. Patrick's parish burdened with debt. He at once set himself to its liquidation, displaying those splendid resources of business tact and energy which ripened in the years of experience that followed. He paid off the debt on the old church, bought the present parochial residence, built the old school in 1865, erected the convent and orphanage attached to the church (the latter in 1855), rebuilt the church after its destruction by fire, and purchased St. Patrick's and Mount St Benedict's cemeteries. He built also an annex to the asylum to be used for an hospital. The financial management of St. Patrick's parish during Father Hughes' pastorate was marked with the same unvarying success that characterized his spiritual administration. It is in every sense a model parish, the most painstaking care being bestowed on every detail connected with its spiritual and temporal well-being.

Father Hughes' sacerdotal career was contemporaneous with the period that has marked the highest progress of the diocese, and he witnessed its growth before and since its division from the coign of vantage of official position.

After forty-three years of devoted labor in the sacred cause of his divine Master, Father Hughes finished his course on August 7, 1895, during the absence of Bishop Tierney in Europe. The large assemblage of priests from this and other dioceses, the concourse of people that thronged the church, the crowds of people who followed sorrowfully the remains to their last resting place—all demonstrated the deep affection of which Father Hughes was the object. The solemn pontifical Mass of Requiem was sung by Right Rev. John Brady, D.D., auxiliary Bishop of Boston, and the funeral oration was pronounced by Right Rev. Thomas S. Beaven, D.D., Bishop of Springfield. The ashes of Father Hughes mingle with those of his brother and sister in Mount St. Benedict's cemetery, Hartford.

The original St. Patrick's church, which occupied the site of the present building, was begun by the Rev. John Brady in 1850. On January 28th of that year, Bishop Fitzpatrick of Boston, who was Administrator of the Diocese of Hartford until the appointment of Bishop O'Reilly, visited Hartford and examined the plans which Father Brady had had prepared for the new church. It was built of rubble stone and was 166 feet long by 75 feet wide. The corner-stone was laid with imposing ceremonies on July 1st, 1850, and the dedication took place on December 14, 1851. Right Rev. Bishop Fitzpatrick, of Boston, was the celebrant of the Pontifical Mass, and the famous Augustinian priest, the Rev. Dr. Moriarty, preached the sermon. The Bishop of Boston also officiated at Vespers, and the discourse was pronounced by Bishop O'Reilly. The latter's comment on the occasion, as found in his Journal, was: "The ceremony was grand, worthy of the church." On January 23, 1875, a conflagration laid this fine edifice in ruins.

With the destruction of the church the people were left without a place for divine services, and the Holy Sacrifice was offered up for the faithful in St. James' chapel, the first Mass in which was celebrated on the morning after the disaster, which was Sunday, while the smoldering fire from the blackened ruins of the church added to the grief of the people. For some time afterwards the 10.30, or Parochial Mass was celebrated in Allyn Hall; but scarcely had the ruins of the old church become cold ere the energetic pastor, Very Rev. Father Hughes, began to take measures for the erection of an edifice, which in beauty of architecture and thoroughness of workmanship would surpass the old one. The work was begun on the 7th of July, 1875, and in the astonishingly short space of three months and twelve days, actual working time, the chancel gable, 88½ feet, the side walls 50 feet high, and the tower and gable to the height of the side walls, were completed.

ST. PATRICK'S CHURCH,

Hartford, Conn.

St. Patrick's church, risen Phœnix-like from the ashes, was solemnly dedicated to the service of God with unusual pomp, accompanied with the most impressive ceremonies of the church, on Sunday, November 19, 1876, by Bishop Galberry. The procession, emerging from the vestry door, moved up Ann street to the main entrance, where it entered in the following order:

Cross Bearer.
Light Bearers.
Acolytes and Altar Boys.
Clergy.
Bishops.
Deacon and Sub-Deacon.
Deacons of Honor.
Assistant Priest.
RIGHT REV. BISHOP GALBERRY, Officiating Prelate.

At the conclusion of the dedicatory ceremonies a Solemn Pontifical Mass was celebrated with the following officers:

*Celebrant*, MOST REV. JOHN WILLIAMS, D.D., Boston.
*Assistant Priest*, REV. F. W. GOCKELN, S. J., St. John's College, Fordham, N. Y.
*Deacons of Honor*, REV. LUKE DALY, New Britain ; REV. E. J. SHERIDAN, Taunton.
*Deacon of the Mass*, REV. FATHER LEO DA SARACENA, O. S. F., Winsted.
*Sub-Deacon*, REV. THOMAS LYNCH, Hartford.
*Masters of Ceremonies*, REV. P. J. MCCABE, Hartford ; REV. D. CREMIN, Hartford.
*Cross Bearer*, REV. P. GOODWIN, East Hartford.
*Book Bearer*, REV. J. J. FURLONG, Rockville.
*Mitre Bearer*, REV. J. CAMPBELL, Manchester.
*Crozier Bearer*, REV. J. RUSSELL, Jewett City.
*Light Bearer*, REV. E. J. O'BRIEN, Middletown.
*Chanters*, REV. J. CAMPBELL and REV. JAMES FAGAN.

The sermon was delivered by Right Rev. Bishop McQuade of Rochester, who selected his text from the eightieth Psalm.

At 7.30 Solemn Pontifical Vespers were celebrated, the following clergymen officiating :

*Celebrant*, RIGHT REV. EDGAR P. WADHAMS, D D., Ogdensburg, N. Y.
*Assistant Priest*, REV. M. BENDER, Cincinnati.
*Deacon*, REV. E. J. SHERIDAN, Taunton.
*Sub-Deacon*, REV. LUKE DALY, New Britain.
*Masters of Ceremonies*, Rev. P. J. MCCABE and REV. D. CREMIN.

The discourse was from Psalm xxv. 8, and was delivered by Right Rev. Bishop O'Reilly, of Springfield. The following prelates honored the occasion by their presence : Most Rev. Archbishop Williams, Bishops Galberry, O'Reilly, Hendricken, De Goesbriand, McNeirney and McQuade. Among the Vicars General present was Very Rev. L. S. McMahon, of New Bedford, Mass., afterwards Bishop of Hartford. Priests had assembled from the New England, Eastern and Middle States to do honor to their esteemed co-worker and friend, the pastor, and to participate in the joy that possessed the hearts of his parishioners.

The crowning glory of St. Patrick's church was its solemn consecration in November, 1885. It was the second church in the diocese to attain this distinction, St. Patrick's, New Haven, being the first. The officiating prelate at the services of consecration was the Most Rev. Archbishop Williams of Boston. Solemn Pontifical High Mass was celebrated by Right Rev. Bishop McMahon, during which the Most Rev. Archbishop Ryan of Philadelphia, pronounced the oration. Right Rev. Bishop Conroy presided at the Vesper service, and Right Rev. Bishop McQuade was the preacher. The ceremonies of the morning and evening services were under the supervision of Rev. M. F. Kelly and Rev. James H. O'Donnell. With the exception of the consecration of the cathedral, the city of Hartford has scarcely witnessed so conspicuous an assemblage of ecclesiastical dignitaries, priests and people. With their pastor the parishioners rejoiced at the realization of their hopes, their noble church edifice relieved of indebtedness; and in recognition of divine blessings received, presented it, a heart offering, to the Giver of all gifts.

On Sunday, September 8, 1895, Very Rev. John A. Mulcahy, Vicar-General, assumed charge of St. Patrick's parish as the successor of Father Hughes. With every promise of a successful career in his new field of labor, Father Mulcahy was stricken down by illness in October, 1897, which has necessitated prolonged absence from home in quest of health.

Before this affliction befell him, however, he gave evidence of his zeal in the erection of a splendid parochial school, the finest in Connecticut, and perhaps in all New England. On September 11, 1894, Father Mulcahy was appointed vicar-general by Bishop Tierney, and who, previous to his departure on his *ad limina* visit to Rome, made him Administrator of the diocese, which position he filled from June 1 to August 18, 1895. During Father Mulcahy's illness the affairs of the parish have been administered by the Rev. John J. Downey, who, faithful to the traditions of the parish, is energetic in promoting the spiritual and temporal welfare of his charge. The assistants at present laboring in St. Patrick's parish are the Rev. J. J. Loftus and the Rev. J. F. Ryan, who is also a professor in St. Thomas' Preparatory Seminary.

Father Mulcahy was born in Ireland and came to this country when quite young. Shortly after his arrival he entered the English and business course of studies in Bryant and Stratton's school at Hartford. Believing himself called to the sacred priesthood, he entered St. Charles' College, Maryland, where he remained six years, completing the course. His philosophical and theological studies were made at St. Joseph's Seminary, Troy, N. Y., where he was ordained to the priesthood on June 17, 1873. His first appointment was as assistant to the Rev. Father Lynch in the parish of the Immaculate Conception, Waterbury, and when Father Lynch was transferred to St. Patrick's parish, New Haven, in August, 1876, Father Mulcahy accompanied him. He labored there until February, 1877, when he was appointed pastor of East Hartford, a mission which included Glastonbury, Wethersfield and Rocky Hill. His labors in this field are eloquent evidences of his zeal and energy. He erected the church at East Hartford and St. Augustine's at Glastonbury, liquidated the debt on the church lot in Wethersfield and collected money for the erection of a church at Rocky Hill. In November, 1878, he was transferred to Thompsonville, which mission then included the present parishes of Hazardville and Broad Brook. For three years he labored in

John A. McLoughlin V.G.

this portion of Christ's vineyard, during which time he purchased new and more eligible sites in Hazardville and Broad Brook and erected upon them substantial churches. His success in Thompsonville is attested by the fact that the parish indebtedness was reduced $9,000, and by the purchase of a lot on which the new church stands. On November 1, 1881, he was appointed pastor of the Sacred Heart parish, New Haven, succeeding the Rev. Stephen Sheffrey, deceased. His four years of earnest and zealous labor there bore rich fruit. The church's indebtedness was reduced $22,000 and sufficient property for a school and convent was purchased adjoining the church on Columbus avenue. On January 1, 1886, Father Mulcahy assumed charge of the parish of the Immaculate Conception, Waterbury. The work accomplished by him from that date to the end of his pastorate will be revealed in part in the history of that parish.

St. Patrick's Parochial School.—"When we consider that the maintenance of the parochial schools of Hartford is wholly by the members of the various Catholic churches, we must one and all admire the cheerful spirit in which these members accept their double school taxation. And again we note with what enterprise they are conducted and with what excellent equipment they are provided. What is good enough for the public school is not any too good for the parochial school, and what advancement is made in education, is as much due to the latter as to the former. They are not 'copyists,' but are originators of the most progressive type. Among their directors are found men of the highest intellectual qualifications and their principals are always priests of thorough scholarly training."

For half a century the children of St. Patrick's parish have enjoyed the blessings of a Christian education. For fifty years have the parents gathered the rich fruits of the Catholic training of their children. Abundant, indeed, have been the graces that have flowed into the parish during these many years. Catholic schools have existed here since 1848. In that year the first parochial school was opened with ten pupils in the basement of the old church. Here the devoted Sisters of Mercy taught an ever-increasing school for ten years. In 1865, Father Hughes erected the school on Allyn street, which in every respect was a model building in those days, and which for over thirty years maintained a high reputation among its sister schools of the city. In September, 1866, the Christian Brothers arrived at the invitation of Father Hughes and assumed control of the boys' department. This school was conducted in part of the building now used as the parochial residence. The growth of the parish made additional school facilities an imperative necessity; accordingly, at Father Mulcahy's advent preparations were immediately begun for the erection of a new school. The property adjacent on Ann street was purchased, and the spacious residence that occupied the site was removed. The work of construction progressed expeditiously, and the building was ready for occupancy in September, 1897. It was solemnly blessed by Right Rev. Bishop Tierney on September 5th, the Rev. James H. O'Donnell preaching the dedication sermon, and opened the day following for the reception of pupils. The ten pupils of 1848 have increased to 1145, the number at present enrolled, and the humble basement has given way to one of the most thoroughly equipped schools in New England. Architecturally, there are schools that present a more striking exterior appearance, but the interior appointments have few equals and no superiors. The system of light and ventilation are unique and leave nothing to be desired in a building in which so many children daily gather. The main building contains eighteen rooms; in the rear, there are two spacious apartments set apart for kindergarten purposes. In this grade there are 175 little ones in attendance. We quote again from the writer whose words begin this sketch: "It is only just that we pay due tribute to the one who has by his indomitable energy and enthusiasm made the erection of this magnificent building possible. This is the present pastor, the Rev. J. A. Mulcahy. Since he took charge of the parish, he has doubled the size of the school, extended the course, added many features of study and in every way made it the equal, if not the superior, of any school in the State."

The success of the pupils in the annual examinations for entrance into the High school attest their proficiency. There are twenty sisters engaged in teaching, under the supervision of the Rev. J. Loftus, to whose efficient management is to be attributed much of the success that attends the sisters' efforts. The members of the parish, the sisters and the clergy have every reason to be proud of their school.

## ST. PETER'S PARISH,

### HARTFORD.

FOR well nigh forty years St. Peter's parish has been faithful to its exalted mission of winning souls to Christ. Zealous in the performance of duty, conscientious in their attention to the spiritual needs of their parishioners, its successive rectors have attained an enviable reputation for priestly energy, and have built up a parish in whose good name its members rejoice.

In September, 1859, St. Peter's parish was set apart from St. Patrick's by Right Rev. Bishop McFarland, and comprised the southern section of the city below Little River. The first pastor of the new parish was the Rev. Peter Kelly, who was ordained to the priesthood on June 13, 1852. Father Kelly had been received into the diocese from the famous Seminary of St. Sulpice, Paris, and spent about nine months completing his theological studies i Bishop O'Reilly's Seminary, Providence. Father Kelly had received the order of sub-deacon on December 13, 1851, and was elevated to the diaconate on the day following. These same orders were conferred at the same time upon the Rev. Patrick Delaney, whose ordination to the priesthood had occurred on December 15, 1851, in St. Patrick's church, Hartford, thus antedating the ordination of Father Kelly six months.

When St. Peter's parish was organized its population was estimated at 1500 souls, chiefly Irish, with a small number of Germans. With characteristic energy, Father Kelly set about securing a fitting place in which his people could attend divine worship, and having secured, through Mr. James Tiernan, an old school building, commonly known as the "Old South Schoolhouse," he had it suitably renovated and appropriately refitted for Catholic worship; and so expeditiously was the work accomplished that the Holy Sacrifice of the Mass was celebrated with joy and thanksgiving on the Sunday following the formation of the parish. As the parish was increasing in numbers, an enlargement of the transformed building became necessary; accordingly, an addition was built, and the structure, as it now stood, was dedicated to God under the patronage of the Prince of the Apostles by Bishop McFarland on December 4, 1859. Father Kelly's next work was the purchase of a frame building north of the church, which he occupied as a parochial residence. A dwelling house south of the church was also secured, and a school erected behind the church. The furniture of this school was of a superior order, and the school itself soon vied with the public schools. Father Kelly accomplished all this work in the brief period of three years. Desiring a different field of labor, Father Kelly was transferred from St. Peter's to St. Joseph's parish, Providence, in October, 1862. He died at Valley Falls, R. I., on February 4, 1868. "Father Kelly was probably the best-known and best-liked man in Hartford. Certainly no person ever lived here to whom our non-Catholic friends would pay their money, by way of subscription, so cheerfully or freely. He was a ripe scholar, an eloquent preacher, and an enthusiast in whatever he undertook."[1]

Father Kelly's successor was the Rev. John Lynch, who came to Hartford from Birmingham, now Derby. In April, 1865, Father Lynch began the erection of the present church edifice. In order not to deprive his parishioners of the privilege of assisting at Mass on Sundays, or to obviate the necessity of removing elsewhere for divine worship, he adopted the plan, hitherto unheard of in church construction, of building the new church up and around the walls of the old, and it was only when the new structure was ready for roofing that the old building was removed; and so scientifically was the work carried on that not for a single Sunday was attendance at Mass interrupted. The corner-stone of the new church was laid in October, 1865, and its solemn dedication occurred on July 26, 1868, Bishop McFarland officiating.

The present rectory was purchased in 1865 from the Hon. Henry Barnard. It was used as a parochial residence for ten years, after which it was occupied for six years by the Sisters of Mercy. After the erection of the convent in 1881, it reverted to the use of the clergy.

Father Lynch gave to the construction of the church his constant and personal supervision. His watchward was "Duty," and the traits that shone conspicuously in his character were exactness, promptness, and love of labor. He watched over the school with truly paternal solicitude, and was ever anxious concerning the educational interests of the little ones of his flock. His love for children was boundless. An accident which occurred while driving through his parish on parochial duties, and which resulted in a fracture of his

[1] *Historical Sketch of the Catholic Church in Hartford.*

collar-bone, necessitated complete rest. Accordingly, he visited Ireland in 1869. The affairs of the parish were administered during his absence by the Rev. John Cooney. The unexpected death of Father Lynch's father rendered the prolongation of his visit a necessity. In June, 1870, the Rev. Lawrence Walsh was appointed Father Lynch's successor as pastor of St. Peter's parish, and upon his return from Europe he was re-appointed to his former charge at Birmingham. An event which rendered Father Walsh's administration noteworthy was the consecration of Right Rev. Bishop Galberry in St. Peter's church on St. Joseph's Day, March 19, 1876. During the pastorate of Rev. Father Walsh the excellent custom was introduced of paying monthly visits to the Connecticut State Prison and saying Mass for and instructing the inmates in Christian doctrine. This work was continued down through successive administrations until the formation of the parish of the Sacred Heart at Wethersfield, whose pastor has the Catholic prisoners under his spiritual charge. The instructions in Christian doctrine were imparted, and are still given by young men of approved character and competency, and the good that has been accomplished among these wards of the State during the past twenty-five years has been incalculable. In July of that year, Bishop Galberry having selected St. Peter's church as his pro-cathedral, Father Walsh, who preached his farewell sermon on Sunday, July 30th, was transferred to the parish of the Immaculate Conception, Waterbury, and was succeeded by the Rev. Thomas Lynch, who served in the capacity of rector until January, 1877. His successor was the Rev. M. A. Tierney, the present bishop of the diocese, who, as pastor, governed St. Peter's parish until June, 1883. During his pastorate, Father Tierney built the convent in 1881. He also erected the third addition to the school, the first part having been built by Rev. Peter Kelly, and the second by Rev. Lawrence Walsh. The splendid organ of the church was put in during Father Tierney's incumbency. It was during this administration that the centennial of the first Mass said in Connecticut was celebrated. This event occurred on June 26, 1881.

Bishop McMahon was the celebrant of the Solemn Pontifical Mass, assisted by the following officers:

*Assistant Priest*, Rev. Augustine F. Hewitt, New York.
*Deacons of Honor*, Rev. Lawrence Walsh, Waterbury, and Rev. E. D Boone, Worcester.
*Deacon of the Mass*, Rev. John J. Furlong, Rockville.
*Sub-deacon*, Rev. John J. Quinn, Hartford.
*Masters of Ceremonies*, Rev. Philip T. McCabe, Hartford, and Rev. Maurice Crowley, Hartford

Right Rev. J. J. Conroy, Bishop of Albany, and Right Rev. J. P. Machebeuf, Vicar Apostolic of Colorado honored the occasion by their presence. A large gathering of priests from this and other dioceses assisted at the impressive and historic ceremony. The oration was pronounced by the Rev. Thomas O'Gorman, C. S. P., the present bishop of Sioux Falls, South Dakota. An appropriate text was selected from *Isaias* v. 2, 3: "*Enlarge the place of thy tent, and stretch out the skins of thy tabernacles. Spare not. Lengthen thy cords and strengthen thy stakes. For thou shalt pass on the right hand and to the left, and thy seed shall inherit the Gentiles and shall inhabit the desolate cities.*" Present at the celebration were Mayor Morgan G. Buckley, with officials of the town and city governments.

When Father Tierney was appointed pastor of St. Mary's, New Britain, he was succeeded in St. Peter's parish by the present incumbent, the Rev. Thomas W. Broderick. Father Broderick's pastorate has been fruitful in works that tend to the advancement of religion and to the upbuilding of the faith of his devoted people. Among the works that have signalized his administration are the renovation of the parochial school and the complete and beautiful redecoration of the church. So thorough was the transformation of the latter and so notable the improvement that the church had lost its former dedication ; in consequence, it was solemnly rededicated by Bishop McMahon in September, 1887.

The people of St. Peter's parish deservedly occupy a high position among their fellows in the political, social, intellectual worlds. They are represented in local, state and national positions of honor and trust. They have given many honored names to the clerical, legal and medical professions, while not a few have attained eminence in commercial, mechanical and industrial vocations. The parish is composed of mixed nationalities, Irish and their descendants, Americans, Poles, Lithuanians and Portuguese, and comprises 4,500 souls.

As a benefactor the name of Patrick Cavanagh stands out in prominence. He left his entire estate in 1897 to be devoted to religious and charitable purposes. Among the notable conversions to the ancient faith within this jurisdiction we may mention Miss Spencer, Miss Hammersly and Mr. Frederick Tudor, all of whom were connected with some of the oldest and most prominent families of Hartford. The last was a descendant of Mr. Samuel Tudor, who treated Bishop Cheverus so courteously at the time of his visit to Hartford in 1823.

The first marriage recorded after the organization of the parish is dated October 9, 1859, and the ceremony was performed by Father Kelly. It was that of Patrick Cullinane and Bridget Glynn, *alias* Mallon. The witnesses were Charles and Ellen Doherty. From this date to July 1, 1898, the number of marriages solemnized was 2,019. The baptismal records in possession of the parish begin at October 2, 1862. From this date to July 1, 1898, the number of baptisms was 7,983.

The clergy who have served as assistants in St. Peter's parish are the following :

Rev. Daniel Mullin.
Rev. Patrick Sherry, 1862.
Rev. P. Grau, March to Dec., 1863.
Rev. Hugh Mallon, Dec., '63—March, '66.
Rev. J. McCarten, April, '66—Oct., '67.
Rev. J. Cooney, Oct., '67—May, '70.
Rev. R. J. Sullivan, Sept., '69—March, '70.
Rev. F. Dent, O. S. F., April, '70—March, '74.
Rev. D. Cremin, Dec., '72—Jany., '77.
Rev. W. T. Slocum, July, '76—Aug., '76.
Rev. J. J. Galligan, Aug., '76—Febry., '79.
Rev. P. F. McAlenney, Jany., '77—July, '81.
Rev. M. J. Crowley, Jany., '79—April, '85.

Rev. J. P. Connelly, July, '81—Oct., '81.
Rev. C. J. McElroy, Oct., '81—Oct., '87.
Rev. W. J. Shanley, April, '85—July, '86.
Rev. R. J. Carroll, July, '86—May, '88.
Rev. J. C. Lynch, Feby., '87—March, '87.
Rev. E. J. Broderick, Oct., '87—   '98.
Rev. J. J. Lynch, May, '88—Sept., '97.
Rev. J. Lee, May, '91—May, '93.
Rev. J. F. Lally, May, '93.
Rev. D. L. Gleason, D.D., Sept., '97—Jany., '98.
Rev. J. J. Laden, Jany., '98.
Rev. Stanislaus Musiel.

Father Broderick has been the Defender of the Marriage Tie in the diocese since 1884; a diocesan consultor since 1886, and is also a member of the diocesan Board of Examiners of the Clergy. In the summer of 1896 he received the public thanks of the governor of the State and a handsome medal in recognition of his services as the Catholic chaplain at the encampment of the National Guard at Niantic.

ST. PETER'S PAROCHIAL SCHOOL.—St. Peter's school is the successor of the school organized by the Rev. Father Kelly in 1860. At that time there were about 200 children enrolled. For some years the school was conducted under the management of the committee of the South school district. The parish furnished the building and furniture, but the district paid the salaries of the teachers. The first teachers of this school were: Mr. John Godfrey, Miss Sarah Kelly, Miss Mary Bows and Miss Hannah Pembroke,[1] all Catholics. Upon the death or resignation of a Catholic teacher, the committee appointed a Protestant teacher in her place. In 1865, during the pastorate of Rev. Father Lynch, a Protestant teacher was appointed who rendered herself objectionable by persisting in reading from a Protestant Bible before beginning the morning exercises. Adhering to the practice despite the protestations of the committee, she was removed, but on appealing to the courts was reinstated over the children she had so persistently offended. Discord only could result from such an arrangement, and the school was closed. After a brief period it was reopened and placed under the control of the Sisters of Mercy. At present the school has eight grades, with 900 pupils, taught by seventeen Sisters, of whom Sister M. Antonius is the directress. It is in a most flourishing condition, and the proficiency of the pupils is demonstrated by the gratifying fact, that for more than ten years the graduating classes have unanimously and with honor passed the competitive examinations for admission to the High School.

An appreciative critic says: "In Hartford no better example of the 'modern school idea' can be found than that offered by St. Peter's Parochial school. Established thirty years ago, it has ever maintained a prominent place in the advance of education in this vicinity. It is the second oldest parish school here and has an annual attendance of 900 boys and girls. It is graded from the kindergarten to the high school course, and the boys and girls, excepting in the kindergarten, are educated in separate rooms. Though the discipline is strict, it is mild and quiet, and the pupils are taught to love rather than to fear their teachers. The Sisters of Mercy preside, and as is their custom, create around them an atmosphere that is sunny, refined and stimulating. There are fifteen rooms devoted to school purposes besides the kindergarten. Two rooms are now utilized in the convent building adjoining the school for the music class and the eighth grade. Both instrumental and vocal music are taught, and a course is provided in needlework and cooking for the girls and in manual training for the boys."

[1] Hist. Sketch of the Catholic Church in Hartford.

## ST. LAWRENCE O'TOOLE'S PARISH,

ST. LAWRENCE O'TOOLE'S parish was organized on February 16, 1885. During the fourteen years of its existence it has accomplished much that has redounded to the honor of religion and the glory of God. The Catholics of this locality were under the jurisdiction of St. Peter's parish from its formation in 1859 until 1881, when they passed under the spiritual guidance of the clergy of the cathedral. This parish is familiarly called "The Rock," from its proximity to a ledge from which for nearly seventy years have been quarried the stones used on the streets of Hartford, and which has furnished employment for the heads of families in this locality. In 1876, the Rev. Lawrence Walsh, then pastor of St. Peter's parish, recognized the necessity of a church in that vicinity, and having obtained from Mr. John Allen the donation of a desirable lot on the corner of Laurel and Wilson streets, 100 by 150 feet, he proceeded to put into execution his contemplated design. Before the work was completed, however, Father Walsh was transferred to Waterbury. The corner-stone was laid on Sunday, September 3, 1876. The Rev. Lawrence Walsh, who began the church, preached the sermon. The construction of the church was prosecuted industriously by his successor, the Rev. Thomas Lynch, rector of the pro-cathedral, and was dedicated on Sunday, December 3, 1876. The officiating prelate was Bishop Galberry. After the ceremonies of dedication, a solemn high Mass was celebrated with Rev. Luke Daly, of New Britain, as celebrant ; Rev. Philip McCabe, of Hartford, as deacon ; Rev. M. Galligan as sub-deacon, and Rev. D. Cremin as master of ceremonies. The sermon was delivered by Rev. Joseph Coleman, O.S.A. Joy and happiness were visible in the countenances of those sturdy sons of toil and devoted children of holy church as they witnessed the celebration of the divine mysteries in a church of their own. From that time Mass was said regularly every Sunday and holy day of obligation by a priest from the mother church until the cathedral assumed charge, when the same facilities for attending divine service were continued.

Recognizing the great spiritual and temporal benefits that would accrue to this section of the city from the presence of a resident pastor, Bishop McMahon organized it into a separate parish, and appointed the Rev. John Lenahan as its first pastor. For ten years Father Lenahan labored unceasingly for the welfare of his flock, and it was with profound regret that they heard the announcement that the relations between him and them were to be dissolved.

The second pastor was the Rev. James Smith, who came hither from Guilford. He continued the excellent work of his predecessor, and among the successes that marked his pastorate of four years was the erection of a finely equipped lyceum for the young men of his parish. Here they were and are provided with every facility for moral, social, intellectual and spiritual advancement. Father Smith preached his farewell sermon in St. Lawrence

O'Toole's church on Sunday, November 21, 1898, and was immediately succeeded by the present pastor, the Rev. Thomas J. Keena, who came to Hartford after many years of faithful and successful labors in St. John's parish, Stamford.

When St. Lawrence O'Toole's parish was organized the census showed a population of 700 souls, principally Irish and Irish Americans. It has since increased to 800.

The priests who served this parish have possessed not only the affectionate regard of their own people, but have also enjoyed the respect and shared in the good-will of their separated brethren, and have done much to dissolve the mists of sectarian prejudice. Father Keena is the Diocesan Director of the propagation of the faith.

St. Lawrence O'Toole's church is a frame building with a solid brick foundation, and is Gothic in style of architecture. It has a front of 40 feet and is 60 feet deep, and will accommodate 300 people. The cost of the church was about $3,500.

## ST. ANN'S (FRENCH) PARISH,

### HARTFORD.

THE first meeting of the French-Canadians with the object of organizing a separate parish with a pastor of their own nationality was held in October, 1888. Mass was celebrated for the first time in St. Joseph's school hall on January 6, 1889, by the Rev. A. St. Louis. The French-Canadian population at that time was 650 souls. The Rev. Father St. Louis was the first pastor of the newly-organized parish, but after a brief term of service he was compelled by illness to retire from his pastoral duties. He was succeeded in March, 1890, by the Rev. P. E. Roy.

Father Roy immediately set himself the task of providing his people with a place of worship. A site was secured at the corner of Park and Putnam streets. Eager to possess a church his parishioners diligently co-operated with him, and in a short time saw their hopes fully realized. Sunday, May 28, 1893, was hailed with joy and delight by the French-Canadians of Hartford, for on that date their new church, whose completion has been awaited with much pleasurable anticipation and longing was dedicated to the service of God with all the imposing ceremonies incidental to such occasions. The dedicatory services began at 10 A. M. with Bishop McMahon officiating. He was assisted by the Rev. M. A. Tierney of New Britain, as deacon, and the Rev. T. W. Broderick of Hartford, as subdeacon. At 10.30 a solemn high Mass was sung, the celebrant being the Rev. J. Bourret of Waterbury; deacon, the Rev. J. E. Marcoux of North Adams, Mass.; subdeacon, the Rev. C. Leddy of Hartford; master of ceremonies, the Rev. W. J. Shanley of the cathedral. The sermon of dedication was delivered by the Rev. J. P. Guinet of the order of Our Lady of La Salette. At the close of the Mass Bishop McMahon imparted the episcopal benediction. At 3.30 vespers were sung with the Rev. E. Cartier of New Haven, as the celebrant. During this service

Bishop McMahon administered the sacrament of confirmation for the first time in the parish to seventy-three children. The bishop addressed the congregation in French in words of encouragement and congratulation upon their fine edifice, the result of their united efforts and generosity. Present at the services were all the priests of the city with many from neighboring parishes.

The church has a seating capacity of 600, and cost $22,000. Above the church is a large hall which is used as a school, wherein the children of the parish obtain instruction in both the French and English languages. The parish numbers at present about 1200 souls.

After nine years of arduous labor which he carried on with commendable zeal, Father Roy severed his connection with St. Ann's parish and with the diocese on Sunday, April 30, 1899. Though laboring within the jurisdiction of the Bishop of Hartford, Father Roy was a subject of the Archbishop of Quebec, not having received dimissory letters from that dignitary. He returned to the archdiocese of Quebec, his mission being to collect funds for the great archdiocesan hospital, the Hotel Dieu. His successor is the Rev. J. E. Sénésac, who assumed charge of St. Ann's on Sunday, May 7, 1899.

## ST. ANTHONY'S PARISH,

### Hartford.

ST. ANTHONY'S is the Italian parish of Hartford. For many years it had been the desire of the Bishops of Hartford to provide ways and means that would enable the rapidly increasing Italian population to receive instruction in the doctrines of our holy faith in their own language. To that end they have been attended for some years by priests set apart for that purpose. In January, 1895, the Rev. Edward Flannery began his ministry among them as assistant to the Rev. Angelo Chicagilione. As the latter returned to Europe on February 27th following, the care of the parish was intrusted to Father Flannery. The present pastor, the Rev. D. L. Gleason, D.D., was appointed on January 1, 1898. In May of the same year, Bishop Tierney purchased from the German Lutheran congregation its church property on Market street. After suitable improvements were made the church was dedicated to St. Anthony on June 5, 1898.

In December, 1898, A. Andretta and P. M. D'Esopo were elected trustees, and on January 11, 1899, the Right Rev. Bishop transferred the church property to St. Anthony's corporation. The census of June, 1898, shows a record of 2,800 names.

## PARISH OF OUR LADY OF SORROWS.

HARTFORD (PARKVILLE).

PARKVILLE originally belonged to the jurisdiction of St. Peter's parish, but latterly it came under that of the cathedral. The present church was erected during the rectorship of Rev. William A. Harty and was attended by the clergy of the cathedral until it was given in charge of the Missionary Fathers of La Salette. The Congregation of La Salette was admitted into the diocese on August 11, 1892, by Bishop McMahon, who granted to the fathers the use of the former episcopal residence on Woodland street. After some necessary repairs Mass was said in the house for the first time on September 19th by Rev. Father Pajot and Rev. Father Vignon. In this year his Eminence, the Cardinal Prefect of the Propaganda, permitted the community to have a novitiate. Rev. Father Pajot was Superior in Hartford from 1892 to 1898. In the latter year, Rev. Father Vignon was appointed Vicar General of the Congregation in America and Superior of the Hartford community. In 1892 the community numbered five priests; there are now eighteen and fifteen professed scholastics.

With the increasing number of priests and students, the house on Woodland street became too small, so that in 1894, the Congregation began preparations for more adequate accommodations. Accordingly, they secured a valuable site on New Park Avenue and began the erection of a new home. The corner-stone was laid on October 7, 1894, by Bishop Tierney, the discourse being delivered by Rev. W. J. Shanley, rector of the cathedral. The seminary is an attractive building 114 x 45, and has accommodations for 100 students. Its cost was about $45,000.

Combined with the seminary is a missionary college embracing the classical and preparatory branches necessary for the ecclesiastical state. Only aspirants to the priesthood in the Order of the Missionary Fathers of La Salette are admitted. There are in this department ten students.

The Fathers of La Salette have pastoral charge of two parishes in the diocese, Our Lady of Sorrows, of which the Superior, Rev. Joseph Vignon, is pastor, and St. James', Danielson, whose rector is Rev. J. P. Guinet. At present all the fathers are French, but it is the avowed purpose to secure vocations among English-speaking young men, who will continue the apostolic work already so auspiciously entered upon. The ten students above mentioned are of this class, which makes the future bright with promise for the enlargement of their field of activity.

The fathers also give missions in French parishes and assist in various parishes on Sundays.

REV. HENRY T. WALSH

REV. PETER H. McCLEAN, S.T.L.

REV. MICHAEL B. RODDEN

REV. WILLIAM J. DOOLAN

REV. RICHARD CARROLL

## IMMACULATE CONCEPTION PARISH,

### HARTFORD.

THE youngest of the parishes of Hartford and one of the most promising is that of the Immaculate Conception. The growth of the Cathedral parish in this section of the city necessitated the erection of a church, which was attended as a mission from the Cathedral until its formation into an independent parish on April 2, 1899. The church was built under the supervision of the rector of the Cathedral, the Rev. Walter J. Shanley. Ground was broken on the feast of Our Lady of Mt. Carmel July 16, 1894. The corner-stone was laid by Bishop Tierney on October 21, 1894, on which occasion the Rev. Thomas W. Broderick preached the sermon. The church was dedicated on May 19, 1895. The celebrant of the Mass, which followed the ceremony of dedication, was the Rev. Thomas Keena, and the preacher was the Rev. Edward Flannery. Previous to its organization into a separate parish, the clergy of the Cathedral celebrated Mass three times here every Sunday, besides offering the Holy Sacrifice of the Mass on holy days of obligation, First Fridays, etc. The Rev. John T. Winters assumed charge of the new parish at the time of its formation. The church is situated directly south, and within three blocks of the State capitol, at the corner of Park and Hungerford streets. It is of Gothic design with spire, and presents an attractive exterior and interior appearance. Its seating capacity is 420.

The church, which was built as a "chapel of ease," is now inadequate to accommodate the parishioners, notwithstanding that four Masses are said every Sunday. This insufficiency of accommodation will necessitate an enlargement of the church in the near future. Father Winters is assisted in his Sunday labors by a priest from the college of Our Lady of La Salette, Parkville. An assistant, however, has been appointed, but has not yet entered upon the discharge of his duties. Father Winters resides temporarily at No. 39 Hungerford street.

The first baptism was administered April 4, 1899. The recipient of the sacrament was Joseph Hood, son of John J. Hood and Delia McMahon. The first marriage was that between Patrick Doran and Elizabeth Brown, April 19th. The first death was that of Mrs. Ann Gilligan of Lawrence street.

The new parish began its career under the happiest auspices and with the brightest prospects of future success.


## ST. JOSEPH'S PARISH,

### BRISTOL.

JAMES SHEEHAN, John Moran, Annie Madden and Mary Moran constitute a little band whose names should be gratefully cherished for their devotion to the church in the days when to be a professing Catholic demanded courage indeed. The working of the North copper mines brought into this locality a goodly sprinkling of Irishmen as stalwart in faith as in physique. Mass was first said here by the Rev. Luke Daly of Hartford, about 1848 or 1849. At the time of the first Mass there were about one hundred Catholics in Bristol. When the copper mines closed and the construction of the railroad began, many Catholics found employment at the work and settled in Bristol Centre. From this time the Holy Sacrifice of the Mass was offered up in a building on Queen street, near John Moran's residence, and also in Gridley's hall.

The church was built by the Rev. Father Daly, in 1855, as pastor of St. Mary's, New Britain, to which Bristol was a mission. The Catholic population at this period had reached two hundred souls. On October 1, 1864, Bristol was made an independent parish, with the Mines and Forestville as dependencies, and the Rev. Michael Rodden was appointed its first resident pastor. Father Rodden's term of service at St. Joseph's was four years. He was succeeded by the Rev. Christopher Duggett, whose pastorate was of three years duration. At the expiration of Father Duggett's administration, Father Rodden returned in 1872, and has administered the affairs of the parish continuously ever since. For many years Father Rodden had the spiritual charge of Plainville, Farmington and Forestville. Plainville was the first mission to be taken from the parent parish, and with Kensington formed a separate jurisdiction. Farmington was attached to Plainville in February, 1885, and Forestville was also annexed on September 20, 1891.

The parish cemetery was purchased in 1868, and solemnly blessed in the same year.

Father Rodden is assisted in his parochial labors by the Rev. Patrick J. O'Leary.

## ST. CATHERINE'S PARISH,

### BROAD BROOK.

THE honor of being among the pioneer Catholics of Broad Brook belongs to Patrick Duffy, James O'Neil, Michael Geary, Patrick McDonald and Patrick O'Reilly. Rev. James Smyth was the celebrant of the first Mass said here, and the house that enjoys this distinction was the residence of Patrick McDonald. But bigotry was rife in those days, and in that section, and Mr. McDonald suffered the penalty of eviction for allowing his house to be used as a temporary chapel. At this time there were about twenty Catholics in Broad Brook, all Irish. In 1856, it passed under the care of the pastor of Rockville, the Rev. Bernard Tully, who met with considerable opposition from fanatics. Being thwarted in his desire to say Mass in the public-school house by the strong anti-Catholic sentiment prevailing, he was rescued from his dilemma by the generosity of the proprietor of the village hotel, a Mr. Hubbard, who placed at the disposal of Father Tully a large room in his house. Mr. Hubbard's generosity and broad-minded principles were still further brought in evidence by the donation of a large lot, upon which the church was afterwards erected.

Cautious to a great degree was Father Tully, as was also his successor in Rockville, the Rev. Hugh T. O'Reilly. They justly feared the burden of debt which the erection of a church would entail, and therefore deferred building. In 1865, Broad Brook was served from Thompsonville, whose pastor, the Rev. Bernard Tully, had been transferred from Rockville. From this time until November, 1882, it continued under the control of the pastors of Thompsonville, being attended every Sunday during the administrations of the Rev. William E. Duffy, Rev. John Cooney and Rev. John A. Mulcahy, and Rev. Patrick Donahoe for a brief period. It was during the pastorate of Father Mulcahy that the church lot was secured and St. Catherine's church erected. In November, 1882, as said above, it passed again under the jurisdiction of Rockville, where it remained until its formation into a separate parish.

The first pastor of the newly created parish was the Rev. Michael J. Daly, who received his appointment in July, 1886. The population of the parish at this time was chiefly—it might be said exclusively—Irish people, and numbered, it was estimated, 600 souls. In 1898 they had declined to 450 souls.

On taking the reins of government, Father Daly entered with zeal upon his labors, and to him is the parish indebted for its handsome rectory and its cemetery. His successor was the Rev. Michael Lynch, who served from August, 1890, to May, 1891. St. Catherine's thereupon reverted to Rockville, whence it was attended until the advent of the present pastor, the Rev. Thomas Dunn, in August, 1891. Father Dunn's systematic labors have borne excellent fruit. What with the liquidation of the debt, improvements made in the church, residence and cemetery, the parish is in a prosperous condition. The people are responsive, devoted to their spiritual guide, and all indications point to a bright future.

From August, 1887, to January, 1898, the records show 205 baptisms and 52 marriages.

## ST. PATRICK'S PARISH,

### COLLINSVILLE.

PROMINENT among the first Catholic settlers of Collinsville the following names stand forth: Peter Myers, Michael Sinnott, Stephen McMahon, James Furlong, Patrick Moore, Patrick Kane, Patrick O'Loughlin, Patrick Tinnian and Walter Lambert. The pioneer priest, Father Brady, of Hartford, being overtaken at night in Collinsville in the winter of 1841, celebrated Mass for the Catholics there resident. Father Brady found the number of people here sufficiently numerous to warrant visitations at frequent intervals; so that Collinsville was faithfully served from Hartford until the appointment of the Rev. Luke Daly to New Britain on May 9, 1849. Father Daly administered the affairs of this congregation until December 10, 1856. It was during Father Daly's pastorate that the church was erected. The lot on which it stands was the generous gift of Mr. Peter Myers, an excellent representative of the Irish Catholic character. When Father Daly remonstrated and suggested to Mr. Myers that the donation was too large for his means, this worthy Catholic, with the grateful feelings of a warm-hearted Christian, made an answer that deserves to be perpetuated: "I have resolved to make this offering to religion and my God; permit me to complete my resolve. I came here poor. God has blessed me with health, the capital with which I have provided what I am possessed of. I will, I trust, ever be grateful to him." The church was dedicated on August 22, 1852, by Bishop O'Reilly under the patronage of St. Patrick. The discourse on the occasion was delivered by the Rev. Thomas Quinn of Winsted. The benefactors to the church who merit remembrance are Bishop O'Reilly, who contributed $100, and Michael Sinnott, whose gift was $150. The total of Mr. Peter Myers' donation was $230. At the time of the celebration of the first Mass in Collinsville the Catholic population was twelve; when the church was dedicated it was 140.

On the 10th of December, 1856, Collinsville was elevated to the dignity of a parish, with Tariffville and New Hartford as dependencies. The Rev. Patrick O'Dwyer was appointed the first resident pastor, and remained in charge till 1861. His pastorate witnessed the purchase, in 1856, and the blessing of the cemetery; the latter event occurred on April 29, 1858, Bishop McFarland officiating, and also preaching an eloquent discourse on the nature of the ceremony, and the spirit of the church in setting aside and blessing spots of earth for the reception of bodies after death. Previous to this ceremony the bishop administered the sacrament of Confirmation to over 100 persons, after the Solemn High Mass, which was celebrated by the Rev. P. J. O'Dwyer, the pastor, assisted by the Rev. Luke Daly of New Britain, as deacon, the Rev. B. Tully of Rockville, as sub-deacon, and the Rev. E. J. O'Brien of New Haven, as master of ceremonies. Present in the sanctuary were the Rev. Thomas Quinn of Meriden; the Rev. Lawrence Mangan of Winsted, and the Rev. Michael O'Reilly of Waterbury. Bishop McFarland preached also at this ceremony from the text Matt. xvi. 18. The succession of priests after Father O'Dwyer was as follows: The Rev. John Fagan, from 1861 to 1868; the Rev. Lawrence Walsh, from 1868 to May, 1870; the Rev. Bernard O'R. Sheridan, from 1870 to 1885; the Rev. Maurice Crowley, from 1885 to 1889. Father Crowley was succeeded by the Rev. John J. Quinn, who still continues in charge. The priests who have served as assistants in this parish are: Rev. William O'Brien, Rev. John Russell, Rev. J. Creedon, Rev. J. Schacken, Rev. T. A. Mulvaney, and Rev. Luke Fitzsimmons.

When St. Patrick's parish was organized in 1856, the population was about 500 souls, principally Irish, and some Canadians. In 1898 it was 1100, comprising 500 Irish, 400 Canadians, 100 Germans and 100 Poles. In the four decades that have elapsed since the organization of the parish, 3298 souls received the priceless gift of faith by baptism, and 544 marriages have received the blessing of the church.

Besides the church and rectory St. Patrick's parish is possessed of considerable property. Regarding no labor too burdensome, and recognizing their obligations to religion, the people are cheerful and earnest in their responses to Father Quinn's appeals, are docile to his authoritative instructions, and stimulated by his zeal and activity in the performance of his duties, are continuing the noble work of their predecessors, and by their profound attachment to the faith are promoting the honor and glory of God—the one thing necessary.

REV. MICHAEL A. SULLIVAN

REV. JOHN J. QUINN

REV. THOMAS J. PRESTON

VERY REV. JOSEPH VIGNON, M.S.

REV. C. SOCQUET, M.S.

## ST. MARY'S PARISH,

### East Hartford.

THE Catholics of East Hartford were organized into an independent parish in August, 1873, with the Rev. Patrick A. Goodwin as the first resident pastor. Previous to that time they had formed part of St. Patrick's parish, Hartford. Before the division land for a church had been purchased through the agency of Mr. Patrick Garvan at a cost of $3,000 The times were then unfavorable, and no attempt was made to build a church. Services were held every Sunday at Elm Hall, on Main street, the Christian doctrine class always preceding the ten-o'clock Mass. A fair held in the fall of 1876, which realized $1,450, infused courage into the people, and they determined to commence the erection of a church. In the meantime, Father Goodwin was stricken with a fatal illness and died on February 15, 1877. Immediately after, the Rev. John A. Mulcahy, who was assistant to Vicar General Lynch at New Haven, was assigned to the pastoral charge of the new parish.

Soon after—such were the desires and the paramount need of his devoted congregation—the energetic young pastor felt obliged to push forward the work of building the church. Accordingly, ground was broken on the 1st day of April, 1877, and on June 3d the corner-stone was laid.

On Sunday, November 11, 1877, the congregation assembled in their new place of worship to witness its dedication to the service of God by Bishop Galberry, who was assisted by Very Rev. Thomas Walsh, Vicar General ; Rev. M. A. Tierney, Rev. T. Synnott, Rev. J. Fitzpatrick, Rev. J. Campbell, and Rev. John A. Mulcahy, the pastor. After the services of dedication, a Pontifical Mass was celebrated, with Bishop Galberry as celebrant ; Very Rev. Thomas Walsh, assistant priest ; Rev. Thomas Synnott and Rev. J. Fitzpatrick, deacons of honor ; Rev. J. Campbell and Rev. John A. Mulcahy, deacon and sub-deacon of the Mass, respectively ; Rev. M. A. Tierney, master of ceremonies. The discourse was preached by Very Rev. James Hughes.

During his pastorate here, Father Mulcahy built also St. Augustine's church at Glastonbury ; liquidated the debt on the church lot in Wethersfield, and collected money for the erection of a church at Rocky Hill. He was transferred from St. Mary's in November, 1878, to St. Patrick's parish, Thompsonville. His successor was the Rev. John T. McMahon, who took control of the parish on November 10th. Father McMahon's administration was marked by many successes, both in the temporal and spiritual order. He was succeeded by the present rector, the Rev. James Gleason, who has labored assiduously in promoting the religious welfare of his flock. When the parish was formed it comprised Glastonbury, Wethersfield, and Rocky Hill. At present Glastonbury only remains with East Hartford. The mission church is 64 feet long by 37 wide. The chancel is 14 feet deep and 24 feet wide. It has a seating capacity of three hundred and fifty persons. Its corner-stone was laid on the 7th of April, 1878, by Bishop Galberry, the Rev. M. F. Kelly, of Windsor Locks, preaching the sermon. The ceremony of dedication took place on Sunday, November 17, 1878, Very Rev. Thomas Walsh, V. G., officiating. The celebrant of the Mass was Rev. James Campbell of Manchester, of which place Glastonbury was formerly an out-mission. The preacher on the occasion was the former pastor, Rev. John A. Mulcahy. The cost of the church was about $3,500.

St. Mary's church, East Hartford, is admirably situated on Main street, and located on a gentle slope off the wide avenue, has a fine sweep of landscape within its view. The edifice is beautiful in design and workmanship, has a seating capacity of six hundred, and is capable of seating seven hundred. At a distance its spire and cross, overtopping and looming up from out of the noble old elms that give grandeur and dignity to the place, harmonize with the Catholic and cultured mind.

## ST. BERNARD'S PARISH,

### HAZARDVILLE.

HAZARDVILLE is situated about three and one-half miles east of Thompsonville in the town of Enfield. Its earliest Catholic residents were William Casey, Martin D'Arsey, John Cunningham, Daniel Bailey and Michael Leary, all of whom are still living. The first Mass said in Hazardville was offered up by the Rev. James Smyth, pastor of St. Mary's parish, Windsor Locks, about the year 1860, in the residence of William Casey. There were at this period about one hundred Catholics here, but scattered over a large extent of territory, and were, for the most part, Irish. Father Smyth visited Hazardville occasionally until the formation of St. Patrick's parish, Thompsonville, in January, 1863, with the Rev. Bernard Tully as its first resident pastor. Father Tully visited Hazardville at monthly intervals and said Mass at William Casey's residence until 1865 when he purchased an old school-house, which was suitably arranged for divine service. Father Tully was succeeded in 1866 by the Rev. William E. Duffy, who said Mass semi-monthly until 1870, when the people began to experience the great blessings of weekly service. Succeeding Father Duffy, the Rev. John Cooney attended Hazardville for eight years, offering the Holy Sacrifice of the Mass every Sunday, visiting the sick and attending to the spiritual needs of the children. His successor was the Rev. John A. Mulcahy, now the Vicar-General of the diocese, who was appointed pastor of Thompsonville and missions in October, 1878. Father Mulcahy began at once the erection of a church. The corner-stone was laid in 1880 by Right Rev. Bishop McMahon, and the discourse on the occasion was delivered by the late Rev. John Duggan, of Waterbury. In the same year the church was dedicated in honor of St. Bernard, the sermon of dedication being preached by the Rev. M. A. Tierney, now Bishop of the diocese. In 1881, the Rev. Patrick Donahoe succeeded Father Mulcahy and continued to serve Hazardville until its erection into a separate parish in January, 1888. The first resident pastor of the new parish was the Rev. John Synnott, who came on January 12, 1888. During his pastorate the parochial residence was built upon land secured by him, a cemetery was purchased and extensive improvements were made in the church. The indebtedness incurred by these works was liquidated by Father Synnott, and a substantial sum was left in the treasury at his departure on May 20, 1894. The cemetery was bought in 1889 by Martin D'Arsey and immediately transferred to the church corporation. It was solemnly blessed in the same year by Right Rev. Bishop McMahon. After a residence of six years in Hazardville, during which he labored actively and successfully for the welfare of his parishioners, Father Synnott was succeeded on May 24, 1894, by the present incumbent, the Rev. Thomas J. Maloney, who has proved a worthy successor of the zealous priests who preceded him in the care of the Catholics of Hazardville.

Among the evidences of his material labors, we may note the introduction of a steam-heating outfit at an expense of $800, the renovation of the parochial residence at an expenditure of $700, and the frescoing of the church.

Among the special benefactors of St. Bernard's parish mention should be made of the Hazard Powder Co., whose donation of $500 infused hope and courage into the hearts of the Catholic people who eagerly desired a suitable place in which to worship God. At the period in which the parish was formed the Catholic population numbered about four hundred souls, chiefly Irish, with a few Canadian families. The growth of the parish has been slow, as its population in 1898 was 425 souls, of the same nationalities and in the same proportion as in 1888. The number of baptisms in the ten years of the parish's existence is one hundred and twenty-five. The first child to receive the sacrament of baptism in Hazardville after the formation of the parish was George Ruschette, January 20, 1888, and the marriage of Clallane Kilba and Catharine Bailey was the first solemnized, September 23, 1888.

St. Bernard's church is a handsome brick edifice with brown stone foundations, and finely situated on the main street of the town. Its attendants are loyal to parochial and diocesan rules and regulations, proud of their faith, patriotic in sentiment and in deed, and generous in their responses to all appeals made in behalf of religion.

### SOMERSVILLE, ALL SAINTS' MISSION.

Somersville is a mission of St. Bernard's parish, Hazardville, and is distant about three miles, in the town of Somers. While pastor of Thompsonville, the Rev. Patrick Donahoe purchased an old Congregational church for the use of the Catholics of Somersville. It was remodeled and appropriately fitted up for Catholic worship by the Rev. John Synnott. Father Synnott paid the indebtedness on the parish, $2,000, and at his transfer left $1,500 in the treasury. The congregation soon outgrew the seating capacity of the building, and early in May, 1897, Father Maloney broke ground for a new church. The corner-stone was laid on July 18th, 1897, by Right Rev. M. A. Tierney, D.D. The Rev. William Gibbons preached the sermon. Among the clergy present were the Revs. John Cooney, Thomas Dunn, Thomas Preston, Richard C. Gragan, and Thomas F. Maloney. Bishop Tierney dedicated the church under the title of All Saints, on January 16th, 1898. A

Solemn High Mass was celebrated, with the Rev. James P. Donovan, D.D., celebrant; the Rev. Thomas Preston, deacon, and the Rev. R. C. Gragan, subdeacon. The dedicatory discourse was delivered by the Rev. Peter McClean. The organ in the church was the gift of Mr. R. Keeney, and Mr. George Keeney has also proved and still continues to show himself a generous benefactor. Somersville mission comprises about 325 souls, the majority of whom are of Acadian descent. Father Maloney offers the Holy Sacrifice of the Mass on every Sunday and holy day of precept, and in other ways assiduously guards the spiritual interests of this portion of his flock. The church is a frame building with stone foundations, and is unencumbered by indebtedness.

## ST. PAUL'S PARISH,

### KENSINGTON.

THE year 1855 witnessed the advent of the first Catholic to Kensington, William Daly. He was followed by John O'Brien, Frank Malloy and Martin Hart in 1856. After this came Peter Hackett, Patrick Roche, James Stafford, John Lynch and John Halloran. It was not, however, until after the Civil War that Catholics came here in any considerable numbers. With the close of hostilities and the return to their homes of the Union's defenders, business interests revived and the factories required additional hands. In consequence of this improved order of things a number of Catholic families came hither in quest of labor, and found it in the factories. It was not until 1872 that Kensington was honored by the offering of the Adorable Sacrifice within its boundaries, the people assisting at Mass in New Britain. In the year mentioned the Rev. Luke Daly said the first Mass in Hart's Hall. At that time there were 350 Irish Catholics in Kensington.

The congregation of St. Paul's continued in missionary relationship until 1881, when the Rev. Paul F. McAlenney was designated as the first resident pastor. He found a church here which had been erected in 1877, but it was in poor condition, unfinished and burdened with a heavy debt.

His dwelling place for the first year of his pastorate was in the sacristy of the church. The church was begun during the pastorate of the Rev. Dr. Carmody, of New Britain. The corner-stone was laid on October 27, 1878, the Rev. M. A. Tierney preaching the sermon. It was dedicated by the pastor in May, 1879. The celebrant of the first Mass in the new church was the Rev. Father Donahoe, and the preacher on the occasion was the Rev. J. H. Ryan, D.D.

Father McAlenney overcame the difficulties with which he was confronted. He finished the church, provided a pastoral residence and liquidated the debt. He severed his relations with St. Paul's parish in February, 1885, and was followed by the Rev. Thomas Shelly, the duration of whose pastorate was eleven years. Father Shelly's success is attested by his promotion to St. John's parish, Cromwell, and his recent advancement to the parish of the Sacred Heart, Waterbury.

The Rev. M. A. Sullivan came in 1896, and still administers the affairs of St. Paul's. When Kensington was elevated to the parochial dignity the Catholic population numbered about 1,000 souls, chiefly Irish and their descendants. At present it is greatly reduced, the number being 500 Irish and 50 Italians.

In two decades, from 1878 to 1898, the sacrament of baptism has been administered 364 times, and in the same period 59 marriages have been solemnized. The first to receive baptism was James McGee, born December 13, 1872. The waters of regeneration were poured upon him in Hart's Hall, where the first Mass was said. The first marriage ceremony performed in the new church was that between John McKeon and Elizabeth Duffy in 1878.

## SACRED HEART MISSION,

### EAST BERLIN.

THE Catholics of East Berlin attended St. Paul's church, Kensington, for many years. They were obliged to travel from four to six miles to assist at divine worship. This was no small inconvenience; and as their numbers increased the need of having a priest to visit them became evident. Rev. Father Shelly said Mass for them in Clark's Hall on June 4, 1893, this being the first time the Holy Sacrifice was offered in East Berlin. He visited this mission thereafter every Sunday, a privilege highly prized by the people, who contributed generously for the purchase of a chalice, vestments, and other articles necessary for the celebration of Mass. Upon Father Shelly's promotion to Cromwell in May, 1896, his successor, Father Sullivan, undertook the erection of a church suitable for the needs of the people.

A generous collection from the parishioners, the sympathy and practical assistance of many non-Catholics, made the task a pleasing one. The contribution of the Berlin Iron Bridge Company, Charles M. Jarvis, president, gave much encouragement and cheered the hearts of their Catholic brethren. A fine site was secured, plans were drawn, and work on the new church was auspiciously begun. The corner-stone was laid by Bishop Tierney on November 8, 1896. An attractive Gothic church, 72 by 42 feet, rose rapidly, and it was solemnly dedicated to God's holy service under the invocation of the Sacred Heart of Jesus, by Bishop Tierney, on Sunday, May 30, 1897. The Mass that followed was celebrated by Rev. M. F. Rigney, with Rev. T. W. Dolan, and Rev. E. P. Sullivan as deacon and sub-deacon, respectively. Rev. N. F. X. Schneider was the master of ceremonies. The dedication sermon was preached by Rev. M. H. Barry, whose theme was, "The Unity of the Church." At the end of the services Bishop Tierney made a felicitous address, in which he congratulated both pastor and people on the happy issue of their labors, and invoked a continuance of the divine favors upon them.

The first child to receive baptism in the new church was James McIntyre, son of Thomas and Mary McIntyre, born on May 30th, the day on which the church was dedicated, and baptized on June 13, 1897. The first funeral services held were over the remains of Mrs. McIntyre, grandmother of the child above mentioned.

The cordial, fraternal relations that exist here between the Catholics and their non-Catholic brethren is very gratifying, and promise well for the interests of religion. Both in Kensington and in East Berlin the bond of union and sympathy between pastor and people is firmly welded, with the natural result that the efforts of both are crowned with success.

## ST. BRIDGET'S PARISH,

### MANCHESTER.

AMONG the earliest Catholics to settle in this vicinity were John Kennedy, James Duffy and Mrs. Gill. The first-named fell a victim to the fell intolerance then prevalent throughout the State. There were some noble exceptions, but these only served to bring out in stronger light the fanaticism of the crowd. Mr. Kennedy had permitted—and rejoiced at the great privilege—Father Brady to offer the Holy Sacrifice in his humble dwelling for the consolation of the few Catholics of this section. For this act he was summarily ejected from his home by his uncharitable landlord, a Mr. Stone. But justice overtook the owner. Indignant at his conduct the proprietor of the mill, Mr. Buell, removed Stone from his employment and restored Kennedy to his position. In Manchester, as elsewhere, the first seeds of faith were, from a human point of view, small and discouraging. Planted in an uncongenial soil, choked and all but stifled by the briars of bigotry and intolerance, they nevertheless germinated into a sturdy growth that astonished those who forgot the divine promises that the gates of hell shall not prevail against the Church.

During the period of his curacy at Hartford, Manchester was visited at regular intervals by Father Smyth, who said Mass in the residence of James Duffy. When Rev. Peter Egan assumed charge of the Catholics of Rockville in 1854, their co-religionists of Manchester passed under his jurisdiction. His pastorate was marked by the purchase of a church lot from Mr. E. Weaver, at a cost of $200. This site was one of the most eligible and commanding in the neighborhood. The Rev. Bernard Tully, who succeeded Father Egan in December, 1856, set about to carry out the designs of his predecessor. On Tuesday, October 19, 1858, the frame of the new church was raised in the presence of a large congregation, most of them Irish-Americans. The Cheney Brothers stopped their mills in order to render all the assistance possible. The dedication occurred on December 5, 1858; 500 persons were present in the church on the occasion. The celebrant of the Mass was the Rev. Father O'Dwyer of Collinsville, and an appropriate discourse was delivered by Rev. Thomas Quinn of Meriden. Thenceforth to 1869, St. Bridget's church was served from Rockville—Father Tully, 1856 to 1863; Father Hugh O'Reilly, 1863 to 1868; Father Tully again, 1868 to October, 1869. At this last date the Rev. James Campbell became the first resident pastor of St. Bridget's parish. Among the material labors that signalized his administration were the purchase of the first rectory and the erection of St. James' church, South Manchester. His pastorate extended to 1890. The Rev. William Doolan

then followed, and after a successful rule of four years was succeeded by the
Rev. Richard Gragan, who served the parish from 1894 to 1897. During this
period the indebtedness of the church was liquidated, a new lot for a church
was secured and a church built at Vernon. The corner-stone of the present
church was laid on August 2, 1896. Bishop Tierney officiated, and Rev.
Thomas W. Broderick preached the sermon. There were twenty-two priests
present and 3500 people. The chapel in the basement was blessed by Bishop
Tierney on Sunday, January 25, 1897. The officers of the Solemn Mass were:
Celebrant, Rev. P. Pajot; deacon, Rev. J. Cooney; sub-deacon, Rev. D. Haggerty; preacher, Rev. P. McClean. On this day Father Gragan announced his
appointment to Stafford Springs. He was followed immediately by the Rev.
Frederick J. Murphy, the present pastor. He has materially reduced the
indebtedness increased by the construction of the church, and is laboring
zealously for the spiritual welfare of his flock.

Attached to St. Bridget's parish is a cemetery of the same name, purchased in 1862 and blessed in 1863. The population of the parish in 1898
was 755 souls, comprising Irish and Americans, while at the time of the first
Mass, in 1854, there were twelve Irish families, or about sixty souls.

## ST. MARY'S PARISH,

### NEW BRITAIN.

AMONG the pillars of the nascent church in New Britain, the vanguard
of that numerous phalanx which is rendering such signal service
in the warfare for Christ and souls, shine out conspicuously the
Celtic names of Patrick Crotty, Thomas Pentilow, Peter McAvoy,
Philip Powers, James Foley, John Haffey, Patrick Brady, John Cusick,
Hugh Fox, and Peter Skelly.

Sixty years ago there were few Catholics in New Britain, and previous
to 1842 the little band had not been visited by a priest. But in July of that
year the Rev. John Brady of Hartford, celebrated the Divine Mysteries in
the house of James Foley, which stood on the site of the Russell & Erwin
screw factory. At this, the first Mass said in New Britain, there were present
about twenty or twenty-five persons. In succession to Father Brady came
the Rev. Edmund Murphy, who labored with great zeal on this mission for
eight months. Father Murphy was a priest of the diocese of Boston, and for
a quarter of a century after his departure from New Britain was pastor of St.
John the Baptist parish at Fall River, Mass. During Father Murphy's brief
pastorate, and for ten years afterwards, Mass was said in private houses,
chiefly in the residences of William Cassidy and Peter Skelly.

When the Rev. Luke Daly assumed charge of this mission in September,
1848, the Catholic population of New Britain numbered about one hundred
souls. His parish comprised New Britain, Farmington, Plainville, Bristol
and the Mines, Forestville, Collinsville, New Hartford, Tariffville, Simsbury,
and Rainbow. His labors in this large field were mainly preaching, catechizing, administering the sacraments, and saying Mass whenever and

wherever he had the opportunity. Father Daly's first Mass in New Britain was celebrated in the building that stands just south of Mr. I. N. Lee's factory, the upper rooms being occupied, the partitions having been removed. Among the congregation at that Mass were Mr. Peter Skelly, Mr. Downs, Mr. Fox, Mr. Gray, Mr. Cassidy, Mr. Brady, and Mr. Haffey. Mr. Cassidy's house was used for a short time, and the second Christmas Mass was celebrated in Humphrey Hall. Though Father Daly was appointed pastor of New Britain in September, 1848, he did not take up his permanent residence there until Wednesday, May 9, 1849. In September, 1850, he began the erection of a church on Myrtle street, 84 feet in length by 45 feet in width. The site which he had secured for the church was purchased for $225. It was the second brick church in the State, the first—old St. James' of Bridgeport—having been erected by Father Smith. The ceremony of dedication took place on August 11, 1853. A contemporary thus wrote of the new church : "There is now here a Catholic church in the early English Gothic style, chaste and perfect in all its proportions. It is the first church of its kind I have seen in which the style is carried out, and is a relief from the barn style, which might be considered the favorite church style in too many sections of our country. The Rev. Mr. Daly is pastor of this, with other missions, to whose energy and labors the good village of New Britain is indebted for this beautiful Gothic church. The congregation is increasing so fast that the church, erected with a view to meet the increasing hosts of Catholicity, is already well filled. The congregation is well spoken of as practical in religion and ever obedient to the monitions of their pastor." In 1851, Father Daly purchased the old cemetery, which was blessed by Bishop McFarland in 1859. He also bought the pastoral residence on Lafayette street in 1857. In September, 1862, Father Daly added to the church a transept 32 feet by 75 feet, and a chancel 42½ feet by 30 feet, which was dedicated by Bishop McFarland on October 11, 1868. The benefactors of this church deserve mention here. Besides Father Daly himself, they were Peter Skelly, William Cassidy, Peter Slain, Joseph Cassidy, Patrick Downs, Patrick Keely, Hugh Fox, Michael Gray, John Haffey, John Bowman, and Patrick Claffey. "We had only poor men to assist us," wrote Father Daly; "but the above gave most towards building the church." In 1866 a bell was purchased for the church and blessed on September 30th of that year by Bishop McFarland. A sacristy, 40 by 20 feet, was also added to the rear of the church. On May 28, 1877, Father Daly began the erection of St. Thomas' Convent, on Lafayette street, the corner-stone of which was laid by Bishop Galberry. Before the convent was completed, however, Father Daly was called to his reward. After thirty-two years of incessant and successful toil in the Master's vineyard, he passed away after a brief illness on June 30, 1878, in the 56th year of his age. Father Daly was born in the County Cavan, Ireland, and was educated at All Hallows' College, a nursery of priests. He was ordained in 1846 by Bishop Tyler, and resided soon after with Father Brady of Hartford. Father Daly's death was a public loss, and the following words of a contemporary testify to the esteem in which he was held :

ST. MARY'S CHURCH.

New Britain

"The flags floating at half-mast on every public building on the eve of the Fourth of July! Every wheel still, and the busy hum of industry hushed in the workshops of a city of 15,000, in Puritan New England, in Protestant Connecticut! Shutters closed on all the business streets! What was the cause of all this public demonstration of respect and veneration? It was because a noble-hearted Catholic priest was dead—a man of no extraordinary abilities, as the world counts genius, but a man whose watchword through life was duty—a priest whose whole life was devoted to the cause of God—a hero of modern times, whose fields of conflict and victory were in the confessional, at the altar, and in the midst of his flock; who had seen New Britain a village and left it a city; who had found the Catholics there few in numbers—about fifty, without strength or reputation—and who left them increased to from 5,000 to 6,000, nearly a third of the population. Well was it that New Britain should mourn; well was it that the church should be crowded; well was it that the chief shepherd of the flock in the diocese and the reverend clergy all over the State should assemble to pay the last tribute of respect to Rev. Luke Daly, New Britain's pastor for nearly thirty years."

The Pontifical Mass of requiem was said by Bishop Galberry, after which the Rev. Dr. Carmody pronounced the funeral sermon and paid this tribute to his departed friend:

"He was a man full of faith, of no pretense. More brilliant priests I have known, but none possessing more priestly traits. He was careful of the neatness, and as time permitted, even of the splendor of the church, devoted to the education of the children, and constant in the confessional. He loved his people and studied both their temporal and eternal interests. He respected those who, although not Catholics, were his fellow-citizens, and was interested in the prosperity of this city."

The Rev. Hugh Carmody, D.D., of New Haven, was appointed the successor of Father Daly on July 16, 1878, and assumed charge of the parish on Sunday, July 21st. His administration was signalized by the completion of the convent, and the purchase of a fine site on North Main street, on which he intended to erect a new church, as the old St. Mary's had become too small for the steadily increasing congregation. Moreover, it was being surrounded by factories. It was unsafe and not in keeping with the dignity and membership of St. Mary's parish. The lot purchased by Dr. Carmody has a frontage of 300 feet, is the same width on Beaver street, and cost $29,000. But death intervened, and the work was postponed. Dr. Carmody passed from earth on April 23, 1883. His last public words about his plans were: "Whosoever will complete the work I began will leave a lasting monument as evidence of the generosity of the Catholics of New Britain." During his administration the parish prospered, and through his efforts the present parochial schools were opened.

The Rev. Michael A. Tierney succeeded Dr. Carmody in May, 1883. He began and carried to completion the work of the church's construction. The corner-stone was laid on June 27, 1886, by Bishop McMahon, Very Rev. A. V. Higgins, O. P., of New Haven, preaching the sermon. The basement was dedicated to the Sacred Heart by the same bishop on September 8, 1889. The preacher was the Rev. Charles McKenna, O. P. Before the main church was dedicated Father Tierney was transferred to a higher position and to weightier responsibilities.

It is of rare occurrence that a bishop dedicates a church which he himself erected as pastor. But on March 4, 1894, Bishop Tierney, with ceremonial the most impressive, solemnly dedicated to God, under the patronage of His ever Blessed Mother, the magnificent edifice upon which he had been engaged for ten years. It was his first public official act as bishop, and a gratifying one it must have been to the devoted people who generously followed his spiritual guidance throughout those years. After Bishop Tierney had concluded the ceremony of dedication, Solemn Pontifical High Mass was celebrated with the following officers:

*Celebrant*, RIGHT REV. JOHN S. MICHAUD, D. D., Coadjutor Bishop of Burlington, Vt.
*Assistant Priest*, The REV. JAMES NIHIL, Bridgeport.
*Deacon*, The REV. JEREMIAH CURTIN, New Milford.
*Sub-Deacon*, The REV. PETER SKELLY, Litchfield.
*Masters of Ceremonies*, The REV. J. CURTIN, New Haven; the REV. M. MAY, New Britain.
*Preacher*, The REV. JAMES C. O'BRIEN, Bridgeport.

Present in the sanctuary were Right Rev. Bishop Beaven of Springfield, and about forty priests. The sacrament of confirmation was administered at 3 P.M. for the first time in the new church to two hundred children and adults. At the Vesper service Bishop Tierney presided, and the Rev. Timothy O'Brien, of Noroton, pronounced the discourse.

St. Mary's church is of Portland brown stone, with rich carvings. Within are three marble altars, one in memory of Father Daly, one in memory of Rev. Dr. Carmody, and the main altar, which is a marvel of workmanship. The ceiling is of ribbed wood-work in artistic colors, the mouldings being of beautiful design. Elegant portraits of twenty saints adorn the panels. The large circular window over the main altar contains pictures of the Twelve Apostles and the Holy Family. There are sixteen stained glass windows portraying leading events in sacred history. Nine large pillars support the roof, and are handsomely decorated. The lights are encircled around these columns. Over the main altar is a handsome group of the Crucifixion. The edifice is Gothic in style, 127 feet long and 80 feet wide. The main auditorium is 100 feet by 80, with a height of 60 feet from the floor to the ceiling. Its seating capacity is 1,500. The chapel of the Sacred Heart, the basement, seats about the same number.

Bishop Tierney was succeeded by the present incumbent, the Rev. William A. Harty, who preached his initial sermon as pastor of St. Mary's parish on Sunday, March 25, 1894. Bringing to his new field of labor ripe experience, reliable judgment, and zeal judiciously tempered with prudence, Father Harty has not only materially reduced the indebtedness, but is keeping the parish on the high spiritual plane established by his predecessors. Father

REV. RICHARD F. MOORE A.M.

REV. N. F. X. SCHNEIDER.

REV. WILLIAM A. HARTY

REV. LUCIAN BOJNOWSKI.

REV. JOSEPH ZEBRIS.

Harty is a diocesan consultor and a member of the Board of Examiners of the clergy.

St. Mary's has two cemeteries. The old burial place was purchased in July, 1851, during the pastorate of Father Daly, and blessed by Bishop Mc-Farland in April, 1859. The new cemetery was bought by Father Tierney in August, 1890, and blessed on May 30, 1893, by Bishop McMahon. Besides the church, rectory and schools, the parish possesses the old parochial residence and grounds on Lafayette street, corner of High, and the sexton's house on Beaver street.

The number of baptisms administered between the years 1849 and 1898 (to June) was 10,724; the number of marriages was 2,313.[1]

The clergymen who have served as assistants in St. Mary's parish are the following:

*With Father Daly:* Revs. Henry Lynch, Thomas Mullen, William Harty, Thomas Smith John H. Duggan, Patrick H. Finnegan.

*With Dr. Carmody:* Revs. John C. Donahoe, James Larkin, J. H. Ryan, M. McKeon, E. McGee, T. J. Hanavan, R. C. Gragan, J. H. Dolan.

*With Father Tierney:* Rev. R. C. Gragan, J. H. Dolan, N. F. X. Schneider, J. W. Lancaster, J. T. McMahon, W. J. McGurk, W. H. Gibbons, Michael May, J. J. Fitzgerald.

*With Father Harty:* Revs. M. May, J. J. Fitzgerald, M. Sheehan, J. Lee, D. A. Bailey, P. J. O'Reilley, J. McLoughlin, D. D.

The estimated population of St. Mary's parish is 6,000 souls, principally Irish, with many French Canadians and a few Italians.

St. Mary's Parochial School.—The first Catholic school in New Britain was built in May, 1862, and opened in the following September, lay teachers being employed. It was about the time the transept was being added. The school building was being constructed at the same time, and the school was organized in the church, classes being formed in the pews. When the school proper opened there were two rooms. The one on the first floor was for the boys and was taught by Mr. Joseph Cullen, now of Waterbury, who was the principal. The girls occupied the second floor, and were taught by a Mr. Grace. Mr. Grace was succeeded by Miss Jennie E. Barnes, who has made teaching her life work and who still resides in New Britain. Mr. Cullen was succeeded by Mr. Thomas O'Dell, a graduate of the New Britain Normal school. In 1871 Mr. John A. O'Brien, A.B., a graduate of St. Francis Xavier College, New York, was called from Providence to succeed Mr. O'Dell. Father Daly inaugurated a Latin School under Mr. O'Brien's tuition, and the class gave to the Church the following priests: Rev. J. J. Curtin, Waterbury; Rev. T. F. O'Brien, Noroton; Rev. J. Curtin, West Haven; Rev. T. J. Mullin, Missouri Valley, Iowa; Hugh McAvoy, Kilkenny, Minn. Rev. P. Skelly, of Litchfield, and Rev. James B. Nihil of Bridgeport, were pupils of this school from its opening. The following table, gathered

[1] For about half of the first decade, *i. e.*, from 1849 to 1854, the marriage and birth entries include the adjacent towns of Farmington, Tariffville, the Mines, Bristol, Berlin, Collinsville, Simsbury, Rainbow, etc.

from authentic sources, will be of interest, as showing the increase in child population for nine years:

| Year | No. of pupils. | Year | No. of pupils. |
|---|---|---|---|
| 1862 | 170 | 1867 | 375 |
| 1863 | 200 | 1868 | 400 |
| 1864 | 300 | 1869 | 450 |
| 1865 | 350 | 1870 | 525 |
| 1866 | 375 | | |

At present there are 1343 pupils, three school buildings, twenty-four Sisters of Mercy, with nine grades. Sister M. Raymond is the superior of St. Thomas convent. Numerically St. Mary's school is the first in the diocese; in point of excellence, in methods of teaching and in the success that attends its graduates, it is second to none. It has sent forth into the world hundreds of young men and women who are loyal citizens of the State and devoted children of the Church. Among the institutions of New Britain that have contributed to the prosperity of the city, in the front rank stands deservedly St. Mary's parochial school.

## ST. PETER'S (GERMAN) PARISH,
### NEW BRITAIN.

AMONG the earliest German Catholics to settle in New Britain were Thomas Schmitt and M. Marron. With few exceptions, the first German Catholics who came hither wandered from the household of the faith. Forming new affiliations they sundered the ties that bound them to the church of their baptism. Into Freemasonry went some of them, into infidelity others. The cause of their apostasy? It is difficult to attribute their defection to any particular cause. Dearth of priests, infrequency of instruction, lack of opportunity to assist at Mass and to frequent the sacraments, pride, association—all have been causes contributing to apostasy. But the history of the Church proves that faith is surrendered only willingly; that those who wish to preserve it, will keep it even at the sacrifice of life itself.

The first Mass celebrated for the Germans of New Britain was said in 1872, probably by the Rev. H. Wendelschmidt, who was appointed in 1868 the first pastor of the German Catholics of New Haven. The first baptism was administered on July 15, 1872. In the spring of 1874, Rev. Father Schale succeeded Father Wendelschmidt at New Haven and assumed charge also of the German Catholics of New Britain. After a short while, however, Father Schale relinquished the New Britain mission to Rev. John Herman Bernard Jaspers, who attended also the Germans of Hartford.

The present incumbent, the Rev. Nicholas F. X. Schneider, received his appointment on July 17, 1889, as pastor of the German Catholics of Hartford and New Britain. Father Schneider resided in Hartford for a year, when he took up his residence in New Britain in July, 1890.

The church, which has not been built beyond the basement, was begun by Father Schneider in 1890. The land upon which it is built was purchased in the fall of this year by Joseph Schilling. On November 23d of that year the corner-stone was laid by Bishop McMahon, the Rev. Boniface Goebbles, a Capuchin Friar, preaching the sermon. The dedication ceremony took place on July 19, 1891, Very Rev. James Hughes, V. G., officiating. The Mass which followed the dedication services was celebrated by Rev. M. A. Tierney, assisted by Rev. T. Shelly as deacon, Rev. J. Lynch as sub-deacon, and Rev. W. Maher, D.D., as master of ceremonies. The preacher was Rev. Father Anastasius, O.M., Cap., of New York. Work on the superstructure was resumed on May 17, 1899, and the edifice is to be completed by January 1, 1900.

When the first Mass was said for the German Catholics of New Britain, in 1872, there were about 100 souls. When the parish was organized in 1889, the number was estimated at 300. At present there are 500.

From July, 1889, to 1898, the sacrament of Baptism was conferred upon 190 persons, and during the same period the marriage ceremony was performed 30 times.

The first piece of land purchased by the German Catholics of New Britain for church purposes was secured in 1873, and on July 2nd of that year the parish was incorporated according to the laws of the State with Right Rev. Francis P. McFarland, D.D., Very Rev. James Hughes, V.G., and Rev. Joseph Schale, as the ecclesiastical members of the corporation, Charles Kemmerer and Frederick Engel being the lay members.

The first death after the formation of the parish was that of Mrs. Ambrose Schmitt, August 6, 1889. The first marriage was solemnized on November 12, 1889, the contracting parties being Frank Benz and Margaret Siering. The first child to receive baptism during Father Schneider's pastorate was Barbara Elizabeth Merget.

The present trustees are Thomas Schmitt and Arthur Volz.

## SACRED HEART PARISH,
### NEW BRITAIN.

IN 1894, the Polish Catholics of New Britain were sufficiently numerous to have assigned to them a priest of their own nationality. On August 10th, of that year, Rev. Thomas Misicki, D.D., the new pastor, said Mass for the first time for his flock in St. Mary's church. At that time his parish had a population of 700 souls, comprising Poles, Slavonians and Ruthenians. Rev. Dr. Misicki remained here a year, when he was succeeded by the present pastor, Rev. Lucian Bojnowski, on September 26, 1895. The present church was begun on April 16, 1896. It is a frame structure, 45 x 100 feet. The upper story is used for divine worship, while the first floor contains a school and the apartments of the rector. The church seats 528 persons. The ceremony of laying the corner-stone took place on July 19, 1896, Bishop Tierney officiating. Present on the occasion were Very Rev. J. A. Mulcahy, V.G., Rev. J. P. Donovan, D.D., Very Rev. P. Pajot, M.S., Rev. W. A. Harty, Rev. R. Moore, Rev. T. Mizotus, Rev. K. Kucharski, Rev. D. Bailey, Rev. J. Fitzgerald, Rev. P. O'Reilly. The Polish societies were present at the ceremony in large numbers. The church was dedicated on October 4th of the same year by

Bishop Tierney in the presence of a large assemblage of the clergy and laity.

When the school was opened forty-two pupils were enrolled. There are now 150, with three grades taught by lay teachers.

The last census of the parish disclosed 1330 souls; 1200 of whom are Poles, 50 Slavonians and 80 Ruthenians. The number of baptisms from the organization of the parish in 1894 to 1898 was 537; the number of marriages for the same time was 172.

Through the zeal of Father Bojnowski, two Protestants and one Jew have received the grace of conversion.

## ST. ANDREW'S (LITHUANIAN) PARISH,
### New Britain.

ON October 1, 1895, Bishop Tierney requested the Rev. Joseph Zebris, pastor of St. Joseph's (Lithuanian) parish, Waterbury, to say Mass every Sunday for the Lithuanians of New Britain. Thereafter, Father Zebris visited New Britain weekly and offered the Holy Sacrifice of the Mass in St. Mary's church, and discharged other duties belonging to his office as pastor. Desirous of possessing a church of their own, they began to make preparations for the accomplishment of the work. Accordingly, on New Year's Day, 1896, the corner-stone of St. Andrew's church was laid in the presence of a large concourse of people. Bishop Tierney addressed the large assemblage in English, and the pastor delivered a discourse to his countrymen. The ceremony of dedication took place on Easter Sunday, 1896, the pastor, Father Zebris, officiating, who also said on that day the first Mass celebrated in the new church. To liquidate the indebtedness thus incurred, the Lithuanians with their pastor collected $3,000.

On July 1, 1896, the Lithuanians received as pastor the Rev. Joseph Masrolas, who remained about six months. St. Andrew's was then attended by the clergy of St. Mary's and Sacred Heart parishes until Father Zebris again assumed charge. He attended New Britain from Waterbury until June 1, 1898, when, at the request of Bishop Tierney, he took up his residence at New Britain, and became the resident pastor of St. Andrew's. In October of that year, Father Zebris built the pastoral residence at a cost of $1,700. The property of St. Andrew's parish is valued at $12,000. The population is 400 souls. The baptisms average thirty-five annually and the marriages fifteen.

## ST. JOSEPH'S PARISH.
### New Britain.

ST. JOSEPH'S parish was organized on April 9, 1896, by Rev. Richard F. Moore, A. M., its first pastor, who celebrated his first Mass here in St. Peter's chapel, Sunday, April 19th, of that year. The estimated number of Catholics when the parish was formed was 1000 Irish, Irish-Americans and a few French. Among those living in this section of the city for any notable time before the formation of the parish are William Stewart, Edward Nihil, John Nolan, Michael Donnelly,

J. and P. O'Sullivan, Judge Roche, P. J. Flannery, Mrs. Devitt, Michael O'Connell, William and Patrick Coughlin, Richard O'Dell and John L. Gardiner.

Father Moore began immediately to make preparations for the erection of a church for his flock. The people responded generously to his appeals for financial aid, and the work progressed so favorably that the corner-stone was soon laid by Bishop Tierney, assisted by Very Rev. J. A. Mulcahy, V. G., and Rev. W. Harty, assistant priests; Rev. N. Schneider, deacon; Rev. J. Lynch, sub-deacon; Rev. J. Fitzgerald, cross bearer; Rev. H. Walsh and Rev. W. J. Dullard, chanters. The sermon was preached by Monsignor T. J. Conaty, D.D. Among the priests present were Rev. M. Rodden, Rev. P. McGivney, Rev. C. McCann, Rev. P. O'Leary, Rev. M. Sullivan, Rev. L. Bojnowski, Rev. A. Mizotus, Rev. D. Bailey and Rev. P. O'Reilly. Five thousand people witnessed the impressive ceremony. On the platform were seated many Protestant ministers, members of the Board of Education, Board of Aldermen, Councilmen and the Mayor. Work on the church progressed under the most favorable circumstances, the enthusiasm of the people increasing as they witnessed the fruition of their labors. On September 19, 1897, the new church was solemnly dedicated to God under the patronage of St. Joseph, patron of the Universal Church. Bishop Tierney officiated at this ceremony, after which a Solemn High Mass was sung, with Rev. J. B. Nihil as celebrant, Rev. H. T. Walsh as deacon, Rev. M. Sullivan as sub-deacon, Rev. R. Early as master of ceremonies; chaplains to Bishop Tierney, Rev. B. O., R. Sheridan and Rev. W. J. Slocum. Rev. W. J. Shanley, rector of the cathedral, preached on "The Beauty of God's House." A number of priests of the diocese were present in the sanctuary. St. Joseph's church has attached to it a school containing four commodious and well-ventilated rooms, which was erected with the church and blessed on the same day. The school, however, has not yet been opened for the reception of pupils. It is the intention of the pastor to convert a dwelling-house of two tenements on the church property into a convent.

The benefactors of St. Joseph's parish are William Stewart, who donated $500 for the main altar; the family of Edward Nihil and that of Mrs. Devitt; Mrs. J. Sullivan, who contributed the Blessed Virgin's altar, and Patrick Mulligan, the sexton, who donated St. Joseph's altar; Michael Donnelly, trustee, and Judge Roche, clerk of the church committee, whose generosity has been made manifest on various occasions. As evidence of the people's coöperation with their pastor, it may be stated that in one collection they contributed $3000 to furnish the church.

The baptisms for the first year numbered twenty-one, for the second, thirty-two. The marriages for the same periods were three and nine respectively.

St. Joseph's parish is in the residential portion of the city; here are the State Normal School and the new High School. Many of its principal members occupy positions of trust in political, business and factory life, while others are an honor to the teaching profession. The young parish has entered upon its career auspiciously and has made enviable progress in the temporal and spiritual orders. Its prospects for a successful future are bright, indeed, if the successes of the past be any criterion.

## OUR LADY OF MERCY,

### PLAINVILLE.

PLAINVILLE in former years was called the "City of the Plains," and is situated about fourteen miles west of Hartford. The town received its name from the fact that its site is one unbroken plain, there being nothing like a hill within the limits of the township. It possesses fine railroad facilities, as both the Highland and Northampton divisions of the Consolidated Railroad pass through it and make it an important junction town. To these may be added the accommodation afforded by the "Third Rail" system and no less than four different trolley lines.

Notwithstanding its attractive and commercial advantages, there are but few large industries located in Plainville, and none of any importance has been introduced in many years. The population of the town has increased but little in twenty years, and the Catholic portion, owing to the few industries, has not increased with that rapidity and steadiness characteristic of large industrial centers.

The pioneer Catholics of Plainville were Luke Doyle, Daniel Kelly, James Prior, Christopher Callen and James McCaul. All of these, with the exception of James Prior, and possibly, Luke Doyle, were long since summoned to their reward, honored by all who knew of their devotion to the faith. The first Mass celebrated in Plainville was said in the residence of Daniel Kelly, about the year 1851, by the Rev. Luke Daly, whose kindly, priestly attentions are still fondly remembered. For some time afterwards Mass was said in "Neal's Hall," the present "Union House," which is under the management of Charles McCaul, the first Catholic child baptized in Plainville. For a number of years the Holy Sacrifice of the Mass was offered up in "Newton's Hall," which was destroyed by fire about a quarter of a century ago. "Morgan's Hall" was then secured, and the faithful band of Catholics attended divine worship here for a few years. At this period, and for some years previous, the spiritual care of the people of Plainville devolved upon the pastor of Bristol, the Rev. Michael B. Rodden.

At the celebration of the first Mass here, probably not more than a dozen Catholics were present, all of whom were Irish. As their numbers increased with the years, they began to discuss the feasibility of erecting a church where their faith could offer suitable homage to the Divine Mysteries. They petitioned the Ordinary of the diocese, Right Rev. Bishop McMahon of blessed memory, with the result that Plainville was taken from the jurisdiction of Bristol and attached to Kensington, both places forming a parish with the Rev. Paul F. McAlenney as its first rector. The work which the new pastor first undertook was the erection of a church, and so generous and constant was the co-operation of the people, that although the parish was formed on July 20th, 1881, the corner-stone was laid in the following December, and the impressive ceremony of dedication took place on September 24th, 1882. The beautiful altar which adorns the sanctuary was the gift of Mr. and Mrs. Frank McDermott.

On February 15th, 1885, the present pastor, the Rev. Henry T. Walsh, was transferred from Stamford to Plainville, as the successor to Father McAlenney. He began immediately the erection of a parochial residence. Again the devoted Catholics of Plainville responded cheerfully to their pastor's appeal for financial assistance, so that within six months a rectory, modern in all respects, was ready for occupancy. But more was yet to be accomplished. A cemetery was imperatively needed, as all burials took place either in Bristol or New Britain. As an evidence of the practical sympathy of the people towards this new project, it may be stated that the first collection taken up for the purpose was more than sufficient to liquidate the indebtedness incurred by the purchase of six acres of land on Farmington avenue. The cemetery was blessed on Sunday, July 12th, 1887, by Right Rev. Bishop McMahon. The sermon on the occasion was preached by the Rev. Richard Moore. The procession, made up of religious and civic societies, which marched to the cemetery on that day, was a revelation to the towns-people, and a parade equal to it has not since been duplicated.

The present Catholic population of Plainville is three hundred and seventy souls, ninety-five per cent. of whom are Irish. The first marriage solemnized here was that between James Prior and Ann Shields. The ecclesiastical property, consisting of the church and parochial residence, which are both lighted by electricity, and the cemetery, are striking proofs of the faith and generosity of the Catholics of Plainville, as well as of the zeal and energy of their pastors. The assistant priest is the Rev. P. F. Daly.

### ST. MATTHEW'S MISSION, FORESTVILLE.

Forestville, formerly served from Bristol, has been attended as a mission from Plainville since September 20th, 1891. For about ten years previous to this change, Mass was said every Sunday in "Firemen's Hall" by Rev. Father Rodden of Bristol. After the transfer of Forestville to the jurisdiction of Plainville, Father Walsh began immediately the erection of a church there. Excavations were begun on November 5th, 1891, and the corner-stone was laid by Right Rev. Bishop McMahon on January 17th, 1892. The work of construction was carried on so successfully that the first Mass was said in the basement by Father Walsh on Sunday, March 27th, 1892. The dedication ceremonies took place on June 12th, 1892, Bishop McMahon officiating. Five years later the superstructure, a beautiful building, was completed and dedicated to God under the patronage of the Apostle, St. Matthew, by Right Rev. Bishop Tierney, on June 27th, 1897. The church is valued at $15,000, is an ornament to the village, as well as a testimony to the faith of the 500 Catholics of Forestville.

### ST. PATRICK'S MISSION, FARMINGTON.

Farmington was detached from Bristol in February, 1885, and assigned to the jurisdiction of Plainville. The first disciples of the faith in this handsome old village were Thomas Smith, Lawrence McCahill, John Reilly, John Brady, Mrs. Mary Skelly and John Flood. The first Mass was said in the early fifties by the Rev. Luke Daly in the present residence of John Flood. The Catholic population of Farmington is chiefly Irish and numbers 200 souls. Mass is said every Sunday in the brick church purchased by Rev. Patrick Duggett and dedicated in honor of St. Patrick.

## ST. JOSEPH'S PARISH.

### POQUONOCK.

POQUONOCK, originally written Paquanocke, is one of the earliest settlements in Connecticut. It was founded in 1635. Its Catholic history dates from 1848, when the first Mass was said within its boundaries by the Rev. John Brady, at the residence of Samuel Conroy.

Poquonock came under the jurisdiction of the Rev. James Smyth, after his appointment as pastor of St. Mary's, at Windsor Locks in 1852. An humble building at the corner of Main street and Maple avenue became the house of worship, and though bereft of all that makes a church a veritable home, a haven of rest to the devout Catholic, it was nevertheless precious to them, for there they could gather before the rudely-constructed altar, and during the celebration of the divine mysteries, petition heaven for needed graces. This first place of worship afterwards came into the possession of the Catholics of Poquonock and was removed to the site of the present handsome edifice. Since the erection of the latter the original church has been transformed into a parish hall.

Before its organization into a separate parish Poquonock continued to be served successively by the Rev. James Smyth, Rev. Michael McAuley, Rev. Michael F. Kelly and Rev. James O'R. Sheridan. During the administration of the last-mentioned, the present fine structure was erected.

Ground was broken in June, 1886, the people co-operating enthusiastically with their pastor, gratified that God had so prospered them that they were soon to possess a church that would be an ornament to the village. Two months later the corner-stone was laid, the orator of the occasion being the Rev. Charles McKenna, O. P. The sacrifices of the people were rewarded and their labors crowned on January 30, 1887, when the new temple, placed under the patronage of the patron of the universal church, St. Joseph, was dedicated with impressive ceremonial. Bishop McMahon officiated on the auspicious occasion, and the dedication sermon was preached by Rev. Thomas W. Broderick, of Hartford.

Poquonock continued under Father Sheridan's jurisdiction for five years longer. The congregation was in a flourishing condition, and contentment reigned among them. The indebtedness had been reduced to $3,000 during Father Sheridan's incumbency, a comparatively small amount when we reflect that the church was thoroughly equipped with all things necessary for the proper and decent celebration of divine worship.

Father Flemming, the first resident pastor of Poquonock, received his appointment thereto in August, 1892, and immediately set about the work of erecting a parochial residence, which he completed at a cost of $2,625. To the liquidation of the indebtedness thus incurred may be added the reduction of the original mortgage debt to $1,000. After five and a half years of unremitting labor in this field Father Flemming was transferred to Bethel, as successor to the Rev. Patrick O'Connell, in the latter part of January, 1898. His successor is an active young priest, a worthy successor, and for many years assistant at St. Francis' parish, New Haven, the Rev. Thomas Shanley.

## ST. GABRIEL'S CHURCH,

### WINDSOR.

ST. GABRIEL'S CHURCH, Windsor, is an out-mission of Poquonock. The church is an old structure and has an interesting history, having been the church of the followers of the famous English clergyman, and friend of Cardinal Newman, Dr. Pusey. Here also the late Right Rev. Mgr. Preston, of New York, officiated as a Protestant clergyman. The church passed into the possession of the Catholics of Windsor during the pastorate of Rev. James Smyth in 1866. It remained under the jurisdiction of Windsor Locks until the formation of St. Joseph's parish, Poquonock, whose pastor has since attended it. Many notable improvements were made on the church and grounds during the pastorate of the Rev. Father Sheridan.

## ST. THOMAS' PARISH,

### SOUTHINGTON.

THE announcement of a sorrowful accident is the first indication we have of the presence in Southington of a member of the Church. The following notice is taken from *The Catholic Press*, Hartford, August 15, 1829:

"Drowned at Southington, Conn., on the 7th inst., Peter Dayle, aged about 44 years. The deceased was a native of Wexford in Ireland, and as he had friends and connexion in this country, editors of newspapers would perform an act of humanity by publishing this notice."

Whether Peter Dayle had compatriots in Southington, it is difficult now to determine. It is not unreasonable, however, to believe, that others from "Sweet Wexford," and, it may be, from elsewhere in the Green Isle, were with him here striving to build up homes in the land to which their youthful aspirations directed them. Bernard Kennedy was here very early, as were also Michael and Thomas Egan, Bernard Curran, John Carmody and Patrick Dolan—these, with their families constituting, as far as the records show, the first Catholic colony of Southington.

In 1852, the Rev. Hugh O'Reilly, of Meriden, offered here for the first time the Holy Sacrifice in the residence of John Cassidy on East Main street in the presence of about twenty-five persons. Southington remained attached to Meriden until 1850, in which year it was attended every third Sunday. In 1860, it was served every second Sunday from Wallingford, reverting to Meriden in 1861. The first resident pastor of Southington was the Rev. Thomas Drea, who assumed charge on September 4, 1862, and remained until October 7, 1867. Rev. Patrick J. Creighton immediately succeeded Father Drea and was pastor of St. Thomas' until his death. His successor was the Rev. William A. Harty, who assumed charge on September 15, 1882. Entering upon his new duties with energy, his zeal was manifested in the thorough renovation of the church and in making many other notable improvements. When he severed his connection with St. Thomas' parish, it was financially and otherwise firmly established. Father Harty's successor was the Rev. Matthew A. Hunt, who came on August 1, 1884. The present rectory was built during his administration. Father Hunt's labors were terminated by death, and his successor, the present incumbent, Rev. William J. Doolan, began his labors on March 26, 1894.

The corner-stone of St. Thomas' church was laid on July 4, 1860, and the edifice was dedicated in December of the same year.

The clergy who assisted the different pastors in parochial work were Rev. J. H. Carroll, Rev. J. J. Quinn, Rev. P. Byrne, Rev. R. Moore, Rev. P. Keating, Rev. P. Dineen, Rev. M. Traynor, Rev. J. Lee, and Rev. P. C. Dunigan.

When St. Thomas' parish was organized there were about 500 souls; at present the population is about 1500, principally Irish and their descendants, with some Italians, Poles, Hungarians and Germans.

## ST. JAMES' CHURCH,

### SOUTH MANCHESTER.

THE early Catholic history of South Manchester is mingled with that of the mother church, St. Bridget's, North Manchester. Mr. John Kennedy, who suffered the penalty of eviction by Landlord Stone, for permitting Father Brady to say Mass in his house, was a resident of this portion of the town. Other pioneers of the faith who performed yeomen's service in the cause of religion are Michael Connors, Denis Dunn, Catharine Moriarty, Catharine Powers, Mrs. John Riley, John and Patrick Connors. With their brethren of North Manchester, they were served from Rockville until the appointment of the Rev. James Campbell, in October, 1869. Until the completion of their own church, the Catholics of South Manchester attended St. Bridget's church in Manchester.

The land on which the church and rectory stand, consisting of one acre and worth $2800, was the generous gift to the parish of the Cheney Brothers, who have at intervals since given substantial contributions to the parish. Begun in 1874, St. James' church was completed and ready for dedication in August, 1876. The solemn ceremony took place on the 20th, with the Right Rev. Bishop presiding. The dedication completed, Solemn High Mass followed, with Rev. Thomas Kane, of Valley Falls, R. I., as celebrant; Rev.

REV. WILLIAM J. McGURK

REV. FRED W. MURPHY

REV. LUKE FITZSIMONS

REV. W. H. REDDING

REV. JEREMIAH DUGGAN

J. J. Furlong as deacon, Rev. P. Mulholland as sub-deacon, Rev. P. McCabe as master of ceremonies. The dedication discourse was pronounced by the Rev. Lawrence Walsh, of Waterbury. The edifice cost $30,000, and has a seating capacity of 750. The centre window represents our Saviour in life size, and was the gift of John Walsh, the builder. The windows on the Epistle side are the donations of Thomas Egan, Oliver Maxwell, Michael Walsh, Thomas Golden; those on the Gospel side were presented by William Dwyer, Denis Dunn, John Shaw and John Sullivan.

Before the church was entirely completed, the most dastardly sacrilege ever perpetrated in Connecticut was committed in St. James' church on the night of the 4th, or the morning of the 5th, of May, 1876. Thirty-five windows were broken, the vestry was ransacked, the altar despoiled of its ornaments and defiled. The altar cloths were afterwards found about a mile from the church, besmeared with blood, apparently from wounds which had been inflicted on the marauders by the broken glass of the church windows. They also attempted to fire the church, and with this object in view, collected a quantity of branches and brambles and placed them in position on the Gospel side of the altar and close to it. They were found in this position in the morning, with the evidences of fire having been applied, as some half-burnt matches were scattered near them. The town authorities promptly offered a reward of $200, to which the trustees of the church added $300 for the apprehension of the criminals. Suspicion, well grounded, at once fastened upon an Orangeman, Nicholas Murray. He had arrived in the town on the evening of the 4th and feigned ignorance of the place and people, but it was disclosed that he was acquainted with the prominent Orangemen and had attended a meeting of the lodge that evening. Murray disappeared immediately after the sacrilege, but was captured on May 19th, in New Hampshire, whither he had fled, having been warned by his Orangemen friends that officers were on his track. He was bound over in the sum of $200 to await his trial in the Superior Court of Tolland county.

Father Campbell, who died in 1890, pastor of St. Bridget's parish, Manchester, was interred in front of the church, South Manchester, where a splendid monument marks his last resting place.

The Rev. Daniel Haggerty was the first resident pastor of St. James' parish, coming here on November 21, 1890. For eight years previous he had been assistant to Father Campbell at Manchester. Father Haggerty built the pastoral residence at a cost of $5,000, towards which the Cheney Brothers contributed $2,000. Other improvements were made which were indicative of good taste and sound judgment. After a month spent in southern climes in search of health, Father Haggerty died at St. Vincent's Hospital, New York, in April, 1898.

His successor, the Rev. William McGurk, is the Diocesan Director of the League of the Sacred Heart, and the success that has thus far attended his ministry, in South Manchester, is a testimony of his sacerdotal zeal and solicitude. The population of St. James' parish is 1,500, principally Irish and their descendants.

The number of baptisms from 1891 to 1898 inclusive was 340; and the marriages for the same period, 97.

## ST. BERNARD'S PARISH,
### TARIFFVILLE.

THE earliest evidence we possess of the presence of Catholics in Tariff-ville is the following record of marriage:

Jas. Kelly            ) "*1842, October 14th:* Married at Tariffville, James Kelly to Rosanna
    and            -    McEllier. Witnesses: Felix Gaffney and Rose McEllier.
Rosanna McEllier )                                             JAS. MCDERMOT."

In October, 1830, Rev. Peter Walsh, the successor of Father Fitton in Hart-ford, reported twenty-four Catholics in Tariffville. The Catholics here con-tinued to be served by the Rev. John Brady of Hartford, until the appointment of the Rev. Luke Daly as pastor of New Britain, in September, 1848. In 1850 a small church was built on the "Mountain Road." Before this, Mass was said in a barn and afterwards in the house of one of the parishioners. This church was destroyed by fire in 1876 and Rev. B. O'R. Sheridan, pastor of Collinsville, purchased a more suitable site upon which to build the second church. Bishop O'Reilly made a visitation here on May 19, 1851, offered the Holy Sacrifice and preached. Tariffville remained under the jurisdiction of St. Mary's, New Britain, until the formation of Collinsville into an inde-pendent parish on December 10, 1856.

Among the early settlers of Tariffville whose names have come down to us, were Thomas Flynn, Neil Lagan, Patrick Timon, John McAleer, James Kelly, Moses Leary and Richard Mulherring. Rev. John Brady of Hart-ford celebrated the first Mass said in Tariffville in 1846; at this period there were about fifteen Catholics here. The first church was built by Father Daly, and was forty by sixty feet in the clear. The Catholic population at the time of the erection of the church was about 100 souls. The principal benefactor of the old church was Bishop Tyler who donated $100 to the building fund.

The priests who successively attended Tariffville until it was set apart as a separate parish were: Revs. James McDermot (and perhaps, Fathers O'Cavanagh and Fitton), Peter Walsh, John Brady, Luke Daly, P. O'Dwyer, Philip Daly, John Fagan, L. Walsh and B. O'R. Sheridan.

About May 1, 1881, Tariffville was formed into a parish with Bloomfield as a mission. Rev. John Quinn was the first resident pastor and remained until his death on December 20, 1890. The present rectory was purchased during his pastorate. On Ash Wednesday, 1892, during the administration of his successor, Rev. James Walsh, a conflagration destroyed the church. A new site adjoining the rectory was purchased and an attractive and com-modious church was erected upon it. The corner-stone was laid by Bishop McMahon in 1892, Rev. T. W. Broderick preaching on the occasion. It was dedicated in May, 1895. On June 1 of that year Father Walsh was trans-ferred and his successor, the present incumbent, Rev. M. C. Cray, immedi-ately assumed charge.

Father Cray attends also the church of the Sacred Heart, Bloomfield. This mission was organized by Rev. Joseph Reid of the cathedral parish, and was subsequently attended by Fathers Kelly and Harty. The church, a handsome structure, was erected during the rectorship of Father Harty. The corner-stone was laid on September 8, 1878, by Bishop Galberry, assisted by Very Rev. T. Walsh, V.G., Rev. Dr. Carmody, Rev. M. Tierney, Rev. M. Galligan, Rev. P. McAlenny, Rev. J. Larkin. The sermon was preached by Rev. Dr. Carmody. The contributions on the occasion realized $440.

The dedication of the church on Sunday, August 17, 1879, was the first public official act of Bishop McMahon, the ceremony taking place one week after his consecration. The celebrant of the Mass, which followed the dedicatory services, was the Rev. M. F. Kelly, and Very Rev. James Hughes, V.G., preached the sermon. At the conclusion of the Mass, Bishop McMahon addressed the congregation as follows:

" My first public act in the Diocese of Hartford, the blessing of this church, was partly by my own choice and partly by circumstances. I am sincerely glad to commence my labors among my people by such an act. The dedication of a new church is an important event of itself, for it is the establishment of a new centre from which should go forth all spiritual graces and blessings ; but I take especial delight in dedicating this particular church because I understand it is practically free from debt. This is a good omen, a happy augury. The Catholics of Bloomfield have, in their act of dedicating a church practically free from debt, given a good example to more wealthy churches elsewhere, and done credit to themselves. I congratulate you and your pastor. You must have been very generous, or you have had good friends to assist you. I presume both suppositions are true. The church is a perfect little gem, complete in all its appointments. As you have done so much now, I hope that you will do still more; that you will make use of the church for the purposes for which it was designed, and then it will indeed prove the means of rich blessings to you and your children."

## ST. PATRICK'S PARISH,

### Thompsonville.

IT is not improbable that the Rev. Father Woodley and the Rev. Father O'Cavanagh visited Thompsonville in 1828, 1829 and 1830, upon the occasions of their periodical trips to the Enfield Canal. The latter was the first resident priest in Hartford, and made frequent visits to the northern section of the State. At any rate, the Rev. James Fitton, Father O'Cavanagh's successor, made a missionary visit to Thompsonville and offered the Holy Sacrifice of the Mass in the house of Richard Murphy in the fall of 1831. Upon his arrival at Thompsonville he arranged to deliver a lecture, which was largely attended by the Protestants of the town, who were moved by curiosity to see a " real live Catholic priest." Throughout this whole section there were about ten disciples of the old faith, and after the lecture they were quietly notified that Mass would be said the next morning before daylight in the house above mentioned. According to appointment, the few Catholics who could possibly attend, assembled in this modest home in the gray dawn of that memorable morning to be present at the Adorable Sacrifice. *There were seven in attendance.* It was not a Sunday morning, and those who came did so at the risk of being summarily discharged by their bigoted employers.

Mass was not said again in Thompsonville for three years. On this occasion the attendance was larger, as a few additional Catholics had come to work in the neighborhood. The marriage register bears testimony to this visit as follows:

"Thompsonville, Conn.

Peter Casey          ) 1834, August 13. Married, Peter Casey to Elizabeth Bachelder.
     and             Witnesses, Patrick and Mary Collins.
Elizabeth Bachelder \                                                  JAS. FITTON."

The small band of the faithful was not again blessed with the presence of a priest until 1837, when it is said a Father Murphy, happening in the vicinity, gladly sojourned a few days with them and ministered to their wants. This priest officiated in the house of James Benson, a worthy pioneer of the faith. In 1838 the Catholics of Thompsonville were consoled by the visits of another priest, the Rev. John Brady, of Hartford, at intervals of three months. So strong was the current of intolerance that Father Brady was compelled to say Mass at *four o'clock in the morning* in Mr. Benson's residence. Having been previously advised by Father Brady, he would carry the glad tidings of his coming visits to the Catholics of the town.

After the arrival of Father Smyth as assistant to Father Brady, he ministered to the wants of the faithful for six or seven years; and a private dwelling being now too small for their rapidly increasing numbers, the town hall was secured and used for divine service once a month. During this period Father Smyth received the occasional assistance of various priests, among whom were the Rev. Father Doherty, of Springfield, Mass.; the Rev. Father Duffy, of Rhode Island, and the Rev. Father Hogan, of Long Island. Increasing numbers brought to the devoted band confidence in their ability to build a church. Accordingly, Father Smyth purchased ground and announced his intention to erect a suitable house of worship. In a short time a fine, spacious and handsome frame structure arose. To this building Father Tully built an addition after a few years, so rapidly did the congregation increase. This edifice, the first Catholic church in Thompsonville, was erected in 1860.

Among the sturdy pioneers of Catholicity, other than those already mentioned, we may note the names of James Donovan, Patrick O'Brien, John Hubbard, Patrick Carroll and Daniel Lawlor.

In Bishop O'Reilly's journal under date of February 9, 1852, is this entry:
"Wrote Rev. Carmody appointing him to the missions of Thompsonville and Windsor Locks; this good young priest was sent to Bridgeport, but left, and begged these missions." Dr. Carmody officiated in Thompsonville on three occasions. His successor in Windsor Locks was the Rev. James Smyth.

The first resident pastor of Thompsonville was the Rev. Bernard Tully, who assumed charge in January, 1863. His term of service was three years, having as successor, the Rev. William E. Duffy, October, 1866. During his pastorate he enlarged the church and built the present convent, though he intended it for a pastoral residence. Having been transferred before the building was completed, the work was carried on by the Rev. John Cooney, who came to Thompsonville in May, 1871. Instead of occupying the new building himself, Father Cooney installed therein a band of Sisters of Mercy, whom he had brought from Hartford. Other substantial evidences of his labors are the parochial school and the present rectory. After a service of eight years he was followed by the Rev. John A. Mulcahy, the present Vicar General, who reduced the parish indebtedness $9,000, besides purchasing the choice lot upon which the present church stands. In October, 1881, the Rev. Patrick Donahoe assumed control of the parish and began the erection of the new church, having disposed by sale of the old buildings that stood on the premises. Father Donahoe also purchased a public-school building, moved it to the lot adjoining the convent, renovated it in a suitable manner and opened it for school purposes. The Rev. Joseph Gleason then came in January, 1889, and immediately took up the work of completing the church. The corner-stone was laid on August 11, 1889. The discourse on the occasion was delivered by the Rev. M. A. Tierney. The work progressed apace, and on October 16, 1892, the basement was dedicated by Right Rev. Bishop McMahon. The celebrant of the Pontifical High Mass was the Most Rev. Archbishop Fabre of Montreal. Other works, such as enlarging the school and the building of a boiler house, closed a pastorate of six years. The present rector is the Rev. Thomas J. Preston, who took charge on December 8, 1895, and with whom the people are cheerfully co-operating to the end, that both may witness the dedication of their magnificent church as a fitting crown to their work. Father Preston's assistant is the Rev. James W. Hoey.

When St. Patrick's parish was organized in 1863, its population was estimated at 500 souls, comprising Irish, Germans and a few French Canadians. In 1898 it was 1700, and of the same nationalities. During the thirty-five years of its parochial existence, 3074 souls have been regenerated by the saving waters of baptism, while during the same period 744 were united in wedlock. Among the generous benefactors of St. Patrick's parish are the Hartford Carpet Company, William Cashman and Mrs. Mary Diedrich. The parish possesses a beautiful cemetery, which was purchased in 1868 by Father Tully, and blessed in the same year by Bishop McFarland.

The assistants who have served in Thompsonville are: Rev. M. F. Kelly, Rev. John H. Duggan, Rev. Thomas Smith, Rev. H. T. Walsh, Rev. Joseph Gleason, Rev. James H. O'Donnell, Rev. W. H. Redding, Rev. R. Walsh, Rev. John Broderick, Rev. D. J. O'Connor, Rev. D. J. Lawlor, Rev. C. W. Morrell, Rev. W. J. Kelly and Rev. James Hoey. The Rev. Father Preston is a member of the Diocesan School Commission.

St. Patrick's school was built during the incumbency of the Rev. Father Cooney. When it was opened it was attended by 200 pupils. At present there are 133 boys and 164 girls in attendance. There are seven class-rooms, six in the main school, and one in the old church building now used for gymnasium purposes. Sister Leo is the Superioress. The educational work accomplished in this school is of a gratifying character, and reflects deserved credit upon the management of it.

## ST. MARY'S, STAR OF THE SEA, PARISH,

### UNIONVILLE.

FOR many years the Catholics of Unionville were faithfully and regularly attended by the Rev. Luke Daly, pastor of St. Mary's parish, New Britain. In 1854 he began to say Mass here, and continued to do so until the appointment to Collinsville of the Rev. Patrick O'Dwyer, early in 1857. He was succeeded in 1861 by the Rev. John Fagan, whose pastorate ended in 1868. Rev. Lawrence Walsh then became pastor of Collinsville and dependencies, and labored in this jurisdiction until May, 1870. His successor was the Rev. B. O'R. Sheridan.

These priests were unremitting in their care for their Unionville charges. They organized them into a compact body, and were zealous in inculcating the necessity and importance of strict adherence to their religious obligations. In 1876 they had become so numerous and had given such unequivocal evidences of their desire and ability to build a church, that a large and attractive edifice was completed and dedicated in that year. At this time the Catholic population numbered about 600 souls.

Their devotion to the church and regular attendance at its various services; their reception of the sacraments and generous contributions to the support of religious and charitable works—all demonstrated to the central authority of the diocese the wisdom of forming the congregation into an independent parish. This was accordingly done to the joy of the people, and the Rev. P. Fox was appointed the first resident pastor. He entered upon his pastorate with the determination to place his new charge upon a solid spiritual and financial basis. The rectory, the many improvements made on the church property, the prudent management of the finances of the parish attest his activity and success.

The present incumbent, the Rev. W. H. Redding, is the second pastor of St. Mary's, and faithful is he in the discharge of the duties which devolve upon him. Having enlarged the parochial residence, beautified the grounds and in other ways enhanced the value of the parish's possessions, he has also guarded the spiritual welfare of his people. St. Mary's parish, which now has 850 souls, consisting of Irish people and their descendants, is in a prosperous condition and is fulfilling its mission of forming devoted children of the church and useful citizens of the State.

## PARISH OF THE SACRED HEART,

### WETHERSFIELD.

THE town of Wethersfield received its name on February 21st, 1636. "It is ordered that the plantacon nowe called Newtowne shal be called & named by the name of Harteford Towne, likewise the plantacon nowe called Watertowne shal be called & named Wythersfield."[1] The boundaries of the town were also then allotted.[2] "Samuell Wakeman and

[1] *Public Records of Conn.*, 1636–1665.        [2] *Ibid.*

Ancient Stoughton doe thinke meete that the boundes of Wythersfield[1] shal be extended toward the Rivers mouth in the same side it standes in to a Tree Sixe miles downeward from the boundes between them & Harteford [marked w^th] N: F: & to [run in an east] & west line, [& over] the great River, the said Wythersfield to begin att [4] the mouth of Pewter pott Brooke & there to runn due east into the Countrey 3 miles & donweward six miles in breadth, w^ch is ordered accordingly . . . The boundes between Weathersfield & Harteford are agreed on the side wherein they stand to be att a Tree m'ked N: F: & to w^ch the Pale of the Said Harteford is fixed, to goe into the Countrey due east & on the other side of the great river from Pewter pott Brooke att the lower side of Hocanno due east into the Countrey, w^ch is nowe ordered accordingly."

This ancient town is rich in Catholic memories. It was in the hospitable "Webb House" that the Count Rochambeau and his staff held a conference with General Washington in May, 1781. At this meeting the plan of campaign was arranged which resulted in the surrender of Lord Cornwallis at Yorktown. In Wethersfield also, it is asserted, was celebrated the first Mass said in Connecticut. This historic event is said to have occurred during the march of Rochambeau's army across the State to join Washington's forces on the Hudson. The celebrant of this Mass, according to tradition, was the Abbé Robin.

As far as can be ascertained, the first Mass said in Wethersfield in recent years was celebrated by the Rev. Peter Kelly, rector of St. Peter's parish, Hartford, about Christmas of 1861. The scene of this offering of the August Victim was the "Chester House," occupied by John Connery. Present at this Mass were Patrick Taffe, James McCarthy, and about twenty-five others. Between this time and the erection of the church, the Holy Sacrifice was offered at various times in the "Chester House," the residence of John Mehegan, the Grand Army hall and in the Town Hall.

Previous to their formation into a separate parish and the appointment of the first resident and present pastor, the Rev. John T. Lynch, on September 1st, 1897, the Catholics of Wethersfield were served by the pastors of St. Peter's parish, Hartford, until the appointment of Very Rev. John A. Mulcahy to the pastorate of East Hartford, when they passed under his jurisdiction and that of his successor, the Rev. John McMahon. When the parish of St. Lawrence O'Toole was organized, Wethersfield was attached to it as a mission and was attended successively by the Rev. John F. Lenihan and the Rev. James Smith. The church was built during the incumbency of the Rev. Father McMahon, and was dedicated to the Sacred Heart on October 31, 1880.

When Father Lynch assumed charge of the newly erected parish, the population numbered 340 souls, Irish and their descendants. Among the benefactors of this parish, John Fitzgibbons, Bridget Galugan, Patrick Taffe, John Mulligan, Michael Riordan and Honora O'Neil, deserve special recogni-

---

[1] The Indian name of Wethersfield was Pyquaagg.

tion. In the short time Father Lynch has been in charge, he has purchased a fine lot, on which he has erected a handsome parochial residence. Besides attending to the manifold duties of his parish, Father Lynch is the Catholic chaplain of the Connecticut State Prison, an office he has held since May, 1888. It is a position that demands a high degree of tact, a good knowledge of human nature, and a heart that sympathizes with the afflictions of others, even when justly imposed; but, during his chaplaincy of eleven years, Father Lynch has so discharged the duties of his difficult office as to merit the high encomiums of the honorable Board of Directors, as well as of his ecclesiastical superiors. As evidence of the tolerant spirit of the prison management, and of the good work he has accomplished, we append Father Lynch's last report:

*To the Honorable Board of Directors of the Connecticut State Prison, James Cheney, president.*

GENTLEMEN: I have conducted religious services for Catholic inmates, at the Connecticut State Prison, every Sunday since my last report to your Honorable Board, one year ago.

On two different occasions during the year several clergymen have assisted me in administering to those foreigners, who can understand and speak only their own language When necessity or occasion required it, I have visited the prison at other times, to administer the consolations of religion to the sick or to those who were preparing to leave this world. Being an advocate of the reform movement recently introduced into our penal institutions, I have endeavored at all times to employ those agencies which are considered the best means of accomplishing that reform, namely, religious instruction and moral suasion. These religious instructions constitute a part of my duties every Sunday. In this work, I am greatly assisted at our Sunday school by a number of self sacrificing men who generously devote their time and labor to this worthy cause. During the past year it has been a pleasure to notice a more uniform and regular attendance at religious exercises, as well as a greater earnestness manifested by the men who attended. As far as our means would allow, I have distributed among the men, every week, a supply of reading matter, with a view to carry on the work of reform spoken of above. By the kindness of the warden a number of books of a Catholic nature have been added to the prison library, and others that had become worn or soiled were replaced by new ones.

To the Sunday-school teachers who have so conscientiously and faithfully assisted me in my work at the prison I am greatly indebted. To Warden Woodbridge and his officers I am also indebted for the courtesy they have at all times extended to me.

Respectfully,                    JOHN T. LYNCH.
WETHERSFIELD, CONN., October 27, 1898.

## ST. MARY'S PARISH,

### WINDSOR LOCKS.

THE Catholics of Windsor Locks were consoled and strengthened by the ministrations of zealous missionary priests very early in our history. Very Rev. John Power, Vicar-General of New York, Rev. R. D. Woodley, and Rev. B. O'Cavanagh, each in succession, came hither, the heralds of glad tidings and the dispensers of the precious graces that flow so abundantly from the Adorable Sacrifice and the sacraments. They watered well the seeds of faith that had been sown in the hearts of those hardy laborers beyond the seas, and God gave the increase. When Father Power had performed the work of mercy that had brought him to the Canal he offered the Holy Sacrifice for the faithful souls there congregated; but the Divine Victim was sacrificed upon no altar of marble. In the open air, upon an humble table with the thick foliage as a canopy, was Christ the Lord immolated for the first time here in Holy Mass. This was in August, 1827. Yielding to their earnest solicitations Father Power returned to the Canal in the October following.

The visits of Father Woodley and Father O'Cavanagh are referred to elsewhere in these pages. Rev. Father Fitton, the successor of Father O'Cavanagh, Father Kiernan, Father Walsh, the third resident pastor of Hartford, also came hither at intervals and gathered the scattered Catholics of the vicinity to assist at Mass and receive the Sacraments. Rev. John Brady then appeared upon the scene. From 1837, when he assumed charge of Hartford, until February 9, 1852, the date of the appointment of the Rev. Hugh Carmody, D.D., as the pastor of these missions. Windsor Locks was served by Father Brady, Rev. John D. Brady, Rev. John C. Brady and the Rev. H. T. Riordan, who had charge of the parish during Father Brady's seven months' absence in Ireland. During these periodical visits the thoroughly Catholic home of John Byrnes was sanctified by the offering of the Holy Sacrifice, save on one occasion, when Rev. John C. Brady said Mass in a dilapidated structure on Grove street, July 4, 1845. Among the early settlers who assisted in laying the foundations of the faith in this parish we note James Coogan, John Byrnes, Patrick Gaynor, Patrick Googarty and William English.

The pastorate of the Rev. Dr. Carmody was of brief duration. He was followed by Rev. James Smyth, then serving as assistant to Rev. Father Brady at Hartford. At first he came here at monthly intervals, but took up his permanent residence on June 24, 1852. For twenty-two years this apostolic priest labored here for the promotion of God's glory and the sanctification of souls. It was his zeal that erected the present church edifice. He had seen the Holy Sacrifice offered amid humble surroundings; it was the all-absorbing desire of his soul to raise aloft a temple to the Most High. On August 17, 1852, ground was broken, and on September 14th following, the corner-stone was laid by Right Rev. Bishop O'Reilly, who also preached the sermon. He was assisted by Rev. James Smyth, the pastor, and Rev. Peter Kelly. The exertions of the faithful people were rewarded by beholding a completed church, within whose sanctuary the first Mass was celebrated on Easter Sunday, 1853. The dedication of the church is said to have occurred on Christmas day, 1853; if so, Bishop O'Reilly did not officiate, as the records of his Journal show that he was in Providence on that day. However, we learn from the same source that the bishop visited Windsor Locks on June 15, 1853; but there is no information as to what, if any, ceremony was performed. It is not improbable that the dedication of the church took place on that occasion. The constantly increasing population made an enlargement of the church necessary; accordingly an addition was built in 1872, which gave the church a seating capacity of well-nigh 2000. In 1853, Father Smyth purchased the original rectory, which stood on the site of the present residence until 1878, and added St. Mary's cemetery to the possessions of the parish, erected a school where the little ones of his flock could receive a Christian education, and in 1869 adorned the church with a valuable organ. Father Smyth died on May 16, 1874, aged eighty-seven years. "His labors were many and arduous; his sacrifices were made for the benefit of the flock he loved so well. Their spiritual wants were well attended to by him, and it might be truly said that he spent his life in their service."

His successor was the Rev. Michael J. McAuley, who governed the parish until his death in March, 1878. On March 16th, the Rev. Michael Kelly was appointed pastor of St. Mary's. The present commodious rectory was built during his period of service. Assigned to Bridgeport in June, 1884, he was followed by the Rev. James O'R. Sheridan. The works accomplished during his ministry were carried forward with characteristic energy. Sparing not himself, he sought only the welfare of his parishioners. Chief among his labors were the complete re-decoration of the interior of the church, including new windows, confessionals and altars; the purchase of a school lot, 240 feet by 160 feet; a home for the Sisters of St. Joseph, whom he introduced, and the erection of a parochial school. After twelve years of successful administration Father Sheridan was followed by the present rector, the Rev. John A. Creedon, on January 8, 1896. Well equipped for the charge assigned him, Father Creedon will faithfully conserve the best interests of his people and lead them in the ways of justice and righteousness. He is assisted in his labors by the Rev. John C. Brennan. The other clergymen who discharged assistant's duties in this parish since its organization are: Revs. P. Fay, T. F. Healy, A. Van Oppen, T. P. Joynt, J. B. Dougherty, J. J. Smith, M. A. Sullivan, W. Lynch, D. Lawlor, John Crowley, J. Cunningham, W. J. Blake.

When St. Mary's parish was established, in 1852, the census disclosed a population of 200 Irish people. In 1898 the estimate is 1600 Irish and about 300 Italians and French. During the forty-five years elapsing between 1853 and 1898, 4559 baptisms and 1095 marriages have taken place. The first baptism was that of Patrick Quirk, January 2, 1853. The marriage of Michael Kelly and Mary Quinn was the first solemnized, August 4, 1850.

### St. Mary's Parochial School.

As stated above, Rev. Father Smyth organized the first Catholic school in Windsor Locks in 1868. It was conducted in the brick building in the rear of the church by lay teachers, Michael Burke, Miss Ellen Maloney and Michael Malone. It closed after a brief existence.

The present flourishing school was founded in 1888 by Father Sheridan. In November of that year the corner-stone was laid, the Rev. William Mulheron, of Auburn, N. Y., preaching the sermon. The Rev. Walter Elliott, C. S. P., was the orator on the occasion of the blessing of the building. The school is taught by the Sisters of St. Joseph, who were introduced into the diocese by Father Sheridan in August, 1889. There are nine sisters teaching, with 328 pupils. The first superior was Sister Mary Ursula; the present directress is Sister St. Hilary. St. Mary's school has all the grades from the primary to the high-school grade inclusive, and is modern both in its material appointments and methods of teaching.

The Order of the Sisters of St. Joseph dates its canonical erection from March 10, 1651. Like many other religious communities it was dispersed in the French Revolution of 1789. Its restoration occurred in 1807. The Order was founded by Mgr. de Maupas and Father Medaille, S. J., at Le Puy, France.

## SACRED HEART (MISSION) CHURCH,

### SUFFIELD.

THE Sacred Heart church, Suffield, is under the jurisdiction of St. Mary's parish. Mass is celebrated here every Sunday. The land on which the church is built was purchased and paid for in 1883 by Rev. Father Kelly. In 1886, during the pastorate of Father Sheridan, the church was erected. It was dedicated on November 31st (Thanksgiving day) of that year, the preacher on the occasion being the Rev. B. O'R. Sheridan, of Middletown. The cost of the church, with the surrounding improvements, was $12,000, all of which was liquidated by Father Sheridan. The church grounds embrace eleven acres.

# FAIRFIELD COUNTY.

## ST. AUGUSTINE'S PARISH,

### BRIDGEPORT.

BRIDGEPORT, known in early times as Fairfield Village, Stratfield, and Newfield, is the county seat of Fairfield county. It was incorporated in 1836. As early as 1657 a portion of the site on which the city stands was known as "Ireland's Brook." The origin of the name is lost in obscurity.

The Catholic history of Bridgeport embraces a period of well-nigh three score and ten years. In 1830, that prince of missionaries and apostolic man, Rev. James Fitton, celebrated here for the first time the Adorable Mysteries in the house of James McCullough, on Middle street. Seventeen souls, of various ages and conditions, formed that first congregation. At this time the following were residents of Bridgeport: Mrs. McLoughlin, Mrs. McConnell, Bernard Kennedy, Peter Carey, John Carey, Michael Sullivan, Joseph Delaney,

James McCullogh, John Reilly, James Gillick, James Ward, Thomas Garey, Edward Lutz, and John Coyle. Father Fitton was of the opinion that Bridgeport had been honored by the presence of a priest before his appearance there; that the sacraments had been administered to a dying child of the faith by a priest from New York. This puts no strain on our belief, for we know that a few years before (in 1827) Very Rev. John Power, Vicar General of New York, attended a sick laborer at Windsor Locks, that he returned again in the same year, and that he said Mass in New Haven. Father Woodley, of Providence, may also have exercised his sacred ministry here, for the records show that he returned to Hartford from the Enfield Canal on July 21, 1829, and on the day following set out for New Haven and New London. It is not improbable that the Rev. Bernard O'Cavanagh, the first resident priest in Connecticut, also visited this section of his extensive parish, as he was on a missionary visit to New Haven on April 17, 1830.

However, Bridgeport was visited by the Rev. James McDermot occasionally from 1832 to 1837, when he was transferred from New Haven to Lowell, Massachusetts. Father McDermot said Mass in Mr. Farrell's residence on Middle street. At the period of Father McDermot's first visitation there were about ninety Catholics in Bridgeport.

The Rev. James Smyth, of New Haven, followed Father McDermot in his attendance upon the Catholics of Bridgeport. For seven years Father Smyth served Bridgeport, coming as frequently as once a month. He erected the old brick church—the first in Connecticut—that stood on the corner of Arch street and Washington avenue. It was dedicated to St. James on July 24, 1843. At this time the number of Catholics had increased to respectable proportions, numbering in 1841, according to Father Fitton, 250 souls. The church measured 60 by 40 feet, had a sacristy, and was adorned with a choir gallery.

On November 18, 1844, the Rev. Michael Lynch, who in 1843 was pastor of Waltham, Mass., succeeded Father Smyth, and became the first resident pastor of the Catholics of Bridgeport. His missions were Norwalk, Stamford, Danbury, Wolcottville and Norfolk. In 1846 Father Lynch estimated the Catholic population of Bridgeport at 300.[1] Father Lynch's relations with the Catholics of Bridgeport closed on August 12, 1852. Rev. Patrick Lamb was attached to St. James' at this time.

In August, 1852, the Rev. Thomas J. Synnott[2] began his pastorate in Bridgeport, which covered a period of thirty-two years. In this new field Father Synnott gave evidence of the possession in a high degree of tact, patience, courage, unconquerable confidence and unusual financial capacity. It was a time when authority had to be exercised firmly, yet withal in a spirit of fatherly kindness. Father Synnott was equal to every demand made upon him, and his conduct of affairs elicited the praise of his Ordinary. On June 5, 1853, Bishop O'Reilly administered confirmation in St. James' church, and under that date he wrote in his Journal: "All matters well in this congrega-

---

[1] Letter to Bishop Tyler, February 16th.

[2] Father Synnott was ordained to the priesthood on April 11, 1851.

ST. AUGUSTINE'S CHURCH,
Bridgeport.

tion." Difficulties which had previously existed were happily adjusted, and with Father Synnott the parish began a new era of prosperity.

Father Synnott was an active laborer in the vineyard of Christ. His works attest his energy. In the first three years of his ministry he enlarged St. James' church, built St. Mary's, situated at the corner of Crescent avenue and Church street, and erected St. Thomas' church at Fairfield.

Old St. James' church continued to be the religious home of the Catholics of Bridgeport until 1864. As far back as July 18, 1852, Bishop O'Reilly had recommended the erection of a new church, and had received some subscriptions to that end. He had examined a contemplated church lot, but was unable to secure it. Notwithstanding the enlargements of the church, first by Father Lynch and afterwards by Father Synnott, it became inadequate for the accommodation of the people. With splendid foresight and judgment Father Synnott purchased a fine lot on the corner of Washington avenue and Poquonock street, and upon this he erected the church which stands a monument to his zeal, one of the ornaments of Bridgeport. The corner-stone was laid on August 28, 1865. It was opened for public worship on March 17, 1869, and dedicated under the title of St. Augustine in June, 1868, by Bishop McFarland. The erection of St. Agnes' magnificent convent next occupied Father Synnott's attention, though he did not live to see it completed. When Father Synnott was attacked by his last illness he was engaged in improving some forty acres of land in the northern section of the city. Among his last acts in the temporal order was the purchase of the Billings property, now used as the parochial residence. Father Synnott died on Wednesday, April 30, 1884, aged 66 years, at the old parochial residence on Poquonock street. The Rev. Augustine Hewitt, C. S. P., pronounced the funeral eulogy. "As a citizen he was upright, honest and sincere; as a priest, he was a firm upholder of the doctrines of the church, and always solicitous for the spiritual welfare of his flock. The cause of education found in him an earnest champion. He was a member of the Board of Education for several years, and during that time not only maintained kindly relations with his colleagues, but endeared himself alike to teachers and pupils."[1]

Father Synnott's successor was the Rev. Michael F. Kelly, a king among men. Father Kelly took up his residence in the house on the Billings' estate, opened the new convent for a select academy, and purchased St. Michael's cemetery, the one in use. The parish has two other cemeteries, St. James' and St. Augustine's. Father Kelly's pastorate was closed by death in September, 1887.

The present rector, the Rev. Denis Cremin, succeeded Father Kelly on November 1, 1887. The first work to which Father Cremin devoted his energies was the renovation of the rectory. At an outlay of $3,000 it was transformed into a model parochial residence; but a conflagration, which broke out on the night of January 18, 1888, destroyed the labor, but not the hopes of the zealous rector. The rectory was rebuilt, the parochial school opened, the church spire was erected in 1894, the interior of the church has been superbly

[1] Orcutt's *History of Bridgeport.*

decorated and the spacious grounds about the church and rectory have been so graded and otherwise improved that they are among the handsomest in the city. Altogether, it is one of the finest and most valuable church estates in New England, and speaks eloquently of the faith, devotion and self-sacrifice of the people, and of the wisdom and courage and ceaseless toil of the pastors. Father Cremin is one of the permanent rectors of the diocese. His assistants are the Rev. William Fitzsimmons and the Rev. John McGivney.

The first Catholic school in Bridgeport was opened in the house of Mr. John Coyle. It was taught by Mary Quigley, and was attended by about twenty-five pupils. In 1874 Father Synnott began the erection of the present school building. It was opened, as said above, as a select school by Father Kelly and as a parochial school by Father Cremin. The school contains nine grades, has 610 pupils, and is conducted by twelve Sisters of Mercy whose superior is Sister M. Colette.

## ST. MARY'S PARISH,

### East Bridgeport.

UNTIL April, 1857, St. Mary's church was attended by the priests attached to St. James'. The first church was a frame building on the corner of Crescent avenue and Church street, now used as a parochial school. It was built in 1854 by Rev. Father Synnott, pastor of St. James', as an accommodation for the Catholics in this section of the city. Previous to its erection into an independent parish it had been served successively by the Rev. Michael O'Neill, the Rev. Patrick Lamb and the Rev. Dr. Wallace. The first resident pastor was the Rev. Peter A. Smith, who assumed charge in April, 1857. He built the rectory and remained in charge until February 10, 1862. His successors were the Rev. Francis J. Lenihan, February 24, 1862; Rev. Richard O'Gorman, January 12, 1866; the Rev. Thomas Drea,[1] October 2, 1867; the present pastor, the Rev. John F. Rogers, who succeeded Father Drea on July 6, 1873.

Father Rogers began the erection of the present fine church edifice in June, 1874. It is situated on the corner of Pembroke and Steuben streets. The corner-stone was laid by Very Rev. James Hughes, V. G., on May 16, 1875, and the church was dedicated by Bishop Galberry on October 14, 1877. Pontifical Mass was celebrated by Bishop Galberry, and the sermon of dedication was preached by the Rev. J. Fitzpatrick, of New Haven. The church is in the Romanesque style, is 74 feet front on Pembroke street and 154 feet in length, with a spire 187 feet in height. The principal feature of the interior is the Roman altar 35 feet high. The edifice cost, when completed, about $100,000. In 1890, on the occasion of the silver jubilee of Father Rogers, a fine bell, worth $1,400, was placed in the tower in honor of the jubilarian. The interior of the church was thoroughly renovated and handsomely decorated a few years ago.

[1] Father Drea was ordained to the priesthood on May 10, 1851, at Hartford, by Bishop O'Reilly.

The present parochial residence was erected in 1881, on a lot adjoining, south of the church. It is a double lot, 240 feet wide on Pembroke street, between Steuben and Sherman, and 200 feet deep on Steuben. Another lot between Sherman and Cedar streets was purchased by Father Rogers, on which it is his intention to erect a convent and parochial school. The population of the parish is about 3200 souls. Father Rogers is assisted by the Rev. William Lynch and the Rev. Peter C. Dunigan.

St. Mary's church is admittedly one of the most graceful and majestic brick structures in the diocese of Hartford, its external beauty arousing the admiration of all beholders. So numerous and ornate are the stone trimmings on front and sides, that it might with truth be affirmed that it is a *stone church with brick ornaments*. The stately spire, which carries its golden cross aloft, like a prayer into the clouds, bears upward the aspiration of both Protestant and Catholic alike that so much of beauty, reared to the honor and glory of the Infinite, may never fail in its exalted and divine mission. The seating capacity is 1300 upstairs and 1350 in the basement. From this it will be seen that 2650 worshipers, including children and adults, can at the same time be assembled for divine service.

The parochial school is held in the old church, and the Sisters of Mercy who conduct it, reside in the rectory built by the first resident pastor, Rev. Peter Smith. At present there are 360 pupils, and ten sisters, whose superior is Sister M. Vincent.

## SACRED HEART PARISH,

### BRIDGEPORT.

THE parish of the Sacred Heart is of comparatively recent origin, its history beginning on November 18th, 1883, when it was organized by the Rev. Denis Cremin, now rector of St. Augustine's parish. It was the second division of the mother parish. From the time Father Cremin assumed charge until the church could be used for divine worship, Mass was said in the Opera House. Having secured a lot on Myrtle avenue near Prospect street, Father Cremin began the project of erecting a church. Ground was broken early in 1884 and the corner-stone of the new structure was laid in the September following. So expeditiously was the work carried on that in January, 1885, the Adorable Sacrifice was offered up in the basement. At the thought of enjoying the happiness of gathering within their own sacred walls to assist at Mass both pastor and people took on new courage, their zeal received new impetus. The work so progressed that on the nation's holiday, July 4th, 1886, the beautiful building was solemnly dedicated to the Adorable Heart of our Lord. The spire was completed and a bell placed in it to ring out the praises of God and to proclaim to the parishioners a welcome to their new temple. This work accomplished, Father Cremin was promoted to St. Augustine's parish on November 1st, 1887. He was followed immediately by the Rev. James C. O'Brien, who is still the rector. The eleven years of his pastorate have been attended with unvarying successes. The church interior was completed under his supervision. A rich-toned organ, two marble side altars, statues and stations of the cross, a handsome vestment case with complete sets of vestments of the prescribed colors in keeping with the dignity of the parish, and the frescoing of the interior—all are works bearing evidence of the thought that the beauty of the temple in which dwells the Lord God should be uppermost in the mind and fill the heart of him who is a dispenser of His mysteries. Yet other works speak of Father O'Brien's activity : the purchase of the rectory at a cost of $15,000, recently almost destroyed by fire, the securing of the convent property adjoining the church at an expenditure of $12,000; the purchase of an acre of land on Park avenue for which he paid $25,000; the erection on this land of a model school which cost, exclusive of furniture, $35,000; the erection of St. Michael's "Chapel of Ease" in the western section of the city. The lot upon which this chapel stands was purchased in 1804. In September, on Labor Day, the corner-stone was laid by Bishop Tierney, Rev. William J. Slocum, of Waterbury, preaching the sermon. It was blessed on January 6th, 1895. The church is a wooden structure with a seating capacity of 700. Its entire cost was $16,500. The clergymen who assist Father O'Brien in parochial work are the Rev. Charles A. Leddy, the Rev. D. P. Hurley, and the Rev. James Clyne.

The Sisters of Mercy were introduced into the parish on December 8th, 1892. After the erection of St. Michael's chapel they opened a school in the rear portion of the building. Here they had three rooms and 125 children, with five sisters. The new school was opened in September, 1896. It contains twelve large and well-ventilated class rooms, has 768 pupils with thirteen sisters, whose directress is Sister M. Petronilla.

## ST. PATRICK'S PARISH,

### Bridgeport.

THE growth of Catholicity in the northern section of Bridgeport convinced Bishop McMahon of the necessity of giving to the Catholics of that locality an independent organization. Accordingly St. Augustine's parish was for the third time divided, and St. Patrick's formed on May 29, 1889. The Rev. James Nihil was appointed the first pastor. Previous to the division Father Cremin had secured property on Lindley avenue known as the Lindley estate.

Upon his arrival among his new flock Father Nihil secured from the Board of Education the gratuitous use of the Grand street school, where for twelve months he gathered his parishioners for divine worship. This courteous action of the school board was an evidence that the narrow religious spirit that formerly prevailed in Connecticut is to be catalogued among the things that were. Believing that the Lindley estate was not sufficiently central to accommodate his parishioners Father Nihil purchased the Eli Thompson estate in April, 1890, for $27,000. No more eligible property could be secured for church purposes. It is 250 by 200 feet, and is bounded by three streets : Thompson and Parallel streets and North avenue. The fine mansion purchased with the property became the parochial residence.

The first shovelful of earth was taken from the site of the future church on May 3, 1890, and the 3rd of August witnessed the laying of the corner-stone. On December 3rd of the same year, Mass was said for the first time in the basement. The basement, which is as far as the work has progressed, is 140 feet long and 64 wide. The interior is 13 feet above the floor, and has a seating capacity of 1000. When the church is completed it will present a truly striking appearance. Its architecture is pure Gothic, will have a clere-story and a spire 175 feet in height. Architecturally it will take front rank among the granite churches of the diocese.

The population of Father Nihil's parish is estimated at 825 souls. Not-withstanding this comparatively small number he has decreased the parish indebtedness nearly $20,000. The amount received from the sale of the Lindley property, first purchased, contributed somewhat to the reduction.

Though numerically small, Father Nihil's parishioners are stimulated to religious endeavors by his example. "To Labor and to Move Onward," is their motto, and they generously co-operate with their pastor in his efforts to advance the interests of religion.

## ST. JOSEPH'S PARISH (GERMAN),

### BRIDGEPORT.

THE earliest German Catholics to settle in Bridgeport were J. Rickel, A. Vorsmeit, Marten Helleman and M. Roerich. St. Joseph's parish was organized in December, 1874, by the Rev. Joseph A. Schæle, of New Haven, who attended it as a mission until July 24, 1886. At first and for some time after the organization Father Schæle said Mass in the hall of the Father Matthew T. A. B. Society, and later in a hall at 449 Main street. In 1877, he began the erection of St. Joseph's church, which was dedicated the following year. On July 24, 1886, the parish was made independent, and the Rev. Theodore J. Ariens appointed pastor. When the parish was organized it contained 700 Germans and 500 Canadians; but the latter were constituted a separate parish in 1893. Father Ariens celebrated his golden jubilee as a priest on October 19, 1895, amidst the universal rejoicings of his people and surrounded by a large number of his brethren of the clergy. Father Ariens was born in Holland on April 14, 1823, and is still active in the discharge of his manifold priestly duties.

## ST. ANTHONY OF PADUA'S PARISH (FRENCH),

### BRIDGEPORT.

THE French Catholics of Bridgeport were organized into an independent parish in 1893, with the Rev. Father Cartier, of New Haven, as pastor. Mass was celebrated in a hall over the post-office. In 1894 Father Cartier began the construction of a church, the corner-stone of which was laid on July 15th of that year by Bishop Tierney. The present pastor is the Rev. Joseph Desaulnier, who succeeded the Rev. J. E. Senesac. The parish population is about 1,000 souls.

## ST. STEPHEN'S PARISH (ITALIAN),

THE first Italian priest to attend to the wants of the Italians of Bridgeport was the Rev. Father Morelli. The Rev. Benjamin Berto was later in charge of them and said Mass in St. Mary's school building. The present pastor is the Rev. George Csaba.

## ST. JOHN NEPOMUCENE'S PARISH (BOHEMIAN),

THE Bohemians and kindred nationalities to the number of about 1,000 were organized into a separate parish by the Rev. Joseph Formanek in 1889. He said Mass and administered the sacraments for them in the basement of St. Mary's church. The church in which the congregation now worships was begun by Father Formanek in 1891; the basement was dedicated by Bishop McMahon in that year.

Father Formanek's successor was the Rev. F. J. Pribyl, who in turn was followed by the present pastor, the Rev. Joseph Kossalko.

## ST. MARY'S PARISH,

CATHOLIC families first settled in Bethel about 1848. In the records of those days we find such names as Skivington, Doyle, Quigley, Hanna, Wixted, Crowe, Doran, Murray, Curtin, Brauneis, Diggins, McLoughlin, Lyman, Mainon, English, McHugh and McGee—all children of the ancient faith.

The Rev. M. P. Lawlor was the celebrant of the first Mass said in Bethel. The historic event took place on January 8, 1882, in the Town Hall, in the presence of about 400 persons. In the spring of the same year the congregation secured Fisher's Hall, in which Mass was said until the church was completed. Before this year the Catholics of Bethel attended Mass at St. Peter's church, Danbury.

In April, 1883, Bethel was separated from the jurisdiction of Danbury and organized into a separate parish, with the Rev. M. Byrne as the first pastor. Father Byrne died after a successful, though brief, pastorate. The main altar of St. Mary's church was donated by his mother as a memorial of her son.

The Rev. Patrick O'Connell succeeded Father Byrne in November, 1883. His period of service was fifteen years. Evidences of his sacerdotal zeal are everywhere visible. The works that signalized his administration were the purchase of the rectory and lot on which it stands, and a cemetery on the line of the Danbury and Norwalk railroad. He furnished the church with a pipe organ and a bell for the tower; erected three sets of granite steps for the entrances of the church; built an expensive property line wall, laid the concrete walks, and graded and beautified the grounds—works which bear testimony to his activity and to the generosity of the parishioners.

The present rector, the Rev. John Flemming, received his appointment as Father O'Connell's successor in January, 1898.

Several years before Bethel was raised to the parochial dignity, Thomas Doran, Patrick Wixted, James Howley, B. Murphy, Michael Branneis, James McGee, Charles Diggins and John Doyle met in conference and resolved to establish a Sunday-school in Bethel. For this purpose a building, owned by Thomas McCorkle, situated in Grassy Plain district, was rented and the school organized. The school was held here as long as the building was for rent, and when the time expired a small building, next to the residence of Mr. B. Morgan, was secured; but the school was soon after discontinued. Not long afterwards, however, *The Catholic Society of Bethel* was organized with John M. Doyle as President and Charles Diggins as Secretary. In the meantime, still determined on continuing the Sunday-school, Thomas Doran and Patrick Wixted purchased the lot adjoining the residence of Mr. E. Farmer from Willis Judd, paying therefor $475. They held this lot for some time, but finally relinquished it to the "Catholic Society" for the same price they had paid for it. Upon this lot the church was afterwards built.

In 1881, it was determined to separate the Catholics of Bethel and Grassy Plain district from the mother church at Danbury. Accordingly, a building committee, comprising Thomas Doran, Michael Branneis and Owen Murray, was appointed, and the work of securing funds for the erection of a new church was auspiciously and successfully carried on. Sufficient money having been collected to guarantee beginning the work, the construction of the church was entered upon with vigor and enthusiasm. The corner-stone was laid on Sunday, September 17, 1882, by Bishop McMahon. The sermon was preached by the Rev. Father Oates, C.S.S.R., of Boston. The ceremony of dedication took place on Sunday, September 16, 1883, Father Byrne, being pastor. Bishop McMahon officiated. The Mass which followed the dedicatory services was celebrated by the Rev. W. J. Slocum, assisted by Rev. M. P. Lawlor as deacon, Rev. H. Lynch as sub-deacon, and Rev. P. M. Kennedy, as master of ceremonies. The discourse was delivered by the Rev. P. P. Lawlor, of New Haven. The church is a brick edifice, Gothic in style with the tower on the side. It is 49 x 88 feet. The basement wall is granite, and the roof imitation clerestory. All the windows are of beautiful stained glass and bear the names of the donors. The distance from the ground to the top of the cross is 138 feet. The seating capacity of the church is 475.

The cemetery was purchased August 19, 1889, and a portion of it was blessed on June 14, 1891, by Bishop McMahon. The sermon on the occasion was preached by the Rev. W. J. Slocum of Norwalk. The number of baptisms administered in St. Mary's parish from 1883, the year of its foundation until 1898, exclusive, was 406; the number of marriages, 81.

The first child to receive baptism after the organization of the parish, as far as the records show, was John Edward Philips. The first marriage recorded is that of Theodore F. Gillooley and Catharine E. O'Connor. The first death on the records was that of Mrs. Mary Crowe, February 27, 1890.

St. Mary's parish is in a flourishing condition. Both pastor and people are one in promoting the interests of religion and in advancing the welfare of the town. They have accomplished much in the past, and if influenced by the memories which previous successes bring, the future will witness still greater things done for God and His holy church.

## REDDING RIDGE MISSION.

ABOUT the year 1879, the building of the church at Redding Ridge was commenced by Father Martin Lawlor, pastor of St. Peter's parish, Danbury, who at that time had charge of this mission. It was shortly afterwards connected with Ridgefield and attended by Father Thaddeus Walsh of that place, who continued the work on the church and completed the superstructure. About 1883, or soon after the death of Father Walsh, the mission was transferred to Father O'Connell and attached to Bethel. Father O'Connell continued attending it till his death. He built an addition to the church, formed a new sanctuary, erected an altar and frescoed the interior, making of it altogether a very pretty and substantial structure. There are about one hundred and thirty souls in this mission. The members of the congregation are Irish and of Irish descent. There are no manufactories in the place. Agriculture is almost exclusively the business of the inhabitants.

## ST. PETER'S PARISH,

### DANBURY.

THE services of the Catholic church were witnessed for the first time in Danbury in 1845, when the Rev. Michael Lynch, pastor of St. James' parish, Bridgeport, offered up the Adorable Sacrifice in the house of James Doyle of Grassy Plains. From his appointment to Bridgeport until 1849 Danbury, with neighboring missions, was attended by Father Lynch at about quarterly intervals. He said Mass alternately at the residence of James Croal, on Deer Hill, and at the house of John Hart, on Franklin street. At the time of the first Mass the Catholic population of Danbury was between sixty and seventy souls. The occasional presence of a priest increased their number. Becoming thus better known, they gradually overcame the prejudices of their Protestant neighbors; so much so, in fact, that they were enabled to secure the use of a building situated near the centre of Main street, the property of Charles Hall, and known as "Union Hall." Services were next held in the academy conducted by a Mr. Erwin. This property afterwards came into the possession of the Catholics, and stood almost opposite the new church on the west side of Main street.

In 1849, Danbury was placed under the jurisdiction of Norwalk, whose pastor was the Rev. John C. Brady. Father Brady continued to hold services in the academy until the appointment of the Rev. Thomas Ryan, who was ordained to the priesthood on March 16, 1851. Father Ryan displayed rare judgment in his administration of affairs, and with diplomacy worthy of a more experienced head, soon secured the use of the court-house for the increasing congregation. Here the Catholics assembled for divine worship

REV. PATRICK FOX.

REV. JAMES B. NIHILL.

REV. HENRY J. LYNCH, P.R.

REV. JOHN FLEMMING.

REV. WILLIAM MAHER, D.D.

until June of 1851, when Father Ryan purchased from the Universalists, for $2750, their building, which stood on the northwest corner of Main and Wooster streets. The manner in which this purchase was consummated throws a light upon the prejudices entertained against Catholics at that time. Bishop O'Reilly was in town on the day of the sale, and during its progress walked up and down the opposite side of the street, an anxious, though an apparently indifferent spectator. To manifest interest openly in the sale would have defeated his purpose, for the Know-Nothing element, then rampant, would not have permitted property to be sold to Catholics, especially for church purposes. Nevertheless the purchase was affected through the shrewdness and liberality of three Protestant gentlemen, William H. Clark, Aaron Seely and Samuel Stebbins, whose names are still fondly cherished by the older Catholics of Danbury. Happy in the possession of a church, though humble indeed, they immediately refitted it in a manner suitable for Catholic worship, and it was dedicated the same year. Father Ryan's pastorate in Danbury terminated on October 10, 1851, having been transferred temporarily to Stonington. His successor was the Rev. Michael O'Farrell, who was ordained a priest on July 12, 1851. At this time the congregation had increased to the respectable number of 400. The arduous labors of this mission soon began to make inroads upon the health of Father O'Farrell, who, after a pastorate of eighteen months, retired to New Haven hospital, where he died. The first cemetery was purchased during Father O'Farrell's pastorate at a cost of $400. His successor was the Rev. John Smith, who came in 1853. The three years of his administration were signalized by the purchase of a lot on the southeast corner of Main and Centre streets, where St. Peter's church now stands, for which he paid $1200, and the erection of a parochial residence upon it at a cost of $3000. Father Smith was followed, in 1856, by the Rev. Peter Kelly, who in turn was succeeded, in 1858, by the Rev. Thomas Drea. At this period Danbury had as dependencies: Brookfield, New Fairfield, Newtown, Redding Ridge and Ridgefield. Father Drea's term of service lasted until 1860, during which time he added largely to the property of the church. A valuable lot of land extending from Main to Foster streets, and including two buildings, the academy already mentioned, and another occupied by the Congregationalists, was purchased for $2500. On Father Drea's transfer to Bridgeport Bishop McFarland appointed the Rev. Ambrose Manahan, D.D., his successor. On September 1, 1860, Dr. Manahan purchased the Congregational church for $600. Father Drea had previously bought the lot on which this church stood. It was remodeled and suitably prepared for Catholic services, and used until the completion of the present church. Dr. Manahan was a priest of fine culture and superior intellectual endowments. He was a polemical writer of great ability, and his book on "The Triumphs of the Church" was one of the standard works of that time. He had gained the unbounded affection of his people, and his death was deeply regretted.

The Rev. Philip Sheridan followed Dr. Manahan in 1865. Four years after his arrival he conceived the design of erecting a Gothic stone church which would not only be an architectural ornament to the town, but a temple worthy of the growing importance of the parish. To this end he removed the pastoral residence to the rear of the lot on the southwest corner of Main street, and on its site began the foundations of the new church. The soil here was sandy and humid, and great difficulty was experienced in securing a solid bed for the foundations. In some places the builders were obliged to grout to the depth of twenty-seven feet. The difficulties were overcome, however, but at an expenditure of nearly $4000. The corner-stone was laid on Sunday, August 28, 1870, by Bishop McFarland, on which occasion the Rev. Augustine Hewitt, C.S.P., of New York, preached the sermon. The priests who assisted Father Sheridan were his brother, Rev. John Sheridan, Rev. John Smith, Rev. Father Plunkett, Rev. Father Bernard, Rev. John Flemming and Rev. Patrick Finnegan.

In July, 1874, the Rev. John Quinn succeeded Father Sheridan. The panic of 1873 had suspended the work on the church; but upon his arrival Father Quinn resumed work on the edifice, and the ceremony of dedication took place on December 13, 1875, Very Rev. James Hughes, V. G., officiating. The celebrant of the Mass following the dedication ceremony was the Rev. H. Glackmeyer, S. J., and the preacher, the Rev. William Hill, LL.D., of Brooklyn, N. Y. The cost of the church, with basement and tower unfinished, was $84,630. With Father Quinn as assistants were Rev. B. Bray and Rev. J. McMahon.

Rev. Martin P. Lawlor was appointed Father Quinn's successor in December, 1876. His assistants were Rev. J. McMahon, Rev. M. Byrne, Rev T. Mulvany, Rev. T. Smith, Rev. T. Walsh, Rev. J. H. O'Donnell and Rev. T. Dunn. Father Lawlor remained in Danbury until 1883, when he was transferred to Meriden.

In August, 1883, Rev. Thomas L. Lynch assumed charge of St. Peter's parish. The works that mark his pastorate were the erection of the school and the purchase and re-fitting of St. Thomas' Convent. Before the school was entirely completed, Father Lynch was summoned to his eternal reward. Father Lynch's assistants were Rev. Thomas Dunn, Rev. Edward O'Donnell and Rev. James B. Nihil.

On December 10, 1886, the Rev. Henry J. Lynch, the present incumbent and the first permanent rector of the parish, was appointed by Bishop McMahon. A brief enumeration of the works accomplished during the past twelve years will bear testimony to zealous, untiring and profitable labor. The first work undertaken was the completion of St. Peter's school. On May 15, 1887, it was dedicated and a sonorous bell blessed for it by Bishop McMahon. A new cemetery was purchased in January, 1887, for $5,000, situated near Lake Kenosia. After being suitably graded and divided into sections and lots, it was blessed by the bishop on September 11th, of the same year, Rev. James Nihil preaching the sermon. His next achievement was the completion of the church by the erection of a sightly spire. A chime of bells costing $5,000, the gift of the ladies of the parish, was afterwards placed in the tower. About this time the basement of the church was finished, and

ST. PETER'S CHURCH,
Danbury.

on September 15, 1889, it was dedicated. The preacher on this occasion was the Rev. James A. Doonan, S. J. On the same day the solemn ceremony of blessing the chimes took place, when the Rev. J. O'Connor, S. J., pronounced the discourse.

The low, swampy and unhealthful grounds about this school were transformed into a fine play-ground by the introduction of a new system of drainage and by scientific grading. The parochial residence, one of the finest in the diocese, was erected in 1891. It stands north of St. Peter's school, fronting on Main street near Elmwood Park. South of the school on the corner of Wooster and Main streets is the handsome convent of the Sisters of Mercy. The corner-stone of this structure was laid by Bishop Tierney on June 29, 1896. Rev. F. J. McCarthy, S. J., preached the sermon. The ceremony of dedication took place on August 15, 1896. In the northern end of this building, entirely distinct and separate from the convent, are four class-rooms, two on the first and two on the second floor. On the third floor is located the parish library. It is abundantly supplied with choice literature and is sumptuously furnished. The library was opened on December 21, 1896. Its chief benefactor is Mrs. J. H. Benedict, a convert, who contributed $500 towards the purchase of books. It will be seen that St. Peter's parish possesses valuable property; but besides that mentioned above, it still owns the old convent property valued at $10,000, and real estate worth $15,000. This latter property was the gift of Mrs. Cunningham, who is regarded as the principal benefactor of the parish.

The zeal of the clergy of St. Peter's is not confined to ministrations among their own parishioners; an average of forty conversions annually to the faith demonstrate the existence there of an apostolate who are stimulated by the words of the Master: "*And other sheep I have, that are not of this fold: them also I must bring, and they shall hear my voice, and there shall be one fold and one shepherd.*"

The number of baptisms administered in the forty years between 1858 and 1898, was 6,143; in the same four decades there were 1,107 marriages.

We have seen that at the time of the first Mass the number of Catholics in Danbury did not exceed 70. The present Catholic population is 6,000 souls, divided into 5,000 Irish and their descendants, and 1,000 of mixed nationalities, Germans, Italians, Hungarians, French, Poles and Slavs.

Twenty-one religious and benevolent societies are under the care of the clergy. Among them are: The Tabernacle Society, Branch of the Eucharistic League, Propagation of the Faith, Immaculate Heart of Mary, for the Conversion of sinners, League of the Sacred Heart, and three T. A. B. Societies.

The estimated value of St. Peter's parish property is $284,000.

St. Peter's school opened in September, 1886, with 400 pupils and eight rooms. At present there are 1,008 pupils, 17 rooms, with 17 teachers and 9 grades. Sister M. Stanislaus is the Superioress of the convent. The standard of this school is above that of the public-schools, as is shown by the annual examinations for admittance into the high school.

The priests who have served with Father Lynch as assistants are: Rev. James Nihil, Rev. Thomas Dunn, Rev. Edward Murray, Rev. Patrick Keating, Rev. Daniel Lawlor, Rev. Richard Walsh, Rev. John Downey, Rev. Richard Shortell, Rev. F. Bedard, Rev. George Synnott, Rev. James Walsh. Those serving the parish at present are Rev. John D. Kennedy, Rev. Matthew Traynor and Rev. Charles Coppens.

Religious harmony prevails and ever has prevailed in St. Peter's parish. Energetic, devoted and self-sacrificing priests have been the leaders, and the generous, devout people have co-operated. Together they have brought the parish to the front rank, where with zeal undiminished and with courage quickened they continue the exalted work of saving souls.

## ST. THOMAS' PARISH,

### FAIRFIELD.

THE Indian name of Fairfield was *Unquowa*, and its discovery was the result of a pursuit of the Pequots in 1637, by Roger Ludlow. Reaching the Iasco, the great swamp of the town, he became enamored of the beauty of the land in the neighborhood and established a settlement.

The Catholic history of Fairfield begins 215 years later, when in 1852 Rev. Thomas Synnott, pastor of St. James' parish, Bridgeport, celebrated Mass here for the first time. It cannot be definitely stated where the first Mass was said. The honor is given to the home of John McKenna and to the residence of Mrs. Sarah M. Jarvis, who had received the precious gift of faith in 1842. It is not unlikely that both houses had the honor of the first and second Masses, and others thereafter, and that tradition has confused the merits of each. Father Synnott visited Fairfield frequently, though the number of Catholics was not large. Deeming it advisable to secure for this little band a house of worship, he began the erection of a church, which was dedicated in honor of St. Thomas Aquinas, on Sunday, June 15, 1854, by Bishop O'Reilly. The Mass which followed the ceremony of dedication was celebrated by Rev. Hugh O'Reilly, of Norwalk, assisted by Rev. James Lynch, of Birmingham, as deacon; Rev. James Kennedy, diocese of Halifax, as subdeacon; and Rev. Richard O'Gorman, of New Haven, as master of ceremonies. The sermon was delivered by Bishop O'Reilly. The church was a frame building, with a seating capacity of about 500. For nearly a quarter of a century the Catholics of Fairfield remained under the jurisdiction of Bridgeport, Rev. Father Synnott pastor. In January, 1876, they became an independent organization with the Rev. Martin P. Lawlor as their first resident pastor. His pastorate was of brief duration, ending in September of the same year. Briefer still was the term of his successor, the Rev. John Quinn, who was succeeded in December, 1876, by the Rev. Thomas Mullen. Like those of his predecessors, the pastorate of Father Mullen was brief, as he died from an affection of the heart under peculiarly sad circumstances. On August 4, 1877, Father Mullen was summoned to administer the consolations of religion to a man who had received fatal injuries during an altercation. The sight of the man's protruding vitals made a deep impression upon Father Mullen, who was naturally of a nervous temperament. After his return home he spoke to his mother of the sad occurrence, dwelling at some length upon the scenes that had fallen under his observation. The following day he was again called to the bedside of the injured man, and the painful impressions caused by the first visit were renewed. After leaving the house of the injured man, he visited another parishioner who was suffering from typhoid fever. Having concluded his duties he returned to the pastoral residence, but the sight of the man's wounds was continually before his mind. Going out in the garden to walk, he was shortly seen to stagger and fall, and by the time help arrived he was breathing his last. Everything that medical science could devise was brought into requisition, but all proved ineffectual. The inexorable fiat of death had been pronounced; his heart had ceased its pulsations. His death occurred on August 5, 1877, in the thirty-second year of his age. His funeral took place on the 7th, the Rev. J. Fitzpatrick, of New Haven, pronouncing the eulogy.

Father Mullen's successor was immediately announced as the Rev. William A. Harty, of St. Mary's church, New Haven, who presided over St. Thomas' parish until Sunday, March 17, 1878. While his administration was also brief Father Harty gave evidence of the possession of the distinguishing faculty of liquidating indebtedness which has characterized his every pastorate since. The week following Father Harty's departure the Rev. Philip McCabe assumed charge. His relations with the parish ceased in September, 1879, when the Rev. Denis Cremin became the pastor. Father Cremin removed the church to another lot, enlarged it, built a basement to it and had it frescoed. It was accordingly rededicated in November, 1880. Father Cremin also purchased a house that stood adjacent to the church, and after thoroughly renovating it, used it as a convent and school. Father Cremin governed St. Thomas' parish four years, during which time he resided in a rented house. The Sisters of Mercy were introduced in 1882 and the school opened. On November 1, 1883, Father Cremin was transferred to Bridgeport. His successor, the present pastor, the Rev. Thomas J. Coleman, followed immediately.

Upon his arrival Father Coleman began the task of erecting a pastoral residence; this he accomplished without incurring any indebtedness. For more than eight years the parish flourished under the pastor's guiding hand. The school's high standard was maintained; the people were united, devout, contented. Suddenly the work of years of patient toil and zeal and self-sacrifice was a pile of smoldering ruins. A conflagration, which broke out on the night of January 19, 1892, destroyed church, residence and convent. But pastor and people were undismayed by the dire calamity. Five days after saw them worshiping in a temporary structure, which strong and willing hands had erected. Work on the present commodious rectory was begun in 1893 and completed before the end of the year. Father Coleman now turned his thoughts to the erection of a church; and his people cordially seconded his intentions. Ground was broken on June, 1894; the corner-stone was laid on July 4th, and the church was dedicated on Thanksgiving day, November 27th, all within the space of a year. Father Coleman also purchased an extension to the cemetery for $1,200.

St. Thomas' Church is a brick edifice, Romanesque in design, with a seating capacity of 650. Its total cost was $22,000. The population of the parish is about 600 souls.

Notwithstanding its reverses, the parish is again in a highly prosperous condition. The future is bright with promise, and pastor and parishioners are grateful to the Giver of all gifts, who has blessed them so abundantly.

## ST. MARY'S PARISH.

### GREENWICH.

WE have seen elsewhere in these pages that one of the original purchasers of Greenwich was an Irishman, Daniel Patrick. His fellow-countrymen, however, did not settle here until about 1845, probably nearer to 1848. Among the first Catholics to seek homes here whose names are remembered were the McCormicks, Barretts, Dorans, Dalys, Egans, Foxes, and Smiths. It has been asserted that the first Mass celebrated in Greenwich was said by the Rev. H. O'Reilly, of Norwalk, in 1854; but it is not improbable that the Holy Sacrifice was offered prior to that year, as in 1854, the number of Irish Catholics in Greenwich was estimated at one hundred souls. Therefore, between 1850 and 1854 the number of Catholics there must have been sufficiently large to require the occasional visit of a priest.

After the formation of St. John's parish, Stamford, in March, 1854, Greenwich passed under its jurisdiction. From that time until 1860, Mass was offered up at intervals in private houses and in the Town Hall. In this year a small church was erected on William street. This was enlarged in 1888. In 1875 the Rev. M. A. Tierney improved the church by the erection of a choir gallery.

During Father Tierney's pastorate provision was made for the near formation of Greenwich into a parish. The first step was the purchase from James Elphich, for $4,200, of one of the finest sites in Greenwich for a new church. To the Rev. William H. Rogers, who was an assistant at Stamford, was intrusted the duty of organizing the Greenwich Catholics, and of beginning work on the new church, retaining in the meanwhile his position at Stamford. Upon the promotion of Father Rogers as the successor of Father Tierney, he relinquished jurisdiction over Greenwich, being followed in January, 1877, by the Rev. Denis J. Cremin. Father Cremin's first work was the liquidation of what debt remained upon the property purchased by Father Tierney. He removed the house that stood on the lot, and having refitted it, occupied it as a rectory. He then began the construction of St. Mary's church. The corner-stone was laid on June 9, 1878, by Bishop Galberry, in the presence of many thousands of spectators. The Bishop was assisted by Father Rogers, of Stamford; Father Meister, of Mammaroneck, N. Y.; Father Walsh, of Waterbury, and the reverend pastor. The sermon was preached by Father Walsh. Miss Anna Caulfield's donation on the occasion was $300, for which generous gift she was presented with the silver trowel used by the Bishop in laying the corner-stone. The handsome edifice was dedicated on May 18, 1878, by the Administrator *ad interim*, Very Rev. Thomas Walsh,

V.G. The mass which followed the ceremonies of dedication was celebrated by Rev. M. A. Tierney, assisted by Rev. John Russell as deacon, Rev. Father O'Brien as sub-deacon, and Rev. P. M. Kennedy as master of ceremonies. The preacher of the occasion was Rev. Lawrence Walsh of Waterbury. Before his transfer to Fairfield Father Cremin had the happiness of seeing his parish free from indebtedness.

The present pastor, the Rev. Thomas Smith, began his pastorate on September 11, 1879. For well-nigh a score of years he has labored faithfully to promote the interests entrusted to him. He introduced the Sisters of Mercy from Middletown, having fitted up the old church for school purposes, and secured the handsome and spacious convent property at an outlay of $9,500. A lot on Greenwich avenue has been added to the real estate already possessed by the parish. The grounds about the rectory and church have been beautified and improved by macadam driveways. In 1884 Father Smith had the church handsomely decorated. St. Mary's church is 107 feet in length and 49 feet in width, and is a frame building.

St. Mary's school was opened with 150 pupils; 204 are now in attendance. There are six grades, with four teachers, whose Directress is Sister M. Philomena. The school maintains a high standard, and its graduates readily pass the required examinations for admission to the Town Academy.

The clergy who have served as assistants to Father Smith are: Rev. Thomas Cronin, Rev. Thomas Maloney, and Rev. John Lee. The present assistant is the Rev. T. W. Dolan.

## ST. ALOYSIUS' PARISH,

### NEW CANAAN.

THE incorporation of New Canaan as a town occurred in 1801. Its Catholic history dates from 1855, when the first Mass was said here by Rev. Father O'Reilly, of Norwalk, in a building on Main street, now occupied by the grocery of Thomas Fairty. Mass was said also in a hall and subsequently in the Town hall by the Rev. Dr. Mulligan at intervals from 1859 to 1862.

The present church was erected in 1863 by the Rev. Peter A. Smith, pastor of St. Mary's parish, Norwalk. It was thoroughly renovated both exteriorly and interiorly, and new altars erected by the Rev. W. J. Slocum during his administration at Norwalk. Priests from Norwalk attended New Canaan regularly every Sunday until May, 1896, when the parochial dignity was conferred upon it by Bishop Tierney, who appointed the Rev. John T. McMahon the first resident pastor. Father McMahon remained here about four months. He had secured a lot for a parochial residence, but was transferred before his designs were realized. His successor was the Rev. Thomas Kelly, whose pastorate of two years was crowned with great success. Upon his promotion to New Milford, he was followed by the present pastor, the Rev. P. Byrne.

When the first Mass was said in New Canaan in 1855, there were about thirty Irish Catholics in town. At present they number 250 Irish and about forty Italians, Poles and Slavonians.

In 1896 and 1897 there were twenty-six baptisms and six marriages. The first child born after the formation of the parish was Mary Kelly, daughter of James and Catherine Kelly, and the first to receive baptism was Maurice Corrigan, son of Joseph and Rose Corrigan. On July 22, 1896, the first marriage was solemnized between Thomas E. Donnillon and Mary Teresa Scott.

## ST. ROSE'S PARISH,

### NEWTOWN.

THE ancient Indian name of Newtown was *Pohtatuck*. The town was incorporated and received its present name in 1708. The first Catholics to reside in Newtown came, not voluntarily, forty-eight years after; they were four Acadians, who were billeted on the town by Act of the General Assembly, January, 1756. The records are silent as to their fate. Perhaps they were among the 240 fortunate exiles who gathered at Norwich in 1767, and were carried to Quebec in the brig " Pitt." But if they remained they and their descendants lived and died without the consoling ministrations of anointed priests.

In 1781 the French army, under the Count Rochambeau, encamped at Newtown on its march from Providence to the Hudson in 1781. They remained here from June 28th to July 1st, and as the latter date fell on Sunday, it may be averred that one or more of the chaplains offered up the Holy Sacrifice of the Mass on that day.

Statements as to the time and celebrant of the first Mass in Newtown vary. Some are certain that the Divine Mysteries were offered here for the first time by Rev. James Smythe, one of the pioneers of the diocese, in 1841, while others contend for six years later. According to the adherents of this latter view, the first Mass was said in Peter Leary's house, which stands now near the Newtown depot on the N. Y. N. H. & H. R. R., and that Rev. John Brady was the celebrant. The first Catholics to establish homes in Newtown were Michael Leary, Peter Leary, John Cavanagh, Patrick Cavanagh, James Carley, William Griffin, Andrew Egan, Daniel Quinlivan, Thomas Bradley, Bernard Donlan, Richard Reilly, Patrick Gaffney.

The first resident pastor of Newtown was the Rev. Francis Lenihan, who organized the parish on August 1, 1859. Previous to the appointment of Father Lenihan Newtown was served by priests from Danbury. Father Lenihan purchased the first cemetery; but it was not blessed until the pastorate of his successor, the Rev. James Daly, who came here in March, 1862. Father Daly served the parish six years, leaving in July, 1868. Rev. John Rogers then became pastor on July 22, 1868, and remained until July, 1873. His successor was Rev. James McCarten, who came about August 1, 1873, and died in January, 1889. The present church was erected during his pastorate in 1882. The corner-stone was laid in May of that year by Bishop McMahon, and the sermon was preached by Rev. Lawrence Walsh. The old church had been a Universalist meeting-house and was purchased by Rev. John Smith about 1858. It was 38 x 48, but an addition enlarged it to 38 x 78. Rev.

Patrick Donahoe followed Father McCarten in January, 1889, and remained until February, 1891. The present incumbent, Rev. P. Fox, became pastor on February 13, 1891. In 1896 Father Fox built the parochial school at Sandy Hook. The corner-stone was laid on June 9th by Very Rev. John A. Mulcahy, V. G., in the absence of Bishop Tierney, who was in Rome on his *ad limina* visit. The sermon was preached by Rev. W. Rogers, of Stamford. The new cemetery was also purchased during Father Fox's pastorate, May 16, 1891. It was blessed by Very Rev. James Hughes, V. G., the Rev. William Maher, D. D., preaching the sermon.

St. Rose's parochial school opened with 125 pupils. It has now 173, with nine grades, taught by six Sisters of Mercy, whose superior is Sister M. Berchmans.

The clergy who have served Newtown as assistants are: Rev. Thomas Mullin, Rev. W. Gibbons, Rev. M. Cray, Rev. M. McCarten, Rev. D. J. Kennedy, Rev. J. J. Loftus, Rev. C. Brady, Rev. P. Daly. The present assistant is Rev. Terence Smith.

The number of Catholics present at the first Mass was about twelve; when the church was bought by Father Smith the number had increased to 100. The present population of the parish is about 1300, all Irish and their descendants.

The first marriage solemnized in Newtown, of which there is record, was that between Jeremiah Cavan and Bridget Hayes, November 4, 1860. The first baptism was that of Charles English, son of William English and Bridget O'Connell, August 2, 1859.

Father Fox and his assistant attend also St. Stephen's church at Stepney twice a month. The church was erected in 1890 by Rev. P. Donahoe. There are about forty souls here and this number is decreasing.

Andrew Egan and brothers are numbered by the grateful parishioners as benefactors of St. Rose's parish.

## ST. JOHN'S PARISH,

### NOROTON.

AMONG the earliest settlers of this mission we may enumerate those who bore the following names: Corrigan, Everett, Kane, Rulihan, Gaffney, Stark, Waterbury, Conboy, Seely, Sheridan, Reilly, Flaherty, Canovan and Wood. Prior to 1888, the Catholics of Noroton went to Stamford to Mass. In that year, permission was asked and obtained to celebrate the Divine Mysteries at the Soldiers' Home, as there were many Catholic veterans, inmates of the institution. A meeting was subsequently held at the Home of the Catholics of Noroton, both resident and visiting. Great enthusiasm prevailed, and it was the sense of the meeting that a church be erected. Accordingly a committee consisting of Rev. William Rogers, Mr. John D. Crimmins and Mr. H. W. Collender, were appointed to carry the work to completion.

A beautiful site of four acres was purchased by Father Rogers from Mr. Francis S. Fitch, for which he paid $5,500; with the land was secured also a house. The property is among the finest in the town and overlooks Long Island Sound.

On August 29th, 1888, ground was broken and the corner-stone laid on November 20th, of the same year by Bishop McMahon. The Rev. Dr. Higgins, O. P., preached the sermon. The beautiful little church was dedicated on December 15th, 1889, by the above prelate. The discourse on the occasion was pronounced by the Rev. Jeremiah Curtin.

Noroton remained under the jurisdiction of Stamford, Father Rogers, pastor, until May 1st, 1895, when the Rev. Timothy M. O'Brien was appointed the first resident pastor. When the parish was formed it contained about 250 souls, Irish and Americans; at present it has about 300, with a few German and Hungarian families. From May 1st, 1895, to 1898, there were forty-five baptisms and twelve marriages.

The permanent Catholic population of Noroton is in character much the same as that which is found generally in rural districts throughout the State, and while a large proportion are in comfortable circumstances, there are none who are wealthy. However, there are in Noroton a number of country homes owned or occupied by wealthy families from New York. These families reside here from four to six months in the year. Attached to the households of the non-Catholic residents in one capacity or another is a goodly number of Catholics, and as a class they deserve recognition, not only as augmenting the congregation for a period of time, but as edifying it by their devotion, and as materially assisting it by their generosity.

St. John's parish is blessed with a number of benefactors, who manifest their interest in the church by their generous contributions; among them mention should be made of Messrs. John D. Crimmins, H. W. Collender, William Rulihan, William Everett, Michael Kane and Felix A. Mulgrew.

The church, which is a handsome structure, is 75 in length and 40 in width, and has accommodations for 350 persons.

Though among the small parishes of the diocese, St. John's is among the most progressive and successful. Co-operation and Unity express the spirit that pervades the parish.

## ST. MARY'S PARISH,

### NORWALK.

THE honor of being the first Catholics to settle in Norwalk belongs to Michael Cooney and family, who came from New York in May, 1828. Mr. Cooney was a hat dyer and lived near the dock on the east side of Water street. William Donahoe followed with his family of six persons, in 1829. He was a chandler by occupation and remained in Norwalk until 1832, returning to New York. Clement Burns then came and boarded with Mr. Cooney. He was a potter and a stanch Catholic. Four years after Mr. Cooney's appearance here the family of Farrell Gillooly and a family, Brennan by name, arrived. Then followed in succession the family of Paul Bresnan and the families of James, John and Edmund Conners.

The Rev. James McDermot, pastor of New Haven said the first Mass

REV. TIMOTHY R. SWEENEY

REV. JOHN J. FITZGERALD

REV. JOHN J. FURLONG, P. R.

REV. THOMAS FINN

REV. D. J. O'CONNOR

offered up in Norwalk, in 1833, at the residence of Michael Cooney. Father McDermot visited Norwalk semi-annually until his transfer to Lowell in 1837, each time celebrating Mass in the front room of Mr. Cooney's house. "Here he met and preached to those poor, hard-working pioneers of our faith, numbering in all about twenty-five persons, at his first coming; he was cheered by their hearty welcome and encouraged on his long and weary mission in the heart of Puritanism by their fervent faith."

The next priest to visit Norwalk was the Rev. James Smyth of New Haven. During his visits here, he said Mass at Mr. Cooney's house, in the basement of George F. Belden's tin-store, and at the residence of Lawrence Martin, on the Newtown turnpike. Afterwards when Mr. Martin had removed to Five Mile River, Father Smyth said Mass in his house there, four or five times.

When Rev. Michael Lynch was given charge of Bridgeport, in 1844, he assumed jurisdiction also over Norwalk and neighboring places. His first Mass here was said in the house of Brian Mahoney, at the foot of Mill hill, on Wall street, and the second, in the summer of 1844, in a large tenement house, occupied by John Connors, John Kelly and two other families on River street. At this second Mass there were present about seventy-five persons. Possessing superior accommodations to other houses occupied by the Catholics, Mass was said here frequently afterwards.

In 1848, a committee, comprising Paul Bresnan, John Hanlon, John Foley, Terrence Reynolds and Farrell Gillooly, was appointed to present a petition to Bishop Tyler for a resident priest. The good Catholic spirit manifested by the petitioners in their letter impressed the Bishop so favorably that he visited Norwalk, said Mass in Marine hall or the Town House, and delighted them with the assurance that he would in the near future send them a priest. Accordingly he appointed the Rev. John Brady to Norwalk with Stamford and other places in the neighborhood as dependencies. The construction of the New York and New Haven Railroad had brought a goodly increase to the original number of Catholics and for their accommodation, Father Brady secured gratis the use of the Town hall for divine services. Before this Mass was said at intervals of four months; now it was said semi-monthly. Father Brady began almost immediately upon his arrival to make preparations to provide his rapidly increasing congregation with a church. A site was purchased by Terrence Reynolds from a Mr. Bailey, on Chapel street, and a church 36 x 40 immediately commenced. Both Protestants and Catholics contributed generously to the erection of the edifice. An anecdote will illustrate the feelings of good-will that prevailed among all classes. "Paul Bresnan and Terrence Reynolds were appointed the committee to solicit from non-Catholics. The most influential man in town was the Rev. Dr. Mead, of St. Paul's Episcopal church. 'He must be got to head the list with his name,' said the committee; so to him they went, and after making their business known, Dr. Mead, who knew the men very well, said: 'Paul, how is it you come to me first; why not go to the Congregational minister, Dr. Hall?' Paul, who was never known to be outwitted, promptly replied : 'Well, Doctor, we know you to be an off-shoot from the parent stock.' The Doctor took the list and headed it generously and was followed by Dr. Hall and many of the most influential citizens of the town." The church was completed in 1851, and on January 28th, of that year, it was dedicated by Bishop O'Reilly. Of this event, the bishop thus wrote in his Journal : "*1851, January 28th.* Made the visitation of St. Mary's church, Norwalk, confirmed about twenty and preached twice. These churches (St. John's, Stamford and St. Mary's, Norwalk) were built by Rev. John C. Brady ; are in debt each about $1,000, but I was pleased with his efforts." Father Brady's residence was on the "Cove Road," near Stamford. In 1852, Rev. Father Kelly was assigned to Norwalk as assistant, and thereafter Mass was said there every Sunday.

In 1853 Father Brady was succeeded by the Rev. E. C. Cooney, but he remained only until March, 1854. Old residents remember him as especially zealous in promoting the cause of temperance. Following Father Cooney came the Rev. Hugh O'Reilly, whose pastorate lasted five years. His first work was the erection of a school, over which he placed Mr. and Mrs. Hession ; but, owing to the great distance and many of the children being obliged to walk, it was soon discontinued. The school was in the rear of the church. Father O'Reilly enlarged the church by an addition of forty feet, and purchased the pastoral residence on Chapel street, known in later years as the "Eldridge Brown House."

Father O'Reilly's pastorate occurred during the years that the Know-Nothing element was triumphant in the State. They manifested their insensate hostility by setting the church on fire, and at another time by sawing off the gilded cross that surmounted the church. In 1858 Father O'Reilly purchased from the Fairfield County Agricultural Association a tract of land opposite the fair grounds for a cemetery. In the same year he was transferred to Providence, and was succeeded successively by the Rev. Richard O'Gorman and the Rev. James Campbell, whose incumbencies were only temporary. On July 18, 1859, the Rev. John Mulligan, D.D., "justly considered one of the most talented and promising clergymen in the Hartford diocese," assumed charge of St. Mary's parish. Among the works he accomplished were the completion of the church at Westport in 1859 ; the organization of St. Joseph's T. A. B. Society ; the establishment of a night school. He had also in contemplation the erection of a church on the present site of St. Mary's, when death closed his brilliant, though brief, career. He died on January 12, 1862. His remains were interred in St. Patrick's Cemetery, Hartford, his natal city.

Dr. Mulligan was followed by the Rev. Peter A. Smith, who came here from East Bridgeport. The works that marked his administration were the purchase of the pastoral residence, which, after many years of occupancy, gave way to the present commodious rectory, and also of the site of the church adjoining. A school was organized in a small building erected on the northeast corner of Orchard street and West avenue, which he placed in the care of a Mr. McGilleck, of New York, and Miss Jane Mahler, of Newtown.

Their successors were Mr. James McGirl, of New York, and Miss Margaret Tierney, of Norwalk. The school was discontinued after an existence of two or three years. Father Smith built the church at New Canaan, began and completed the present church, with the exception of the spire. The corner-stone was laid in 1869, and on the same day of this ceremony Bishop McFar-land blessed the new cemetery. When the basement of the church was ready for occupancy the old church was sold to S. E. Olmstead. Though the church cost $85,000, there was only an indebtedness of $20,000 on it when dedicated in 1870. It is a Gothic structure, 60 x 130, and has a seat-ing capacity of 1,200 persons. Father Smith's death occurred on December 16, 1875, after a most successful pastorate of thirteen years. His remains rest in St. Mary's cemetery, by the side of his brother, Rev. John Smith, who died on November 5, 1869.

The Rev. P. O'Dwyer succeeded to the pastorate of St. Mary's in January, 1876. His term of service was brief, though replete with works that redounded to the spiritual welfare of the parish. He founded many religious societies, and erected the memorial tablet to the deceased priests of the parish in the vestibule of the church at a cost of $350. He died on June 7, 1878, and was buried in Ansonia, where he had been pastor from 1870 to January, 1876.

The Rev. John Russell followed Father Dwyer and assumed formal charge of St. Mary's parish on June 30, 1878. The duration of his pastorate was five years, during which period he built St. Mary's parochial school, purchased the convent and introduced the Sisters of Mercy from Meriden into his parish. In April, 1883, he was transferred to St. Patrick's, New Haven, and his successor was the Rev. William J. Slocum. The works accomplished during his pas-torate attest his activity. Besides adding to and beautifying the convent he built the present parochial residence, purchased a valuable piece of property in the rear of the church, added a large tract to the cemetery, which was greatly improved, completed the church by the erection of a spire, put in marble altars, liquidated the indebtedness, and to the joy of his parishioners had the church consecrated, a heart offering of his people to God. During his incumbency St. Mary's parish was raised to the dignity of a permanent rectorship.

He was transferred to the Immaculate Conception parish in succession to Very Rev. John A. Mulcahy, V. G., in September, 1895. His successor, the Rev. J. B. A. Dougherty, assumed control on September 19th. The term of his pastorate was one year. He was succeeded by the present rector, the Rev. John Furlong, who began his administration on October 12, 1896. Recognizing the importance of a suitable place where the young of his parish could spend their evenings profitably, Father Furlong purchased a site opposite the church on which stood a dwelling-house, which he converted into a club-house and established the Catholic club in January, 1897. Plans are being drawn for a more commodious building, which no doubt will be an ornament to the town, as well as a source of social, intellectual and spiritual profit to its attendants.

St. Mary's school is one of the most proficient in the diocese. There are

486 pupils with eleven Sisters. Sister M. Clare is the superior. The trustees, John Fahy and James Clavin, have held this office for upwards of thirty years, and have been pew-rent collectors for the same period of time.

The population of St. Mary's parish is 3100 souls, and comprises among this number physicians, merchants, expert mechanics and a number of public-school teachers.

## ST. MARY'S PARISH,

### RIDGEFIELD.[1]

IT is a well-established fact that James Brophy and family were the first Catholics to stand upon the soil of Ridgefield. They came here on Thanksgiving Day, November 30, 1848. After them in succession we meet the familiar names of Whalen, Kirwin, Purcell, Kelly, Murphy, Cahill, Fitzgerald, Short, Mulhall, Gallagher, Halpin, Cullen and Enright. In a few years the number so increased that from fifty to seventy-five persons would gather about the humble altar when it would be known that a priest was to visit Ridgefield.

The house of James Brophy was the first to harbor a priest in Ridgefield. Returning to his home at Danbury, Father Ryan stopped at Ridgefield and administered the last sacraments to two of Mr. Brophy's relatives who were dangerously ill. His successor in the pastorate of Danbury, Rev. Father O'Farrell, becoming cognizant that there were a number of Catholics in Ridgefield and vicinity, arranged to pay visits at monthly intervals. Coming on Saturday evenings he would hear confessions and say Mass on the following morning at Mr. Brophy's residence. Father O'Farrell's successors, Rev. Fathers Smith, Kelly and Drea, continued to serve the Catholic people of Ridgefield. The number of Catholics increasing, it became necessary to secure the old Town hall for divine services, paying at each visit five dollars for the privilege.

On November 23, 1867, the site upon which the first church was built was purchased from George R. Scofield for $975, James Enright and James Walsh acting as agents for their Catholic brethren. A frame dwelling-house stood on the lot at the time of the purchase and for a time served as a church. It was destroyed by fire in 1868. The destruction of this building was a severe blow to the devoted little band. It made a return to private houses and the Town hall necessary, and in this struggling condition they remained for nearly nine years. But their courage revived. They eagerly desired a church, and their faith and self-sacrifice provided the means. Generous souls contributed, $20, $30 and $50. Thus stimulated they bent their energies to the task before them, and in due time had the happiness to see their long-desired church erected—small, indeed—but their own, and when the work was completed, the financial manager of the work, Thomas McGlynn, presented to the pastor, Rev. M. P. Lawlor, of Danbury, a bill receipted in full payment for all debts that had been contracted.

---

[1] The Indian name of Ridgefield was *Caudatowa*, a name signifying *High Land*. It was incorporated in 1708.

Some time after the completion of the church, Ridgefield was taken from the jurisdiction of Danbury, and transferred to that of Georgetown, which had been made a parish with the Rev. Thaddeus Walsh as the first resident pastor. Redding Ridge was also served from Georgetown. In 1880, Father Walsh transferred his residence to Ridgefield, Georgetown becoming the mission, where Mass is said by Father Shortell every Sunday and holyday in the church of the Sacred Heart. This church was built during the administration of Father Walsh. Father Walsh died in 1886 and was immediately followed by Rev. P. Byrne, who in turn was succeeded six years later by Rev. Joseph O'Keefe. After a pastorate of ten months ill health compelled him to retire. Brief as was his pastorate he left in the treasury, the result of his efforts, $535, as a nucleus of a building fund.

The present pastor, the Rev. Richard E. Shortell, assumed charge of St. Mary's parish on May 30, 1893. Father Shortell immediately began preparations for the erection of a new church. The first step to this end was the purchase from Jacob M. Lockwood for $2,750 of the site on which stand the present handsome church and fine pastoral residence. The rectory was built early in 1894 and was free from indebtedness when completed. Work on the church commenced in May, 1896, and the corner-stone was laid on July 4th of that year by Bishop Tierney. The church was dedicated under the patronage of the Mother of God on July 5, 1897. The sermon was preached on the occasion by the Rev. T. J. Kelly. Says a local chronicler: "Realizing that this first little church was inadequate in size, undesirable in locality, their zeal prompted them to renewed efforts, and then was called forth that generosity which gives them to day one of the most desirable places in the village of Ridgefield for a church worthy to be called a House of God."

St. Mary's cemetery was purchased by Rev. Father Walsh in August, 1882; it was blessed on October 13, 1883, by Bishop McMahon.

When St. Mary's parish was formed it comprised about 200 souls, all Irish and their descendants. The number at present is 270.

## ST. JOSEPH'S PARISH,

### SOUTH NORWALK.

S T. Joseph's parish was formed September 1, 1895, by cutting off the southern portion of St. Mary's parish, Norwalk. It comprises all of South Norwalk and extends north to Cedar street. The first pastor was the Rev. John Winters, who offered his first Mass for his new parishioners on September 8, 1895, in Music Hall, South Main street. This hall was rented for church purposes at a rental of $500 per annum. When the parish was organized it comprised 1200 Irish people, 200 Hungarians and 100 Italians.

Work on the church was begun in October, 1896. The corner-stone was laid on Sunday, April 4, 1897, by Bishop Tierney, in the presence of 8,000 citizens of both Norwalks. The preacher on the occasion was the Rev. William Maher, D.D., of Milford.

St. Joseph's parish began its career with $1,750 in the treasury, the gift of the Rev. W. J. Slocum. They possess a very valuable property on South Main street. Two separate properties, side by side, were purchased and united, the one serving for a church site, the other for a rectory. The building on the rectory site has been re-modeled and is used as a pastoral residence. The house on the other property was removed to make way for the new church. The rectory property cost $6,000, and the church lot with building, $4,750. The erection of the handsome brick church and the thorough renovation of it exteriorly and interiorly and the improvements made in the grounds, make this property the chief ornament of South Main street and the pride of the Catholic population.

The number of baptisms administered during 1896 and 1897 were 166, and the marriages solemnized during the same time were 32. The first baptism was that of Helen Kindilien; the first marriage was that of John Kennedy and Mary Lynch.

The Catholics of South Norwalk enjoy the esteem and good will of all classes and creeds, and under the patronage of St. Joseph are prospering. Politically, they are divided between the two great parties; socially, they are the peers of their neighbors; intellectually, they are recognized as influential elements in the population.

The week after Easter Sunday, 1899, witnessed the transfer of the Rev. Father Winters from South Norwalk to the newly organized parish of the Immaculate Conception, Hartford. His successor is the Rev. William Maher, D. D., formerly of Milford.

## ST. JOHN'S PARISH.

### STAMFORD.[1]

THE services of the church were held for the first time in Stamford in September, 1842, in the house of Patrick H. Drew in West Stamford. The celebrant of the Mass on that occasion was the Rev. James Smyth. Three families comprised the Catholic population at that time. Mass was said here at stated intervals until 1846. When Mr. Drew removed to the old "Webb Place" on South street, the Divine Mysteries were there celebrated, first by Bishop Tyler. In this house and in the Town hall services were held until the completion of the church on Meadow street in 1851.

Writing to Bishop Tyler under date of February 16, 1846, the Rev. Michael Lynch of Bridgeport said: "I was at Stamford on the 8th and 9th inst., and administered the Sacraments to 12 or 14 persons there; said Mass for them and baptized two children. This makes eleven visits to them these three years past, most of them on Sundays."[2] In the same letter he gave the number of Catholics of Stamford as "15 to 25." Besides Stamford, Father Lynch attended from Bridgeport, Norwalk, Danbury, Wolcottville and Norfolk also. Despite his almost quarterly visits—and it is difficult to see how he could go more frequently with missions as widely separated as Norfolk, Wol-

---

[1] *Rippowams* was the original name of Stamford. It was purchased for "twelve coats, twelve hoes, twelve hatchets, twelve knives, two kettles and four fathom of wampum."

[2] The 8th and 9th of February, 1846, fell on Sunday and Monday.

ST. JOHN'S CHURCH.
Stamford, Conn.

cottville and the others—complaints were made to Bishop Tyler that Father Lynch had "despised and forgotten our Catholic brethren in the locality of Stamford." This formal accusation was drawn up, it should be known, by one who "would not submit to the rules of this diocese," and who, refusing to obey the law concerning the proclamation of the banns, was married in New York.

The people finally appealed to the priests of St. John's College, Fordham, for assistance. The following official correspondence will throw much light on the status of Catholicity in Stamford at this period :

ST. JOHN'S COLL., FORDHAM, Aug. 12, 1846.

*Right Revd. Sir :* [1] Mr. J. Lynch, a good Catholic of Stamford, Conn., applied to us some time since to know if we could send, once every six weeks, one of our F.F. (Fathers) to Stamford, which, he said, can receive but very seldom the visit of a clergyman. I answered him that as soon as I had ascertained the possibility of doing so I would write to your Lordship, in whose jurisdiction the place is.

Our intention is not and cannot be to establish there one of us as parish priest, nor to attend the sick calls; but merely to say Mass, hear confessions, and give instructions to that good people twice in three months, until your Lordship may provide better for them.

If this demand meets with your approbation, I will immediately answer affirmatively to Mr. Lynch, and at the beginning of next month one of our gentlemen will go to Providence to receive your blessing and acquaint himself with your desire.

I have the honor to be, Right Revd. Sir,

Your Most Obt. Servt.,

AUG. J. THEBAUD, S. J.

To this note Bishop Tyler sent the following reply :

PROVIDENCE, Aug. 18, 1846.

*Rev. Dear Sir :* I have received your letter of the 12th inst. I wish certainly that the good people of Stamford may enjoy all the benefits of religion and as frequently as possible. They are now under the care of Rev. Mr. Lynch, who resides mostly at Bridgeport.

More than a year ago I received a letter signed by —— and several others, complaining of being neglected and requesting, not in the most humble terms, to be better provided for. I wrote to Rev. Mr. Lynch upon the subject, and after that when I saw him, spoke to him more fully about it. It was not difficult to perceive that an unfortunate misunderstanding existed between a considerable portion, at least, of the Catholics of Stamford and their pastor. They charged him with neglect and want of attention to them, and he accused them of requiring of him things that were unreasonable, and refusing to contribute a proper sum towards his support,[2] and to enable him to procure things required for the decent celebration of the sacred mysteries.

That their demands upon him were in some cases unreasonable was manifest to me from their own letter, and I do not doubt that when they began to entertain an unkind feeling towards him they also withheld their contributions. Such a state of things is deeply to be deplored. It is out of my power to remedy it. I have no other priest to send them,[3] and even if I had I doubt whether they would give him a support.

Perhaps some of your good Fathers may do good in the case. If so, I shall be very happy. But you can easily perceive that it will not do for them to go there, as it were, rivals of Rev. Mr. Lynch. They should rather appear as his assistants, and of course

[1] Bishop Tyler.

[2] In his letter to Bishop Tyler, quoted above, Father Lynch said that from his eleven visits to Stamford he "got very little from them, sometimes nothing, at other times hardly what would pay my expenses."

[3] Beside Father Lynch there were only three other priests in Connecticut, Rev. John Brady, Rev. Jas. Smyth and Rev. John Brady, Jr.

should first have a good understanding with him ; unless, indeed, you could take the whole care of the place, which you intimate is impossible.

I will write immediately to Rev. Mr. Lynch upon the subject, and if one of you good Fathers will see him and have an agreement with him upon the subject, and do something for the spiritual welfare of those poor people you will have not merely my thanks, but will have the merit of promoting the great object which your society has always in view—the honor and glory of God and the salvation of souls.

With sincere respect, I am, Dear Sir,

Yours in Christ,

REV. AUG. J. THEBAUD, S.J.,                                                    † WM. TYLER.
St. John's College, Fordham, N. Y.

In accordance with Bishop Tyler's wishes, a priest of St. John's College held a conference with Father Lynch at Bridgeport, the results of which will be seen from the following letters :

BRIDGEPORT, Sept. 23, 1846.

*Right Revd. Bishop :* The Revd. Mr. de Luynes, one of the priests of St. John's College, called here last week to make arrangements for visiting Stamford. I told him he might come there, with your approbation, as often as he pleased, provided he did not interfere with my visits once in every three months; or, with your consent, that he might take the entire charge of that place and the adjoining towns. I presume Rev. Mr. Thebaud will write to you again. I submit the matter to your lordship for adjustment, and await your decision.

Wishing your Lordship health and happiness, I remain,

Your Lordship's most Obt. Servant,

M. LYNCH.

Father Thebaud wrote :

ST. JOHN'S COLL., Sept. 28, 1846.

*Right Rev. Sir :* Last week Father de Luynes, one of our gentlemen, went to see Revd. Mr. Lynch, of Bridgeport, to hear from him, if he would have any objection to our visiting periodically the Catholics of Stamford. Mr. Lynch said that he was willing, provided we should take altogether the charge of that part of his congregation and attend the sick calls. This we cannot do, chiefly on account of the distance, and the difficulty of the roads in winter. We give up, therefore, the idea we had of obliging those poor people, and I think it proper to inform your Lordship of it. It may be, nevertheless, that, at least, in summer, some of us may go occasionally to Stamford, as Rev. Mr. Lynch said he had no objection to it, and I hope you will grant us for those occasions, the power of hearing confessions and administering other sacraments in that portion of your diocese.

I have the honor to be, Right Rev. Sir,

Your Obt. Servt,

AUG. J. THEBAUD, S.J.

After Bishop McFarland's ordination to the priesthood, on May 18, 1845, he was assigned to St. John's College as professor. He did not remain here long, as on May 6, 1846, he was appointed pastor of Watertown, N. Y., and dependencies. Previous to this he had done parochial duty in New York city. While professor at Fordham, Father McFarland often attended sick calls at Stamford. His visits antedated the application mentioned in Father Thebaud's first letter to Bishop Tyler, and may, indirectly, have been the cause of the petition being made to the college.

In 1849, the Rev. John C. Brady was appointed pastor of Norwalk, with Stamford, Danbury, New Milford and Canaan as missions. Father Brady took up his residence on the Cove road a short distance from the town. On July 4, 1849, he broke ground for a new church on Meadow street. It was a one-story frame structure, 60 by 40 feet. The church was dedicated on January 26, 1851. On that occasion Bishop O'Reilly also made a visitation of the parish, administered confirmation and preached three times.

In March, 1854, the Rev. E. J. Cooney succeeded Father Brady. During his pastorate the church was enlarged by an addition of twenty feet. Father Cooney made many other improvements in and about the church. The next pastor and the first resident priest of Stamford, was the Rev. James Reynolds. His term of service began in November, 1857, and ended by his death in October, 1858.

The Rev. James H. O'Neill immediately succeeded Father Reynolds. Finding the labors of the parish too arduous to be borne alone, as the number of souls had increased from a few hundred to over a thousand in less than ten years, he received as assistants the Rev. Edward O'Neill, who served from 1860 to 1864; Rev. Christopher Duggett, 1864 to 1866; Rev. James Ward, 1866; Rev. James Charleton, 1867, and Rev. Eugene Gaffney. Recognizing the importance of Catholic schools Father O'Neill in 1860 built a school on Meadow street, and procured effective teachers in the persons of Mr. P. Reilly and Miss B. Clancy, who retained their positions until 1876, when the old church having been converted into school-rooms, and the pastoral residence into a convent, the Sisters of Mercy assumed charge of the schools. During these years Greenwich was a mission of Stamford, and so continued until the fall of 1876, when it attained the dignity of a parish, with the Rev. W. H. Rogers as the first pastor.

The Rev. John Fagan was appointed the successor of Father O'Neill upon the death of the latter in October, 1868. One of the great needs of the parish at this time was a new cemetery, as the little burial ground around the old church had only a few untenanted graves. A tract of thirty-six acres in Springdale, about two and one-half miles from Stamford, on the line of the New Canaan R. R., was purchased. Father Fagan had this surveyed and laid out for cemetery purposes. He built a massive stone wall along the front, planted trees and otherwise beautified the grounds, so that with its graveled walks and driveways, its shrubs and flowers, gentle undulation and stream of water running along its western border, Springdale cemetery is a place of great beauty. As the congregation had increased to 3000 souls, Father Fagan was not long in recognizing the necessity of a larger church. Accordingly, a short time after his appointment, he took steps to secure an eligible site. He purchased the present site on Atlantic street from Mr. A. J. Bell for $12,500. Work on the church was immediately begun, but Father Fagan lived to see the work completed only to the water table. He died on December 5, 1873. Father Fagan's assistants were: Rev. James Daly, from April to October, 1871; Rev. Thomas Lynch, from October, 1871, to April, 1872; Rev. Thomas Healy, from April, 1872, to September, 1873; Rev. John A. Mulcahy, from June until September, 1873, and Rev. W. H. Rogers, appointed September, 1873.

The Rev. Michael A. Tierney assumed charge of St. John's parish on February 1, 1874, pushed on the work of the church vigorously, roofed in the building and completed the basement, which was ready for divine services on Thanksgiving day, 1875. Very Rev. James Hughes, administrator of the diocese, officiated at the dedication ceremonies, and the sermon was preached by the Rev. Matthew Hart. The evening discourse was pronounced by the Rev. P. A. Murphy. In the meantime Father Tierney had purchased the present pastoral residence on Atlantic street from Mr. J. A. Condon for $18,500, had fitted up the old church for school purposes, and brought the Sisters of Mercy to take charge of the schools.

Father Tierney was followed in the pastorate by the present rector, the Rev. William H. Rogers, in 1877. Father Rogers continued the work on the church until its completion. The ceremony of dedication was performed by Bishop McMahon on May 30, 1886. The preacher was the Rev. Dr. Horstmann, the present bishop of Cleveland. The orator at the evening services was the Rev. Edward McGlynn, D. D.

The Rev. Thomas Coleman served as assistant here from July, 1876, to the following September; Rev. Joseph Gleeson from January, 1877, until November, 1878; Rev. H. J. Walsh from November, 1878, to February, 1885; Rev. P. Skelly from February, 1885, to April, 1886; Rev. Thomas Keenan from February, 1886, to November, 1897; the Rev. E. A. Flannery from January, 1898, to September, 1898. Rev. J. T. Lynch and Rev. E. Sullivan are the present assistants.

The property of St. John's parish was recently increased by the purchase of the house and land adjoining the rectory for $8500. In four decades the Catholic population of Stamford has increased from 100 to 4000 souls. The value of the church property is near a quarter of a million dollars.

The parochial school is in a very prosperous condition. There are 463 pupils and eleven sisters, of whom Sister M. Alexius is Superioress.

St. John's church is of grey stone with granite trimmings throughout. It is of Gothic design, cruciform with clerestory. The dimensions are: extreme length, 176 feet; width of nave and aisles, 68 feet; breadth of nave at intersection of transepts, 92 feet; transepts, 16 x 50; height of nave, 50 feet; vestibule, 16 x 50; height of spire, 225 feet. The architect was Mr. James Murphy, of Providence, R. I.

### LIST OF EARLY CATHOLIC NAMES OF
#### STAMFORD.

| Families | Whole number of souls | Families. | Whole number of souls |
|---|---|---|---|
| Drew, Patrick, wife and six children | 8 | O'Brien, Patrick, wife and three children | 5 |
| Kenney, Timothy, wife and two children | 4 | Murphy, James, wife and two children | 4 |
| Dwyer, Robert, wife and three children | 5 | Shaughnessy, Patrick, wife and four children | 6 |
| Hogg, Peter, wife and two children | 4 | | |
| Gilfoyle, Mrs., and five children | 6 | Hogg, Michael, and wife | 2 |
| Deagan, John, wife and child | 3 | Eagan, Felix, and wife | 2 |
| Muldoon, John, wife and five children | 7 | Edell, Madame, and one child | 2 |
| Fitzgerald, Thomas, wife and one child | 3 | | |

#### STILLWATER DISTRICT.

| | | | |
|---|---|---|---|
| Kennedy, John, and wife | 2 | Guider, John, and wife | 2 |
| Sullivan, John, and wife | 2 | Brown, Mrs. Rose, and four children | 5 |

ST. JOHN'S CHURCH,
Stamford, Conn.

ROXBURY.

| Families. | Whole number of souls. | Families. | Whole number of souls. |
|---|---|---|---|
| Crowley, Patrick, wife and two children | 4 | Shea, Patrick, and wife | 2 |
| Crowley, Timothy, and sister | 2 | Welsh, Thomas, wife and child | 3 |
| O'Brien, Michael, wife and one child | 3 | | |

DUMPLING POND LOCALITY.

| | | | |
|---|---|---|---|
| O'Neil, Edward, wife and one child | 3 | O'Brien, Thomas, wife and four children | 6 |
| Power, John, wife and two children | 4 | Karney, Michael, wife and one child | 3 |

STANAVE LOCALE.

| | | | |
|---|---|---|---|
| O'Connell, Timothy, wife and two children | 4 | Ryan, John, wife and three children | 5 |
| | | O'Brien, Patrick, wife and four children | 6 |

Whole number of souls . . . . . . . . . . . . . . . . . . . . . . 117
Whole number of families . . . . . . . . . . . . . . . . . . . . 30

STAMFORD.

| | | | |
|---|---|---|---|
| Daniel Lahy. | Edward Ryan. | James Brennan. | Michael Lynch. |
| Francis O'Neill. | William Murphy. | James Kelly. | Martin Gillespie. |
| Michael Kennedy. | Edward Kavenagh. | James Herbert. | Francis Lee. |
| Lawrence Walsh. | Michael Conly. | Joseph McNamara. | James Keenan. |
| Daniel Doolan. | John Hickey. | Peter McGowan. | Michael O'Donnell. |
| Charles Downey. | John Ryan. | Cornelius Cavanagh. | Francis McGarvey. |
| Michael Mangen. | Patrick Cavanagh. | Patrick Lynch. | Bernard Kehoe. |
| | Patrick Powers. | Peter Nugent. | |

STILLWATER.

| | | | |
|---|---|---|---|
| Martin Flinn. | John Foley. | John Foley, Jr. | Timothy McDonald. |
| William Collins. | John Murphy. | John Harrison. | John Terry. |
| Timothy Conroy. | Miles Riley. | James Mulkey. | Daniel Duffy. |
| | John McMahon. | | |

ROXBURY.

| | | |
|---|---|---|
| Thomas Blute. | Patrick Rourke. | Thomas Dacey. |

DUMPLING POND.

| | | | |
|---|---|---|---|
| Thomas Buckley. | James Magee. | Jeremiah O'Brien. | Michael Kennedy. |
| Edmund Clute. | James McLaren. | Patrick Gannan. | James Lynch. |
| | Peter Kennedy. | | |

STAMFORD.

| | | | |
|---|---|---|---|
| Bridget Langen. | Ann Nugent. | Ellen O'Neill. | Ann Smith. |
| Catherine Donavan. | Mary Gorman. | Mary Brady. | Margaret Smith. |
| Mary Moran. | Mary Shean. | Margaret Collins. | Mary Fitzpatrick. |
| Sarah Berresford. | Bridget Conelly. | Ellen Malone. | Catherine Dougherty |
| Ann Mack. | Margaret Doran. | MaryMcCahey. | Margaret Flannigan. |
| Bridget Kelley. | Rosey Nugent. | Cecilia O'Shaughnessy. | Margaret Lee. |
| Bridget Lynch. | Mrs. Simox. | Mary Sanderson. | Ann O'Neill. |
| Ellen Crowley. | Rosanna Flood. | Jane McGrath. | Bridget Connelly. |
| Catherine Connors. | Mary Curran. | Bridget Kehoe. | Rosanna Riley. |
| | Mrs. Sullivan. | Catherine Smith. | |

Also a number of others whose names could not be easily ascertained.

Thirty families numbering . . . . . . . . . . . . . . . . . . . . . . 117
Unmarried persons as far as could be learned . . . . . . . . . . . . 93

Total . . . . . . . . . . . . . . . . . . . . . . . . 210

There is no date on the original paper from which the above was copied, but it is a very old list. Its probable date is about 1850.

## PARISH OF THE ASSUMPTION,

### WESTPORT

THE town of Westport was incorporated in 1835. Eighteen years after, on November 21st, was offered up for the first time in Westport the Holy Sacrifice of the Mass. The celebrant was the Rev. John Brady, of Norwalk, and the chapel for the occasion was the Universalist church, on Main street. The priests of Norwalk continued to serve the Catholics of Westport until a short time previous to its formation into a parish.

In 1860, the church was built by the Rev. Dr. Mulligan, and dedicated on August 15th of that year. When Rev. M. P. Lawlor began his pastorate at Fairfield, in January, 1876, he took charge also of Westport. Father Lawlor's pastorate was of short duration, at the end of which Westport was made an independent parish. The Rev. Patrick Keating was appointed the first resident pastor, and in January, 1877, purchased the pastoral residence. Among the other material works effected was the decoration of the church. Father Keating ministered to the wants of the Westport Catholics with commendable zeal until May 10, 1885, when the Rev. John H. Carroll was appointed his successor. His thirteen years of service here were productive of gratifying results in the material and spiritual order. For many years Father Carroll served on the Board of Education, and was also the chairman of that body, a fact which strongly attests the existence of the spirit of fraternity between Protestants and Catholics; and, that this spirit does exist, is due in no small degree to the prudent, and withal manly course adopted and steadily pursued by the clergy. Father Carroll preached his farewell sermon on Sunday, October 9, 1898, and on the following Sunday assumed charge of the parish of the Holy Trinity, Wallingford. He was succeeded by the Rev. James P. Ryle, who came here from Montville.

The church of the Assumption is a frame structure, whose seating capacity is 500.

# LITCHFIELD COUNTY.

## ST. JOSEPH'S PARISH,

### WINSTED.

THE first Mass said in Winsted, or, as it was then called, Clifton, was offered by the Rev. James Lynch, of Birmingham, in the west district school-house, in 1851, in the presence of about forty persons. An old resident, however, is authority for the statement that the first Mass was said in 1850 by a Father Tucker. One who was present at Father Lynch's Mass, Mrs. Gabriel Grinnan, is still living, and has vivid recollections of the same. Mr. Peter Dardis came to Winsted in 1849. At that time, he says, there were about twelve Catholic families here. In 1851 land was purchased for a church. In 1852 the Rev. Thomas Quinn entered upon his duties as the first resident pastor of Winsted. Soon after his arrival he began the erection of the church, the corner-stone of which was laid in 1853. Until the church was ready for occupancy, divine services were held in Camp's Hall. In 1853 Father Quinn was succeeded by the Rev. Philip Gillick, who came from the diocese of New York. He completed the church, in the basement of which he took up his residence. Rev. Thomas Hendricken came in 1854. Serving here about one year, he was followed by the Rev. Richard O'Gorman in 1855. Rev. Lawrence Mangan came next, and remained three years. While traveling in Europe Father Mangan was drowned. Rev. Daniel Mullen was appointed pastor in 1860, but at the outbreak of the Civil War he resigned to accept the office of chaplain of the Ninth Connecticut Volunteers. "Father Mullen was a man of literary culture," says the *Annals of Winchester*, "and earnest patriotism, who served at Baton Rouge and Chackaloo Station, La., and Deep Bottom, Va. He was compelled by ill health to resign on the 26th of August, 1862." Father Mullen's successor was the Rev. Philip Sheridan, who a few years later was followed by Rev. Father Leo da Saracena, O. S. F., who had taken Father Mullen's place as chaplain of the Ninth Regiment. During his first administration this parish was thoroughly organized. Father Leo received his appointment as rector of St. Joseph's parish on January 1, 1865. In August, 1870, the Rev. Father Anacletus, O. F. M., became pastor, but was transferred in the following year to allow Father Leo to resume charge of the parish, which he continued to govern till 1877. From 1877 to 1880 he was Custos Provincial of the order, and resided at Allegany in St. Bonaventure's seminary, of which he was the president for three years. Father Leo was followed by Father Ubaldus da Rieti, who held the position of rector until 1878, when he was succeeded by the Rev. Bonaventure Fox, O. S. F. He remained until 1879, when he returned to Santa Barbara, California. In 1879, Fathers Jerome, Daniel, and Francis labored here as well as on the outmissions. At the expiration of his term of office at Allegany in 1880, Father Leo returned to Winsted. With the exception of a tour through Europe and the Holy Land in 1891 and 1892, Father Leo labored continuously in the parish until summoned to his reward on November 3, 1897, in the sixty-fifth year of his age and the forty-second of his priesthood. His successor, the Rev. Alexander M. Hickey, O. S. F., was appointed by the Custos Provincial, Very Rev. Joseph Butler, with the approbation of Right Rev. Bishop Tierney, and is still in charge of the parish.

Among the works that distinguished Father Leo's administration were the purchase from a Mr. Philips of a dwelling-house; the providing the Sisters with a building which they used as an academy and convent; the opening of a parochial school in the basement of the church on August 15, 1865; the purchase of a piece of land in 1866 west of the church, and the erection on it of a spacious brick monastery; the securing of the property in the rear of the church, known as the Grove; the building, in 1876, of the convent of St. Margaret of Cortona, which, with the beautifying of the grounds, cost over $15,000. The corner-stone of the convent was laid on September 17, 1876, and on December 3, of the same year, it was dedicated ; the new convent bell was blessed on this occasion. The Holy Sacrifice of the Mass was celebrated by Rev. E. J. O'Brien, assisted by Rev. C. Hughes, of Providence, Rev. Father Boniface and Rev. Father Leo. The discourse at the morning service was pronounced by Bishop O'Reilly, of Springfield, and Bishop Galberry preached the sermon in the evening. In 1883 Father Leo remodeled the church by adding a transept and chancel, and had it thoroughly renovated exteriorly and interiorly — the whole work at an expense of $15,000. The church was dedicated on June 13, 1883, the Rev. Charles McKenna, O.P., preaching the dedicatory sermon. In 1887 the energetic pastor built St. Anthony's school, a fine brick edifice, with a stone basement. The school was blessed by Bishop McMahon on December 11, 1887. He was assisted by Rev. J. A. Mulcahy, now Vicar-General, and Rev. T. W. Broderick. The oration was pronounced by Mgr. Thomas J. Conaty, D.D.

The cemetery attached to the parish was purchased during the pastorate of Rev. Father Mangan, about 1858 or 1859. It was secured for the parish by a Mr. McGuire, and cost $400. A portion of it was blessed by Bishop McFarland before the departure of Father Mangan, and the remainder when Father Leo was pastor, before 1876. Prior to the purchase of this cemetery the parishioners buried their dead in the Catholic cemeteries of New Hartford and Norfolk.

According to the deed by which Bishop McFarland conveyed the entire property to the Franciscans, the people of the parish must have the use of the church ; and it may excite surprise that they have *only the use of it.* This may be accounted for thus : that the people who visit a church of the Friars Minor on the 1st and 2d of August, other conditions being complied with, may gain the indulgences granted by the Pope. The circumstance affects the people indifferently, because all the property held in the name of the Friars Minor belongs to the Holy See.

When Father Leo took charge in Winsted he had as dependencies Colebrook, New Boston, Torrington, Litchfield and Norfolk. Of these missions Colebrook alone remains. The estimated number of Catholics in Winsted, when the parish was formed, was 250, principally Irish. The number at present is about 2,000. Father Hickey is assisted in his parochial labors by Rev. Father Lewis, O.S.F., and Rev. C. Ryan, O.S.F.

Among the benefactors of St. Joseph's parish mention may be made of Mr. Harvey Wakefield, who died on July 24, 1884, bequeathing $1,000 to the church.

St. Joseph's school is taught by the Sisters of St. Francis, nine in number, of whom Mother Leo is the Superioress. The school has nine grades, with an attendance of 314 pupils, and is among the best in the diocese.

From 1867 to the present there have been twenty-nine assistants, and among them was Rev. Father Diomede Falconio, O.S.F., now an archbishop in Italy, and recently appointed Apostolic Delegate to Canada.

REV. MICHAEL MANN O.F.M.

REV. JAMES H. O'DONNELL.

REV. P. KEATING.

REV. TIMOTHY F. BANNON.

REV. JOHN LEE.

## ST. MARY'S PARISH,

### LAKEVILLE.

NTIL the appointment of Rev. H. Lynch in 1875, the pastors of the missions included within this jurisdiction resided at Falls Village, as here was the parish church. Mass was said for the first time in Falls Village in 1849 by Rev. John C. Brady, pastor of St. Mary's parish, Norwalk. Previous to this the Holy Sacrifice had been offered in North Canaan on Christmas Day, 1848, in the house of Patrick Lynch by Rev. John Smith of Albany, N. Y. The total Catholic population of North Canaan at this time consisted of three families, the Lynch's, McCarthy's and Gorman's. The first Mass celebrated in Lakeville was said on July 4, 1849, under a tree near the Davis Mine by Rev. Father Howard of Poughkeepsie, N. Y. Father Smith came from Albany at stated intervals and said Mass in Mr. Lynch's residence and elsewhere as opportunity provided.

When Rev. Christopher Moore, the first resident pastor of Falls Village, assumed charge in 1850, his jurisdiction embraced Canaan (Falls Village), Goshen, Salisbury (Lakeville), Sharon and Cornwall. Having no church in which to gather his flock, he said Mass and administered the sacraments in houses most convenient for the people. At the time of his arrival, about 800 men were employed at Ames' Iron Works; for their accommodation Mass was frequently said in the school-house at Amesville. One Sunday morning, however, they found the door of the school locked by the authorities against them, so that divine services were resumed in private houses and in the open air, "an apple tree standing on Beebe Hill furnishing them shade on one fine Sunday morning in June." Rev. Peter Kelly succeeded to the pastorate of Falls Village in 1851. Here he built St. Patrick's church in 1854, as well as churches at Goshen and Cornwall. Before St. Patrick's church was dedicated it was paid for, Father Kelly's mother in Ireland contributing generously for the purpose. St. Patrick's church enjoys the distinction of never having been in debt, although it is the oldest church on the railroad line between Bridgeport and Pittsfield.

In 1887 Father Kelly was transferred to Hartford and was followed by Rev. Dr. Mulligan, who remained two years. Then Rev. Richard O'Gorman was appointed pastor. His pastorate was of short duration, having been succeeded by Rev. Philip Sheridan in 1860. After serving three years, Rev. J. Couch came, but remained for a short time only. The pastorates of his successors, Father O'Reilly and Father O'Farrell, were also brief. The latter died at Falls Village in 1868. Early in 1868, Rev. John J. McCabe assumed charge, but was followed in September, 1869, by Rev. Joseph O'Keefe. During his pastorate in 1871 he built St. Joseph's church in North Canaan. After four years of labor here Father O'Keefe gave way to Rev. Stephen Sheffrey, whose pastorate was of one year's duration, having been sent to New Haven in February, 1875. Immediately following Father Sheffrey came Rev. Henry Lynch, who remained pastor of these missions until December, 1886. Father Lynch built St. Mary's church in Lakeville, and erecting a pastoral residence also, moved his residence here and constituted Lakeville the parish. The corner-stone of St. Mary's church, Lakeville, was laid on the feast of Corpus Christi, May 27, 1875, by Very Rev. James Hughes, Administrator, and it was dedicated to divine worship by the Rev. Luke Daly, on January 16, 1876. Falls Village then became a mission. At this time his jurisdiction embraced Lakeville, Falls Village, Canaan and Cornwall, with Catholics at Huntsville and Lime Rock. Father Lynch built the splendid St. Mary's convent and parochial school in 1882, and introduced the Sisters of Mercy from Hartford to conduct an academy for young ladies and to teach in the school. The academy was discontinued, but the school continues with three sisters and seventy-one pupils. Sister Euphemia is the Superioress of the convent. Father Lynch's pastorate ceased in December, 1886, when the Rev. P. Fox was appointed pastor. His success in this field, wherein he had been assistant to Father Lynch, was marked by a notable reduction in the indebtedness of the parish. Father Fox was transferred to Newtown in February, 1891, and was succeeded by the Rev. P. Donahoe, who died here on July 12th of the same year. From this date the present pastor, the Rev. Timothy F. Bannon, has been the pastor of St. Mary's. Father Bannon is assisted in his parochial labors by the Rev. William Kiernan. It was in Lakeville, in the residence of Father Bannon, that Right Rev. Bishop McMahon died.

The population of St. Mary's parish is about 700 souls, including the missions, Falls Village and Canaan, where Mass is said every Sunday.

The chief benefactors to the parish were Jonathan Scoville, who donated $3,500 to St. Mary's, and the Hon. William H. Barnum, who was ever a generous and consistent friend, giving freely of his substance to further the interests of religion as represented by St. Mary's parish.

St. Patrick's cemetery, Falls Village, was purchased in the fall of 1853, but was not blessed until the episcopate of Bishop Galberry, July 17, 1876. Rev. Father Glackmeyer, S.J., preached on the occasion. St. Joseph's cemetery, North Canaan, was bought in the spring of 1889, and in the following September was blessed by Bishop McMahon, Rev. J. J. Quinn preaching the sermon. St. Mary's cemetery, Lakeville, was purchased early in 1885, and was solemnly set apart for burial purposes by Very Rev. John A. Mulcahy, V.G., in the same year. On this occasion Rev. J. J. Curtin pronounced the discourse.

Father Bannon labors unceasingly, not only to promote the spiritual interests of his flock, but also to reduce the indebtedness of the parish; and in this arduous task he has been eminently successful.

## ST. ANTHONY'S PARISH,

### LITCHFIELD.

THE section now comprised in the town of Litchfield was known to the Indians as *Bantam;* it was incorporated in 1724 as Litchfield. The first minister in Litchfield bore the familiar name of Timothy Collins. He was a native of Guilford, and a graduate of Yale college in 1718. Another suggestive name found in the early records of this historic old town is Mark Kenney, who saw hard service in the French and Indian war. The first

Catholics to come within the confines of Litchfield were three Acadians, the victims of English oppression. Sybil Shearaway, one of them, married Thomas Harrison in 1764, and their descendants are still residents of Litchfield. The town records of January, 1759, disclosed the manner in which these poor people were treated. On this date it was "voted that the selectmen may provide a house or some suitable place in the town *for the maintenance of the French;*" and in the county treasurer's book this entry is found: "To paid John Newbree for keeping William Dunlap *and the French persons,* 54s. 6d., which the county allowed, and R. Sherman, justice of the quorum, drew an order dated April 25, 1760, as per order on file." As the proselytizing spirit was then rife in Connecticut, it is almost certain that if the elder Acadians did not sacrifice their faith, their descendants were taught to believe that nothing good could come out of Rome.

From this time on we find no trace of Catholicity in Litchfield until the period when Irish emigration was at its height. Irish people settled here in the rural districts and devoted themselves to the pursuits of agricultural life. "The celebrated ' Echo Farm,' known the world over," says a local historian, "as a most thoroughly scientific agricultural institution, is a glorious example of their success in this branch of industry."

The first priest to visit Litchfield was the Rev. John Smith, of Albany, who made a missionary tour through this section of the State in 1848 on horseback, seeking out and ministering to the Catholics whom he might find here. On one of these tours he tarried at Litchfield and said Mass, but where, has passed from remembrance.

Bishop O'Reilly visited Litchfield on February 25, 1851, as his journal informs us; but the entry is silent concerning the Holy Sacrifice. It is probable, however, the bishop traveled on these missionary tours provided with all things necessary for celebrating the divine mysteries. Missionary priests did so; why not missionary bishops?

The second Mass was said in the house where Henry Ward Beecher was born. It was the house of John Ryan, on Mill street, and is now a portion of Buell's Retreat. This historic Mass was said by Rev. Philip Gillick in 1853, in the presence of twenty persons. At this time, or at least in the same year, was solemnized the first Catholic marriage in Litchfield, Father Gillick officiating.

The Rev. Thomas F. Hendricken was the next priest to visit Litchfield. In 1854, when pastor of Winsted, he ministered to the spiritual wants of the Catholics in the residence of Peter Vogin. Father Hendricken was succeeded in Winsted by Rev. Richard O'Gorman, who in turn was followed by the Rev. Lawrence Mangan in 1856. Father Mangan visited Litchfield and said Mass in the Academy. The year following Rev. Peter Kelly gathered the Catholics of this section about him in the residence of Joseph Fanning, on North street.

During all these years that Litchfield was honored by the visits of priests, there was no settled place for divine worship. In different private houses the faithful little band gathered to listen to the voice of the priest. But as the congregation grew, it became necessary to secure more adequate accommodations than afforded by private houses. Moreover, the pastors, energetic and willing as they were to meet the demands of their people, could not, as a rule, visit them oftener than quarterly. What was to be done for them, especially for the children, between visits? God provided the ways and means to keep alive the faith of his children here. A convert to the faith, born in Litchfield, Miss Julia Beers, became a ministering angel to her co-religionists.

She purchased from her father in 1858 a small building, which is now a part of the pastoral residence; the room which she suitably arranged with altar and seats, is the dining-room of the rectory. Here the devoted congregation assembled at frequent intervals until 1861, when increasing numbers necessitated removal to the court-house, where they worshiped until the old church was completed in 1868. During these years and until 1882, the pastors of Winsted served the people of Litchfield. The old church was begun by Rev. Father Leo, O.S.F., in 1867, and the first Mass was offered up in the new edifice on New Year's Day, 1868. Father Leo also purchased a cemetery about this time.

On September 8, 1882, Litchfield was made an independent parish with the Rev. M. Byrne, as its first resident pastor. During his brief pastorate here he occupied apartments for a time with that pioneer of Catholicity in this section, Mrs. Fanning. Father Byrne was transferred to Bethel on April 4, 1883, leaving in the treasury $2,700, which he had collected for a building fund. His successor was the Rev. Joseph Gleeson. Entering upon his work with enthusiasm, Father Gleeson, secured for his people the present rectory, paying therefor $6,000. After two years of service Father Gleeson was followed by the Rev. Timothy M. Sweeney, in November, 1885. His administration was distinguished by the erection of the beautiful church that is the pride of all who gather within its walls, at a cost of $23,000. The old church was removed to the rear and the grounds were beautified and fine walks laid about the church and parochial residence.

In March, 1889, the Rev. Patrick Finnegan was appointed rector of St. Anthony's in succession to Father Sweeney. Father Finnegan's pastorate was signalized by the most gratifying successes. In a few years he liquidated the entire indebtedness of $9,000, and placed a sweet-toned bell which cost $700 in the tower. Ill health brought to a close a pastorate as successful in spirituals as in temporals. Father Finnegan, to the grief of his devoted people, resigned his parish on October 15, 1896.

The present pastor, the Rev. Peter Skelly, was then appointed rector of St. Anthony's. Since his advent to Litchfield, Father Skelly has accomplished much for his people. The young are the special objects of his affection. For their improvement he has established an indoor and outdoor gymnasium. The athletic field has been improved by the removal of the old church, and on its site a fine lawn-tennis court has been made. In this field his young men gather for trials in athletic sports and the old saw, "a sound mind in a sound body," has nowhere a better illustration than among the enthusiastic devotees of this field.

As auxiliaries to the pastors of St. Anthony's parish, Miss Julia Beers and

Miss Emma Deming, both converts, labored zealously in season and out of season to promote the spiritual interests of their co-religionists. In the intervals between the visitations of the priests these self-sacrificing women taught the young the salutary truths of our holy religion, while all gathered at their homes to assist at devotions. Their disinterested, faithful and laborious work for souls has left an impress upon the Catholic hearts of Litchfield which time will never erase. Their names are spoken with reverence by a grateful people, and from the hearts of child and parent fervent prayers are ever ascending for their devoted benefactors. They were a host in themselves, and the full measure of the good they accomplished for religion here will not be known until the pages of the Book of Life are revealed at the Final Day. Blessed, indeed, is the parish that possesses such heroic, saintly souls—souls, who, keeping ever in mind the divine injunction : "Seek first the Kingdom of God and His justice," have all things else added unto them.

## ST. THOMAS OF VILLANOVA,

### GOSHEN MISSION.

FOUR miles from Litchfield is the town of Goshen, a dependency of St. Anthony's parish, Litchfield. It was incorporated as a town in 1749. Catholics were residents of Goshen as early as 1831. The following record tells a story of interest :

"GOSHEN.

Henry Briordy *1831. June 7.* Married Henry Briordy to Elizabeth Rosen. Witness, and Peter King.
Elizabeth Rosen

JAS. FITTON."

In 1837 other Catholics found homes here and gave evidence of the faith that was in them by traveling to Norfolk to assist at Mass, when they would receive notice of the coming of the priest to that station. In 1854, however, the Rev. Peter Kelly said the first Mass celebrated in Goshen, in a private house, unless we suppose that Father Fitton offered the Holy Sacrifice on the occasion when the above marriage took place, which is very probable. In 1856, Father Kelly converted a private residence into a chapel where Mass was said by the pastors of Falls Village for seventeen years. On December 1, 1873, Goshen passed under the jurisdiction of Rev. Father Leo, O.S.F., who visited it at monthly intervals. While in his charge Father Leo built St. Thomas' church. The pastors of Winsted continued to serve Goshen until Rev. M. Byrne assumed charge of Litchfield as its first resident pastor. During his brief pastorate Father Byrne liquidated an indebtedness of $800 on the church and left $300 in the treasury. His immediate successor, Father Gleeson, renovated the church, and his successors have labored indefatigably for the well-being of this portion of their flock.

## IMMACULATE CONCEPTION PARISH,

### NEW HARTFORD.

THE first Catholic to reside within the limits of the present parish was an Irishman, a farm hand, and it is traditional that his advent created such a stir that the old residents came from miles around to see what "a real live Irishman looked like." He was here early in the forties, and no doubt, if he resembled his fellow-countrymen and co-religionists of that period, was fully competent to give a reason for the faith that was in him. After him, in 1847, 1848 and 1849, came John Mangan, John Creuss, John Henry, Robert Smith, Joseph McManus, John O'Connell, John Smith, James Cummings, Joseph Hagarty and Timothy Buckley. In 1850, 1851 and 1852, we meet the names of John and James O'Keefe, Patrick Keegan, James Donovan, John Cahill, John McNamara, Thomas Ryan, Patrick and John Whalen, Daniel Mulcondry, Michael Young, H. Lynch, Patrick Donovan, Luke Mc-Cabe, Cornelius Danalvy, J. Sheehan, Timothy Mulcondry, Martin Walsh, Mrs. Gorman and Mrs. Tuite.

In the residence of John Mangan in 1849, was offered the first Adorable Sacrifice in New Hartford, in the presence of about 30 persons. The celebrant was the Rev. Michael O'Neill. Two months later a second Mass was said by the Rev. Luke Daly, then assistant to the Rev. John Brady, Hartford. At intervals of two or three months thereafter until 1851,[1] Father Daly visited New Hartford, and said Mass in the house of John Henry and other places. Father Daly gained the affections of the people of this mission to a high degree, and so zealously did he labor for their spiritual welfare that his name is yet held in benediction. After him New Hartford was attended by the pastors of Winsted, Rev. Thomas Quinn, in 1852; Rev. Thomas F. Hendricken, and Rev. Richard O'Gorman, who had charge in 1856 and 1857. When Collinsville received its first resident pastor in the person of the Rev. Patrick O'Dwyer in 1858, New Hartford passed under his care,[2] and was served successively by Rev. John Fagan and Rev. Lawrence Walsh, his successors, who said Mass here twice a month until 1870, when the Rev. B. O'R. Sheridan began his administration. When Father Sheridan secured an assistant the Catholics of New Hartford were blessed with holy Mass every Sunday thereafter. It has been handed down that the Rev. Father Gillick was among the earliest priests to attend New Hartford; that, in fact, he was the successor of Father Brady and the predecessor of Father Quinn. This would make the time of his service between 1851 and 1852. But Father Gillick had not been received into the diocese up to March 1, 1852. He had previously applied for admission, but at this date his application was refused. Moreover, the *Catholic Almanac* for 1852, gives New Hartford as being attended from West Winsted, Rev. Thomas Quinn pastor. However, there is nothing to militate against the supposition that Father Gillick exercised

---

[1] Father Daly was in charge of this mission as late as August, 1851.

[2] The exact date of his appointment is not known, but it is certain that he was pastor of Collinsville as early as May, 1858.

here temporarily the sacred ministry pending the granting of or the refusal of his petition.[1]

The project of building a church for the Catholics of New Hartford was inaugurated by the Rev. P. O'Dwyer, who took up the first collection for it. His successor purchased the land and built the basement. The corner-stone was laid June 10, 1869, by Bishop McFarland. Rev. Lawrence Walsh completed the church, and it was dedicated by Very Rev. James Hughes, V.G., on March 27, 1870. Rev. B. O'R. Sheridan cleared it of indebtedness and purchased three acres of land adjoining the cemetery; on this lot there was a house which served as a rectory for nine years. This last purchase was also paid for except a mortgage note of $800.

The church is situated in the most elevated and picturesque part of the village. The land upon which it stands was bought of Mr. E. D. Curtis, M.D., on March 11, 1867, by Henry T. Smith, who transferred it to Father Fagan. The purchase of a site for a Catholic church in those days required a discreet, tactful and responsible man, and Mr. Smith proved equal to the emergency.

The present pastor, the Rev. Luke Fitzsimmons, received his appointment on August 15, 1881. During his administration the church was frescoed in water-colors, new stained-glass windows put in, besides being otherwise much improved interiorly and exteriorly. At the ceremony of re-opening the church on September 26, 1886, Bishop McMahon officiated, and Rev. John H. Duggan, of Waterbury, pronounced the oration. The church was frescoed the second time in oil, and a large handsome altar erected. At the celebration of this event, August 13, 1893, Bishop McMahon presided, and Rev. B. O'R. Sheridan preached the sermon. This was Bishop McMahon's last public function. Other works which are evidences of Father Fitzsimmons' zeal are the grading and enlarging of the cemetery in 1883; the grading and beautifying of the grounds of the school, convent and rectory; the completion and furnishing of the three buildings at a cost of $22,000, nearly all of which has been paid. Truly a record of cheerful co-operation and generous self-sacrifice, of zeal, faith and confidence.

When the Immaculate Conception parish was formed, its population numbered about 1,000 souls, 600 Irish and 400 Canadians. The latest census disclosed about 1,300 souls: Canadians, 700; Irish, 457, and Slavonians about 150.

The parish cemetery was purchased in 1852 from Henry Seymour by a committee comprising John Cruess, Joseph McManus, James Cummings and Santy Cruess. It was enlarged and the new part blessed on June 4, 1883, by Bishop McMahon.

The parochial school was begun in 1888, and on September 9 of that year the corner-stone was laid by Bishop McMahon. The preachers on the occasion were Rev. M. J. Lavelle, LL. D., of New York, and Rev. T. J. Dunn, of Dayville, Conn. The building was completed in 1889. The con-

[1] The *Catholic Almanacs* of 1850 and 1851 assign the Rev. Philip Gillick to St. Paul's church, Belleville, N. J., diocese of New York. In 1853 he was in Winsted. In 1855 he was at Greenville, R. I.

vent was finished in 1890 and the rectory in the year following. On September 7, 1890, the school, convent and school bell were blessed by Bishop Mc-Mahon, Rev. J. J. Quinn preaching the English discourse, and Rev. J. A. Bachand, of Canada, delivering the sermon in French.

In August, 1890, Father Fitzsimmons introduced the Sisters of St. Joseph, whose mother-house is in Chambery, France, and placed them in charge of his school. There are four Sisters with 102 girls and 81 boys. Sister Mary Amedine is the local superioress. The Sisters engage also in Sunday-school work and visit the sick.

## ST. FRANCIS XAVIER'S PARISH,

### New Milford.

LIKE many other stations within the limits of the diocese, missionary priests came hither occasionally to celebrate Mass, administer the sacraments and to minister in other ways to the spiritual wants of the scattered Catholics of this section.

According to reliable traditions, the first Mass celebrated here was after the completion of the railroad. This Mass was said at the residence of Matthew Dunn, who resided near the railroad station, but the name of the celebrant is not known ; probably it was the Rev. James Smyth, of New Haven. In 1850 Rev. Father Brady and Rev. Father Ryan visited New Milford and said Mass at quarterly intervals during that year. Father Ryan said Mass in Wright's Hall, on Main street. In 1851 Father O'Farrell, of Danbury, celebrated the Divine Mysteries at the residence of Edmond Finn. The next priest to visit New Milford was the Rev. John Smith, of Falls Village, who said Mass for the first time on Sunday, July 3, 1853. His period of service here was four years. In succession to Father Smith, Fathers Kelly, Mulligan and O'Gorman ministered to the Catholics of New Milford. In the fall of 1858, Rev. Father Lenihan, of Newtown, assumed spiritual control of the Catholics of New Milford, and remained until 1862. During Father Lenihan's pastorate the site of the present church was purchased from Messrs. Beach and Canfield, on May 21, 1860. Upon the premises was an old saw mill which was remodeled into a church, and divine services were held here in the following October. This humble house of prayer and sacrifice was dedicated to St. Francis Xavier by Bishop McFarland. Succeeding Father Lenihan came Father Daly, also of Newtown, whose term of service was four years. It was during his administration that the cemetery was purchased. The Rev. John Rogers then assumed charge of Newtown and served the Catholics of New Milford from 1866 to 1871. The Catholics of New Milford were honored with a resident pastor on May 21, 1871, in the person of Rev. P. G. McKenna. The first trustees of the new parish were Michael A. Kelly and John Dolan. Father McKenna died after two years of successful labors in July, 1873.

In succession to Rev. Father McKenna, Rev. Fathers M. O'Herr, M. P. Lawlor, W. Hart, P. Finnegan, B. Bray, J. Gleason, J. C. O'Brien, C. McElroy, J. J. Curtin, T. Crowley, and T. Kelly faithfully and zealously discharged their duties as pastors of their widely scattered flock. During

Father Finnegan's pastorate the rectory was built. The work which marked the administration of Father Bray was the interior decoration of the church, and the purchase of horses and vehicles for use on the missions. Father Gleason materially reduced the indebtedness of the parish, besides making marked improvements in the property.

In 1886 Father O'Brien enlarged the church, adding a spire, chancel and sacristy; the interior was also handsomely frescoed, and a new altar erected. The renewed temple was dedicated by Bishop McMahon on Tuesday, August 13, of that year. Father McElroy's pastorate was signalized by putting in a splendid pipe organ, a heating apparatus in the basement of the church, re-shingling the spire, and by making other improvements in church and rectory. In 1892, during Father Curtin's administration, a parcel of land in the rear of the church was purchased, upon which were erected horse-sheds for the accommodation of the parishioners. Father Crowley liquidated the church indebtedness, enlarged the rectory, and left a substantial sum in the treasury. Rev. Father Crowley preached his farewell sermon in New Milford Sunday, September 18, 1898, and was succeeded in the following week by the present rector, Rev. Thomas Kelly. The first High Mass celebrated in New Milford was sung by the Rev. William Hart, on Christmas Day, 1874. No pipe organ was there to add dignity nor lend solemnity to the occasion; but the devout parishioners listened to the familiar *Adeste Fideles and Venite Adoremus* with as much joy and gladness as though discoursed by a cathedral instrument.

The dependencies of New Milford were formerly Bridgewater, Kent, Warren, Washington and Roxbury. In Bridgewater Mass was celebrated first in the Town hall and afterwards at the house of Mr. Thomas Halpin. Services here were discontinued upon the removal from the town of the hatting industry. The property purchased by Father Lenihan, whose intention it was to erect here a church, was sold by Father McKenna in November, 1872. In 1883, Kent and Warren were attached to Cornwall Bridge, but Brookfield was added to New Milford. In 1874, the missions of Woodbury and Southbury were placed under the jurisdiction of New Milford, by whose pastors it was served for thirteen years. These missions were assigned to the Watertown jurisdiction in 1887. Previous to Father McKenna's pastorate divine services were held at Roxbury only at irregular intervals. Being desirous of providing a place of worship for this portion of his flock, he secured the consent of Mr. Lenihan and Mr. Michael Pickett to say Mass in their residences. It was reserved, however, to the Rev. Father O'Brien in April, 1885, to purchase a lot in Roxbury Center, upon which he erected a church which was dedicated in August of the following year in honor of Ireland's Apostle. On September 21, 1890, the church at Washington Depot was dedicated under the title of "Our Lady of Perpetual Help," during the administration of Father McElroy. Emulating his predecessors Father Curtin erected a church at Brookfield, which was dedicated under the patronage of St. Joseph in November, 1892. The labors of Father Crowley were attended with gratifying success; indebtedness liquidated, the relations of pastor and people firmly cemented; and under the present administration the spiritual status of the entire jurisdiction is faithfully maintained.

## IMMACULATE CONCEPTION PARISH,

### NORFOLK.

THE town of Norfolk was incorporated in 1758. It is the highest land reached by railroad in Connecticut. The scenery in this vicinity is unsurpassed by any in New England.

It is traditional among the Catholics of Norfolk that Bishop Cheverus, of Boston, visited here in the discharge of his missionary duties. This is not improbable, as in 1823 he made an extensive tour through the State. Another interesting tradition has a Father Plunkett, of Boston, as a visitor to Norfolk before 1829.

The introduction of Catholicity into Norfolk as a part of the town's life dates from 1836. In March of that year Matthew, John and Charles Ryan and Edward C. Ryan, a convert to the faith, settled here and engaged in the woolen industry. In this year Patrick Burke, father of the Rev. Charles E. Burke, of North Adams, Mass., established his home here. Mr. Burke was present at the first Mass known to have been said here. It was in 1836, Rev. James Fitton, of Hartford, officiating, in the home of Matthew Ryan, now occupied by Michael Whalen. About twelve persons assisted at the Mass.

Father Fitton's extensive territory, which must needs be visited, precluded frequent visits to Norfolk. The Ryan family, in the absence of the priest, proved faithful and worthy auxiliaries. In a room in the woolen mill they would gather the handful of Catholics, and in prayer petition the Giver of all gifts for the grace of perseverance. They practiced their devotions earnestly, faithfully, and if Christ the Lord is in the midst of two or three gathered together in His name, we may well believe that this little band were partakers of the divine favors.

The successor of Father Fitton, the Rev. John Brady, also came to Norfolk when possible, and offered the Holy Sacrifice in the wool-sorting room or at the house of John Ryan. Rev. John D. Brady, Rev. John Brady, Jr., and Rev. James Strain also exercised the ministry here, though their visits were necessarily infrequent owing to the difficulties of travel. The old residents still speak of Father Brady's experience in being snow-bound for a week in Norfolk.

The first Catholic marriage solemnized in Norfolk was that of Patrick Burke and Ann O'Neil on October 9, 1842, the Rev. John D. Brady officiating.

The generosity of the Ryans was not confined to providing a place for divine services; they also purchased a piece of land for cemetery purposes, which they transferred to the congregation. In this spot rest the remains of pioneers from all that section of the State.

In 1846 the Catholics of Norfolk were attended by the Rev. Charles O'Reilly. On June 22d of that year he thus wrote from Waterbury to Bishop Tyler: "Yesterday was my second Sunday here; the people seem anxious to have a church; the foundation is cleared, some brick are on the spot and almost as much cash on hand as will pay up to this time. But to commence building would require a considerable sum, which these people cannot procure, except I become security, and I have had a considerable degree of repugnance at all times to have myself involved in money matters, and how to proceed I am really at a loss to know. Employment in this locality is very precarious. . . . . There is a great deal of labor and inconvenience in attending Norfolk and this place (Waterbury), there being no decent mode of travel between them. A person must either go by Bridgeport or Hartford and stop a night in either place, as the stages do not run all the way on the same day, so that there is considerable expense incurred and great loss of time. . . . The Norfolk people have made no move yet with regard to building; they seem content to have Mass, but I will not be content with saying Mass in a shanty."

When Falls Village was organized in 1850 with Rev. Christopher Moore as the first pastor, Norfolk became its mission. On March 2, 1851, Bishop O'Reilly visited Norfolk and made arrangements for a church, and on the 31st of the same month he appointed the Rev. Thomas Quinn to the pastoral charge of Norfolk and dependencies. Father Quinn's successor was the Rev. John Smith, who received his appointment to the Norfolk Mission on February 9, 1852. On this date Bishop O'Reilly wrote: "This is a most difficult mission."[1]

Under date of February 27 and 28, 1854, Bishop O'Reilly wrote in his Journal: "*27th*. Leave (Winsted) at 10 A. M. for Norfolk, where I arrive before noon and stop with Mr. Edward Ryan. I make this evening an arrangement with the Ryans for the building of a church on the lot they presented me. This will be effected, I hope, next spring."

"*28th*. Say Mass in Ryan's hall; it was full; published the regulations for Lent; said a few words to the people and left in Ryan's carriage for Falls Village, where I arrive at 11 A. M."

In 1859 the church of the Immaculate Conception was built, but in 1865 it had not yet been dedicated. In the meanwhile, the successors of Father Moore in Falls Village celebrated Mass and administered the sacraments over the store of Matthew Ryan, now occupied by M. N. Clark. In 1856 Norfolk was under the jurisdiction of Winsted, from which it was attended once a month. It so remained until the summer of 1889, when it was formed into an independent parish, with the Rev. P. Keating as the first pastor. At this time the Catholic population of Norfolk was 380 souls. Upon his arrival Father Keating secured apartments in the village, where he resided until the completion of the present commodious rectory. The work accomplished by Father Keating here is sufficient evidence of his activity. He graded the property about the church, which he remodeled and frescoed and adorned with new stained glass windows, beautiful Stations of the Cross and organ, all at an expenditure of $1400. In 1898 he purchased a lot for cemetery purposes, which was immediately paid for.

In 1891 Father Keating began to attend Stanfield in the diocese of

[1] *Bishop O'Reilly's Journal.*

Springfield at the request of Bishop O'Reilly. After two years of regular attendance he discontinued his visits, as nearly all of the Catholics had removed elsewhere.

Much of the prosperity that has attended the parish of the Immaculate Conception is due to the sturdy faith, the good example and the generosity of the Ryans. In practice they were Catholics as well as in name, and though more than half a century has elapsed since they moved upon the scene, the influence of their lives is still visible in their successors. Numerically small, the Catholics of Norfolk are strong of faith, and their devotion to religion was manifested by their donation to Bishop McMahon of the Tabernacle of the main altar of the cathedral.

## ST. BERNARD'S PARISH,

### SHARON.

THE township of Sharon was surveyed in 1732, and settlements were begun in 1739. The first white man to settle here was Daniel Jackson. In 1826 we find settlers bearing such names as Butler, Bailey and Donovan residing here. Two Catholics came into the town late in the thirties, and the following Catholics settled here in the early forties: Michael and Mrs. Henry, Mary Mannion, Bernard and Mrs. McDonald, Bridget Craven, Michael and Mrs. Curley, Mary Henry, Patrick and Mrs. Dunning, Sarah Henry, Thomas and Mrs. Kelly, Mary Moran.

From 1826 to 1840 there occur on the records names which investigation shows to have been borne by persons who were originally Catholics, viz.: Smith, Brown, Riley and Walsh. The descendants of these early settlers are not of the household of the Catholic faith, though one of them has admitted his Catholic ancestry.

In a small house, so small as to be almost concealed from view, though just beside the road on a declivity, was the first Mass said in Sharon. It was the humble home of a good Catholic woman, Mrs. Bridget Dunning. It was in the spring of 1845, and the celebrant of the Mass was the Rev. Michael Lynch, of Bridgeport. About thirty Irish Catholics knelt reverently around that humble altar.

Before Cornwall, the original parish, was formed into an independent organization, it was under the jurisdiction of Lakeville. In 1883 it received parochial honors, and the Rev. W. O. R. Sheridan was appointed the first resident pastor. In the following year Father Sheridan completed St. Bridget's church, which had been started by Father Lynch, of Lakeville. Father Kelly built the church at Cornwall about 1854: it is now a dwelling house. It was the first church within the limits of the present parish. Father Sheridan was succeeded by the Revs. W. J. Doolan, Maurice J. Sheehan, Michael F. Rigney, Michael C. Cray, J. T. Walsh and John Lee, the present rector. Father Doolan's pastorate was of four years' duration; Father Sheehan's, three; Father Rigney's, two; and Father Walsh's, three. All of the above-named pastors labored faithfully to advance the interests of their scattered flock. Among the benefactors of Sharon we may mention Mr. Wheeler, who offered a site for a church on the principal street of the town, but the offer was not accepted; however, he is still a generous friend to the parish. When the parish was first organized it numbered 450 souls, chiefly Irish, with some French. At present the Catholic population is about 300 souls, including five French families. It is a sad reflection that about 40 French families of Sharon have departed from the faith of their fathers. The parish possesses a beautiful cemetery. The number of baptisms administered in the parish, the missions included, from 1884 to 1898, was 199. The total number of marriages solemnized within the same period was 46. In January, 1896, Rev. Father Walsh purchased the new parochial residence in Sharon, and in the same month transferred his residence here. St. Bernard's church was then made a parish church. St. Bridget's church at Cornwall Bridge, until then a parish church, became a mission of Sharon. Mass is said in Cornwall Bridge every other Sunday. At present there are about 100 souls here, but the Catholic population is rapidly decreasing, as the furnaces have been closed for over four years. Cornwall Bridge also has a beautiful cemetery. The first marriage recorded in the town records was between Thomas and Sarah Rogers, September 14, 1855, Rev. Father Kelly officiating. Among the first births recorded were those of Ann Kenney, Michael Kenney and P. J. Kenney. The first death on record in Sharon was that of James Davis, March 10, 1857. The Rev. Father Lee has charge also of the Sacred Heart mission in Kent. The church was erected in 1884 by Father Sheridan. It was dedicated by Very Rev. James Hughes, Administrator, during the absence of the Bishop at the Baltimore Council. Mass is said here every other Sunday. The Catholic population is about 90 souls, and, like Cornwall Bridge, is declining, owing to the closing of the furnaces.

## ST. THOMAS' PARISH,

THOMASTON.

THE following entries are extracted from the early marriage records of Hartford:

PLYMOUTH.

Ber'd Mount and Neom Braynard ) *1831.* April 17 : Married Bernard Mount to Neoma Braynard. Witnesses, Den's Ryan and Owen Right.

JAS. FITTON.

Den's Ryan and Rosina Braynard ) *Ibid:* Married Dennis Ryan to Rosina Braynard. Witnesses, Ber'd Mount and Owen Right.

JAS. FITTON.

These felicitous events are evidence that Catholics were early settlers here. What is now known as Thomaston was formerly called *Plymouth Hollow.* It is probable that, besides the above named Catholics, others were here to share their lot. It is not improbable that the above marriages were solemnized during an historic visit of Father Fitton to Plymouth. Traveling from Hartford to Wolcottville (now Torrington) Father Fitton was compelled to remain at Plymouth over Sunday, as there existed a law against traveling on that day. April 17, 1831, fell on Sunday. Eager to exercise his sacred ministry, Father Fitton obtained permission to preach in the school building, the belief being that he was a Protestant clergyman; but upon the discovery that he was a priest, he was violently assailed with abuse by the audience. The undaunted priest received their revilings with calm dignity and succeeded in so overcoming their opposition that he not only finished this sermon amid the silence of the assemblage, but received applause at the end.

Among the first Catholics to arrive and reside here, besides the persons who were married by Father Fitton, was Martin Claffin (or Claffey), afterwards janitor of the city hall, Waterbury. Then followed at various intervals, Denis Hogan, Garret Burns, Michael Higgins, Michael Ryan, William Dunlay, Eugene O'Connell, Bartholomew Gleason, Jeremiah Hurley, John Kelly, David Harrigan, Jeremiah Howard, Thomas Claffey, John Penders, James McDermott, Thomas Joy, William Hoard, Edward Stuart, Farrell Foy, John Murphy and Farrell Sheridan.

The Holy sacrifice of the Mass was offered up for the first time in Thomaston, in 1854, in Michael Ryan's residence on Railroad street, by Rev. Michael O'Neil of Waterbury. At this time there were about fifty Irish Catholics in the town. Father O'Neil visited Thomaston at monthly intervals, saying Mass and administering the sacraments at Mr. Ryan's house, until they secured Academy Hall. When Father Hendricken was appointed pastor of Waterbury, in 1855, in succession to Father O'Neil, he visited Thomaston regularly or sent his assistants, Rev. Father Bohan and Rev. Father Rodden. When the Bristol church was organized with Father Rodden as first resident pastor, in 1863, he assumed charge also of Thomaston, which remained under the jurisdiction of Bristol until 1871.

Father Rodden's successor, Rev. Christopher Dugget, began the erection of St. Thomas' church, upon a site, which had been donated by Aaron Thomas, and the foundations had been laid when Rev. Eugene Gaffney was appointed the first resident pastor in 1871. Within his jurisdiction were also Terryville and Watertown. Father Gaffney had apartments at the house of Mr. Curtis, but soon secured a house from Mr. Bradley, in which he lived until the erection of the present rectory. He completed the church, purchased the original cemetery and erected churches also in Terryville and Watertown. Father Gaffney died on August 30, 1884. Until the appointment of his successor, the affairs of the parish were conducted by Rev. Joseph Fones.

Father Gaffney's successor was the Rev. Michael J. McGivney, who came here in November, 1884. For six years he administered the affairs of the parish with commendable zeal and gratifying success. He provided the church and parochial residence with electric lights and laid walks about both. While Father McGivney was zealous in promoting the interests of all his flock, he was particularly devoted to the younger element of his parish, and they reciprocated his affection. He died on August 14, 1890, and his remains rest in the family plot in St. Joseph's Cemetery, Waterbury.

The present rector, the Rev. Michael J. Daly, began his administration on August 17, 1890.

Father Daly furnished the pastoral residence with steam heat, improved the old cemetery, besides enlarging it by the addition of four acres, built a new and fine entrance thereto, and provided the church with new vestments of all the prescribed colors. The new cemetery was blessed by Bishop Tierney, on which occasion the sermon was preached by the Rev. Edward Brennan. On July 9, 1898, Father Daly increased the temporal possessions of the parish by the purchase of the splendid Woodward property with dwelling-house, and barn, situated on the corner of Main and East Main streets. On this site it is the intention to erect a church and rectory which will be a worthy crown to the generous and constant efforts of the Thomaston Catholics in the sacred cause of religion.

When St. Thomas' parish was organized its population was 700 souls, chiefly Irish. At present it is 1000, comprising Irish, Germans and Poles.

The clergy who have labored as assistants here are Revs. Joseph Fones, E. J. Murray, T. M. Crowley, R. J. Early, C. W. Morrill, M. Byrne, and C. McGowan. The present assistant is the Rev. John F. Donahoe.

The first child to receive baptism in this parish was James Torrance, and the first marriage was that of William Trihey and Helen Burns.

St. Thomas' church is a neat and graceful structure, and adorns the eastern slope of the hill convenient to the railroad depot.

It was erected by the united and generous efforts of a handful of poor but devoted Catholics. It was solemnly dedicated on October 15, 1876, by Bishop Galberry, who made his first visitation to Thomaston on that occasion. The ceremony of dedication was followed by a solemn High Mass *Coram Episcopo*, with the Rev. James Fagan as celebrant, Rev. Father Isaias, O.S.F., as deacon, Rev. B. O'R. Sheridan as sub-deacon and Rev. M. Rodden as master of ceremonies. Rev. Hugh Brady preached the sermon, his theme being the "Eucharistic Sacrifice." In the afternoon Bishop Galberry administered the sacrament of Confirmation to 139 persons.

## IMMACULATE CONCEPTION MISSION,

### TERRYVILLE.

ATTACHED to Thomaston is the mission of the Immaculate Conception, Terryville, where Mass is said every Sunday and holyday of precept. The mission has 350 souls, and, like the mother parish, is in a most prosperous condition.

The first Catholic to settle in Terryville was Denis Ryan. He came in 1843, and his brother, Philip C. Ryan, in 1845. There were giants of Catholicity in those days, and Philip Ryan was one of them. Not infrequently he walked to New Haven, a distance of thirty-seven miles, to assist at the Holy Sacrifice.

Closely following Denis and Philip Ryan came William Roach, Martin Kearney, Thomas Keefe, John Byron, John McNamara, Timothy Keefe, Thomas Higgins and Timothy McNamara.

Early in 1848 Father O'Neil paid a missionary visit to Terryville, and

II—20

celebrated the divine mysteries in Philip Ryan's house. In subsequent visits the school-house was secured for divine services. Terryville was regularly served by the clergy of Waterbury until the formation of the Bristol parish, in 1863. In 1862 the cemetery was purchased by Philip Ryan, who transferred it to Father Hendricken for the congregation.

Terryville became a dependency of Thomaston upon the formation of that parish in 1871. The present church was built in 1882. In 1884 it became a mission of Watertown, when Rev. Joseph Fones was appointed pastor of that parish, but in 1886 it reverted to the jurisdiction of Thomaston during the pastorate of Rev. M. J. McGivney.

Father Daly has had the church beautifully decorated within, a new altar has taken the place of the former holy table, and a new set of Stations of the Cross has been erected. The cemetery has been improved and the church lawn beautified. After the completion of the work on the church the renewed edifice was dedicated by Bishop Tierney on June 20, 1897. The Rev. Luke Fitzsimmons was the preacher on the occasion.

The successes achieved by the pastors and people of Thomaston and Terryville are a fine illustration of the familiar maxim that in union there is strength.

## PARISH OF ST. FRANCIS OF ASSISI.

### TORRINGTON.

THE township of Torrington received its name at the May session of the General Assembly, 1732. Torrington, formerly Wolcottville, named after Oliver Wolcott, Esq., formerly governor of the State, was incorporated as a borough at the January session of the Legislature, 1887.

The introduction of the holy services of the church into Torrington dates from 1835, when that apostolic missionary, Rev. James Fitton, offered the Holy Sacrifice of the Mass in a brick building, now occupied by O'Brien's bakery, south of the bridge on South Main street. There were but few children of the faith here at that time to profit by the ministrations of the pioneer priest. Among the early settlers, we find the names of Timothy Fanning, William Grant, John Looby, Edward Kelly, Timothy Hennessy, James Batters, Daniel Burns, Owen Cummings, John Cummings, Martin Hennessy, Richard Carroll and James Kent.

Seven years after Father Fitton's visit, his successor, Rev. John Brady, gathered the scattered Catholics at the home of one of the Messrs. Hennessy on the west hill. Five or six families and a few unmarried persons constituted the little congregation. Father Brady, and after him, Father Lynch, of Bridgeport, visited Torrington once a year until 1847, when Rev. Michael O'Neil was appointed pastor of Waterbury and the missions of the Naugatuck Valley.

After Father O'Neil's first visit to Torrington he perfected arrangements whereby he was enabled to hold divine services in a three-story brick building, sometimes used as a place of worship and as an academy. Two other religious bodies used "that old union meeting-house." Father O'Neil visited Torrington twice annually. In February of 1851 Bishop O'Reilly made a visitation of Waterbury, Litchfield and Wolcottville, his visit to the last place taking place on the 26th. No doubt the bishop strengthened and consoled the good people here by saying Mass, preaching and administering the sacraments. In this year, Rev. James Lynch, of Birmingham, assumed spiritual charge of Torrington and made one or two visits. From 1852, beginning with the pastorate of Rev. Thomas Quinn, Torrington was attended from West Winsted. His successors, Rev. Fathers Gillick, Hendricken, O'Gorman, Mangan, Mullen, Sheridan and Leo, continued to render faithful service to the Catholics here, "each doing his work earnestly for the improvement of his people."

In 1851, a lot opposite the Congregational church on Main street was secured by Father O'Neil for a church. Father Lynch paid for the lot by collecting therefor $400, and transferred the property to the bishop. Work on the church was not begun until the fall of 1859, during the pastorate of Father Mangan. It was completed in July, 1860, and the indebtedness incurred by its erection, $3000, was liquidated by Father Mangan.

"About the time the church was built there was considerable prejudice manifested toward the Catholics, and against the building of the church, and whether there were threats made or not, the Catholic people felt it necessary for a time to station a watchman at the church during the nights, to give the alarm if an attempt should be made to burn the building. This was a decided mistake, if any occasion was given for such fear, for if religious liberty is good, then it is as good for one as another, and it is not good unless it will apply to all the heathen as well as Christians. The Catholics are a Christian people. But all the disposition, if ever there was any, to hinder the success of the Catholic church in the town is thoroughly removed, all persons knowing that it is far better for them, as well as all other people, to go to church, hear the gospel and obey it, than to neglect such duty and privilege. It is also true that the Catholic people know that there is no occasion for fear, so long as they do as they heretofore have done, respect the rights of others as well as their own, and that they are now held in respect by those who differ from them, in religious belief." [1]

In 1866, Father Leo built an addition to the church at a cost of $1500, and beautified the interior. In 1870, the Coe Brass Company sold to Father Leo, through Owen Cummings, for $1000, six acres of land, near the Redfield and Rice manufactory, for cemetery purposes, and it was blessed by Bishop McFarland Mr. Oliver Coe donated $100 towards its purchase.

The first resident pastor of Torrington was a Franciscan priest, the Rev. Father Isaias, who received his appointment in October, 1874. He secured the Patterson property on Prospect street, which he remodeled and occupied as a parochial residence. St. Francis' parish at this time numbered 120 families ; 115 children attended Sunday-school. The laymen who constituted the first church committee were Edward Kelly, Andrew Harty, Richard Carroll and William Grant.

Father Isaias was succeeded in November, 1877, by the Rev. John H. Duggan, who in turn was followed by the present rector, the Rev. Patrick Duggan, in May, 1879. Father Duggan purchased, in 1884, all the property at present occupied by the parish, save the piece of land purchased in 1851 by Father O'Neil. In 1886 plans were accepted for a new church more in keeping with the growing importance of the parish. The first collection for this purpose brought the splendid sum of $11,000, yet the parish census placed

[1] *Orcutt's History.*

the number of souls at 1376. The work of construction was begun at once, and the corner-stone was laid by Bishop McMahon on September 5, 1886, Rev. John H. Duggan, of Waterbury, pronouncing the discourse. Two thousand dollars were realized in a collection on that occasion. The generous Catholic spirit of the people was shown in the following year by the contribution of $12,000 to the building fund. When St. Francis' church was completed it was free from financial encumbrance, and both pastor and people united in consecrating it to the service of God forever. The solemn services of consecration took place on November 13, 1887. The consecrating prelate was Right Rev. L. S. McMahon. The Mass which followed this impressive ceremony was celebrated by Very Rev. James Hughes, V. G., assisted by Rev. Father Leo, as deacon, Rev. J. H. Duggan, as sub-deacon, and Rev. James H. O'Donnell and Rev. T. Crowley as masters of ceremonies.

The next work that engaged Father Duggan's attention was the erection of the pastoral residence; this was built on the site of the former church in 1888. Three years later the convent and school, both handsome structures, were erected. Notwithstanding the great material works accomplished in these years there was no indebtedness when the last building was completed. Father Duggan disposed of the former rectory by sale in 1892. The school was blessed in September, 1893, by the Administrator of the diocese, Very Rev. James Hughes, V.G., Rev. W. J. Slocum preaching the sermon. When the school was opened it received 391 pupils; at present there are 605, with nine grades and eleven Sisters of Mercy, of whom Sister M. Dominic is the Directress. St. Francis' parish enjoys the proud distinction of having all its children, who attend school, taught within the walls of the parochial school, and the standard of scholarship here maintained is of such excellence that its graduates are admitted into the high school without examination.

When St. Francis' parish was organized in 1874, its population was estimated at 800 souls. At present there are 3600, of mixed nationalities, comprising Irish, French, Germans, Poles, Lithuanians, Slavs, Hungarians and Italians.

The number of baptisms administered between 1874 and 1899, exclusive, was 1867; the number of marriages solemnized within the same period was 376.

The assistants of St. Francis' parish were: Rev. T. Brady, Rev. T. Whelan, Rev. M. Barry, Rev. S. Musiel. The present assistants are Rev. E. Brennan and Rev. N. Brommenschenkel.

St. Francis' parish enjoys an enviable reputation among its sister parishes of the diocese. If the success achieved in the material order has been gratifying, not less consoling have been the results in the spiritual.

## ST. JOHN'S PARISH,

### WATERTOWN.

THE ancient town records of Watertown contain many names that have a distinctively Celtic flavor, but whether their owners were of Irish birth or descent is conjectural; much less is it known what creed they professed. However, the names themselves lead us to the not unreasonable conclusion that they were borne by children of Holy Mother church, whatever may have been their subsequent spiritual fate. Some of these names copied from the records are : Seth Blake (1769); Eunice Collins (1777); Love Higgins (1780); Rhoda Finn (1779); John Brien (1780); Lucy Brien (1785); Annie Flynn (1788); Joseph Finn (1805); Richard Finn (1813); Thomas Finn (1818).[1] John O'Brian and Polly Matthews were married on December 12, 1802; Henry O'Bryan and Cordelia McDonald, on June 6, 1825; Timothy Richards and Sally Daly, on October 28, 1827. The above family names are unmistakably Irish, while the baptismal names indicate mixed marriages, or, as was frequently the case in the early days, a change of Irish into Puritan baptismal names, so as not to leave too many traces of Irish origin.

The first Catholic, known to be such, to reside in Watertown was Michael Dunn, who came here about 1841. Three years later he was reinforced by two others, Anna Gaffney and Patrick Doherty, the latter of whom still resides here. In 1853, the entire Catholic population of the town numbered about a dozen souls. It comprised Patrick Doherty, Patrick Drum, James Godsell, John Kane, Robert Torrence, and John McGowan with their families.

Previous to 1855, no priest had visited Watertown. In that year Mass was said for the first time by the Rev. Michael O'Neil, of Waterbury, in the residence of John McGowan. Robert Torrence's house was the scene of the second Mass, and Mrs. Harvey's had the honor of the third. At first, the Catholics of Watertown were attended every three months, but as their numbers increased Father O'Neil and his successors made monthly visits. The first death of a Watertown Catholic was that of Patrick Fitzpatrick, who died late in 1853. The first baptism was that of an infant of Patrick Drum.

After Father Hendricken had assumed charge of the Catholics of Watertown, he offered the Holy Sacrifice of the Mass monthly in what was known for years as "Citizens' Hall," a former Episcopalian church. Father Rodden and Father Bohen, of Waterbury, also made periodical visits here. As pastor of Bristol, Father Rodden attended Watertown, but only for a brief period; it then reverted to Waterbury. On April 9, 1871, it was assigned to the care of Rev. Eugene Gaffney, of Thomaston, under whose jurisdiction it continued until 1884.

In 1877, the site now occupied by the residence of Mrs. James Dunigan, was purchased from the Dayton estate for $375; but as it was found to be unsuitable for church purposes, it was sold and the present beautiful site bought for $600. Father Gaffney began at once the erection of a church, the corner-stone of which was laid in November, 1877. On March 24, 1878, Bishop Galberry dedicated it in honor of St. John the Evangelist. The High Mass which followed the dedicatory services was sung by the pastor, Father Gaffney, and the sermon was preached by the Rev. Patrick Fay of Colchester. The church, though small, is an architectural gem and cost $7,000. Patrick Dunigan and John Kane were the first trustees.

In November, 1884, Watertown was separated from Thomaston and formed into a parish with Terryville as a mission. Rev. Joseph Fones was appointed the first resident pastor. During his administration of two years,

[1] The name of Finn appears in 1770.

Father Fones accomplished much for his parish, among the material works completed being the parochial residence. In November, 1886, the Rev. James W. Lancaster assumed charge of the parish. An eloquent and active priest, a man of deeply sympathetic nature he labored here for six years, beloved by his parishioners. Father Lancaster died on April 28, 1892, and was succeeded by the present pastor, the Rev. James H. O'Donnell, on May 15, 1892.

Father O'Donnell has thoroughly renovated the church and rectory, within and without, laid concrete walks about both, introduced a new heating apparatus and electric lights, and liquidated the entire indebtedness of the parish.

On February 24, 1896, he purchased three and one-half acres of land for cemetery purposes, paying therefor $700. This transaction was distinguished by the town donating $300 towards the purchase. Mt. St. James' cemetery was blessed by Bishop Tierney on Sunday, July 26, 1896. The sermon was delivered by Very Rev. John A. Mulcahy, Vicar-General.

The parish, which comprises Oakville, numbers about 475 souls, Irish and their descendants and French Canadians.

The present trustees are Thomas Shields and John Doherty.

## SACRED HEART (MISSION) CHURCH,

### SOUTHBURY.

IN the beautiful Pomperaug valley is situated the Sacred Heart church, Southbury, a mission of Watertown. The Rev. James Bohen celebrated the first Mass said here in 1862, in the house of Francis Grant. There were present about forty persons. After this, Mass was said at intervals by priests attached to the church of the Immaculate Conception, Waterbury. From Waterbury it passed under the jurisdiction of New Milford. For many years the Catholics of Southbury joined with their brethren of Woodbury and worshiped in the town hall of the latter village. In 1884, there were about forty families in Southbury, and the pastor of New Milford, the Rev. James C. O'Brien, began the erection of a church. The site was donated by Denis Houlihan. In November of that year the corner-stone was laid by Very Rev. James Hughes, V. G., assisted by Revs. H. T. Brady, Ansonia; P. M. Kennedy, Birmingham; J. Fagan, Naugatuck; J. M. McCarten and M. Cray, Newtown. The sermon was preached by Rev. W. A. Harty, and Rev. Fathers Kennedy and Fagan discharged the office of chanters. The work on the building progressed so favorably, that Mass was said in it for the first time on Christmas day, 1884. During the pastorate of the Rev. Father Lancaster, Southbury was attached to Watertown, whence it is still attended. Father Lancaster purchased the cemetery which was blessed by Bishop McMahon in the summer of 1890. The sermon on the occasion was preached by Father O'Donnell, then of Waterbury. Mass is said here twice a month. The number of Catholics in Southbury is about seventy-five.

In the summer of 1892 the church was artistically frescoed, the sanctuary re-carpeted and the altar re-decorated. Vestments of all the prescribed colors were recently added to the possessions of the church.

Woodbury is another mission of Watertown where Mass is said semi-monthly. Woodbury was first attended by priests from Birmingham, then from Waterbury until it was assigned to New Milford. During the administration of the Rev. Father Fones, it was attached to Watertown. About thirty Catholics reside here and Mass is said in the Town hall. In 1895, the town generously donated a cemetery lot to the Catholics, which was blessed on November 21st of that year, by Bishop Tierney. The congregation owns a valuable lot upon which it is the intention to erect a church.

The first Catholics to reside in Woodbury were nine Acadians, but the names of four only have come down to us, viz: Peter Beaumont, Henrie Sciscean, Alexander Pettigree and Philemon Cherevoy. In 1760 we meet the name Philemon Way. Was he an Acadian, also? It is probable. Other names copied from the ancient records indicate the probable presence in Woodbury of Catholics in the last century. Mary Lacey appears in 1704. In the adjoining town of Roxbury, we find such names as Mary Ward (died September, 1760), wife of Thaddeus Lacy (died May 12, 1764), and Mary Hunt (died May 6, 1782). In Woodbury there was a John Runnolds (Reynolds) in 1759, and a Timothy Mitchell in 1768. Joshua Guitteau died in 1746; Francis Guitteau in 1760; David Guitteau in 1774, and Jerusha Guitteau in 1783. A Joseph Tooley died in 1778.

Members of the Acadian family of Cherevoy died, Philemon, March 1, 1801, aged 52 years; Nathaniel, April 29, 1813, aged 28 years; a child of Philemon, August 22, 1790; Rachel, widow of Philemon, January 14, 1831, aged 77 years; Elizabeth, May 5, 1850, aged 75 years.

The first Catholic marriage that took place in Woodbury, of which there is any record, was that between Stephen Collins and Bridget Dolan, October 26, 1856. Rev. James Lynch of Birmingham performed the ceremony. The first birth recorded is that of a female child of Patrick and Mary Collins, April 2, 1852. In 1849 occurred the first death, Charles Birney; the second, May 27, 1852, Mary Ann Quirk.

# MIDDLESEX COUNTY.

## ST. JOHN'S PARISH,
### MIDDLETOWN.

MIDDLETOWN, the Indian name for which was *Mattabesett*, was invested with town privileges in September, 1651, and received its name in November, 1653. The historian Barber says, that in 1654 there were about thirty families, and in 1670, fifty-two. From a list given by the same author, we extract some names that are unmistakably of Irish origin. The list is dated March 22, 1670, and the names represent proprietors of Middletown with their estates: John Ward, William Ward, Anthony Martin, Samuel Collins, Nathaniel Collins, John Savage, John Kirby, Philip Mortimer and Captain Gleason. The city of Middletown was incorporated in 1784.

Middletown received its quota of French Neutrals, according to the disposition made by the General Assembly in January, 1756. Sixteen of the exiles were assigned to this town. They were the first Catholics, known to be such, to reside within the borders of the town. Did they remain faithful to the church, to the faith of their baptism? The elders did, no doubt; but what of their descendants? Did the memories of childhood keep alive the sacred flame, or did human considerations smother the fire that later burned, perhaps, but dimly?

The first priest to visit this section was the Rev. R. D. Woodley, of Providence. In July, 1829, he was directed by Bishop Fenwick to visit Middletown. In this same month he had visited the Enfield Canal, New Haven and New London. As Father Woodley and all other early missionaries always traveled prepared to say Mass when the opportunity was favorable, it may be reasonably inferred that the Holy Sacrifice was offered in Middletown during this visit.

The Rev. James Fitton informs us in his *Sketches* that he attended Middletown and Portland in 1830, when Mass was said and the sacraments administered in private houses. "The extensive work at the brown stone quarries of Portland," says the missionary, "gave employment to several laborers, the majority of whom, with their families, were members of the church, who, after their week's toil, had occasionally the privilege of Mass on Sundays, or before their day's work on other occasions." Father Fitton visited Middletown on Thursday evening, November 10, 1831, delivered a lecture which had been previously advertised, and no doubt said Mass and performed other religious functions during this visit. In July, 1832, religious services were held in Westfield, a few miles north-west of Middletown. We quote from the *United States Catholic Press*, July 12, 1832:

"Seldom did we witness a more pleasing sight than that afforded us on Sunday, the 8th inst. The Catholics employed on the Enfield Canal were visited, agreeably with previous arrangements, by their pastor, *it being the first time that the holy services* of our Church were performed in this section of our country. The concourse of those who attended from the neighboring towns, some of them coming from eighteen miles distant, was so great that no room could be found sufficiently spacious to accommodate all; they assembled in the nearest woods, called Cedar Swamp, where the Holy Sacrifice was offered under the spacious boughs of a large tree. The scene was impressive and truly edifying, similar to that which was exhibited on the discovery of America by the Catholic Columbus; as then, so now, the holy altar was erected and sacrifice offered to the living God of the universe. The multitude of those who were present, to their credit be it said, behaved with propriety and becoming respect. Though the Holy Sacrifice of the Mass, as it often happens, was a subject of much mystery to our Protestant brethren of various denominations, who were present, yet they were attentive and duly respectful. The discourse, both morning and afternoon, was listened to with much apparent interest, and though hours were necessarily employed in establishing as well as vindicating the truths of the Catholic religion, still the pastor was called upon to visit and preach in another section of the country the same evening. Many on this occasion attended to their religious duties; some were baptized, and one family presented themselves for other instructions, that they might be admitted into the communion of the Catholic church."

Among the first Catholics to settle in Middletown to establish homes were Thomas Condon, Michael Ahern, James Sheridan, Martin Deegan, Michael Byrnes, James Barry, David Geary, Edmund Higgins and John Dunn. These were probably here in 1835, and it may be, earlier, as about that time labor was in great demand in the quarries at Portland. Those who located at Middletown, Portland and Cromwell, formed a not inconsiderable body, and therefore, like their countrymen who settled elsewhere in the State and throughout New England, were eager to possess the benefits of religious services. Accordingly, the Rev. James McDermot, of New Haven, was notified of the presence in this neighborhood of a goodly number of Catholics. In response to their request, he visited Middletown in the summer of 1835 and offered the Holy Sacrifice in Mr. Taylor's house on East Court street. The successor of Father Fitton of Hartford, Rev. Peter Walsh, came in 1836, and held divine services at the house of Michael Ahern. He continued his visits at regular intervals until August, 1837, when he was succeeded in Hartford by the Rev. John Brady. In September of that year, Father Brady began his missionary visits here, and for four years said Mass at monthly intervals at Mr. Ahern's residence. The increase in numbers made search for a larger place for worship an imperative necessity. A small building on the " Sand Bank " was purchased from Thomas Condon, and was appropriately fitted for Catholic worship. In this humble chapel they gathered for their religious devotions until the erection of the brick church in 1843.

The little church soon became inadequate to the needs of the congregation. Therefore, in the year above mentioned, Father Brady began his quest for an eligible site for a church in Middletown. There were at this time about thirty families in the parish. The result of his efforts was the obtaining of the land on which the church now stands on November 18, 1841. The lot was owned by Mr. Charles R. Alsop, who asked $500 for it. A Catholic lady, Mrs. Richard Alsop, generously donated this amount, and the contract was closed. Father Brady began immediately to raise funds for the prosecution of the work of building the church, and in a short time his people experienced the happiness of witnessing the realization of their hopes. The church was 65x40 feet. This building is still standing. The exterior, with the exception of the cross, which was removed, is the same as when erected. The interior was remodeled and fitted up as a tenement house.

The Catholic population having increased in 1845 to nearly 400 souls, a petition was forwarded to Bishop Tyler, praying for a resident pastor. It is as follows:

MIDDLETOWN, April 2, 1845.

RIGHT REV. AND DEAR SIR :—

We, the undersigned as a Committee, do hereby most respectfully solicit your kind and immediate attention to the spiritual wants of the Catholics of Middletown and Portland in Connecticut.

It would be impossible for us to set forth in this communication all the spiritual wants which the Catholics of this portion of your diocese suffer, or to make you acquainted with the numerous disadvantages under which they labor, in consequence of their not having a priest reside here amongst them.

In the absence of any personal acquaintance with you, we deem it most applicable to the object, which we have in addressing you, to state such facts as we think best calculated to command your kind and immediate consideration.

We presume that you are well aware that we have through the extraordinary charitable exertions of the Rev. Mr. Brady, of Hartford, got a church built in Middletown which contains at present 48 or 50 pews, each pew calculated to contain 5 or 6 persons, for which the people agree to pay the sum of, say, men, $6, and women, $4 each per seat quarterly.

We can confidently state to you that there is at present a number of Catholics sufficiently large to occupy the above-mentioned number of pews to the utmost extent for which they are calculated to accommodate.

In addition to the above facts we have good reasons to suppose from personal knowledge and observation on the increased activity of business that there will be a great increase in the number of Catholics here in course of the ensuing summer.

As the Catholic population of Middletown and vicinity is composed of Irish laborers, with very few exceptions, we are unable to state their exact number; but we will state without any pretensions to accuracy, however, that in the course of the ensuing summer their number will not fall much short of four hundred.

The Rev. Mr Brady told us on the last Sunday he gave service here, that it was impossible for him on account of his health, and his obligations to his people in Hartford, to come here much longer.

This letter, we as a committee in the Catholic name of the people of Middletown and Portland, present to your Reverence with the most profound respect, and subscribe ourselves                    Your most faithful servants and Catholics,

| | | | |
|---|---|---|---|
| JOHN DRENNAN, | JAMES GEARY, | J. BARRY, | MICHAEL KEEFE, |
| MICHAEL HOGAN, | P. CAVANAGH, | MARTIN DEEGAN, | JOSEPH MAGNER, |
| M. BYRNE, | JOHN CARR, | WILLIAM DOUGE, | M. HANEGAN. |

Bishop Tyler honored this petition by the appointment to Middletown in the same year of the Rev. John Brady, Jr. The stream of immigration that flowed into Connecticut between 1845 and 1850 increased to a great extent the Catholic population of Middletown, Portland and Cromwell. These hardy sons of toil found employment in the quarries at Portland. The new church became too small to accommodate the congregation. Father Brady, therefore, set about the erection of a church which would meet all future demands. Learning of this determination, admiring the spirit it disclosed and recognizing the salutary influence exerted by religion over their employees, the owners of the quarries generously donated all the stone necessary for the construction of the church; the money which paid for the building was collected almost entirely among the parishioners. A unique means of raising funds was employed in building both churches. In 1843, a piece of land in the rear of the church was laid out in burial lots, and every parishioner who contributed $20 towards the erection of the church received in return a lot in the cemetery. When the new church was projected by Father Brady, the same method was adopted of giving a whole lot in the cemetery to those contributing $20 and a half lot to those who gave $10. So enthusiastic were the people over the prospect of a new church that the lots were disposed of in a short time.

In the meantime Bishop O'Reilly made a visitation of Middletown on May 11, 1851, administered confirmation to 116 persons and preached three times.

The new church was dedicated to the service of God under the patronage of St. John, on Sunday, September 5, 1852. Bishop O'Reilly arrived at Middletown on the 4th, and remained until the 8th. The ceremony of dedication was as edifying as it was interesting. Bishop O'Reilly officiated at the service, at the conclusion of which a Solemn High Mass was celebrated by the Rev. Thomas Quinn, of Winsted, assisted by the Rev. Edward O'Brien, of New Haven, as deacon; the Rev. Hugh O'Reilley, of Meriden, as sub-deacon, and the Rev. Thomas Daly, of Albany, N. Y., as master of ceremonies. The preacher at the morning service was the Rev. Dr. Moriarty, and at the Pontifical vespers Rev. Bernard O'Reilly, S. J., of St. John's College, Fordham, pronounced the discourse, his theme being, "The Priesthood." In the morning Bishop O'Reilly administered confirmation to a large number of persons, and preached. Commenting on the ceremonies of this day, a contemporary wrote:

"Dedications of churches to Catholic worship are now almost of weekly occurrence throughout the country, but nowhere more so than in the diocese of Hartford, a proof of the untiring enterprise of our Bishop and the zeal of our priesthood. Localities in this State where, five or six years since, a Catholic priest was a rare sight, are now supplied with churches, pastors and congregations, a proof of the inherent vitality of Catholicity and the divine mission of its teachers. Although the Rev. Mr. Brady has been a comparatively short time with us, he has, through his indomitable energy and fervent desire to promote the glory of God, erected a temple which will live after him; within whose walls many generations will enter, and worship, and go out, and which will endear his memory to many a pious soul for whose benefit he has provided a temple and erected a tabernacle in which the God of Heaven may be worshiped in spirit and in truth."

Father Brady's relations with St. John's parish ceased on April 21, 1855. As was not infrequently the case in those days, his retirement caused no little excitement among the people. Some adherent of the pastor, with more zeal than respect for authority, nailed the following notice on the principal entrance of the church on the evening of the 21st: "*Let no man take this down till the Bishop gives a reason for removing Mr. Brady from his beloved congregation. Let no man dare to.*" The Rev. Louis Mangan, who had accompanied Bishop O'Reilly to Middletown, and who became the successor of Father Brady, saw the notice on the door as he approached to say Mass on the morning of the 22nd. News of the placard had spread through the town, and the people began to gather very early, discussing among themselves the propriety of such proceedings. Father Mangan tore the notice off the door and asked the reason of it. An elderly man in the crowd told him that the Bishop's course was disapproved by the congregation, as they did not wish to part with Father Brady. He had been with them ten years, had built them up to what they were, and that to remove him without giving a reason to the congregation was an outrage, he said, to their feelings. Father Mangan procured a hatchet, pried off the boards which had been nailed across the doors and opened the church for divine service. Some of the people entered, while others remained outside, but all were quiet and orderly. Father Mangan addressed the people in a calm, dignified and conciliatory manner, which tended to allay the excitement which had been aroused by a few misguided leaders. Excitement had run high and passion was deep. There was a disposition to rebel against ecclesiastical authority, and to censure the Bishop for exercising what was inalienably his right. He was the object of severe condemnation at the time; but, as was becoming his office, he remained silent. But in the interests of truth and historic justice, I believe he should now speak after a silence of fifty-four years. From Bishop O'Reilly's Journal: "*1855, April 20*, Leave (Hartford) in the evening for Middletown, arrive there at 8 p.m., and put up at the McDonough house.

*21.* "Go to the church to say Mass at half-past 6 a.m. Send to Rev⁴ Brady for the key of the church; the messenger informs me that Father Brady will bring the key in a few minutes. He shortly appears accompanied with his man of all business, Mr. Cody, and presents me his resignation in writing; this act of his, whilst his resignation or his right to resign was of no consideration, was most acceptable. He asked me if I accepted it; I answered yes, and treated him most courteously."

Here, in a few words, is the plain, unvarnished account of a transaction which threatened at the time to disrupt the congregation. It is within a Bishop's province, as it is his bounden duty, to warn, reprimand and to punish with censures, if necessary, his clergy, who are negligent, or who prove a stumbling block to their people, and this duty of giving warning Bishop O'Reilly had performed on the preceding 1st of March, the outcome of which was the voluntary resignation of Father Brady.

Father Brady founded the first parochial school in Middletown in 1849. Mr. Andrew Cody, a classical scholar from Fermoy College, County Cork, Ireland, was the first master of the school, which position he retained until his death, in 1866. He was assisted for many years by two sisters, Isabella A. and Helen G. Fagan.

Rev. Louis Mangan became the pastor of St. John's parish on April 22, 1855. He maintained this relationship until his death in November, 1857, when the Rev. James Lynch, "a man of ability and enterprise," was appointed his successor. For fifteen years Father Lynch was the faithful, devoted pastor of St. John's. In that time he liquidated the debt of the church, completed the spire in 1864, placed a large bell in the tower, and had the church frescoed in the most artistic manner. He erected the parochial residence and convent, introduced the Sisters of Mercy as teachers of the school, and purchased the cemetery. This tract of land was on Johnson street, and was secured from Michael H. Griffin in 1865, and blessed in the same year. Father Lynch's kindness and zeal, his unobtrusive manner, and his profound sympathy with the people won for him an abiding place in the hearts of all. When he was transferred to Waterbury, to succeed Father Hendricken, who had become Bishop of Providence, he was followed early in 1873 by the Rev. Edward J. O'Brien, who resigned his pastorate in 1876. His successor was the Rev. Francis P. O'Keefe. Father O'Keefe organized the mission at Cromwell and remodeled the main altar of the church.

The Rev. Denis Desmond followed Father O'Keefe in October, 1881. Father Desmond liquidated the debt that remained on the cemetery and spire, introduced steam heat into the church, convent and pastoral residence, had new and beautiful stained-glass windows put in the church, and in 1883 secured the tract of land south of the cemetery, which he had laid out for burial purposes. After a successful pastorate of three years and seven months Father Desmond died at Middletown in April, 1885.

The present incumbent, the Rev. Bernard O'Reilly Sheridan, succeeded to the administration of St. John's on May 1, 1885. In July of that year Father Sheridan began the work of thoroughly renovating the church, within and without. The roof was reslated; new stained-glass was placed in every window, even the smallest; handsome altars were erected in place of the former ones; and new pews and confessionals added to the beauty of the interior—all accomplished at an outlay of $25,000. The renewed edifice was reopened with impressive ceremonies on October 12, 1885. Pontifical Mass was celebrated by Bishop McMahon.

The zeal of Father Sheridan was now directed to the entire liquidation of the indebtedness which the recent extensive improvements had entailed. Having accomplished this end, the crowning event of his pastorate, as it is the crowning event in the life of any pastor, came on September 10, 1886, when his beautiful church, unencumbered by financial obligations, was with great pomp and solemnity consecrated forever to divine service. It was a day on which the faithful people truly rejoiced and were glad, for they were the possessors of a temple upon which no profane hand would ever fall.

The Most Rev. M. A. Corrigan, Archbishop of New York, officiated at the ceremony of consecration, and the Rev. Edward McGlynn, D.D., preached the sermon. Of the Pontifical Mass which followed, Bishop McMahon was the celebrant, with the following clergy assisting: Very Rev. James Hughes, V. G., arch-priest; Rev. Thomas Broderick, deacon; Rev. Luke Fitzsimmons, sub-deacon; Rev. Michael F. Kelly and Rev. James H. O'Donnell, masters of ceremonies at the consecration services and at the Mass. Right Rev. Bishop Conroy officiated at Pontifical Vespers, with Very Rev. M. McCabe, of Woonsocket, as assistant priest.

The handsome and commodious parochial school was begun in 1887. The corner-stone was laid by Bishop McMahon, and the oration on the occasion was pronounced by Rev. H. Kinnerney, of Pawtucket, R. I. The blessing of the new school took place in September, 1888, the officiating prelate being Bishop McMahon, and the orator the Rev. Dr. Conaty, at present rector of the Catholic University of America at Washington. The school was erected at a cost of $30,000, and when opened was free from debt. Besides these greater works, Father Sheridan erected a brown-stone chapel in the cemetery on the site of the old brick chapel, built an archway between the church and school, placed a handsome granite coping and new flagging around the rectory grounds, purchased a new house for the janitor and another dwelling east of the convent, improved and beautified the convent property, renovated the rectory and purchased several lots on north Main street—works that speak eloquently for the activity and the financial ability of the pastor.

St. Coleman's church at Middlefield, a mission church, was also built during Father Sheridan's administration in 1887, site and building costing $3500, all of which was liquidated when the church was completed. Mass is said here every Sunday. The Catholics of Middlefield number about 100 souls.

As stated above, the first Catholic school in Middletown opened in 1849, in charge of lay teachers. This arrangement continued until 1866, when it passed under the direction of the Board of Education, thus becoming one of the public schools of the city. On May 10, 1872, during the pastorate of Father Lynch, seven Sisters of Mercy from Ennis, County Clare, Ireland, came to Middletown at the invitation of Bishop McFarland, and took possession of the new convent. They assumed charge of the parochial school, and opened an academy for young ladies which acquired a just fame for the high standard of scholarship there maintained. The parochial school at present has 568 pupils, with twelve grades. Mother M. Aloysius is the Superioress of the convent. Results the most gratifying are secured in St. John's school. Its graduates pass with no difficulty to the high school, and while there, reflect honor on the school that laid the foundation upon which their higher education is builded.

The clergy who assist Father Sheridan in his parochial labors are the Rev. P. J. McGivney and the Rev. J. H. Walsh.

When the first Mass was said in Middletown there were between thirty-five and forty Catholics to kneel before the altar; when the church was built in 1843 the Catholic population had increased to 300 or 400; at present the number of souls is estimated at 3700, comprising Irish, French, Germans, Poles, Portuguese and Italians.

The baptismal records of St. John's parish show that from 1845 to June, 1898, the sacrament of baptism was administered 8949 times; and the marriage records testify that 1897 marriages were solemnized within the same period.

## ST. JOSEPH'S PARISH,

### CHESTER.

CHESTER was incorporated as a town in 1836. In 1850 we note the beginnings of Catholicity. Among the pioneers who settled here about this time were John Barry, David Flynn, John Baker, Leonard Baker, Daniel Duggan, William O'Connor and John Daily. In 1850 these sons of Holy Church invited the Rev. John Brady, of Hartford, to come and minister to them the consolations of religion. He visited Chester in response to their urgent call and said Mass in a private house in the same year; about twenty-five persons received the blessings of that service. The house in which this Mass was said was afterwards owned and occupied by Fisk Shailer. Rev. Peter Kelly came in 1851, and the people having secured Rechabite Hall, through the liberal dispositions of its owners, said Mass there for the first time. The privilege of holding divine services in this hall was a boon highly prized and for which the Catholics have ever been grateful. Rechabite Hall was used until the erection of St. Joseph's church.

REV. RICHARD C. GRAGAN

REV. ANDREW F. HARTY

REV. JOHN WALSH

Having been informed of the presence here of this congregation, Bishop O'Reilly appointed the Rev. John Lynch their pastor in 1852, with Saybrook, Clinton and Branford as dependencies. In 1853 there were ten Catholic families in Chester and about forty unmarried persons.

In the fall of 1852, Father Lynch secured through the agency of Judge Vinal the present church lot, paying therefor $600, and in 1855 began the erection of old St. Joseph's church, which was completed in the same year. During these years, Father Lynch's residence was on Maple street. About the end of 1856, he transferred the pastoral residence to Guilford, from which Chester, Branford and Clinton were attended. In 1856, Chester was under the jurisdiction of Branford, the pastor of which was the Rev. William Clarke. In 1865 it was severed from Colchester by the Rev. P. Creighton, who attended it for about two years, when late in 1867 it reverted to the jurisdiction of Branford. The pastors of Branford visited Chester frequently until 1876, when the Rev. Philip Sheridan was appointed the first resident pastor with Saybrook as a mission. His period of service ended with his death in 1883. His successor was the Rev. Joseph Synnott, who assumed charge in April of the same year. Father Synnott built the pastoral residence and St. John's church at Saybrook, at an expenditure of $9,500, the former at $5,000 and the latter at $4,500; and when in April, 1886, he was transferred to Ansonia, he had not only liquidated the indebtedness incurred by the construction of these two buildings, but left to his successor a balance in the treasury.

The Rev. Father Skelly became Father Synnott's successor. Among the material works which marked his administration, were the erection of St. Peter's church at Higganum; the removal of old St. Joseph's church and the construction on its site of the present edifice in 1891; the purchase of a lot north of the church property, which he transformed into a park. When Father Skelly was transferred to Litchfield, the present rector, the Rev. Andrew F. Harty, became his successor on October 19, 1896. Father Harty attends also the churches in Saybrook, Essex and Higganum. Mass is said in Saybrook three times a month, in Essex and Higganum once. The population of the missions is chiefly Irish and is constantly decreasing. When Chester was organized into a parish, the number of Catholics here was about seventy-five; at present there are about 125 souls.

The parish owns a fine cemetery which was purchased in 1873 and blessed by Bishop McFarland.

Arduous, indeed, but consoling withal, are the labors of these missions. Higganum is ten miles, Saybrook nine and Essex four, from the home parish. What with the Sunday work at these distant missions—saying Mass, preaching, instructing the children and administering the sacraments, the long drives soon make inroads upon a priest's health. But zeal for God's honor and glory recognizes no fatigue; to spend and to be spent are the all-absorbing desires of the priest who is a true father to his flock; but when the labors of the pastor are recognized with such grateful appreciation as at Chester, no work is too exhausting, no sacrifice too great.

## ST. JOHN'S PARISH,

CROMWELL.

FIVE years before Cromwell received its civic incorporation Catholic settlers had established homes here. Michael Dowling, Elizabeth Kelly and Patrick Byrne arrived in 1846, and of this trio, Elizabeth Kelly still survives. Of the Germans, John Myer was the first Catholic resident, coming in 1857. In 1847 was solemnized the first Catholic marriage in Cromwell, that of John Ryan and Mary Moran, and their daughter, Sarah, was the first Catholic child to receive baptism, April 10, 1848. In their family, also, occurred the first death, that of their infant daughter, Anna, in 1860.

As Cromwell originally belonged to the jurisdiction of Middletown, the Catholics of this place attended divine services at St. John's church, until June 3, 1877, when the first Mass celebrated in Cromwell was said by the Rev. Francis P. O'Keefe in Stephens' Hall. At that time there were about 350 Catholics in Cromwell, of Irish and German extraction, in the proportion of about four to one. Besides the attendance given by the pastor to the Catholics of Cromwell, the Sisters of Mercy from Middletown became efficient auxiliaries in teaching the children the salutary truths of faith.

The Rev. John H. Ryan, D.D., became the first resident pastor in February, 1880, with jurisdiction over Rocky Hill and Kensington. According to the census taken that year, there were 400 souls in the parish. The people continued to gather in Stephens' Hall for divine services under Dr. Ryan's administration. He purchased the present church property, remodeled the house that stood on the premises, and had begun the excavation of the basement of the new church, when he was succeeded by the Rev. John F. Murphy in July, 1881. In that year the corner-stone of the church was laid, and the ceremony of dedication was performed by Bishop McMahon on April 22, 1883. The church is an attractive, substantial structure with a seating capacity of 500. Father Murphy's work in Cromwell may be estimated when it is stated that, besides building the church, he erected the present handsome pastoral residence, and made other improvements which greatly enhanced the value of the parochial property.

Rev. William Gibbons succeeded Father Murphy, who was transferred to Mystic, in September 1895. Remaining eight months, he was followed by Rev. Thomas Shelly in May, 1896. Father Shelly served the parish eighteen months, when he was appointed to the pastorate of the Sacred Heart parish, Waterbury. His successor is the present incumbent, the Rev. John Fitzgerald. The population of St. John's parish is 513 souls, of Irish and German extraction, in the proportion of three to one. Since his advent Father Fitzgerald has liquidated the indebtedness of the parish.

In the first decade after the organization of the parish, the number of baptisms was 250 and the marriages 55 ; in the second decade 200 baptisms were conferred and 31 marriages solemnized.

The members of St. John's are chiefly engaged in agricultural pursuits, devoted to the church and most attentive to their religious duties.

Rocky Hill, formerly attached to East Hartford, is attended by Father Fitzgerald, as it had previously been served by his predecessors from the formation of the Cromwell parish. The church here, a frame building with brick basement, was erected during the pastorate of Father Murphy, and dedicated in honor of St. James in 1880. Its seating capacity is 300. Free from financial obligations, the church is a splendid testimony to the faith and generosity of the people. Mass is said here every Sunday.

In the home of Michael Kelly, Rev. Louis Mangan celebrated the first Mass said in Rocky Hill. No little uncertainty surrounds the dates of the first marriage, baptism and death. John Halligan was the first child born and baptized here, and John Grimes the first child claimed by death. The oldest residents assign these events to the year 1848. The baptismal records show seventy baptisms and nineteen marriages in the first decade.

## ST. MARY'S PARISH,

### PORTLAND.

CHATHAM, now Portland, was part of Middletown until October, 1767. In that year it was granted separate rights and given the name Chatham, after the town in England of that name, famous for its shipbuilding.

The earliest Catholic services in this vicinity were held at Portland. The second priest to reside in Connecticut, Rev. James Fitton, said Mass and discharged in other ways his priestly office in Portland in 1830. His successor in Hartford, the Rev. Peter Walsh, came to Middletown in the spring of 1836, with the intention to arrange for monthly services. He arrived on a Sunday afternoon at Middletown, and learning that the greater number of Catholics resided across the river, he went to Portland to secure a suitable place in which to assemble the people. Being unsuccessful in his search for a house or a hall, he finally secured the use of a barn from a Captain Worthington on Main street. With his devoted little band he repaired to the place on the following morning, but found the doors of the barn bolted against them. Receiving no reasons for this change of attitude, Father Walsh was about to gather his flock, as his brethren in the priesthood had done before in those days, beneath the overspreading boughs of a large tree, when a neighbor of Captain Worthington, Joseph Myrick, graciously extended the hospitality of his house. Here the Divine Mysteries were celebrated. The Divine Victim of the sacrifice rewarded his servant for his generous act, and Joseph Myrick became the first convert to the faith in Middlesex county.[1] From this time till 1845, Father Walsh, Father Brady, Sr., and Father Brady,

---

[1] In this connection the following marriage record will not be without interest:

Benjamin J. Myrick      "*August the 7th, 1831:* Married, Mr. Benjamin James Myrick,
         to          of Chatham, Ct., to Mrs. Eleanor Strong, of Hartford. Witnesses
Mrs. Eleanor Strong.    present, Mr. Daniel Donevan and Lady.      B. O'CAVANAGH."

The reader will notice that this marriage took place nearly five years before the above-mentioned event.

Jr., visited Portland frequently, until the appointment of Rev. John Brady, Jr., as the first resident pastor of Middletown. Thenceforth until 1872, the Catholics of Portland went to Middletown to Mass and were attended by the pastor of that place. The first marriage solemnized by Rev. John Brady, Sr., is the following taken from the record of marriages preserved at St. Patrick's church, Hartford.

" CHATHAM

1850. *January 28.* Married, Martin Degan to Bridget Ryan. Witnesses: Martin Degan and Bridget Mulhern.                                        JOHN BRADY."

St. Mary's parish was formed in 1872, and the first resident pastor, Rev. William E. Duffy, assumed charge on August 8th of that year. Father Duffy secured Waverly Hall, in which he held divine services for some time; afterwards moving to a building owned by John Bransfield, where the congregation worshiped until the church was completed. It was Father Duffy's purpose to build a church, and to this end he had purchased the site on which the present edifice stands; but death intervened. Father Duffy died on August 30, 1876.

The Rev. Denis Desmond was appointed Father Duffy's successor, and on October 1, 1876, assumed charge. The erection of the church first occupied Father Desmond's attention, and within a month after his arrival ground was broken. The corner-stone was laid on April 15, 1877. Bishop Galberry officiated at the ceremony assisted by Very Rev. Thomas Walsh, of Meriden, and Rev. Flor. De Bruckyer, of Willimantic, as deacons of honor. The sermon was preached by Rev. M. A. Tierney, of Hartford.

The church was completed and dedicated during the administration of Father Desmond, who built also the pastoral residence. His successor, the Rev. John Flemming, followed on September 2, 1881. St. Mary's cemetery was purchased during his pastorate, which terminated in 1885. Rev. Joseph Gleeson then became pastor of St. Mary's. Father Gleeson introduced the Sisters of Mercy into the parish, organized the parochial school, purchased a fine estate adjoining the parish property and transformed the dwelling thereon into a home for the Sisters. Appointed to Thompsonville, Father Gleeson was followed by the present rector, the Rev. Timothy R. Sweeney, on January 31, 1889.

Among the parochial works which Father Sweeney has accomplished are the liquidation of the indebtedness, which he found on assuming the pastorate, $3,400; the remodeling of the pastoral residence, and otherwise improving the parish buildings; the grading of the grounds about the church and rectory; the placing of an $800 bell in the church tower on May 8, 1890, on which occasion Rev. T. W. Broderick, of Hartford, pronounced the oration; the erection of a parochial school, which was blessed by Bishop McMahon, Rev. Walter Elliott, C.S.P., preaching the sermon, on November 27, 1890.

With its sister schools of the diocese, St. Mary's is doing splendid work for the church and the state. Its graduates reflect honor upon their instructors and serve well the state of which they become useful citizens. The training they here receive qualifies them to enter into the battle of life well equipped against the dangers that surround them. Five sisters are in charge, having under their tuition 178 pupils. Sister M. Ignatius is the superioress of the convent.

## ST. PATRICK'S (MISSION) CHURCH,

### East Hampton.

THE Rev. Patrick Creighton, of Colchester, was the first priest to attend the faithful of East Hampton. He began his visitations in 1857 and offered the Holy Sacrifice of the Mass in the house of William Wall. The name of Patrick O'Connell appears prominent among the early Catholics, as on May 23, 1865, he transferred to Bishop McFarland a half acre of land for $100, upon which St. Patrick's church was built. The church was completed during the pastorate of Father McCarten in 1869. East Hampton became a dependency of Portland in 1872, during the pastorate of Rev. Father Duffy. Father Desmond enlarged the church in June, 1878, and on August 11th of that year, it was dedicated by Bishop Galberry, assisted by Very Rev. Thomas Walsh, V.G., Rev. J. S. Fitzpatrick, and Rev. Flor. De Bruckyer. The Solemn High Mass which followed the dedication ceremonies was celebrated by Father De Bruckyer, and the sermon was preached by Father Fitzpatrick. Over 2,000 persons assisted at the ceremony.

In 1895, Father Sweeney purchased a fine lot, and having paid the cost of it, $5,000, began the erection of the church on May 1, 1896. The new edifice was dedicated on February 14, 1897, by Bishop Tierney; the sermon was delivered by Rev. Thomas Campbell, S.J., president of St. John's College, Fordham. The church was filled to its utmost capacity, one half of the congregation being non-Catholics. After the ceremony Bishop Tierney addressed words of congratulation to the parishioners upon the self-sacrificing spirit manifested in the erection of the church, after which he imparted to the assemblage his benediction.

St. Patrick's church is 98 x 47 feet with a spire 104 feet high, and accommodates 400 persons.

---

# NEW HAVEN COUNTY.

NEW HAVEN COUNTY is bounded on the north by Litchfield and Hartford Counties; on the east by Middlesex County; on the south by Long Island Sound; and on the west by Litchfield County and the Housatonic river. From north to south it is about 21 miles in width, and its length from east to west is about 26 miles. It contains 546 square miles, or 345,600 acres. The population of the county in 1820 was 39,616; in 1830, 43,847; in 1890 it was 209,058. The cities and towns in which there are Catholic parishes are the following:

| | | |
|---|---|---|
| NEW HAVEN, | GUILFORD, | SEYMOUR, |
| ANSONIA, | MERIDEN, | SOUTH MERIDEN, |
| BRANFORD, | MILFORD, | WALLINGFORD, |
| DERBY, | MOUNT CARMEL, | WATERBURY. |
| | NAUGATUCK, | |

## NEW HAVEN.

NEW HAVEN was known among the Indians as *Quinnipiac*, and by the Dutch, who were here some years before the English, as *Red Mount*, so called from the appearance of East and West Rocks.[1] In 1637 Mr. Eaton and others made a tour of exploration to Connecticut. Selecting Quinnipiac as the place of their settlement, they spent the winter in a miserable hut at the corner of Church and George streets.[2] In the following year, on March 30th, the Rev. John Davenport, Theophilus Eaton and others sailed from Boston to Quinnipiac, where they arrived on April 18th. Rev. John Davenport was a vigorous opponent of the Catholic church, as were the Puritans of his day. They deemed it a privilege in their public declarations to associate "Popery" with the devil, tyranny and idolatry. Nevertheless, John Davenport's nephew, Christopher Davenport, renounced Puritanism, entered the Catholic church, became a student at the famous seat of learning, Douai College, in 1651, entered the novitiate of the Flemish Franciscans at Ypres, October 7, 1657, and was enrolled, October 18, 1658, as a Franciscan Friar, taking the name in religion of Francis a Sancta Clara.[3]

Thirteen years after the advent of John Davenport there came into New Haven the first Catholics to tread the soil of Connecticut. One was a priest of the Society of Jesus, the Rev. Gabriel Druillettes; the other a legal luminary, Mons. Godefroy. They, with their retinue, all Catholics, arrived in New Haven about September 2d or 4th, 1651, and remained some days in convention with the venerable Commissioners of the United Colonies of New England, to whom they had been sent as ambassadors from Canada.

The expedition against Cape Breton in 1745 resulted in the capture of that place with a large number of prisoners, many of whom were brought to New Haven and placed in the custody of Samuel Miles. By an act of the General Assembly of July of the same year, Miles was ordered to convey his prisoners to the care of Joseph Whiting, Esq., also of New Haven. These prisoners were Catholics; but it is of no practical benefit to speculate as to their spiritual fate. The legislation of the time, and the spirit then prevailing, were hostile to the faith they professed, and though every means, no doubt, were employed to estrange them from their cherished belief, yet it is our privilege, as it is our hope, to believe that they remained steadfast to the creed of their baptism.

Eleven years later New Haven received nineteen Acadians—all children of the ancient Church—its quota, as established by the General Assembly of January, 1756. They were faithful, devoted Catholics, otherwise they would not have been exiles; but deprived of priest and church, of the Mass and the sacraments and instruction, living in the midst of a people antagonistic to their dearest possession, their faith, a sense of fear steals over us that, though

[1] Barber's *Historical Collections*.
[2] *Historical Collections*.
[3] Very Rev. Dr. Shahan's Pamphlet, *Christopher Davenport*.

the fathers and mothers were not attracted by an alien creed, their children eventually yielded to influences which, taken in every respect, were bitterly and inexplicably anti-Catholic.

Thenceforth, the records are silent concerning the presence of Catholics in New Haven until January 28, 1796. As told elsewhere in these pages, a French priest visited here and took up lodgings at Mr. Azel Kimberley's residence on Chapel street, probably to care for the spiritual interests of the numerous French refugees who had gathered here, as well as at New London and Hartford, at the end of the last century, victims of the San Domingan insurrection. It may be inferred that this priest said Mass during his sojourn in New Haven, and that the published notice of his presence brought a goodly number who profited by his ministry.

Bishop Cheverus, of Boston, active, ceaseless in labor, an apostolic man, seeking ever the extension of the Kingdom of God on earth, was the next representative of the priesthood to visit New Haven. He came in 1823, and offered the Holy Sacrifice of the Mass on York street, at the residence of a French professor of Yale College. Catholicity had now come to stay, to remain a permanent and beneficent factor in the city's life. The prayer of the saintly bishop that religion might flourish here has received an answer which even those who cannot see may read.

The next priest to visit New Haven was Very Rev. John Power, Vicar-General of the diocese of New York. He had ministered to the spiritual wants of the Catholics on the Enfield Canal near Windsor Locks, in August and October, 1827, and on his return from one of these visits remained over Sunday in New Haven. At this time there stood near the head of Long wharf a little chapel, which had been erected and used by the Protestants as a seamen's Bethel. The committee who had charge of the building were appealed to for permission to occupy it at an early hour on Sunday. The application was refused with the reply: "We have no Popery now in New Haven, and we don't want any." In this emergency the Catholics secured the only available building, *a bar-room:* the bar was closed and concealed from view by blankets, and a few benches were brought in as seats for the little congregation; amid these humble surroundings was the Holy Sacrifice offered by the Vicar-General of New York.

On July 13, 1829, Rev. R. D. Woodley, of Providence, set out from Hartford for New Haven, and on the following morning said Mass and administered the sacraments in a barn which stood on the corner of Chapel and Chestnut streets, then called "Sliny's Corner." "The barn was in such a dilapidated condition that the wind whistled through the crevices of the walls, and the good people thought it miraculous that the candles on the altar were not extinguished by the lively gusts. Here some of our leading Catholic residents were baptized." During this visit Father Woodley baptized two persons. About this time, there came to New Haven one who had acquired no little degree of local celebrity, George Gabriel. He was of Catholic antecedents, no doubt, as he was a descendant of a Frenchman who came over with Lafayette. He opened a grocery store near the college, but afterwards engaged in the fancy goods business. He accumulated a fortune, chiefly by mending canes, umbrellas and parasols, at which trade he was very proficient. He bequeathed $10,000 to Yale College, $15,000 to Yale Divinity School, besides leaving large sums to various charities.

The Rev. Bernard O'Cavanagh, who took up his residence at Hartford on August 26, 1829, as the first resident priest of Connecticut, visited New Haven on Sunday, December 21, of that year, and said Mass in the house of a Mr. Newman. Father O'Cavanagh returned to New Haven on December 31, and on January 1, 1830, celebrated Mass, preached and administered the sacraments at the residence of a Mr. McGrath. He remained here three days, intending to visit New London, but circumstances called him to Hartford on January 4th. Father O'Cavanagh's next missionary visit was on Saturday, April 17, 1830, when he said Mass and preached twice in Union church, near the city, heard the confessions of many and baptized two children. On June 17th he united in marriage Patrick Shea, of New Haven, and Hulda Catharina Whaley, of Waterbury. In its issue of October 30, 1830, *The Catholic Press* contained this notice:

"The Catholics residing at New Haven will be visited by their pastor on Friday, the 5th of November."

And on December 18th, it published that

"The Catholics at New Haven will be visited by their pastor on the 23d inst."

The earliest recorded marriages of Catholics solemnized at New Haven are the following, taken from the Marriage Record. The entries are in the beautiful penmanship of Father Fitton, but are signed by Father O'Cavanagh.

Philip Slevin
and
Ann McGrath.
} *1831, January 10th.* Married, Philip Slevin to Ann McGrath. Witnesses: John McGrath, Daniel and Mrs. Donevan.

B. O'CAVANAGH.

Rog' Kennedy
and
Bridget McGrath.
} *January 27th.* Married, Roger Kennedy to Bridget McGrath. Witnesses: Daniel and Mrs. Donevan.

B. O'CAVANAGH.

The trials experienced by the pioneers of Catholicity in New Haven are thus described by one of them in a letter to a friend: "When we heard that a church had been purchased at Hartford, and was about to have a priest, we were delighted. The appointment gave us an opportunity of having Mass at New Haven about once in three months, and happy we then were for so great a privilege. Hearing for the first time that the priest was about to visit us, we were at a loss to know where we could find a place for offering the Holy Sacrifice. After many efforts to secure a respectable and suitable place, we were in the end necessitated to take up with an old barn, which we swept and fitted up the best we could. (This was on the occasion of Father Woodley's visit, July 13, 1829). By the next visit of his Reverence we rented a room from a German, he not knowing for what purpose we intended it. We next needed a few benches; but the joiner, hearing what we wanted them for, refused positively to make them, saying that 'they—his fellow-townsmen—were determined to put down that religion, at least in Connecticut, whether or no.' We succeeded, at length, in finding one who made us a few, not suspecting the place for which they were intended; but as soon as as he found out, declared 'he would not have made them for fifty dollars a piece if he had known it in time.' " [1]

It had been announced in *The Catholic Press* that Father Fitton would visit New Haven on December 24, 1831, and that midnight Mass would be celebrated on Christmas morning at 12.30 at the residence of a Mr. Finnegan. The writer above quoted, thus wrote of that historic event: [2] "Whenever we expected the priest we all came together to receive him. One Saturday, in particular, it was the eve of Christmas, and, anticipating midnight Mass, we were all at our accustomed place of meeting, awaiting his arrival; but he did not come. We were certain he would not disappoint us, whilst, at the same time, we could not account for his delay. At length we concluded to go and see if we might not meet him. We did so, and met him on the road, about four miles outside of New Haven. The sleighing from Hartford had been good part of the way, and then failed, till nothing remained but bare ground, and his horse gave out; the distance from Hartford to this city is about thirty-four miles; but the good priest, not wishing to disappoint us, determined to walk the rest of the way. When we met him he had his valise, containing his vestments, etc., on his shoulders. The walking being rough and frozen, his shoes were nearly worn out, and when he arrived that night he was scarcely able to preach, though he did so at the end of Mass, after which we secured a conveyance to leave him where he had left his horse, for he had to return and say another Mass at Hartford the same day." [3]

The writer thus concludes his reminiscences: "There is another little incident that occurs to my mind in connection with the early establishment of our religion at this place. As our members began somewhat to increase, I called upon a certain gentleman who owned an old building that we thought might be fitted up for church purposes, but neither for love nor money would he listen to our proposition, declaring that he would not encourage Catholicity in any way. We felt disappointed, and my reply to him was: 'Sir, I hope that you and I may live to see Catholic churches in this city with spires as high as any of yours.' He doubted it; but, thank God, it has come to pass; and he has lived to see our splendid churches all well filled, and even crowded, every Sunday."

Rev. James Fitton, who succeeded Father O'Cavanagh as the second pastor of Hartford, attended New Haven, among other places, at regular intervals until the appointment of the Rev. James McDermot as resident pastor of New Haven. Among the marriages solemnized by him, and the first marriage ceremony by him performed at New Haven, was recorded as follows:

Corn. Driscoll \
and } *1832, May 28th.* Married at New Haven, Cornelius Driscoll to Jennet \
Jen't Twitchell. } Twitchell. Witnesses: Ricard England and Mary Bowen.

JAMES FITTON.

[1] Father Fitton's " *Sketches.*"    [2] *Ibid.*    [3] *Ibid.*

Other dates on which Father Fitton visited New Haven are, Monday, February 13, 1832; Easter Monday, April 23d, and May 27th. On this last occasion services were "at 10 o'clock, where they were performed on last visit near the New Green."

The first resident pastor of New Haven was the Rev. James McDermot. He offered his services to Bishop Fenwick on September 2, 1831, was accepted and sent to Montreal, where he made his philosophical studies. He received Minor Orders on February 24, 1832, and in the same year received sub-deacon-ship, deaconship and priesthood on August 16th, 17th and 19th respectively. His first assignment was as an assistant to Father Fitton at Hartford, where he arrived on September 18th. After a brief term of service in this capacity he was appointed to New Haven, with Bridgeport, Waterbury, Derby, Norwalk, Danbury, Meriden, Middletown, Goshen, Tariffville and other stations as dependencies. Among the prominent Catholics who resided here about this time were James Callaghan, John Connor, James Hayes, an engineer on the Farmington canal, Charles Fagan and Patrick Murphy, of State street; in all they formed a congregation of about 200.

It was Father McDermot's desire, as it was the ambition of his people, to build a church in which they could assemble regularly and with comfort for divine worship. To this end a lot on the corner of York and Davenport streets, on which St. John's church now stands, was secured through the instrumentality of Mrs. Driscoll, a Protestant, whose marriage record is given above. The sum paid for this lot was $100, and on May 14, 1833, Bishop Fenwick received the deed for the same. The New Haven town records show other real estate transactions. On May 9, 1833, a transfer of a lot on the corner of Whiting and Hill streets was made by Adolphus Michael Bagne-lin to Bishop Fenwick, the consideration being $450. On September 24, 1833, this piece of land was given to Timothy Alling in exchange for a lot on the corner of York street and Davenport avenue, "adjoining the land owned by Jannett Driscoll." A portion of this land was set apart and became the first Catholic cemetery in New Haven.

On the lot secured on May 14, 1833, was erected the first Catholic church in the city. It was a frame building, sixty by thirty-five feet, exclusive of sacristy, twenty-two feet high to the plates, exceedingly neatly furnished inside and out, and contained one gallery. The feast of the Ascension, May 8, 1834, was the date assigned for its dedication. Bishop Fenwick arrived at New Haven at noon on May 7th, and as he notes in his Journal, "Was courteously treated by a servant in the hotel, named Daniels." During the ceremony of dedication a distressing accident occurred, which the Bishop thus described: "May 8. Said early Mass and gave communion. A great concourse was assembled at 10 o'clock, consisting of Catholics from all the adjacent country, and a very great number of Protestants who were attracted merely to witness the ceremony, from New Haven. I went to the church at 10; found Fathers McDermot and Fitton there; dressed and prepared for the ceremony. After making the circuit of the church, returned to the altar; was hardly arrived when the gallery behind gave way and fell with all its incumbents upon the mass of people below. One boy, fourteen years old was instantly killed, and several others were dreadfully wounded; of these one died in the course of the day. Both of these were converts." The boy who was killed was Abraham Lloyd Bryan; the other victim was his grandfather, Mr. Hardyear, of West Haven, both brought into the Church, as converts, through the agency of the famous convert, Calvin White. As the blood of Hardyear mingled with that of his grandson in the church, his dying request was that they should be interred in the same grave. They were buried on the day following in the cemetery adjoining the church. A large concourse of people of all denominations followed the remains to the grave and manifested profound sympathy. Among the sufferers of this calamity were John Conner, of Derby, and James Callaghan, who was on the point of removing to New York, but delayed his journey to witness the ceremony. Their escape from being crushed was almost miraculous, for they were both caught by the falling gallery near the spot where the greatest pressure was. Of the Protestants who were present and received serious injury, were a Mr. Tomlinson, Mrs. Hinman, wife of Deacon Scovill Hinman, Miss Taylor, daughter of Solomon Taylor, and a daughter of Daniel Collins, all of New Haven. The cause of the disaster was ascribed to the carpenter who had constructed the gallery. According to the original plan, it was intended there should be two Gothic columns to support it. The carpenter, however, deemed these unnecessary, and in lieu thereof undertook to support the gallery by trussing.

Fifteen persons had been prepared to receive confirmation on this fatal day, but only two presented themselves after the accident, and were confirmed privately. They were Michael Thomas Cooney and Elizabeth Mead. On the Sunday following the disaster, May 11, the church having been cleansed, the Bishop celebrated early Mass, previous to which he blessed the church, giving it the title of "Christ's Church." At the Mass which was celebrated at half-past ten, and said by Father McDermot, the Bishop preached and administered confirmation to four persons, Margaret Finnegan, Margaret O'Leary, Ann Reynolds, and Bridget Toohey. Christ's church cost $3,000, and was without exception the most beautiful little Gothic church in New England. The debt at the time of the accident was $500, which the disaster increased. To encourage the disheartened congregation Bishop Fenwick donated $50 to the treasury.

The disaster, awful as it was, while it evoked the profound sympathy of the majority of non-Catholics, gave to some editors of religious journals an opportunity to display their fanaticism. We extract the following editorial from *The Jesuit*, May 31, 1834:

"Under the head of 'A Solemn Providence,' we find an article in *Zion's Herald* of May 21st, of this city (Boston), which purports to have been copied from the *Religious Intelligencer*, of New Haven, in reference to the distressing accident which occurred there in the breaking down of the organ gallery of the new Catholic church on Ascension day. While the editors of the other papers of the city, one and all, as far as we have ascertained, expressed themselves on this melancholy event as they should and with much delicacy to the feelings of Catholics, who were the principal sufferers by it, he of the *Intelligence* alone, in the true spirit of a fanatic, must come out with his '*Solemn Providence.*' The article which he penned on that occasion commences thus: 'On the 8th inst. the Roman Catholic church lately erected in New Haven was to have been consecrated, *whether to the Virgin Mary or to God we know not.*' The fanatic! Why did he not inquire to which? There were enough present, even of his own people, to inform him correctly. Why did he not go himself to the church? The walk was but a moderate one; he could have there seen and read on the very frontispiece of it,

## 'CHRIST'S CHURCH,'

in characters sufficiently large, too, as to have been read, even without spectacles, at the distance of 200 yards, at least, to whom it was to have been dedicated. But is it quite certain that the gentleman, the religious editor, was not there, and that he did not read the above glowing characters before he penned the article in question? . . . The least grain of his charity, let it be ever so cold, should have suggested to him the propriety of not bearing false witness against his neighbors, and of not throwing out a hint, without the least grounds for it, to induce the public, as far as he had any control over it, to believe that the Catholics were a superstitious race, who were in the habit of dedicating their churches to the Blessed Virgin instead of dedicating them to God."

In October, 1834, Christ's church was broken into, the altar stripped of its ornaments, and the crucifix and the silver chalice stolen; but the Protestants of New Haven deprecated the outrage, and presented the church with a handsome silver chalice to replace the one taken.

A census taken in 1836 gave New Haven 300 adult Catholics; Derby, 25; Bridgeport, 100; Norwalk, 25, and Waterbury 30. On June 4, 1837, Bishop Fenwick administered confirmation for the second time at New Haven, and twenty-one males and twenty-three females were the recipients of the sacrament. The Easter communions of this year in New Haven were 301.

On June 15, 1837, Father McDermot severed his relations with the Catholics of New Haven, having been transferred to Lowell, Mass., all the New England States at that time being under the jurisdiction of the Bishop of Boston. His successor was the Rev. William Wiley, who remained only until August 24th of that year. Bishop Tyler, Father Fitton, and Father Wiley received the orders of sub-deacon and deacon on December 21 and 22, 1827, respectively. Fathers Fitton and Wiley were ordained priests on December 23rd of the same year, while Bishop Tylor was ordained to the priesthood on June 3, 1829. Father Wiley died at East Boston on April 19, 1855, aged 51 years. The Rev. Father Haskins preached the funeral sermon, which we herewith append.¹ It shows in the most graphic manner the trials and hardships

---

¹ From the *Freeman's Journal*, June 2, 1855, copied from the *Pilot*.

Father Wiley experienced in youth, and reveals his steadfastness in aiming at and reaching the holy priesthood:

William Wiley was born in the city of New York, in the year 1803 or 1804. He was deprived of both his parents during his infancy, so that he had no recollection of ever having seen either of them. His earliest recollections were of an aunt who had the charge of him, and who did not treat him well, and of a sister who was under the same roof. After having suffered much harsh treatment for, as it then seemed, a long time, he was at the age of five or six years placed in a Protestant Orphan Asylum. Here he was kindly treated, and here he went to his first school. At the age of ten or eleven years he was apprenticed to a shoemaker, who, unfortunately for the boy, was one of that class to whom parents would not entrust their children, and who are therefore compelled to seek their apprentices among friendless orphans. He proved a hard master, and when the boy, after having patiently borne many cruel whippings, at length dared to remonstrate, his master returned him to the asylum, as a stubborn and refractory child. A short time after he was apprenticed to another shoemaker, 150 miles from the city of New York. This new master proved even worse than the first. Poor William was nearly starved, and was reduced to almost a skeleton. He was but scantily clad with clothing, and what little he had was in tatters. Moreover he was covered with disease caused by neglect and want of food. So one morning, while all were asleep, he took his resolution and escaped from the house of his master, and walked a distance of fifty miles, stopping only to repose by the wayside, or to eat that which was given him by charitable housekeepers. He had now reached a town on the Hudson river, where he fortunately met a man who had seen him in the asylum, and who, when he heard his story, put him on board a vessel bound for New York, where he arrived the following day, and immediately presented himself at the door of the orphan asylum, and related the story of his escape. His story, and still more, his wretched condition, his altered looks, his neglected and tattered clothes, corroborating every word of it, excited the pity and indignation of the guardians of the institution, and they received him at once, and clothed and nursed him until he was again strong enough to be apprenticed.

Then there came one day to the asylum a rich farmer in search of an apprentice. He selected William Wiley, and took him to his residence in Waterford, in the State of New York, where he faithfully served his new master for the space of about two years. During the week he labored on the farm, and on Sunday he drove the farmer and family to meeting, which he attended very devoutly himself; for, educated though thus far a Protestant, he firmly believed many of the truths of Christianity, and had an ardent desire to love and to serve God and gain heaven. At length by the mercy of God, he formed the acquaintance of a Catholic—the first he had ever met. He was an Irishman—a devout and exemplary Christian—who conversed frequently with him upon Catholic doctrine, and lent him the "Poor Man's Catechism." This was his only book of study for several months. It was his constant companion after the labors of the day, and on Sunday he would sit for hours devouring its contents.

At length his master and mistress perceived the change that had been wrought in him, discovered the cause, seized the book, and concealed it, remarking that he should read no popish trash in their house. From that moment his existence was embittered. Ever after, when he drove them as usual to meeting, they took every occasion to ridicule and abuse those who professed the Catholic faith, and on their return would regale each other with thanks to God that they were not worshipers of the Virgin, and that the minister had given them no popish mummeries. He forbore as long and as patiently as he could, and then determined to leave them. So one Sunday morning after he had driven the family to meeting, he returned to the house, and first searched every place he could think of till he had found his book—his beloved treasure—with which he immediately ran to the good Irishman in order to return it to its rightful owner. Next he searched the drawers of his master's desk till he found his indentures, which he incontinently committed to the fire. Then he made up his little bundle, which consisted of an old gray coat and a Protestant Bible, and in the middle of winter, on foot, he started off for Boston, because the Irishman had told him that there was a Catholic church and a Catholic bishop there. He walked as fast as he could for fear of being overtaken. He sold his Bible for seventy-five cents, but that was soon exhausted. One bitter cold day, as he was pelting through the storm, the stage-coach overtook him. It was on runners; and he looked for a chance to ride, and looked imploringly at the driver, for he was cold and hungry. The driver was a good-natured soul and stopped his coach and said: "Get inside, my boy," and he drove him to the end of his route, and then consigned him to the care of the next driver, and so he made a good piece of his journey. However, a benevolent old gentleman in the coach perceived that the boy never got out at meal times, but always remained gathered up in a corner of the coach. So at length he suspected the true reason, and when all the passengers had gone in to dinner, he went back to the coach—this benevolent old gentleman—and asked the boy where he was going. "I am going to Boston," he replied; "to try if I can find my sister, or half-sister" (he never knew which). This was no falsehood, for he would indeed have been very glad to have found her, or any one else related to him, for he felt so lonely in the world. The kind old gentleman was moved to compassion for the boy, and put his hand into his pocket and took out some silver and did not stay to count it, but thrust it into the boy's hand, and bade him go straight into the tavern, and call for whatever he wanted.

At last, however, there came along a surly driver, who declared gruffly, that he wasn't going to drive boys that didn't pay. "So get out here, boy, and go along on foot." Poor William obeyed, of course. He had no other alternative. He walked on till he came to Bennington in Vermont. Here some kind person took him in and kept him for a day or two; and then he started off again, inquiring the way to Boston. It seemed to him as if he were going around the world, the journey was so long. At length, hungry, weary and penniless, he reached Boston, and continued to walk about the streets, till by repeated inquiries he found Franklin street and the Catholic church. He contented himself with merely looking at the outside of it, not feeling himself worthy of entering so holy a place. Walking up Broomfield Lane, now called Broomfield street, he discovered a stable, which he entered and asked for employment, offering to work for his board and lodging. But the proprietor refused him, and with others who stood by jeered at him and called him some runaway thief. William made no reply, but burst into tears, and was walking quietly away, when the stable man relented, and called after him and took him to his house, and took the kindest care of him for several days, during which he went frequently to an intelligence office, to seek a situation and means of support. One day while standing among a crowd of other applicants, a venerable-looking man came in and asked for a boy, and engaged William Wiley. This gentleman was the late President Kirkland, President of Harvard University. He lived with the president till the latter broke up housekeeping, when he recommended William to a friend of his in Boston, Benjamin Fessenden, Esq., with whom he remained several months, and was then employed by a Mr. Hill. While with Mr. Fessenden he called on Father Larisey, the first and only priest he had ever yet seen. By him he was instructed, baptized and received into the Catholic church. In August of the year 1820, he was confirmed by Bishop Cheverus, and made his first communion the same month. He was then about 16 or 17 years of age. It was at this time that he first conceived the idea of studying for the priesthood, though he revealed his intention to no one. He immediately commenced taking lessons in private in Latin of Master Pemberton, the distinguished teacher of the Boston Latin School. He also applied himself to the study of the French language and read all the books he could obtain. Many of the old Catholics of Boston still live, who remember well how constantly and piously he assisted at Mass every day of the week in the Cathedral Church at this time.

All his thoughts were now upon the holy ministry. He felt himself called to consecrate himself without reserve to God; but how to accomplish it was his great embarrassment. He fervently prayed to God for light and to his blessed Mother for aid. At length, hearing that Dr. Jarvis, Protestant Rector of St. Paul's Church, was about making a tour to Europe, he offered to go with him in the capacity of a servant, in order, as he had candidly avowed, that he might get into France and study for the priesthood, under the Rt. Rev. Dr. Cheverus, who was at that time Archbishop of Bordeaux. Dr. Jarvis received his application with due consideration and kindness, and applied to the Rev. Mr. Burns, then stationed at the Cathedral, for the character of the young man, and informed him of Mr. Wiley's application and intentions for the future.

The Rev. Mr. Burns at once informed Bishop Fenwick of the nature of Dr. Jarvis's interview, and the bishop immediately sent for Mr. Wiley, and after an interview with him in which he was perfectly satisfied of his vocation, offered to receive him as a student of theology, which he did at once, and placed him to board in the family of Mr. Thomas Murphy, who occupied a portion of the episcopal residence.

With a zeal and industry characteristic of himself he pursued his studies, and in December, 1827, was elevated to the priesthood. There are many thousands living who can attest to the fidelity and charity with which he discharged its duties, and many more who have departed will rise again on the final day and call him blessed. Many a broken heart has he healed; into many a wound has he poured the balm of consolation; many an orphan's tear has he dried; and many a widow's heart has he made to sing for joy.

He served the Cathedral parish for several years, and it was here that I had the happiness of first forming his acquaintance. I was at that time a Protestant myself, but called at the bishop's house to find a priest to assist a poor woman who was very ill. The Rev. Mr. Wiley answered the call. I can never forget this, my first interview with a Catholic priest, nor the eloquence, earnestness and unction with which he extolled the beauties of the Catholic faith, and portrayed the horrors and deformities of heresy and schism. He compromised nothing. When I asked him if he did not think that I could be saved as an honest and sincere Episcopalian he answered that it was impossible. That there was no possibility of salvation out of the Catholic church—that there was but one Lord, one Faith and one Baptism—that the believer would be saved, and the unbeliever damned. This was my first lesson in Catholic doctrine, and I never forgot it. It made so strong an impression upon me that when I left the house I made a vow, which was registered in Heaven, that I would faithfully examine and diligently seek the truth, and that if I found it where Father Wiley said it was, I would at any risk embrace it. And thanks—eternal thanks—to God, I kept that vow. It was Father Wiley who found me wandering about, and lost in the mazes of falsehood and error, and speeding fast to my eternal ruin, and kindly warned me of my danger, and took my hand and led me into the paths of peace and safety. Oh, my Father, my Father! I shall see thee no more. But I do fervently ask for the gift of thy mantle, that I may live as the just man, and my last end be like this.

The Rev. James Smyth, who had been ordained to the priesthood by Bishop Fenwick on October 17, 1835, came to New Haven from Waltham, Mass., as successor to Father Wiley, on August 24, 1837.

Father Smyth enlarged Christ's church, of which Thomas Darcy McGee wrote on August 30, 1843: "Whilst speaking of churches, I begin to bethink me of New Haven. This well-known and admired model of neatness has been enlarged, through the laborious zeal of the Rev. Mr. Smyth, its pastor, and now stands in the form of a perfect cross. Its dimensions are 85 by 75 feet, and both interiorly and outwardly, it is just now a unique piece of church architecture, yet the fairest in the diocese."

The following letter, written by Father Smyth to Bishop Tyler, will throw some light upon a portion of his extensive parish.

NEW HAVEN, April 15, 1845.

My Lord :—

The number of marriages in my mission in 1844 was 30, and of that number three were from Waterbury and two from Derby. I registered all the baptisms under the head of New Haven; the total number for 1841 was 103. As near as I can ascertain there are in Waterbury adults, that is men and women, married and single, about 100, and about 60 children. There are thirty-four married couples; about the third part of that number came there the past year. Derby, about 60 adults and about 60 children. I have not got the land for a church in that place as yet. I hope to get it ere long. I have got the land in Waterbury; it cost $275; it is paid for and the deed taken out as you directed. We have about $60 collected after paying for the land.

On Sunday night, June 11, 1848, the Catholics of New Haven experienced a severe loss in the destruction of their beautiful church by fire. It was supposed at the time to be the work of an incendiary. The church was valued at between $8,000 and $9,000, and was insured for $5,500.

After eleven years of arduous and faithful labor in New Haven, Father Smyth was transferred to Windsor Locks in July, 1848, where he died on May 16, 1874, aged 87 years. His successor was the Rev. Philip O'Reilly. After the destruction of the church divine services were held in a tent until December of that year, when the building occupied by the Congregationalists on Church street was purchased from Sidney M. Stone. After being suitably fitted up for Catholic worship it was dedicated under the title of St. Mary's on December 18, 1848. Of this ceremony the *Journal and Courier* the following morning said: "The Catholic society assembled for the first time at their place of worship which they purchased some months since. Rt. Rev. Bishop Tyler officiated. At the close of the ritual, Bishop Tyler addressed the assembly, congratulating them on the auspicious circumstances under which they were again permitted to meet after having been scattered by the disastrous fire which reduced to dust the beloved temple of their faith. The cost of the edifice was $13,000, of which sum there yet remain to be raised $700." Two entries in Bishop O'Reilly's Journal indicate a numerous congregation in New Haven at this time and disclose as well the zeal and activity of the Bishop.

"*1851, February 4th:* Arrived at New Haven, where I heard confessions the remainder of the week from 6 A. M. to 11 P. M., and preached each evening.

"*9th:* Made a visitation of this congregation, confirmed 671, gave Holy Communion to over 1000 and preached five times."

Father O'Reilly's pastorate ended on May 12, 1851. His removal from St. Mary's was the subject of no little comment at the time and evoked the following correspondence:

"NEW HAVEN, June 20, '51.

"TO THE EDITOR OF THE CELT:

"The Right Rev. Dr. O'Reilly has been in town for some days past, making arrangements for the immediate commencement of another Catholic church, which is to be located on Grand street, in the lower part of the city. It is to be built of stone, and in the Gothic Style. When completed it will be one of the largest Churches in the State. It will be the endeavor of the entire Catholic population of this city to make it an ornament to the city, and a structure as near worthy, as their means will allow, of the great object to which it is to be dedicated.

"Owing to the removal of Rev. Mr. O'Reilly, our former Pastor, from this diocese, the Bishop has appointed the Rev. Mr. O'Brien pastor, with the Rev. Messrs. Sheridan and Tevin as assistants. To Mr. Sheridan is committed the superintendence of the building of the new Church."

This communication brought out the following letter:

NEW HAVEN, June 30, 1851.

*Dear M. Gee*—I have noticed in the last number of the *Celt* that your informant from our city has led the many readers of it astray, by stating that Rev. Mr. O'Reilly was removed from this diocese, which I am happy to inform you is not the case. That Rev. Mr. O'Reilly has resigned the pastoral charge among us, is alas, too true; a circumstance which has caused extreme regret among his friends here, who wish him God speed wherever Providence shall see fit to place him. A FRIEND TO TRUTH.

About sixty-two years ago the first Catholic school of New Haven was opened. An humble beginning it was, in very truth, but then were laid the foundations of a school system that has no superior in Connecticut, and which is the joy and pride of its devoted adherents. In 1834 Peter McDermot, a brother of the first pastor, opened a school in the sacristy of Christ's church. He was followed by Mrs. Rosanna Toole, who gathered her pupils at her house, on the corner of Fair and Wooster streets. Her school was afterwards moved to Church street. In 1838 a school was conducted in the vestry of Christ's church by a Mr. John Smith. In 1848 a Mr. Looby and Miss Elizabeth Meagher took charge of the school, which had been opened on the ground floor of St. Mary's church. On September 19, 1849, Patrick Morrissey, a name held in veneration in New Haven, began his career as a teacher here. He was "then a vigorous young man just from Tipperary county, Ireland, who in his career of twenty years has taught the greater part of the young men of New Haven, some of them priests to-day." The status of the school conducted by Mr. Morrissey and Miss Meagher, who became Mrs. Morrissey, was defined in a "report of the Board of School Visitors of the First School Society of New Haven, at the annual school meeting, held at the Lancasterian school-house, October 5, 1850."

"The board have twice," said the report, "within the last three months visited the two schools, one for boys and the other for girls, of the Catholic denomination, which are under the general supervision of Rev. Mr. O'Reilly, and which are kept beneath the audience room of the Catholic church. The committee were, of course, aware that they had no legal rights there, but they doubted not that they would be kindly received and afforded every opportunity desired for such observations as would either gratify their curiosity or afford them information. The superintendent expressed himself not only willing to comply with our request to see his little flock, but was highly gratified that we had made it. Our first visit was so satisfactory that we obtained the consent of Mr. Lovell, of the Lancasterian school, to unite with us in a second and more thorough examination. We found the higher classes in both of the schools to be in a most excellent condition and far surpassing our expectations. In grammar, reading, spelling, speaking and defining there was throughout the exercises great promptitude and surprising accuracy. One little girl, between four and five years of age, took her station at the maps and passed most triumphantly a close examination in geography, answering correctly for some fifteen or twenty minutes nearly every question put to her. The teacher of the girls' school is Miss Eliza Meagher, and the teacher of the boys' school is Mr. Patrick Morrissey. These accomplished instructors were educated in Ireland, their native country."

The child who went through the ordeal so successfully, was Miss Nellie McGuire, for many years a teacher in the public schools of New Haven, and leading soprano singer of St. Patrick's choir.

On May 12, 1852, four Sisters of Mercy, of whom Sister M. Camillus was Superior, arrived at New Haven from Providence, brought hither by the Rev. Edward J. O'Brien, pastor of St. Mary's parish. They assumed charge of the girls' school, while Mr. Morrissey continued in charge of the boys' until July 20, 1860. The first home of the Sisters was on George street, near Broad. They remained here until the summer of 1854, when they took up their residence in a new convent adjoining old St. Mary's church on Church street. In the summer of 1875 they took up their abode in a house near the new St. Mary's. In July, 1860, the Sisters assumed charge of both boys and girls. The basement of the new St. Mary's church became the school in the fall of 1875, and in the following year a dwelling in the neighborhood was secured in which the school was continued.

The first Catholic cemetery of New Haven was a part of Christ's church lot, near the corner of York street and Davenport avenue. Here the Catholics of New Haven were interred until 1851. On June 28th, of this year, Mr. Bernard O'Reilly purchased from Mr. Gerard Hallock, at one time editor of the New York *Journal of Commerce*, a parcel of land near the "West Bridge," avowing it as the intention to dispose of it in small lots. The "small lots" proved to be cemetery lots, to the chagrin of Mr. Hallock, who was noted for his hostility to the Catholic church. This tract of land was blessed as St. Bernard's cemetery on September 1, 1851. In 1858 an additional tract of eighteen acres was purchased, which, with a small piece of land secured in August, 1876, made a cemetery of about twenty-five acres. On November 22, 1887, the deeds to the Bronson farm were conveyed to Rev. John Russell, who had purchased it for cemetery purposes in the name of the corporation. This tract of land contains fifty-two acres and lies southwest of the city and town boundary line in the town of Orange, and the price asked was $10,000. On June 22, 1888, the new cemetery received the name of St. Lawrence's cemetery; it was solemnly blessed on Sunday, October 4, 1890, by Bishop McMahon, Rev. B. W. Bray preaching the discourse.

In the summer of 1851 the Rev. Edward J. O'Brien[1] became the pastor of St. Mary's in succession to the Rev. Philip O'Reilly. He had as assistants the Rev. Bernard Tevin, Rev. John Sheridan, who had been commissioned to build St. Patrick's church, and Rev. Matthew Hart. On April 18, 1858, Bishop McFarland visited St. Mary's church and administered the sacrament of Confirmation to over 300 persons.

In 1868 negotiations were begun for a site for a new church. The old church had become the centre of commercial firms, and in consequence had become ill suited as a place for divine worship. A number of sites were in-

---

[1] Father O'Brien was the first priest of the diocese to receive ordination at St. Mary's Seminary, Baltimore, Md. He was ordained by Archbishop Eccleston in 1850.

ST. MARY'S CHURCH,
New Haven, Conn.

spected, among them one on the corner of Elm and High streets, another on Meadow street, and a third on the corner of Elm and York streets. The first of these was almost purchased, but Bishop McFarland's objection to the location brought the negotiations to an end. The site on which the church was subsequently built was then secured in a manner thus related by a local writer:

"There is some disagreement as to the circumstances attendant on the purchase of the lot on which the church was in reality afterwards built. According to one story Mr. John Kennedy, of Branford, had something to do with the negotiations. Another, which is worth giving in detail, is to the following effect: As soon as Father O'Brien learned positively that he could not obtain the Elm street lot, he sorrowfully turned his steps towards the City Hall, where he met City Clerk William Downes, who was the only Catholic lawyer in the city at the time. He told Mr. Downes his story. The latter thought a while, and then turning to the priest inquired, 'Why don't you buy that lot on Hillhouse avenue, next to Dr. Hillhouse's place? It is the prettiest spot in the city for a church, and not many years will pass by before it will be one of the most convenient for the Catholics of St. Mary's.' Father O'Brien answered that there was no sense in talking of that lot, for the residents would not permit the erection of a church there. Mr. Downes suggested that they go over to the avenue and look at the lot. They agreed upon its desirability. 'Now,' said Mr. Downes, 'you agree to take the lot if I secure it?' Father O'Brien so agreed. The city clerk immediately approached the agent who had the sale of the lot. The agent inquired whether Mr. Downes intended to build immediately, and was answered in the affirmative. The price was agreed upon. Mr. Downes drew up a deed, brought back to the agent $100, and thus sealed the bargain."

This lot had been transferred by Dr. Hillhouse to Chauncey O. Crosby on February 11, 1867, with this proviso in the deed: "This deed is, however, on the express condition that said Crosby, his heirs and assigns, shall not hereafter at any time erect or maintain dwelling houses or buildings for manufacturing purposes upon that part of said land which fronts upon Temple street, nor more than two dwelling houses upon that portion of said land which fronts upon Hillhouse avenue." The records show that the property was transferred by Mr. Crosby to William Downes on June 13, 1868, with the above provision, and that he conveyed it to St. Mary's parish on June 15, 1868, the conditions remaining the same. The price paid was $16,000. A building committee, comprising Charles Atwater, Francis Donnelly, John and Patrick Maher, P. Wood, M. Fahy, J. McLaughlin and Edward Downes was immediately organized, and the services of James Murphy, architect, secured. The ground plan of the church was accepted on June 27th. The sentiment of the neighborhood was opposed to the erection of the church. It was feared that the seclusion it had so long enjoyed, and which was so much desired, would be broken in upon by the crowds who would attend divine worship, and so powerful was this influence that many Catholics so far yielded as to suggest other sites. Wiser counsels, however, prevailed. At a meeting, on

September 15, 1868, at which Bishop McFarland presided, it was decided that not more than $120,000 should be expended on the contract. It was a stupendous undertaking for the parish, and fears were entertained as to the success of the enterprise. It was the wish of some of the parish that the administration of affairs be placed in the hands of a religious congregation, and, on May 8, 1869, Judge William Robinson suggested to Bishop McFarland, Father Hecker and Father O'Brien the advisability of the Paulists being called to assume charge.

The construction of the church began under the supervision of Father O'Brien, and the corner-stone was laid on September 22, 1870, by Bishop McFarland in the presence of thirty priests from this and neighboring dioceses and of several thousand spectators. The preacher on the occasion was Very Rev. I. T. Hecker, of New York. Among the prominent guests were the Rev. Dr. Bacon of Center church, President Woolsey of Yale College, Judge Bradley, Charles Atwater, Mayor Lewis and ex-Mayor Welch. The assemblage contributed $906.

The work of construction then ceased by order of Bishop McFarland. The magnitude of the work discouraged Father O'Brien, and knowing his want of capacity as a financier, he urged the Order of Preachers, the Dominicans, to take charge of the parish. In May, 1872, Father O'Brien relinquished the heavy burden, and the Rev. Patrick A. Murphy became the pastor of St. Mary's. In July of that year work on the church was resumed, the people co-operating enthusiastically with the new pastor. A series of monthly collections inaugurated brought into the parish treasury over $1,000 a month for some time. At length the church, one of the finest in New England, was dedicated on October 25, 1874. At this time there were five Catholic parishes in the city, St. Mary's, St. Patrick's, St. John's, St. Francis' and St. Boniface's. Following the ceremony of dedication, Pontifical Mass was celebrated by Right Rev. Bishop O'Reilly, of Springfield. The assisting clergymen were Very Rev. James Hughes, who, after the death of Bishop McFarland, had been appointed Administrator of the diocese, assistant priest; Rev. Hugh Carmody, deacon; Rev. James Fagan, sub-deacon; Rev. Edward J. O. Brien and Rev. Matthew Hart, deacons of honor; Rev. Thomas Griffin, of Springfield and Rev. Francis O'Keefe, masters of ceremonies. The bishops and priests in attendance and assisting at the ceremony were:

> Right Rev. Bishop O'Reilly, Springfield, Mass.
> "      "       " Lynch, Charleston, S. C.
> Very Rev. James Hughes, V. G., Hartford.
> "      " Wm. Quinn, New York.
> Rev. Dr. Carmody,
> " James Finnegan,
> " Matthew Hart
> " Frank O'Keefe,
> " Patrick H. Murphy,      New Haven.
> " P. Mulholland,
> " James Fagan,
> " John McMahon,
> " Thomas Lynch,
> " E. J. O'Brien, Middletown.

Rev. Thomas Griffin, Springfield.
  " J. F. Campbell, D D., North Manchester.
  " T. Synnott, Bridgeport.
  " Patrick J. O'Dwyer, Ansonia.
  " Peter Smith, Norwalk.
  " Dr. McGlynn, St. Stephen's church, New York.
  " James Lynch, Waterbury.
  " Charles McCallian, Ansonia.
  " H. Brady, Naugatuck.
  " E. Gaffney, Thomaston.

The sermon was preached by Right Rev. Bishop Lynch, Charleston, S. C. Taking his text from Hebrews xiii. 10, the preacher began by complimenting the people of the parish on the beauty of their church and the generosity and faith they had manifested in building it. All had done their part—their late pastor who had the courage to begin the work, and the younger man, his successor, to whom he had transferred the task of completing it. All had contributed of their means. The widow had given her mite, and the little children what they could bring. The day was a joyful one for them now that they took possession of a church which was more beautiful than any other in the diocese. The preacher then said that sacrifice was the crowning act of all true religion, and had been so from the earliest times. Prayers could be and were shared by others than God, but to Him alone could sacrifice be offered. Sacrifice was the distinctive mark of the Church, and therefore from the earliest ages, in the Catacombs, in the far East, every church had its altar. Though nothing could add to the dignity of that sacrifice, which was the same under the dome of St. Peter's as in the rude chapel of the poor missionary, it was nevertheless fitting that beautiful churches should be built. In an eloquent passage, the preacher spoke of the myriad stars that adorned the heavens, and were to us as we gazed upon them lamps of lights; so to the saints and angels in paradise looking upon the world, foul and dark with sin and evil, the churches appeared like stars amid the blackness.

In the evening, Right Rev. Bishop Lynch was celebrant at the vesper service. The Rev. Dr. McGlynn, of New York, was the preacher. His text was the following: "Truly this is the house of God and the gate of heaven."

After the erection of the church, the work of completing St. Francis' Orphan Asylum devolved upon Father Murphy. He had charge also of St. Bernard's cemetery. "But while his youthful energy was laughing at the heat of the fray, and while great and delicately manipulated real estate transactions were on his hands, there came the great financial panic. The sources of the church's income almost dried up. His ability was of no avail. His eyes lost their lustre and his cheeks paled. Night and day for some years longer he struggled with the frightful incumbrance of debt, then about $165,000."

Father Murphy died on May 19, 1879. The impressive funeral services were held in St. Mary's church on the 21st. The officiating clergymen were: Rev. Father Lynch, of Thorndike, Mass., celebrant; Rev. Fathers O'Keefe,

Harty, O'Connell and Dougherty as deacon, sub-deacon, and masters of ceremonies, respectively. Rev. L. Walsh, of Waterbury, delivered the panegyric.

The successor of Father Murphy was the Rev. Patrick P. Lawlor, who assumed charge of St. Mary's parish on Sunday, June 29, 1879. Father Lawlor was an exemplary and energetic priest. Few priests in the diocese possessed greater executive ability. He was immediately confronted with an enormous debt. He was no visionary, or dreamer, or sentimentalist. Of an exceedingly practical bent of mind, he employed all his energies to the diminishing of the indebtedness. The first step to this end was the gentle forcing of the bankers to reduce their rate of interest from 7 to 5 per cent. Every year witnessed a diminution of the financial burden. But the weight of seven years of arduous and exacting labor brought his pastorate and his life to an end. Father Lawlor died on March 20, 1886. Funeral services the most imposing were held in St. Mary's church on the 23rd. Bishop McMahon presided at the ceremony. The officers of the Mass of requiem were:

> Celebrant—Rev. J. Cooney, New Haven.
> Deacon—Rev. P. Mullholland, New Haven.
> Sub-Deacon—Rev. J. A. Mulcahy, Waterbury.
> Master of Ceremonies—Rev. J. E. Dougherty.
> Chanters—Rev. T. Kennedy, Rev. John Fagan, Rev. J. Joynt.

The Rev. M. A. Tierney, of New Britain, preached the funeral sermon, of which the following is a brief extract:

"I have known Father Lawlor for nineteen years, ever since his ordination. The first of his priestly labors were spent among you in St. John's parish. Many of you here to-day remember him and know him as well as I do. I need not speak to you of his labors in Mystic, Rockville, and New London. The same noble characteristics which marked him here ever followed him throughout his sacerdotal life.

"When it became necessary for some one to take charge of this church, there was not a priest in the diocese who was willing to take upon himself the burden. You may then judge for yourself of Father Lawlor's priestly character when he was willing to respond to the call of God, leave a comparatively comfortable life, which he had made so by his indefatigable labors, and come here to St. Mary's, upon which such an enormous debt rested. For the last seven years, therefore, he has labored among you with a success that few men could attain. His one ruling thought was to liquidate this debt. Is it any wonder that he succumbed under this heavy load? Many there are who look upon a priest from a worldly point of view. They look to his oratorical powers, his talents, etc. But few there are who look to the inward life of a priest. He has his sorrows and his joys. His heart is filled with heavenly comfort when he beholds the flock intrusted to his care following out the truths which are expounded to them. He is filled with sorrow when he sees the little ones growing up without faith, and when he knows that before God he is responsible for them. In conclusion, I would ask you to pray for the repose of the soul of Rev. Father Lawlor, because of the awful responsibilities that were his. But I would have you pray not without hope."

After the death of Father Lawlor, the Rev. Michael Daly, now of Thomaston, administered the affairs of the parish until the arrival of the Dominican Fathers on May 16, 1886. On that date, St. Mary's passed under a new *regime*, a new era in its history was entered upon. On the feast of St. Joseph the sons of St. Dominic began their career in New Haven. Their first public service was a solemn High Mass, with the Rev. Father Hartigan as celebrant, the Rev. Father Kent as deacon, and the Rev. Father O'Connell as sub-deacon. The sermon was preached by the Rev. Father Lilly, and was in part as follows:

"Last Sunday, my friends, it was announced to you by your acting pastor that the Bishop had given over this church and parish to the Dominican Fathers, and that they would make their first public appearance among you to-day. In accordance with that announcement we are here to-day to take formal possession of the church and to begin the work of our spiritual ministrations in the parish. We have been called here by your Bishop, not for the purpose of remedying any defect in the administration of previous pastors, for no defect has ever been attributed to them, except perhaps an excessive zeal which sapped the foundation of their health and brought at least two of them to premature graves. But if this be a fault, surely it is a noble one in a priest. How can the change be construed into a reflection on the temporary government of your late acting pastor, for all the evidence goes to prove that he worthily emulated the energy and zeal of his predecessors and discharged the delicate functions of his vicariate with rare tact and prudence. Far be it from us to utter any words on this occasion other than those of commendation of the zealous and worthy men who have gone before us. On the contrary, the very first duty that we would inculcate among you is that of constantly and gratefully remembering the arduous labors of those devoted priests.

"No, my friends, the presence of a religious order in New Haven is not due to any such narrow-minded views as those to which I have referred. The counsels that called us to this diocese and to this parish were cast in a larger mould. Catching his inspiration from the encyclicals of the Sovereign Pontiff himself, your chief pastor has concluded that it would be to the interest of religion in his diocese to secure the co-operation of another religious order, whose members would hold themselves ever in readiness to assist him and his devoted clergy in the great work of caring for the souls committed to his charge, and in making his choice amongst the different religious organizations, I hope I may be pardoned the seeming egotism in asserting that he chose wisely in selecting that grand old order, whose record during six centuries of the church's history has gained for itself the proud distinction, the glorious title of 'The Order of Truth,' upon whose teachings the greatest of modern popes relies to bring back the world from the mazes of extravagance and error to the pure, simple, yet sublime, precepts of the Gospel. Whether for weal or woe, however, the choice has been made, and though there may be some who might doubt as to whether your Bishop has chosen wisely, there is not, in the diocese of Hartford, an individual, knowing the man, who would dare assert that he has not chosen conscientiously. And though we are comparative strangers to you here in New Haven, we are well known in other portions of the diocese. During the last two decades our Fathers have been called by various pastors to assist them in their labors by giving missions amongst their people, and I am vain enough to believe that our position amongst you to-day is in some measure at least an acknowledgment and a recognition of the work that we have done.

"Your Bishop has been frank enough to declare that he expects 'great results' from this new foundation of the Dominican Fathers in his diocese. Henceforward it will be our highest aim and our chief ambition to bring those hopes of our common Father to their fullest and maturest realization. But to succeed in this we need the co-operation of the people; and in assuming the burden to-day—for we do not conceal from ourselves the fact that it is a burden whose weight is charged with having borne two of your pastors to untimely graves—in assuming this burden we are sustained by the glowing reports which come to us from every quarter of the admirable disposition and spirit of the people of this parish."

When the Dominican Fathers assumed charge of St. Mary's parish in May, 1886, the indebtedness was over $150,000; on January 1, 1888, it was

$130,000; on January 1, 1886, it had been reduced to $120,000. In 1889 the old Church street property was sold for $55,000, which, being applied to the debt, reduced it to $65,000. After thirteen years of arduous and self-sacrificing labor the indebtedness has been reduced to $21,000. In the meantime, the chapel property has been acquired at an outlay of $12,500, and is free from debt.

The population of St. Mary's parish is about 5,000 souls, chiefly Irish and their descendants. The priests who serve the parish are Very Rev. Hugh F. Lilly, O.P., P.G., Vicar; Revs. J. C. Gilroy, O.P., T. H. Justin, O.P., L. J. Lockingen, O.P., M. A. McClellan, O.P.

## ST. PATRICK'S PARISH,

### NEW HAVEN.

ST. PATRICK'S parish is a portion of the original mission established in New Haven by the Rev. James McDermot in 1832. The formation of St. Patrick's parish was the earliest division of St. Mary's, the eldest of the New Haven parishes. In 1851, the Rev. E. J. O'Brien, pastor of St. Mary's, in anticipation of the approaching needs of the lower part of the city, purchased the site upon which stand the present church, parochial residence and schools. The land having been secured, Bishop O'Reilly appointed the Rev. John Sheridan an assistant to Father O'Brien, but with the commission also to build the new church. The work on the church progressed rapidly, and the corner-stone was laid on August 31, 1851.

A contemporary thus wrote of this interesting event:

"NEW HAVEN, September 1, 1851.

"Yesterday was a day long to be held in grateful remembrance by the Catholics of this city. The imposing ceremony of laying the corner-stone of a new church was performed according to the ancient usage and solemn rites of the church of God. At three o'clock in the afternoon, a large procession was formed at St. Mary's church, Church street, headed by a cross-bearer and numerous acolytes, bearing lighted tapers, followed by the children of the female and male schools, the Rev. clergy of the city, the choir of St. Mary's, members of the Hibernian and Montgomery Societies, and the Catholic population generally. It proceeded through several streets to the site of the edifice about to be erected, where was performed, by the Right Rev. Dr. O'Reilly, assisted by the clergy, the sacred rite of blessing the foundation and laying the corner-stone, in which were deposited several American coins of recent date, and a manuscript in Latin, of which the following is a literal translation:

✠

"'In the name of Our Lord Jesus Christ. Amen.

"'In the year of our Lord 1851, the thirty-first day of August, the twelfth Sunday after Pentecost, in the seventh year of the Pontificate of our Holy Father Pius the Ninth, in the first year of the Episcopacy of Bernard O'Reilly, Bishop of Hartford, in the seventy-sixth year of the Independence of the United States, Millard Fillmore being President of the United States, Thomas H. Seymour being Governor of the State of Connecticut, Aaron N. Skinner being Mayor of this city, (New Haven); this, the first stone of this new temple, was laid in honor of God, under the invocation of St. Patrick, by the aforesaid Bishop of Hartford, James Fitton, Edward J. O'Brien, Bernard Tevin, John Sheridan, assisting priests—the members of the Hibernian and Montgomery Societies, besides a great concourse of Catholic people and others, being present. Sidney M. Stone, of this city, architect.'

REV. JOHN D. COYLE.

REV. MICHAEL J. DALY.

REV. JOHN RUSSELL P.R.

REV. JEREMIAH CURTIN.

REV. WILLIAM J. DULLARD.

"The ceremonies being over, the bishop and priests ascended the platform, and taking for his text the passage of Scripture embraced in the 10th to the 22nd verses of the 28th chapter of Genesis, the bishop preached a most eloquent and impressive discourse. He observed that the passage he had read was the record of the first dedication of a place for the worship of Almighty God. He traced the historical records of the blessing of places and things to be used in divine worship as contained in Holy Writ; it has been observed in the Christian church by sacred rite since the first dawn of freedom, in the same manner and form as his audience had witnessed on the present occasion. He explained the doctrine which will be preached and maintained in the temple about to be built. The religion which there will be taught, will be the religion which received its commission from the Son of God. The religion which alone of all others has converted and civilized the world with no other weapons but those of its Divine Master, Truth and Faith.

"But it would be impossible to give even a synopsis of his masterly discourse with anything like justice to the Right Rev. Prelate. It occupied about three-quarters of an hour in delivery, and was listened to with the greatest attention by the vast audience, which was estimated by good judges as near seven thousand persons.

"The choir having sung in an excellent manner 'Hail Glorious Apostle,' the *Te Deum Laudamus* and several other chants of the church, and the bishop having given the solemn benediction, the vast concourse retired with grateful hearts; nothing occurred to disturb the solemnity of the occasion.

"The church is to be built in the style of the eighth century—the Romanesque—and is expected to be ready for divine service by Christmas day.

"This morning the Right Rev. Bishop, assisted by the Rev. Messrs. O'Brien and Tevin, consecrated with solemn rite and ceremony the new Catholic cemetery. It is beautifully situated on the northern bank of a small river, which forms the southern boundary of the city."

The corner-stone laid and the foundations finished, Father Sheridan was succeeded by the Rev. Matthew Hart, who had also been an assistant at St. Mary's until December, 1852, when he took up his residence among his new parishioners. Father Hart himself is authority for the statement that he offered the first Mass said within the limits of the present parish on December 19, 1852. With the Rev. Michael O'Farrell, Father Hart was ordained subdeacon, deacon and priest on July 16, 19 and 20, 1851, respectively. Upon his appointment to St. Patrick's the work of construction was prosecuted with vigor until the church was ready for dedication. This event took place on October 9, 1853. The ceremony was performed by Archbishop Bedini, Papal Nuncio to Brazil, assisted by Bishop Fitzpatrick of Boston, Bishop Timon of Buffalo and Bishop O'Reilly. Archbishop Bedini celebrated Pontifical Mass, at which the Bishop of Boston pronounced the discourse. At Vespers in the afternoon, the Bishop of Hartford preached, and in the evening a discourse was delivered by Bishop Timon. The church was 120 by 65 feet and was built of brown-stone. At the time of the dedication, the parish numbered about 1500 souls.

Father Hart continued his arduous labors, reducing the indebtedness and assiduously guarding the spiritual interests of his increasing flock. He erected the pastoral residence, two school buildings, the first in 1853 and the second in 1858, and the convent in 1870. In 1867, the desire of his heart was realized, the wishes of his people were fulfilled. The church was freed from financial encumbrance and was ready for consecration. This ceremony was performed by Archbishop McCloskey, of New York, on October 15th of the above year, assisted by two other bishops, in the presence of a large attendance of the clergy and laity.

In January 1875, a fire destroyed the roof of the church and severely damaged the interior of the edifice. The church was practically rebuilt and is a mixture of Gothic and Romanesque styles of architecture. Father Hart did not live to witness the completion of the church. Having been taken ill in the latter part of June, 1876, he went to St. Vincent's hospital, New York, on July 5th, where he suddenly expired on the morning of the 9th, in the fiftieth year of his age. "The announcement of the death of their beloved pastor was received with the most touching demonstrations of grief by his parishioners in New Haven. He had endeared himself to them by every tie that can bind a priest to his people, and no one but a Catholic can fathom the unbounded love which a Catholic people hold for a priest to whom they have become attached. He lives but for them and their welfare ; he knows every one of them personally and is at once their father, brother, friend, physician and counsel; he has joined them in the holy bonds of matrimony; he has baptized their children and watched with the zealous care of a pastor the young souls committed to his guidance; he has comforted them in affliction and wept with them in sorrow; he has rejoiced with them in their joy and gloried in their glory ; he has supported and strengthened the weak and encouraged the strong ; he has buried their dead and assuaged their grief for the loved one gone, by the soft and holy accents of the hope of a blessed reunion above. He has grown into and around their very heart-strings, and the sundering of the earthly tie that binds them to him, causes anguish and heart-rending too deep for expression. Such a priest was Father Matthew Hart—a priest beloved by all and whose memory will be long sacredly cherished with the deepest reverence." [1]

The remains of Father Hart were brought to St. Patrick's on their arrival from New York, but the funeral services were conducted at St. Mary's church, on July 12th. The Solemn Mass of Requiem was celebrated by Very Rev. James Hughes, assisted by Rev. James Lynch of Waterbury as deacon, Rev. P. Mullholland of New Haven as sub-deacon and Rev. Francis O'Keefe of Middletown as master of ceremonies. Bishop Galberry and Bishop Hendricken were present in the sanctuary. The funeral oration was pronounced by the Rev. Hugh Carmody of New Haven in the course of which he said : "For five and twenty years he labored among you with a success which few men can expect, and we take it as a sign that God's blessing was on his labor. To all of us, and to the diocese of Hartford, death has brought a great loss.

"He was sent by Bishop O'Reilly to found a new parish, and God only knows what trials and struggles, sleeplessness and care were his. He had great difficulties to contend with, but he left his parish one of the first in the State. He built his church, parsonage, and school, and was engaged at the time of his death in the project of the orphan asylum. His heart was with the little orphans. During the twenty-five years of his residence here,

[1] Connecticut Catholic Year Book, 1877.

he was esteemed by Protestants and Catholics alike, as a useful and one of our foremost citizens.

"His deep knowledge of canon law and church discipline was soon discovered by the late Bishop McFarland, of blessed memory, who reposed such confidence in his judgment that he made him his theologian, and in that capacity he accompanied the Bishop to the Ecumenical Council at Rome, and only a short time ago the venerable head of the diocese appointed him one of his counsellors."

The successor of Father Hart was Very Rev. James Lynch, Vicar General, who preached his first sermon as pastor of St. Patrick's parish on Sunday, August 6, 1876. With this appointment came also his elevation to the office of Vicar General. Father Lynch was accompanied to New Haven by Rev. John A. Mulcahy, the present Vicar General. Father Lynch's pastorate was of only five months' duration.[1] His final illness began on November 17th, with a stroke of paralysis, occasioned by an accident, which injured his spine. From that date he lingered until December 6th, when he peacefully expired, aged fifty years. A striking coincidence attending the final moments of Father Lynch, was that on the eve of his death, the 5th inst., the Holy Viaticum was administered to him by one of his assistants, Rev. William J. Slocum, whom nearly twenty six years before he had himself baptized in Winsted, while there shortly after his ordination. The funeral services were held at St. Mary's church on Saturday, the 9th, the following clergymen officiating:

*Celebrant*--Rev. Thomas Synnott, Bridgeport.
*Deacon*--Rev. Luke Daly, New Britain.
*Sub-deacon*--Rev. E. J. O'Brien, Middletown.
*Master of Ceremonies*--Rev. W. A. Harty, New Haven.

Present in the sanctuary with a large assemblage of priests were Bishop Galberry, of Hartford, and Bishop Lynch, of Charleston, S. C., the latter of whom pronounced the eulogy on the departed priest. Bishop Lynch said in part: "Sorrow has fallen on your community. One of the chief churches of this city has lost its beloved pastor; the body of the clergy has lost a reverend brother and one of its brightest ornaments; the diocese loses its kind Vicar General. . . . Shall I tell you of his call to the service of the altar; how that young heart answered the promptings of Divine grace and from his earliest years devoted himself to God, to the service of His church? . . . The day came to him, as it came to us, his brethren of the clergy, when in the sanctuary he lay prostrate before the altar and offered to God all the days of his life to do His work. And he never drew back. . . . Shall I speak of the twenty-six years of his priesthood or of his character for earnest piety? Years ago I was struck with his sweetness of disposition, by his zeal and assiduity in the performance of works of charity. I have seen children's eyes gladden

[1] From Bishop O'Reilly's Journal:
"*1851. March 11.*—Recd. Revd. James Lynch from All Hallows.
"*11.*—Revd. Hugh O'Reilly arrived from the Seminary of All Hallows.
"*31.*—Appointed Revd. James Lynch to the pastoral charge of Birmingham and its dependencies."

as they caught sight of his form, and his untiring exertions in behalf of those little ones, prone to evil, but easily led to good, are matters well known. Wherever he labored he increased the schools and the facilities for teaching his Catholic children the doctrines of our holy faith. Throughout his whole life he sought not distinction nor renown, but what he did seek with all his soul was to fulfill the vows taken at his ordination, and he labored faithfully and zealously among the population to which he was sent. Witness the congregation at Middletown, where for nearly sixteen years he worked tirelessly and gained the hearts of all. Witness the congregation at Waterbury, where for four years he was idolized by the people. And in this city, during his short sojourn, with what love, affection and reverence has he not inspired those to whom he had become as a father!

"But called to his reward, dying in the discharge of his duty, we may mourn for him, but not without hope. Such a life as his is happily terminated with such a death."[1]

The Rev. Jeremiah S. Fitzpatrick became the successor of Father Lynch and entered upon his duties Sunday, December 24, 1876. Father Fitzpatrick brought to his new field of labor reliable judgment, ripe experience acquired from pastoral labors elsewhere and from study and observation and a determination to maintain the high standard of material and spiritual excellence established and sustained by his predecessors. He entered upon his labors confident both of the divine assistance and the co-operation of his people. Success followed his labors, and his pastorate promised the full measure of honor and glory for the Divine Head of the church when a serious and protracted illness compelled his retirement after an administration of five years.

It was during Father Fitzpatrick's pastorate that St. Patrick's remodeled church was dedicated. After its partial destruction by fire in 1875, Father Hart embraced the opportunity to considerably enlarge the edifice and to improve its appearance, both interior and exterior. The work designed and pushed forward by Father Hart was continued vigorously by his successor,

---

[1] In the three years previous to the death of Father Lynch the diocese lost by death sixteen of her ablest and most indefatigable workers, namely :

1. Rev. John Fagan, Stamford, December 5, 1873.
2. Rev. P. McKenna, New Milford, August 27, 1874.
3. Rev. J. B. Reynolds, Jewett City, December 30, 1874.
4. Rev. W. F. O'Brien, Middletown, January 8, 1874.
5. Rev. J. Smyth, Windsor Locks, May 16, 1874.
6. Rev. T. Drea, East Bridgeport, July 11, 1874.
7. Right Rev. F. P. McFarland, Hartford, October 12, 1874.
8. Rev. T. F. Healy, Windsor Locks, August 26, 1875.
9. Rev. Peter Smith, Norwalk, December 20, 1875.
10. Rev. William Hart, Naugatuck, March 10, 1876.
11. Rev. John O'Brien, Hartford, March 27, 1876.
12. Rev. Matthew Hart, New Haven, July 9, 1876.
13. Rev. W. E. Duffy, Portland, August 30, 1876.
14. Rev. F. Duggett, Waterbury, August 29, 1876.
15. Rev. R. O'Gorman, Naugatuck, December 3, 1876.
16. Very Rev. James Lynch, New Haven, December 6, 1876.

Very Rev. Father Lynch. The honor of completing the work so well begun and advanced fell to Father Fitzpatrick. The impressive ceremony of dedication took place on Sunday, January 21, 1877. Bishop Galberry officiated at this ceremony, and at the Pontifical Mass following. At the latter ceremony he was assisted by

> Very Rev. James Hughes, Archpriest
> Rev. H. Carmody, D.D., and Rev. P. J. O'Dwyer, Deacons of Honor.
> Rev. P. A. Murphy, Deacon.
> Rev. P. Kennedy, Sub-deacon.
> Rev. E. J. O'Brien and Rev. J. A. Mulcahy, Masters of Ceremonies.

The Rev. Michael O'Farrell of St. Peter's church, New York, preached the sermon, taking his text from the Apostles' Creed: "I believe in the Holy Catholic Church." In the evening Bishop Galberry officiated at Pontifical Vespers, and Rev. H. Brady, of Ansonia, preached the sermon.

Father Fitzpatrick's assistants at this time were Rev. John A. Mulcahy and Rev. W. J. Slocum.

The first service held in the church after its re-dedication was a " Month's Mind " Mass for the late Very Rev. James Lynch, V. G., which had been postponed owing to the unfinished condition of the church.

Upon the retirement of the Rev. Father Fitzpatrick the parish was administered by the Rev. W. J. Slocum until the appointment of the Rev. John Russell in April, 1883. What with the erection of new schools, the liquidation of the parish's indebtedness, the supervision of the great cemetery interests of the Catholics of New Haven, and the guarding of the manifold spiritual interests entrusted to his care, Father Russell has witnessed results that speak of zeal and priestly solicitude on the one hand and of confidence, appreciation and co-operation on the other. St. Patrick's parish is at the zenith of its prosperity, temporal and spiritual, a potent factor in the intellectual, financial and spiritual life of New Haven. Father Russell found an indebtedness of $65,000, which was paid within ten years. A large lot was purchased and a new school building erected upon it, and the old buildings were renovated. The debt incurred by these improvements has also been liquidated. A handsome marble altar and new stations of the cross have been erected in the church. An extensive addition has been built to the convent, so that this structure is one of the most imposing convents in the diocese.

The schools of St. Patrick's parish enjoy the distinction of being under the direction of the School Board of the city of New Haven. One thousand one hundred and eight pupils are taught by sixteen Sisters of Mercy, of whom Sister M. Patricia is the Directress.

Father Russell is one of the permanent rectors of the diocese. His colaborers are Rev. E. O'Connell, Rev. Jeremiah Duggan, Rev. M. J. O'Connor.

## ST. JOHN'S PARISH,

### New Haven.

ST. JOHN'S PARISH is the second offshoot of the mother parish, St. Mary's. In 1857 Rev. John Smith, of Danbury, was appointed by the Very Rev. Administrator, William O'Reilly, to proceed to New Haven and collect funds for the erection of a church on the site of old Christ's church, destroyed by a conflagration in 1848. The growth of the Catholic population in that section of the city rendered a new house of worship necessary. Moreover the people were desirous of seeing a church erected on the spot hallowed by the memories of the old historic edifice. Arrived at New Haven, Father Smith took up his residence with Father O'Brien at St. Mary's.

Entering upon his mission with enthusiasm, and cordially assisted by his parishioners, Father Smith began the second period of his pastorate when the corner-stone of the church was laid on Sunday afternoon, April 18, 1858, under the title of St. John, the Evangelist. The Catholic population, with many others, formed in procession at St. Mary's church and proceeded to the site of the new church, where the stone was placed in position, in the presence of 12,000 people. Bishop McFarland performed the ceremony and preached on the occasion, selecting as his text the words of the royal psalmist: "Unless the Lord build the house, in vain do they labor who build it." The donations of the assemblage amounted to over $1,000. On Sunday, September 28th, of the same year St. John's church was dedicated by Bishop Mc-Farland. The church was the first of the kind built in the United States, being of the Celtic style of architecture, which prevailed throughout Ireland in the 11th and 12th centuries. The architect was P. C. Keeley. Father Smith's pastoral relations with St. John's were severed by death, in 1864, the Rev. Hugh Carmody, D.D., becoming his successor. The church had been built, but much was to be done towards furnishing it. Dr. Carmody put in stained glass windows, erected the main altar and a commodious gallery. In 1874 the convent building on South street was built at an expense of $30,000, exclusive of the cost of the site. The pastoral residence was also erected during his administration at an expenditure of $15,000. Dr. Carmody was extensively interested in educational matters, and the South street school, built and owned by the parish, was leased to the school district. He purchased, also, the church known as "Hallock's church," which became the church of the Sacred Heart, with Father Sheffrey as its first rector. Dr. Carmody's fourteen years' pastorate came to an end on July 16, 1878, when he received notification of his appointment to St. Mary's parish, New Britain, as the successor to the Rev. Luke Daly. He preached his farewell sermon to his sorrowing parishioners on Sunday, the 28th, saying:

"My relations to the people of this parish have been so intimate and endearing during the past fourteen years that it is not surprising that there should be pain at parting. I do not desire to leave you, but it is the wish of the bishop, who makes changes and does what he thinks best for the interest of the diocese. I cannot look forward to such ease and comfort in my new station, for although much has been done by the saintly priest who has passed away, there is much yet to do. I can only offer up my prayers in your behalf. In the fourteen years of my life with you I have always been treated with love and kindness. The greatest harmony has existed between us. Twenty years ago, this year, St. John's church was first opened for divine worship, and all its prosperity and all it has achieved is owing to God's blessing. Your new pastor has been placed over you by the bishop, and, with your hearty co-operation in all good works, God's blessing will be upon you. God has wonderfully blessed your parish, and I would ask you to give your prayers, your powers, your interest and your sympathies to the schools of the parish. The bishop says there are no better schools in the diocese. In a few years we elder ones will have passed away, and the children are the only hope of Catholicism in the future. Indeed, I do not know what to say on this occasion. Usually, I am not at a loss for words, but to-day I am. The majority of my priestly life has been spent in this parish. You have aided my work in all ways. You have given what I have asked, and given freely and generously. You have upheld my hand and my heart in all good works. I wish I could say more to you to day, but I cannot do so From my inmost heart I pray God to bless you, and your families, and the church of God—the church so dear to us all."

In succession to Dr. Carmody came Rev. John McMahon, Rev. John Cooney, Rev. Bernard Bray and the present rector, Rev. John D. Coyle—all animated with zeal to extend the kingdom of God on earth, all fully cognizant of their responsibilities, devoted to the interests of Christian education, conservative yet progressive—they have achieved successes in the great cause of the Divine Master, that redound to the welfare of souls, and to the honor of the parish whose influence is ever expanding. Father Cooney assumed charge of St. John's in December, 1878. His administration was marked by mildness and pastoral solicitude for all, but especially for the children to whom his heart went out in its fulness.

In February, 1887, Rev. Bernard Bray succeeded to the pastorate of St. John's. The sacristy was enlarged and the church redecorated during his pastorate. The present rector, Father Coyle, assumed charge in May, 1895. Since his advent the school has undergone a complete transformation, the convent has been renovated and the grounds beautified. A piece of land, north of the rectory, has been purchased, which enhances the value of the church property. The schools of the parish maintain their efficiency, and the pupils go out therefrom well equipped to engage the enemies which so sturdily assail youth upon their entrance into practical life. Success after success has attended the self-sacrificing labors of the devoted pastors of St. John's, but the material achievements were not secured at the sacrifice of higher and holier interests. Societies for mutual aid, religious confraternities, associations for the promotion of the virtue of temperance, institutes for the moral, intellectual and spiritual advancement of youth have been founded, and are accomplishing in a gratifying manner the results anticipated from their organization. Thirteen Sisters of Charity, under the direction of Sister M. Geronimo, are efficient auxiliaries to the pastor in the training of the youth of the parish. Four hundred and fifty-nine children receive daily the benefit of their experience and come under the salutary influence which flows from the presence of a religious garb ; so that the parish, solidly established financially and spiritually, has still brighter prospects in the children who are now being so religiously nurtured.

From 1858, to January, 1890, the number of baptisms in St. John's parish was 8,607 ; for the same period there were 1,543 marriages. The first marriage was that between Cornelius Leonard and Mary Collins, October 3, 1858, and the first baptism recorded was that of James John, son of Maurice and Mary Farraher, September 26, 1858.

Assisting Father Coyle in his parochial labors are Rev. Francis Murray and Rev. James Keating.

## SACRED HEART PARISH,

### New Haven

ON December 20, 1874, the Rev. John McMahon, an assistant in St. John's parish, celebrated the Divine Mysteries in what had been a Congregational and Presbyterian church for twenty-three years.

The cross that surmounted the original structure was raised on December 18, by the Rev. Dr. Carmody and Major Patrick Maher. The church was originally built by the Congregationalists in 1851, and the chapel in the rear in 1852. The chief contributors to the building fund were Girard Hallock, Thomas R. Trowbridge and brothers, Sidney M. Stone and Amos Smith. In 1855, Mr. Hallock purchased the shares of Messrs. Stone and Smith, and in 1864 those also of Messrs. Trowbridge, thus becoming sole owner.

An ecclesiastical society was organized on November 8, 1852, and the two buildings, the South church and the South church chapel, were offered to it for the rental of a barleycorn a year. This nominal rental was faithfully paid until the church passed into other hands. After many vicissitudes the property was transferred to the Dutch Reformed church of New York, a Presbyterian organization, on April 30, 1869. The Board of Domestic Missions paid a rental of $2000 per annum, and the formal transfer was made on October 21, 1874. The property had been in the market for sale, and three days after the transfer to the Board, it was purchased by Rev. Hugh Carmody, D.D., pastor of St. John's parish. On November 10, 1874, he received the deed transferring the property.

In the meantime, Dr. Carmody had been energetic in the endeavor to collect funds sufficient to make the enterprise an assured success. Forty thousand dollars, price down, was the amount asked for the property. The warranty deed was eventually executed and a mortgage secured. Among those who supported Dr. Carmody by suggestion and advice, but, particularly, by financial assistance, were John R. Gildea, Patrick Eagan, Bernard Reilly, John Starrs, Thomas Deskin, Charles McConville, William Kearney, Dr. Barry, Thomas F. Stackpole, Edward Boylan, Michael Herrity, Lawrence Curtis, Thomas Kelley, David O'Donnell, Michael Reynolds, Francis Coyle, Patrick Maher and Martin Kennedy.

The new acquisition was refitted and prepared for Catholic services. It was attended by the clergy of St. John's church until Sunday, February 14, 1875. On that day, the Rev. Stephen P. Sheffrey began his administration as pastor of the newly formed parish. When Father Sheffrey assumed charge of the parish the prospects of a successful pastorate were dark indeed. Not a dollar was there in the treasury, nor was there a parochial residence. His lodgings for a time were in the old South church chapel. It was his mission to unite his people, and to instill a love for the parish that had been formed in honor of Him whose adorable heart had been pierced on Calvary. His it was to assuage the grief that had been caused by the severance of time-honored ties. Twelve months after his arrival, Father Sheffrey secured the house on Columbus avenue, opposite the church, which was used as a pastoral residence until the erection of the present rectory. Exacting were the duties of Father Sheffrey, arduous his labors. The burden became greater than he could bear, and he yielded to its weight. The prospects of success which he had conjured up had faded and the hopes upon which he had builded were shattered. Illness, from which he never recovered, followed, and on October 1, 1881, Father Sheffrey obeyed the final summons. He was "mourned sincerely by a congregation which at last had become unified through his ministrations," wrote one who knew him, "and every member of which loved him for the goodness of a patient heart which had endured much uncomplainingly. His memory remains green as the turf beneath which he sleeps in the churchyard."

In November, 1879, Rev. Thomas Coleman was appointed administrator of the Sacred Heart parish, and in this capacity he served until the appointment of Rev. John A. Mulcahy. To Father Coleman belongs the honor of paying the first thousand dollars of the parish indebtedness. The priests who served with Father Sheffrey as assistants were Rev. Luke Fitzsimmons, Rev. Thomas Mulvaney and the Rev. Thomas Coleman. Serving with Father Coleman during his administration were Rev. J. Dougherty and Rev. R. C. Gragan.

The successor of Father Sheffrey was the Rev. John A. Mulcahy, the present Vicar-General of the diocese, who began his pastorate of four years on November 1, 1881. Father Mulcahy was confronted with an indebtedness of $39,000, but when his pastorate terminated, this burden had been reduced to $14,000. He also added to the parish possessions by the purchase of sufficient land on Columbus avenue for a school and convent. Father Mulcahy was assisted in his parochial labors by Father Coleman and Father Gibbons.

Upon the transfer of Father Mulcahy to Waterbury, the Rev. M. McKeon assumed charge of the parish on January 1, 1886. Evidences of his zeal and success abound. He enlarged and remodeled the church, and decorated the interior in the most artistic manner at an expense of $30,000. The cornerstone of the new addition was laid in May, 1888, by Bishop McMahon, attended by the clergy of all the churches of the city. Rev. Father Mulcahy pronounced the discourse on the occasion. The old church was 64 by 90 feet, and had a seating capacity of 1000. The chapel in the rear was razed, and on its site the walls of an addition were erected, wider than that of the church proper by ten feet, and sixty-five feet in length, making the edifice a total length of 155 feet. The renewed church is in the Romanesque style of architecture. The altar is of the purest marble, is an artistic piece of workmanship, one of the most beautiful in the diocese, and cost $4000. It is made of various kinds of marble, foreign and domestic. The quarries of France and Italy, as well as those of Vermont and Tennessee, furnished its material. It is twenty-five feet from the sanctuary floor to the top of the cross, while the table is twelve feet in length. Father McKeon purchased at a cost of $5500 two lots on Liberty street in the rear of the church, 70 feet on Liberty and 120 feet on Portsea street, upon which he erected a commodious pastoral residence. In 1894 he erected a school that is an honor to the parish and which has few equals in the State; it was blessed in 1895. The handsome convent was built a year later, and blessed in 1897.

Having, in the meantime, liquidated the indebtedness on the church, Father McKeon resolved to solemnly consecrate it forever to the service of God. The impressive ceremony took place on Sunday, September 27, 1889, Bishop McMahon officiating, assisted by Revs. James H. O'Donnell and John D. Coyle, masters of ceremonies; Rev. F. Murphy, thurifer; Rev. J. Lawless, cross-bearer; Rev. J. Synnott, bearer of relics; Rev. P. McAlenney, bearer of holy oils; Rev. B. Bray, deacon of the door. The Pontifical Mass which followed the ceremonies of consecration was celebrated by Right Rev. Matthew Harkins, D.D., Bishop of Providence, with the following assistants: assistant priest, Very Rev. James Hughes, V. G.; deacon, Rev. P. Mullholland; sub-deacon, Rev. J. Russell; masters of ceremonies, as above. The oration was pronounced by the Rev. Father McCarthy, S. J. Bishop McMahon presided at the Vesper services, and Rev. Richard Burke preached the sermon.

In his parochial labors Father McKeon has been assisted by Rev. W. Gibbons, Rev. William Maher, D.D., Rev. J. Curtin, Rev. R. J. Early. The present assistants are Rev. G. Sinnott and Rev. J. J. Fitzgerald.

A sad occurrence, resulting in the death of a Sister of Mercy, cast a gloom over the parish. On June 29th, of this year (1899), a fire broke out in the convent, during which Sister Mary Aloysius died from suffocation. Twenty Sisters were in the building at the time, but the others escaped injury. The damage to the convent was $3000.

The religious societies attached to the church, and which are accomplishing much for religion are: the Confraternity Society, with a membership of about 300; the Sodality of the Children of Mary, 150; the Holy Angels' Sodality, 300; the Sacred Heart T. A. B. Society, 200; the Sacred Heart Cadets, 180; the Catholic Club, 175; the Holy Name Society, 200; the Junior Holy Name Society, 150; Infants' Sodality, 200; Junior Sodality, 150.

The population of the parish is about 5000 souls.

The material successes that have attended the labors of the rectors of this parish are evidence that its spiritual status is of a high standard, and are eloquent attestations of the fidelity of the people to instruction and of co-operation with their spiritual guides.

REV. EDWARD MARTIN.

REV. CHARLES J. McELROY.

REV. PETER M. KENNEDY.

REV. JOHN CORCORAN

REV. JOHN D. KENNEDY.

## ST. FRANCIS' PARISH,

### New Haven.

NTIL 1867, the Catholics of Fair Haven, so called, attended divine services at St. Patrick's church, the Rev. Matthew Hart, pastor. In that year Father Hart secured a piece of land upon which the first resident pastor of St. Francis' parish, the Rev. Patrick A. Gaynor, built the church. Its dimensions were 100 by 60 feet. After a pastorate of two years Father Gaynor died in 1869, and was succeeded by the Rev. Patrick Mullholland. When Father Mullholland assumed charge of St. Francis parish its population numbered about 1,500 souls. With their young pastor they entered enthusiastically into the work of promoting the great interests of the parish. His will was their law. Obedient to his wishes, even anticipating them often, both forces accomplished results that are visible to-day, and which will serve to keep the memory of Father Mullholland green for generations to come. Active, responding to the demands of his high calling, sparing not himself when the interests of others were at stake, faithful to the promises made to the ordaining prelate, Father Mullholland's career in St. Francis' parish produced results which his colleagues might pardonably envy, and which no doubt merited a benign sentence from the Supreme Pastor when he stood before the Throne to receive judgment. The school and convent, an enlarged and beautifully decorated church, a remodeled rectory, the institution of parochial societies, the purchase of valuable pieces of property, and other works redolent of zeal and priestly solicitude, all are reminders that a strong hand was at the helm. The people of St. Francis' revere his memory; the children, for whom he ever had a father's love, hold his name in benediction; all recognized that when Father Mullholland responded to the final summons, there went forth a devoted friend, a wise counselor, a faithful pastor, one who wore himself out in the service of his Master.

Father Mullholland died in October, 1897. Bishop Tierney celebrated the Pontifical Mass of Requiem, and the Rev. J. Creedon, of Windsor Locks, preached the panegyric.

The Rev. Peter M. Kennedy, the present incumbent, assumed the burdens laid down by his predecessor on October 26th, of the same year. Assisted in the labors of his parish by Rev. D. O'Connor, Rev. W. J. Blake and Rev. D. F. Baker, Father Kennedy not only maintains the parish upon the grade of efficiency established by those who went before, but is increasing its power as a spiritual force in the city. Thirteen Sisters of Mercy, under the direction of Sister M. Bonaventure, render invaluable assistance in instructing 700 children in the parochial school. Here, humanly speaking, are the hopes of the church, the future props of society, and the Sisters, realizing their responsibilities, are faithful to the trust imposed upon them.

## ST. BONIFACE'S (GERMAN) PARISH,

### New Haven.

THE following correspondence which appeared in the New York *Citizen* discloses the fact that harmony did not reign among the early German Catholics of New Haven. It shows that a disturbing element, under the name of religion, sought to sow the seeds of discord among the faithful:

### The German Catholics of New Haven.

In our last number we copied from a contemporary a preamble and resolutions, purporting to express the sentiments of the German Catholics of New Haven. We have since received the following correspondence on the subject:—

GREENWICH STREET, NEW YORK, February 9, 1855.

To the Editor of the Citizen:

Sir—In looking over your good paper, the *Citizen*, of this week, I see a preamble and resolutions purporting to be the wishes of all the German Catholics of New Haven. Sir, perhaps the enclosed true preamble may be worthy of your insertion, and confound these infidels. Yours, etc., A GERMAN CATHOLIC.

NEW HAVEN, February 15, 1855.

To the Editor of the New York Herald:

In your issue of the 30th ult., you published certain resolutions said to have been adopted at a meeting of the "German Roman Catholics" of New Haven. I am sure you will not hesitate to make the correction which justice demands, when I make known to you that it was nothing else than a hypocritical trick to injure us in the estimation of our fellow-Catholics. The accompanying resolutions, as published in the New Haven *Palladium*, and which were adopted by the Catholic Germans, will explain. They read thus:

At a meeting of the Catholic Germans of New Haven, the following preamble and resolutions were unanimously adopted:

"*Whereas*, certain persons calling themselves 'German Roman Catholics,' have wrongfully usurped the right of speaking for us, against our will; and whereas, they have published resolutions in direct opposition to our feelings—said resolutions being drafted by a committee made up of one Jew, one Protestant and one who publicly professes himself to be an infidel, believing all religion 'a humbug,' and adopted by a meeting of the same class of men. Therefore—

"*Resolved*, That we Catholics deny having any part in the proceedings; that we denounce the statements made by them as being wicked and injurious to us; more like 'His blood be upon us and upon our children,' than the sentiments of true Catholics. We despise the hypocrisy of the Jew, infidel or Protestant, who would call himself Roman Catholic for an evil purpose.

"*Resolved*, That we do want a priest who can preach the Gospel to us in our native language, and who will find that we do not yet deny the 'one faith' taught us carefully by our parents, and which we shall never renounce for mammon.

"*Resolved*, That we hail Rev. Mr. Hender's advent among us with joy and gratitude; that Bishop O'Reilly be requested to make this city his residence, and that we shall do everything in our power to sustain him and make him comfortable.

"*Resolved*, That a copy of these resolutions be published in all the papers that circulated the late calumny on our good name.

"Signed on behalf of meeting,

"JOSEPH AUGRICK, President.

"ANDREW KLAFFKI,
"JOHN RATT,
"FREDERICK THESING,
"GASPER FINK,    } Vice-Presidents.

CHRISTIAN GERGEN, Secretary."

The upshot of the former resolutions was this : Bishop O'Reilly sent a priest to take charge of the German Catholics of this city, about two hundred in number. The German Jews and infidels, who are trying to establish a society which would acknowledge no other God than nature, took this amiss. They saw the projected society in danger, and consequently determined to oppose the priest. For this purpose they called a meeting, inviting a great many, whilst they kept the object of the meeting a secret. Some Catholics, myself amongst the number, went there to see what was going on, but when the object leaked out, most of them left, and were it not that a few stopped to watch the proceedings, the brotherhood would have been "alone in their glory." The meeting itself was an admirable burlesque on the use of reason ; and he who would be so foolish as to believe in God, Christ or the Bible, got a place among the long-eared tribe At length, after much trouble and any amount of confusion, three individuals were appointed a committee to draft Roman Catholic resolutions ; and they did draft them.

CHRISTIAN GERGEN, Secretary.

On July 21, 1868, the Rev. H. Wendelschmidt assumed charge of the German Catholics of New Haven. The parishioners assembled in a hall in Gregson Alley for divine services, and here they worshiped every Sunday until 1873. In April of this year St. Boniface's church was begun on a lot which had been previously secured. The corner-stone was laid on May 11, 1873, by Bishop McFarland, the Rev. Dr. Schrader, of New York, preaching the sermon. Father Wendelschmidt's pastorate terminated on December 29, 1873, his successor, the present incumbent, Rev. Joseph Schale, assuming charge on May 15, 1874.

At the formation of the parish its population was about eighty souls ; at present it numbers about 800. St. Boniface school was organized in September, 1896, with 143 pupils. It is conducted by the Sisters of St. Francis, has eight grades, with 163 pupils. In addition to the church, school, convent, and rectory, the parish owns Germania Hall.

The number of baptisms administered during the past three decades was 1773, and the number of marriages solemnized during the same period was 390. The first baptism conferred was that of Wilhelmina Reinpherd, and Joseph Dunbar and Gertrude Jansen were the first to receive the sacrament of matrimony, October 18, 1868.

## ST. LAWRENCE'S PARISH,

### WEST HAVEN.

THE earliest Catholics to settle in this section of New Haven were James, Peter, and Bernard Gaffney, Patrick Morrissey, James and Thomas Leddy, John Slater, Denis Boyle, Edward McCabe, Lawrence Riley, George McDermott, David Monahan, Denis Kennedy, Paul Kehoe, Peter English, Philip Cronan, John Ennis.

The first Mass celebrated in West Haven was said by the Rev. James Larkin, of Milford, in April, 1886, in the Borough Officer's room of Thompson's block, in the presence of about forty persons, though at this time there were about two hundred Catholics in this section. West Haven remained under the jurisdiction of Milford from 1886 until May 1, 1895, when the Rev. J. Curtin was appointed the first resident pastor. Previous to 1886 the people attended Mass at the Sacred Heart church, New Haven, and still earlier at St. John's.

St. Lawrence's church was built by Father Larkin in 1885. The corner-stone was laid in November of that year by Bishop McMahon during a heavy rainstorm in the presence of two thousand people. The clergy present were Rev. Fathers Russell, Lawlor, Maloney, Gibbons, Mulcahy, Mullholland, Smith, Murray, Rogers, and Murphy. The preacher was the Rev. W. A. Harty, of Waterbury. He said in part:

"We are gathered here to-day to witness the solemn exercises of laying the corner-stone of another new church. It is eminently proper that there should be no difference in the ceremony for the church that is built in the village and the most gorgeous cathedral in the world. Each one is entitled to our respect and to our admiration. Each one should have our best wishes and our watchful care. And so may we repeat, 'How terrible is this place, it is no other than the house of God.' It is eminently proper, then, that we should gather here to-day, though the elements are against us, to join in these solemn services, and bid God speed to the people who are so nobly spreading our glorious religion. This is none other than the foundation of the house of God. Here in this church the poor will be as welcome as the rich, and the low will occupy positions as lofty as the high. Here the blessed Gospel will be preached alike to old and young, to the rich and to the poor. Here in this church, the corner-stone of which has been laid to-day, that awful Sacrifice that was transacted on Calvary will be explained, and its truths and lessons expounded. Here will be renewed the old story, and from here the Bread of eternal life will be disseminated. Here, brethren, standing around these unfinished walls, will God's own words be fulfilled: 'Behold, I am with you all ages, even to the consummation of the world.' Again, I say, this is truly God's house, and no gate of bigoted opposition can destroy it. It is the house of God, and not the house of man. The country towns are especially dear to God's heart. It was in Bethlehem, not in Jerusalem, that He was born; in Nazareth, not in imperial Rome, He lived. There is not a village in Connecticut, having twenty Catholic families, that has not a Catholic church. On every hand Catholic churches are springing from the soil. During the six years and five months of the administration of our beloved bishop, half of the one hundred and twenty churches in this diocese have either been built or completely renovated."

The church is 40 by 70 feet, with a spire 130 feet high, and cost $12,000. Over $2,000 was contributed on the occasion of the laying of the corner-stone. The ceremony of dedication took place in 1895.

Among the benefactors of St. Lawrence's parish mention should be made of John Anderson, Edward Kimberley, Donaldson Thompson, and James Graham. Handsome windows were donated by P. Morrissey, S. Boyle, James Gaffney, 1st; James Gaffney, 2d; Bernard Gaffney, Peter Gaffney, Margaret Leddy, Maria, Rose, and Julia Murphy, David Monahan, James McCarthy, Lawrence Reilly, Bernard and Lottie Farrell, and the Rev. James Larkin.

The population at the formation of the parish in 1895 was about 500 souls; it is now about 600, chiefly Irish and their descendants. The number of baptisms conferred from 1895 to 1898 was 83, while 11 marriages were solemnized in the same period.

Attached to St. Lawrence's parish, and attended by its pastor, is St. Joseph's mission, Westville. Previous to the formation of St. Lawrence's parish, the Westville Catholics were attended by the pastors of St. John's, New Haven. The first Mass celebrated in Westville was said by the Rev.

Hugh Carmody, D.D., in 1871, in Franklin Hall, on Fountain street, now St. Joseph's Lyceum and T. A. B. Society Hall. A lot for a new church was purchased on Hill—now Emerson—street from E. W. Cooper for $1,400. Ground was broken in 1872, and the corner-stone was laid in the same year by Bishop McFarland, the Rev. M. Hart preaching the sermon. The cost of St. Joseph's church was $7,500.

The first Mass offered up in the new church was celebrated by the Rev. Dr. Carmody in the fall of 1872. The first baptism recorded is that of Annie T. Powers, and the first to receive the sacrament of matrimony were Thomas Elliott and Annie Mullen, the Rev. P. Keating officiating. Martin Heath and Michael Sarsfield were the first pew-rent collectors.

Dr. Carmody's successor was the Rev. John McMahon, who remained only for a brief period. Rev. John Cooney, his successor, served St. Joseph's five years, during which time he frescoed the church, erected new stations and adorned the edifice with handsome statues. Rev. B. Bray was the next pastor, serving also five years. During his administration new stained-glass windows were put in the church, and concrete walks laid.

The principal benefactors of St. Joseph's parish were the Messrs. Beecher, who donated $300 to the building fund.

## ST. LOUIS' (FRENCH) PARISH,

### NEW HAVEN

THE history of the French Canadian Catholics of New Haven, as an organization, dates from May 25, 1889, when they assembled before the altar in St. Patrick's school to assist at the Holy Sacrifice offered by the Rev. J. E. Bourret. About 600 persons assisted at this Mass. In this year Father Bourret purchased a chapel, which was dedicated by Bishop McMahon in July, 1890. Father Bourret's term of service expired in May, 1890. His successor, the Rev. J. E. Cartier, came in August of this year, and remained as pastor until December, 1897. The priests who served as assistants in St. Louis' parish were Revs. J. E. Cartier, L. Mayeur and J. E. Ferran. The Rev. J. E. Sénésac followed Father Cartier in the pastorate, and in turn was succeeded by Rev. H. Chapdelaine, the present pastor.

The present population of the parish is about 1,000 souls.

## ST. MICHAEL'S (ITALIAN) PARISH,

### NEW HAVEN.

THE Rev. Vincent Asterri, M.A., was the first resident pastor of the Italian Catholics of New Haven. He organized his fellow-countrymen into a parish in 1889. His successors were Rev. Orestes Alussi, Rev. Francis Becherini, Rev. Vincent Sciolla, Rev. Peter Lotti. The present pastor is the Rev. Aloysius Lango. The priests, who have served St. Michael's parish as assistants were Rev. Vitterio Sovilla and Rev. Father Battaglia.

St. Michael's church was dedicated with unusual pomp on Sunday, April 24, 1890. Among the ecclesiastical dignitaries, who graced the occasion by their presence was the Apostolic Delegate, Most Rev. Sebastian Martinelli. He was accompanied by his secretary and the Rev. Francesco Zibolio, of New York, and the Rev. Giacommo Zambero, of Boston, Provincial of the Order of San Carlo Borromeo, and the Rev. Paulo Novati, of Providence, R. I. All the Italian societies of the city with two bands, a drum corps, and a great crowd of people, escorted the distinguished prelate from the station to St. Michael's rectory. The Papal Delegate was received at the depot by Bishop Tierney, Rev. John Russell, Rev. M. McKeon, Rev. John D. Coyle, Rev. John Corcoran, and the rector of St. Michael's church.

Following the ceremonies of dedication a Solemn High Mass was celebrated by the Rev. Orestes Alussi, of New York, assisted by the Rev. James Gambera, the Rev. C. H. Victor Tiene and the Rev. J. P. Donovan, D.D. The discourse was pronounced by the Rev. Paulo Novati. During the vesper services Bishop Tierney administered Confirmation to 150 persons.

During the first year of the parish's existence there were 55 baptisms and 20 marriages. In 1897, the baptisms were 308 and the marriages 165. The Italian population of New Haven is about 11,000.

The limits and regulations of the English-speaking parishes of New Haven are shown by the following circular dispatched by the Very Rev. Administrator in 1878:

MERIDEN, Oct. 19, 1878.

REV. DEAR SIR: —You will please notify your congregation at all the Masses on Sunday, the 20th inst., of the parochial regulations adopted at the late Synod. As applicable to New Haven, they are as follows:

1. The parish limits lately established by our lamented bishop will be strictly observed. These limits are the following:

### LIMITS OF ST. MARY'S PARISH.

St. Mary's parish comprises that part of the city which lies between the east side of Meadow street, commencing at the N. Y. & N. H. Railroad Depot, to the junction of Meadow street with George, the north side of George street and Derby avenue, to the bridge over West river, and thence northerly along West river to town line, the west side of Olive street from the harbor to the junction of Olive street and State street, to Mill river, and thence along Mill river to Lake Whitney.

### LIMITS OF ST. PATRICK'S PARISH.

St. Patrick's parish includes that part of the city which lies between the east side of Olive street from the harbor to the junction of Olive street and State, the southeast side of State to Mill river, and thence southerly to the harbor.

### LIMITS OF ST. JOHN'S PARISH.

St. John's parish embraces that part of the city which is situated between the south side of George street from its junction with Congress avenue, and the south side of Derby avenue to West river, and the northwest side of Congress avenue to West river, with that part of the town of Orange which lies north of the Milford turnpike.

### LIMITS OF SACRED HEART PARISH.

Sacred Heart parish comprises that part of the city which lies between the west side of Meadow street from the New York Depot to the junction of Meadow street with Congress avenue; the south side of Congress avenue to West river; and that part of the town of Orange that is situated south of the Milford turnpike.

CHURCH OF THE ASSUMPTION, B. V. M.
Ansonia.

### LIMITS OF ST. FRANCIS' PARISH.

St. Francis' Parish includes all Fair Haven and the town of North Haven.

2. No pastor or assistant pastor shall administer the sacraments or perform any sacred function in another parish, without the permission of the pastor thereof. From this rule confession alone is excepted.

3. Funerals must be attended by the pastor of the parish in which the deceased lived. The funeral service, unless in prohibited cases, must take place in the parish church.

4. Persons holding sittings in any church may retain the sittings until they can conveniently change. In the meantime they must apply to the pastor of the parish in which they live for the administration of the sacraments and other sacred functions, and no sitting for the future will be rented to a person living outside of the parish.

5. The marriage ceremony must be performed by the pastor of the parish in which the female party resides; and baptism by the pastor of the parish in which the parents reside.

6. No collection shall be made in any parish without the permission of the pastor.

These regulations are now in full force.

VERY REV. T. WALSH, *Administrator.*

## PARISH OF THE ASSUMPTION,

### ANSONIA.

ANSONIA enjoys the distinction of being the youngest town in New Haven county, having been separated from Derby in the spring of 1889. There is a well-grounded tradition that it was visited by priests soon after it became a village in 1845, as some Irish people were attracted here by the promise of employment on the public works. Ansonia remained in the relation of a mission to Birmingham until the pastorate of the Rev. Patrick O'Dwyer. It was attended successively by the Rev. James Lynch, the Rev. John Lynch, the Rev. John Sheridan and the Rev. P. J. O'Dwyer. In 1864 Father Sheridan conceived the design of erecting a church, and to that end purchased a piece of land on Atwater avenue. This project, however, did not mature, and the lot was sold. Nothing daunted, Father Sheridan, in 1866, secured from Phelps, Dodge & Co., the lot on which the old church stands, and generously donated it to the congregation. Encouraged by the possession of so eligible a site, his successor, Father O'Dwyer, resolutely entered upon the work of building a church. Bishop McFarland laid the corner-stone on August 15, 1867, when Rev. T. F. Hendricken preached the sermon. The church was dedicated in 1868. Its entire cost was nearly $20,000. On June 25, 1870, Father O'Dwyer severed his relations with Birmingham and became the first resident pastor of Ansonia, which now began a new epoch in its history. When Father O'Dwyer assumed charge of Ansonia he found 1,000 souls. His first work was the purchase of the house on Factory street which became his residence. Father O'Dwyer's term of service expired in January, 1876. He was followed by the Rev. Hugh T. Brady, who came here from Naugatuck. Among the achievements of Father Brady's pastorate were the enlargement of the church and the erection of the present pastoral residence, and the introduction of the Sisters of Mercy from Meriden, who occupied the former rectory. In the spring of 1886, Father Brady retired from the active duties of the ministry, and a few months later died in New York. He was buried in the West Ansonia cemetery.

His successor, the Rev. Joseph Synnott, became pastor on Holy Thursday, 1886. Father Synnott is signalizing his pastorate by the erection of one of the finest church edifices in New England. In August, 1888, he secured a beautiful site from Charles H. Hill on North Cliff street, paying therefor $25,000. A fine residence still stands on the premises, the home of the Sisters; two other buildings that adjoined were sold. On April 4, 1889, ground was broken for the new church. On Sunday, September 6, 1891, Very Rev. James Hughes, V.G., laid the corner-stone, assisted by Rev. M. Mulholland, of New Haven; Rev. P. M. Kennedy and Rev. T. F. Finn, of Birmingham. The preacher on the occasion was the Rev. Walter Elliott, C.S.P., of New York. Work on the church is still in progress. The walls will be of granite, and will be more than 46 feet high. The length of the building is 183 feet, the front width 96 feet and the rear width 138 feet. The tower will be 156 feet high. The seating capacity of the superstructure will be 1,200. The plans were drawn by Architect Keeley, of Brooklyn.

The assistant priests of the parish of the Assumption are the Rev. John Fleming and the Rev. John J. McLoughlin, D.D. The estimated population of the parish is 4,000 souls.

The first Catholic school in Ansonia was organized by the Rev. James Lynch in 1853. It was conducted in an old building that is now a Methodist church. Its duration was about seven years, and had as teachers a Mrs. Morgan, Michael McDonald and a Mr. Conway. The present school is conducted in the spacious convent and is attended by 52 boys and 75 girls, who are taught by six Sisters of Mercy. The sister Superior is Sister M. de Pazzi. The school is in a highly flourishing condition, and sends annually a class to the High School.

Ansonia has a congregation of Greek Uniats, whose pastor is the Rev. Anthony Bonezewsky.

## IMMACULATE CONCEPTION PARISH,

### BRANFORD.

AMONG the pioneers whose names have come down to us, who materially assisted in the up-building of the Catholic faith in Branford, we note Francis Harding, Edward Rice, Thomas Fitzgerald and Michael O'Brien, Michael Scanlan, John and Bartholomew O'Brien, David Sliney, Thomas Carter, Edward Mulvey, John O'Donnell, James, Thomas and John Carney and Daniel Driscoll. In the house of the first named was celebrated the first Mass said in Branford. Tradition has given the honor of this Mass to the Rev. John Sheridan of New Haven, and also places the year at 1851. In 1852 the priests serving in New Haven were the Rev. Edward J. O'Brien and the Rev. Bernard Tevin at St. Mary's, and the Rev. Matthew Hart at St. Patrick's. Father Hart, of New Haven, broke the ground for the church which was completed in 1854 by Rev. John Lynch. At this time Branford was under the jurisdiction of Guilford, whose pastor was the Rev. John Lynod. About 1859 Branford became the residence of a pastor, the Rev. William Clarke, who attended Chester, Clinton, Guilford and Haddam. Father Clarke said Mass every third Sunday in Branford. Rev. James Bohen succeeded Father Clarke in 1861. On November 6, 1861, the Rev. Thomas Quinn succeeded Father Clarke, and served until August, 1864; and in turn was followed by the Rev. James F. Campbell, who came here from Waterbury on February 18, 1865. Father Campbell enlarged the church. Father Campbell's pastorate terminated in September, 1869, and was followed by Rev. John Sheridan on October 3d, of the same year. The Rev. Thomas Mullen succeeded to the pastorate in October, 1873. The term of his administration closed on September 1, 1876, when the present rector, the Rev. Edward Martin, assumed charge of the parish. The Catholic population of Branford is about 1200 souls, principally Irish, with a few Poles and Hungarians.

The parish possesses two places of burial. The old cemetery, purchased and blessed in 1858, is in the northern part of the town and is nearly filled. The new cemetery purchased in 1889 for $2,500 contains fourteen acres and is east of the village.

During the recent temporary pastorate of the Rev. Bonaventure Broderick, D.D., the parish purchased a most eligible site upon which it is intended to erect a handsome church in the near future. From January 1, 1887, to the end of the decade there were 570 baptisms and 90 marriages.

## ST. MARY'S PARISH,

### DERBY.

THE original name of Derby was *Paugasset*. The first purchase of land made here was in 1653, followed in 1654 by a few settlements. In October, 1675, it received town privileges, as well as its present name. On March 17, 1775, there was born in Derby a child with a familiar name, Keeney, to whom the parents gave the name of Ethel. Like many other towns of Connecticut, Derby received its quota of the hapless Acadians—four. They were, no doubt, the first Catholics here, but all trace of them has long since been lost. The earliest Catholic of whom anything is known to come to Derby (1760), was a Frenchman, Claude Bartheleme, who was made a prisoner at Fort Niagara. He married a Protestant lady, but his offspring were reared in the Catholic faith. The following letter, written to his brother in France, will throw some light on the history and religious character of this remarkable man.

DERBY, IN THE COLONY OF CONNECTICUT, AMERICA.

*Sir and My Very Dear Brother:—*

This is to inform you of my very humble respects, and to inquire after the health of my friends. I am still in good health, thanks be to God. I should inform you that, after quitting you to make a tour of France, I engaged in the Regiment Royal Rossilon in the year 1756. Some of us embarked for Canada. I continued in good health until we arrived on the bars of Newfoundland; there a malady broke out on board the vessel. . . . In 1757 we went to besiege Fort George, which surrendered after a siege of nine days, when we made eighteen scores of savages see the expediency of surrendering. . . . In 1758 we gained a victory over the English, who were ten thousand men strong, we having only three thousand men, who sustained for five hours by the clock a strong fire and conquered. In the year 1759, in the month of May, we set out for Niagara, near which 170 of us found a health house. . . . After having been three months at Niagara, the English began the siege, and after sustaining it for twenty days we were obliged to surrender. Afterwards we were brought to New England, where I married a girl in 1762, by whom I had three children, two girls and one boy. I built me a house in which I dwelt, and afterwards another log house, in which I lived as well, thank God. In the year 1762 I learned to read and write English, and in 1768 I learned to write French. I desire to thank God that you may hear from me. Also, I thank God for His Holy Spirit and for the gift of His Son. This faith so pure, so full of joy to one who believes in Christ. . . . My dear brother, I entreat you to pray for me, a poor sinner, who is able to make to you his salutation.

(Signed) CLAUDIUS BARTHELEME.

Claudius Bartheleme died in 1824, faithful to the end, we may rest assured, to the Catholic faith. His descendants in Derby are for the most part Protestants.

The presence in Derby of other French people, and probably Catholics also, is evident from this entry taken from the old town records:

"Louis de Lamarquesie, son of Bernard de Lamarquesie, Esq'r.,—and major in the Continental service,—and Mary Anne de Lamarquesie, was born on the 10th day of March, 1719."

A prominent Catholic, a convert, of early Derby, was the Rev. Calvin White, whose span of life reached from 1763 to 1853. In 1833 Irish Catholics began to settle in Derby; in that year we find the sturdy names of John Phalen, William Quigley, William Foley, John O'Connor and Matthew Kellady. This little band was shortly after increased by Michael Stokes, George Wallace, Patrick Quinn, John Reynolds, John Ryan and Farrell Riley. In 1833 Father McDermot, of New Haven, visited Derby, and for the first time Mass was celebrated here in the "Old Point" house, which was situated near the site of the National Bank on Main street. Two of the persons injured by the falling of the gallery of Christ church, New Haven, 1834, were residents of Derby. Derby continued to be served from New Haven by Father McDermot until his removal to Lowell in 1837. Occasionally Mass was said at the residence of Bernard Reilly on Hawkins street.

The next priest to visit Derby was the Rev. James Smyth, of New Haven, who attended this portion of his flock at regular intervals until 1847. It was during his term of service, 1845, that the first Catholic church in Derby was built, the spacious site having been donated by Anson G. Phelps. The dimensions of this church were 50 by 33 feet. The building was enlarged, first by the Rev. James Lynch, and secondly by the Rev. John Lynch. After the first enlargement the church was solemnly dedicated to God under the patronage of the Blessed Virgin, on May 2, 1852. The ceremony of dedication was performed by Bishop O'Reilly, after which a Solemn High

Mass was sung, the pastor, Rev. James Lynch, being the celebrant, Rev. M. O'Neil, deacon, and Rev. Christopher Moore, sub-deacon. Bishop O'Reilly preached the dedication sermon. After vespers the Bishop administered the sacrament of confirmation to 120 persons.

In 1847 the Rev. Michael O'Neil assumed jurisdiction, but after a sojourn of a few months took up his residence in Waterbury, retaining, however, charge of Derby. The number of Catholics had so increased that Derby was erected into a parish with the Rev. James Lynch as the first resident pastor, March 31, 1851. Father Lynch added to the lot donated by Mr. Phelps and purchased another piece of land with a house from John Cross in 1853. The four succeeding pastors ruled over St. Mary's parish as follows: Rev. John Lynch, November 1, 1857, to November 2, 1862; the Rev. John Sheridan, November 2, 1862, to December 31, 1866; the Rev. Patrick O'Dwyer from January 1, 1867, to June 25, 1870; the Rev. John Lynch (the second time) from June 25, 1870, to September of 1878. In 1870 Ansonia was separated from Derby and formed into a parish with Father O'Dwyer as the first pastor.

The successor of the Rev. John Lynch was the Rev. Peter M. Kennedy, who began his duties here on October 1, 1878. Among the works that marked his administration were the removal of the old rectory to College street, and the building on its site of the present fine pastoral residence; the erection of the church; the purchase of the convent property; the introduction of the Sisters of Mercy from Meriden (1885); the purchase of thirty-one acres of land for a cemetery and the erection in 1881 of the church at Milford, then a mission of Derby. Work on the present church was begun in March, 1882; the corner-stone was laid on June 25th of the same year, by Bishop McMahon; and on the 21st of November, 1883, it was dedicated. Bishop O'Reilly, of Springfield, preached the sermon on this occasion. The seating capacity of the church is 1,058. The main altar is a masterpiece of workmanship, over 1,000 pieces of various stones entering into its construction. The tower is equipped with a fine bell.

The present rector, Rev. Charles McElroy, succeeded Father Kennedy on February 1, 1891. Conspicuous among his achievements in the interest of his parish are the renovation of the exterior of the church; the remodeling of the convent and the grading of its surroundings; the improvement and enlargement of the cemetery; the purchase of a lot adjacent to the church property; the reduction in a very gratifying degree of the indebtedness; the erection of a handsome parochial school.

The old or first cemetery was purchased by Farrel Riley from Joseph P. Smith on August 27, 1847, and transferred to Bishop O'Reilly on September 4, 1851. The lot was in the section of the town known as "Bare Plains." It was blessed in the fall of 1858. A child of Thomas Maher was interred here in December, 1847. This was the first burial of a Catholic in a Catholic cemetery in Derby. A new tract of land was bought by Rev. John Lynch on August 9, 1861. It was consecrated by Bishop McFarland on January 12, 1864, during the pastorate of Father Sheridan. Mt. St. Peter's cemetery, purchased by Father Kennedy, was blessed by Bishop McMahon on May 8, 1887, the Rev. Dr. Higgins, O. P., preaching the sermon.

When the first Mass was said in Derby in 1833 the number of Catholics was 28. When the church was built in 1845 the Catholic population was about 100. In 1890 it was estimated at 3,500, and in 1898 the number is 4,000, comprising many nationalities, viz.: Americans, Irish, Germans, French, Greeks, Poles, Slavonians, Hungarians, Bohemians, Italians and a few English.

The clergymen who have served St. Mary's parish as assistants are the following :

| | | |
|---|---|---|
| Rev. C. Duggett, | Rev. T. Shelly, | Rev. J. Dolan, |
| Rev. P. G. McKenna, | Rev. M. Keane, | Rev. M. Barry, |
| Rev. M. McAuley, | Rev. E. McGee, | Rev. T. Finn, |
| Rev. Jas. Gleeson, | Rev. Jas. Nihil, | Rev. J. Fogarty. |
| Rev. Wm. O'Brien, | Rev. C. McGowan, | |

Prominent among the benefactors of the parish were Edward Shelton, Anson G. Phelps, Sheldon Bassett, Peter Phelps, F. Smith, Messrs. Canfield and Downs, and Messrs. Tomlinson and Smith.

The first Catholic marriage ceremony in Derby was performed about 1837. The contracting parties were George Wallace and Ann Reilly, the Rev. James Smyth officiating at the residence of Bernard Reilly on Hawkins street, between what is now Eighth and Ninth streets.

A festival day for St. Mary's parish was December 8, 1895, the fiftieth anniversary of the erection of the first church. The golden jubilee was impressively celebrated in the presence of a large concourse of people. Bishop Tierney graced the occasion by his presence, and the Solemn High Mass, celebrated *Coram Episcopo*, was sung by the Rev. Henry Walsh of Plainville, assisted by the Rev. Thomas Coleman as deacon, and the Rev. John Fitzgerald as sub-deacon. The jubilee oration was pronounced by Very Rev. Father Pardow, S.J. The sermon in the evening was delivered by the Rev. William Maher, D.D.

The first Catholic school in Derby was organized in 1852, and was taught by lay teachers. It was held in the basement of the church. The first teacher was Mr. Cain, whose term began on June 14, 1852 and expired on February 6, 1854. Mr. Nicaloi then taught for a year and was followed by Miss Gossin, who began her duties on February 10, 1855. She was succeeded by Miss Rathbone in the spring of 1856. Mr. Michael McDonald was also a teacher in this school. The school closed after a career of five years. In September, 1885, after the introduction of the Sisters of Mercy, Rev. Father Kennedy opened a school in the basement of the church. It contained seven rooms and was attended by 350 children.

The corner-stone of the present fine school was laid on May 16, 1897, by Bishop Tierney. Right Rev. Mgr. Joseph Mooney, Vicar-General, New York City, delivered the discourse. On September 11, 1898, it was blessed by Bishop Tierney, the Rev. James H. O'Donnell preaching the sermon.

The attendance is 225 boys and 219 girls; there are twelve Sisters, whose Superioress is Sister M. Columba. The members of St. Mary's parish are proud of their school and rejoice at the successes achieved by the pupils. It ranks among the first schools of Derby, which position it is the intention of the management to maintain.

## ST. GEORGE'S PARISH,

### GUILFORD.

THE first appearance of Catholicity in Guilford as an organized force, was in 1854, when priests from St. Patrick's parish, New Haven, ministered to the spiritual wants of the Catholic people here residing. The Adorable Sacrifice was first offered in that year in the presence of a few persons, in a stone house, at one time the residence of the Rev. Henry Whitfield.[1] The occasional visits of priests were productive of good results. Desirous of possessing a chapel of their own, the little band purchased a store on Whitfield street in 1860. After being suitably remodeled, Mass was said in the new chapel for the first time on Sunday, March 4, 1860. In January, 1861, there were seventy-five Catholics in Guilford, and of these, less than a dozen were children of Sunday-school age. The congregation continued to worship in this chapel until 1876, when the Rev. Edward Martin, pastor of St. Mary's parish, Branford, erected the church on the corner of Whitfield and High streets. The corner-stone was laid on November 12, 1876, by Very Rev. James Lynch, Vicar-General, assisted by the Rev. P. Mullholland and the Rev. Father Rogers. The sermon was preached by the Rev. J. Lynch. Over 2,000 persons were present at this ceremony, 500 of whom were from New Haven. At the time of the completion of the church the Catholic population of Guilford had increased to about thirty families. The congregation of St. George's remained under the jurisdiction of Branford until March 1, 1887, when the Rev. John Dolan was appointed the first resident pastor of Guilford and dependencies, Clinton,[2] Madison, Leete's

---

[1] In connection with this house where Mass was first said in Guilford, the following will not be without interest:

"It is believed to be the oldest house now standing in the U. S. (1838). This building was erected by the company who first settled the town, about the year 1640. The leader or head of the company was Henry Whitfield, a minister of the church of England, and one of the number of those who were called Non-Conformists. This house was built for him; the stone of which the building is constructed was brought on hand barrows, from a ledge some considerable distance from the place where the house stands; the cement used in building the walls is said now to be harder than the stone itself. The walls were plastered 15 or 20 years since. Mr. Whitfield and several others of the company who came to this place in 1639, returned to England in 1649. This house was used by the first settlers as a kind of fort for some time, to defend themselves against the hostile savages. The first marriage which took place in this town, was solemnized in this building. The supper which was provided for the occasion consisted of pork and beans."—Barber's *Historical Collections.*

[2] This entry is found in Bishop O'Reilly's journal: "*October 16, 1851:* Sent Rev. Drae to Clinton, Connecticut, to open a mission there."

Island and Stony Creek. Father Dolan's pastorate was of short duration, as he died on July 3, 1888. He was buried in the new cemetery on the Durham turnpike, which had been consecrated a short time previous.

The Rev. James Smith succeeded Father Dolan on July 21, 1888. In 1890 the number of Catholic families in Guilford and missions was estimated at sixty-seven, distributed as follows: In Guilford, 41; Madison, 7; Clinton, 5; Stony Creek, 5; Leete's Island, 9. In 1888 Mr. John Beattie built a hall at the latter place, where Mass is said for the accommodation of its residents as well as for those who attend from Stony Creek.

Father Smith's successor was the Rev. William J. Dullard, who received his appointment in August, 1893; after a successful administration of two years he was followed by the present pastor, the Rev. James Degnan, in September, 1895. A notable convert to the faith in Guilford in its early days was Mr. George Hill, who was an active auxiliary to the priests attending this mission. To him belongs the honor of organizing the first Catholic Sunday-school in Guilford.

## PARISH OF ST. ROSE OF LIMA,

### MERIDEN.

THE first glimpse we catch of Catholics in Meriden is in 1839; a few laborers, humble, unknown, men of brawn, but like their fellow-countrymen of that period whom emigration brought to our shores, men of faith and profoundly attached to the creed of St. Patrick.

A dilapidated barn, recalling the night when a multitude of angels filled the air with heavenly chant nineteen centuries ago, was the temple in which Mass was first celebrated in Meriden. The old structure stood on Holt's Hill, below South Colony street. The year was 1843 or 1844, and the celebrant the Rev. Father Smyth, who was on his way from New Haven. Mass was subsequently said in 1846 by Rev. Philip O'Reilly and Rev. Bernard Tevin. The latter offered the Adorable Sacrifice in the residence of Robert Clarke on Broad street. Among the pioneers who resided in Meriden at this period were James Connolly, John Flynn, James Collins, Robert Clarke, John Slane, Patrick and James Carroll, John Cassidy, Bernard Brady, Patrick Reynolds, Michael Moran, Patrick and Francis Carlin, Frank Maloney, William Hagarty, John McCaffrey, Thomas Fahey, Hugh McCauley, Thomas Hickey and John McKinley.

Father Tevin was followed by the Rev. James Smyth, who secured the old Episcopal church which stood on the corner of Broad and Olive streets; the price was $1,450. In two years, notwithstanding their small number, this indebtedness was liquidated. Mass was said in this building for nine years. On March 31, 1851, the Rev. Hugh O'Reilly became pastor of Meriden, with Wallingford, Cheshire and Southington as missions. During Father O'Reilly's pastorate Bigotry showed its hideous head on more than one occasion and at times when serious consequences might have resulted. Father O'Reilly purchased St. Patrick's cemetery on South Broad street, as well as

REV. JOHN H. CARROLL.

REV. MICHAEL F. RIGNEY.

REV. JOHN COONEY, P.R.

REV. JAMES P. DEGNAN.

REV. JAMES CUNNINGHAM.

the land occupied by the cemetery and old church in Wallingford. Father O'Reilly had lodgings with James Lynn on High street.

His successor was the Rev. Thomas Quinn, whose pastorate began on June 4, 1854. In 1855 he organized the first Catholic school in Meriden. It was conducted in the basement of the church on the corner of Broad and Olive streets by Professor P. Smith. Among the pupils who began their education here is the present pastor of St. Edward's parish, Stafford Springs, Rev. R. C. Gragan. Father Quinn about this time purchased the lot on Center street for the church which was in contemplation. The pastoral residence was the humble little building that stood south of the church for many years, and in which Very Rev. Thomas Walsh breathed his last.

St. Rose's church was begun and completed in 1856. Very Rev. William O'Reilly, Administrator, officiated at the ceremony of laying the corner-stone, and the Rev. Dr. Cummings of St. Stephen's parish, New York, preached the sermon. The same orator pronounced the discourse at the dedication of the church which took place towards the end of the same year.

In May, 1858, the Rev. Charles McCallion came to St. Rose's as assistant to Father Quinn, and remained in this capacity until the following December. While at Meriden Father Quinn became involved in a lawsuit, which attracted no little attention at the time. A woman, one of his parishioners, married a divorced man whose wife was still living. Realizing that, according to the laws of the Church her marriage was invalid, she submitted the matter to Father Quinn, who informed her that her reconciliation with the Church could be effected only by a complete separation. The husband brought suit against Father Quinn, claiming $10,000 damages.

Very Rev. Thomas Walsh began his administration of St. Rose's in January, 1859, with a church burdened with a heavy debt. Among the achievements of his successful pastorate were the purchase of a piece of land from a Mr. Fuller, adjoining that secured by his predecessor, the acquisition of all the church property on Center street, save one lot in the rear of the garden, the purchase of a new cemetery in 1864, the erection of a spire and the placing therein of a bell. The impressive ceremony of blessing the bell was performed by Bishop McFarland on November 1, 1866, assisted by Very Rev. James Hughes, Rev. E. J. O'Brien, Rev. Thomas Walsh and Rev. J. Smith. The preacher on the occasion was Bishop McFarland. The Solemn Mass which followed was celebrated by Rev. E. J. O'Brien, with Father Hughes as deacon, and Father Smith as sub-deacon. It was during Father Walsh's pastorate, also, that the Sisters of Mercy from Ennis, Ireland, were introduced into the diocese. They arrived at Meriden on May 7, 1872, and on that day four Sisters took possession of their new convent home on Liberty street, which Father Walsh had purchased from Mr. F. H. Williams for $8,300. The first Superioress of the convent was Mother Teresa, who is the only survivor of the original band. In 1875 the Sisters took up their residence in the new school, which had been built in the previous year at a cost of $20,000; here they remained until the erection of the convent in 1877. At the laying of the corner-stone of the convent Bishop Galberry officiated, and the Rev. T. W.

Broderick preached the sermon. In 1876 St. Bridget's convent was elevated to the dignity of a Mother-house, Sister M. Teresa Perry being appointed the first Rev. Mother. Father Walsh was appointed Vicar-General of the diocese in succession to Very Rev. James Lynch, who died on December 6, 1876.

In the spring of 1883, Father Walsh began the erection of a pastoral residence. For thirty-four years he had been content with the comforts afforded by the humble home which the new and more commodious residence was destined to replace. He had completed the church, built a spacious school and provided the Sisters with a convent. A new rectory was necessary to complete the series of handsome structures that had grown up on Centre street. He would cheerfully have remained in the old home, as he was a priest of simple habits and of retiring disposition; but he overlooked his own desires in his thoughts for others. But Divine Providence did not permit him to witness the completion of the work. Seized by a sudden illness, the Vicar-General expired, after a few days' sickness, on Monday, July 2, 1883. The funeral services, at which Bishop McMahon officiated, and Rev. Lawrence Walsh preached, were attended by over 100 priests and a concourse of people that taxed the capacity of the church to its utmost.

"The expressions of sympathy and regret manifested by all classes and denominations in the city revealed the happy relations which the good pastor had maintained with all, by whom he was universally respected. Meriden mourned his loss as one of her best citizens and most respected members of society."

The month following the demise of Very Rev. Father Walsh witnessed the advent of his successor, the Rev. M. P. Lawlor. During his brief pastorate the rectory was completed, but ill health compelled his retirement in January, 1885.

The present rector, the Rev. Paul F. McAlenney, became pastor of St. Rose's on February 22, 1885. The works that have signalized his administration are evidence of sacerdotal zeal and of lay co-operation: the two schools were remodeled and renovated; St. Patrick's cemetery was beautified and improved by additional walks and driveways; on June 15, 1885, a handsome monument was completed in the cemetery, erected to the memory of Very Rev. Thomas Walsh, V.G.; the church organ was enlarged one third its original dimensions, and the capacity of the sanctuary increased; the confessionals were reconstructed and made conformable to the interior architecture of the building, and necessary changes were made in the means of exit. Father McAlenney purchased in 1886 from Mrs. Lucy Mather a piece of land on the east side adjacent to the church property, and later secured a tract of land on the corner of North First street and North avenue. A farm was also purchased from a Mr. Godey. In 1889 a tract of land comprising thirty acres was secured for cemetery purposes, but it did not receive episcopal blessing until 1893. In that year it was solemnly set apart for burial purposes by Bishop McMahon, Rev. J. J. Curtin preaching the sermon.

As the old chapel had become inadequate to the wants of the Sisters, Father McAlenney assumed the labor of erecting a chapel that would be in all respects a suitable place for the sisters to gather for divine worship. The result was the construction of St. Rose's present spacious and elegant chapel. It adjoins and forms part of the convent, and its general architecture conforms to that of the main building.

The construction of a boiler-house also engaged the attention of the rector. Previous to this the buildings were heated by apparatus put in as each one was erected. To concentrate this force would lessen labor and expense, and secure more satisfactory results. The new boiler-house is 30 by 40 feet.

In March, 1895, Father McAlenney put into execution a plan he had under contemplation for some time, the securing of a "chapel of ease" in the western section of the city. He purchased a brick building from the Trinity-Methodist Society, transformed it into a well-equipped chapel, and named it in honor of the Sacred Heart. It is attended by the clergy of the mother church, who say two Masses there every Sunday.

With so much accomplished for God and His church, with so many evidences of material and spiritual prosperity abounding, the rector and his devoted parishioners celebrated the golden jubilee of the parish on Sunday, September 4, 1898. The joyful occasion brought together a large number of priests, many of whom were children of the parish, and received here the rudiments of their education. The chief feature of the occasion was the Solemn High Mass, with the Rev. J. P. Donavan, D.D., as celebrant; Rev. M. P. McCarthy, as deacon; Rev. Denis Hurley, as sub-deacon; Rev. E. Lamontagne, as master of ceremonies. The Rev. Walter Elliott, C.S.P., pronounced the oration. Bishop Tierney was present in the sanctuary, having as attendants Revs. John Russell and Richard C. Gragan. Besides the officiating clergymen, twenty-two other priests of the diocese assisted at the imposing ceremony. The evening service was a fitting crown to the day's jubilation. At the solemn vespers Rev. R. C. Gragan officiated as celebrant; Rev. T. J. Preston, as deacon; Rev. J. H. Broderick, as sub-deacon; Rev. M. P. McCarthy, as master of ceremonies. The preacher was the Rev. Denis P. Hurley, who spoke from the divine words: "The kingdom of heaven is like a grain of mustard seed."

The priests who received their early education in St. Rose's parish were Revs. Peter M. Kennedy, the first to receive this distinction; Richard C. Gragan, Maurice J. Crowley, James Connolly, Daniel Haggerty, Thaddeus Walsh, Andrew Haggerty, Denis P. Hurley, James P. Donovan, D.D., Michael McCarthy, Earnest Lamontagne.

Nineteen young ladies, members of the parish, embraced the religious life, and retiring from the world, entered various religious orders: Harriet McNamara, Miss Waldron, Mary Mulligan, Annie McCabe, Margaret Ames, Lizzie Dooley, Mary Martin, Mary Breen, Minnie Burk, Margaret O'Brien, Katie O'Brien, Mary O. Johnston, Mary J. Byrnes, Fannie Garvey, Jennie Brock, Lizzie Johnston, Rose Johnston, Mary McFarland, Mary Quinn.

Before the arrival of the Sisters of Mercy in Meriden, the schools were conducted by lay teachers. As stated above, Father Quinn instituted the first Catholic school in Meriden, with Prof. P. Smith as the first instructor.

Father Walsh organized his school in the basement of the present church, which was taught successively by the following teachers: Miss Grogan, of Hartford, from 1860 to 1861; Miss McDonough for a brief period; Miss Mulvyhill, from September, 1861, to March, 1863; James Yates, from March, 1863, to September, 1865; from this date to 1866, Timothy Sweeney; Miss Spellman for a short time; the Misses Grundelle, Yates, and Mulville, from 1868 to 1871; F. J. Lamb and Miss Mulville, from 1871 to 1872; Miss Mary Daly and Miss Mary Liddy, from 1872 to 1874, as the Sisters did not assume charge of the boys and girls together until 1874. In 1872 they began to teach the girls in a two-room school on Liberty street, in the rear of the convent. Additional room becoming necessary, a coach-house was secured, refitted, and here were gathered the younger children of the school. The building was afterwards removed to Center street.

The priests who served as assistants in St. Rose's parish are:

*Pastorate of Very Rev. Thomas Walsh:* Revs. E. O'Connor, T. Smith, B. O'R. Sheridan, B. Plunkett, J. A. Fitzsimon, J. B. Reynolds, J. Russell, T. W. Broderick, T. P. Joynt, M. C. McKeon, T. J. Preston, T. Sweeney, A. J. Haggerty, M. Costello, W. T. Doolan, T. M. O'Brien.

*Pastorate of Rev. M. P. Lawlor:* Revs. W. J. Doolan, T. M. O'Brien.

*Pastorate of the Rev. P. F. McAlenney:* Revs. W. J. Doolan, T. M. O'Brien, J. Walsh, J. H. O'Donnell, J. H. Broderick, J. T. Crowley, James Degnan, D. P. Hurley, C. McCann, F. Murphy, John Lee, R. Early, L. Guinan.

As St. Rose's parish fulfills all the requirements to constitute a permanent rectorship, Bishop McMahon conferred this dignity upon it with Father McAlenney as its first permanent rector.

## ST. LAURENT'S (FRENCH) PARISH,

### Meriden.

PRIOR to June 6, 1880, the French Canadians worshiped at St. Rose's church, where the 9 o'clock Mass was set apart for their benefit. Their spiritual interests were in charge of Rev. John Russell and his successors at St. Rose's, Rev. T. W. Broderick and Rev. T. P. Joynt. Becoming too numerous to be accommodated with one service, steps were taken to organize the French Canadians into a separate parish organization. Accordingly, a meeting which had been duly warned at the parochial Mass on the Sunday previous, was held in the hall of the Y. M. C. A., on June 2, 1880. A president and secretary were chosen by the parishioners then and there present, a church committee was appointed and two trustees were legally elected by said committee. With the Canadians were a number of Germans, Poles and Italians; but the Canadians and Germans being the most numerous, it was thought at first to form both under one corporation; by an agreement of both parties, however, it was determined, before organizing into a corporate body, to form the new corporation under the name of the "French Canadian Catholic Church," while the Germans were to enjoy all the spiritual privileges of the same. At this meeting, attended by two hundred persons, a few collectors, who had taken up a census, reported that 1100

French-speaking people resided in Meriden. The announcement filled all present with enthusiasm, and before the meeting adjourned $3,500 was pledged by the French Canadians towards the building of a church.

Among the earliest French Canadian settlers in Meriden were Narcisse Anger, L. Loissell, O. Raby, P. and O. Belcourt, L. Gouin, W. and E. Dubord, D. A. Dolbec, V. Besurchaine, N. Lisee, T. and J. Chalifoux, R. Dessurean, T. and A. Felix, E. Cossette, F. Cossette, O. Duplessis, Mons. Brunelle, M. Des Rosiers, M. Bibeau, M. Turcotte, N. P. Lamontagne and U. Neven.

The first Mass celebrated before the newly organized parish was said by the new pastor, the Rev. A. Van Oppen, on June 6, 1880, in the Grand Army hall; but for the following nine months, the people attended divine services in the City Hall. Work on the excavation of the cellar for the new church began on July 5th, 1880, and so numerous were the workers, and so vigorously did they ply pick, and spade, and shovel, that the excavation was completed that evening. The scene was enlivened by music by the city band, and so enthusiastic were the toilers at the success of their labors that they organized an impromptu procession and marched through the city, the men shouldering their picks and other implements of toil.

In November, 1880, work on the basement was begun, and on Palm Sunday, April 10th, the following year, the corner-stone was laid by Bishop McMahon, who also blessed the basement, which had been completed, on the same day. The morning discourse was pronounced by Right Rev. Bishop Shanahan, of Harrisburg. The celebrant of the Mass was the Rev. Flor. De Bruycker, and the master of ceremonies, the Rev. E. J. Vygen. Rev. L. G. Gagnier preached at Vespers. The basement structure, including the furnishings, cost $11,000.

The congregation worshiped in the basement until the completion of the superstructure, work on which had been resumed in the spring of 1886. On November 4, 1888, the church was solemnly dedicated to God in honor of the martyr, St. Lawrence, Bishop McMahon officiating. Right Rev. L. F. Lafleche, D.D, Bishop of Three Rivers, P. Q., preached the French sermon, and Rev. W. Stang, D.D., delivered the discourse in German. On the corner-stone are these inscriptions: "*Eglise de Saint Laurent, 1880;*" "*Laurentio Auspice, pie fidelium obolis exstructa, 1880.*" The dimensions of St. Laurent's church are, length 118 feet, width 60 feet; the exterior is 60½ feet high, and the interior, 45½ feet; when completed, the tower will rise 165 feet.

At the time the parish was organized in 1886 there were 1150 French Canadians in Meriden; when the church was dedicated in 1888 the number was 1300; the present population of the parish is 1700 souls.

St. Laurent's school was opened in September, 1893, with 200 pupils, under the guidance of the Sisters of the Assumption, whose Mother-house is in Nicolet, P. Q. The French and English languages are taught. There are at present 325 pupils in eight grades taught by six Sisters, of whom Sister Felicite is the Superioress. The rector, Rev. Father Van Oppen, is a member of the Diocesan School Commission.

Since the organization of the parish in June, 1880, to 1898, 1658 baptisms have been administered and 360 marriages solemnized.

## ST. MARY'S PARISH,

### MERIDEN.

THE German Catholics of Meriden attended services at St. Rose's church with the French Canadians previous to June 6, 1880. On that date they became part of St. Laurent's parish. When the church was dedicated in 1888 the German Catholic population of Meriden numbered 400 souls. They remained under the jurisdiction of St. Laurent's until December 6, 1891, when they took possession of their own church, St. Mary's, with the Rev. Ignatius Köst, as the first pastor, who is still in charge. Three Sisters of Notre Dame, Baltimore, Md., whose Superioress is Sister Helena, teach 212 pupils.

## PARISH OF OUR LADY OF MOUNT CARMEL,

### MERIDEN.

AS far as can be ascertained the first Italian Catholics to settle in Meriden were S. Gentile, G. Mancano, G. Conco, J. Materese, S. Larese, and B. Ponzillo. Like other nationalities, the Italians worshiped in the mother church, St. Rose's, until June, 1880, when they came under the jurisdiction of the pastor of St. Laurent's parish, the Rev. A. Van Oppen. The first Mass said for them by a clergyman of their own nationality was in St. Laurent's church in October, 1892, the celebrant being Rev. Angelo Chiariglione. About sixty-five Italians attended that Mass.

The first resident pastor was Rev. Felice Morelli, who remained from May, 1894, until September of the same year. His successor was the Rev. Dr. Falcotill, who served until February, 1895. Father Becherini then became pastor, which office he held till May of that year, when the present pastor, Rev. Vittorio Sovilla, assumed charge.

The corner-stone of the church of Our Lady of Mount Carmel was laid early in 1894, Bishop McMahon officiating. The ceremony of dedication was performed by his Eminence, Cardinal Satolli, in the presence of a host of people who gathered to witness the impressive ceremony and to render respect to the venerable Apostolic Delegate.

When the parish was formed the Italian population numbered about 400; a census recently taken enumerates about 600 souls.

## ST. STANISLAUS' PARISH,

### MERIDEN.

THE Polish Catholics of Meriden were organized into a parish in the spring of 1891. They held divine services in the basement of the church, which was generously set apart for their use, until October 30, 1892, when the corner-stone of their new church was laid during the pastorate of Rev. Father Kelaniter. Remaining about eighteen months, he retired. Until the appointment of his successor, Father McAlenney, assisted by Rev. Father Havey, administered the affairs of the parish. The present pastor is the Rev. C. Kucharski. The school attached to the church has sixty pupils and is taught by a lay teacher.

## ST. MARY'S PARISH,

### Milford.

IN February, 1685, Colonel Thomas Dongan, the Catholic governor of New York, visited Milford to confer with Governor Treat of Connecticut, about the agreement of the Commissioners selected to determine the boundary line between the two colonies. On the 23rd of the month the report was assented to and ratified by both governors. On this occasion, Governor Dongan received the salutes proper to his dignity. In firing one of the great guns, a Samuel Adkins was injured, on account of which he petitioned the General Court for damages; he was awarded five pounds. It is not improbable that Governor Dongan's retinue comprised a goodly number of Catholic officials.

The construction of the New Haven railroad brought a great influx of Irish laborers to Milford, those sturdy sons of the Church, who craved the presence of a priest, and whose fellow-countrymen in scores of places in Connecticut laid strong and deep the foundations of what their descendants enjoy. In 1848, they experienced the great happiness of assisting at a Mass celebrated by a visiting priest in the house of John Lyons. Being informed of the presence here of children of the church, the Rev. Edward J. O'Brien of St. Mary's parish, New Haven, administered to them the consolations of religion, occasionally saying Mass in the houses of John Lyons or of Mrs. Sullivan.

Yielding to the importunities of the people and pleased with the sustained interest manifested, Father O'Brien, in 1853, erected a church on a lot, ninety feet wide, bought from Mrs. Sullivan, southeast of the cemetery. From the directories we learn that in 1856 and 1857, Milford was served from St. James' parish, Bridgeport, the Rev. Thomas Synnott, pastor; in 1859–60–61, from St. Mary's, New Haven, by the Rev. Peter A. Smith; from 1865 to the first year of the pastorate of the Rev. John Rogers, from St. Mary's, East Bridgeport, when the Rev. John Lynch, pastor of Birmingham, assumed charge of the Milford mission.

Milford owes its present church to the energy of Rev. P. M. Kennedy, the successor of Father Lynch at Birmingham. In 1881, Father Kennedy bought a fine lot on the corner of Gulf street and New Haven avenue from Judge Fowler, for which he paid $500. He began the work of construction immediately, and the corner-stone was laid in December of that year. It was dedicated on June 25, 1882, by Bishop McMahon. The Rev. Lawrence Walsh, of Waterbury, preached the sermon. The church has a seating capacity of 400 and cost $12,000, not a heavy burden when we consider the willingness of the people to make generous sacrifices in behalf of the faith to which they were devotedly attached, and the sacerdotal zeal that inflamed the hearts of their spiritual leaders. So prosperous in fact had this mission become, that it was deemed advisable to erect it into an independent parish. Accordingly in April, 1895, it was separated from the mother parish and the Rev. James Larkin was appointed the first resident pastor. He assumed charge also of West Haven and Stratford as dependencies. His seven years pastorate was marked by works which will long survive him. Two churches are evidence of his activity—St. James' at Stratford, and St. Lawrence's at West Haven. The erection of the pastoral residence is also his work; he renovated the old church, which is used for various parochial purposes. Father Larkin entered into his reward on July 25, 1892.

The Rev. William Maher, D.D., began his duties as pastor of St. Mary's parish on October 23, 1892. During Dr. Maher's illness, which occurred in December following his appointment and continued until June, 1893, the affairs of the parish were administered by the Rev. John T. Kennedy of New Haven. Though deprived of the manufacturing industries that are of such incalculable assistance to many parishes, St. Mary's parish is in a flourishing condition, the result of sustained co-operation on the one hand and of unremitting labor on the other.

St. Mary's, Milford, is the headquarters of the Hartford Apostolate.

St. Mary's cemetery is situated on Indian river, south of the N. Y. and N. H. R. R. Though purchased in 1868, when Milford was served from East Bridgeport, it was not blessed until about 1878.

Stratford is the out-mission of Milford and is attended every Sunday.

## ST. MARY'S PARISH,

### Mt. Carmel (Hamden).

WHEN the Rev. Matthew Hart, of New Haven, celebrated the first Mass said in Hamden in September, 1852, there were about thirty Catholic people in the town. At intervals of a month they were privileged to assist at Mass said by priests from New Haven. In 1856 Hamden was under the jurisdiction of Rev. E. J. O'Brien, of St. Mary's. The increasing number of Catholics prompted him to secure a suitable house of worship. In the above-mentioned year Father O'Brien bought a lot, to which he moved an old building purchased from the Axle Company. This was suitably remodeled for divine worship. An enlargement became necessary in 1867. For thirty-four years was this humble but well-beloved church used by the Catholics of Hamden. The directories inform us that Hamden was attended from St. Mary's, New Haven, until 1860, when it was served from Wallingford. In 1865 it was in charge of the pastor of Southington, the Rev. Thomas Drea. On August 11, 1867, it reverted to Wallingford, and was taken in charge by the Rev. Hugh Mallon. There were at this time 225 Catholics in Hamden. Alone at Wallingford, Father Mallon could not give weekly services in Hamden; but after the appointment of the first assistant in 1878, Mass was said regularly there every week. In 1890 the Catholics of Hamden had increased to 500; so that the old church was insufficient to accommodate the congregation. To encourage his people, to stimulate their faith and to provide them with a church suitable to their aspirations, Father

Mallon purchased a lot between Centreville and Mt. Carmel, south of the old church. Work on the foundation was begun in 1888, and the church was dedicated in the summer of 1890 under the title of Our Lady of Mt. Carmel. It is an imposing structure, the most prominent church in the town, and when completed and furnished, cost $20,000. The architecture is Gothic.

The church of Our Lady of Mt. Carmel continued in the care of the Rev. Father Mallon until April 22, 1891, when Bishop McMahon bestowed upon it parochial honors and appointed the Rev. John Winters the first resident pastor. For over four years Father Winters labored in this portion of the Vineyard, accomplishing much for his people both in the spiritual and temporal orders. The sightly rectory was built by him and other improvements of a substantial character were effected. On September 1, 1895, he was transferred to South Norwalk, and was immediately followed by the present incumbent, the Rev. William Dullard.

## ST. FRANCIS' PARISH.

### NAUGATUCK.

THE first Catholic settlers in Naugatuck were Patrick Maher, John Kelly, Andrew Moran, George Burns, Patrick Conron, Patrick Butler, Walter Healy, Thomas and John Campbell and John Hyne. Though it is not improbable that Naugatuck was visited by Father Fitton and Father McDermot in their periodical tours through this section, the first Mass said here, as far as is known, was offered up by Father O'Neil of Waterbury, in 1847 in the Naugatuck hotel. There were about fifty Catholics here at this time. Anterior to this date the sacraments were administered to people in Naugatuck by Father Smyth of New Haven. Mass was said later in the residences of Patrick Conron and Patrick Boylan. In 1857 five men, public spirited and strong of faith—Patrick Maher, Thomas Campbell, John Donovan, Edward Conroy and Patrick Conron—purchased a lot on Water street, for which they paid $400. At this time Naugatuck was served from Birmingham, whose pastor was the Rev. James Lynch. Father Lynch began the erection of a church, which was continued by his successor, the Rev. John Lynch. In the meantime the Holy Sacrifice was offered up semi-monthly in Nicholas' hall. Mass, however, was said in the new church before it was entirely completed. In 1858, Naugatuck was given in charge of Father Hendricken, of Waterbury, who completed the church and purchased a cemetery about 1859. He continued in charge until 1866, when Naugatuck was elevated to the dignity of a parish. The Rev. Hugh T. Brady was appointed the first resident pastor. The duration of Father Brady's pastorate was nine years. He purchased a house on Arch street from George A. Lewis for $5,000, which became his pastoral residence. Upon his transfer to Ansonia, he was succeeded by the Rev. William Harty, who died on March 19, 1876, five weeks after his appointment. He was followed by the Rev. Richard O'Gorman, who died on December 3d, after a pastorate of six months.

The Rev. James Fagan was appointed pastor on December 17, 1876. As the congregation was increasing it became evident to Father Fagan that a new church was a necessity. Accordingly, in 1877, he purchased the Hine property on Church street, and, after the necessary renovations, occupied the house on the premises as a rectory. The indebtedness incurred by this transaction was liquidated in less than a year. Father Fagan then established a building fund and so actively did he labor and so generously did his people coöperate with him that in a dozen years the fund reached the sum of $20,000.

Ground was broken for the present beautiful church on April 7, 1882, Father Fagan digging the first shovelful of earth. Right Rev. Bishop McMahon laid the corner-stone on July 23d, in the presence of the largest concourse of people ever gathered in Naugatuck up to that time. The Rev. Lawrence Walsh, of Waterbury, preached the sermon.

The collection on that occasion added to the building fund the munificent sum of $5,000. The basement, with a seating capacity of 1100, was soon ready for occupancy. On Sunday, August 19, 1883, Mass was said in the old church for the last time, and on the Sunday following the basement chapel was dedicated by Bishop McMahon. The solemn High Mass, *Coram Episcopo*, which followed the dedication services, was celebrated by Very Rev. James Hughes, Hartford, as celebrant; the Rev. James Campbell, Manchester, deacon; the Rev. Thomas Beaven (now Bishop of Springfield), sub-deacon; the Rev. Peter M. Kennedy, Birmingham, master of ceremonies. The discourse was delivered by the Rev. John H. Duggan, of Waterbury. The congregation worshiped in this chapel until November 30, 1890, the date of the dedication of the main church. A striking architectural feature of the edifice is the tower on the right hand corner; it is modeled after that of St. Gertrude's in Louvain, Belgium. Father Fagan's labors did not cease with the construction of the church. This work accomplished, he purchased a fine tract of land of over thirty acres, which, in November, 1892, was consecrated to burial purposes under the patronage of St. James. When Father Fagan took up the reins of government, St. Francis' parish had not one thousand souls, and the value of the church property was estimated at $10,000. At the time of his death, August 1, 1893, the property valuation was $110,000, with a population of three thousand. An appreciative contemporary thus wrote of Father Fagan: "Father Fagan is warmly interested in all matters pertaining to his parish, which are constantly calling forth his best efforts; but in his relations to the community at large he is liberal and progressive. . . . . His zeal and energy were largely manifested in the erection of the new St. Francis' church, which is a grand and imposing monument to the Catholic faith and the sacrificing devotion of his parishioners."

Father Fagan's successor was the Rev. John F. Lenahan, who came here from Hartford. Brief as was Father Lenahan's pastorate, it was replete with good works. The Spring property, adjacent to the church, was purchased in 1895, and the grounds improved and beautified. Father Lenahan was summoned to his eternal reward in December, 1895. His successor is the present rector, the Rev. James O'Reilly Sheridan. Early in his pastorate the parish was visited with a severe loss in the almost total destruction of the basement interior; the altar, two confessionals, and two statues only were saved from the wreck. The damage was caused by defective drainage, which resulted in a flood. As a consequence, an improved and modern system of drainage was introduced; and the chapel, thoroughly renovated, was transformed into a new and elegant place of worship, all at an expense of $10,000. On February 20, 1897, Father Sheridan introduced the Sisters of Mercy from the Mother-house of Middletown, and installed them in the residence purchased by his predecessor, where they conduct a select school for girls. Other evidences of Father Sheridan's activity are to be found in the improvements made in the new cemetery, and the erection therein of necessary buildings. At the present writing, plans are being considered for a school, which exteriorly and in its interior appointments will be in keeping with the dignity of the parish.

Among the recent benefactors of St. Francis' parish are Thomas Neary, who donated the chandeliers in the church, valued at $1,000; Miss Mary Shields, whose gift was a statue of the Sacred Heart; Richard Neary, who gave a statue of St. Patrick. The assistant priests are the Rev. William Gibbons and the Rev. William Fanning.

## ST. AUGUSTINE'S PARISH,

### SEYMOUR.

THE original name of Seymour was *Nau-ko-tunk*, which signifies *one large tree*, so called from a large, stately tree which formerly stood near Rock Rimmon. To the stream on which Seymour is situated was given the English pronunciation of the above name *Naugatuc*. *Nau-ko-tunk* subsequently gave way to Humphreysville in honor of David Humphreys, whose manufacturing establishment was incorporated in 1810.

Fifty-five years ago Seymour (which received its present name in 1850) had only six Catholics, Nicholas and Daniel Brockway, Thomas Gaffney, Nicholas Cass, James Quinlan and Patrick Gaffney. In 1844, Father Smyth, of New Haven, celebrated the first Mass said in Seymour in a building known as the "Old Long House," which was situated on the site of the engine house on Raymond street. The construction of the railroad brought a goodly increase to the Catholic population, and at the appointment of Rev. Michael O'Neil, to Waterbury, Seymour—or Humphreysville—passed into his charge. During the interval between the first Mass and this period the Catholics of this mission assisted at Mass either at Derby or New Haven; at the former when Father Smyth would visit it. Upon the assumption of the pastoral charge of Birmingham in 1851, Rev. James Lynch also assumed control of Seymour. On September 24th of that year, he purchased a fine lot for a church from Alfred Blackman, paying therefor the sum of $400. In the fall of 1855, work on the new church was commenced, and it was dedicated under the patronage of St. Augustine in the fall of 1856. Seymour continued to be served from Birmingham until the transfer of Father O'Dwyer to Ansonia in 1870, when it began mission relations to the latter place. In October, 1885, it was organized into a parish with the Rev. John McMahon as the first resident pastor. On May 1, 1886, he was followed by the Rev. Richard C. Gragan, whose period of service terminated on April 1, 1894.

For some time after his arrival Father Gragan had lodgings at a private house and at the hotel. Having liquidated an outstanding indebtedness of $1,000, he began the erection of a church more suitable to the needs of the population of the parish. On May 4, 1888, ground was broken, and on July 15th, the corner-stone was laid by Bishop McMahon, the Rev. M. A. Tierney, of New Britain, preaching the sermon. Divine services were held in the new church on Christmas day, 1889, for the first time, and on May 18, 1890, it was solemnly dedicated. The Mass which followed the ceremony of dedication was sung by the Rev. T. Kelly, assisted by the Rev. M. Mulholland as deacon and the Rev. Father Walsh as sub-deacon; Rev. J. Synnott as master of ceremonies; the preacher was the Rev. James C. O'Brien. The cost of the edifice was $13,000. When the parish was formed the population was estimated at 650, consisting of Irish, Germans and Poles. When the church was dedicated, the number was about 700. After the completion of the new church, Father Gragan converted the old one into a parochial residence.

The present rector, the Rev. Michael Rigney, succeeded to the pastorate of St. Augustine's on April 1, 1894. His success attests his activity. What with renovating the basement, beautifying the grounds, improving the cemetery and purchasing a sweet-toned church bell, his zeal has been expended in promoting the interests of his parish. The ceremony of blessing the bell took place on May 7, 1895, Bishop Tierney officiating, and Very Rev. John A. Mulcahy, V.G., preaching the sermon. St. Augustine's church has a seating capacity of 600 and cost $13,000. The present population of the parish is 500. St. Augustine's cemetery was purchased in 1863 and blessed by Bishop McMahon on June 25th of that year, the Rev. J. Fitzgerald of Cromwell delivering the discourse.

From 1885 to 1898 exclusive, the sacrament of baptism has been administered 270 times; while 98 marriages have been solemnized. The first baptism conferred after the organization of the parish, was upon Charles Parsons, December 6, 1885; the first marriage ceremony performed was between John Cassidy and Elizabeth Frazier, November 26, 1885.

Father Rigney attends also two stations, Beacon Falls and Oxford.

The Beacon Falls Rubber Company recently donated to the Catholics of Beacon Falls a fine tract of land upon which a church will be built in the immediate future.

## HOLY ANGELS' PARISH,

### SOUTH MERIDEN.

SOUTH MERIDEN is about two miles distant from Meriden and was formerly a part of St. Rose's parish, Meriden. For many years the Catholic people attended the mother church, but Father McAlenney, recognizing that on stormy Sundays and during the winter months, it was a trying task to walk this distance, sought and obtained permission from Bishop McMahon to erect a church, suitable for the people's needs, in South Meriden. Selecting a fine site opposite Hanover Park, Father McAlenney broke ground for the new church in December, 1886. The corner stone was laid on Sunday, April 3, 1887, by Bishop McMahon, Rev.

John Russell, of New Haven, preaching the sermon. On July 17, 1887, the first Mass was offered up in the newly dedicated church. Holy Angels' church continued to be served from St. Rose's, until January 10, 1880, when the Rev. Richard Moore was appointed the first resident pastor. Upon his advent into the parish, Father Moore lived in a house that recalls the residence of Bishop Tyler in Providence, described elsewhere, which could be carried about by a pair of oxen. In this humble, yet cheerful home, Father Moore lived until the completion of the rectory which now ornaments the parochial property. Successfully fulfilling his mission here, Father Moore was promoted to a new parish in New Britain, St. Joseph's, and the Rev. P. Byrne became his successor. After a brief administration Father Byrne was transferred to New Canaan and was followed by the present rector, the Rev. Thomas Cronin.

Father Cronin attends also St. Bridget's church, Cheshire, among the pioneer churches of the diocese. As early as 1852, Rev. Father Tevin and others visited Cheshire to say Mass, administer the sacraments and instruct the faithful. The residence of Michael Garde was one of the first in which divine services were held. The attendants at Mass at this time were principally miners. Later the Holy Sacrifice was offered in Baldwin's Hall by Rev. Hugh O'Reilly of Meriden. Not long after a room in Martin Brennan's hotel was secured for divine worship, and here the Catholics of Cheshire worshiped until the church was built.

In the meantime the number of Catholics was increasing, and Father O'Reilly began to make preparations for the erection of a church. He secured an acre of land from Michael Garde in the northern part of the town, which he intended for church and cemetery purposes. The corner-stone of the church was laid in the summer of 1859, during the pastorate of Father Quinn of Meriden. The first Mass said in the new church was celebrated on Christmas day of the same year by Rev. Charles McCallion, assistant to Father Quinn. The church was beautified and improved in 1883, a small tower was added and stained glass windows were put in. So notable were the improvements made at this time that the church was rededicated by Bishop McMahon on November 4, 1883 St Bridget's church was attended at different times from Meriden, Wallingford and Southington. In 1888, it came under the jurisdiction of South Meriden. At one time it had a resident priest, the Rev. Thomas Drea, who resided in the Beadle place and attended Hamden and Southington. The Catholic population of Cheshire is about twenty-five families, or 100 souls.

## HOLY TRINITY PARISH,

### WALLINGFORD.[1]

IN 1840 there were only three Irish Catholics in Wallingford, James Hanlon, Michael Mulligan and Mark Daly. Seven years later, on December 22d, Mass was said for the first time in Wallingford by Father McGarisk, an Illinois missionary, in the house of James Hanlon, at the corner of Main and High streets. Among those who were privileged to assist at this Mass were James Hanlon, Mrs. O'Connor, Mrs. Leonard, Mrs. Logan

[1] For some of the details of this sketch, I am indebted to Mr. John Phelan's admirable History of this parish.

and Charles Logan, about a dozen persons in all. Previous to this, the Catholics in order to hear Mass were obliged to go to New Haven where the nearest church was located.

The Rev. Philip O'Reilly, of New Haven, was the second priest to visit Wallingford. He also said Mass in the home of James Hanlon, who was then residing on Academy street. When Meriden was organized into a parish, Wallingford became attached to it as a mission and was attended by the Rev. Bernard Tevin, who offered the Holy Sacrifice in the residence of Martin Owens at frequent intervals. Father Tevin performed the first Catholic marriage ceremony witnessed in Wallingford. The historic date is May 12, 1850, and the contracting parties were Philip McCabe and Ellen Maloney.

Father Tevin was followed by the Rev. Hugh O'Reilly, who had arrived at Providence on March 14, 1851. He was an alumnus of All Hallows' College, Dublin. Father O'Reilly continued to say Mass at the home of Martin Owens; and here also he established Wallingford's first Catholic school. Desirous of providing a house of worship for his people, Father O'Reilly purchased three choice lots from Philip McCabe, on May 29, 1852, paying therefor $280. Land had been offered gratis to the people, but their locations were unsuitable for church purposes. Meriden still continued to serve Wallingford, which was visited regularly by the Rev. Thomas Quinn from 1854 to 1856.

His successor and the first resident pastor of Wallingford was the Rev. M. A. Wallace, LL.D., who assumed charge in 1857. He said Mass in Union Hall. The Catholic population at this time had increased to 150, and the people felt they could bear the burden of a church. They would make the necessary sacrifices to see in their midst a church, how humble so ever, in which they could commune with their Heavenly Father. The project was auspiciously started, many non-Catholics generously contributing. The work progressed so favorably that the corner-stone was laid on November 23, 1857, the Rev. Father Quinn officiating. The church was a small structure, 60 feet in length by 40 feet in width; but it was a church, nevertheless, and their own. It was built on the lot previously purchased by Father O'Reilly.

Before the completion of the church, Wallingford passed again under the jurisdiction of Meriden—Father Quinn still pastor. In April, 1858, the floor of the church fell, while Father Quinn was saying Mass. Though no lives were lost, the accident resulted in the serious injury of many persons. From the directories we gather that the Rev. Father Sheridan was resident pastor of Wallingford in 1860 with Cheshire and Hamden as missions. From the same source we learn that his successor in 1861 was the Rev. Charles McCallion, whose pastorate here was very brief, owing to the outbreak of hostilities between the North and the South, which so unsettled financial matters as to render the maintenance of a separate parish organization well nigh impossible. Accordingly, Wallingford was again taken in charge by Meriden, under whose jurisdiction it remained from 1862 to 1867. In that year, on August 11th, the Rev. Hugh Mallon received his appointment as resident pastor of Wallingford.

Father Mallon's first success was the purchase of a fine piece of land near the center of the town, on which he purposed to erect a church that would accommodate his growing congregation ; and the future justified the wisdom of his course. The old church was improved by the addition of galleries, but the accommodations remained inadequate.

Ground for the new church was broken in 1875, and on September 24, 1876, Bishop Galberry laid the corner-stone in the presence of 8,000 interested spectators. From this time on the work advanced slowly, the height of the water-table being reached three years later. On August 9, 1878, a tornado struck Wallingford and spread desolation everywhere. The old church was swept out of existence, thirty persons were hurled into eternity and thirty-five were seriously injured, the majority of them being members of Father Mallon's parish. The dead were laid in the school-house, on the steps of which Mass was offered up on August 11, 1878, for the repose of their souls.

The heart of the pastor was crushed with grief at the calamity that had fallen upon his people ; but Father Mallon rose equal to the emergency. A temporary basement was fitted up by roofing the walls of the new church, and here the congregation worshiped until the following spring. The first Mass said in the temporary chapel was celebrated by the Rev. Father Harding. Father Mallon made a tour of the diocese, collecting funds for the completion of his church. Generously did he receive. The work of construction was resumed, and in August, 1879, it had reached such a state, that it could be used for divine service. In November, 1879, the basement was ready for occupancy, and here services were held until the dedication of the church on November 24, 1887, by Bishop McMahon. The church is built in cruciform style ; its extreme length is 148 feet ; the width of the transepts is 104 feet, and of the nave 72 feet. The side walls are 29 feet high, and from the floor to the apex of the roof the height is nearly 50 feet. The spire is 190 feet high, and the gilt cross that surmounts it is 12 feet in height.

The rectory adjoining was also built by Father Mallon. It is a handsome structure and, with the church, presents an attractive view. The entire parish property is evidence, if any were needed, that a man of wisdom was at the head of affairs, and that his people nobly seconded his efforts to place and to maintain the parish upon a high spiritual and temporal plane.

After thirty-one years of faithful, diligent, and successful labor, Father Mallon laid down the burden on September 27, 1898. He was succeeded on October 15th following by the Rev. John H. Carroll, who came here from Westport.

## PARISH OF THE IMMACULATE CONCEPTION,

### WATERBURY.

ACCORDING to the testimony of those who may claim the longest residence here, the Catholic who is justly entitled to be named the pioneer of his race and faith in Waterbury was Cornelius Donnelly, who lived on West Main street, near Crane street, about 1832. Others gradually found their way here, until Waterbury embraced within its limits a colony composed of the following Irishmen:

In 1837 and earlier : Cornelius Donnelly and family, James Martin and wife, Christopher Casey, John Flynn, John Connors, John Corcoran and wife, M. Neville and sister, (later Mrs. William Moran), Michael Corcoran, William Corcoran, Timothy Corcoran and wife,[1] John Galvin and wife, James Byrne, James Grier.

In 1838: Michael Donohue, Patrick Donohue, Patrick Martin, Patrick Reilly and sister.

In 1839, 1840 and 1841: Patrick Delavan, Matthew Delavan, Finton Delavan, Thomas Delaney, Thomas Kilduff and wife, Timothy Whalen and wife, Thomas Claffey.

The Rev. James Fitton was the first priest to visit Waterbury, and it may be safely asserted that he said Mass during his periodical visitations here. So little impression did his visit make, however, that his name is not remembered by any of the old people now residing here.

The Rev. James McDermot, of New Haven, also visited Waterbury, and celebrated Mass. The precise date cannot be determined, but the place was the dwelling house of Cornelius Donnelly. So anxious were the Catholics of Waterbury to have the Holy Sacrifice of the Mass offered for them, and to receive otherwise the consolations of their religion, that they generously presented Father McDermot with a handsome horse, saddle and bridle, in the hope that, being provided with his own means of travel, he might occasionally find opportunity to visit them. But the good donors were doomed to disappointment, as he was unable to return, owing to a multitude of missionary duties. In the summer of 1837 he was transferred to Lowell, Mass.

The Rev. James Smyth officiated in Waterbury from 1837 to the fall of 1847. During these years Waterbury was connected with St. Mary's parish, New Haven. In these days traveling was either by stage coach or private conveyance, and Father Smyth generally traveled with a large sorrel horse that was about as well known as the priest himself.

His first reception in Waterbury was not very encouraging. When he arrived he went to the same house at which Father McDermot had stayed, but was informed that he could not be received there, as the owner had been notified by his employers that if he entertained the priest he would be discharged from his work. He then went to the old Franklin House, and immediately sent word of his situation to Michael Neville, who lived in the eastern part of the borough. Mr. Neville at once went to his assistance and offered him the hospitality of his home.

From 1837 to 1845 Father Smyth offered the Holy Sacrifice of the Mass at the residence of Michael Neville on East Main street. The building is standing now, a precious landmark for the Catholics of Waterbury. In 1845 Washington Hall, on the corner of Exchange Place and West Main street, was secured from Dr. Jesse Porter. Dr. Porter was an intelligent citizen, but his views in regard to Catholics were similar to those held by a good many

---

[1] It appears from the records of the town that " Timothy Corcoran, of Ireland, and Sarah Glover, of Birmingham, England," were married January 7, 1831. Their first child, James, was born January 7, 1833.

CHURCH OF THE IMMACULATE CONCEPTION,
Waterbury, Conn.

others at that time. Although he granted the use of the hall, he insisted that
the rent should be paid before the doors would be opened. The handful of
devout worshipers were not at all disconcerted at this turn in the proceedings.
Worship they would, so they climbed into the attic through a trap-door.
Divine services were usually held in this hall until the Catholics secured a
church of their own.

A short time previous to Father Smyth's departure the Catholics, constantly increasing in number, determined to secure a fitting house of worship,
one that might be solemnly set apart solely for religious uses. The possession
of a church had been their controlling desire, the aim of all their labors, and
God rewarded their fidelity and perseverance. In 1847 they purchased the
lot on the corner of East Main and Dublin streets, prejudice having again
interfered to prevent the purchase of one more centrally located. The lot
secured, the question of building a church became the all-absorbing topic.
The financial means of the Catholics were limited. At this time the Episcopalians were seeking larger and better accommodations for their increasing
flock, and the Catholics bought their church and began preparations for removing it to the lot on the corner of East Main and Dublin streets. The old church
cost $1,500, of which Father O'Neil paid $600 in the course of nine weeks.
When the building had been moved to a point in the street opposite the present church, the contractor (Major D. Hill, of Hartford), became convinced that
he could not get it over the high ground a short distance ahead. The original
plan was abandoned, and the lot on which St. Patrick's hall now stands was
purchased from Elizur E. Prichard, by Michael Neville, acting as the agent
of the Catholics. The sum paid for it was $650.

In the midst of these transactions Father Smyth was removed from New
Haven, and placed in charge of St. Mary's church, Windsor Locks.

Except on the occasions when Father Smyth visited Waterbury, baptisms, marriages and funerals took place in New Haven. Among the earliest
marriages recorded are the following:

Patrick Delaney and Mary Delaney, April 9, 1837. (Their first child,
John, was born in Waterbury, February 11, 1838.)

William Moran and Bridget Neville. (Their first child, Catherine, was
born in Waterbury, May 11, 1837.)

Michael Donohue and bride, July 7, 1839, and Patrick Reilly and bride,
the same date.

The first children of Catholic parents to receive baptism in Waterbury
were, Thomas Donohue and James H. Riley. The sacrament was administered
by Father Smyth at the residence of Michael Neville. Funerals were always
largely attended, the entire Catholic community accompanying the remains
to the cemetery at New Haven. The last funeral to go to New Haven was
that of Captain Bannon. In 1847, Bishop Tyler, through John Galvin as
agent, purchased the lot south of Grand street, adjoining the old burying
ground, for burial purposes. The price paid for the land (about an acre) was
$50. In 1890 the property, with that adjoining, was condemned by the city, as
it was required for public uses. The Catholic section was valued by the city

at $12,000, which amount was distributed among the Immaculate Conception, St. Patrick's and Sacred Heart parishes.

It would be impossible to speak of all those whose struggles in the early days built up a flourishing parish, and whose influence for good, always potent, is now unquestionable. Besides those previously named we will be pardoned for mentioning William Moran, Patrick Delaney and his brother, Andrew Moran, Thomas Matthews, Finton Riley, John Burns, Captain Bannon and John Reid, all honored in their day and generation. Many of them have entered into their reward. Others still remain, happy in the enjoyment of the respect of their fellows, and proud of the achievements of the past. In the evening of their lives they may well rest from active participation in parochial affairs. It is for their children to sustain what they established.

About October, 1847, the Rev. Michael O'Neill arrived in Waterbury. He was the first resident Catholic pastor. His first work was to put the church recently purchased, in order. He placed it under the patronage of St. Peter. So energetically did he labor and so generously did his flock co-operate with him that on Christmas day, 1847, he had the happiness of offering for the first time within its walls the Holy Sacrifice of the Mass. It was an appropriate day on which to crown the self-sacrificing labors of those sturdy pioneers, and many recollections are still affectionately entertained of it. The young pastor was full of vigor and the personification of zeal. With pardonable pride he rejoiced in the completion of his work, and his parishioners shared in his enthusiasm. Divine services were held in this church until 1859. Here in 1851 Bishop O'Reilly administered, for the first time in Waterbury, the sacrament of Confirmation. On that occasion 200 children were made soldiers of Jesus Christ. Bishop Tyler had previously visited Waterbury, and promised to return when his engagements would permit and administer the sacraments. But he was soon after called to his eternal reward. On December 29, 1854, while a large congregation was attending divine service, a fire broke out in the church. The coolness of the pastor and the efforts of the men present prevented what might have been a serious conflagration.

From his arrival in Waterbury until the autumn of 1850, Father O'Neill resided with the family of Michael Neville, on Dublin street, opposite the cemetery gate. In 1850, he rented a house on East Main street from John Sandland, now the property of James Lunney. On November 11, 1851, he purchased from George Root the property on which the church of the Immaculate Conception now stands. He occupied one of the old houses then on the property until July, 1855, when he was transferred to East Bridgeport.

Like many another pioneer missionary, Father O'Neill had his trials. Anti-Catholic prejudice was strong then. There were some who did not look with favor upon the rapid increase of Catholicity, and who in consequence sought to stem the tide of its progress. Obstacles great and numerous were thrown in the way of the priest's labors, and to the annoyances from individuals, to which he was forced from time to time to submit, were added not infrequently the complications of legal tribunals. In November, 1855, after his transfer to Bridgeport, the case of Blakeslee versus O'Neill came before the Superior Court at New Haven, and attracted unusual interest owing to the attendant circumstances. Alfred Blackman and N. J. Buell appeared for the prosecution, and R. J. Ingersoll and J. W. Webster for the defense. The suit was brought on an action of trespass on the part of Father O'Neill, who in the discharge of his duty as pastor had endeavored to administer the last rites to Blakeslee's wife, who was a Catholic (her maiden name was Helen Lynch), and after her death to read the funeral services of the Catholic church. This was in accordance with the wishes of the deceased; but Mr. Blakeslee, who was an Irish Protestant, remonstrated against the execution of the wishes of his dying wife; hence the suit. During the trial attempts were made to coerce Father O'Neill to divulge the secrets of confession. A record of the case says: "The judge is taking time to consider whether he shall be made to answer;" but the priest very properly refused to disclose what had transpired between him and his penitent. His reply was: "I will burn first." The result of the trial was that Father O'Neill was convicted and sentenced to pay a fine of $150 and costs. The judge in his charge stated that he did not require Father O'Neill to divulge the secrets of the confessional, as he did not consider that it affected the merits of the case, but said that if it had been important his priestly office would have been no shield against the usual punishment.

In July, 1855, Father O'Neill severed his connection with the Catholics of Waterbury and went to East Bridgeport. He died at New Haven, February 25, 1868, aged forty-nine years. His remains rest in Waterbury, the city he loved so well and served so faithfully. The Catholic people of Waterbury loved him, and to show their affection and to perpetuate his memory among their children, erected a handsome monument over his grave in St. Joseph's cemetery. We can truly say of him, that he was a man without guile— "with charity for all and with malice towards none."

The Rev. T. F. Hendricken arrived in Waterbury in July, 1855. He came from Winsted. He was ordained at All Hallows College, Dublin, Ireland, April 25, 1853.

The first work to which he devoted his energies was the erection of the present church of the Immaculate Conception. On Sunday, July 5, 1857, he had the happiness of seeing the corner-stone laid in the presence of a large concourse of people. The ceremony was performed by the Very Rev. William O'Reilly, administrator of the diocese. The priests assisting were the Very Rev. James Hughes, of Hartford, Rev. Luke Daly, the Rev. C. Moore, the Rev. Dr. Wallace, the Rev. James Lynch, the Rev. Fathers Aubier, Charaux, Bede and Hendricken. A procession, in which were two hundred Sunday-school children, marched from the pastoral residence to the grounds. The sermon was preached by the Rev. Thomas Quinn, of Meriden.

On December 19, the church was solemnly dedicated under the patronage of the Immaculate Conception of the Mother of God. The ceremony of the dedication was performed by the Right Rev. Bishop McFarland, who also

II—25

preached the sermon. Pontifical Mass was celebrated by the Right Rev. John Loughlin, D.D., Bishop of Brooklyn, assisted by the Rev. Fathers Regnier and Lynch as deacons of honor, the Rev. Fathers Hughes and Delaney as deacon and sub-deacon respectively, the Rev. Thomas Quinn as thurifer, and the Rev. James Lynch as master of ceremonies. At the evening service the preacher was Bishop Loughlin. At the close, Bishop McFarland addressed the congregation, congratulating them on the completion of their splendid church, and paying a deserved compliment to the zeal of their pastor. The architecture of the church is purely Gothic. It presents the following dimensions: Extreme length, 162 feet; extreme breadth, 65 feet; interior height, 65 feet; height of the spire, 200 feet.

At the time the church was dedicated, and for some time after, Father Hendricken resided in the brick building directly opposite the present pastoral residence. The dedication of the church marked an epoch in his life in Waterbury. Between that event and his election to the episcopal see of Providence, his was an extremely busy life. What with the building of the parochial residence, the founding of the young ladies' academy of Notre Dame, and the purchase of eight valuable pieces of property in the heart of the city, his time was advantageously employed. It was during his administration that the parish of the Immaculate Conception was incorporated under the laws of the State.

The news of Father Hendricken's elevation to the bishopric of Providence was received in Waterbury February 22, 1872. While his devoted parishioners were loath to part with him, yet they experienced feelings of pardonable pride in the fact that their parish had given to the church a worthy prelate. Many were the expressions of sorrow at his prospective departure, and sincere the testimonies to his worth not only as a churchman, but as a citizen interested in the welfare of his city.

Dr. Hendricken left Waterbury for his new field of labor in March, 1872, followed by the good wishes and blessings of the entire city of Waterbury. His faithful assistant, the Rev. Robert Sullivan, followed him to Providence soon after, having preached the farewell sermon on Sunday, April 22nd.

Coming to Waterbury a young man, Father Hendricken was full of zeal and willing to spend himself to advance the spiritual and temporal interests of the people. He was a man of marked faith and piety, and soon gave evidence of possessing superior executive ability. His enthusiasm knew no bounds, and his constant aim was to build up a parish second to none in the diocese. That he succeeded is a fact of history. For seventeen years he labored unceasingly in the cause of temperance, and the fruits of his labors in this field were numerous and are still manifest. Not less earnestly did he struggle for Catholic education. The seed sown by Father Hendricken is now bearing rich fruit. It is true that some feared that he was in advance of his time, and that a few of his undertakings were more or less hazardous. But he was a man who had implicit confidence in divine Providence. He believed that God's work must succeed, notwithstanding temporary difficulties. He saw far into the future and acted according to the light vouchsafed

REV. JOSEPH M. GLEESON.

REV. JEREMIAH J. CURTIN.

REV. WILLIAM J. SLOCUM, P.R.

REV. FARRELL MARTIN, D.D.

REV. TIMOTHY M. CROWLEY.

him, and the result justified his actions. The name of Father Hendricken and the parish of the Immaculate Conception are inseparable. The history of the one in its brightest pages is a history of the other. He built the present church and parochial residence, established a parochial school in the old church, purchased the property of the convent of Notre Dame, erected the convent hall, and bought the magnificent property on which St. Mary's school now stands. Though a great deal of that property has been sold from time to time, it is at present unquestionably the finest school lot in Connecticut. Dr. Hendricken's influence in Waterbury was recognized by the whole community. He was the head of a parish daily growing in numbers and influence. Following his wise guidance it attained an enviable position among the parishes of the diocese. The poor were his special charges, and those whose temptations led them into the path of intemperance found in Dr. Hendricken a kind, considerate and sympathetic friend. He was particularly fond of children. In their company he was as one of them, and it is needless to say they reciprocated his affection. Many of them have now attained to manhood and womanhood, but time does not dim their recollections of Father Hendricken.

On Sunday, April 22, 1872, the Rev. James Lynch preached his farewell sermon to his flock in Middletown, and during the week following arrived in Waterbury as the successor of Bishop Hendricken. Having witnessed for seventeen years the zeal, ability and foresight of their pastor, and knowing that under his administration the parish of the Immaculate Conception stood peerless in the Naugatuck valley, and ranked with the foremost Catholic parishes of New England, the parishioners dared not hope to find in Bishop Hendricken's successor the combination of qualities adequate to conserve and render permanent the prosperity they had attained. A few months, however, sufficed to show that the mantle of Bishop Hendricken had fallen upon worthy shoulders.

When Father Lynch arrived in Waterbury he was in the prime of life, being about forty-four years of age. Like the majority of priests of that day in charge of English-speaking congregations, he was born in Ireland. At an early age he prepared himself for the sacred ministry. Ordained to the priesthood at All Hallows College, Dublin, he intended to devote his services to God in the diocese of Toronto, Canada. On his way hither he stopped at New Haven to visit his sister, and his brother Thomas, a respected member of the Waterbury parish. Bishop O'Reilly, who was very favorably impressed with the young priest, requested him to remain and labor in this portion of the Lord's vineyard. The Vicar-General of the diocese, the Very Rev. Father Hughes, fully shared the views of the Bishop, and prevailed upon Father Lynch to make Connecticut his home.

Endowed by nature with an amiable disposition which was nourished and purified by years of unselfish devotion, gifted with prudence garnered from varied and arduous missionary labors, filled with zeal born of his own good impulses, and quickened by the knowledge of the rich spiritual harvest that awaited him, Father Lynch entered upon his duties as pastor of the Immaculate Conception parish. By careful management combined with strict economy he paid the parish debt of $38,000 in an incredibly short space of time. And the wonder was how it was accomplished. Apparently he devoted no time to financial matters, yet his annual statements of the financial condition of the parish were agreeable surprises.

On August 1, 1876, having received the appointment of Vicar-General, Father Lynch left Waterbury to assume charge of St. Patrick's parish, New Haven. He died there December 6, 1876, from an accident that had befallen him a short time before.

Father Lynch's successor, the Rev. Lawrence Walsh, was born at Providence, April 10, 1841. Evincing in his early youth marked tendencies towards the priesthood, he was sent by Bishop McFarland to St. Charles's College, Ellicott City, Md. Graduating with honor from this famous institution, he was sent to the Grand Seminary, Montreal, to complete his studies. He was ordained a priest in 1866. His first appointment was to Woonsocket, R. I., as assistant. From there he was transferred to Hartford as assistant to the Very Rev. James Hughes, then pastor of St. Patrick's parish. His first pastorate was at Collinsville. From Collinsville he was appointed pastor of St. Peter's church, Hartford, where he remained until his appointment to Waterbury in August, 1876.

Here he displayed the same love for souls that shone so conspicuously in his former missions. His devotion to the old land abated not a jot nor tittle. His voice and pen were always at the service of the oppressed mother country. His labors for the Irish cause made his name a household word throughout the United States and Ireland. While pastor of the Immaculate Conception parish Father Walsh occupied the honored and responsible positions of president, secretary and treasurer of the National Land League. As treasurer, over $1,000,000 passed through his hands.

Father Walsh embodied in his character the noblest qualities of the priest, and the sterling traits of the patriot. His love for, and practical charity to the poor were boundless. A larger-hearted priest was never ordained. There was not a selfish fibre in his body. He lived for his church and for the land of his ancestors. But his constant and arduous labors, both as pastor of a large congregation and as an official in the Land League, soon began to make inroads upon his health. He realized that a transfer to another field of labor was necessary in order to preserve his strength for the accomplishment of the work to which he had dedicated his life. After seven years of zealous labor in Waterbury he was transferred to Westerly, R. I., and on Sunday, July 29, 1883, he bade an affectionate farewell to his parishioners. His removal from Waterbury was at his own request, and his sudden death occurring soon after, justified his grave apprehensions regarding the state of his health. While on a visit to Boston in 1884, he was stricken with apoplexy and died suddenly at the Commonwealth hotel on January 3d. The news of his death was a shock to the Catholics of the entire city. In life he was deeply loved, in death sincerely mourned. His remains rest in St. Francis' cemetery, Providence. His tomb contains the dust of "one whose life-work as a priest, citizen and patriot has received the benediction of his fellow countrymen."

The successor of the lamented Father Walsh was the Rev. William A. Harty, whose successful pastorate began on August 4, 1883, and terminated January 1, 1886.

Although the period of his residence here was brief, he accomplished much. Prominent among his works were the purchase of property east of the city for a cemetery and the renovation of the interior of the church. This latter work is an evidence of his excellent taste and correct judgment in matters of art, and an illustration of his ability as a financier.

The renovation of the church cost over $15,000, and yet it was accomplished within a year, without the addition of a dollar of debt to the parish. The church was reopened for divine worship on Sunday, September 28, 1884. The services consisted of a Solemn Pontifical Mass celebrated by the Right Rev. Lawrence S. McMahon, Bishop of Hartford, assisted by the Very Rev. James Hughes, Vicar-General, arch-priest, the Rev. Thomas Broderick, of Hartford and the Rev. Michael Tierney, of New Britain, deacons of honor; the Rev. Father Leo, O. S. F., of Winsted, deacon; the Rev. M. P. Lawlor, of Meriden, sub-deacon, and the Rev. James H. O'Donnell, of Waterbury, master of ceremonies. The sermon was preached by the Rev. John H. Duggan, pastor of St. Patrick's church. In the evening, Solemn Pontifical Vespers were sung, Bishop Hendricken officiating. Vicar-General Hughes was assistant priest, and the sermon was preached by the Rev. Thomas Shahan, D.D.

Father Harty was succeeded, January 1, 1886, by the Rev. John A. Mulcahy. On April 18, 1887, Father Mulcahy sold to Irving C. Platt the property known as St. Patrick's chapel, formerly the Methodist Episcopal church. On August 7, 1889, by virtue of a vote of the trustees at a meeting held two days before, he leased to the sisters of the Congregation de Notre Dame of Montreal, the convent property, so called, at the corner of South Elm and Union streets, for 999 years, from September 1, 1889. Upon the acceptance of certain conditions by the lessees, the delivery of the lease was approved by Bishop McMahon. The granting of the lease was only carrying out the intentions of Dr. Hendricken, the founder of the convent. On September 1, 1895, Father Mulcahy severed his relations with the parish of the Immaculate Conception to succeed Rev. James Hughes as pastor of St. Patrick's church, Hartford. The successor of Very Rev. Father Mulcahy was the Rev. William J. Slocum, who assumed charge on September 8, 1895, and is the present incumbent. Father Slocum has zealously maintained the high spiritual standard of the parish secured by his predecessors. Among the material works accomplished during his administration have been the beautifying of the old St. Joseph's cemetery and the purchase of a fine tract of land on Dublin street for a new cemetery. This new burial place has been finely graded and laid out in plots and solemnly blessed by Bishop Tierney on September 25, 1878. The clergymen who have assisted Father Slocum are Rev. John McMahon, Rev. Patrick Finnegan, Rev. Patrick Kennedy, Rev. James McGuane, Rev. James O'Brien.

## ST. MARY'S SCHOOL.

The first of the great works inaugurated by Father Mulcahy was the erection of St. Mary's School. Its corner-stone was laid by Bishop McMahon, on August 29, 1886. The sermon on the occasion was preached by Father Harty, rector of St. Joseph's Cathedral, Hartford. A large number of clergy assisted at the ceremony, and it was witnessed by an immense concourse of people. On September 3, 1888, the school was solemnly blessed by the Bishop, and on the day following was opened for the reception of pupils. The building is an imposing structure, and there are few school edifices in Connecticut superior to it. The rooms, twelve in number, are large, well lighted, and furnished with an excellent system of ventilation and heating. They are all of equal size, twenty-five by twenty-nine feet.

The school was placed in charge of the Sisters of Charity from Convent Station, N. J. The first superior was Sister Rosita. After she had served the school for two years, failing health necessitated her transfer to another field of labor. She was succeeded by Sister Marie Agnes, and the present superior is Sister Claudine. On January 4, 1888, occurred the first death among the teachers. The deceased was Sister Rachel Cronin, aged twenty-four years. She had been stationed in Waterbury only four months, but in that time had won the esteem not only of the pupils of the school, but of the entire parish. She was interred in the sisters' plot in St. Joseph's cemetery.

An event of great interest in the history of the school was the presentation of a large and handsome American flag by the four local divisions of the Ancient Order of Hibernians, May 13, 1890. It was the first flag-raising over a school in Waterbury.

## ST. PATRICK'S HALL.

The work of demolishing the old church on East Main street was begun in May, 1888. For many years it had served the purpose of a public school, but time made sad havoc with the venerable structure, and it was deemed advisable to remove it, and in its place to erect a building that would be an ornament to the city and a benefit to the younger portion of the parish. St. Patrick's Hall, as the new building was called, is another evidence of the zeal of Father Mulcahy and the generosity of the people. In building it, the interests of the youth of the parish were chiefly considered. The object was to provide them with a place for divine worship and Sunday-school, and to furnish a gymnasium and reading-room for the improvement of mind and body. On Sunday, April 11, 1889, the Sunday-school room was opened, the celebrant of the first Mass within its walls being the Rev. James H. O'Donnell. It was the aim of Father Mulcahy to have a reading-room in St. Patrick's Hall second to none in the diocese. His interest in the enterprise may be inferred from his presentation to the library fund of $1,150, the amount donated to him by his parishioners on his return from Europe, in September, 1890.

The hall is built in the Romanesque style of architecture, and presents a massive but graceful appearance. The building measures a little over 57 feet on East Main street, and is about 100 feet deep. The East Main street front is of White Vermont granite, trimmed with brown stone, and presents a striking appearance. The cornice is of brown stone, and the dormer roofs of blue slate, with terra-cotta crestings.

### ST. MARY'S CONVENT.

St. Mary's convent, adjoining St. Mary's school, was ready for occupancy on November 27, 1889. The building measures 50 feet by 60, and has accommodations for over one hundred pupils. The establishment, including the school building proper, embraces fourteen class-rooms, with sittings for eight hundred and fifty children.

The convent walls are built of pallet brick; the roof is of Bangor slate, and has an iron cresting. The tower over the main entrance rises high above the roof, and is surmounted with a gilt cross.

The entire cost, including the grading of the grounds and the laying of the asphalt walks, was $20,000, everything having been constructed with a view to excellence and permanency.

The number of Sisters in St. Mary's convent is seventeen.

### ASSISTANTS AND PRIESTS BORN IN THE PARISH.

The following are the priests who have served as assistants in the parish of the Immaculate Conception, including those who have served it temporarily:

*With the Rev. Michael O'Neill, from 1847 to 1855*—Rev. Peter Cody.

*With the Rev. Dr. Hendricken, from 1855 to 1872*—Revs. Peter Cody, M. O'Riley, Charles McCallion, J. Sheridan, P. F. Glennon, J. A. Couch, J. O'Farrell, J. Smith, J. Bohan, J. J. McCabe, J. Daly, Michael Rodden, J. Campbell, John Fagan, Daniel Mullen, John Lynch, Phillip O'Donahue, Thomas Walsh, J. Reynolds, P. A. Smith, J. Mulligan, Richard O'Gorman, R. J. Sullivan, C. Lemagie, Thomas Kane, A. Princen, Bernard Plunket, Maurice Herr.

*With the Rev. James Lynch, from 1872 to 1876*—Revs. Richard O'Gorman, Maurice Herr, M. J. McCauly, J. A. Mulcahy, James Fagan.

*With the Rev. Lawrence Walsh, from 1876 to 1883*—Revs. J. B. Creeden, J. O'R. Sheridan, Patrick Finnegan, Patrick Duggan, Michael Donahoe.

*With the Rev. William Harty, from 1883 to 1886*—Revs. P. J. Finnegan, J. O'R. Sheridan, Michael Donahoe, James Walsh, James H. O'Donnell, Frederick Murphy.

*With the Rev. John A. Mulcahy, from 1886 to 1894*—Revs. P. J. Finnegan, James Walsh, Frederick Murphy, John Flemming, James H. O'Donnell, P. F. Dinneen, Patrick Kennedy, William Lynch, J. J. Downey.

The parish of the Immaculate Conception has given to the Church the following priests:

| | | |
|---|---|---|
| William Hill, | Patrick P. Lawlor,[1] | Thomas Shanley, |
| F. H. Kennerney, | Christopher McAvoy, O.S.A., | William Lynch, |
| Jeremiah Fitzpatrick,[1] | Michael J. McGivney,[1] | Patrick McGivney, |
| Thomas Galvin,[1] | John Donahoe,[1] | Arthur McMahon, O.S.D., |
| Joseph Read,[1] | John Tennion, | John McGivney, |
| Martin P. Lawlor, | William White, | Joseph Heffernan, O.S.D. |

[1] Deceased. J. Delaney may be added, who died a deacon.

## St. Joseph's and Calvary Cemeteries.

On December 1, 1857, Father Hendricken bought St. Joseph's cemetery, paying for the same $2,000. The first person interred there was John Rice, whose funeral took place October 17, 1858.

Calvary cemetery comprises about sixty-seven acres. In 1885 the Rev. William A. Harty purchased fifty-three acres, and the Rev. John A. Mulcahy the remainder in August, 1891. The first interment in Calvary cemetery was that of Thomas Harry, infant son of P. J. Bolan, June 22, 1892. The cemetery was consecrated by the Right Rev. Michael Tierney, May 24, 1894. The sermon on the occasion was preached by the Rev. James H. O'Donnell, of Watertown.

## ST. PATRICK'S PARISH,

### Waterbury.

AMONG the early Catholic settlers in this section of Waterbury, we note Michael Spellman, William Luddy, Mr. McEvoy, father of the Rev. Christopher McEvoy, O. S. A., Michael Begnal, Thomas Claffey, Thomas Mellon, Thomas Russell, Michael McNamara.

On February 1st, 1880, the Rev. John H. Duggan, who was then pastor of the Catholic parish of Colchester and the outlying missions, was directed by the Right Rev. Lawrence S. McMahon, D.D., to proceed to Waterbury and purchase land for a new church and its future dependencies in the southwest part of the city, known as Brooklyn district. On February 19, 1880, Father Duggan purchased nearly three acres of land from J. C. Booth and N. J. Welton for $5,200, the last installment of which was paid July 25, 1881. In the following April he was instructed by the Bishop to go to Waterbury again and commence the organization of a parish, of which he was appointed pastor. On his arrival, about the middle of April, he was received at the pastoral residence of the Rev. Father Walsh, who on the preceding Sunday had officially announced the contemplated division of the parish of the Immaculate Conception. He announced that for some time past the Catholic population of the city had been outgrowing its facilities for providing for its spiritual wants. He had laid before Bishop McMahon, he said, the situation and the necessities involved in it, and they were promptly recognized and acted upon.

Father Walsh afterwards defined the boundary lines of the new parish, and having submitted them to Bishop McMahon, they were announced in the church of the Immaculate Conception as follows :—

"Commencing at the city limits in the direction of Thomaston, the line will run south along the Naugatuck railroad to the West Main street crossing, thence along the middle of West Main street to the New York and New England railroad, and down the railroad to the north end of Meadow street, thence along Meadow to Grand street, through the middle of Grand street across Bank street to South Main street, along the middle of South Main street to Clay street, through Clay and along Mill street to Liberty street,

ST. PATRICK'S CHURCH,
Waterbury, Conn.

then across the bridge over Mad river, and thence in a straight line through the Abrigador and over the hill in the direction of St. Joseph's cemetery."

That part of the city lying west and south of this line was to constitute the new parish. By a census taken in 1881, it was found to contain 3000 souls. Father Walsh, on behalf of the Immaculate Conception parish, gave the use of the old Methodist church, on the corner of East Main and Phœnix avenue, then called St. Patrick's chapel, as a temporary place of worship for the members of the new parish, and they worshiped there until the basement of their church was ready, in December, 1882. The parish was placed under the patronage of St. Patrick.

The corner-stone of St. Patrick's church was laid on October 16, 1881. Fully 10,000 persons were present. The ceremony was performed by Bishop McMahon. The Rev. J. C. O'Brien was cross-bearer, and the Rev. P. M. Kennedy and the Rev. James Fagan as chanters. The Rev. Philip McCabe was master of ceremonies. In the corner-stone was deposited a parchment record containing the names of the President of the United States, the Governor of Connecticut, the mayor of the city, the selectmen of the town, the Sovereign Pontiff, the officiating bishops, the pastor and his assistants, the trustees of the new parish, the architect and the mason; also the name of the patron saint and the title of the new church, together with copies of the local and other newspapers, various curious coins, and other articles of interest.

The sermon was preached by the Right Rev. M. J. O'Farrell, Bishop of Trenton, N. J. The contributions on the occasion amounted to $5000. The Roman Catholic Total Abstinence and Benevolent society donated $150, the Young Men's Catholic Literary association $100, the St. Aloysius society $100, the Temperance Cadets $110, the Children of Mary $113, and the Convent of Notre Dame $50.

St. Patrick's church is situated on high ground in a lot containing nearly three acres. It fronts on Charles street and overlooks the city, commanding a beautiful view. St. Patrick's church would have been completed sooner, had not the Rev. Father Duggan determined to avoid, as far as possible, paying interest on borrowed money. In the meantime, the congregation has had a comfortable place of worship in the basement of the edifice, which was fitted up for church use.

Father Duggan was called to his reward on November 10, 1895; his remains rest in front of the church which will be his monument. His successor is the Rev. Joseph Gleeson, who came to Waterbury on December 2nd, following. He completed the splendid parochial residence begun by his predecessor, and is now engaged in completing the church. The plastering is finished, the statues, made on the premises, are completed, and the beautiful Stations of the Cross, purchased in Munich, are erected. Father Gleeson is now negotiating for the construction of the organ, altars, pews and confessionals, all of which will be worthy of the magnificent edifice. Besides the church and rectory the parish possesses St Patrick's Lyceum on Porter street, purchased by Father Duggan, to which Father Gleeson built an addition, making the seating capacity 900, and St. Michael's convent on

Bank street, secured by Father Gleeson for the Sisters of St. Joseph, whom he introduced into the parish.

The present estimate of the population of the parish is 3500, Irish and their descendants. From April, 1880, to June, 1898, there have been 3812 baptisms and 348 marriages. The first baptism was that of Catharine Mulcahy, May 30, 1880, and the first marriage solemnized was that of Patrick Cronan and Margaret Madden, May 31, 1880.

The successful accomplishment of the work thus far accomplished is chiefly due, under God's providence, to the strong faith and religious zeal of the parishioners, who have heartily co-operated with the efforts of their pastors. Though principally of the working-class they constantly and voluntarily contributed of the means which God gave them to the erection of a church that would redound to His glory and the advancement of religion.

The parishioners were buoyed up with the hope, often inculcated, of sharing in the merit that would accrue from the many holy works that were to be accomplished within this sacred edifice, namely, the preaching of the divine word, the offering of the Holy Sacrifice of the Mass, the sacraments that would be administered, the souls which would be regenerated, strengthened, consoled and sanctified. They will leave to their descendants in St. Patrick's parish enduring memorials of what the strong faith that begets Christian zeal and genuine self-sacrifice can accomplish when strengthened by the all-powerful grace of God.

ASSISTANT PASTORS.—The Revs. James Birracree, Jeremiah Curtin, Edward O'Donnell, Farrell Martin, D.D., Dominic Brown, James B. Lawless, William Gibbons and F. A. Jordan.

## ST. MICHAEL'S (MISSION) CHURCH,

### WATERVILLE.

WATERVILLE is a suburb of Waterbury, and, until the advent of the Rev. Father Gleeson, the Catholics of that district were attended from the church of the Immaculate Conception. The first Catholic settler of this mission was John McCarthy, who took up his residence in 1854. He was followed soon afterwards by Charles Shepley and Hugh O'Donnell. When Father Gleeson assumed charge of St. Patrick's parish, Waterbury, he took at the same time control of Waterville as a mission. The first Mass said under the new regime was celebrated in Ford's Hall, on January 19th, 1896, by Father Gleeson. For a time this arrangement was continued, until the growing membership made it necessary to provide a place of worship of their own. An eligible site was secured, centrally located on the main street, directly in the heart of the thriving village. The corner-stone of the new church of St. Michael was laid in the presence of fully 3,000 people on Sunday, June 20th, 1897. Bishop Tierney officiated, attended by a number of priests. The sermon was preached by the Rev. Michael J. Daly, of Thomaston, whose text was, "And this stone which I have set up for a title shall be called the house of God," *Gen. xxviii. 22.* "And whosoever shall fall on this stone shall be broken; but on whomsoever it shall fall, him will it grind to powder." *Ibid.*, 43.

At the conclusion of Father Daly's address, Bishop Tierney spoke words of congratulation upon the work which the people had accomplished, and exhorted them to remain steadfast to the teachings of Holy Church, after which he imparted the episcopal benediction.

St. Michael's church was dedicated on Sunday, August 8, 1897, by Bishop Tierney, with impressive ceremonies. A Solemn High Mass followed, with the Rev. Joseph Gleeson, pastor, as celebrant, the Rev. M. J. Daly as deacon, the Rev. Luke Lawlor as subdeacon, and the Rev. J. L. McGuinness as Master of Ceremonies. The preacher was the Rev. William Gibbons, who selected the following text: "I will bring them to my holy mountain, and make them joyful in my house of prayer . . . for my house shall be called a house of prayer for all the people."

The new church faces the west and is directly opposite the largest school in the village.

The first baptism in Waterville as a mission of St. Patrick's was that of Charles Humphrey, March 8, 1896, and the first marriage in the chapel was that of Frederick Doll and Margaret McConnell, June 22, 1898.

## THE SACRED HEART PARISH,

### WATERBURY.

SECOND of the daughters of the mother church, the parish of the Sacred Heart is discharging faithfully its appointed task, and realizing the fondest hopes of its founders. Like all other young parishes, it has had its struggles and trials, but with steady purpose it has held to its course, and has seen the greater part of its material work accomplished.

On Sunday, February 15, 1885, Rev. William Harty, rector of the parish of the Immaculate Conception, made the formal announcement that the Right Rev. Bishop McMahon had erected a new parish in the city. The announcement was not entirely unexpected, as rumors of the intended division had been current for some time. The new parish was to comprise East Main street east of Dublin street, all of Dublin street, the east side of Welton street, Walnut street and all of the streets east of these points, and would include between 1,500 and 2,000 souls. The Rev. Hugh Treanor, who for six years had been the efficient assistant pastor of St. Mary's church, Norwalk, was appointed by Bishop McMahon pastor of the new parish. A short time after the division the lots, on which the church now stands, were purchased by Father Treanor from the estate of Horace Porter for $4,440. A piece of property north of the church, and six acres on the east, were subsequently added.

On Sunday, February 22, Father Treanor preached his initial sermon to his new flock in the church of the Immaculate Conception. On March 1, the members of the Sacred Heart parish held divine services for the first time as a distinct congregation in St. Patrick's chapel. Services were held here until the blessing of the basement of the new church, March 14, 1886.

Bringing to his new field of labor earnestness, zeal and a spirit not easily subdued by real or apparent difficulties, Father Treanor began immediately the task of providing his parishioners with a temple of worship that would be not only suitable to their present and possible future requirements, but an ornament also to the city. And this was no light undertaking. For years Father Treanor's parishioners had contributed generously to the support of the mother parish. Many of them had been pew-holders since the dedication of the church. The memories of many went back to the days when, but few in number, comparatively speaking, they reverently knelt around the altar in old St. Peter's. To begin again the erection of a church and its necessary adjuncts was the task which the central authority of the diocese called upon them to perform. They cheerfully obeyed. With the courage, perseverance and self-sacrifice so characteristic of Catholic people in the cause of religion, they bent their energies to accomplish the will of the bishop, which they regarded as the will of God. Generously they co-operated with their pastor, giving freely of their time and money. In the furtherance of their purpose they received generous assistance from their former fellow-parishioners. So successful were their efforts that in seven months almost from the day that Father Treanor assumed charge of the parish, his congregation had the happiness of witnessing the laying of the corner-stone of their church with the impressive ceremonial of the Catholic ritual. That day, which meant so much for the parishioners of the Sacred Heart parish, was Sunday, August 16, 1885. The corner-stone was laid by Bishop McMahon, in the presence of an estimated attendance of 8000 persons. The sermon was preached by the Rev. Francis Delargy of the Order of Redemptorists. The handsome silver trowel used by the Bishop during the ceremony was presented to the Rev. John Russell of New Haven, who was the largest contributor on the occasion.

The first mile-stone on the journey of the young parish had been reached and passed successfully. The future was bright with promise, as the past had been fruitful in blessings. Redoubling their efforts the members of the parish began to look anxiously forward to the day when they could worship within the walls of their own church home. This happiness was vouchsafed them on March 14, 1886, when the basement of the church was blessed and formally opened for divine worship. Bishop McMahon graced the occasion by his presence. The Rev. John Russell was the celebrant of the Mass, and the sermon was preached by the Rev. William J. Slocum, of Norwalk. At the vesper service confirmation was administered for the first time to a class of over sixty children.

Thanksgiving day (November 28), 1889, witnessed the crowning of the good work, a fitting day on which to give to God a holy temple wherein His name should be praised. On that day the new edifice was solemnly dedicated under the patronage of the Sacred Heart of Jesus by the Right Rev. Bishop McMahon. The celebrant of the Mass was the Rev. Michael Tierney, of New Britain. The sermon was preached by the Rev. Thomas Broderick, of Hartford. At the evening services, the Rev. James Fagan of Naugatuck officiated.

The cost of the church was $55,000. The architect was P. C. Keeley, of Brooklyn, N. Y.

During 1893 and 1894 the attention of the parish and its pastor was largely occupied with the erection of a parochial residence, on Wolcott street, adjoining the church. It is a substantial and commodious three-story structure, built of pallet brick, with Dummerston granite and terra cotta trimmings. The entire inside finish is of brown ash, and the floors are of quartered oak and southern pine. The architect was Augustus J. Smith.

On November 15, 1897, Father Treanor's pastorate ended with his appointment to St. Patrick's parish, Norwich. He was immediately succeeded by the Rev. Thomas Shelley, who has gained the affection of his flock by his active and paternal interest in their welfare. The membership of the parish is between 1,800 and 2,000 souls.

The clergy who have assisted in the labors of this parish are the Rev. Frederick Murphy, the Rev. Robert Egan, and the present assistant, the Rev. Bernard Bray.

## ST. ANNE'S PARISH (FRENCH-CANADIAN),

### WATERBURY.

IN April, 1886, the Rev. Joseph Fones, while pastor of St. John's parish, Watertown, was requested by Bishop McMahon to assume pastoral charge also of the French Catholic population of Waterbury. He began at once to organize his new flock. The old Universalist chapel on Grand street (known as Trinity chapel) was secured for divine worship. Mass was celebrated in this building for the first time on Sunday, May 2, 1886. At this time the population was 500 French Canadians and 40 French. The first marriage ceremony performed in it, and the first after the erection of the parish, took place on May 5, 1886, Father Fones officiating. The congregation continued to worship here until the dedication of their present church, January 6, 1889. Previous to their organization into a separate parish the French Catholics attended divine service in the churches of the district in which they resided.

Father Fones continued to reside in Watertown, visiting St. Anne's every Sunday. In November, 1886, he relinquished the charge of his Watertown parish and took up his residence in Waterbury. During his short pastorate in Waterbury he accomplished much for the spiritual and material welfare of his parishioners. From a scattered folk they became a compact and influential organization. In April, 1887, he bought from the estate of A. C. Porter the lot on the corner of Clay and South Main streets, for $10,000. In July, 1888, he purchased from E. C. Lewis the former parochial residence, with its spacious grounds, the price being $22,500. St. Anne's church was built on this lot at a cost of $10,000. The corner-stone was laid on September 2, 1888, by Bishop McMahon, and the sermon was preached by Rev. J. M. Emard, now Bishop of Valleyfield, Canada. The dedication of the church under the patronage of St. Anne took place on January 27, 1889.

For some time before his death Father Fones had been in declining health. He realized that his course was well-nigh run. Two weeks before the end came he retired to Pawtucket, R. I., his birth-place. He died May 18, 1890, at North Attleboro, Mass. His remains were interred in the Roman Catholic cemetery in Pawtucket.

On May 15, 1890, the Rev. J. E. Bourret began his duties as pastor of St. Anne's parish. The purchase of the two pieces of property already referred to and the erection of the church entailed considerable debt. But with characteristic energy, and confident of the co-operation of his parishioners, Father Bourret set himself at once to the task of reducing the burden. Not less diligently has Father Bourret labored for the spiritual interests of his flock. The number of religious societies in his parish attests his zeal in this respect.

In 1895 Father Bourret erected a school, which has eight grades taught by the Sisters of the Congregation of Notre Dame. Beginning with 175 pupils it has now 400. In the same year a commodious rectory was built on South Main street. The old residence, having been removed to the rear and suitably refitted, serves as a convent. The present church is a temporary structure which will be transformed into a school when the new church is erected. The present school building will be converted into a convent, as it is admirably built for that purpose.

The number of souls who have received the infusion of divine faith by baptism in St. Anne's parish from 1886 to 1898, exclusive, is 1,401; the number of marriages, 275.

The population of the parish is about 3,500 souls. The clergymen who have served the parish as assistants are: the Rev. Eugene Roberge, the Rev. A. Mailhiot, the Rev. J. A. Cadotte, the Rev. J. E. Senesac, the Rev. J. J. Papillon, the Rev. F. Bedard.

## ST. CECILIA'S PARISH (GERMAN)

### WATERBURY.

THE Catholic Germans of Waterbury were organized into the Society of the Holy Family at a meeting held in St. Patrick's hall, April 24, 1892. The charter members were Thomas Hermann, Herman Herringer, Charles Martin, Jacob Daniels, John L. Saxe, Irwin Straub, Michael Dietz, Franz Schell, Louis Strobel, Michael Block, Anton Hoefler, John Wieker, Henry Schild, Sr., and others. A committee of these, consisting of Herman Herringer, Jacob Daniels and Irwin Straub, were empowered to wait upon Bishop McMahon and to solicit the formation of the German Catholics of Waterbury into a separate organization. The committee was instructed to organize and secure a suitable site for a church. Accordingly, a lot was purchased on Scoville street by the Society for $7,500. The Rev. Farrell Martin, D.D., who had been appointed an assistant to the rector of the Immaculate Conception parish, had received instructions from the Bishop to organize the German Catholics. He addressed them for the first time in St. Patrick's hall on October 9, 1892, and on November 18th, Dr. Martin was appointed pastor of the newly organized parish.

The Sisters of the Congregation of Notre Dame having donated the use of their convent hall to Dr. Martin, the first Mass after his appointment as pastor was said there on November 20, 1892. On January 1, 1893, the corporation was formed with Herman Herringer and Carl Martin as the lay trustees. The church property, held by the Holy Family Society, in all valued at $12,000, was transferred to the corporation.

Dr. Martin applied himself at once to the erection of a church for his people. The work of construction commenced in May, 1894, and the corner-stone was laid on July 29th following. Bishop Tierney officiated, the Rev. Wilhelm J. Remmper, S.J., preached in German, and the Rev. S. B. Hedges, C.S.P., in English. The work progressed so rapidly that the ceremony of dedication took place on November 18, 1894, Very Rev. John A. Mulcahy, Vicar-General, officiating. After the dedication a solemn High Mass was celebrated with Father Mulcahy as celebrant, the Rev. John H. Duggan as deacon, the Rev. William Lynch as sub-deacon and the Rev. James H. O'Donnell as master of ceremonies. The English sermon was delivered by the Rev. L. A. Delurey, O.S.A., and the discourse in German was pronounced by the Rev. John Roser, O.S.F.

The parish property consists of church, rectory and a lot. The number of baptisms in the parish from 1892 to 1898 was 184, and the marriages 32. The first baptism administered was that of Rudolph August Gauthe, March 26, 1892. The first marriage took place on January 29, 1893, the contracting parties being Frederick Stubenrauch and Margaret Eagan.

The members of St. Cecilia's parish are of different political affiliations, of good social standing, and in occupation are mostly factory employees. They number about 800 souls.

## ST. FRANCIS XAVIER'S PARISH,

### WATERBURY.

THE territory comprised within the limits of St. Francis Xavier's parish, with the exception of a few streets, was under the jurisdiction of the Rev. John H. Duggan from the time of his appointment to St. Patrick's parish in April, 1880, till his death in 1895. It is that section of Waterbury known as Washington Hill, with about 200 souls from the parish of the Immaculate Conception parish. The first Catholics to reside within the present limits of the parish were Michael Donahue and Patrick O'Reilly. They came to Waterbury about 1836, but settled in this section of the town a few years later.

The first and present pastor, the Rev. Jeremiah J. Curtin, came here from New Milford. He received his letter of appointment to Waterbury on November 30, 1895, and arrived among his new charge on December 3rd, the feast of St. Francis Xavier; it was this circumstance that determined the selection of the patron saint. Father Curtin took up his temporary abode at the rectory of the Immaculate Conception, and began to cast about him for a suitable place in which to assemble his people for Mass and instruction. The Auditorium, a public hall, on South Main street, was secured, and on December 8, 1895, the members of St. Francis Xavier's parish assembled for the first time as a distinct organization; on this day, the feast of the Immaculate Conception, the pastor said two Masses for his people. At this time the population of the parish was 2,800, or 565 families. The new parish was enthusiastic and determined to vie with their pastor in securing a place of worship of their own, and more centrally located than the Auditorium; and when both forces were active and generous the object of their hearts' desires was soon accomplished. On December 30, 1895, Father Curtin took possession of the present parochial residence on the corner of Washington and Baldwin streets, and in the reception-room of which on January 2, 1896, was offered the first Mass said within the boundary lines of the parish. In this room and on the same date the Rev. Peter Skelly administered the sacrament of Baptism to Thomas Murphy and Ellen Kearns. Father Curtin used this room for week-day Masses and baptisms until May 29, 1896. On the feast of St. Blase, February 3, 1896, 5,000 people passed through this room after having received the blessing of the throat given on that day. Thus began the sacred functions of religion in St. Francis Xavier's parish.

The formal and complete organization of the parish into a corporation took place on January 19, 1896, when the following church committee was formed: John Havican, John E. Finley, James Coughlin, Francis Reed, John C. Allman, Thomas Halpin, William Delaney, Timothy Meehan, Emmet Riordan, Thomas McEvoy, James Tiernan and John Galvin. The lay trustees elected by this committee on that evening were James J. Cassin and James Coughlin.

The parish was now thoroughly organized and the enthusiasm continued unabated. As an earnest of the people's co-operation with the designs of their pastor, the first collection taken up on February 9, 1896, reached the gratifying amount of $3,390. The first step towards the consummation of their hopes was the purchase of a piece of land on the corner of Washington and Baldwin streets from the Waterbury Buckle Company. The deeds of the property were conveyed to the corporation on February 12, 1896. Thereupon a contract for a temporary church was signed, and the work of construction given to Mr. Charles O'Connor. The first Mass said in the new church was offered upon April 22, 1896. On this occasion Father Curtin solemnized the marriage of Nicholas J. McEvoy and Elizabeth Wall. On May 30, 1896 (Memorial Day), the church was dedicated by Bishop Tierney. After the ceremonies of dedication a solemn High Mass was celebrated, with the Rev. J. O'R. Sheridan, celebrant. The Rev. Peter Skelly preached the dedication sermon. On October 25th confirmation was administered for the first time in this parish, 174 persons becoming soldiers of Jesus Christ. On this occasion Bishop Tierney solemnly blessed the statues of Our Lady and of St. Joseph, the preacher being the Rev. James J. Eagan. In November, 1896, Father Curtin's parishioners gave further evidence of their willingness to co-operate with him by contributing $3,722 net at a fair. And if still further evidence were needed to show the ability of the pastor and the generosity of the people, it may be stated that the receipts of the first year of the parish's existence were $20,657; furthermore, there is in the treasury a balance of nearly $20,000 on hand with which to begin the erection of a church worthy of the dignity of the parish. This work has been unavoidably delayed owing to the extreme difficulty of securing a desirable site. The assistant pastor is the Rev. J. E. Clark, appointed in January, 1896.

Among the benefactors of St. Francis Xavier's parish may be noted Right Rev. Bishop Tierney, who donated the first and most highly prized property of the parish, a chalice of beautiful design; and Mrs. Ann Weis, who presented the large pipe-organ now in use.

From the formation of the parish to 1898 exclusive, the baptisms have numbered 281 and the marriages 46.

The first baptism was that of Thomas Shea, December 5, 1895. The first marriage was between P. F. Cunningham and Catharine A. Saults, January 15, 1896.

The first death occurred on December 11, 1895, Ann Honors. The first child to receive confirmation was Thomas J. Coogan, October 25, 1896.

The population of the parish at present is 3,000 souls, Irish and their descendants.

The Rev. J. J. Curtin is a member of the Diocesan School Commission.

## ST. JOSEPH'S (LITHUANIAN) PARISH,

### WATERBURY.

ST. JOSEPH'S parish, comprising the Lithuanian Catholics of Waterbury, was organized in 1894. The Rev. Joseph Zebris was appointed pastor, and entered upon his work on March 28th. The first Mass was celebrated on April 1st, in Mitchell's block on Bank street.

On September 28th, the Dreher property, with a frontage of 200 feet on James street and 220 feet on John street, was purchased at a cost of $7,000, and the erection of a church was begun on October 6th. On Thanksgiving day, November 29, 1894, the corner-stone was laid with the usual services. Vicar-General John A. Mulcahy performed the ceremony, the Rev. B. Molejkatys acting as deacon, and Dr. Farrell Martin as sub-deacon. The address of the occasion was delivered by the Rev. Joseph Jaksztys, first in the Lithuanian and then in the Polish language. He afterward addressed the other clergymen in Latin, and was followed by Vicar-General Mulcahy in an address of congratulation to the Lithuanian people.

At the time of the laying of the corner-stone, the exterior of the little church was already completed. It was ready for occupancy on December 16th. The building has a seating capacity of 300, besides the galleries over the vestibule. The dedication of the church took place on December 25th, the pastor, Father Zebris, officiating. When the parish was formed, its population was estimated at 478 souls. In 1898 the number had increased to 1,000, including the Lithuanians of Union City and Naugatuck and about 250 Poles in Waterbury and dependencies. From 1894 to 1897 the number of baptisms was 250 and the marriages 74.

II—26

The present church is designed to serve as a school-building, when a larger and more imposing church shall have been erected. The present pastor of St. Joseph's parish is the Rev. Peter Saurasaitis, who began his pastoral duties on May 28, 1898.

## THE ITALIAN CATHOLICS,

### WATERBURY.

A RECENT estimate places the number of Italian Catholics in Waterbury at 1,500. As yet they have no church organization, although laudable efforts are being made to erect a parish for them. In 1894 a mission was conducted by two Italian priests at the church of the Immaculate Conception from which good results followed. For some time the question of securing for themselves a church has been under consideration by the Italian Catholics, and no doubt the near future will witness the realization of their hopes. With this end in view, the Right Rev. Bishop Tierney appointed the Rev. Dr. Martin, pastor of St. Cecilia's parish, to the pastoral charge of the Italian Catholics of Waterbury. He assumed this additional labor in October, 1894. Since then Italian clergymen have given missions to the people, with a view to the permanent organization of a parish. For the benefit of the Italians, a sermon in their language is preached at the first Mass in St. Cecilia's church every Sunday. The first baptism since the Italians came under Dr. Martin's jurisdiction was that of Maria Oriano, October 21, 1894; the first marriage was between Ciro Carangelo and Benedetta Lanze.

## ST. THOMAS' PARISH,

### WATERBURY

O FFICIAL notice of the formation of the new parish of St. Thomas was given by the Rev. William J. Slocum, rector of the mother parish of the Immaculate Conception, on Sunday, September 18th, 1898. The boundary lines were announced as follows: Beginning at the intersection of Walnut and Ward streets, and going westward along Ward and Vine to Grove street, along Grove, taking in the north side of that street, to Cooke; the north side of Cooke street from Grove to Buckingham, along Buckingham to Pine, from Pine to Columbia avenue, and from there to the city line. The Rev. Timothy M. Crowley was appointed pastor of the new parish. He preached his first sermon and assumed formal charge of the parish on Sunday, September 25th, on the occasion of the dedication of the church. When the construction of a church in this section of the city was proposed, it was intended that it should be a portion of the old parish, a "chapel of ease;" but the need of a separate parish was soon recognized. The church was begun and completed by Rev. Father Slocum, who paid over half of the indebtedness which its construction entailed.

The corner-stone of the new edifice was laid on Saturday, September 24th, and the ceremony of dedication was performed on the day following. Bishop Tierney officiated, assisted by a number of priests of the city and neighboring parishes. This ceremony was followed by a Solemn High Mass, with the Rev. James O'R. Sheridan as celebrant; Rev. W. A. White as deacon; Rev. M. Daly as sub-deacon; Rev. P. Kennedy as master of ceremonies. The dedicatory sermon was preached by the new pastor, Rev. T. M. Crowley.

The church stands at the corner of Crown and Beacon streets, and is an imposing structure. It has a seating capacity of 700. The parish population is about 1800 souls, chiefly Irish and their descendants. Father Crowley is assisted by the Rev. William Kennedy. The work of erecting a parochial residence is in progress.

# NEW LONDON COUNTY.

EW LONDON COUNTY is bounded on the north by Windham, Tolland and Hartford counties, on the east by Windham county and Rhode Island, on the south by Long Island Sound, and on the west by Middlesex county. From east to west the length averages 26 miles, and its average breadth is about 20 miles. The cities and towns in which there are Catholic parishes are the following:

| | | | |
|---|---|---|---|
| NEW LONDON, | COLCHESTER, | MONTVILLE, | NORWICH, |
| BALTIC, | JEWETT CITY, | MYSTIC, | TAFTVILLE, |
| | VOLUNTOWN. | | |

## ST. MARY'S—STAR OF THE SEA—PARISH,
### NEW LONDON.

EW LONDON was settled by the English in 1646. Its Indian name was *Nameaug*, otherwise known as *Towawog*. In March, 1658, the General Assembly gave the town its present name; "that they might leave to posterity the memory of that renowned city of London, from whence we had our transportation, (we) have thought fit in honor to that famous city, to call the said plantation New London." At the same time the Pequot river became the Thames.

Elsewhere in these pages we have written of the presence in New London of 400 Acadian exiles in January, 1756, of the San Domingan refugees, who gathered here at the end of the last century, of the arrival and death of Father Duprè from the island of Gaudeloupe, of Thomas Allen's inn, of the visit of Bishop Carroll to this portion of his flock, and of other events of historical interest that occurred in and about New London. We have now to deal with the Catholic life of New London as a permanent force in the upbuilding of the city's welfare.

After Bishop Carroll's visit in 1791, thirty-two years elapsed before New London was honored by the presence of another bishop. Bishop Cheverus, active, alert and solicitous for the welfare of his vast diocese, visited New

London in June, 1823, and on the first of the month, among other priestly functions, baptized two children. The record is:

"*1823, June 1*—Baptized Thomas, born January 4, 1821. Sponsor: J. B. Walbach.
"Honora, born December 4, 1822. Sponsor: John O'Brien.
"Both children of Richard and Catharine Morris.     † J. Cheverus."

A local historian says of Bishop Cheverus' visit: "There was at the time, we believe, but a single family of Roman Catholics in the town—that of Colonel Walbach, who was commandant at the fort for many years. He had a pew at St. James' (Protestant), and himself and family were regular attendants upon its services, joining in the worship of the church with apparent interest and devotion. A priest of their own profession came to visit them occasionally, and give them the rites of their church. The Roman Catholic bishop of Boston at that time was Dr. Cheverus, a man whose amiable, pure and benevolent character secured the respect of men of all creeds and conditions. On one occasion he came to New London to pass a Sunday with the family which has been mentioned. The rector took occasion to invite him to preach at St. James' in the afternoon. He accepted the invitation, and at the usual hour of service came to the church in the costume of his office, and after reading some English prayers from the desk, preached a sermon from the pulpit. A crowded congregation assembled to hear him, for in those days a Romish bishop, in the attire of his office, was a lion indeed. Fortunately, to secure us against any charge of tendency to Popery, our Congregational neighbors invited him to preach for them also at a later hour. It was a long summer day. A crowd assembled at the appointed hour. The bishop came again in his robes, and after offering an extempore prayer, delivered a sermon upon Martha and Mary from the pulpit of the Congregational church." During this visit Bishop Cheverus said Mass at the fort, the guest of Colonel Walbach.

The Rev. R. D. Woodley, of Providence, was the next ecclesiastic to visit New London. He ministered to the wants of the Catholics here in 1826, in the week beginning with July 12, and also in October of the same year. From his report to Bishop Fenwick of his visitations we learn that during those missionary tours he baptized two children, besides performing other duties incident to his office.

The first resident pastor of Hartford, who had all Connecticut in his jurisdiction, the Rev. Bernard O'Cavanagh, attended New London in April, 1830. He offered the Holy Sacrifice of the Mass in the residence of Mr. P. Mitchell, and baptized one infant, having on the evening previous heard a number of confessions. The name of Father Fitton now became associated with New London, as we gather from the following record of marriages:

"New London.

JOHN BALDWIN  )    *1830, Oct. 14*: Married John Baldwin to Matilda Dunn. Witnesses, John and Mary Dunn.
   AND     ) 
MAT'T DUNN.   )                                      JAS. FITTON."

¹ The bell of this church "was brought from the West Indies, and had originally hung in some French church or convent. It was small, but its tone was sweet and musical."—*Annals of St. James'*, New London.

ST. MARY'S STAR OF THE SEA CHURCH,
UNLEDGE, CONN.

Another entry in Father Fitton's handwriting is :

| | |
|---|---|
| MATH. HIGHLAND<br>AND<br>ESTHER MURPHY. | "*1830, Oct. 19th :* Married Matthew Highland to Esther Murphy, both from New London. Witnesses, Lawrence McGuire and Ann McGuire. JAS. FITTON." |

Of his experiences in New London Father Fitton thus writes : "To be hooted and occasionally stoned by urchins who had imbibed the prejudices of their parents was not an uncommon occurrence in former days. But deep-rooted as was the prejudice of the majority of the people, there were not a few found better informed at New London, who were inclined to liberality and toler-ance, and who allowed the use of the court-house for occasional preaching."[1]

Notwithstanding the great influx of Catholics into New London at the close of the last century the number found here by Father Fitton was small. Deprived of priests, surrounded by hostile influences, the descendants of those who adhered to the ancient faith fell away and became believers in creeds that held the doctrines of their ancestors in abhorrence. And some of the New London families who boast of their Puritan ancestry are not of Puritan extraction, but are the descendants of men and women of Irish, French, Spanish and Portuguese ancestors—children of the Catholic faith. Their names are a part of the public records of New London, and the story of some of them is told in the pages of this history.

Of the status of Catholicity in New London, during his period of service, Father Fitton wrote in a record-book, preserved in St. Mary's church : "The Catholics of New London in 1831 numbered about three families and five unmarried persons. These were attended from time to time by the clergy-man from Hartford (himself). This number even, small as it was, dimin-ished, and then as gradually began to increase till 1842, when an appropria-tion having been made for repairs on Fort Trumbell, a number of mechanics and laborers came with their families to the place. About this time an upper room of a small building near the southwest corner of Long Bridge (now Bank street) was rented for the purpose of divine worship. Here the Catholics assembled on Sundays, and were attended monthly from Worcester, Mass., by the clergyman formerly of Hartford (himself). In January, 1843, a lot of land was purchased for a church and deeded in trust to Rt. Rev. Benedict Fenwick and the foundation immediately commenced, which, by the energy and persevering zeal of the little flock, was so far advanced as to be ready to have the Holy Sacrifice of the Mass offered up in it the following April." Father Fitton paid a missionary visit to New London on April 9, 1832.

From the marriage register preserved at St. Patrick's church, Hartford, we take the following additional entries.

"NEW LONDON, CONN.

| | |
|---|---|
| PETER WHITTEN<br>AND<br>ANN PHALEN. | *1835, Sept. 21 :* Married Peter Whitten to Ann Phalen. Witnesses, Jas. Rargen and Elizabeth Crandell. JAS. FITTON." |

"*Sept. 22 :* Married John Barry to Margaret Donoghue. Witnesses, Jas. Fitzgibbons and Bridget Ford. JAS. FITTON."

[1] "*Historical Sketches.*"

Upon Father Fitton's transfer to Worcester he attended New London from that place at monthly intervals, saying Mass in an upper room of a small building on the southwest corner of Long Bridge. The growth of the Catholic population soon made more ample accommodations necessary, so that a lot was purchased by Father Fitton on Jay street in January, 1843. The work of constructing a church was begun immediately, and so vigorously was it pushed that the building was ready for occupancy in the following April. Of this little church Father Fitton wrote: "Although it was anticipated at the time that this edifice would prove too limited for increasing numbers, yet it was considered that the fact of the proprietors of the houses right and left being good Protestant fellow-citizens, would be the best insurance against casualties that otherwise might happen." Bishop Fitzpatrick, of Boston dedicated the church on May 13, 1850, and administered Confirmation on the day following. Among those confirmed on that occasion was Lieutenant Deshon.

In 1852 the church had become inadequate to the wants of the parish; it was determined to erect a more commodious house of worship. A site on Truman street was obtained, and the work of building was begun without delay. This church was dedicated by Bishop O'Reilly on May 13, 1855, the Bishop also preaching the sermon. "The church was well filled," wrote the bishop, "and the ceremony most edifying." In June, 1860, the church was furnished with an organ. Its seating capacity was 700, and the whole property was valued at $12,000.

In the meantime New London had been attended by a number of priests. In August, 1845, it passed under the jurisdiction of Rev. John Brady, of Hartford, who remained in control until September, 1848, when the Rev. James Gibson assumed charge. He attended to the spiritual wants of the Catholics here until 1850, when they began to be served by the Jesuit Fathers from Holy Cross College, Rev. William Logan and Rev. Peter Blenkinsop. Father Logan died here in 1850, a victim of smallpox.

The first resident pastor, Rev. Peter Duffy, came in 1851, but remained only for a brief period. His successor, the Rev. Thomas Stokes, officiated until October, 1852. Rev. Thomas Ryan followed as pastor. During his pastorate, which was of six years' duration, St. Patrick's church, on Truman street, was built and dedicated. The original church on Jay street still remains the property of the parish and was used for Sunday-school purposes.

The next pastor of St. Patrick's parish was the Rev. P. J. Gaynor, who came in 1858. He administered the affairs of the parish for eight years, having been transferred to St. Francis' parish, New Haven, in 1866. Then the Rev. Bernard Tully came, and during a short pastorate of a few months purchased the lot on the corner of Washington and Huntington streets, on which the present church edifice stands. Father Tully was followed in August, 1867, by the Rev. Philip Grace, D.D., who began the erection of the present church.

In 1867, Dr. Grace was succeeded by the Rev. Edmund A. O'Connor, who laid the corner-stone of the church under the title of St. Mary's, Star of

REV. FRANCIS P. O'KEEFE.

REV. THOMAS JOYNT

REV. PATRICK J. KENNEDY.

the Sea, August 15, 1870. The exterior of the church had been almost completed when the clerestory fell, entailing a great financial loss. Father O'Connor died here in 1871, the Rev. John Furlong succeeding temporarily to the pastorate. In May, 1872, the Rev. Michael A. Tierney took up the reins of government, and remained as pastor until late in 1873. Father Tierney organized the Star of the Sea Total Abstinence Society, and continued the work of the construction of the church. About January 1, 1874, his successor, the Rev. Patrick P. Lawlor, became pastor. Resuming work on the church, he brought it to a successful completion. The solemn dedication took place on Sunday, May 7, 1876, with elaborate ceremonial. After the ceremonies of dedication Solemn Pontifical Mass was celebrated by Rt. Rev. Bishop Galberry, the orator on the occasion being the Rev. Michael O'Farrell, of St. Peter's church, New York. In the evening Solemn Pontifical Vespers were sung by the above-mentioned prelate, and the Rev. Father O'Farrell again pronounced the discourse before an audience that taxed the seating capacity of the church to its utmost. Father Lawlor remained pastor of St. Mary's until June, 1879, when he was transferred to St. Mary's parish, New Haven. A local historian says that "Father Lawlor was a very popular man, and had a high reputation for executive ability."

Father Lawlor's mantle fell upon the shoulders of the Rev. Thomas W. Broderick. Among the works which signalized his administration of four years was the reduction of the parish indebtedness by over $10,000, and the artistic grading and beautifying, and otherwise improving, the valuable property about the church and parochial residence. On May 28, 1883, the present incumbent, the Rev. Thomas P. Joynt, assumed pastoral charge of St. Mary's. Father Joynt has continued the excellent work of his predecessors, manifesting great zeal and priestly activity in promoting both the temporal and spiritual interests of his people. In July, 1891, he purchased a beautiful residence on Franklin street, which, suitably remodeled, has become the home of the Sisters who are the teachers of the children of his parish. This purchase was made at the expenditure of $6,000. In May, 1892, the Young Ladies' High School, contiguous to the church, was secured at a cost of $10,000. In addition to these works, Father Joynt has reduced the indebtedness every year, so that the financial condition of St. Mary's is surpassed by few parishes in the diocese. Father Joynt is assisted in his parochial labors by the Rev. David O'Donnell and the Rev. John F. Quinn. St. Mary's school is taught by nine sisters of Mercy, of the Meriden community, Sister M. Xavier, superioress, who began their efficient labors in New London in August, 1892. The school is attended by 369 girls. A new parochial school is in the course of construction and will be ready for the ceremony of dedication on Sunday, September 3d, of the present year.

Attached to New London is the mission of Rocklawn, whose church is dedicated in honor of Our Lady of Good Counsel.

On Sunday April 30, 1893, the Catholics of New London observed the fiftieth anniversary of the erection of their first church in that city. The Solemn High Mass on the occasion was celebrated by the Rev. Michael Tierney assisted by Rev. John Lenehan, deacon; Rev. Timothy R. Sweeney, sub-deacon; the Rev. Michael H. May, master of ceremonies. Right Rev. Bishop McMahon occupied a throne in the sanctuary with the Rev. J. P. Dougherty of New York and Rev. Thomas W. Broderick of Hartford as attendants. The oration was pronounced by the Rev. V. A. Higgins, O.P., S.T.M., of New Haven. His subject was "The Benefits Conferred by the Church." The day's celebration was fittingly closed by Solemn Vespers sung *coram episcopo*, with the Rev. J. J. Furlong as celebrant, Rev. J. H. Fitz-maurice as deacon, the Rev. M. Cray as sub-deacon, Rev. M. H. May, master of ceremonies. The chaplains to Bishop McMahon were Rev. T. W. Brode-rick, Hartford, and Rev. J. E. Leonard of Troy. The discourse was pro-nounced by Rev. John A. Mulcahy of Waterbury. At the close of the ser-vices Bishop McMahon in a felicitous manner addressed words of congratula-tion to the congregation. Among those present on this joyous occasion, who attended the first church a half century before, were Michael Gaffey, Stephen Hayes, William Sheridan, Mrs. Daniel Hogan, Mrs. Edmund Sweeney, Mrs. Maurice McDonald and Mrs. John Ferguson.

## IMMACULATE CONCEPTION PARISH.

### Baltic.

BALTIC is located in the town of Sprague, and is built on both sides of the Shetucket river. Besides the village proper, the parish com-prises the outlying villages of Franklin, Scotland and Hanover.

As early as 1840, a small band of Irish Catholics located in Baltic and vicinity, and were generally occupied in farm work. Among the early settlers we note Denis P. Sheahan, Jeremiah Donovan, Jeremiah Curtin, and Peter Hartnett. Their number was increased by the building of the Provi-dence and Hartford railroad. It was, however, the building of a large cotton mill by the Spragues of Rhode Island, which brought the first great influx of Catholics to reside at Baltic. This necessitated the speedy erection of a church.

In the meantime, the Catholics of Baltic experienced the happiness of assisting at the Holy Sacrifice for the first time in the summer of 1852, the Rev. Michael McCabe being the celebrant. When Father McCabe assumed charge of Danielson his jurisdiction included also Willimantic, Baltic, Colchester, Stafford Springs and Putnam. The successors of Father McCabe to attend Baltic were Rev. H. O'Reilly, 1860 to 1863; Rev. Daniel Mullen, January 7, 1863, to May, 1863; Rev. Flor. De Bruycker, May, 1863, to September 1, 1869.

The first Catholic church in Baltic was built in 1860, during the pastor-ate of Father O'Reilly. It was 77 x 38 feet. Father O'Reilly also purchased the cemetery in 1860, which was blessed on November 1, 1861. Father O'Reilly's successor was the Rev. Flor. De Bruycker, as when Willimantic received its first resident pastor Baltic became a dependency. During his administration, Father De Bruycker enlarged and renovated the church at an expenditure of $15,000. The enlarged structure was 120 x 60 feet.

The first resident pastor of Baltic was the Rev. G. Joseph Van Laar, who entered upon his duties in September, 1869. Zealous to a great degree, religion made rapid strides during Father Van Laar's pastorate. St. Joseph's school was opened on May 15, 1870, with 70 pupils. To meet pressing spiritual needs, he purchased in 1871 a piece of ground upon which he intended to erect a convent, school and chapel; but the sweeping away of the mill dam delayed, but did not prevent the continuance of the work. In the erection of the convent, which contained four stories, Father Van Laar devoted not only his time, but contributed $8,000 from his personal income towards its completion. It was completed in 1874. In the spring of 1876, Father Van Laar resigned his charge and entered the Congregation of the Oblate Fathers.

His successor was Rev. John Van der Noort, who took up the great work left by his predecessor and brought it to a successful completion. Under his guidance religious education began to show forth its fruits. The school, erected at such sacrifices, abundantly proved that it had not been built in vain. Though the number of children attending the school had become reduced from 240 to 30, owing to a large number of people leaving the town on account of the freshet, yet the Sisters persevered and God so blessed their labors that it became necesssary to build an addition to the school. A fine chapel was also added to it. Other works did Father Van der Noort accomplish which made for the honor and glory of God and His church. With him were associated in parochial labors, Revs. James Lancaster, John T. McMahon, John Synnott and James Degnan. Having served with signal success in Baltic until October, 1889, Father Van der Noort was promoted to Putnam, and Rev. John Synnott was appointed his successor. Father Synnott's labors in this field as pastor were those of a priest, zealous and single-minded, one whose sole ambition is the spiritual and temporal welfare of his parishioners. For this were his labors unremitting and productive of excellent results. On September 1, 1897, his ecclesiastical superior called him to a higher sphere of labor and appointed him President of St. Thomas' Preparatory Seminary, Hartford. His successor is the present pastor, Rev. Terrance Dunn.

When the first Mass was celebrated in Baltic in 1852, there were in the vicinity 300 or more Catholics, laborers on the Providence and Hartford railroad. When the church was built in 1860, the number had increased to 800. But the temporal status of Baltic has not kept pace with the years. Thirty-six years ago the Catholic population was about 2000 souls; at present it numbers about 500.

## ST. ANDREW'S PARISH,

### COLCHESTER.

THE first settlement of Colchester began about 1701. Its average length from east to west is about nine miles, about four miles in breadth, and comprises an area of about forty-three square miles. The first Catholic settlers to reside here were Patrick Gardland, John Murphy, Patrick Henry, Thomas Sheridan, John English and James Kelleher and families. As far as can be ascertained, the first Mass celebrated in Colchester, was said in 1851 at the residence of John Murphy, by the Rev. Christopher Moore. About fifty Irish-Catholics were present at that Mass. The first pastor who attended to the wants of the Catholics here was the Rev. Michael McCabe, of Danielson, coming once a month. Rev. Hugh O'Reilly of Willimantic was his successor, and visited Colchester also at monthly intervals. The Rev. Patrick Creighton was the first resident pastor. Following him came in succession Rev. James McCarten, Rev. Patrick Fay, Rev. John Duggan, Rev. B. W. Bray, Rev. John Cooney, and the present rector, Rev. Michael H. May.

St. Andrew's church was built about 1854, by the Rev. Michael McCabe. The first Catholic marriage solemnized in Colchester was that of Martin Minnick and Ann Kearns, Rev. Christopher Moore performing the ceremony. The school was erected during the administration of Father Fay, and is conducted by lay teachers, whose salaries are paid by the town. The school is under the full control of the pastor of St. Andrew's, and has at present 145 children. The present population of St. Andrew's is 600 souls, all Irish and their descendants. The priests who have labored in St. Andrew's parish in the capacity of assistants are the Rev. J. Winters, the Rev. J. Lee, Rev. D. Bailey, Rev. P. McClean, Rev. J. Sheehan, Rev. P. Daly and Rev. C. McCann.

Within the jurisdiction of St. Andrew's are three out-missions, St. Bridget's, Moodus, ten miles distant. The church was built in the seventies and is attended by about 400 souls, for whom Mass is celebrated every Sunday. The Catholic population is chiefly Irish, though there are some Poles. Attached to St. Bridget's is a cemetery.

St. Mary's church, Bozrahville, was built in 1880, six and a half miles from Colchester. Mass is also said here every Sunday. The estimated number of Catholics of this mission is 200 souls. St. John's church, Fitchville, was built by Rev. John Cooney in 1894, and is ten miles from the parochial residence. The population here also is chiefly Irish, and numbers 300 souls. They also receive every Sunday the benefits of the Holy Sacrifice. At the ceremony of laying the corner-stone of St. John's, the Rev. Michael Sullivan preached the sermon. The church was dedicated by Bishop Tierney, the Rev. John Winters preaching the discourse.

The marriage and baptismal records of the mission churches are preserved in the registers of the mother parish. The first recorded marriage is the following: "November 1, 1860, married, James Fenton and Anna Sullivan. Witnesses, John Murphy and Mary Shea. (Signed) P. J. Creighton."

The first recorded baptism is: "October 25, 1860, baptized, Timothy, born 17th October, of John Sullivan and Mary O'Kiely. Sponsors, Michael Gormley and Julia Sullivan, by proxy for Catherine. (Signed) P. J. Creighton."

## PARISH OF OUR LADY OF THE ROSARY,

### JEWETT CITY.

THE first Catholics to reside in Jewett City were John Dolan and Philip O'Reilly, in whose houses the Holy Sacrifice of the Mass was offered about once a month. The first Mass, however, offered within the boundaries of Jewett City was celebrated in 1857 by the Rev. Michael McCabe, pastor of Danielson. At this time the Catholic population numbered 25 families, all Irish. After the organization of Moosup into a parish, Rev.

Fathers Daly, Quinn and Belanger made frequent visits to Jewett City. Becoming too numerous to have divine service in private houses, the Rev. Father Quinn purchased from the Congregationalists in 1864 their house of worship, remodeled it, and suitably prepared it for Catholic worship. In 1868 and 1869 the Catholics of Jewett City were attended by the Rev. Father Mullen of Norwich. Soon after it passed again under the jurisdiction of Moosup. The first resident pastor of Jewett City assumed charge in 1872, and was the Rev. James B. Reynolds appointed by Bishop McFarland. His parish embraced also the missions of Taftville, Occum and Voluntown. Father Reynolds remained here until his death in 1875, having in the meantime secured the Samuel Cole estate for a pastoral residence. His successor was the Rev. John Russell, who served from February, 1875, to June, 1878. His administration was marked by the enlargement of the seating capacity of the church at Jewett City, and by the erection of churches in Taftville and Occum. Following Father Russell came the Rev. Thomas P. Joynt, whose period of service here began in June, 1878, and terminated in June, 1883. Father Joynt built the church at Voluntown and the rectory in Jewett City.

In June, 1883, the mission relationship that existed between Taftville and Occum and Jewett City ceased, and the two former places were erected into independent parishes. The Rev. Francis P. O'Keefe at this time began his pastoral labors in Jewett City, having within his jurisdiction Voluntown and Glasgo. Recognizing that the future would bring new and greater needs, Father O'Keefe with wise foresight purchased the Enoch Hawkins estate, which will be used as the necessities demand. The church at Glasgo was built during his pastorate, mainly through the financial and other assistance of Mr. Lucius Briggs of the town, who donated the land and contributed $500 to the building fund. In February, 1892, Voluntown and Glasgo were separated from Jewett City and elevated to the parochial dignity, with Voluntown as the place of residence.

The assistant priests who served at various times in Jewett City were Revs. Thomas Broderick, Joseph Fones, John Synnott, Daniel M. Lawlor and Patrick Kennedy. When the parish was formed in 1872, its population was estimated at 80 families, chiefly Irish; at present there are 550 Irish people, and 1,100 Canadians.

The cemetery owned by the parish was blessed in 1883.

## ST. JOHN'S PARISH,

### MONTVILLE.

THE Rev. James P. Connolly was the first resident pastor of St. John's church, Montville. He began his parochial labors here on March 1, 1887. Prior to this date the Catholics of this town were served by the clergy of St. Mary's parish, New London. Father Connolly's pastorate terminated by death in October, 1890, and his successor was the Rev. Charles E. McGowan, serving until December 10, 1894. Father McGowan gave way to Rev. James P. Ryle, who assumed charge on that date. Shortly after his arrival here he remodeled the rectory, renovated and re-furnished the church, erected horse sheds and a barn, liquidated the mortgage indebtedness, and paid, moreover, $1,000 of floating debts. After a successful pastorate of nearly four years, he was transferred to Westport on October 15, 1898. He was succeeded by Rev. Charles Morrill, who died here in June, 1899. His successor, the present incumbent, the Rev. Patrick J. Kennedy, immediately followed in succession on June 14th.

The parochial residence was built by the first resident pastor, and the church was enlarged during the pastorate of Rev. T. W. Broderick, of New London, by the addition of a transept. Originally a part of New London, Montville was incorporated as a town in 1876. It was noted as the home of the famous Pequot chief, Uncas.

## ST. PATRICK'S PARISH,

### Mystic.

THE first Catholics to reside in Mystic were exiles, being eight of the four hundred Acadians who were landed at New London and distributed throughout the State in 1756. No trace of Catholics is discovered after, until the ship-building interests brought some Irish-Catholics hither. Among the first Irish people to settle here were James Brahan and Denis Cradie. The few Catholics in Mystic attended divine worship at Stonington until September, 1870, when St. Patrick's church was purchased by Rev. Patrick Sherry, of Westerly, from the Methodists. After making necessary repairs, the church was dedicated on October 30, 1870, by Bishop McFarland. In November, 1871, Father Sherry was called to his reward. Mystic and Stonington were then erected into a parish on December 19, 1871, with the Rev. Patrick P. Lawlor as resident pastor.

At this time the Catholic population numbered about 450 souls ; at the time of the first Mass in Mystic, there were about fifty members of the ancient faith in the town. Father Lawlor's pastorate ended on November 18, 1872, and he was succeeded by the Rev. William Hart. On April 9, 1873, the Rev. John Flemming assumed charge, continuing in office until his successor, the Rev. J. B. Dougherty, came on September 11, 1881. Rev. John F. Murphy, the present rector, began his pastorate on September 19, 1895.

St. Patrick's church has a seating capacity for 400 people, its original dimensions being 50 by 35 feet. The splendid organ which adorns the choir-gallery, was put in during the administration of Father Dougherty.

Father Murphy's jurisdiction embraces, besides Mystic, Stonington, West Mystic, and Noank. The entire church property, church rectory and cemetery has been free from financial encumbrance for many years. Writing in 1871, of Mystic, the Rev. Father Lawlor said, "The only other fact of interest that strikes me often, is, that, while almost every other place is prospering and increasing in population, this is decreasing. Six months ago there were 450 Catholics in Mystic, to-day there are about 300."

REV. J. F. MURPHY.

REV. AMBROSE BRISCOE.

REV. MICHAEL H. MAY.

## ST. MARY'S (MISSION),

### STONINGTON.

THE first Catholic settlers in Stonington were all Irish, and bore the familiar names of McCarthy, Sullivan, Kirby, Gilmore and Carr. The three first came here about 1829, and the other two in 1836. Kirby was a brother to the Most Rev. Archbishop Kirby, late rector of the Irish college at Rome. Kirby taught a select school. Mass was first said in Stonington by Rev. Father Fitton, about 1840, offering the Holy Sacrifice frequently at the home of Mr. Kirby. The first resident pastor of Stonington was the Rev. Patrick Duffy. Prior to his arrival, the people were served by the Rev. John Brady of Middletown. St. Mary's church was erected by Father Duffy in 1851; its dimensions were 60 by 40 feet, and it was dedicated by Bishop O'Reilly, on October 5, 1851. On October the 10th, Bishop O'Reilly sent the Rev. Thomas Ryan to Stonington, giving him $425, to pay the mechanics who did the carpenter work on the church. On the 16th of the same month, the Bishop sent the Rev. Father O'Dowd here, as we gather from his journal. Following these clergymen, came in succession, the Rev. Thomas Drea, Rev. Peter Kelly, Rev. John Sheridan, and Rev. Michael O'Reilly. The term of Father Drea's pastorate was about five years, that of Father Kelly a few months only. Father Sheridan assumed charge in November, 1858, and served until 1859. Father O'Reilly removed the pastoral residence from Stonington to Westerly in 1861, with which Stonington assumed mission relations. Thereafter for ten years, until the death of Father Sherry, and for a brief period by Father Fitzpatrick, Stonington was attended by the clergy of Westerly. In December, 1871, Stonington was attached to Mystic, and since then has been served by the pastors thereof.

During Father Dougherty's pastorate the church was partially destroyed by fire, but was rebuilt and beautifully renovated. The Stations of the Cross were erected and a fine organ placed in the church, also by the Rev. Father Dougherty. Like their brethren of Mystic, the entire church property of the Catholics of Stonington is free from indebtedness.

It will not be without a degree of interest to append herewith a list of the contributions paid to Bishop Tyler on January 14, 1848, as a nucleus of the building fund:

| | | |
|---|---|---|
| John Gorman..............$1 00 | Margaret McMahon....$1 00 | John Drinen...............$1 00 |
| James O'Brien............ 1 00 | John Keegan.............. 1 00 | Peter Ducey.............. 1 00 |
| Felix McCarthy......... 1 00 | Thomas Gilmore........ 1 00 | Ann Gearm.............. 1 00 |
| John Corcoran............ 1 00 | Thomas Donnelly...... 1 00 | Owen Hore............... 1 00 |
| Eliza Gorman............ 1 00 | Walter Simons........... 25 | Thos. Cosgrove......... 1 00 |
| John McCarthy.......... 1 00 | Bridget O'Neil.......... 50 | Charles Mealy........ ... 1 00 |
| John Murphy............. 1 00 | Julia Shaw................ 50 | Jas. Gilmore........... ... 1 00 |
| Catherine Cune......... 1 00 | Thomas Fay.............. 1 00 | Owen McCloskey....... 1 00 |
| Richard Lynch........... 1 00 | Ellen McDonald......... 1 00 | Ann Burns................ 1 00 |
| Patrick Murphy. ....... 1 00 | Patrick Carpenter...... 1 00 | |
| Patrick Maher............ 1 00 | Edward Cox ............. 1 00 | |

## ST. PATRICK'S PARISH,

NORWICH, like many of her sister towns in Connecticut, had Catholic people residing within her limits in the last, as well as in the beginning of the present century. Though such names as Tracy (1687), Kelly (1716), Kirby (1721), and Kennedy (1730) appear on the town records, there is no evidence that their owners professed the Catholic faith. In January, 1756, the first Catholics, certainly known to be such, came here, not voluntarily, but by virtue of legislative enactment. They were a part of the 400 Acadians who were landed at New London. Nineteen were assigned to Norwich, but as 240 of these exiles were taken back to Quebec in 1767, it is probable they were among the number returned. The historian of Norwich, Miss M. F. Caulkins, asserts that a priest was with the Acadians at Norwich, and returned to Canada with them; if so, the Holy Sacrifice was probably offered by this faithful shepherd for his exiled flock.

Eleven years after the return of the refugees to their former home we note the presence of a large body of Catholics in Norwich. In 1778 a detachment of the French army spent fifteen days here on account of illness that had broken out among them.[1] "They had their tents spread upon the plain, while the sick were quartered in the court-house. About twenty died and were buried each side of the lane that led into the old burying ground. No stones were set up, and the ground was soon smoothed over so as to leave no trace of the narrow tenements below." Lafayette and De Lauzun were here during the Revolution, and the former visited Norwich on August 21, 1824.

The Rev. John Thayer, formerly a Congregationalist minister, now appears upon the scene. He came hither as a missionary priest, seeking the few Catholics who were scattered throughout the State. His visit to Norwich is thus described by a local newspaper of November 14, 1793:

"On Friday last, Mr. John Thayer, Catholic missionary, delivered to a large audience at the Rev. Joseph Strong's meeting-house in this city, a learned and ingenious discourse, in which he undertook to prove that the Catholic church was the only true church of Christ. On Sunday evening following, at the same place, he delivered a discourse on the propriety and true piety of invoking departed saints and the utility and efficiency of addressing prayers to them."

The Catholics who next entered Norwich came like the Acadians, under compulsion. They were refugees from San Domingo and were brought hither as prisoners of war.

"In September, 1800, the U. S. ship 'Trumbull,' Captain Jewett, returning from a cruise against the French, came into New London harbor with a prize vessel of ten guns, called 'La Vengeance,' which had been taken near the port of Jacquemel in the West Indies, with 140 persons on board. These were delivered over to the authorities as prisoners of war, and seventeen of them sent to prison, where they remained about six months.[2]

[1] *History of Norwich.*

[2] Eighty-four were sent to Hartford; the remainder were retained in New London.

REV. JOHN SYNNOTT.

REV. HUGH TREANOR.

REV. JAMES J. SMITH.

"The terrific war of the races, French, Spaniards and Africans struggling for dominion, had made fearful havoc in St. Domingo, and at this period Gen. Rigaud was at the head of one party and the African chief, Toussaint of the other. The latter had laid siege to Jacquemel, which was about to surrender, and many of the inhabitants, apprehensive that an indiscriminate sack and slaughter would follow, fled with what little property they could carry with them to the vessels in the harbor for safety. It was one of these vessels endeavoring to reach Cuba with its throng of exiles that was taken by the 'Trumbull.'

"The prisoners were natives of St. Domingo, partly of French origin, but with a large admixture of African blood. They were mostly civil officers, captains of barges, merchants and their servants, and though nominally of Rigaud's party, they had taken no active part in the contest, and might reasonably have expected that an American ship would humanely favor their flight, rather than plunder them of their goods and carry them into captivity.

"The prisoners sent to Norwich were treated with compassionate kindness. They had the privilege of the gaol limits and were allowed to stroll from house to house. Wholesome food and comfortable winter garments were provided for them. Dr. Philemon Tracy, who attended them as their physician, apprehending that they would suffer from the rigors of a cold climate, made great exertions to procure their immediate release. It was not, however, till March, 1801, that the government virtually condemned their capture by ordering their free discharge and furnishing them with transportation home.

"Some of these exiles were men of education and ability. One of them had been a justice of the peace; another, a young mulatto of manly and dignified deportment, was afterward the able and discreet President of the Republic of Hayti. He was then about twenty-four years of age, and having already attained considerable rank in the order of Freemasons, he was boarded while in Norwich, at the expense of the Masonic Lodge, in a private family. Most of his leisure time he employed in perfecting himself in the English language, and at his departure he cut from a piece of his linen his name, marked at full length, *Jean Pierre Boyer*, and gave it to one of the young members of the family that had assisted him in his lessons. 'Keep this,' he said, 'and perhaps, some day, you may send it to me in a letter, and I will remember you.'

"The lad lost his mark, but nearly twenty years afterward, President Boyer, then at the head of the Haytien Republic, made inquiries of certain Norwich ship-masters respecting his former friends, and sent a handsome gratuity to the two families in which he had been treated with special kindness."[1]

Thenceforth, we find no trace of Catholics in Norwich until 1824, when we discover the name of Edward Murphy, the only Irishman in a population of 4000. Probably he was the first of the Catholics of later days to come to Norwich.

It is traditional that the Rev. James Fitton paid a missionary visit to Norwich in 1831. The tradition places no strain upon our belief, as the energetic priest visited this section of the State, New London, on October 19, 1831, and on September 21, 1835. It is not unreasonable to infer that on one, and, perhaps, on all of these visitations, Father Fitton sought out the few Catholics of Norwich also. However, there are records extant which prove the presence of Father Fitton in Norwich in 1838. The first record of baptism administered here is that of Catharine, daughter of John and Eleanor Connolly, born June 8, 1835, and baptized May 15, 1836, Father Fitton performing the ceremony. The sponsors were Thomas Connolly and Judy Donnelly. The first male child to receive baptism was James, son of David and Johanna

[1] *History of Norwich.*

Shaughnessy, born on August 18, 1836, and baptized on the 21st. The first marriage ceremony performed by Father Fitton here was on June 30, 1840, the contracting parties being John Savage and Mary Melvin.

Upon the transfer of Father Fitton to Worcester in 1836, Norwich was attended from there by this pioneer missionary. He came at stated intervals, saying Mass and otherwise ministering to the spiritual wants of his flock. The building of the Norwich and Worcester railroad considerably augmented the Catholic population here. Father Fitton informs us that he held religious services on the Norwich road "in shanties or in groves and but few permanent stations were established."

In 1843,[1] the number of Catholics had so increased that Father Fitton determined to erect a house of worship. He selected a lot "midway between" Norwich and Greenville in order to accommodate the people of both places. The foundations were laid in September, 1844, and the building was sufficiently completed to permit the offering of the Holy Sacrifice of the Mass on December 25th, of that year. Two hundred and fifty persons assisted at this service. Work on the church was continued, and its permanent occupancy began on March 17, 1845. The church was dedicated in honor of the Mother of God, under the title of St. Mary's.

In May, 1845, Father Fitton severed his relations with Norwich, which again passed under the care of Hartford, Rev. John Brady, pastor, who attended it until 1848, when Bishop Tyler came in person for a brief period. The Bishop relinquished personal care of Norwich in November of that year, and Rev. William Logan, S. J., and Rev. Peter Blenkinsop, S. J., of Holy Cross College, received charge of St. Mary's, the former serving until May, 1850, the latter from this time until August, 1851. In the meantime, the Catholic population was increasing rapidly, so that when Rev. Daniel Kelly succeeded Father Blenkinsop as the first resident pastor, the Catholics numbered well nigh 3000 souls. In 1854, Father Kelly enlarged the church which had been erected in 1843. On June 26, 1853, Bishop O'Reilly made a visitation of Norwich and administered confirmation to 190 persons. In the following year, April 22, the Bishop arrived at Norwich for another visitation, of which he thus wrote in his journal: "*23rd, Tuesday:* Confirmed at Norwich 75 and preached four times; succeeded in settling difficulties between the pastor and a few of the people; all reconciled. Was much pleased with this visitation; a pastoral residence has been purchased since the last visitation at the expense of $900; debt on church about $1300."

The difficulties mentioned by Bishop O'Reilly were renewed in the following year with greater intensity of feeling. Visiting Norwich on May 15, 1855, the Bishop again became involved in the controversy between the pastor and a few of the parishioners. We quote again from his journal: "*16th:* Wrote a petition to the legislature adverse to the prayer of seven poor Catholics who petitioned for a change in the tenure of the church prop-

---

[1] The building of the Norwich and Worcester road brought the first permanent settlers to Norwich, who built settlements of shanties, the ruins of which are yet to be seen on the line of the road, the *extrema vestigia* of the first sad exodus of the famine days.

erty." The trouble had its origin in the disposition of the moneys received from the sale of lots in the cemetery which was contiguous to the church. Like church property in general, this burial ground was purchased with money contributed by the parishioners. The price of lots four feet wide by eight feet long was $8.00, except the purchaser was one of the original contributors, in which case he was entitled to a reduction of $1.00 on the price mentioned. The pastor, Rev. Father Kelly, used a portion of the money thus received for legitimate church purposes, but the seven malcontents—none others gave countenance to their protest—sought to control this money in ways conformable to their own ideas. Another source of the difficulty was the renting of pews at the two Masses.

Bishop O'Reilly's counter petition to the Legislature was as follows:

To THE HONORABLE THE GENERAL ASSEMBLY OF THE STATE OF CONNECTICUT, NOW IN SESSION AT HARTFORD :

The undersigned, citizens of Norwich, and members of the Catholic Church, in that city, have been apprized through the newspapers, that a petition is now pending before your honorable body, signed by William T. Brown, and six other persons, styling themselves Catholics, and praying for the enactment of a law changing the tenure by which the property of that Church is now held in this State : and they take this method to remonstrate against the granting by your honorable body of the prayer of said petition.

The signers of said petition are nominally members of the Catholic denomination, but are, we conscientiously believe, hostile to its best interests and inimical to its prosperity and advancement. It is, we think, in that spirit, and not from any sincere regard for the Catholic religion or the welfare of the Catholic Church, that they have brought their petition before you. Excepting them, we know of no person calling himself a Catholic, in this city, who does not deprecate the attempt which they are making to procure through your interposition, a change in the tenure by which the property of the Catholic Church is now held.

We would also call your attention to the fact that notwithstanding the said petition prays for legislative action in regard to the entire property held for the benefit of the Catholic Church in this State, even to the extent of vacating the titles under which the same is held, no notice of the intention to prefer the petition was ever given to the public, nor was the same ever served upon any of the parties whose rights are by the petitioners sought to be invaded, if not entirely destroyed. It seems to us that such notice ought as a matter of justice to have been given in order that those who are interested in the question might have appeared before you in a suitable state of preparation, to show reasons why the prayer of the petitioners should not be granted. And we think, moreover, that the tenth section of " An Act relating to the General Assembly," requires such notice to have been given. In this state of things we cannot believe that your honorable body will take cognizance of a petition like the one under consideration, signed as it is, by only seven persons, in opposition to the wishes and feelings of the great body of our Church, especially as by doing so a serious wrong will be inflicted upon us.

We believe that the change in the law contemplated by the petitioners would be productive of no good, but would work serious injury to us as a religious body. This is the view entertained by every member of our communion who has the good of our Church at heart and claims to be called a Catholic. In remonstrating, therefore, against the granting, by your honorable body, of the passage of said petition, we ask nothing more than that we may be permitted as heretofore to manage our Church affairs in our own way, and in the manner which we may deem most beneficial.

*Norwich*, May 16, 1855.

This remonstrance was signed by several hundred parishioners, thus

II—*27*

showing that the great majority of the members of the parish were not in sympathy with the alleged reform movement.

Father Kelly remained at Norwich fifteen years, leaving in August, 1866, having been transferred to Providence, R. I., in exchange with the Rev. Peter Kelly. Father Kelly's death occurred at Thomasville, Georgia, February 19, 1877. "To say that Father Kelly was universally beloved by the people of Norwich," wrote a contemporary, "who were for years under his charge, is to express but feebly and imperfectly the affection, veneration and esteem with which they regarded him. During his long residence here his existence was completely merged in that of his people. Their welfare was his; their interests his; their sorrows his. He never complained of too great or of too onerous labors, although he frequently undertook more than one mortal could possibly accomplish in a life-time. While his inclination often out-stripped his strength, he was never wholly baffled. His hands were ever tendered to lift his people's burdens; his sympathies were ever ready—

'To fly East or West
Which ever way besought them.'

"His actions were constantly characterized by that sincere charity which is ever indissolubly allied to kindness. To elevate and refine his congregation, religiously and socially, was through life his highest aim. He constantly endeavored to appreciate and suitably reward the meritorious, while his benevolent aid was never withheld from any person by whom it was sought. In his exhortations to his people, mildness and force were invariably mingled. Towards offenders his deportment was so firm, but withal so tender, that even his checks and frowns had grace and favor in them." [1]

Shortly after Rev. Peter Kelly's arrival in Norwich he purchased two lots on Church street commanding the Thames river, paying therefor $10,000. Intending to erect a suitable church for the growing needs of his congregation, he broke ground on March 17, 1867; but as the ecclesiastical authorities deemed the site unsuitable, it was abandoned. Father Kelly's pastorate ended on July 27, 1867.

Though Father Kelly's administration in Norwich was but of a year's duration, he had gained the profound affection of all his parishioners. "Ovid's line,

'Non illo melior quisquam, nec Amantior aequi et Vir fuit,'

most appropriately defines Rev. Peter Kelly's character in life. Love of justice and right were the distinctive qualities of all his deeds. A kind and genial disposition, unsullied purity and simplicity of manners; unaffected wisdom and inward greatness, combined with the most persuasive eloquence, won for him subtle influence over all hearts, which rendered his mission in Norwich so satisfactory and successful."

After the retirement of Father Kelly he was succeeded for brief periods by the Rev. Bernard Tully, whose pastorate was of a few months' duration only, and the Rev. Michael Tierney, then Chancellor of the diocese, who

[1] *Connecticut Catholic Year Book, 1877.*

ST. PATRICK'S CHURCH,
Norwich, Conn.

remained in charge until January 20, 1868, when the Rev. Daniel Mullen succeeded to the administration. Father Mullin had been chaplain for a time of the Ninth Regiment of Connecticut Volunteers.

The erection of a new church was the all-absorbing topic among the parishioners. Project after project was abandoned and the people began to lose hope of witnessing the fulfillment of their desires. Father Mullen, however, having given the matter mature consideration, and acting for the best interests of the parish, made selection of a lot on Broadway, which with the buildings on the premises, was secured for $17,000. "This location was chosen, not only on account of its beautiful surroundings, but also because of its being so near the centre of the scattered parish, which extended from the village of Yantic on the north to Thamesville on the south and west, and Greenville and a portion of the town of Creston on the east."

Work was begun immediately by the breaking of ground on March 17, 1870, Very Rev. James Hughes, V. G., taking out the first shovelful of earth in the presence of the pastor, the city and town officials, and a large concourse of people. A building fund was then established in order to render more certain a continuation of the work, and on Good Friday, April 7, 1871, the men of the congregation, preceded by a band of music, with horses and carts, shovels and picks and other implements of labor, marched to the site of the church and commenced the work of excavation. The work on the cellar was completed after three days of unremitting toil. Work on the foundations now began, and the corner-stone was laid under the patronage of St. Patrick, on July 13, 1873, in the presence of the civic dignitaries and many thousands of spectators. The contributions on this occasion realized over $10,000, the largest ever received at a similar ceremony. The work of construction was pushed vigorously until the death of Father Mullen, which occurred on March 3, 1878. The funeral services were held in St. Patrick's church, Hartford, on Tuesday, the 5th, the following clergymen officiating: Celebrant of the Mass, Very Rev. James Hughes; deacon, Rev. P. Fay, Colchester; sub-deacon, Rev. T. Coleman, Norwich; master of ceremonies, Rev. M. Galligan, Hartford. The Right Rev. Bishop of Springfield pronounced the funeral oration from the text—"Lord, the servant whom Thou loved, is dead." The absolution was pronounced by Bishop Galberry. Previous to the celebration of the Mass a delegation from Norwich waited on Bishop Galberry, expressing the desire of their congregation to have Father Mullen's remains interred in their cemetery. The bishop replied that it was Father Mullen's expressed wish to be buried in Hartford. Father Mullen's remains rest among those of his relatives in Mt. St. Benedict's cemetery, Hartford.

The Rev. P. P. Shahan then became pastor of St. Mary's and took charge of the parish on Sunday, March 17, 1878. When Father Shahan became pastor the church walls, roof and towers were completed to the ridge-pole. He immediately entered upon the work of completing the entire church. The first Mass offered up in the new temple was celebrated upon St. Patrick's day, 1879, and the solemn ceremony of dedication was performed on September 28th of the same year. The dedicatory services were conducted by

Bishop McMahon, assisted by Very Rev. T. Walsh, V.G., and Very Rev. P. V. Kavanagh, C. M. Solemn Pontifical Mass was celebrated by Bishop McMahon, with the Revs. James Campbell and T. P. Joynt deacons of honor, Very Rev. Thomas Walsh, V.G., assistant priest; Revs. Denis Daley, Suspension Bridge, N. Y., deacon; Peter Kennedy, Birmingham, sub-deacon; Fathers Murphy and Farrell, masters of ceremonies; Father Russell, Norwich, censer bearer. His Eminence, Cardinal Gibbons, Archbishop of Baltimore, preached the sermon, taking his text from the fourth chapter of St. Paul's epistle to the Ephesians. Solemn Pontifical Vespers were celebrated by Bishop McMahon, and the discourse was pronounced by Bishop Shanahan, of Harrisburg

During the evening services, Rev. James Fitton, the missionary pioneer, gave some interesting reminiscences of the early growth of Catholicity in Norwich, a part of which we herewith append:

"A pastor (himself) once had for his parish the districts lying between Boston and New York, and was occasionally called to visit the sick in New Hampshire, Vermont, and Rhode Island, and while thus traveling abroad in 1833 he discovered two or three Catholics in Norwich. It was not so encouraging then to build a church as now. But I notice that where you find one Catholic, you will soon find another, and so here they went on increasing until there were twelve, when a priest first came here and offered Mass in a house. The first Mass was said in the third story of an old building so weak that the weight of the congregation gave rise to apprehensions that we should all fall through to the cellar, and this fear prompted us in buying a lot, and, that there might be no jealousy, we secured it in the middle of the parish. We paid $300 for the lot and put up a shanty with the earth for the floor, and then there was no danger of falling through. This was in a place now called Toumeytown. The subscription books were opened, and $163 was subscribed the first day. William Toumey was a devoted Irish Catholic, the richest among the first congregation. He subscribed $30; the next in wealth $10, and some $1 each. The church and lot cost $1,300. We had shutters to the windows, and there was no danger of the glass being broken. On December 25, 1842, the first holy Mass was offered in a church in this town, and it was not much like the present edifice, yet we were glad that we had a church; and from that date Catholicism has gone on spreading itself, not by the power of wealth, but by the grace of God."

After Vespers Right Rev. Bishop McMahon and the visiting prelates were serenaded at the pastoral residence by the Norwich City Band, and an address of welcome was delivered by Judge Shields.

Other works than the completion of the magnificent church edifice signalized the pastorate of Father Shahan, such as the purchase of the present parochial residence, the transforming of the old rectory into an academy, the erection of St. Patrick's parochial school and convent at an outlay of $43,000, the grading of the church grounds and the laying of walks, which contribute materially to the beauty of the parochial property.

After a pastorate of fourteen years he was succeeded by the Rev. Peter M. Kennedy on February 1, 1892. Father Kennedy converted the old pastoral residence that adjoined St. Mary's church, in Greenville, into a primary school, sufficiently large to accommodate over 150 children. The church indebtedness was reduced during his administration many thousand dollars The old historic church, St. Mary's, was served with two Masses every Sunday, and the succursal chapel of the Sacred Heart, in Norwichtown, was also attended. Father Kennedy's assistants were Rev. John Neale, Rev. F. M. Murray, Rev. R. J. Fitzgerald, D.D. The present assistants are Revs. John P. Neale and W. Bellerose. Father Kennedy's successful pastorate of over five years expired on November 21, 1897. The present rector, the Rev. Hugh Treanor, assumed control of the parish on November 26th, of the same year. Since Father Treanor's advent the Sacred Heart chapel, Norwichtown, which was begun under the pastorate of Father Kennedy, was dedicated. It is an attractive edifice of pressed brick and is adorned with a beautiful marble altar, the donation of a lady of St. Patrick's parish.

## ST. JOSEPH'S (MISSION) CHURCH,

### Occum.

THIS mission comprises the two villages of Occum and Versailles, the former being on the right bank of the Shetucket river, and the latter on the left. Occum is located in the town of Norwich, and Versailles in the towns of Lisbon and Sprague.

In 1845 four or five Catholics came to labor on a dam which was being built at Occum, but remained only a short time. At this period an inexcusable prejudice against Catholics existed here, and though few, and as intelligent and loyal as their tormentors, they were given to understand that their departure would be a boon highly prized.

The earliest Catholics to settle in Occum were John McCarthy and Mrs. Margaret Reilly, who came in 1847. With their families they came to labor in a small cotton factory, which had been built in Versailles about this time by a Mr. Bachelor. In 1864 a cotton mill was built in Occum, and soon afterwards Catholics came here and established homes.

The first Mass said in this mission was celebrated at Versailles, in the town of Lisbon, in the residence of J. McCarthy, by Rev. Father De Bruycker, of Willimantic, early in January, 1867. About fifty persons were present at this Mass. For some time after this Mass was said here every three months by the pastor of Willimantic. On the intervening Sundays the faithful assisted at divine worship at Baltic.

The first Mass offered up in Occum was celebrated by Rev. J. Reynolds in Parent's hall, in January, 1873. Mass was said in this hall afterwards every two weeks until the erection of the church. When Father Russell was appointed pastor of Jewett City he began preparations for the erection of a church in Occum. The people were unanimous in declaring for the project, and contributions of the most encouraging kind began to flow in. The church was completed and dedicated by Bishop Galberry on September 22, 1878, under the patronage of St. Joseph, the Rev. Thomas Joynt preaching the sermon in French, and Rev. Flor. de Bruycker in English. At this time

Occum had passed under the jurisdiction of Baltic, Rev. Father Van der Noort, pastor. The extreme length of the church is 78 feet; the distance between the altar-rail and the inner door is 55 feet; the extreme width is 39 feet.

The first resident Catholics of Occum were under the spiritual jurisdiction of the pastor of Norwich. When a resident pastor was appointed to Willimantic, Occum was assigned to his care. It was detached from Willimantic and added to Jewett City, when the first resident priest of the latter place, Rev. Father Reynolds, was appointed on January 15, 1873. Father Reynolds died on January 1, 1875.

In succession to Father Reynolds, Rev. John Russell was appointed pastor of Jewett City on January 20, 1875. After the transfer of Father Russell to Norwalk, Occum reverted to the care of Father Van der Noort, the pastor of Baltic.

On February 8, 1886, Occum was made a parish by Bishop McMahon, who appointed Rev. John Synnott pastor. In the same year an attractive and substantial parochial residence was erected. Owing to the closing of the Versailles woolen mill, and the consequent loss to the parish, Occum was again united to Baltic in October, 1889. The Rev. John Synnott was then transferred to Baltic and the re-united churches were placed under his charge.

Revs. M. McCarten, M. H. May and F. J. O'Neil assisted Father Synnott in his parochial labors.

On September 1, 1897, Rev. T. Dunn succeeded Father Synnott as pastor of Baltic and Occum. Mass is said in the latter place on Sundays and holydays of precept.

The Catholic population of Occum is about 400 souls.

## SACRED HEART PARISH,

### TAFTVILLE.

THE earliest Catholics to settle in Taftville were both Irish and French, namely, Thomas Kelly, Hugh McLaughlin, John Sullivan, Michael Clifford, Patrick O'Neil, Daniel Day, Nazaire Lafleur, Joseph Massé, Kearn Nolan, Joseph Marsin.

The first Mass said in Taftville was celebrated in the school-house by the Rev. Daniel Mullen, of Norwich. From that time until the appointment of Rev. James B. Reynolds, as pastor of Jewett City, the people attended Mass at St. Mary's, Greenville, when it was not celebrated in Taftville. Father Reynolds was appointed pastor of Jewett City in May, 1872, at which time Taftville became one of his dependencies. After the death of Father Reynolds, which occurred in January, 1875, the Rev. John Russell attended Taftville as pastor of Jewett City. From that time Mass was celebrated at stated intervals in the school-house, and occasionally at Occum.

In the fall of 1875 work on the church was begun. It was completed in 1876 and dedicated by Bishop Galberry March 24, 1877. Upon his removal to Norwalk Father Russell was succeeded by the Rev. Thomas P. Joynt, who also attended Taftville until June, 1883, when Taftville and Occum were separated from Jewett City, and the Rev. James J. Thompson appointed first resident pastor of Taftville. A census taken at that time disclosed a Catholic population of 1630 souls, whereas the census of 1887 showed a membership of 2340. In January, 1885, Rev. Maurice J. Sheehan was appointed assistant to Father Thompson. The convent and school were commenced in April, 1886, and completed in March, 1887. Father Thompson's period of service terminated with his death, in January, 1894, his successor being the Rev. Terrence Dunn, who remained till the May following.

The present incumbent, the Rev. John Synnott, began his labors here on May 16, 1894. Among the achievements that distinguish Father Synnott's administration are the liquidation of the parish indebtedness of $7,100, the erection of a chapel and community room for the sisters, the renovation of the school, the purchase of a tract of land on October 30, 1897, 200 by 512 feet, and the building thereon of a handsome parochial residence. This new property and rectory are valued at $15,000. Father Synnott also put in a metal ceiling in the church. The entire parish property comprises church, convent, school, rectory, about 2¼ acres of land on Providence street and about two acres on School street, and a cemetery which was purchased in 1886 and blessed by Bishop McMahon in May of the same year. The Catholic population of Taftville is 2,300 souls, one-third of whom are Irish and the remainder French.

The Sacred Heart school is conducted by ten Sisters of Our Lady of Charity, Mother of Mercy, Sister M. Benoit, Directress. When opened 300 children presented themselves for enrolment. There are now in attendance 400 pupils distributed through eight grades.

The clergy who assisted the pastors in parochial work, were the Rev. Fathers Fones, Sheehan, Cartier, Mailhot, Senesac, Chapdelaine, and Perrault. Rev. Father Synnott is a member of the Diocesan School Commission.

## ST. THOMAS' PARISH,

### VOLUNTOWN.

WHEN the Rev. James B. Reynolds was appointed pastor of Jewett City, in 1872, Voluntown was assigned to him as an out-mission. St. Thomas' church was built during the administration of the Rev. Father Joynt, who succeeded Father Russell as pastor of Jewett City. Voluntown remained a dependency of the latter place during this and the pastorate of Rev. F. O'Keefe, until February, 1892, when, with Glasgo, it was organized into an independent parish, with the Rev. Edward Chapdelaine as first resident pastor. The duration of his pastorate was sixteen months. The next pastor of St. Thomas' was the Rev. L. Mayeur, who remained in office two years and a half, receiving as a successor the Rev. J. E. Senesac, whose pastoral labors terminated six months later. The Rev. J. L. Desaulniers administered the parish for eighteen months, when the Rev. J. H. Chapdelaine was appointed. During the last illness of the first resident pastor, Rev. Edward Chapdelaine, the parish was in charge of the Rev. Pierre Cardin, from Canada. The cemetery attached to St. Thomas's was purchased and blessed in 1895. The present population of the parish is about thirty families, mostly French, with three Irish and one American family.

Since the organization of the parish the sacrament of baptism has been conferred on 88 persons; the number of marriages within the same period being 17. The first baptism in the newly formed parish was that of Ovila Russi; the first marriage, February 28, 1892, was that between Napoleon Jacques and Amelie Contu. The first death recorded occurred on July 27, 1894, and was that of Rosa DeLina Grenier.

Father Chapdelaine attends St. Ann's church, Glasgo, every Sunday, where the Catholic population is about 200 souls. From 1892 to 1898, exclusive, the number of baptisms here were 80, and the marriages, 14. The first baptism recorded in St. Ann's is that of Eva Daigneault. The first marriage ceremony was performed on October 1, 1892, the contracting parties being Arthur Pepin and Amanda Labarre. The first death occurred on the 24th of March, 1894, that of Adeline Jolicoeur.

---

# TOLLAND COUNTY.

TOLLAND COUNTY was formed from Hartford and Windham Counties, and was incorporated in 1876. Its form is irregular, and is bounded on the north by Massachusetts, on the east by Windham County, on the south by New London County, and on the west by Hartford County. Its greatest length is thirty miles; its northern breadth is twenty miles; while its extreme southern breadth is only five miles. The cities and towns in which there are Catholic parishes are:

ROCKVILLE,    SOUTH COVENTRY,    STAFFORD SPRINGS.

## ST. BERNARD'S PARISH.

### ROCKVILLE.

THE first Catholic, as far as is known, to settle in Rockville was James McAvenney. He came in 1842, but afterwards wandered into a strange fold. In 1848, about fifteen Catholics assembled at the first Mass celebrated in Rockville. The place where divine services were conducted was a house owned by the paper-mill company, then occupied by Christopher Carroll and family. The celebrant of the Mass was the Rev. John Brady, of Hartford. Among the attendants at that first Mass were Christopher Carroll, Patrick Quinn, Edward Gorman, Thomas McDonnell, Denis O'Donnell, James Conner, Philip Kiernan, Matthew Fay, Eugene Kiernan, Patrick Duffy, Martin Flood, John Moore and Michael Lawlor.

It was deemed advisable afterwards in 1849, that regular visitations should be made. This duty devolved on the Rev. James Smyth, one of the patriarchs of the diocese. He officiated here at monthly intervals at the Albert Lamb house, where Patrick Quinn resided. He said Mass also in the Dean house on Mountain street, where Martin Flood and family then lived.

In 1851, more commodious quarters being necessary, a large room was secured in the "Brick Tavern" up-stairs on the west side. The altar used here was in the keeping of Michael Regan in 1888. Father Smyth also organized a Sunday-school at which both old and young were obliged to assist. Mass was said in the "Brick Tavern" for a couple of years, when a hall was secured on Market street over the Rockville meat market. This hall was used in later years by the St. John's Young Men's society. It was afterwards destroyed by a conflagration. Mass was said here by Father Smyth and others until March 15, 1854, when the Rev. Peter Egan assumed charge as the first resident pastor, with Manchester, Stafford Springs, Broadbrook and Mansfield as dependencies.

In the course of time, the arrival of strangers in quest of employment, made it evident to the Catholics that a site and a building of their own would become a necessity. But the financial means of the Catholics were meagre; moreover, a deep-rooted prejudice existed in Rockville against Catholics and Irishmen. However, by a strict adherence to the teachings of their church, they gave evidence of the possession of Christian charity, and this overcame existing prejudices. A more friendly disposition soon became manifest. One of the first to evince freedom from prejudice was Hanly Kellogg, a druggist, who conducted his business on the terrace. He offered his entire property to the Catholics on terms satisfactory to them, and they quickly availed themselves of the opportunity presented. The store on the premises was moved back to School street and was known afterwards as the Blake house. Work on the new church was at once begun and rapidly advanced. Before its completion, Father Egan removed to Lee, Mass., on November 12, 1856. Father Egan purchased also the cemetery on the Tolland road consisting of five acres in September, 1854. Owing to the death of Bishop O'Reilly, who was lost with the ill-fated steamer *Pacific*, the corner-stone of the new church was laid by a priest, probably Father Egan, assisted by Fathers Daly, Smyth and O'Brien.

The Rev. Bernard Tully was Father Egan's successor, coming in December, 1856. During his administration the church was finished and embellished. It was dedicated by Bishop McFarland. After a pastorate of six years Father Tully was transferred to Thompsonville in January, 1863.

The Rev. Hugh O'Reilly became the third pastor of Rockville, immediately following Father Tully. He enlarged the sanctuary, had the church beautifully frescoed and built the main portion of the rectory. The Rev. John Rogers, the present pastor of St. Mary's parish, Bridgeport, was Father O'Reilly's assistant and remained with him until February 26, 1868. After a pastorate of five years, Father O'Reilly went to Valley Falls, R. I., where he labored until his death.

To the great gratification of the Catholics of Rockville Father Tully returned to his former charge February 20, 1868. His second pastorate was of brief duration. While on a journey to Ellington he expired suddenly in his carriage on July 20, 1869. In testimony of the love and esteem in which he was held, a splendid marble monument, whose estimated cost was $1,600, was erected by the people of Manchester and Rockville over his grave in front of the church. Father Tully's assistant was the Rev. William Halligan, who died recently at Pawtucket, R. I.

The Rev. James Quinn began his labors as the fifth pastor of Rockville in September, 1869. He died December 1, 1872. He was assisted for a few months prior to his death by the Rev. Thomas L. Lynch. His remains rest in the cemetery at Rockville.

Rev. Patrick P. Lawlor succeeded Father Quinn in November, 1872. He re-organized the parish, liquidated the indebtedness, and built an addition to the vestry at an expense of $1,700. After the shortest period of any of his predecessors, having remained but one year, he was transferred to New London.

The Rev. John J. Furlong assumed charge of St. Bernard's parish January 24, 1874, though he was appointed on December 25, 1873, an illness preventing an earlier assumption of the reins of authority. In the meantime, the affairs of the parish were administered by the Rev. T. L. Lynch. Father Furlong's first work was to improve the cemetery. In 1875 he placed a new altar in the church. To provide better accommodations for his people the church was moved back forty feet and raised six feet, while a new front with a tower was added. The interior was handsomely decorated, a new organ put in the choir gallery, new pews placed in the body of the church and beautiful stained-glass windows inserted. Among the benefactors at this time mention should be made of the Hon. E. S. Henry, who contributed $500. The renovated church was re-dedicated on January 20, 1878, Bishop Galberry officiating. Rev. Father Ryan, C. S. P., of New York, preached at the morning service, and Rev. Father Deshon, C. S. P., in the evening. At both morning and evening ceremonies Rev. M. A. Tierney was the celebrant. In February, 1886, Father Furlong purchased the Johnson site on Park street, paying therefor $8,000. The house was fitted up for a convent and a chapel was arranged therein. To this eligible property was soon added the Cogswell lot adjacent. The school lot, on which the present handsome school building stands, was also secured by Father Furlong for $16,500. On this lot was the old building which Father Egan had removed to make room for the church. This was remodeled for the Sisters, who moved thereto from Park street May 15, 1895.

In October, 1895, Father Furlong, in recognition of his successful labors in Rockville, was transferred to the permanent rectorship of St. Mary's Norwalk. His successor is the present incumbent, the Rev. John Cooney, who is assisted by the Rev. Thomas Murray.

The Rev. Arthur O'Keefe was the first native of Rockville to be elevated to the priesthood; he was ordained on December 18, 1883.

Father Furlong introduced the Sisters of Mercy into Rockville on November 3, 1886. Four constituted the first band, Sister M. Columba, Sister M. Clara, Sister Mary Alphonsus and Sister M. Ursula. The basement of the church was fitted up for school purposes and opened on May 2, 1887, with five grades and over 300 children. In 1894, Father Furlong began the erection of the new school building, which is 65 by 68 feet. The corner-stone was laid on August 11, 1895, by Very Rev. John A. Mulcahy, V. G., on which occasion the sermon was preached by Rev. William Rogers, of Stamford. On September 10th, the same year, the new school was opened. Its entire cost was $22,000. There are eight Sisters, Sister M. Gabriel Superior, with 156 boys and 163 girls. The success of the pupils in the annual examination for the High School is evidence of the excellence of the course of studies and the proficiency of the disciplinary management.

## ST. MARY'S PARISH,
### South Coventry.

IN 1859, Jeremiah Crowley had the distinguished honor of having said within the walls of his home the first Mass celebrated in South Coventry. The celebrant of the Holy Sacrifice was the Rev. Michael McCabe, under whose jurisdiction were the three counties of Tolland, Windham and New London. Upon the accession of the Rev. Hugh O'Reilly to the pastorate of Willimantic, South Coventry came under his care. Father O'Reilly served this mission at occasional intervals, offering the Holy Sacrifice in private houses, as the Catholics here were few in number and poor in the goods of this world. Early in 1863, Father O'Reilly was transferred to Danielson and was succeeded in Willimantic by the Rev. Daniel Mullen, afterwards of Norwich. Father Mullen remained in Willimantic only three months, during which period he made about three visits to South Coventry. His successor was the Rev. Florimond DeBruycker, who began his administration on May 11, 1863. Within his jurisdiction were Stafford Springs, Baltic and South Coventry. The Catholic population of South Coventry was increasing and Father DeBruycker, anxious to secure for them a public house of worship, purchased the old Methodist church on Monument Hill, near Lake Wangombog. In this humble edifice the Catholics attended divine services, until the appointment of the Rev. P. P. Shahan, as first resident pastor of Stafford Springs in 1872. Father Shahan purchased the site known as the Wilson property and began excavations for a new church on Good Friday, 1877, the men of the congregation coming in a body to assist in the laudable work. Work progressed so rapidly and auspiciously that the corner-stone was laid amid impressive ceremonies, by Very Rev. Thomas Walsh, V.G., on June 10, 1877. The church was dedicated under the title of St. Mary's on Thanksgiving day, Nov. 29, 1877. The officiating prelate was Bishop Galberry, assisted by the Revs. P. J. Garrigan, D.D., of Fitchburg Mass., Denis Desmond of Portland, Thomas Smith of Thompsonville, John Russell of Taftville, Thomas Broderick of Meriden, J. J. Keegan of Harrisville, R. I., J. Van den Noort of Baltic, R. Van Wersch of Willimantic, J. Furlong of Rockville, and the pastor Rev. P. P. Shahan.

Solemn High Mass was celebrated after the dedication, with Rev. Thomas Broderick, celebrant ; Rev. Denis Desmond, deacon ; Rev. J. Russell, subdeacon ; and Rev. J. Keegan, master of ceremonies. The orator of the occasion was the Rev. Dr. Garrigan. St. Mary's church is 75 feet in length and 33 feet in width.

On the promotion of Father Shahan to St. Mary's parish, Norwich, he was followed by the Rev. Thomas Broderick as pastor of Stafford Springs. Serving only eighteen months, during which he regularly attended this mission, he was succeeded by Rev. Patrick Donahoe, who resold the old Methodist church which had been used for many years by the Catholics, to the Methodists, who transformed it into a rectory for their minister, the Rev. J. O. Dodge. This building has a curious history: first, a Methodist meeting-house, afterwards a Catholic church, then a Methodist parsonage; finally it was rented by the Catholics of South Coventry for a parochial residence, until the construction of a new and permanent rectory in 1887, during the pastorate of Rev. J. J. Quinn. The Rev. M. McKeon succeeded to the pastorate of Stafford Springs in November, 1881, and continued his attendance upon South Coventry, and liquidated the parish indebtedness.

After many years of mission relationship, South Coventry was honored with parochial privileges on January 2, 1886, with the Rev. J. J. Quinn as first resident pastor. Beside South Coventry, Father Quinn had within his jurisdiction Eagleville, Mansfield, Merrow Station, South Willington, Andover and Hop River. The Catholic population of all these missions was about 85 families at the formation of the parish. As stated above, the pastoral residence was erected during Father Quinn's period of service, and after three years of faithful administration he was followed by the Rev. J. H. Fitzmaurice, who purchased a tract of land for a cemetery. Five years later, in February, 1894, Rev. W. H. Gibbons became pastor of St. Mary's, and on the 9th of September of the same year the cemetery was blessed. The Rev. M. H. May became Father Gibbons' successor in September, 1895, and he in turn gave way to Rev. T. J. Dunn in October, 1896. After a pastorate of a year's duration, Father Dunn was succeeded by the Rev. Thomas J. Cronan on September 1, 1897. Father Cronan was succeeded by the Rev. Richard Carroll who is at present in charge. Father Carroll attends Hop River as a station.

## ST. EDWARD'S PARISH,

### STAFFORD SPRINGS.

THE first Catholic settlers to arrive in Stafford were Stephen Jackson, Jeremiah O'Brien, Thomas Hassett, Timothy Desmond, Daniel Hurley, William Tracy and their families. They came in 1849. In November of this year the Rev. Luke Daly said the first Mass in Stafford, and a second was celebrated by the same missionary on March 2, 1850. In 1851 the small congregation was augmented by the arrival of Stephen Collins, Wm. D. Brennan, Wm. I. Brennan, Peter Murphy, Thomas Warren, John Stewart, John Swanton, with their families. In this year the Rev. Michael McCabe visited Stafford as often as the opportunity permitted, and ministered to the wants of the Catholic people. In 1853 the Rev. Father Smyth, of Windsor Locks, began to look after the spiritual interests of Stafford, which he continued to do at quarterly intervals for two years. His successor here was the

Rev. Peter Egan, of Rockville, who for two years served Stafford bi-weekly. Father Egan offered the Holy Sacrifice, preached and administered the sacraments in Oronoco Hall. Previous to this Mass was said in the district school house, and in private dwellings. In 1857 the Rev. Bernard Tully began his service of six years, offering the Holy Sacrifice once every two weeks in the above-named hall. The Rev. H. J. O'Reilly in 1855 took charge of this portion of Rockville's jurisdiction and attended it for one year and seven months, making his visits as did his predecessors every fortnight. When the Rev. F. L. De Bruycker became pastor of Willimantic, Stafford Springs became part of his charge. In October, 1866, he began the construction of a church in which his people here could gather for divine worship. The land upon which the church was subsequently built was purchased from Lewis Parkess for $100 by a committee consisting of Daniel Hurley, Stephen Jackson and William Brennan.

The church was completed in November following, and the first Mass offered up within its walls was said on the 24th of that month. It was dedicated on March 10, 1868, under the patronage of St. Edward.

The increase of the Catholic population in twenty years may be seen from the following brief table:

1851—40 persons.   1857—200 persons.   1871, Sept. 15—550 persons.

Up to this date (September 15, 1871,) the benefactors of St. Edward's parish were the following:

| | | | |
|---|---|---|---|
| E A. Converse and Sons | $ 50 00 | G. M. Ives | $50 00 |
| Charles Fox | 100 00 | Lieut.-Gov. Hyde | 25 00 |
| Howe & Converse | 75 00 | M. B. Harvey | 20 00 |
| P. P. Corner, Ridgefield, Ct | 50 00 | | |

In 1872 the first resident pastor, the Rev. P. P. Shahan, began his six years administration of St. Edward's parish. In this period Father Shahan made notable improvements in the church's surroundings, remodeled the edifice itself, erected a pastoral residence, founded the parochial school, over which he placed the Sisters of Mercy from Hartford, purchased a tract of land, consisting of 30 acres, a part of which belonged to the Parley Converse estate, which was blessed and set apart for cemetery purposes. Father Shahan built also the chapel in Staffordville. All these works entailed an expenditure of over $15,000, yet his successor, the Rev. T. W. Broderick, found an indebtedness of only $8000. Father Broderick's labors of eighteen months resulted in a marked diminution of this debt; his successor, the Rev. Patrick Donahoe, also reduced the financial burden, purchased a fine residence on High street, which the Sisters have since used as a convent. During the administration of the Rev. M. McKeon, which began in November, 1881, the entire indebtedness was liquidated, and a thousand dollars left in the treasury to his successor, Rev. John D. Coyle, who succeeded to the pastorate from the position of assistant at St. Edward's for four years, on January 1, 1886. Among the first works that engaged Father Coyle's attention was the erection of the present commodious school, with which is connected a hall having a seating capacity of 400. In 1887 he began the construction of the present St. Edward's church, the corner-stone of which was laid on November 6, 1887. The Rev. Thomas W. Broderick pronounced the discourse at this ceremony. The Right Rev. Bishop McMahon presided at the service of dedication on October 14, 1888, the sermons being delivered, in the morning by Very Rev. A. V. Higgins, O. P., S. T. M., and in the evening by the Rev. James Coyle, of Newport, R. I. The next work accomplished was the construction of the rectory. Father Coyle closed his pastorate in Stafford Springs in May, 1895, and was followed by the Rev. Daniel H. Lawlor, on the 20th of that month. Father Lawlor died January 11, 1897, and the Rev. Richard C. Gragan was appointed his successor on February 1, 1897. During his pastorate thus far Father Gragan has reduced the parish indebtedness $1500, besides laboring with zeal to promote the spiritual welfare of his flock. The clergy who served in the capacity of assistants in this parish are the Revs. John O'Connell, Edward P. McGee, John Donahoe, John D. Coyle, M. P. McCarthy, and A. Dykmans.

When St. Edward's parochial school began its educational career, the names of 75 children were enrolled; at present there are four Sisters teaching, whose Directress is Sister Marie, with four grades, and 190 children.

The population of St. Edward's parish is estimated at 1750 souls, comprising 750 Irish, 900 Canadians, and 100 Italians.

The baptismal register of St. Edward's parish from 1864 to 1897, inclusive, discloses 1603 baptisms. The marriage records inform us that 338 marriages were solemnized between 1865 and 1898.

Father Gragan attends also St. Joseph's mission church, Staffordville, where Mass is said every Sunday.

# WINDHAM COUNTY.

MASSACHUSETTS bounds Windham County on the north, the State of Rhode Island on the east, New London County on the south, and Tolland County on the west. Its average length from north to south is twenty-six miles, and it is about nineteen miles in width.

Windham county was originally a part of Hartford and New London counties, and received its incorporation as a county in May, 1726. In 1820 its population was 31,684; in 1830 it had decreased to 27,077. The Catholic parishes of Windham county are the following:

| | | | |
|---|---|---|---|
| WILLIMANTIC. | DANIELSON. | DAYVILLE. | GROSVENORDALE. |
| MOOSUP. | PUTNAM. | WAUREGAN. | WEST THOMPSON. |

REV. FELIX J. O'NEILL.

REV. JOHN H. BRODERICK

REV. FLOR. DE BRUYCKER.

REV. ARTHUR O'KEEFFE.

REV. EUGENE O'CONNELL.

## ST. JOSEPH'S PARISH,

THE historian of Windham county, writing of the early Catholic settlers, said: "The first colony of Irish Catholics came to locate in Willimantic in the summer of 1847. But few representatives of that nation were then living here, and the little band of twenty foreigners, with but little of this world's goods to incumber them, was visited with much curiosity, and their coming was the subject of considerable excitement. They came at the instance of the Windham Manufacturing Company, who sent for five persons, but their call was responded to by four times that number. The greater part of them, however, were employed by the company, while the balance readily found work at the other factories in the village. This was the opening wedge of Irish labor, which has grown by frequent accessions to be one of the most powerful elements in the industry of this community."

Catholicity in Willimantic had an humble beginning, as its history elsewhere frequently began amidst humble surroundings. When the first Mass was offered here by Rev. John Brady, Jr., of Middletown, in March, 1848, about twenty Catholics, the entire number in the town, gathered before an humble altar in a kitchen of the Lathrop house, which stood on the corner of Washington and Main streets, and was occupied by Arthur McDonald and his family. Among the pioneers present at that first Mass were Owen Thompson, John Gates, Thomas Anderson, Arthur McDonald and their families. In the fall of 1849 Franklin Hall was secured for divine services, and the Rev. Father Brady and his successor, Rev. Michael McCabe, at monthly intervals until 1857 occupied the same building for public worship. In the meantime, Father Brady had, in 1848, secured a tract of land on Jackson street, upon which the present church was subsequently erected.

During Father McCabe's attendance upon Willimantic he and his devoted people were annoyed by exhibitions of bigotry which all good men to-day disavow. Intolerance was prevalent at that time in many places in Connecticut, and both priests and people were made to feel the heavy hand of fanaticism. On one occasion Father McCabe went as usual to Franklin Hall to celebrate the Divine Mysteries, and found the door locked against him. But, determined upon offering the Holy Sacrifice, he led his little congregation to the lot which Father Brady had previously purchased on Jackson street, and upon a rudely-constructed altar offered the Divine Victim. At another time, having ministered to the spiritual wants of his little flock, he started to drive for Baltic, which was in his jurisdiction, but had gone but a short distance on his journey when one of the carriage wheels came off, throwing the priest to the ground. Investigation disclosed the fact that the bolts, screws and nuts of the carriage had been removed, with the intention, evidently, of causing serious injury to Father McCabe. Realizing the seriousness of the case Father McCabe remarked to a by-stander, "The one who did this will come to an untimely end." Verified soon after was the prophecy, as the guilty person was suddenly killed in a railroad accident.

In 1857 Father McCabe purchased an old Baptist meeting-house, and removed it to the lot purchased in 1848 by Father Brady. This building was 60 by 32 feet. Later additions enlarged it to 75 by 50. Having remodeled it as far as the means of the congregation would permit, and arranged it in a manner suitable for Catholic worship, Father McCabe blessed it and placed it under the patronage of St. Joseph. At this time there were about eight Catholic families in Willimantic, and as an instance of their poverty, as well also of the anti-Catholic spirit then prevailing, an attachment was served on the building for a debt of a few dollars only, before the blocks were removed from it.

Upon the death of Father McCabe in Danielson in 1860, the Rev. Hugh J. O'Reilly became the first resident pastor of Willimantic. His first work was the erection of a parochial residence, and in 1863 he secured a tract of land for cemetery purposes. Upon Father O'Reilly's appointment to Danielson, his successor became the Rev. Daniel Mullen, who labored here only four months, when his successor, the present incumbent, assumed charge on May 11, 1863. When Father De Bruycker succeeded to the pastorate of Willimantic Stafford Springs, Baltic and South Coventry were also assigned to him, and faithfully and with signal success did he discharge his duties to these missions, all of which have had resident pastors for some years. In 1864 Father De Bruycker secured about thirty acres of land for a new cemetery, the old burial place having become inadequate to the needs of the congregation ; the remains of those who reposed in the first cemetery were reverently and with due solemnity transferred to the new one on Good Friday of the same year. The new tract of land received solemn blessing in November, 1875, a portion of it only having been previously set apart by private blessing.

In the meantime, the growth of the congregation rendered the repairing, refitting and enlarging of the church necessary, but nevertheless, it soon became inadequate to accommodate the congregation. Accordingly, in 1892, Father De Bruycker took the first step towards the erection of a church edifice that would meet all future demands. He purchased a house and lot, west of the old church, and having removed both church and rectory in May, 1873, from Jackson to Valley street, began immediately to lay the foundations for a new structure. As evidence of the progress made on the work of construction, it may be stated that the corner-stone was laid on August 17, 1873, by Bishop McFarland, which was the last public act of this prelate. Assisting Bishop McFarland were Rev. Fathers Walsh, Schale and Dent, of Hartford; Van Laar, of Baltic; Mullen and Desmond, of Norwich ; Lawlor, of Rockville ; Desoulniers, of Canada ; Campbell, of Manchester ; Reynolds, of Jewett City. The address was delivered by Rev. Lawrence Walsh, of Hartford. The contributions realized $3,000. On November 17, 1874, the church was dedicated by Right Rev. Bishop McQuaid, of Rochester, N. Y.

St. Joseph's Church is Gothic in design ; length, 156 feet ; width, 64 feet ; and from the floor to the highest point of the ceiling, 75 feet. From the curbstone it is 175 feet to the top of the spire. The high altar is of Munich construction, and a notable work of art. The church will accommodate 1,200 people, and when completed cost over $80,000.

## ST. JAMES' PARISH,

DANIELSON.

THE first missionary priest to exercise his ministry permanently in Windham county was the Rev. Michael McCabe, a Franciscan friar from Ireland. Previous to his advent Jesuit priests from Worcester, Mass., visited this section of the State at irregular intervals, perhaps semi-annually, or at most, quarterly, and ministered to the wants of the people whom they found in their missionary journeys. Father McCabe entered upon his ministry here in 1850 and offered the Holy Sacrifice of the Mass for the first time in a private residence on Franklin street. Bacon's Hall was afterwards secured for Divine Worship. Father McCabe's pastorate in Danielson terminated with his death in 1860, and he was succeeded by the Rev. Philip B. Daly, whose period of service was of short duration. The Rev. James Quinn succeeded Father Daly, taking up his residence at Moosup, Danielson becoming a dependency. On August 20, 1864, Father Quinn purchased an old Second Adventist chapel, with the lot on which it stood, of Sally D. Brown. This, the first Catholic church in Danielson, became afterwards the transept of an enlarged edifice. Father Quinn added the front part of the edifice and also secured additional property on the north of the church from Elisha Chamberlin on July 3, 1866. On this land Father Quinn erected the parochial residence. In September, 1869, Danielson again became the residence of a pastor in the person of the Rev. A. Princen. Father Princen enlarged the church again by the addition of the sanctuary and vestry. His pastoral relations were severed by death in April, 1883. Rev. Thomas J. Preston began his administration of St. James' upon the death of Father Princen. The works which marked his pastorate were the renovation and remodeling of the church; the liquidation of the $6000 indebtedness and the erection of a parochial school at an expense of $11,000, including the lot, which comprises two and one-half acres, and purchased on March 7, 1877, of Betsy H. Ely. The school is a spacious and an attractive structure and was opened in September, 1889. It will accommodate about 350 pupils and is conducted by the Sisters of St. Joseph. Instruction is imparted in the modern languages, and also in music, drawing and fancy work. The present enrolment of pupils is 245, with four sisters, of whom Sister M. Theophane is the Directress.

At the time St. James' parish was organized a census of the Catholic population gave 800 souls, Irish and Canadians. During Father Preston's administration the estimated number was about 1300 French-Canadians and 500 Irish and their descendants.

Father Preston's administration closed in 1895, when St. James' passed under the jurisdiction of the missionary Fathers of Our Lady of La Salette, Hartford, with the Rev. C. F. Socquet, M.S., as pastor. In 1898 Father Socquet gave way to the Rev. J. P. Guinet, M.S., who is still in charge.

The priests who served here as assistants are the following: Revs. John Van den Noort, T. J. Preston, Father Finnegan, Joseph Gleeson, James Thompson, Andrew Haggarty, Arthur O'Keefe, P. Fox, A. L. Dusablon,

F. Bedard.   The present assistants are Rev. J. Blanc, M.S., and the Rev. T. Roux, M.S.

Besides the church, rectory, school and convent, the parish possesses a tract of land on which it is the intention to build a new church and parochial residence.

The difficulties which existed between the pastors and parishioners of St. James' and to which the English-speaking portion of the congregation were no party, and which, furthermore, may have been the result of a lack of proper appreciation of the genius of our institutions, are now, we trust, happily adjusted, and that the memory of them will never again arise to disturb the peace of the parish.  Refusal to acknowledge legitimate ecclesiastical authority, especially when such refusal leads to seeking relief in the civil courts, cannot but exercise a deleterious influence upon those not of the household of the faith, while at the same time it tends to weaken, if not to utterly destroy, the faith of those who claim the Catholic church as their mother.

In the early days of Catholicity in this, as in other dioceses, difficulties between bishops and priests and people were not of infrequent occurrence; but they sprang, not always from a desire to rebel against their lawful superiors, but were rather the outcome of the unsettled condition of ecclesiastical laws. Moreover, priests and people came not so frequently into contact with one another as at present, owing to widely-separated missions and the scarcity of priests.  The people, therefore, were, to a certain extent, under the influences of designing men who sought the advancement of self, and who, therefore, endeavored to curtail the power of the priest with his people, and sometimes to destroy it altogether.  This was a potent factor in many quarrels, the memory of which is becoming dim as time advances.  But at present, with our means of enlightenment, with our numerous priests and Sisters, with our bishops, who are no respecters of persons, ever active and willing to conserve the spiritual interests of all their flocks, irrespective of race conditions, resistance to legitimately established authority, under what pretext soever, seems an anachronism, is utterly to be condemned, and to be repudiated by all who have the welfare of the church and the honor and glory of God at heart.

During the three decades of the parish's existence the sacrament of Baptism has been conferred 335 times; in the same period 72 marriages were solemnized.

The clergy of St. James' attend also one mission, Hampton, where Mass is said every other Sunday, and two stations, Brooklyn and Chestnut Hill, which are attended once a month.  Hampton was incorporated in 1786.  In 1720 it was known as *Kennedy, or Windham Village,* so called from a Mr. Kennedy who, with his family, were the first settlers here.  The cornerstone of the Hampton church of Our Lady of Lourdes was laid on Thursday, the 15th of November, 1877, by Bishop Galberry, during the administration of Rev. Father Princen.  The priests assisting the bishop were the Rev. Fathers De Bruycker, as deacon; Rev. Daniel Mullen, of Norwich, as subdeacon; and Rev. Thos. J. Preston, of Danielson, as master of ceremonies.

Other priests present were Fathers Van den Noort, Van Oppen, Martial, Van Wersch, Shahan, Russell, and Kennedy. The sermon was delivered by Rev. Father De Bruycker.

An acre of ground had been donated to the Catholics of Hampton for the site of a church by ex-Governor Cleveland. The church was dedicated the following spring. The cost of the building when completed was about $4,000. At that time there were thirty-four families professing the Catholic faith in Hampton. The number has decreased to eighty souls, the present population.

## ST. JOSEPH'S PARISH,
### DAYVILLE.

BESIDES Dayville, St. Joseph's parish embraces within its jurisdiction Williamsville, Attawaugan and Ballouville. Dayville was formerly attached to Danielson as an out-mission, and for some years the Rev. A. Princen said Mass in Sayles Hall In 1873 St. Joseph's church was built, and was dedicated by Very Rev. Jas. Hughes, V.G., Administrator, in May, 1875. The lot on which the church stands, containing about three acres, was donated by Sabin L. Sayles. Dayville remained a mission of Danielson until September 1, 1881, when the Rev. Theodore Ariens was appointed first resident pastor. Father Ariens built the parochial residence, and also the church of the Five Wounds, in Ballouville. Father Ariens served five years, when the Rev. Terrence J. Dunn was appointed his successor. On February 7, 1894, the present incumbent, Rev. Jas. H. Fitzmaurice, was appointed pastor of St. Joseph's. In 1898 the Dayville Woolen Co. became a benefactor of the parish by the generous donation of a tract of land to serve as an addition to the cemetery, which had been previously given by Mr. Sayles.

The site on which the church of the Five Wounds, Ballouville, stands was presented by the Attawaugan Company. The estimated number of Catholics in Dayville at the present time is 1,400, of whom the majority are French Canadians, the remainder being Irish and their descendants.

## ST. JOSEPH'S PARISH,
### GROSVENORDALE.

THE early Catholic residents of the two Grosvenordales attended divine services at Putnam and Webster, Mass. The first priest to minister to their spiritual wants was the Rev. William E. Duffy, of Pascoag, R. I., who had Putnam in his jurisdiction. When Putnam received a resident pastor in September, 1866, Thompson was attached to it as a mission, with the Rev. Eugene J. Vygen as pastor. Father Vygen purchased in 1872 twelve acres of land between Grosvenordale and North Grosvenordale, and immediately began preparations for the erection of a church. Having matured his plans, St. Joseph's church, a frame structure of Gothic design, was built at an outlay of $10,000. The church was dedicated by Right Rev. Bishop McFarland, on September 29, 1872, the Rev. Father Martial, of Putnam, delivering the address.

In January, 1873, St. Joseph's was elevated to the parochial dignity, having in its jurisdiction the whole town with the exception of Mechanicsville, West Thompson, and *Quaduc* or *Quanduc.* The estimated population of the parish at that time was about 900 souls. The first resident pastor was the Rev. H. Martial, and the lay trustees were Patrick Kelly and Louis P. Lamoureux. Father Martial built the parochial residence in the same year, and in the year following the cemetery was blessed by Very Rev. James Hughes, V.G., Administrator, on June 15th. Six years later the limits of the parish were extended to embrace the whole town, and Rev A. J. Haggarty was appointed assistant. During this year the church of the Sacred Heart at West Thompson was erected, and dedicated by Bishop McMahon. Upon the death of Father Martial the affairs of the parish were administered by Rev. Father Flannagan until February 14, 1883, when Rev. Thos. Cooney began his administration. Soon after entering upon his labors Father Cooney extended his missionary sphere to New Boston and Quinnebaug. Mr. Eben S. Stevens, of Quinnebaug, moved by generous impulses and desirous of advancing the interests of religion, donated a piece of land for church purposes, and added $300 to this donation. The church was erected in New Boston and dedicated in honor of St. Stephen by Bishop McMahon on March 30, 1884. The edifice cost $3,000. St. Joseph's parochial school, an attractive, substantial and commodious structure, embracing also the convent and hall, was erected in 1881, at an expense of $12,000. The school was placed in charge of the Sisters of the Holy Cross and of the Seven Dolors, and was opened for the reception of pupils on January 2, 1882. On that day 300 children presented themselves for enrolment. At present 473 pupils are taught by nine sisters, whose Directress is Sister M. St. Beatrice.

The Congregation of the Sisters of the Holy Cross was founded in the city of Mans, France, in 1837, by the Very Rev. Basil Moreau, C.S.C. The Congregation is at present divided into three branches, each having a superior and a government of its own. The Mother-house of the Marianites of Holy Cross is the cradle of the institution of Mans, France. The American branch has its Mother-house at Notre Dame, Ind., the title of the community being Sisters of the Holy Cross.

The Canadian branch to which the Sisters of Grosvenordale belong has its Mother-house at St. Laurent, near Montreal, and the official title of the community is Sisters of the Holy Cross and of the Seven Dolors. In April, 1881, Rev. Father Martial, pastor of St. Joseph's, first broached the question of a parochial school to his parishioners. Generous subscriptions were offered immediately, the St. John Baptist society, Cadets of Temperance, the Dramatic Club, and the parishioners vying with one another in their contributions. Encouraged by these marks of good will on the part of his people, Father Martial visited Montreal during the same month, and through the intervention of the Bishop of that See, secured the services of six Sisters of the Holy Cross from the Mother-house at St. Laurent. On his return to Grosvenordale, Father Martial began the building of the convent and school, which were completed in November of the same year. The convent is a substantial wooden structure, 48 by 39 feet, and three stories high. The school adjoins the convent, is two stories high, 98 by 29 feet, the largest portion being used as a public hall. The Sisters arrived in Grosvenordale on December 21, 1881, and were cordially received by the ladies of the parish. On Sunday, Christmas day, Mr. Joseph Magnan, at an assemblage of the parishioners, addressed the Sisters in behalf of the French-Canadians, and Mr. Patrick Kelly, in behalf of the Irish members of the congregation.

Of late years, the building has been enlarged and improved, and the work begun by Father Martial is continued by his zealous and energetic successor, Father Cooney.

## ALL HALLOW'S PARISH.

### Moosup.

ABOUT sixty-six years ago (1833), the first little band of Catholics settled in Moosup in the persons of Michael Smith, Sr., Andrew Smith, James McCaffrey, and James Meehan. Like their fellow-countrymen of those trying days, whom immigration brought to our shores, they yearned for the presence of those who could administer to them the consolations of religion and dispense the graces of the sacraments. Though deprived of priestly ministrations for some years they, nevertheless, held fast to the faith once delivered to the saints and rejoiced when, about 1848, the first Mass in Moosup was offered up in the house of Michael Smith, Sr., now occupied by Terrence Coughlin. The celebrant of this historic Mass was the Rev. William Logan, S.J., of Holy Cross College, Worcester, who about this time had charge of New London, Norwich and several adjoining stations. On his way from Worcester, he may have heard of the presence here of some Catholics and sojourned amongst them to offer up the Holy Sacrifice. About this time there were between twenty and thirty Irish Catholics in Moosup. Following Father Logan, Moosup was attended at intervals of three months by the Rev. Peter Blenkinsop, also of Worcester, until the appointment of Rev. Michael McCabe to the pastorate of Danielson. Father McCabe's visits were made at intervals of two or three months, and on these occasions he said Mass in private houses. His services continued until the appointment of the Rev. Philip Daly, whose pastorate terminated in June, 1861, when the Rev. James Quinn succeeded him. Father Quinn served until the appointment of the Rev. J. J. McCabe in October, 1869. The next pastor was the Rev. Ferdinand Belanger, who came in April, 1870. His successor was the Rev. John Quinn, who received his appointment in November, 1872. Rev. Denis Desmond then followed in July, 1874, and remained until October, 1876, when Rev. P. M. Kennedy took up the reins of government. His pastorate terminated in October, 1878, and the Rev. John A. Creedon became pastor of All Hallow's. Upon the translation of Father Creedon to Windsor Locks, in January, 1896, the present incumbent, Rev. John H. Broderick, became his successor.

All Hallow's church was built in 1859-60, by Rev. Philip Daly. So enthusiastically did the people set about to witness the realization of their hopes that the site of the church and parochial residence was soon purchased from M. S. Bennett. The corner-stone of the church was laid by Bishop McFarland in the same fall, Rev. Thomas Quinn delivering the address. The same prelate dedicated it under its present title in the following spring. During the pastorate of the Rev. Father Belanger the old pastoral residence and lot were secured. All Hallow's parish embraced at one period the towns of Sterling,[1] Plainfield, Griswold, Canterbury, Hampton and a part of Killingly. When the parish was organized, the population was estimated at about 500 souls, chiefly Irish. At present it numbers about 1,500, comprising Irish and French Canadians. During Father Creedon's period of service, in 1889, the church was practically rebuilt, extensive improvements having been made both within and without. A conflagration in May, 1893, destroyed the old rectory, and the present attractive and spacious parochial residence arose from its ashes. Since the arrival of Father Broderick the reduction of the debt has been steady and gratifying, both to pastor and people, new land has been acquired, the grounds about the church and rectory have been greatly improved, and hopes are entertained of beginning the erection of a new church in the near future.

The old cemetery is in the church-yard, and was first used in 1861, but it has ceased to be used as a place of burial for well nigh fifteen years.

The priests who have served All Hallow's as assistants are the following: Rev. A. Bernard, from July, 1869, to September, 1869; Rev. T. Sweeney, from November, 1880, to January, 1882; Rev. T. J. Dunn, from March, 1882, to June, 1886; Rev. T. H. Shanley, from November, 1886, to October, 1890. The present assistant pastor is the Rev. E. J. Broderick.

The baptismal records disclose 5,402 baptisms from 1869 to 1898; in the same period the marriage ceremony was performed 773 times.

Oneco, a town on the N. Y., N. H. and H. R. R., formerly the New England railroad, is attended from All Hallow's as a station.

" The parish is prosperous, its numbers on the increase and the Catholic portion of the community, with its usual generous and self-sacrificing spirit, is determined to keep fully abreast of the times."

## PARISH OF ST. MARY'S OF THE VISITATION,

### PUTNAM.

AS far as can be ascertained from existing records, the first Catholic in Putnam was a French-Canadian, Peter Donough, who came in 1843, with a large family. After the opening of the great factories, in 1848, other Canadians came and soon formed a comparatively numerous colony. Among the other early Catholic settlers of this mission, were Nicholas Cosgrove, James Rafferty, Francis Madden, James Bracken, Matthew Ragan, John Conway, Jean Baptiste Lapointe, Francois Piché, Menis Bibeault, M. Champeau, Ambrose Lapointe, and Thomas Luby.

---

[1] Sterling was named after an Irishman, Henry Sterling, M.D., who was a resident of the State during the Revolution.

REV. JOHN H. FITZMAURICE.

REV. JOHN VAN DEN NOORT.

REV. THOMAS COONEY.

REV. J. P. GUINET. M.S.

The Rev. William Logan, S. J., of Worcester, celebrated the first Mass said in Putnam, in the residence of Nicholas Cosgrove, on July 8, 1849. His successor was also a Jesuit priest of Holy Cross College, Rev. Peter Blenkinsop, who celebrated Mass in the house of Mr. Ambrose Lapointe. The Rev. Michael McCabe came next and celebrated his first Mass here in a private house, but afterwards secured Morse's Hall. The presence of Catholics, however, in this hall was displeasing to the Know-Nothing element, and Father McCabe and his congregation were ordered to discontinue their services there. Determined to build a church for his people, if possible, Father McCabe purchased an acre of ground from Edward Wilkinson. But the financial means of the people not corresponding to their own nor to their pastor's desires, they secured Quinnebaug Hall, where divine services were held once a month. In 1858, Putnam was attended from Pascoag, R. I., whose pastor was the Rev. William E. Duffy. In the year following he began the erection of the first church in this section of Connecticut. It was a small frame building, and cost when completed and furnished about $2200; its dimensions were 60 x 24. Father Duffy was succeeded in 1866 by the Rev. Eugene J. Vygen, who became the first resident pastor. When Bishop McFarland appointed him to this mission he said to him : " Putnam is a poor missionary field, and will not be able to support you ; but go there, board at the hotel and do the best you can." " Sent to administer the sacraments at Putnam, he was greatly moved by the spiritual destitution of the people without resident priest, schools or burial ground; it was no marvel that 'scandals became frequent and the church of God suffered.' The keen-eyed young missionary saw at a glance the great capabilities of the field. Some half dozen large manufactories in Putnam and Thompson were bringing in hundreds of Catholic families. Putnam village gave promise of becoming an important business centre, and was a natural church home of this increasing Catholic population. With much earnestness Father Vygen laid the need and opportunity before the Bishop of the diocese, and was allowed to enter upon the Putnam pastorate."

The first work accomplished by Father Vygen was the purchase of a residence from a Mr. Tanner ; he then secured five and a half acres of land which he laid out for cemetery purposes, and had it consecrated by Bishop McFarland in 1868. He then added to the church's possessions by purchasing additional property, and soon after erected a pastoral residence near the church at an expense of about $4,000. But Father Vygen's ambition, and a laudable one it was, was directed to the building of a church more adapted to the growing importance of his congregation. Before entering, however, on the project he visited the various capitals and other cities of Europe, making a tour of inspection of the chief church edifices. With this experience and having secured financial aid among his European friends, he returned with a determination to begin and prosecute the work to a successful completion. To this end he purchased additional property from Messrs. Morse and Wilkinson, and removed the old church. The new edifice, an impressive brick structure, was dedicated by Bishop McFarland on November 24, 1870. The dimensions of this church were 160 by 93 ; transept, 90 feet. But Father Vygen's labors were not yet finished. Early in 1873 he began the erection of a school and convent, and in April, 1874, the former was opened under the direction of the Sisters of Mercy.

But Father Vygen and his devoted people were to be tried in the crucible of affliction. On February 6, 1875, a conflagration destroyed the church, and what had been "the pride of the Catholics of Putnam, was a charred and blackened mass of ruins." The fire spread so rapidly that the sacred vessels, the vestments, the altar and organ, and a valuable library of a thousand volumes —in a word, all the treasures of the church were consumed. Among the precious articles destroyed was a gold chalice presented to Father Vygen by his parents on the day of his ordination. The church with its treasures was valued at $85,000, and was insured for $48,000. Of this amount $32,000 was spent in the liquidation of the debt on the school and convent. Undismayed by this severe loss, Father Vygen began immediately the erection of a chapel, his people worshiping in the meantime in Quinnebaug hall. Within a year after the conflagration St. Joseph's chapel was dedicated, on November 1, 1876, by Bishop Galberry. The dimensions of the chapel were 95 by 65 feet, and it had a seating capacity of 800.

Father Vygen celebrated his silver jubilee in March, 1889. He was summoned to his reward in October of the same year. His had been a most useful and active life, and his memory is honored by Protestants and Catholics alike. A contemporary paid him this tribute : "Father Vygen is much beloved by his people and respected by all for his consistent Christian character, and faithful labors in behalf of temperance, morality and all salutary enterprises."

The present rector of St. Mary's, the Rev. John Van den Noort, became his successor.

In 1849, when the first Mass was said in Putnam, about thirty-five persons were present. When the first church was built the Catholic population was estimated at 1,000, probably a high estimate. When the church which was destroyed by fire was completed, a census showed the presence in Putnam of 2,500 Catholics. The present population of the parish is 3,400 souls, of mixed nationalities.

In 1874 when the school was opened, 400 pupils asked for admission. The present number of pupils is 586, taught by nine sisters, whose Superioress is Sister M. Paula.

The assistants who served in St. Mary's at various periods were the Revs. H. Martial, T. Joynt, A. Van Oppen, T. Cooney, W. Flannagan, T. Cronan, E. Broderick, E. Chapdelaine and J. Papillon.

Among the special benefactors of the parish mention should be made of Bishop McFarland, Rev. Eugene Vygen, Rev. F. DeBruycker, Rev. Van Laar, and Rev. A. Princen, Michael McGuirk, Maria McDerby, Wm. Mullen, Augustin L'Esperance, Misael Desrosiers, Francois Bibeault.

The most remarkable conversion to Catholicism within the jurisdiction of Putnam was that of Mrs. Clara Thompson, of Pomfret, the authoress of several Catholic works of great value. She had formerly professed the Episcopalian faith.

## SACRED HEART PARISH,

### WAUREGAN.

HE earliest known Catholics to settle in Wauregan were Thomas Gibbons, P. Flanagan, James Riley, Louis Charon, Pierre Girard and Alexis Jetté. To them belongs the distinction of keeping alive the sacred flame of faith in this vicinity at a period when a Catholic was scrutinized as the representative of a foreign despot, whose ambition it was to enslave the human family, and as the embodiment of superstition, idolatry and disloyalty. Of inferior clay he was supposed to be, and as "an ignorant foreigner," was held in contempt, a sentiment which in this enlightenment age provokes rather pity than anger. Sons of the Emerald Isle and children of France, the fervent disciples of St. Patrick and of St. Louis, of Columba and of Genevieve, came hither to cast their lot with others more prosperous in the goods of earth and to assist in laying strong and deep the foundations of the Church in this portion of our beloved land.

Missionary priests from Holy Cross College, whose jurisdiction extended as far south as New London, exercised their ministry here between 1848 and 1850, consoling the faithful by the graces of the Mass and the sacraments, and strengthening them against the spiritual dangers which are ever present to the soul when deprived of the holy ministrations of God's anointed.

The Rev. Michael McCabe, a pioneer missionary of north-eastern Connecticut, visited Wauregan in the early fifties. When the church of All Hallows was built at Moosup in 1859–60, by Rev. Philip Daly, the Catholics of Wauregan attended divine services there, many of them making the journey on foot. But the inconvenience attendant upon these journeys was eliminated when, in 1870, Rev. Ferdinand Berlanger, pastor of Moosup, began the erection of a church at Wauregan, which was completed by his successor, Rev. John Quinn. The corner-stone was laid by Very Rev. James Hughes, V. G., and the church was dedicated to the Sacred Heart of Jesus by Bishop McFarland. The church property, which is situated in West Wauregan in the town of Brooklyn, was purchased from Mr. James Atwood, manager of the Wauregan Mills, for $1000.

The priests who attended Wauregan in succession to Father Berlanger were Revs. John Quinn, Denis Desmond, Peter M. Kennedy, John Creedon.

The jurisdiction of Moosup over Wauregan ceased on May 20, 1889, when Bishop McMahon organized the latter into a parish and appointed Rev. Arthur A. O'Keefe the first resident pastor. Father O'Keefe entered upon his new sphere of labors with characteristic activity, and, his parishioners cheerfully co-operating, has accomplished results that make for the temporal and spiritual welfare of his people and the honor of the church. Among other material works, mention may be made of the erection of a parochial residence, and other buildings, barn, horse-sheds, etc. A new cemetery was purchased and blessed on May 17, 1891, the grounds about the church and rectory have been improved and beautified, and an abundant water supply introduced into the parochial residence and outer buildings. The total extent of the church property is twenty-five acres.

When the parish was organized, its population was estimated at 1350 souls, of whom 1100 were French and 250 Irish; the latest census gives 1200: French Canadians, 1000, Irish, 200.

The baptismal register, beginning in 1889, discloses 452 baptisms to have been administered to 1898; while 97 marriages were solemnized within the same period. The first birth, as well as the first baptism, was that of Mary Ellen Fallon. The first marriage ceremony was performed on June 24, 1889, the contracting parties being Joseph Lefevre and Aglae Boivin. The first death was that of Ludger Gauthier, a child of two years.

## SACRED HEART PARISH,

### West Thompson.

**M**ECHANICSVILLE began its existence as an independent parish on February 2, 1886, the Rev. W. E. Flannagan having been appointed by Bishop McMahon its first resident pastor. The pastoral residence was built in 1887, at an outlay of $3,000. In 1889, Mechanicsville and West Thompson were assigned as dependencies of Grosvenordale. In that year the church of the Sacred Heart was built, the principal benefactor being Mr. Thomas D. Sayles, who donated the site and $500 additional to insure the inception of the edifice.

The present pastor is the Rev. James Cunningham.

Attached to West Thompson is the mission of Pomfret, church of the Holy Trinity.

First settled in 1686, Pomfret was granted the privileges of incorporation in 1713. In this vicinity is Putnam's "Wolf Den," famous in Connecticut history, as the scene of the great American's encounter with a she-wolf in which the former was victorious.

Previous to the erection of the church divine services were held in Pomfret Hall. A class in Christian doctrine was also conducted. Work on the construction of the church was begun early in 1885, and Mass was said in it for the first time on Easter Sunday, 1887. Shortly after it was dedicated.

An efficient auxiliary to the clergy in religious and charitable work, a munificent benefactor to the parish, Mrs. Clara Thompson, a convert from the Episcopal faith, was a power for good among her co-religionists, devoted and zealous, withal prudent, enjoying the confidence and affection of all classes. She passed among them a striking example of the sweet and precious influence of the Catholic religion upon a soul who realizes its relationship with its Creator, who recognizes that, not earthly pleasure, nor preferments nor wealth, is the goal towards which man should tend, but that his destiny, a supernatural end, is the eternal possession of God, and who from a heart craving for divine love, cries out with St. Augustine: "Our hearts know no rest, O God, until they find rest in Thee."

## ST. MICHAEL'S PARISH,

WESTERLY, R. I. (P. O.).

THE Holy Sacrifice of the Mass was first offered up in Westerly in 1835, by the Rev. James Fitton, in the house of a railroad contractor which was situated about a mile and a half from Pawcatuck bridge. After this visit Father Fitton returned to this neighborhood twice each year to offer the Holy Sacrifice and otherwise minister to the spiritual wants of the Catholics engaged on the railroad. But in 1837, when this work was completed, these sturdy laborers sought homes elsewhere, so that in 1838 only two Catholics remained in this vicinity, namely, John Ryan and Andrew Lahey. Besides these mentioned other Catholics were here early in Westerly's history, among whom we notice the Celtic names of Murphy, Keegan and Fay.

After Father Fitton's transfer to Worcester he continued his visits through this section of Connecticut, and about the year 1845 said Mass on one occasion in what was known as Babcock's Woods, under a spreading oak tree. During his subsequent visits for some time thereafter Mass was said in the open air. Recognizing the devotion of the apostolic missionary and of his little congregation to their faith, who were willing, if needs be, to worship God beneath the azure sky, the trustees of the Union meeting-house finally offered him the use of this building for divine worship.

The Rev. John Brady, of Hartford, succeeded Father Fitton in his attendance upon Stonington, Westerly and adjoining stations, and served them as well as his manifold labors would permit.

The Rev. Patrick Duffy became the first resident pastor of Stonington, and Westerly was assigned to it as a dependency. During his visits here he offered the Holy Sacrifice and performed other priestly functions in the residence of Mr. John Murphy, as did also his successor, the Rev. Thomas Drea. Owing to the steady increase of the Catholic population of Westerly, Father Drea visited this place at monthly intervals.

In 1857 the Rev. Peter Kelly assumed charge in succession to Father Drea, and shortly after his assumption of the pastorate purchased the property on which St. Michael's church now stands, as further use of the Union meeting-house was denied him. After a pastorate of brief duration in Stonington, Father Kelly was succeeded by the Rev. John Sheridan, who, serving but a short time, was followed in the same year by the Rev. Michael O'Reilly. Immediatiely upon his accession to the pastorate Father O'Reilly began preparations for the erection of a church, and the first step to this end was the purchase of a piece of land in Pawcatuck, upon which the church was built. The corner-stone was laid in August, 1860, and the church was dedicated in May, 1861. The dimensions of this building were 40 x 60. At this time the Catholic population of Westerly numbered about 100. After the erection of the church in Pawcatuck Father O'Reilly disposed of the rectory at Stonington and took up his residence in Pawcatuck. Attached to Pawcatuck at this time were Mystic and Stonington, in Connecticut, and Wakefield and Carolina, in Rhode Island.

In succession to Father O'Reilly came the Rev. Patrick Sherry, in the fall of 1863, and five years later he repaired and enlarged the church sufficiently to accommodate 1250 persons. Father Sherry died here in 1870, and in December of this year the Rev. Jeremiah Fitzpatrick assumed charge. Shortly after his arrival the mission dependencies were separated from the mother church. In 1873 Father Fitzpatrick, having secured an eligible site, built thereon a convent and parochial school. Father Fitzpatrick was transferred to St. Patrick's, New Haven, in December, 1876, and his successor became the Rev. Thomas L. Lynch.

In the meantime, the diocese of Providence had been erected with the Right Rev. Thomas Hendricken as its first bishop. Though Westerly was a part of Rhode Island, which was within the new See, the bishops of Hartford and Providence mutually agreed that it should remain a part of the jurisdiction of the former.

Father Lynch's relations with Westerly ceased in 1883, but during his administration the old rectory was disposed of by sale, moved elsewhere, and the present parochial residence was commenced, but not completed. His successor was the Rev. Lawrence Walsh of Waterbury, who came in August, 1883. Father Walsh's pastorate was of brief duration, ending after five months by death.

His successor, the present rector, Rev. Ambrose Briscoe, assumed charge on January 19, 1884. In May, 1885, Father Briscoe's parish was divided, the Westerly portion passing under the jurisdiction of the Bishop of Providence.

In 1893, Father Briscoe built St. Michael's school, a wooden structure having six spacious rooms. The school is taught by five Sisters of Mercy, of whom Mother M. Ambrosia is the Directress, with 259 pupils.

The parish cemetery was purchased in 1856.

Free from financial burdens, the pastor zealous and the parishioners generously co-operating, St. Michael's parish is fulfilling its mission: *Ad Majorem Dei Gloriam.*

## SACRED HEART (GERMAN) PARISH.

### HARTFORD.

THE Rev. Joseph Schale was the first German priest to reside in Hartford. He came in the summer of 1872, at the invitation of Bishop McFarland, with whom he resided, attending to the spiritual wants of the German Catholics on Sundays at St. Peter's church. In August of 1872, Bishop McFarland organized the Germans into an independent parish under the title of the Sacred Heart, and purchased a lot on the corner of Winthrop and Ely streets. Business depression followed, and the project of building a church was abandoned for the time. In 1874 Father Schale was given charge of the German Catholics of New Haven and Bridgeport.

On Pentecost Sunday, 1886, Bishop McMahon reorganized the parish in St. Peter's school hall, and the Rev. Nicholas Schneider, of New Britain, was appointed pastor. As soon as circumstances permitted, the erection of the church was commenced, and the corner-stone was laid on September 4, 1892, by Bishop McMahon. The same prelate dedicated the present basement on April 9, 1893. Father Schneider continued to attend the German Catholics of Hartford until January 1, 1897, when the Rev. H. Dahme, the present rector, assumed charge. The present rectory, a brick building with brownstone trimmings, was completed on November 1, 1898. Services are held for the present in the basement, and it is expected to have the superstructure finished in about two years.

---

In the preceding sketches mention is made particularly of the labors and successes of the clergy in the temporal order. There is no intention of exalting the temporal above the spiritual, nor of conveying the impression that a pastor's success is solely to be measured by the amount of property purchased or indebtedness paid. But, circumstanced as the Catholics have been (and as they are still in many places) their pastors were obliged to exhibit in some degree the qualities that lead to success in temporals, as well as those of faithful shepherds of souls. At the same time it is gratifying to place on record the fact that the spiritual interests of the people have always been faithfully conserved. For this priests were ordained, and for this placed in their responsible positions. That in the midst of so many and so trying difficulties their spiritual labors have been crowned with success is a source as well of wonderment as of joy and thankfulness. To implant the seeds of strong faith and to extend the kingdom of Christ among men was the goal of their ambition, and their divine Master has bestowed the reward.

If the historical details of some of the parish sketches appear meagre, it is because they were inaccessible; or in a few instances, having been received, were found untrustworthy and were rejected. In other cases, repeated attempts to obtain information having failed, the writer was obliged to make use of the data at his disposal.

---

## THE INSTITUTIONS OF THE DIOCESE.

---

### ST. FRANCIS ORPHAN ASYLUM,

#### New Haven, Conn.

#### Established 1852, incorporated 1865.

ITS PROPERTY.—The Asylum consists of a large brick building, three stories high, which contains the dormitories, school rooms, recreation halls, refectories and chapel, and of out-buildings used for laundry, bakery, barn and storage purposes. Surrounding these it owns about thirteen and one-quarter (13¼) acres of excellent land, so that there is sufficient room for all its needs. The building proper is well heated, lighted and ventilated; and provided with baths and all else necessary or conducive to cleanliness and health. The various departments of the asylum, even to the small farm, gardens and grounds, are kept in perfect order and cleanliness, and bear marks of excellent management.

OBJECTS.—To support, maintain and educate orphan, half orphan, homeless, destitute and indigent children.

GOVERNING AUTHORITY.—This body consists of a Board of Trustees originally named in the charter, and authorized thereby to appoint associates and successors.

MEMBERS.—The members of the corporation are: First, the pastors of all the Catholic parishes of the St. Francis orphan asylum district and their successors in the pastorate; second, three laymen from each of the Catholic parishes of the City of New Haven. The original St. Francis orphan asylum district, outlined at the time of its incorporation in 1865, has never been changed. As appears from the records of the orphanage, all that portion of the original Hartford diocese, which after the division of 1872, comprises the present diocese of Hartford, constitutes the aforesaid asylum district. From the parishes formed within said territory the orphans have constantly been sent, many of the parishes, too, having been assessed, as they might be assessed again, if necessary, to help it in its work, and the asylum has always depended on its said district for support. Thus fostered, therefore, and supported by the bishops, priests and Catholic laity of the present diocese of Hartford, the orphanage from a private parish charity has not only grown into an excellent diocesan asylum, but has become one of the most attractive charitable institutions in this State.

OFFICERS.—President, vice-president, secretary, treasurer and fifteen managers, whose duties are prescribed in the by-laws of the corporation. The Right Rev. Bishop of the diocese is *ex officio* president of the corporation; the vice-president, secretary and treasurer, each elected annually by ballot, are *ex officio* members of the board of managers in addition to the fifteen managers above provided for.

*President.*—Right Rev. M. Tierney, D.D., 140 Farmington avenue, Hartford,

*Vice president.*—Rev. John Russell, 640 Grand avenue, New Haven.

*Secretary.*—William M. Geary, 479 Orange street, New Haven.

*Treasurer.*—Rev. John F. Corcoran, who resides at the asylum.

*The Board of Managers.*—The managers are selected by the trustees; and they attend to the financial and secular affairs and details of the orphanage.

The internal management of the asylum is intrusted to the Sisters of Mercy, whose practical knowledge of institutional household duties and domestic economy along the line of what is useful, comfortable and necessary, without luxury, is only surpassed by their methodical system of training and educating children, both boys and girls and young ladies, in the religious and secular departments of education, which make for soul and body, and by example and precept teach their pupils to keep the commandments of God and to practice the Christian virtues. The Sisters of Charity had ably managed the institution for about eighteen years— from June 2, 1864, to July 1, 1882—when the Sisters of Mercy re-assumed charge of the work which they had so favorably begun in 1852, and so creditably continued till June 2, 1864. On January 1, 1899, the Sisters of Mercy had spent more than twenty-eight years in the management of the orphanage, and they are still doing their good work for their little charges.

THE SCHOOLS.—The children attend school in the main building, where they enjoy the advantages of six large and well appointed school rooms. They are taught by the sisters, and the schools are under the direction of the local Board of Education. The classes are graded in the same manner as the public schools, and the Sisters who teach are paid by the Board of Education. The children,

ST. FRANCIS ORPHAN ASYLUM,
New Haven.

according to their age and capacity, are also taught to make themselves generally useful about the house, farm, garden and grounds. As soon as funds permit, manual and industrial training especially adapted to the inmates will be supplied by the establishment of two trade schools, one for the boys and one for the girls, wherein such as cannot be provided with suitable homes, may be taught some useful trade or handicraft by which they may earn an honest livelihood after leaving the institution.

The number of children cared for from May 12, 1852, to September 17, 1898, is 3,763, of whom 2,162 were girls and 1,601 boys; the orphanage from 1852 to 1875 admitted girls only, but from that year the institution has taken care of both boys and girls.

The number of children, representing about twelve nationalities, cared for during the year 1898, was 517; remaining January 1, 1899, 312 – boys, 197, and girls, 115.

ADMISSIONS IN 1898. —New-comers, 141; previous inmates, 77; total, 218.

QUALIFICATIONS FOR ADMITTANCE. —Orphans, half-orphans, homeless, destitute, indigent, or dependent children, healthy and of sound mind, between the ages of two and twelve years, are received from all parts of the State. Unless for special reasons, those living outside of Connecticut are not eligible. As the laws of Connecticut do not permit children of tender years to be kept in almshouses, many such children (none under two years of age being received up to the present) belonging to parents of the poorer classes are sent to the asylum if Catholic, and there provided for by the Board of Managers. Children suffering from contagious or infectious diseases are not admitted. Epileptic, idiotic, insane, crippled, blind, deaf, and dumb children, as well as all vicious, incorrigible, or ungovernable boys or girls are not eligible for admission.

APPLICATION. —In regard to "church children," that is, such as are subjects of Catholic charity in the various parishes throughout the asylum district, application is to be made to the pastor of the child or children deserving the care and protection of the asylum, or to the Receiving and Dismissing Committee, residing at the asylum, every application to be passed or acted upon by the foregoing Committee, in accordance with the asylum's charter and rules, and the authority of the Committee on Admission and Discharge of Children.

The institution is empowered by its charter to place out the children on its "disposable list" in families or homes by legal adoption, indenture, or special contract; but the usual practice is to place its disposable children out in good Catholic families or homes, according to opportunity, on terms and conditions deemed just and reasonable, expedient for the best interests of the child, and agreeable to its intrustee, every child thus disposed of being subject to the supervision of the pastor in whose parish the little one has found a home. The priests of the asylum district have always been interested in finding good homes for the asylum's charges, in recommending the most respectable applicants of their parishes, and in reporting, when requested to do so, the condition of the asylum's little people living in their parishes. The asylum also, in every case, reserves the right, whenever its officials shall think proper, to have any placed-out child returned to its care, or removed from any family or home at any time. All children, moreover, whether sent to the orphanage by counties, cities, towns, parishes, or guardians, are committed subject to the charter and rules of the institution.

The asylum is supported chiefly from pensions paid for the care of a number of its children. Other means of support are derived from the school sisters' salaries, from the annual appropriation of $2,000 from the city of New Haven, in return for the good work done by the orphanage, which cares for a number of children committed to it by the city authorities, from the income of its invested funds received from time to time in the form of bequests, from occasional legacies, from the surplus cemetery moneys of the St. Bernard and St. Lawrence Cemetery Association of New Haven, and from its yearly "donation day" subscriptions of cash and contributions of generous gifts.

## HISTORY.

The institution whose property, objects, officers, work, etc., are thus narrated had its beginning on Friday, May 12, 1852. On that day, four Sisters of Mercy from Providence, R. I., arrived at New Haven. The Rev. Edward J. O'Brien, pastor of old St. Mary's parish, New Haven, had concluded arrangements with the Right Rev. Bishop O'Reilly and Rev. Mother Xavier Warde, Superior of the Convent of Mercy, Providence, to establish a convent of the order in his parish, and having accompanied the Sisters from Providence to New Haven, conducted them to their new home.

The building first occupied by the Sisters of Mercy, who were the first of any religious sisterhood to settle in the Elm City, was a handsome brick private residence, with brownstone trimmings and imposing entrance, situated near Broad street, on George, convenient to St. Mary's church and school. It was in this temporary convent that on May 12, 1852, the very day of the arrival of the Sisters of Mercy in New Haven, two little orphan girls put in an appearance. They had come to live in this new convent home, where they were kindly welcomed, as the Sisters themselves had been welcomed but a short hour before.

The nucleus of the first Catholic orphan asylum in the City of Elms thus formed, the Catholic orphan children, pending the erection of St. Mary's new convent, directly north of and adjoining old St. Mary's church, on Church street, were, for about two years, cared for, under the direction of Father O'Brien, by the Sisters of Mercy, till they and their little charges, in 1854, vacated the George street house, and removed into the new St. Mary's Orphan Asylum, on Church street, the convent and the asylum both being in the one new brick building.

There, in the heart of the city, the asylum existed as a private parochial institution until the year 1864.

The location of the convent and asylum on Church street, a very busy portion of the city, though the best that could then be selected, was found in the course of time to be ill-adapted to the purposes of a growing institution. The Sisters' work becoming daily more extensive, they needed the spacious rooms of the convent; the number of orphan girls was steadily increasing, and the accommodations grew so limited that a new site for the asylum became a pressing necessity.

Accordingly, on the 6th of April, 1864, the land together with all the buildings thereon, on which the asylum now stands, running 300 feet east on Whitney avenue, 300 feet west on Prospect street, and 1,000 feet south on Highland street, was purchased from the Hon. Thomas H. Bond, by Rev. E. J. O'Brien and Rev. Matthew Hart, for the sum of $19,500. The cottage which stood on the grounds was enlarged, and the building made ready for the use of the orphans. The institution was now called, "The St. Francis Orphan Asylum of New Haven," in honor of Rt. Rev. Francis P. McFarland, D.D. In the administration of Bishop

McFarland, the foundations of the asylum's present main building were laid. It was Bishop McFarland also who authorized the purchase of the Whitney avenue property, and who, in 1873, approved the erection of the first brick structure on its newly acquired grounds. St. Francis, the Seraph of Assisi, selected as the patron saint of the new orphanage, and all things prepared, the institution was placed under the charge of three Sisters of Charity, from Mount St. Vincent, on the Hudson, New York.

On the arrival of the Sisters, June 2, 1864, the orphan girls, forty-four in number, were transferred from their old residence, St. Mary's Orphan Asylum, to their new abode, the successor of their former temporary home on Church street.

In the May session of the Legislature of 1865, the petition of the Rev. Edward J. O'Brien and others, praying, for reasons therein stated, for an act incorporating the St. Francis Orphan Asylum of New Haven, was presented to the General Assembly; and on June 22, 1865, the act of incorporation was approved, whereby Francis Patrick McFarland, Edward J. O'Brien, Matthew Hart, Hugh Carmody, Thomas F. Hendricken, Thomas Synnott, John Sheridan, Charles Atwater, jr., Edward Downes, Patrick Morrissey, Thomas W. Cahill, William Geary, Bernard Reilly, William Downes, John Starrs, and their associates and successors, were constituted a body politic and corporate by the name of the St. Francis Orphan Asylum of New Haven.

The number of the orphans constantly increasing, and room for male orphans for whom no provision had hitherto been made, being very much needed, the corporation, at a meeting held in February, 1873, determined on the erection of the first new main brick building, which when completed would provide ample room for both boys and girls for many years. Rev. Dr. Carmody, the pastor of St. John's parish, New Haven, was charged with the supervision of the work, and under his direction the foundations were laid, in the year 1874. In the spring of 1875, Dr. Carmody having resigned his charge on account of a necessary absence from home, the Rev. Matthew Hart, pastor of St. Patrick's parish, took charge of the building of the new asylum. He pushed on the work of construction, and had brought the edifice nearly to completion, when his death occurred in July, 1876. Rev. Father P. A. Murphy, pastor of St Mary's, was substituted in his place, and the building was made ready for use in November, 1876.

From 1876 to 1896, owing to the steady increase in the number of its inmates, the asylum again became so inadequate to meet the needs of the home that it was found necessary to enlarge the house by the addition of another large wing. Plans were submitted and approved early in 1894 for this enlargement of the institution; and in the spring of 1896 this new "South Addition," built of red brick, with brown-stone trimmings, at a cost of about $40,000, with a capacity for 200 children, extending nearly 180 feet along Highland street, was completed and occupied, Rt. Rev. M. Tierney, D.D., Bishop of Hartford, afterwards blessing the new structure, on the afternoon of June 7, 1896.

The whole brick asylum building, a substantial structure, with appointments most complete, beautifully situated, is most favorably located for the health, training, occupation and recreation of its inmates. It stands on an elevated ledge of rock, commands an extensive view of the eastern portion of the city, and from the summit of East Rock, on which its neighbor, the soldiers' monument, is erected, it presents a very imposing appearance.

The institution is prosperous, its inmates happy, and its trustees gratified with the work accomplished. The Sisters of Mercy, likewise, who for so many years, have without worldly recompense, given their life and labor to the work of the orphanage, though they look for a higher reward, may not disdain the testimony of the Board of Trustees concerning the admirable manner in which they perform the onerous duties devolving upon them.

In this noblest of charities—the care, protection and education of the poor orphan—St. Francis' Orphan Asylum is a splendid monument to the Catholics of Connecticut, as well as a beautiful memorial of the grateful and generous people who, without distinction of religion, as friends of its little helpless ones, have their names associated with a great work, and whose countless deeds of true charity are written by angelic instead of human pen.

The first resident chaplain of the asylum was the Rev. James Hilary Harding, who entered upon the discharge of his duties on January 6, 1878. During his period of service here, Father Harding had the spiritual charge also of the jail and of "Springside Home." Father Harding was a native of Kilkenny, Ireland, and was born in 1812. His early education was obtained in his native town, and after a period of study and travel in France, came to this country, where he completed his theological studies at Villanova College, near Philadelphia. Thenceforth he labored in the archdiocese of Dubuque, Iowa, until, having obtained the requisite permission, he became affiliated with the diocese of Hartford.

Among the works that absorbed most of the time and all of the fortune of Father Harding was the construction of the Protectory for wayward boys on Fair Haven Heights. The corner-stone of the building was laid by Bishop McMahon on June 12, 1881. The site of the Protectory was purchased in April, 1879, from Francis Donnelly and a Mr. Shipman, and comprised three acres. The building, however, was never completed. Father Harding died at the asylum on May 25, 1889, in the seventy-seventh year of his age. His remains rest in the priests' lot, St. Bernard's cemetery, New Haven. The funeral services were held at St. Mary's church, where a Pontifical Mass of Requiem was celebrated by Bishop McMahon, assisted by the following clergymen: Assistant priest, Rev. John Furlong; deacons of honor, Revs. John Cooney and M. McKeon; deacon, Rev. M. A. Tierney; sub-deacon, Rev. F. O'Keefe. The panegyric was preached by Rev. W. J. Slocum.

The successor of Father Harding as chaplain of the asylum was the Rev. John Francis Corcoran, who is still in charge, and is also the treasurer of the corporation. Father Corcoran had been an assistant for nearly six years to Very Rev. James Hughes, V. G., Hartford, when, at the urgent request of Bishop McMahon, he gave up the parochial work of the ministry to assume that of the chaplaincy of the asylum. Father Corcoran began his successful career in this field of sacerdotal zeal on October 9, 1889. The new south addition was erected and dedicated during Father Corcoran's tenure of office, on June 7, 1897. The new chapel, school rooms, chaplain's apartments, and dormitories for the Sisters and children are in this addition, which cost $50,000.

The first regular attending physician was Charles A. Gallagher, M. D. He held this position until his death, which occurred on May 9, 1878. Dr. Gallagher's successor is the present attendant physician, Matthew Charles O'Connor, M. D.

The principal benefactors of St. Francis' Orphan Asylum were Philip Marett and the Hon. James Edward English, formerly Governor of Connecticut.

The history of the Asylum would be incomplete were the names of the zealous

Sisters of Charity and the Sisters of Mercy, who labored to care for, protect and educate the orphans, omitted.

The following Sisters of Mercy were superiors of St. Mary's Orphan Asylum, from 1852 to 1861: 1852, Sister M. Camillus; 1854, Sister M. Josephine Lombard; 1859, Sister M. Liguori; 1861, Sister M. Borgia.

On June 2, 1864, the Sisters of Charity assumed charge. They came to St. Francis' Orphan Asylum. Sister M. Ulrica was the first superior, and associated with her were Sister Stephen, Sister Zita and Sister Inez.

Sister Felicita was the second superior, and her companions were Sister Agnes, Sister Edwin, Sister Josephine, Sister Corsina, Sister Victor, Sister Bernardo, Sister Everilda, Sister Ann Alexis, Sister Ferdinand, Sister Vincenti, Sister Maria Bernard and Sister Anthony. Sister Ulrica was superior for about three years. Sister Felicita was superior for about fifteen years—to July 1, 1882, when the Sisters of Mercy re-assumed charge of the institution.

Mother M. Rose was superior during the months of July and August till the appointment of Mother M. Angela, who from August 16, 1882, continued in office until her death, February 8, 1888. She was succeeded by Sister M. de Sales, who remained in charge till August 15th, of the same year, when Mother M. Agnes was appointed. Mother M. Agnes continued in control for three years—till August 15, 1891, when she was succeeded by Mother M. Rose, whose term expired September 2, 1893.

Sister M. Borromeo became superior September 2, 1893, and remained in office till September 2, 1898.

Sister M. Dionysius succeeded Sister M. Borromeo on September 2, 1898, and is the present superior.

The names of the other Sisters of Mercy who were stationed at different times at the Asylum, are here appended:

Sister M. Colette, Sister M. Jerome, Sister M. Euphrasia, Sister M. Athanasius, Sister M. Julianna, Sister M. Margarita, Sister M. Borgia, Sister M. Alice, Sister M. Mark, Sister M. Adrian, Sister M. Cletus, Sister M. Winifred, Sister M. Matthew, Sister M. Catherine, Sister M. Euphemia, Sister M. Eleanor, Sister M. Mildred, Sister M. Aquinas, Sister M. Sylveria, Sister M. Chrysostom, Sister M. Pauline, Sister M. Geraldine, Sister M. Louis, Sister M. Augustine, Sister M. Clare, Sister M. Francesca, Sister M. Christina, Sister M. Calasanetius, Sister M. Gervase, Sister M. Eucharia, Sister M. Veracunda, Sister M. Cephas, Sister M. Irmine, Sister M. Laura, Sister M. Bennett, Sister M. Kotska, Sister M. Florentine, Sister M. Macarius, Sister M. Alcantara, Sister Margaret Mary, Sister M. L'Esperance, Sister M. Carmelita, Sister M. Andrew, Sister M. Rufina, Sister M. de Monfort, Sister M. Emeline, Sister M. Evangelista, Sister M. Xavier, Sister M. John, Sister M. William, Sister M. Gertrude.

## ST. JAMES' ORPHAN ASYLUM,

### HARTFORD.

ST. JAMES' Asylum for boys, situated at 93 Church street, was founded by the late Very Rev. James Hughes, V. G., on May 6, 1864. In the beginning of its career, and for many years afterwards, it had the names of over a hundred boys on its rolls; but the founding of St. Francis' Orphan Asylum of New Haven has diminished this number considerably, so that the average number of boys at present cared for at St. James' is about thirty. The institution is in charge of the Sisters of Mercy,

Connected with St. James' is St. Catharine's Asylum for girls, also founded by Father Hughes. About thirty girls here find shelter.

## ST. THOMAS' PREPARATORY SEMINARY,

### 352 COLLINS ST., HARTFORD, CONN.

THE Preparatory Seminary of St. Thomas of Aquin, founded by the Rt. Rev. Michael Tierney, D.D., Bishop of Hartford, is the youngest Catholic seminary or college in New England. It was a long cherished desire of Bishop Tierney that there might be established in his diocese an institution wherein the highest grade of education should be furnished, and where, at the same time, the principles of religion should be made the beginning and end of the students' ambitions and efforts. He was enabled to realize this wish by securing the estate located at 352 Collins street, Hartford.

This property was purchased from Patrick B. Donovan, by Bishop Tierney, on the Feast of the Presentation of the Blessed Virgin, November 21, 1896. The land measures one hundred and forty-six (146) feet on the north, two hundred and ninety-nine (299) feet on the east, one hundred and ninety (190) feet on the south, and three hundred and seventeen (317) feet on the west.

Besides the fact that a sufficient tract of land was at his disposal in his episcopal city, the healthfulness of the location, and the beautiful and retired section of the city, in which it is situated, were controlling factors in inducing the bishop to have his seminary in Hartford.

The building is a large brick structure erected according to the ideas of modern architecture, and is admirably adapted for college purposes. The first floor is taken up with the study-hall, class-rooms, refectory and parlors. The chapel, dormitory and professors' quarters are on the second floor. On the third floor are the large dormitory, infirmary, library and private rooms. The domestic department and the infirmary are under the efficient care and direction of the Sisters of St. Joseph.

The bishop called the diocesan clergy to take charge. At first there were but three resident professors: Rev. John Synnott, president and bursar; Rev. Robert F. Fitzgerald, D.D., vice-president, and Rev. F. X. Mullville, prefect of studies. Besides these the following professors, who resided in the city, attended: Revs. Paul E. Roy, Hubert V. Dahme, D. J. Gleason, D.D., and John Ryan. On February 23, 1898, Dr. Gleason was appointed rector of the Italian church, and was succeeded by Rev. B. F. Broderick, D.D., who took up his residence at the seminary. On September 6, 1898, Mr. A. J. Plunkett was called to the seminary as prefect of discipline and librarian.

Classes were organized in St. Thomas' Seminary on September 7, 1898, when thirty-seven students—fifteen boarders and twenty-two day-scholars— were entered on the roll.

On the following day, September 8th, after the celebration of Mass, the Rt. Rev. Bishop, assisted by the Rev. President and the Chancellor, Rev. J. P. Donovan, D.D., blessed the chapel and seminary. Others who were present at the blessing were Rev. W. J. Shanley, Rev. T. S. Duggan, Rev. E. A. Flannery, Rev. B. Broderick, D.D., and the whole student body. The chapel is located in the west side of the seminary, and, besides its altar of white and

ST. THOMAS' PREPARATORY SEMINARY,
Hartford (Front view).

gold, possesses a fine painting of the Sacred Heart, statues of the Blessed Virgin and St. Aloysius, which have been donated, and an organ.

On April 1, 1898, the Rev. President erected canonically the Stations of the Cross, in accordance with the beautiful ceremonial prescribed by the Roman Ritual.

Before stating the special object of the preparatory seminary it may be well to relate briefly the history of seminaries and the attitude of the Church towards them. The history of seminaries may be divided into two periods, one prior and the other subsequent to the Council of Trent. Some canonists trace episcopal seminaries to the very beginning of the Church; some to the Council of Nice (A.D. 325), and some to St. Augustine. It cannot be disputed that seminaries existed in the 6th century, for the Council of Toledo (A. D. 531) ordained that boys dedicated by their parents to the service of the Church, should be brought up under the tuition of a director, in a house belonging to the cathedral, and under the eye of the bishop. Nor was ecclesiastical education confined solely to seminaries. Many of those destined for the Church, as early as the 6th century, received their education in the houses of the clergy. About the 8th century universities began to take the place of seminaries. The Council of Trent re-established seminaries and placed them on a more solid basis. The following are some of the enactments of this council in regard to seminaries: 1. A bishop is bound to have at least one seminary, unless the poverty of the diocese makes it impossible. 2. Those only should be received into seminaries whose character and inclination afford a hope that they will always serve in the ecclesiastical ministry. 3. Not only students of theology, but also of classics, should be admitted.

In our own time the Fathers of the Councils of Baltimore promulgated many canons respecting seminaries in the United States. The Third Plenary Council of Baltimore decreed that every diocese should, if possible, have its own major and minor seminary set apart exclusively for the education of ecclesiastical students. Where this is impossible one higher and one preparatory seminary should be established in each province. How important preparatory seminaries appeared to the Fathers of the Third Plenary Council is apparent from the fact that they allow aspirants to the priesthood to study the classics in secular schools and colleges only in places where, owing to lack of means, preparatory seminaries, exclusively for clerical students, cannot as yet be established.

Inspired by the wise and weighty words of these Councils, Right Rev. Bishop Tierney planned to found in his diocese a preparatory seminary devoted exclusively to the training of youth destined for the priesthood.

In his circular to the clergy the Right Rev. founder announced the object of St. Thomas'; he said, "We have always looked forward to the time when we could have a seminary in our own diocese, where candidates for the priesthood would grow up under the eye of their bishop, and be trained to meet the especial wants of the field in which they are called to labor." Other inducing motives were:

1. That boys having a vocation to the priesthood may immediately enter the seminary after completing the course of studies in the parochial school instead of entering the high school, where their vocation may be endangered, and, as experience proves, is often lost. For a vocation, however true it may be, is no guarantee that a youth may not fall into sin, contract evil habits, and event-

nally lose his calling. For, once the character of a boy is formed, no discipline can produce any lasting results. This formation of character takes place during the period of transition from youth to young manhood,—from the thirteenth to the seventeenth year of a boy's life. Just then a boy is apt to enter a secular school or college, where he will mingle with others, who are led on by mere worldly motives, and, as a result, in his tastes and enthusiasm he will imbibe a spirit wholly alien to the priestly character. The Fathers of the Council of Baltimore had this fact in mind when they said: "These seminaries are to shield, from their earliest years, boys against the influence of bad example and mingling with the world during the time in which they prepare themselves for the theological seminary."

2. That the dispositions and habits of the young men may be carefully studied; that those whose habits unfit them for the priesthood may become known to the bishop, and may thereby be prevented from entering the sacerdotal state, where they would likely do much harm to souls.

3. That judgment may be passed upon the capacity of the students, in order that they who may be deficient in the abilities requisite for the priesthood, may be informed as soon as possible and permitted to withdraw from the seminary, ere they have wasted several years.

The cost of maintaining a seminary is naturally very great. The necessity of meeting it generally falls upon the students who are, for the most part, poor. Bishop Tierney, in founding his seminary, resolved to change this method, and to reduce to a minimum the expenses to be incurred by the students. In this he has been successful. Matters have been so arranged that the day scholars receive their tuition free, while the resident students pay but a small sum—one hundred and fifty dollars—for board, tuition, etc. So that poor boys need no longer feel that they are debarred from studying for the ministry on account of lack of means.

The course of studies embraces a period of five years. The course is strictly classical, including, besides a thorough grounding in the Latin, Greek and English languages, a systematic training in French and German; a complete course in mathematics and the natural sciences, Christian doctrine and history.

Each student is required to pass an entrance examination, after which he will be assigned to the class for which he is fitted. No applicant will be admitted who has not made some progress in study, and who has not successfully completed his studies in what is commonly known as the "Grammar Grade." Thence he will pass, by graduation, to the higher classes throughout the remainder of the course.

There are three examinations a year—the first, before the Christmas holidays; the second, before the Easter recess; and the third, immediately before the close of the academic year in June.

The first examination was held on the 20th, 21st, 22nd and 23rd of December, 1897; the second included the first five days of April, 1898; and the third examination was held in June, from the 22nd to the 27th, 1898. On the 28th of June, 1898, the first annual commencement of seminary was celebrated, and it will be remembered by those participating as a most happy and auspicious day for the young seminary.

On September 7, 1898, the portals of St. Thomas' were again thrown open to receive a body of students to the number of 38—22 boarders and 16 day-scholars. It is evident from the increase of resident students, that the

PREPARATORY SEMINARY,

boys appreciate the advantages to be derived from living at the seminary, where the kind treatment they receive and the regularity of life enable them to progress more easily in their studies.

The library, which at present contains over 700 volumes—all donated by Bishop Tierney—was opened for general use on November 4, 1897. Efforts are being made to increase the number of books by securing, by gift or purchase, all the best modern works in literature, science, history, philosophy, and theology. It is also desired to make of the seminary library a diocesan institution, in which may be deposited old documents and manuscripts and such old additions of books as are of value when deposited in such a place, but which are almost worthless when relegated to trunks and attics.

On November 4, 1898, a literary society was organized by the students. The object of this society is to promote a deeper interest in the study of the English classics, and to cultivate a high literary spirit among the students. Bishop Tierney was chosen first honorary president, the prefect was selected as moderator, while all the other offices were filled by the students.

That the students may be rounded into good strong men is a wish dear to the Bishop and faculty. For this purpose the best possible facilities have been furnished. A brick building, 30 feet high, 25 feet wide, and 40 feet long, has been fitted out with modern gymnastic apparatus; a double hand-ball court has been built close by the gymnasium, while the grounds around the seminary are extensive enough to afford the students ample opportunity for tennis, cricket, and the more vigorous games of base ball and foot ball. These sports, however, are never encouraged to the extent of injury to studies.

Education, rightly understood, means not alone mental and physical development, but also moral training. And while every effort is being made to educate the mind and to strengthen the body, a much greater care is exercised over the moral culture of the students. In an institution of ecclesiastical lore, the moral development is considered of most importance, and at St. Thomas' it holds the first place, as it should in every well-arranged system of education. The students are expected to approach the sacraments once a week, and to attend High Mass and vesper service on Sundays at the cathedral, where they cannot fail to imbibe a love for the beautiful ceremonial of the church.

Instruction in Christian doctrine is given daily. Private devotion is likewise encouraged, and sodalities exist for fostering it.

The League of the Sacred Heart was established in the seminary on the 1st of October, 1897.

The Society of the Holy Rosary was organized on the feast of the Holy Rosary, October 2, 1897. Its object is the fostering of filial devotion to the Mother of God, and the practice of virtue and piety among its members.

## SEMINARY OF MT. ST. JOSEPH,

### HARTFORD.

MT. ST. JOSEPH'S SEMINARY was founded in 1873 by the Rt. Rev. Bishop McFarland. His purpose was to provide a school in which the young ladies of the diocese might perfect themselves in the higher branches of a liberal education hallowed by religion.

The seminary is situated on one of the most beautiful sites in Hartford on Farmington avenue, adjoining St. Joseph's magnificent cathedral. The building, a massive one, possesses much architectural beauty, and was erected with a special view to the wants of a first-class boarding-school. The grounds are extensive and laid out with much taste. Every incentive is offered to induce sufficient exercise in the open air. In their system of education the Sisters endeavor to combine mildness with firmness, and their constant aim is to instill into their pupils those principles of religion which are the only safeguard through life. The Sisters require from the pupils an exact observance to the rules of the school, as they are convinced that submission to lawful authority and respect for the rights of others are as necessary for the good of the individual pupil as for that of the entire institution. The course of studies embraces all grades from the primary to the academic, and a careful training in the French, German and Latin languages is received. There are also musical, business and art departments.

"It is a noteworthy fact that the Sisters of Mercy have, in all their teaching, pursued a systematic course of instruction leading up to practical results. They aim to instruct their pupils so they can utilize their knowledge in practical pursuits. The result is that many young ladies from this seminary are now engaged in business offices, and also as successful teachers, while many have been prepared here for higher colleges. At the Normal schools of the State the certificate of Mt. St. Joseph is accepted in lieu of an entrance examination.

"That the Sisters of Mercy have taken a foremost part in the educational work of Hartford no one familiar with its history will deny. They have taught in every grade from the alphabet of the English language to the most advanced classics. Their teachings hallowed by religion have been productive of much good, and fortunate is he or she whose education is wholly or in part received under their guidance."

## ACADEMY DE NOTRE DAME.

### WATERBURY.

THE fame of this educational institute is not confined to the limits of the city in which it is located, but has gone throughout the diocese and beyond. To the late Bishop of Providence, Right Rev. T. F. Hendricken, D.D., then pastor of the Immaculate Conception parish, Waterbury, is due the honor of introducing the Sisters de Notre Dame from the mother-house, Villa Maria, Montreal, into Waterbury, where they arrived in 1869. The foundation of the convent occurred during the episcopate of Bishop McFarland, and on the occasion of his last visit in 1873, he remarked to the sisters: "The day is not far distant when the little house on the hill will spread its wings to shelter hundreds." The bishop's prophecy has been fulfilled. A handsome and stately edifice has replaced the humble building in which both Sisters and pupils spent many happy and profitable years. The new building has been justly designated as "one of the ornaments of the city." It was erected during the pastorate of the Rev. John A. Mulcahy, who supervised its construction.

Before the sisters arrived in Waterbury no little difficulty was experienced in securing a suitable house which would become for them a convent home, owing to the anti-Catholic prejudices, then prevailing in certain quarters. However, they purchased through the agency of a third party a dwelling-house from Anson G. Stocking, for which he received $11,000. The Sisters had not been long established before their services to the community were recognized with the result that more pupils asked for admission than they could adequately accommodate. Accordingly the convent was enlarged by the erection of what has since become known as Commencement Hall; at the same time the grounds were beautified by the planting of shrubs and the laying of concrete walks.

As to location the Academy de Notre Dame is highly favored. It is built on an eminence in an elevated portion of the city and its pupils enjoy the salubrious air for which this part of Connecticut is famous. The course of studies is thorough and complete; its study-halls and class-rooms are equipped with every aid for the acquisition of knowledge, and not only can those who aspire to the acquisition of a solid and refined English education attain the goal of their ambition, but, as well also, those who seek to become proficient in music, both vocal and instrumental, drawing, painting, sewing, etc. The pupils are also taught French, and as it is the language of the house, soon become proficient in its use.

The first Directress of the convent was Madame St. Cecilia. Her successor was Madame St. Gabriel. She was followed by Madame St. Mary, who in turn was succeeded by the present Superioress, Madame St. Stanislaus.

"A prominent trait in the management is the deportment and behaviour of the young ladies who have had the good fortune to spend some time at this school; and so conspicuous is this feature that an eminent educator who usually spends his summer vacation in this beautiful town, and who once had ample opportunity for forming a correct judgment, said: 'For true lady-like bearing, for that easy and refined yet unaffected manner which should be one of the chief aims of a polite education, the pupils of Notre Dame are the peers of any in the land.'"

## NOTRE DAME ACADEMY,

### PUTNAM.

THIS institution of learning, the fame of which is well known, is situated in the most beautiful part of Putnam, on a rising eminence, which insures pure air and commands an extensive and superb scenery. This fine edifice has been erected with a special view to the wants of a first-class boarding school, well heated by steam and supplied with hot and cold water, and all modern improvements and conveniences. The building is of pressed brick with elaborate granite trimmings; the water tables, the buttress, caps and belts are also of granite, thus showing the solidity of its character. A graceful tower with chime of bells rises on its side; the distance from base to apex being 112 feet.

The exterior surrounding corresponds well with the interior. Beautiful grounds, evergreen shrubbery, marble statuary, circular concrete walks, fountains sending up their sparkling jets and surrounded by flower beds, draw the attention of all who have any love for the beautiful. On the right of an extensive avenue is the Grotto of Lourdes, an excellent imitation of the French original. Pleasant verandas, shrines, summer houses, form a delightful resort for pupils during leisure hours. Electric lights enhance the beauty of the evening scene. The beautiful shrine of St. Ann in front of the façade has become a centre of attraction for pilgrims far and near. Besides this favorite park the young ladies may also enjoy the woodland dale.

About a mile distant is a shady grove, on the banks of the Quinnebaug, known as "St. Joseph's Island." Here is a lofty retreat, a seclusion for the tired students, and a charming spot for the merry-hearted school girl.

The past history guarantees the promise for the future. The Alumnæ have added lustre to the reputation of Putnam. The moral and intellectual education of the pupils is attended to with the greatest solicitude, and the most devoted attention is paid to their domestic comforts. While the solid studies are regarded as the more important, great attention is given to the graceful accomplishments which throw a charm over domestic life and tend toward elevating society.

## ACADEMY OF THE HOLY FAMILY,

### BALTIC.

THIS academy holds high rank among the educational institutions of Connecticut. It is under the supervision of the Sisters of Charity of Our Lady of Mercy, who were introduced into Baltic by Rev. Father Van Laar, at the request of Right Rev. Bishop McFarland, on October 15, 1874.

Situated in a beautiful location in Baltic, the academy affords a most picturesque view of the surrounding country, and on account of its high and beautiful position is admirably adapted for educational purposes. The extensive grounds of the institution afford every facility for open-air exercise, which the pupils are required to take at all seasons. The curriculum of the academy embraces all the studies generally followed in schools of the highest rank. Six Sisters formed the first community in Baltic.

The object of the Sisters of Charity of Our Lady of Mercy is the santification of its members by the practice of works of charity. These include the education of young girls in boarding schools, orphanages, public and private schools, hospital work, care of the aged of both sexes, and of the deaf and dumb, and blind. The care of male insane persons, and the education of boys beyond the primary grades are the only works of charity forbidden by the Congregation. Dispensation to teach boys in grammar grades has been granted to the Congregation in England and America. The constitutions and general rules of the Congregation were approved by his Holiness Pope Gregory XVI., on December 18, 1843, and five years later, in 1848, the Congregation itself was approved by his Holiness Pope Pius IX. The mother-house is in Tilburg, Holland, in the diocese of Bois le-Duc. The chief direction of the Congregation is confided to a Mother-General and four sisters. The Congregation has ninety-five convents. The greater number are in Holland and Belgium; three in England under the patronage of the Earl of Denbigh; three in America, two in the East Indies, and one in South America. This last foundation was due to the efforts of Bishop Wulfingh, C.S.S.R., of Paramaribo, Dutch Guiana. Being anxious to obtain Sisters to care for the lepers of his diocese, the bishop laid the matter before the Holy Father, Pope Leo XIII. His Holiness expressed the wish that the Sisters of Charity of Our Lady of Mercy should take charge of the leper colony. Considering the self-abnegation necessary for such a sphere of labor, Mother General Smarius declined to appoint Sisters for the work. Consequently a circular was sent to the different convents of the Congregation asking for volunteers. Three hundred applications were immediately received. From this number six Sisters were chosen to form the neckeus of the South American colony. They arrived at Paramaribo, on September 29, 1894.

The academy at Baltic opened with two teachers and two pupils. At present, there are twelve teachers and seventy-five pupils. The Alumnæ number about one hundred.

The Directress of the convent and academy is Mother M. Aloysio.

## ST. AUGUSTINE'S VILLA,
### HARTFORD.

THIS institution is under the direction of the Sisters of Mercy and is in a beautiful and healthful location. The Villa, an attractive and substantial structure, was purchased by the Sisters for its present purposes in September, 1877, and in 1883 a wing was added to the main building to accommodate the increasing number of pupils. On Thanksgiving day of the same year the school was blessed with impressive ceremonies by Bishop McMahon, assisted by a number of clergymen. The Villa stands on an eminence, is commodious, thoroughly ventilated, and furnished throughout with all modern improvements. The grounds are extensive, and afford ample means of exercise. The school has accommodations for about seventy boys, who are received between the ages of four and fourteen. The curriculum followed is preparatory for entrance either to High school or college. "Everything conducive to the health, happiness and advancement of the pupils receives constant and conscientious attention. The discipline is maternal and uniform and the course of instruction thorough and extended. In such a healthful atmosphere as this the boy gains in physical vigor and at the same time has his mind cultivated by a carefully planned system of education. That St. Augustine's is capable of turning out boys thoroughly prepared for their after-work is proved by the many who have gone from here to higher institutions and have graduated with honor."

St. Augustine's school was founded by Mother M. Angela, and the present Superioress is Sister M. Genevieve.

## ST. MARY'S HOME FOR THE AGED,
### HARTFORD.

THIS most worthy, charitable and benevolent institution was founded on October 18, 1880, by the Rev. Mother Angela Fitzgerald. Three Sisters of Mercy took possession of the building which had been purchased in November, 1880. Two men and three women were the first recipients of the charity of the Sisters. Now sixteen men and sixty-five women receive the gentle ministrations of seventeen Sisters.

The increase in the number of inmates made the construction of another building necessary, the corner-stone of which was laid on May 19, 1895. The building, a handsome, commodious and substantial structure, was completed and dedicated on April 8, 1896, by Rt. Rev. Bishop Tierney.

Since its foundation, St. Mary's has registered about 120 inmates. The Home is beautifully situated on a farm of 116 acres near the city line of Hartford. The farm is well stocked, and is well cultivated, yielding nearly the full supply of vegetables used in the institution. It was formerly the property of Mr. Terry, father of the gifted poetess, Rose Terry Cooke.

## ST. FRANCIS' HOSPITAL,
### HARTFORD.

ST. FRANCIS' HOSPITAL, was founded by Right Rev. Bishop Tierney, and was opened for the reception of patients on September 1, 1897. With the exception of contagious and infectious diseases all classes of disease are received here. During the first year of the institution's existence, *i. e.*, from September 1, 1897, to September 1, 1898, 314 patients were treated; the mortality was 14, making a percentage of deaths to the whole number received, 4½ per cent. Of the 14 patients who died, 10 were incurable when received. Of the need in Hartford of such an institution of Christian charity and benevolence, the President of the Medical Staff said in his first annual report:

"The wisdom and urgent need of such an institution as St. Francis' Hospital, I think, is established beyond any question of doubt, from the loyal support and cordial endorsement it has received from the majority of the profession in our own city and from those in surrounding towns in the county, and as it is not intended to antagonize in any particular way with the work of the older hospital, but is supplying a long-felt void in our city, I feel assured that it will grow in favor and receive the support and endorsement of the profession at large, and the approval of the vast majority of the best people of our city and State."

The officers of the Board of Directors of St. Francis' Hospital are: President, Rt. Rev. Michael Tierney, D.D.; Vice President, Very Rev. John A. Mulcahy, V. G.; Secretary, Rev. Walter J. Shanley; Treasurer, Mother Valencia.

*Board of Directors.*—Rt. Rev. Michael Tierney, D.D., Very Rev. John A. Mulcahy, V.G., Rev. Walter J. Shanley, Rev. Thos. W. Broderick, Rev. James Smith, John O'Flaherty, M.D., George C. Bailey, M.D., Daniel F. Sullivan, M.D., Hon. Thos. McManus, Hon. Patrick Garvan, James Ahern, John W. Coogan, Capt. Cornelius Ryan, Matthew Hogan.

### HOSPITAL STAFF.

*Officers of the Medical Board.*—President, John O'Flaherty, M.D.; Vice-president, John Dwyer, M.D.;[1] Secretary, Wm. J. Lynch, M.D.; Consultants, W. F. Bacon, M.D.; S. B. St. John, M.D. Medical Board—Nathan Mayer, M.D., John O'Flaherty, M.D., John Dwyer, M.D.,[1] and Joseph H. Cahill, M.D. Surgical—P. P. Carlan, M.D., M. M. Johnson, M.D., O. C. Smith, M.D., D. F. Sullivan, M.D., J. F. Dowling, M.D., M. A. Bailey, M.D., and J. A. Boucher, M.D. Gynæcologists—G. C. Baily, M.D., and A. J. Wolff, M.D. Neurologist—T. D. Crothers, M.D. Bacteriologist— John B. McCook, M.D. Doctor of Dental Surgery—James McManus, D.D.S. Oculist and Aurist—F. T. Waite, M.D. Visiting Physicians—John O'Flaherty, M.D., Nathan Mayer, M.D., P. P. Carlan, M.D., Joseph H. Cahill, M.D., and William J. Lynch, M.D. Visiting Surgeons—M. M. Johnson, M.D., D. F. Sullivan, M.D., O. C. Smith, M.D., J. F. Dowling, M.D., J. A. Boucher, M.D., and M. A. Bailey, M.D.

The hospital is in charge of the Sisters of St. Joseph, from Chambery, France, and true to their exalted vocation are angels of mercy to their stricken brethren who come under their influence and care. Imitating Him whose spouses they are, they go about doing good; healing the sick, strengthening the weak, consoling the sorrowing, imparting cheerfulness and warmth and happiness in the midst of the gloom that often attends illness, carrying heavenly favors everywhere with their presence; a noble vocation is theirs and thrice holy.

### SUMMARY.

#### INSTITUTIONS IN CHARGE OF SECULAR CLERGY.

HARTFORD.—*St. Thomas' Preparatory Seminary*—Very Rev. John Synnott, rector; Rev. R. F. Fitzgerald, D.D., vice-rector; Revs. B. Broderick, D.D., J. F. Ryan, Hubert Dahme, Frank Mulville and Mr. A. Plunkett, professors.

[1] Deceased.

ST. FRANCIS HOSPITAL,
Hartford.

#### INSTITUTIONS IN CHARGE OF RELIGIOUS ORDERS.

HARTFORD.—*Missionary College of Our Lady of La Salette and Theological Seminary*— Both conducted by the Missionary Fathers of La Salette.

#### RELIGIOUS COMMUNITIES IN THE DIOCESE.

##### ORDERS OF MEN.

Dominican Fathers (Eastern province).
Franciscan Fathers (Friars' Minor).
Jesuit Fathers (New York; Maryland Province).
Missionaries of La Salette (Grenoble, France).

##### ORDERS OF WOMEN.

Sisters of the Assumption (Nicolet, P. Q.).
Sisters of Charity (Convent Station, New Jersey).
Sisters of Charity of St. Vincent de Paul (Mt. St. Vincent, on Hudson).
Sisters of St. Joseph (Chambery, France).
Sisters of Charity of Our Lady, Mother of Mercy (Tilburg, Holland).
Sisters of St. Francis (Allegany, N. Y.).
Sisters of St. Joseph (Flushing, L. I.).
Sisters of Mercy (Hartford, Mother-house).
Sisters of Mercy (Meriden, Mother-house).
Sisters of Mercy (Middletown. Mother-house).
Sisters of the Congregation de Notre Dame (Villa Maria, P. Q.).
Sisters of the Holy Cross and of the Seven Dolors (St. Laurent, P. Q.).
School Sisters of Notre Dame (Baltimore, Md.).

### SOCIETIES.

THE oldest society of Catholics in Connecticut was the Hibernian Provident Society of New Haven, incorporated in 1841 for benevolent purposes by Bernard Riley, Michael Coogan, Michael Martin, and others. The next in order of time was St. Patrick's Society, Hartford, incorporated in 1842 by Rev. John Brady, Thomas Keeney, John Hickey, James McManus and Michael Byrnes. St. John's Sick and Burial Society, Hartford, followed in 1848, with James McManus, Edward McGuire, John Lake and James Mulligan as charter members. The Montgomery Benevolent Society of New Haven was incorporated in 1849 by William Downes, James Reilly, and others, but it does appear to have been a religious organization.

### THE ANCIENT ORDER OF HIBERNIANS.

THE first Division of the Ancient Order of Hibernians in Connecticut was organized on March 6, 1869, at Bridgeport. James Davitt was the first President, and the records show that seventeen members enrolled themselves on that occasion under the white banner of Friendship, Unity and Christian Charity. The present membership is 5,600, an increase of 105 from January 1, 1898, to January 1, 1899. The present State officers are: State President, James P. Bree; State Secretary, John D. Cunningham; State Treasurer, P. D. Ryan; State Chaplain, Rev. B. O'R. Sheridan.

The principles of the A. O. H. are embodied in the motto of the order. The intent and purpose of its members is to promote friendship, unity and charity. They maintain the aged, the sick, the blind and the infirm. The Golden Rule receives practical illustration in the charity the order dispenses, in the intimate bond of union which exists among its members, and in the good-will which the sons of this organization have for their brethren of what race or creed soever. Practical Catholics only, that is, men who comply with the religious obligations imposed by the church, are eligible for membership; and should a member fail in this necessary requirement; should he fail to give edification and become a rock of offence, he becomes amenable to the law which decrees expulsion as the penalty. The rules of the order call for a chaplain in each county, who will be named by the Bishop, and to him must all questions pertaining to morality or religion be submitted before action is taken.

Faithful is the A. O. H. to the divine injunctions:

"*Let love be without dissimulation, hating that which is evil, cleaving to that which is good.*

"*Loving one another with the charity of brotherhood, with honor preventing one another.*"—Romans xii. 9, 10.

"*But above all things have charity, which is the bond of perfection.*"—Colossians iii. 14.

"*Let the charity of the brotherhood abide in you. And hospitality do not forget.*"—Hebrews xiii. 1, 2.

## THE KNIGHTS OF COLUMBUS.

THIS organization, named in honor of the immortal discoverer of America, was organized at New Haven on February 8, 1882, by the Rev. Michael J. McGivney, assistant pastor of St. Mary's parish, New Haven, and incorporated on March 1, 1882. Its first officers were: Supreme Knight, James T. Mullen; Deputy Supreme Knight, John T. Kerrigan; Financial Secretary, Rev. Michael J. McGivney; Recording Secretary, William H. Sellwood; Lecturer, Daniel Colwell; Chancellor, James T. McMahon; Physician, Matthew C. O'Connor, M.D; Treasurer, Michael Curran.

The order was founded upon *Union* and *Charity*.[1] Unity in banding Catholics together for mutual comfort and aid in time of sickness and at death, who are physically and morally fit, between the ages of eighteen and forty-five, and for the highest development and elevation of its members in all that pertains to the best in moral, social and literary acquirements. Charity, in causing a keener interest in the attainment of all commendable undertakings, and by force of precept, example, or other proper means, to enable each to share in the world's prosperity, and to become of the best and noblest in morals and citizenship; by administration of Christian consolation to those bereft, in time of sickness and death; by lawful contributions to the order for the benefit of the beneficiaries of deceased members, thereby in life assuring each of fraternal brotherhood, and in death appeasing the pangs of poverty and despair consequent upon its visitation. The order is Catholic throughout, and has (although not a church society) the sanction of the clergy and bishops of the diocese where the same exists.

The membership for Connecticut is 5,750. The order is now established in all the New England States, and also in New York, New Jersey, Pennsylvania, Delaware, Maryland, Ohio, Illinois, Michigan, Minnesota, District of Columbia, Virginia, Kentucky, and the Province of Quebec.

There are two classes of members, insured and associate. The membership of the former is 22,005; of the latter, 20,257—42,262.

[1] Prospectus.

The national officers are Supreme Knight, Edward L. Hearn, Boston, Mass.; Deputy Supreme Knight, John J. Cone, Jersey City, N. J.; National Secretary, Daniel Colwell, New Haven, Conn.; National Physician, Wm. T. McMannis, New York City; National Treasurer, P. D. Ryan, Hartford, Conn.; National Advocate, P. J. Markley, New Britain, Conn.; National Chaplain, Hugh Treanor, Norwich Conn.; National Warden, M. McNamara, New London, Conn.; National Organizer and Director of Ceremonies, Thomas H. Cummings, Boston, Mass.

When Cardinal Satolli was at the head of the Apostolic Delegation at Washington, the ritual of the order was submitted to him for inspection. In his letter of approval the Cardinal said: "We also wish to express our great pleasure, after learning the merits of this great Catholic organization, that in the present active period of social and practical alliance in America, there exists a society of practical Catholics, which offers them the best advantages of insurance, benevolence and fraternity professed by the most popular secular societies without any of the disadvantages of prohibited companionship."

## THE CATHOLIC BENEVOLENT LEGION.

THE first Council of the Catholic Benevolent Legion in Connecticut was instituted on October 15, 1883, in St. John's parish, Stamford. The officers chosen were: President, John Conniff; Secretary, F. W. Herrgen; Treasurer, Edward Duffy; Collector, John White.

The Connecticut State Council, Catholic Benevolent Legion, was instituted on March 1, 1892, at Hartford, with the following officers: President, Jeremiah J. Desmond, Norwich; Secretary, James Scanlon, New Britain; Treasurer, P. Hanrahan, Stamford.

The present officers of the Connecticut State Council are: President, John F. O'Brien; Secretary, James Scanlon; Treasurer, Miles McNiff.

The Connecticut membership of the Catholic Benevolent Legion is about 1,100.

The objects of the Legion are:[1] 1st. To unite fraternally for social, benevolent and intellectual improvement, only male Catholics, personally acceptable, of sound bodily health, between the ages of eighteen and fifty-five years at the time of admission. 2d. To afford moral and material aid to its members and their dependents by establishing a fund for the relief of its sick and distressed members 3d. To establish a benefit fund from which, on the satisfactory evidence of the death of a member who shall have complied with all its lawful requirements, a sum not exceeding $5,000 shall be paid to his legally designated beneficiary or beneficiaries. And from which benefit fund a sum not exceeding $2,500 may be paid to a member, who shall have become permanently disabled from attending to business or gaining a livelihood, and who, having complied with all its lawful requirements, has arrived at the age of expectancy as fixed by law.

The Catholic Benevolent Legion was incorporated under the laws of the State of New York on September 5, 1881. The first officers were John C. McGuire, President; John D. Carroll, Secretary; Thomas Cassin, Treasurer. The present officers of the Supreme Council are:

Spiritual Adviser, Rt. Rev. Charles E. McDonald, D.D., Brooklyn; President, John C. McGuire; Secretary, John D. Carroll; Treasurer, John D. Keiley; Medical Examiner-in-Chief, George R. Kuhn, M.D.

[1] Constitution and By-laws.

## THE CATHOLIC TOTAL ABSTINENCE UNION OF CONNECTICUT.

THIS organization was founded in 1870. The objects of the Union as disclosed in its Constitution are the promotion of the cause of Total Abstinence by united effort; to establish and maintain Total Abstinence Societies in every parish in the diocese; to develop a broad spirit of co-operation and friendly intercourse among such societies and their members; to enlist the sympathy and practical aid of those who do not belong to the movement by means of public meetings, addresses and the distribution of documents.

The officers of the Union for 1898-99 are: Spiritual Director, Rt. Rev. M. Tierney, D.D., Hartford; President, Rev. Walter J. Shanley, rector of St. Joseph's cathedral, Hartford; First Vice-President, Edward F. Cavanaugh, Wallingford; Second Vice-President, Mrs. Harriet Gragan, Meriden; Secretary, John G. McGowan, New Haven; Treasurer, Charles Fitzgerald, Middletown; Editor Thomas F. Fitzgerald, Winsted.

Board of Directors for 1898-99: New Haven County, J. Edmund Miller, New Haven; Henry A. Hayden, Waterbury; New London County, Felix Callahan, Norwich; Hartford County, James J. Bohan, Hartford; Joseph M. Holleran, New Britain; Fairfield County, Paul G. Schultze, Jr., South Norwalk; Tolland County, William J. Devine, Rockville; Middlesex County, Patrick Foley, Portland; Litchfield County, Walter Peters, West Winsted; Windham County, Rev. M. P. McCarthy.

The Catholic Total Abstinence Union of Connecticut has entered upon the thirtieth year of its existence, and is the oldest union in the national movement. Its membership as reported on September 5, 1898, was 6,699.

## ADDENDA.

THE following entries are taken from the Record of Interments of Calvary Cemetery Office, New York City. The dates given are those of the day of burial.

Elizabeth Murphy, May 31, 1817, born in Connecticut, 1778; 39 years old. She was buried from Gould street, New York.

1825, Deborah Walker, died in Cross street; born in Connecticut, 1779; 46 years old.

May 8, 1821, Ann Hurley, died in Chatam street; born in Connecticut, 1782; 39 years old.

November 19, 1823, Elizabeth Kerney, died in Clark street; born in Connecticut, 1790; 33 years old.

May 6, 1829, Sarah Rochelue, died in Anthony street; born in Connecticut, 1797; 32 years old.

June 19, 1846, Margaret Welsh, born in Ireland, 1811; died in Connecticut; aged 35 years.

October 27, 1846, James Coughlin, one year and nine months old; born in New York; died in New Milford, Connecticut.

December 1, 1846, Thomas Gibney, born in Ireland, 1827; died in New London; aged 19 years.

December 3, 1846, Lawrence Kelly, born in Ireland, 1802; died in New London; aged 44 years.

May 1, 1847, Margaret E. Gently, four years old; born in New York; died in Fairfield, Connecticut.

The above records are additional evidence of the presence of Catholics in Connecticut very early in the history of the State.

## ST. MARY'S PARISH.[1]

### NORWICH.

THE history of St. Mary's parish is the history of Catholicity in Norwich down to September 28th, 1879, when St. Patrick's Church was dedicated to God with solemn ceremony. The Norwich land records show that the site of St. Mary's Church was purchased from the Norwich Water Power Company on September 4th, 1844. The erection of a church, 65 feet by 40 feet, was immediately begun, and the first Mass within its walls was offered on the feast of the Nativity of the same year. It was dedicated on March 17th, 1845.

After the occupancy of St. Patrick's Church, an effort was made to close St. Mary's, as the authorities wished all the parishioners to worship in one edifice; but the people's affection for the venerable building, within whose walls they were united in holy wedlock, wherein their little ones had received the waters of regeneration, and through whose portals their beloved dead had been borne to their final resting place, was too deeply rooted to brook a separation. Accordingly, they petitioned for the reopening of their church. Their prayer was finally granted, and St. Mary's was opened in 1883 as a mission of St. Patrick's, in which condition it remained until the appointment of the present pastor, the Rev. James Smith, who assumed charge November 27th, 1897. His first assistant was the Rev. W. Becker, who was succeeded by the Rev. Joseph Culcowski, February 1st, 1900.

At the time of the division, the district which comprises the present parish contained about 2500 souls, mainly Irish people and their descendants, with some French and Poles. The old parochial residence was converted into a primary school by the Rev. Peter Kennedy, wherein 185 children are being instructed by three Sisters of Mercy. The older pupils, to the number of seventy, attend the school attached to St. Patrick's Church.

The first marriage to be solemnized after the organization of the new parish was that of Charles McSheffrey and Rose Ward. The first child to receive baptism was Hanora Alice, daughter of Denis and Bridget Driscoll.

St. Mary's parish is in a flourishing condition, and all indications point to a successful future. Many improvements are contemplated, among which is the purchase in the near future of new church property.

[1] See pages 414-421.

# APPENDIX.

SINCE the publication of the first edition of this History many religious events of importance have transpired in the diocese, which give evidence of the virility of the faith among us and speak forcibly for the activity of the diocesan clergy and the co-operation of the laity under the fostering care, the prudent guidance and encouragement of the Ordinary, Right Rev. Bishop Tierney. Every section of the diocese has contributed to the marvelous results accomplished. All have responded to the call of the bishop for earnest, continued and unremitting efforts in the exalted labor of bringing souls to Christ. Village and city have witnessed the walls of church and school ascend heavenward, and where before was naught but tree and shrub and rock, the cross, the symbol of man's redemption, now glistens in the sunlight, proclaiming hope and salvation in the Crucified.

The number of churches and schools erected or in course of construction, the erection of our diocesan seminary and its neighbor, the new hospital, the ordination of many young men to the holy priesthood and the numerous solemn professions of Sisters, the splendid, undeviating attendance of the faithful at the Holy Sacrifice of the Mass and their edifying reception of the Sacraments — all testify to the religious devotedness that pervades the diocese; are indubitable signs that religion forms no small part of the people's life, and that the ancient faith within our borders is still pure and vigorous. Daily proofs are not wanting to show that this portion of the Lord's Vineyard is tilled by earnest and skilled laborers, and that the seed, sown in good soil, is bringing forth abundant fruit. Two hundred and seventy-two priests are active in ministerial labors, while no less than seven hundred and sixty religious women are devoting their lives to charitable and educational work. These forces, engaged in God's cause and working in harmony, must succeed despite the obstacles that from time to time confront them. Financial difficulties are overcome where faith is strong and devotion loyal. Sacrifices cheerfully made are abundantly rewarded by Him for Whom they are made; and when obedience is joined with sacrifice, the Heart of the Invisible Head of the Church will be moved to shower lavishly His blessings upon His people. It is here we find the key to the great successes which are daily chronicled in the diocese. "Sacrifice and Obedience" is the watchword of the clergy and laity of the diocese of Hartford. Inspired by the records of the past and guided by the sage counsels of their bishop, they will go on to other victories, and bring grace to men and glory to God.

In brief, the record since August, 1899, is as follows:

## 1899.

August 27th. Right Rev. Bishop Tierney laid the corner stone of the Church of the Immaculate Conception, Branford, the Rev. Edward Martin pastor. The sermon was preached by the Rev. Walter J. Shanley, rector of the Cathedral, Hartford.

August 27th. Celebration of the forty-seventh anniversary of the founding of St. Patrick's parish, Collinsville, the Rev. John Quinn pastor. The Rev. B. O'R. Sheridan was the celebrant of the Solemn High Mass, the Rev. Luke Fitzsimmons, deacon, and the Rev. J. Quinn, sub-deacon. The preacher was the Rev. Father Quinn.

September 3rd. The dedication of the new parochial school of St. Mary's Star of the Sea parish, New London, the Rev. Thomas Joynt pastor, Bishop Tierney officiating. Solemn High Mass was celebrated by the Rev. John Russell, P. R., of New Haven, assisted by the Revs. John Coyle, New Haven, and J. F. Quinn, of New London, as deacon and sub-deacon respectively. The Rev. David O'Donnell, New London, was master of ceremonies. The preacher on the occasion was the Rev. James J. Dougherty, LL.D., New York.

September 4th. The blessing of the new cemetery at Norfolk by Bishop Tierney, the Rev. P. Keating pastor. The address was delivered by the Rev. Edward Brennan, of Torrington.

September 8th. The Rev. J. C. Moussier, M. S., the Rev. C. Glattigny, M. S., the Rev. M. E. Michael, M. S., were ordained to the priesthood in St. Joseph's Cathedral by Right Rev. Bishop Tierney.

September 10th. The placing of the corner stone of St. Francis' parochial school, Naugatuck, Bishop Tierney officiating, the Rev. James O'R. Sheridan rector. The sermon was preached by the Rev. Walter Elliott, C. S. P.

September 17th. The laying of the corner stone of the Church of the Assumption, the Rev. James Ryle rector, by Bishop Tierney. Preacher of the day, the Rev. Peter H. McClean, S. T. L., Superior of the Hartford Apostolate, Milford.

November 19th. Bishop Tierney placed the corner stone of St. Michael's Church, Beacon Falls. The Rev. M. A. Sullivan, of Kensington, preached the sermon. Beacon Falls is attended by the Rev. M. F. Rigney, pastor of St. Augustine's parish, Seymour.

November 19th. The dedication of the Church of Our Lady of Lourdes, Waterbury, by Bishop Tierney. The building was originally a private residence and is situated on South Main Street. The church is attended by the Italian Catholics, who, previous to their occupancy of this building, assembled for divine worship in a hall on Canal Street. The Rev. M. A. Karam is the pastor.

## 1900.

March 11th. The dedication of St. Michael's Church, Beacon Falls, and the blessing of its bell by Bishop Tierney. Celebrant of the Solemn High Mass, the Rev. Michael F. Rigney; deacon, the Rev. C. McElroy; sub-deacon, the Rev. J. Curtin. The discourse was pronounced by the Rev. Joseph A. Rigney, of Washington, N. J.

April 22nd. Right Rev. Bishop Tierney dedicated the Church of the Assumption, Westport, the Rev. Thomas Shanley rector. High Mass was celebrated by the Rev. John H. Carroll, of Wallingford, and the

Rev. William Maher, D.D., of South Norwalk, preached the dedicatory sermon. The church occupies a commanding sight on Riverside Avenue and cost upwards of $20,000.

April 29th. The Rev. Michael J. Daly, formerly of Thomaston, assumed pastoral charge of the newly erected St. Joseph's parish, New Haven, with the Rev. John F. Donahoe as assistant. The parish was formed by portions taken from St. Mary's, St. Patrick's and St. Francis' parishes.

May 14th. The appointment of Very Rev. John Synnott, President of St. Thomas' Seminary, Hartford, as Vicar-General in succession to Very Rev. John A. Mulcahy.

May 30th. St. Joseph's Church, South Norwalk, dedicated by Bishop Tierney. Celebrant of the Mass, the Rev. John Winters, Hartford; deacon, the Rev. Francis P. Havvey, St. Joseph's Seminary, Dunwoodie, N. Y.; sub-deacon, the Rev. T. Crowley, Waterbury. The preacher on the occasion was Very Rev. William O'Brien Pardow, S. J. Pastor, the Rev. William Maher, D.D.

June 3rd. The laying of the corner stone of the Church of the Sacred Heart to replace the building destroyed by fire in the preceding January, the Rev. James Cunningham rector. The Rev. John F. Boland, of Chicopee Falls, Mass., preached the sermon.

June 3rd. Right Rev. Bishop Tierney placed the corner stone of St. James' Church, Danielson. The Rev. Joseph Vignon, M. S., preached the sermon in French and the Rev. Arthur O'Keefe pronounced the English discourse.

June 17th. Bishop Tierney dedicated the chapel of the new Church of the Assumption, Ansonia, the Rev. Joseph Synnott rector. Solemn High Mass was celebrated by the Rev. John Walsh, of Middletown, assisted by the Rev. James Nihil, of Bridgeport, as deacon, the Rev. Thomas Kelly, of New Milford, as sub-deacon, and the Rev. John Flemming, of Ansonia, as master of ceremonies. The sermon was preached by the Rev. William O'Brien Pardow, S. J. The discourse at the evening service was pronounced by the Rev. Father Valentine, C. P.

July 1st. Right Rev. Bishop Tierney laid the corner stone of St. Michael's Church, Hartford, the Rev. John J. Downey acting pastor. The Rev. Walter J. Shanley, of Hartford, was the preacher of the day.

July 4th. The placing of the corner stone of the new St. Francis hospital, Hartford, by Bishop Tierney, the Rev. John J. Fitzgerald, of New Britain, being the orator of the occasion.

July 7th. The Rev. Andrew J. Plunkett, the Rev. John M. Sullivan, the Rev. E. X. Cruveiller, M. S., the Rev. H. Galvin, M. S., the Rev. A. R. Chapignac, M. S., were ordained to the priesthood in St. Joseph's Cathedral by Right Rev. Bishop Tierney.

July 22nd. Right Rev. Bishop Tierney laid the corner stone of the mission Church of St. Mary Magdalene, Oakville, the Rev. James H. O'Donnell pastor. The preacher on the occasion was the Rev. Walter J. Shanley, of Hartford.

July 22nd. Mission of Noank organized with John E. McDonald and John Fitzpatrick as trustees. A lot was secured on Spicer Avenue, and ground was broken for a new church on November 13th. It will be a frame building, 67 feet long and 36 feet wide, with a seating capacity of 350. When completed, the edifice will cost about $8000. The Catholics of Noank, who number about 400 souls, formerly attended the parish church at Mystic, the Rev. John F. Murphy pastor.

July 29th. Bishop Tierney officiated at the dedication of the Church of the Sacred Heart, West Thompson, the Rev. James Cunningham rector. The Rev. John J. Fitzgerald, of New Haven, delivered the dedication address.

July 30th. The Rev. James A. Broderick, the Rev. Bernard Donnelly and the Rev. John Kennedy were ordained to the priesthood in the Cathedral, Hartford, by Bishop Tierney. The sermon was delivered by the Rev. Felix O'Neil, of Hartford.

August 1st. Right Rev. Bishop Tierney blessed the bell of the Church of the Sacred Heart, East Berlin, the Rev. M. Sullivan rector.

August 5th. The corner stone of the Church of the Sacred Heart, Taftville, was laid by Bishop Tierney, the Rev. Walter J. Shanley, of Hartford, preaching the English sermon and the Rev. P. Roux, M. S., of Hartford, pronouncing the French discourse. The Rev. John Synuott is the rector.

September 2nd. St. Michael's Church, Hartford, was dedicated by Bishop Tierney, the Rev. John J. Downey pastor. The celebrant of the High Mass was the Rev. P. J. Kennedy, of Montville; deacon, the Rev. R. C. Gragan, of Stafford Springs; sub-deacon, the Rev. C. Leddy, of Bridgeport; master of ceremonies, the Rev. C. McCann, of Hartford. The Rev. John T. Lynch, of Wethersfield, delivered the discourse.

September 2nd. Bishop Tierney laid the corner stone of St. Thomas' Seminary, Hartford, the Rev. R. F. Fitzgerald, D.D., Vice-President of the Seminary, preaching the sermon. The building is in the form of the letter " L." The longer arm, or the main building, is 150 feet by 50 feet, and the shorter arm, or extension, is 85 feet by 36 feet. The Seminary is four stories in height with a basement.

September 3rd. St. Francis' parochial school, Naugatuck, the Rev. James O'R. Sheridan pastor, was blessed by Bishop Tierney. The oration was pronounced by the Rev. William O'Brien Pardow, S. J.

September 23rd. Bishop Tierney laid the corner stone of St. Mary's Church and St. Mary's parochial school, Greenwich, of which the Rev. John J. Fitzgerald is rector. The address was delivered by the Rev. Walter J. Shanley, of Hartford. The new church replaces the old one destroyed by fire on May 16th.

October 7th. Right Rev. Bishop Tierney dedicated the Church of St. Mary

Magdelene, Oakville, and blessed its bell, the Rev. James H. O'Donnell pastor. The sermon was delivered by the Rev. Peter McClean, of Milford, Superior of the Hartford Apostolate. The celebrant of the Mass was the Rev. E. X. Cruveiller, M. S.

November 10th. Dedication of St. Mary's Convent, Bridgeport, Bishop Tierney officiating, the Rev. John Rogers rector.

November 18th. Dedication of the chapel of St. Mary's Church, Greenwich, the Rev. John J. Fitzgerald rector, Bishop Tierney officiating. The celebrant of the Mass was the Rev. John J. Elty, and the Rev. James C. O'Brien pronounced the discourse.

November 25th. The dedication of the Chapel of the Sacred Heart, Taftville, the Rev. John Synnott rector, Bishop Tierney officiating. Celebrant of the Solemn High Mass, the Rev. James Smith, Norwich; deacon, the Rev. Thomas Joynt, New London; subdeacon, the Rev. U. O. Bellerose, Norwich; master of ceremonies, the Rev. J. P. Perrault, Taftville. The French discourse was pronounced by the Rev. U. O. Bellerose, and the English address by the Rev. Charles McElroy of Derby.

December 2nd. Reopening of St. John's Church, New Haven, the Rev. John D. Coyle rector. The Rev. James Coyle of Taunton, Mass., pronounced the oration at Mass, and the Rev. William H. Coyle, S. J., preached the sermon at solemn vespers.

----

## APPOINTMENT AND TRANSFER OF PASTORS IN THE DIOCESE SINCE JUNE, 1899.

### 1899.

Rev. P. J. Kennedy from assistant at the Immaculate Conception, Waterbury, to St. John's, Montville, June 14th.

Rev. Vittorio Sovilla removed from Our Lady of Mt. Carmel, Meriden, to Syracuse, N. Y., July 30th.

Rev. Pamphilus Ennis, O. F. M., to St. Joseph's, Winsted, October 5th.

### 1900.

Rev. Witold Becker from assistant at St. Mary's, Norwich, to St. Michael's (Polish), Bridgeport, February 1st.

Rev. C. F. Socquet, M. S., to Our Lady of Sorrows, Hartford, February 2nd.

Rev. John J. Fitzgerald from St. John's, Cromwell, to St. Mary's, Greenwich; assumed charge February 7th.

Rev. Thomas Dunne from St. Catherine's, Broadbrook, to St. John's, Cromwell; appointed February 7th.

Rev. John C. Lynch, assistant at St. John's, Stamford, to St. Catherine's, Broadbrook; assumed charge February 8th.

Rev. Thomas H. Shanley from St. Joseph's, Poquonock, to the Church of the Assumption, Westport; assumed charge March 29th.

Rev. F. Lally from assistant at St. Peter's, Hartford, to St. Joseph's, Poquonock; assumed charge March 29th.

* Rev. Michael J. Daly from Thomaston to St. Joseph's (new parish), New Haven.

* Rev. Timothy M. O'Brien from Noroton to Thomaston.

* Rev. D. O'Connor from assistant at St. Francis', New Haven, to Noroton.

* Rev. John P. Neale from assistant at St. Patrick's, Norwich, to Terryville (new parish).

Rev. John D. Kennedy from assistant at St. Peter's, Danbury, to St. John's (new parish), Westville; assumed charge June 10th.

Rev. Hubert Dahme from the Sacred Heart, Hartford, to St. Joseph's, Bridgeport, July 1st.

Rev. M. N. Brommenschenkel to the Sacred Heart, Hartford, July 2nd.

Rev. Joseph E. Senesac from St. Ann's, Hartford, to St. Ann's, Waterbury, July 13th.

Rev. F. Bedard from assistant at St. Ann's, Waterbury, to St. Ann's, Hartford, July 14th.

Rev. Father Michael, O. F. M., to St. Joseph's, Winsted, August 22d.

Rev. John J. Downey from acting pastor of St. Patrick's, Hartford, to St. Michael's (new parish), Hartford, September 2nd.

Rev. Paul F. McAlenney from St. Rose's, Meriden, to St. Peter's, Hartford; assumed charge September 9th.

† Rev. William H. Rogers from St. John's, Stamford, to St. Patrick's, Hartford.

† Rev. James C. O'Brien from the Sacred Heart, Bridgeport, to St. John's, Stamford.

† Rev. Timothy R. Sweeney from St. Mary's, Portland, to the Sacred Heart, Bridgeport.

† Rev. Richard C. Gragan from St. Edward's, Stafford Springs, to St. Mary's, Portland.

† Rev. Felix O'Neil from assistant at St. Ann's, Waterbury, to St. Edward's, Stafford Springs.

† Rev. John T. Lynch from the Sacred Heart, Wethersfield, to the Sacred Heart (new parish), Meriden.

† Rev. Jeremiah Duggan from assistant at St. Patrick's, New Haven, to the Sacred Heart, Wethersfield.

† Rev. John Walsh from St. Augustine's Villa, Hartford, to St. Patrick's (new parish), East Hampton.

¶ Rev. John Cooney from St. Bernard's, Rockville, to St. Rose's, Meriden.

¶ Rev. Luke Fitzsimmons from the Immaculate Conception, New Hartford, to St. Bernard's, Rockville.

¶ Rev. Michael J. Cray from St. Bernard's, Tariffville, to the Immaculate Conception, New Hartford.

¶ Rev. Richard Carroll from St. Mary's, South Coventry, to St. Bernard's, Tariffville.

¶ Rev. James B. Lawless from assistant at St. Patrick's, Waterbury, to St. Mary's, South Coventry.

---

* Formally assumed charge of their respective parishes Sunday, April 29th.
† Assumed formal charge on September 23rd.
¶ Assumed formal charge on September 30th.

** Rev. James Cunningham from the Sacred Heart, West Thompson, to Holy Angels', South Meriden.

** Rev. Eugene O'Connell from assistant at St. Patrick's, New Haven, to the Sacred Heart, West Thompson.

** Rev. Thomas Kelly from St. Francis Xavier's, New Milford, to St. Michael's (new parish), Bridgeport.

** Rev. Thomas Cronin from Holy Angels', South Meriden, to St. Francis Xavier's, New Milford.

The following deaths occurred during the year 1900:

Rev. Thomas Smith, at Greenwich, January 9th.

Very Rev. John A. Mulcahy, V. G., at Hartford, January 13th.

Rev. Henry A. Stokes, at Bridgeport, January 25th.

Rev. James P. Ryle, at Westport, March 23rd.

Rev. Maurice J. Sheehan, at Kenton, Ohio, May 16th.

Rev. Terrence W. Dolan, at Albany, N. Y., July 6th.

Rev. Thomas W. Broderick, at Hartford, August 12th.

Rev. M. P. McCarthy, at Branford, September 19th.

Very Rev. Pamphilus Ennis, O.F.M., at Winsted, October 1st.

Rev. Joseph O'Keefe, at West Hartford, October 14th.

---

** Assumed charge in first week of October.

An old Spanish church bell cast in 815, probably the oldest witness of its kind to the antiquity of the faith in the United States. It is the property of St. Stephen's Episcopal Church, East Haddam, Conn. It was part of the plunder taken from the churches of Spain by Napoleon when he devastated that country. It was brought to America about 1835, with many other bells, to be sold to bell manufacturers to be recast. It was purchased by William Wyllis Pratt, a New York ship-chandler, and by him presented to the parish. It now stands on a stone wall in the rear of the church.

The following is the inscription incised on the bell:

A NO      DE      S 1 5
CONCEPE DE ESPIRITV SANTO
SI EN  Do PRIOR ELV PDS
MIGVEL VILLA NVEVA
PROC  RA   DOR EL VP Dn JOSEF
ESTEVAN
CORRALES ME  H I  T O

Lightning Source UK Ltd.
Milton Keynes UK
UKHW031433220520
363714UK00003B/295